Believers Church Bible Commentary

Douglas B. Miller and Loren L. Johns, Editors

"1 & 2 Kings are not dry, dusty history, but the dynamic story of Israel's and Judah's kings and their people all too often snubbing the Deuteronomic call for justice and the human vocation given all at creation. Jost skillfully explains these writings with a perceptive eye to how they address the contemporary world."
—Gerald Gerbrandt, president emeritus and professor emeritus of Bible, Canadian Mennonite University

"This commentary leads us to the end of the prophetic narrative of humankind that begins at creation. This is not just the account of the demise of one nation; it is the story for all civilization. Jost clarifies the obscure details of 1 & 2 Kings and bring focus to the human vocation. The fundamentals of human life have not changed. In 1 & 2 Kings are lessons to live the life of faith in the events of current time."
—August H. Konkel, professor of Old Testament, McMaster Divinity College

"Preaching is a daunting endeavor in these tumultuous times. We'd do well to gather around 1 & 2 Kings and learn what it means to faithfully follow God in the midst of social, political, and religious upheaval. Jost is just the one to help us preachers listen, listen deeply, and gather God's people around these ancient texts made fresh again—living wisdom for these wanton times."
—Chris Neufeld-Erdman, pastor of Davis (Calif.) Community Church and author of *Ordinary Preacher, Extraordinary Gospel: A Daily Guide for Wise, Empowered Preachers* (Lloyd John Ogilvie Institute of Preaching)

BELIEVERS CHURCH BIBLE COMMENTARY

Old Testament

Genesis, by Eugene F. Roop, 1987
Exodus, by Waldemar Janzen, 2000
Leviticus, by Perry B. Yoder, *forthcoming*
Numbers, *forthcoming*
Deuteronomy, by Gerald Gerbrandt, 2015
Joshua, by Gordon H. Matties, 2012
Judges, by Terry L. Brensinger, 1999
Ruth, Jonah, Esther, by Eugene F. Roop, 2002
1-2 Samuel, by David Baker, *forthcoming*
1-2 Kings, by Lynn Jost
1-2 Chronicles, by August H. Konkel, 2016
Ezra-Nehemiah, by Steven Schweitzer, *forthcoming*
Job, by Paul Keim, *forthcoming*
Psalms, by James H. Waltner, 2006
Proverbs, by John W. Miller, 2004
Ecclesiastes, by Douglas B. Miller, 2010
Isaiah, by Ivan D. Friesen, 2009
Jeremiah, by Elmer A. Martens, 1986
Lamentations, Song of Songs, by Wilma Ann Bailey and Christina A. Bucher, 2015
Ezekiel, by Millard C. Lind, 1996
Daniel, by Paul M. Lederach, 1994
Hosea, Amos, by Allen R. Guenther, 1998
Joel, Obadiah, Nahum, *forthcoming*
Micah, Habakkuk, Zephaniah, by Dan Epp-Tiessen and Derek Suderman,
    forthcoming
Haggai, Zechariah, Malachi, by Patricia Shelly, *forthcoming*

New Testament

Matthew, by Richard B. Gardner, 1991
Mark, by Timothy J. Geddert, 2001
Luke, by Mary H. Schertz, *forthcoming*
John, by Willard M. Swartley, 2013
Acts, by Chalmer E. Faw, 1993
Romans, by John E. Toews, 2004
1 Corinthians, by Dan Nighswander, 2017
2 Corinthians, by V. George Shillington, 1998
Galatians, by George R. Brunk III, 2015
Ephesians, by Thomas R. Yoder Neufeld, 2002
Philippians, by Gordon Zerbe, 2016
Colossians, Philemon, by Ernest D. Martin, 1993
1-2 Thessalonians, by Jacob W. Elias, 1995
1-2 Timothy, Titus, by Paul M. Zehr, 2010
Hebrews, by Estella Horning, *forthcoming*
James, by Sheila Klassen-Wiebe, *forthcoming*

1-2 Peter, Jude, by Erland Waltner and J. Daryl Charles, 1999
1, 2, 3 John, by J. E. McDermond, 2011
Revelation, by John R. Yeatts, 2003

Old Testament Editors

Elmer A. Martens, Mennonite Brethren Biblical Seminary, Fresno, California
Douglas B. Miller, Tabor College, Hillsboro, Kansas

New Testament Editors

Howard Charles, Anabaptist Mennonite Biblical Seminary, Elkhart, Indiana
Gordon Zerbe, Canadian Mennonite University, Winnipeg, Manitoba
Loren L. Johns, Anabaptist Mennonite Biblical Seminary, Elkhart, Indiana

Editorial Council

David W. Baker, Brethren Church
W. Derek Suderman, Mennonite Church Canada
Christina A. Bucher, Church of the Brethren
John R. Yeatts, Brethren in Christ Church
Gordon H. Matties (chair), Mennonite Brethren Church
Jo-Ann A. Brant, Mennonite Church USA

Believers Church
Bible Commentary

1 & 2 Kings

Lynn Jost

HERALD PRESS

Harrisonburg, Virginia

Herald Press
PO Box 866, Harrisonburg, Virginia 22803
www.HeraldPress.com

Library of Congress Cataloging-in-Publication Data
Names: Jost, Lynn, 1954- author.
Title: 1 & 2 Kings / Lynn Jost.
Other titles: Believers church Bible commentary ; vol. 34
Description: Harrisonburg, Virginia : Herald Press, 2021. | Series: Believers church
    Bible commentary; vol. 34 | Includes bibliographical references and index.
Identifiers: LCCN 2021031452 (print) | LCCN 2021031453 (ebook) | ISBN
    9781513802633 (paperback) | ISBN 9781513802640 (ebook)
Subjects: LCSH: Bible. Kings—Commentaries. | BISAC: RELIGION / Biblical Commentary
    / Old Testament / General | RELIGION / Biblical Commentary / General
Classification: LCC BS1335.53 .J67 2021 (print) | LCC BS1335.53 (ebook) |
    DDC 222.507—dc23
LC record available at https://lccn.loc.gov/2021031452
LC ebook record available at https://lccn.loc.gov/2021031453

BELIEVERS CHURCH BIBLE COMMENTARY: 1 & 2 KINGS
© 2021 by Herald Press, Harrisonburg, Virginia 22803. 800-245-7894.
    All rights reserved.
Library of Congress Control Number: 2021031452
International Standard Book Number: 978-1-5138-0263-3 (paperback);
    978-1-5138-0264-0 (ebook)
Printed in the United States of America
Cover by Merrill Miller
Interior design by Merrill Miller and Alice Shetler

25 24 23 22 21   10 9 8 7 6 5 4 3 2 1

To my wife, Donna,
who for fifty years has remained my fiercest critic
and staunchest support.

Abbreviations

ANE	ancient Near East(ern)
ABD	*The Anchor Bible Dictionary.* Edited by David Noel Freedman. 6 vols. New York: Doubleday, 1992.
ANEP	*The Ancient Near East in Pictures Relating to the Old Testament.* 2nd ed. Edited by James B. Pritchard. Princeton, NJ: Princeton University Press, 1969.
ANET	*Ancient Near Eastern Texts Relating to the Old Testament.* Edited by James B. Pritchard. 3rd ed. Princeton, NJ: Princeton University Press, 1969.
art.	article
AT	author's translation
BCE	Before the Common Era
ca.	circa, around
CE	Common Era
cf.	*confer*, compare
ch(s).	chapter(s)
d.	died
DtrH	Deuteronomistic History
DtrN	Deuteronomic texts on law (*nomos*)
DtrP	Deuteronomic texts on prophetic matters
Dtr1	Deuteronomic optimism (hopeful)
Dtr2	Deuteronomic pessimism (colored by the exile)
e.g.	*exempli gratia*, for example
emph.	emphasis
EN	Explanatory Notes
Eng.	English
esp.	especially
etc.	*et cetera*, and so forth, and the rest
Heb.	Hebrew
i.e.	*id est*, that is
JSOTSS	Journal for the Study of the Old Testament Supplement Series
KJV	King James Version
LXX	Septuagint, the Greek Old Testament
MT	Masoretic Text of the Hebrew Bible
NASB	New American Standard Bible
NEB	New English Bible
NIV	New International Version (2011)
NRSV	New Revised Standard Version
NT	New Testament

OT	Old Testament
par.	parallel(s)
pl.	plural
RSV	Revised Standard Version
SBL	Society of Biblical Literature
SN	Succession Narrative
TBC	The Text in Biblical Context (in Contents as *)
TLC	The Text in the Life of the Church (in Contents as +)
vol.	volume
×	times, such as 3×

Transliteration of Hebrew Consonants

Sign	Name	Letter	Sound
ʾ	ʾalep	א	glottal stop
z	zayin	ז	z sound
ḥ	ḥet	ח	kh sound as in loch
ṭ	ṭet	ט	t as in bet
ʿ	ʿayin	ע	ahyeen (guttural with a vowel)
ṣ	ṣade	צ	ts as in bets
ś	śin	שׂ	s
š	šin	שׁ	sh

Contents

Series Foreword

The Believers Church Bible Commentary series makes available a new tool for basic Bible study. It is published for all who seek more fully to understand the original message of Scripture and its meaning for today—Sunday school teachers, members of Bible study groups, students, pastors, and others. The series is based on the conviction that God is still speaking to all who will listen, and that the Holy Spirit makes the Word a living and authoritative guide for all who want to know and do God's will.

The desire to help as wide a range of readers as possible has determined the approach of the writers. Since no blocks of biblical text are provided, readers may continue to use the translation with which they are most familiar. The writers of the series use the New Revised Standard Version and the New International Version on a comparative basis. They indicate which text they follow most closely and where they make their own translations. The writers have not worked alone, but in consultation with select counselors, the series' editors, and the Editorial Council.

Every volume illuminates the Scriptures; provides necessary theological, sociological, and ethical meanings; and in general makes "the rough places plain." Critical issues are not avoided, but neither are they moved into the foreground as debates among scholars. Each section offers "Explanatory Notes," followed by focused articles, "The Text in Biblical Context" and "The Text in the Life of the Church." This commentary aids the interpretive process but does not try to supersede the authority of the Word and Spirit as discerned in the gathered church.

The term *believers church* emerged in the mid-twentieth century to define Christian groups with direct or indirect connections to the

Radical Reformation, a distinctive faith expression that arose in Europe during the sixteenth century. These believers were concerned that the church be voluntary and not be aligned with political government. *Believers church* has come to represent an identifiable tradition of beliefs and practices that includes believers (adult) baptism; a voluntary fellowship that practices church discipline, mutual aid, and service; belief in the power of love in all relationships; and a willingness to follow Christ by embracing his cross as a way of life. In recent decades the term has sometimes been applied to church communities informed by Anabaptism, evangelicalism, or pietism, such as Brethren Church, Brethren in Christ, Church of the Brethren, Mennonite Brethren, and Mennonites, as well as similar groups. The writers chosen for the series speak from within this tradition.

Believers church people have always been known for their emphasis on obedience to the simple meaning of Scripture. Because of this, they do not have a long history of deep historical-critical biblical scholarship. This series attempts to be faithful to the Scriptures while also taking archaeology and current biblical studies seriously. Doing this means that at many points the writers will not differ greatly from interpretations that can be found in many other good commentaries. Yet these writers share basic convictions about Christ, the church and its mission, God and history, human nature, the Christian life, and other doctrines. These presuppositions do shape a writer's interpretation of Scripture. Thus this series, like all other commentaries, stands within a specific historical church tradition.

Many in this stream of the church have expressed a need for help in Bible study. This is justification enough to produce the Believers Church Bible Commentary. Nevertheless, the Holy Spirit is not bound to any tradition. May this series be an instrument in breaking down walls between Christians in North America and around the world, bringing new joy in obedience through a fuller understanding of the Word.

—*The Editorial Council*

Introduction to 1–2 Kings

The situation: Citizens, including political and intellectual leaders, exiled through war and conquest. Government buildings in ruins. An economic system where the rich get richer and the poor get poorer. The power of the state used to damage and silence political opposition. Government policies favoring the cronies of the political establishment and suppressing any opposition. Mushrooming expenditures by the military-industrial complex, creating huge budget deficits and endangering the economy. Growing xenophobia, with foreigners exploited or denied entry. Leaders following the advice of cronies rather than experts. Citizen being divided from citizen, fomenting hatred and distrust. Nations destroyed by their superpower neighbors. Are these contemporary headlines, captions from the books of 1–2 Kings, or both? The question of justice to protect the marginalized or policies to enrich the powerful runs through today's news feeds and the biblical books of Kings. No biblical books address contemporary readers with more urgency than 1–2 Kings.

Kings is the final installment of a national narrative that not only analyzes the tragedy but also explores the deepest purpose of human existence. The exiles mentioned at the end of Kings face critical issues of identity: retribution (evil as punishment for sin), theodicy (why bad things happen to good people), leadership (kings, priests, or prophets), and worship (religious faith without a temple). These significant issues pale next to the question, What is the purpose of humans created in the image of God? Written in the crisis of the Babylonian exile, 1–2 Kings grapples with the question, What has God called humans to do in the world?

Just as Harry Potter aficionados make sense of the seventh novel after reading the first six in the series, so readers of Kings need orientation to enter Israel's story generations after it begins. Moses' last will and testament, Deuteronomy, establishes Yahweh's covenant, which sets conditions for Israel's success or failure in the land of Canaan (the geographical area often called Palestine). Joshua, Judges, and Samuel narrate the ups and downs of entry, land possession, and establishment of the monarchy. Then 1–2 Kings provides the last installment of the national narrative of life in Palestine, from the glorious reign of Solomon, through the divided kingdom, and ultimately exile for both Israel (722 BCE) and Judah (586 BCE).

Here 1–2 Kings also completes a story that begins with creation. God creates humans in the image of God, blessed to represent God and fulfill God's purposes (Gen 1:27-28). God renews the blessing to Abraham and articulates the whole human vocation—to keep the way of the Lord by doing righteousness and justice (Gen 12:3; 18:19). The Kings narrative explores the outcome of the creation mandate and explains how and why Abraham's descendants ended in exile.

Though this narrative ends in exile, the Deuteronomic covenant foresees this outcome. Anticipation of the event demonstrates that exile is not the end of life—and proves that national institutions are penultimate to God's universal human vocation (Deut 4:25-31; 30:1-5). All humanity is to demonstrate covenant love for God by imitating God's love for marginalized people (10:12-21). What is required? *Fear, love, and serve Yahweh your God with heart and soul, keep the LORD's commandments, and walk in all God's ways* (cf. 10:12-13). This vocation to imitate Yahwistic justice offers meaning when institutions disintegrate.

Composition

Occasion for Writing Kings

Readers of 1–2 Kings find themselves about twenty-five years after the destruction of Jerusalem in 586 BCE (the most important date for OT interpretation, says Brueggemann [1997: 614; 2014b: 4–5]). Thus 1–2 Kings probes the question posed by Yahweh to Solomon: *Why has the LORD done such a thing to this land and to this house?* (1 Kings 9:8; cf. Deut 29:24). Within the question lie several issues of theological tension within 1–2 Kings. Foremost is the question of how to understand the exile. Does this exile result from divine judgment or from other national political and military power? The perspective of Kings is that the exile is the result of God's judgment on faithless people—not the superior power of the empires and their gods. The precise nature of that unfaithfulness has been grounded in several issues. Improper worship, including the idolatrous *sins of Jeroboam* and worship on the high places (in Judah), transgresses the Deuteronomic stipulation of worship in a single place chosen by the Lord (Deut 12; 2 Kings 17:7-23). Alliances with foreign powers, including emptying the treasury or taxing the populace to pay tribute, transgress the Deuteronomic prohibition on alliances (Deut 7:1-5). The issue about whether God's promises are unconditional (as they were for David: 1 Kings 11:36) or conditioned on obedient faithfulness (1 Kings 9:4-9) factors into the question of exile. The question of the most important institution involves the relative significance of the land, the Torah, the priesthood, the temple, the monarchy, the wisdom of the sages, and the prophets.

Objective of Kings

The thesis of this commentary is that the purpose of 1–2 Kings is to refocus the human vocation. The place of Kings as the climax of the grand creation-to-exile story narrated from Genesis to Kings substantiates this claim. The Creator blesses human creation with the mandate to represent God as the image of God by practicing justice and righteousness (Gen 1:27-28; 18:19). The Deuteronomic covenant rests in a relationship of love and obedience most clearly demonstrated by the practice of justice and righteousness for the marginalized (Deut 10:12-21). The Kings narrative evaluates human faithfulness to this vocation. Read in the context of Deuteronomic theology, 1–2 Kings offers hope that the human vocation is even greater than Israelite identity or prosperity. God renews the call to practice justice.

As the concluding chapter in both the creation narrative and the story of Israel in the Promised Land, Kings demonstrates that the future of God's people does not depend on monarchy, priesthood, temple, life in the land, or even the Torah. Rather, God calls all humanity to live in covenant by practicing justice for the marginalized. The radical hospitality stipulated in Deuteronomy for all marginalized people, including strangers outside the bounds of Israel, is demonstrated in the Kings narrative, particularly the Elijah-Elisha narratives.

Authorship and Date

Clues to authorship and date of Kings come from its contents. Second Kings 25:27-30 reports contemporaneous events in 562 BCE in Babylon. Debate about the provenance of Kings is inconclusive, but this commentary assumes a Babylonian exilic audience wrestling with the identity questions listed above. Kings is the final installment of Israel's epic narrative known as the Former Prophets in the Hebrew canon (Joshua, Judges, Samuel, Kings). Informed by the covenant of Deuteronomy, these books are known as the Deuteronomistic History (DtrH) [*Kings in the Hebrew Canon: Kings in the Deuteronomistic History, p. 453*].

Though the "author" of the final form of Kings (and DtrH) is likely an editorial school or tradition shaped by Deuteronomy, resolution of the question is tentative. Noth theorized that DtrH was composed by a single individual living in Palestine early in the exile (about 560 BCE), using written and oral traditions. Cross postulated two editions of DtrH: Dtr1, written with optimism during Josiah's reign; and Dtr2, a final form, rewritten in the pessimism of exile (Cross; Nelson 1981a: 127–28). The Scandinavian school theorizes three editorial layers: an original exilic author (DtrH), edited in a prophetic (DtrP) outlook, and later revised with a nomistic perspective (DtrN, concerned with law; Smend, Dietrich, and Veijola). Other scholars theorize that a synchronistic narrative history was written during the reign of Jehoshaphat, that the negative Jehuide perspective regarding the Omride dynasty was incorporated by the scribes of Hezekiah and Josiah as apologetic pieces supporting their reigns, and that an exilic edition of 1–2 Kings was a final form (Halpern and Lemaire: 151–53). Steven McKenzie, in reviewing these alternatives, describes "the tension between Dtr's imagined role as author and editor" as "a point of ambivalence" in modern scholarship "from the start" (McKenzie 2006: 526).

Among related issues are whether the author(s)/editor(s) were from the Levites (country preachers), of a prophetic school, the people of the land, or leaders in Jerusalem influenced by northern materials and whether they lived in Palestine or Babylon (Fretheim 1983: 17; Geoghegan: 118). Nicholson theorizes that northern Levites came to Jerusalem, were proclaiming the Mosaic covenant, and supported the reforms of Hezekiah. Based on her reading of Jeremiah 39, 52, and 2 Kings 24–25, Dutcher-Walls suggests that factions within the royal-priestly administration debated policy based on opposing theological convictions. The Jeremiah faction, based on the conditional covenant anticipating divine judgment, lost the policy battle (favoring accommodation to Babylon) but prevailed in DtrH (Dutcher-Walls 1991: 92).

Because 1–2 Kings incorporates material contemporaneous with events that traverse nearly four centuries, a primary question about authorship has to do with use of sources. More radical scholars (e.g.,

P. Davies, Thompson) read 1-2 Kings as fiction created centuries later, with little concern for the historical events; yet the reading offered here presupposes a series of editions of the history of Kings, each incorporating and reworking inherited material, completed by an author or editor (or several) who bequeaths us a document much like canonical 1-2 Kings.

Structure and Purpose

Kings accounts for the failure of the kingdoms of Israel and Judah in theological terms. Exile is primarily understood not as a result of political factors but as an act of God in response to human behavior. The structure of the book reinforces this.

First Kings opens with Solomon's reign over a united Israel and Judah under the Davidic dynasty. A positive perspective of Solomon's initial rule shows a faithful, wise heir of the exemplary David (2:1-4; 3:3-7, 14; 11:6, 33-39). This perspective views the narrative centrality of Solomon's temple building and dedication as evidence of divine blessing (8:9-13). The perspective followed in this commentary deems Deuteronomic, Yahwistic justice as the primary measure of faithfulness and perceives a sometimes subtle critique of Solomon's monarchic administration (justice, Heb. mišpaṭ, pronounced "mishpat"), one that often follows another Davidic mandate (2:5-9) [Mišpaṭ, p. 461]. The sometimes subtle (or perhaps ambivalent) characterization of Solomon explodes into unambiguous negative evaluation of kings that follow in the divided monarchy (1 Kings 12 to 2 Kings 17).

The stylized structure of the divided-kingdom narrative follows the framework of the opening and concluding royal formulas [Chronology: Synchronization, p. 440]. More significant is that all the northern kings (in Israel) are evaluated as having failed to serve the Lord, nearly all for the sins of Jeroboam, exchanging Torah obedience and temple worship for the idolatry of monarchic injustice. The ledger of the southern kings of Judah is mixed, with the more positive evaluation of having done what was right in the sight of the LORD as David had done (1 Kings 15:11), though with the caveat except in the matter of Uriah the Hittite (15:5) as a subtext. The Southern Kingdom, though politically and militarily subordinate to the Northern Kingdom, is spared for the sake of the Lord's servant David (2 Kings 8:19) despite permitting hill shrines to prevail until the reforms of Hezekiah (ch. 18) and Josiah (chs. 22-23). Though frequent regime changes characterize the Northern Kingdom, David's line continues almost unbroken (see 2 Kings 11).

The prophetic word and its fulfillment are significant in Kings, beginning with the prophecy of Ahijah (1 Kings 11) [Prophets, p. 465], but the Elijah-Elisha prophetic centerpiece in 1 Kings 17–2 Kings 13 interrupts the royal prominence. In their extended critique of the monarchy, Elijah and Elisha call for just rule to protect the marginalized (ch. 21; 2 Kings 4). Jehu's reform receives limited Deuteronomistic approval for cutting off the Baal-inspired injustice of Omri's dynasty (2 Kings 10:30). After the Judah-Israel alliance engineered by Ahab, the royal dynasty in the Southern Kingdom has a mixed ancestry of the righteous David and the worst of all kings, Ahab (1 Kings 16:31-33). The first of two climactic narrative moments offers the report and explanation of the exile of Israel in 722 BCE, attributing that exile to the people rejecting the prophetic calls to Yahwistic justice (2 Kings 17:7-23), with the lengthy following description of the mixed mišpaṭ of Yahweh and the nations (17:24-41). The Southern Kingdom survives for more than a century longer, but when the son of the reformer Hezekiah (chs. 18–20), who is also grandfather of the reformer Josiah (chs. 22–23), commits the sins of Ahab and the nations that preceded Israel in the land (21:2-3), Manasseh seals the fate of Judah, and they, like Israel, are taken into exile in 586 BCE (ch. 25).

The author/editor arranges the material to demonstrate the Lord's justice, which prevails despite human injustice. Even the often exemplary David falls short in the important "matter of Uriah." Though offered life and prosperity (1 Kings 9:2-4; 11:38), neither kingdom practices Deuteronomic justice. The message of 1–2 Kings reiterates the call to live in the image of God by practicing justice in imitation of the Lord (Gen 1:27-28; 18:19; Deut 10:12-21). The structure of the report reinforces this call.

Theological Themes

To grasp the objective of Kings requires that the reader be alert to theological themes. These themes are essential building blocks for the message and purpose of the book.

Justice

Kings contrasts two opposed views of justice, the exercise of power, especially in the economic and political sphere (J. P. Walsh: 31) [Economics, p. 444]. The Lord's justice provides for and incorporates the marginalized, often identified as orphans, widows, and strangers. This is the primary measure of doing justice in 1–2 Kings. Justice is more than fair law enforcement or even providing for the marginalized. Justice is the generous way of Yahweh, contrasted with the grasping ways of the nations and their gods (2 Kings 17:24-41). In contrast, royal justice, the *way of the kings*, has the king amassing wealth and power at the expense of the populace, despite the law of the king limiting accumulation (Deut 17:14-20; 1 Sam 8:10-18) [*Law of the King, p. 456; Mišpaṭ, p. 461*].

Idolatry

Illicit idol worship on high places and in Baal temples characterizes evil kings and results in exile (2 Kings 17:21-23). More than cultic unfaithfulness, idolatry describes the royal ideology of royal (in)justice. The cult of Baal and other gods replaces egalitarian generosity with hierarchical social organization (the king represents the gods). Humans are reduced to pawns. Idolatry is the ideological base for royal accumulation of power, wealth, and human resources, including forced labor, military service, and large harems [*Idolatry, p. 449*].

Covenant

Deuteronomy, composed in the covenant form, presents the covenant stipulations (laws), blessings, and curses that become the language of 1–2 Kings. The covenant presents justice as the primary mandate for covenant people. Human behavior is rewarded with blessings or curses, depending on covenant faithfulness. Reformer kings renew covenant (2 Kings 11:17; 23:1-3), promising to be faithful to the Lord. The covenant offers life, anticipates exile, and promises return from exile for repentant people. The covenant promise transforms exile from a pessimistic and hopeless outcome to an invitation to renewal and repentance [*Covenant in Kings, p. 443*].

Provoking the Lord to Anger

Influenced by Deuteronomic theology, Kings unapologetically attributes imperial invasions and natural disasters to the Lord's wrath. This perspective recognizes Yahweh's sovereignty over history, including the powerful empires that attribute their conquests to their own deities. If it is the Lord's wrath that brings exile, Israel need not fear imperial deities. Further, if exile results from God's reaction to human injustice, human repentance and obedience promise life; human agency influences outcomes. Barton suggests that Kings is a liturgical confession of sin, acknowledging God's justice in sending Israel to exile (33). Modern readers find retribution theology troubling because it suggests that calamity comes as divine judgment because of sin. Some find helpful the notion that God's wrath is built into the cosmos and that injustice often ends in disaster. Other readers are unable to reconcile divine retribution with the God who in Jesus suffers with those crushed by injustice [Provoke the Lord to Anger, p. 470].

Kings and History

The books of Kings interpret Israel's past, specifically its engagement with other kingdoms from King Solomon in Jerusalem in about 960 BCE through to Jehoiachin's release from prison in Babylon in 562 BCE (2 Kings 25:37-40). Using the assumptions of ancient history writing, Kings examines the causes of present circumstances. Unlike modern history, Kings recognizes God as an active character in control of history. In God's covenant with Israel, God promised life in the land on the condition that God's people keep the covenant's call for justice. Military defeats and regime changes occur because kings and people provoke God's wrath by breaking covenant, following idols, and rejecting the Old Testament law.

History as Event

Political history focuses on events concerning nations and heads of state. Kings is structured with royal formulas that report the opening and closing of each king's reign, including information about the contemporary ruler in the other Israelite kingdom. King Solomon rules over a united Israel and Judah for about forty years (1 Kings 11:42; ca. 961–926 BCE). His son Rehoboam loses sovereignty over Israel when Solomon's supervisor of forced labor leads a rebellion against Solomon's policies (ca. 925 BCE). The northern kingdom of Israel features conspiracies, assassinations, and new rulers, with only two dynasties of four generations: the Omride dynasty (ca. 879–840) and the Jehuide dynasty (ca. 839–748). After the Assyrian conquest and Israel's exile (722 BCE), Judah continues, ruled by the house of David until its exile to Babylon (586 BCE). While an exact chronology is uncertain, for reference purposes this commentary follows that of Hayes and Hooker [Chronology, p. 439].

Judgments regarding biblical historicity are based on several factors, including archaeological finds. Archaeologists do not agree on how archaeological discoveries are associated with the story of Israel [Archaeology, p. 436]. Their analysis ranges across a spectrum from "minimalists" to "maximalists." Minimalists minimize the value of Scripture in determining facticity of events and find minimal archaeological evidence to support the biblical record. Maximalists maximize Scripture in recovering historicity and tend to identify artifacts that support the historical reliability of the Bible. The spectrum includes scholars who reject the extremes, holding to the basic historicity of the story line without necessarily accepting details in the biblical record. This text is written with sympathy for the judgment that "information regarding the historical integration of Judahite and even Israelite history is . . . generally reliable" and "recollection of foreign kings . . . is also accurate" (Halpern and Lemaire: 136).

One example illustrates judgments regarding historicity. Avraham Biran found a ninth-century BCE inscription referring to "the house of David" and the "king of Israel" at the ancient site of Dan. Maximalists saw evidence that David's kingdom was well known throughout Palestine, proving the historicity of the biblical text. Minimalists raised questions about that interpretation partly because missing letters from the inscription fragment needed to be supplied to arrive at the interpreters' conclusion. Based on both their differing interpretations and their presuppositions, they rejected the find as evidence regarding the David of the Bible. Though a middle-of-the-road approach may prevail, archaeological finds in themselves are insufficient to prove the historicity of the events described, much less to support the interpretation given to those events by the biblical narrative.

Typical of Hebrew narrative, the plot is often carried by dialogue attributed to the characters [Literary Criticism, p. 457]. Among the factors that increase verisimilitude (plausibility) is the story line, running uninterrupted for more than four centuries, with references to source material such as the Book of the Acts of Solomon (1 Kings 11:41), the Book of the Annals of the Kings of Judah (e.g., 14:29; 15:7, 23; 22:45) and of Israel (e.g., 14:19; 15:31; 16:5, 14). Chronological data presented in the opening and closing royal formulas of each king keep time in the story. Synchronistic data correlating reigns of the kings of Israel and Judah present problems explained by using overlapping reigns, coregencies of sons with fathers, and differences in the calculation of a king's first year (Wray Beal 2014: 42–45). One proposed dating system is presented in a table, but dates of reigns are not included in the body of this commentary [Chronology, p. 439].

History as Report

There is a difference between "history as event," driven by the actual events themselves, and "history as report," which is in the hands of the writer, who has control over what is included or excluded and the order in which the material is placed within the text. This distinction was noted by John in the last verse of his gospel: "But there are also many other things that Jesus did [events]; if every one of them were written down [reports], I suppose that the world itself could not contain the books that would be written" (21:25).

While Kings uses the historical context described in the previous section, "History as Event," the text itself is ancient history telling a narrative with such conventions as giving reasons for events, incorporating divine causes, and attributing military outcomes to divine intervention. This "history as report" selects material in line with its perspective and goals, particularly supporting the conclusion that the exile results from the endless idolatry of the people. One distinctive feature of Kings is the prophetic narrative featuring Elijah and Elisha (1 Kings 17–2 Kings 13). Unlike the parallel history of Chronicles, these stories often narrate events from a nonroyal perspective. Another distinguishing feature is that here the reports of Kings Solomon and Manasseh end in disgrace, in contrast to the apparently later interpretation of the Chronicler (Konkel 2016: 24).

History as Evaluation

As noted above, the understanding of history has changed over time. Unlike historiography of the ancient Near East—including Kings, which attributes political events and natural disasters to divine intervention—modern history writing limits analysis to natural causes. Both literary and historical analysis regard literature as reflecting the perspective of both its author and its reader. In this commentary we note that much of the report of Solomon's reign reads like promonarchic propaganda, with the kingdom established in the hand of Solomon (1 Kings 2:46); all Israel in awe of the king, because they perceived that the wisdom of God was in him, to execute justice (3:28); and Judah and Israel . . . ate, drank, and were happy (4:20). We suggest an against-the-grain reading of the pro-Solomonic texts, noting that a faithful reader would raise suspicion about much that the propagandist lauds, such as making a marriage alliance with Pharaoh (3:1), conscripting forced labor (5:13), and accumulating large numbers of horses and chariots (4:26-28; 10:26-29). Our reading of 1-2 Kings focuses on literary and theological issues, with occasional references to "history as event."

Kings and the New Testament

Kings plays an important role within the Bible as a whole [Kings in the Hebrew Canon, p. 453], including in the New Testament, so it is of relevance to contemporary Christians. Jesus fulfills the human vocation to do justice and thus reverses Israel's exile. Matthew introduces Jesus as the son of Abraham and the son of David. As Abraham's son, Jesus ends the exile and fulfills the human vocation (Matt 1:1-25; Gen 18:19). As David's son, Jesus is the new and faithful reformer king (Matt 1:23; fulfilling Isaiah's prophecy to Ahaz, the father of the reformer Hezekiah, Isa 7:14) [Wisdom in Kings, p. 484].

Deuteronomy guides Jesus against Satan's temptations in the wilderness (Matt 4:1-11; Luke 4:1-13). Citing Deuteronomy, Jesus rejects the imperial temptations for economic accumulation (stones to bread; Deut 8:3), idolatrous exercise of political power (worshiping the devil; 6:13), and sensationalistic compromise with popular culture (falling from the temple; 6:16). Though the return to Jerusalem had reversed the geographical exile, Israel remained in theological exile (Wright: 538). Israel had not realized the Deuteronomic promise of abundant life (Deut 30:5). Jesus reverses the exile by fulfilling the divine vocation.

Jesus announces the arrival of God's reign, a new kingdom that transforms the Israelite royal system (Matt 4:17). He cites Elijah (mentioned twenty-seven times in the Gospels) and Elisha to demonstrate that the year of the Lord's favor extends beyond ethnic boundaries (Luke 4:17-30). Jesus refers to prophets from 1–2 Kings to establish direction for his ministry.

In the Sermon on the Mount, Jesus inaugurates God's reign (Matt 5–7). He blesses those for whom God makes justice: the poor in spirit are the orphans, widows, and strangers (5:3; Deut 10:17-19). Jesus fulfills Torah and the Prophets (including 1–2 Kings) by doing justice (NT Greek translates the Hebrew words for righteousness and justice with the single term dikaiosynē; Matt 5:17-20). Jesus contrasts the worry associated with Solomonic royal justice with pursuit of God's righteous rule, which stores up treasure by giving alms (6:19-34). Jesus claims to be greater than Solomon and recalls the queen of Sheba, who reminds Solomon that God has placed him on the throne to do justice (12:38-42; 1 Kings 10:9).

Malachi predicts that the Lord will send the prophet Elijah to announce the day of the Lord (4:5). Jesus confirms that John is Elijah (Matt 11:14; 17:10-12; Mark 9:11-13), though John himself rejects the identification (John 1:21). Jesus' ministry leads some to speculate that Jesus is Elijah (Matt 16:14; Mark 6:15; 8:28; Luke 9:8, 19). Elijah is a forerunner of Jesus and thus a herald of salvation.

On the Mount of Transfiguration, Jesus meets Moses and Elijah (Matt 17:1-9; Mark 9:2-8; Luke 9:28-36), who represent the Law and the Prophets. God confirms that Jesus is the Beloved Son, who is fulfilling the human design. In his resurrection appearances, Jesus uses the Scriptures to interpret his ministry (Luke 24:27, 44-47). He fulfills God's call to humans to do justice. God has brought an end to exile through Jesus.

The letter of James encourages hearers to ask for wisdom, much as Solomon had done (1:5-8). James calls for hearers to practice justice by caring for orphans and widows (1:27). He teaches that godly wisdom yields a harvest of righteousness and peace (3:13-18). James uses Elijah to show that prayer is powerful and effective (5:16-18).

The Relevance of Kings Today

The text of Kings describes the final era in Israel's grand epic, which begins with creation in Genesis and is renewed in Deuteronomy with covenant stipulations for life in Canaan. Creation issues the vocational call to all humanity to represent God's purposes for justice and righteousness (Gen 1:28; 18:19). As the preacher who addresses Israel on the eve of entry into the land, Moses reissues the call, reminding the people of their history as strangers and calling for care of the marginalized (Deut 10:12-19). Never has this vocational call addressed a greater socioeconomic political crisis than the world faces today. Despite his dominating accumulation of wealth, power, and even wisdom, Solomon fails to practice divine justice and forfeits the united kingdom. Thereafter both kingdoms pursue the idolatry of self-determined unjust imperial ideologies that put self first, without regard for others.

The theology of Kings may appear problematic because of its teachings of retribution (reward and punishment) and the frequent reminder that human evil provokes divine wrath. This perspective recognizes both that human actions have real consequences and that God's sovereignty limits human injustice even by employing evil imperial powers to bring judgment [Theology of Exile, p. 479].

Political rulers are held accountable for policies of violent domination. Shedding innocent blood brings the downfall of both kingdoms, a descriptor that invites contemporary readers to a pro-life stance from cradle to grave. The universal scope of God's sovereignty rules out the politics of discrimination and calls for hospitality to the poor and to noncitizens. Jesus cites the actions of the prophets of Kings to extend the good news beyond national boundaries (1 Kings 17:7-21; 2 Kings 5; Luke 4:18-29). These prophets immerse themselves in impoverished communities to practice community development. The final kings of Judah are judged for building opulent residences but failing to practice justice as their reformer father King Josiah had done (2 Kings 22-25; Jer 22:16).

The writer of Kings makes use of texts that have the veneer of royal propaganda, but the careful reader discovers a less obvious critique of royal "justice." The contemporary reader is invited to consider how the subtlety might guide prophetic proclamation today. One problem in the text is the suggestion that God uses deceptive communication (1 Kings 13, 22; 2 Kings 3). The reader is reminded that God's purposes may be worked out in ways not limited by human morality.

Finally, 2 Kings 25:27-30 places Judah's king at the imperial dinner table—leaving the door to the future ajar. Read within the canonical context (Deut 4:25-31; 30:1-10), the ending reminds readers that God's political vocation does not promote, or depend on, political institutions or economic systems such as theocracy, monarchy, temple sacrifice, or even Torah observance. Practicing justice supersedes political systems and parties. Even exile does not eliminate hope. In every circumstance people of God practice godlike hospitality that extends beyond differences of nationality, race, gender, sexual orientation, and economic class. Since these same concerns, and a continuing lack of their actualization, are all too evident in today's world, Kings continues to offer relevant and even vital instruction for nations as well as individuals.

Our Approach

In this commentary we read 1-2 Kings while using various interpretive approaches. Within the biblical canon, 1-2 Kings explores distinct theological perspectives. Read as political history, the text illuminates competing sociological, political, and psychological forces. Literary approaches discover artistic design based on rhetoric, form, or reader response.

The factual narrative of Solomon's reign can be read from at least two perspectives. "Reading with the grain" views Solomon as blessed by God with wisdom, riches, honor, and peace. Judah and Israel flourish. Reading with the grain takes the royal report of Solomon (and perhaps such kings as Jehu and Josiah) at face value. In contrast to this sympathetic reading, we also suggest "reading against the grain" of the text to explore how power plays within the text advance powerful positions. Within the biblical canon, DtrH *[Kings in the Hebrew Canon: Kings in the Deuteronomistic History, p. 453]* traces human faithfulness to God's call to righteousness and justice *[Mišpaṭ, p. 461]*. The egalitarian Deuteronomic perspective reads against the grain of typical royal wisdom, criticizing the accumulation of power and possessions at others' expense. From this perspective, 1 Kings 3–10 is a propagandistic report of Solomon's court history that communicates to the far-flung regions of his empire.

Reading with the grain in 1 Kings 10:14-29 accepts the grandeur of Solomon without suspicion, but an against-the-grain reading notes that Solomon's wealth transgresses the law for the king (Deut 17:14-20) and anticipates the clearly anti-Solomonic evaluation in 1 Kings 11. Reading against the grain identifies subtle features that in some cases may be inserted by suspicious scribes seeking to undercut the royal perspective. Reading against the grain may also identify readings that deconstruct promonarchic material by noting literary and ideological inconsistencies. Using several of these approaches can inform one's interpretation, though some are more compatible than others [Reading Strategies: Reader-Response Criticism, p. 475].

The standard translation used for Scripture quotations in this commentary is the New Revised Standard Version. Translations of 1–2 Kings are italicized, including those of the author (AT); yet a simple change to present tense in the flow of this commentary may not be flagged. When English verse numbering varies from that of the Hebrew (MT), English versification is given.

Parts of the Commentary

Part 1: Solomon as King, 1 Kings 1:1–11:43

Part 2: The Divided Kingdom to Israel's Exile, 1 Kings 12:1–2 Kings 17:41

Part 3: The Southern Kingdom to Judah's Exile, 2 Kings 18:1–25:30

(See Contents in the front of the commentary and the Outline of 1–2 Kings in the back of the book.)

Part 1

Solomon as King

1 Kings 1:1–11:43

OVERVIEW

Ordinary holograms encode a three-dimensional image on a two-dimensional surface, creating a puzzle solved by staring intently into the surface image until the more profound image is perceived. The Solomon narrative can be interpreted like a hologram puzzle. The story of King Solomon's reign is bracketed by an introduction describing his rise to power and a conclusion recounting his loss of power (1:1–2:46; 11:14-43). On its surface the text portrays Solomon's reign as Israel's golden age, a time of peace and prosperity. With wisdom and wealth from the Lord (3:11-14), Solomon fulfills promises made to the ancestors, to Moses, Joshua, and David [Prophets: Prophetic Word, p. 469]. The story of Solomon's reign reads like propaganda disseminated throughout the kingdom to reassure a satisfied populace that they can "let the good times roll."

The narrative of Solomon's enthronement and consolidation of power (1 Kings 1–2) has been attributed to the hand of an author answering the question, Who will succeed David as king (2 Sam 9–1 Kings 2)? The provenance and purpose of the Succession Narrative, as the document has been identified, is debated. Because the narrative ends with Solomon in power, some have theorized a pro-Solomonic perspective. Because Solomon's rise to power includes dubious power plays and extreme violence, some detect an anti-Solomon origin. The exquisitely told tale of power and intrigue makes for fascinating reading.

The narrative of Solomon's reign (1 Kings 3:1–11:13) has a pro-Solomonic veneer, reading like contemporary propaganda written to glorify a powerful monarch. The story opens with a dream narrative claiming divine authority and blessing with untold wisdom (3:1-15), followed by a juridical tale demonstrating the use of wisdom in the defense of justice (3:16-28). Lists of officials, court details, and encyclopedic wisdom complete the first section of the story (4:1-34). The centerpiece of the reign is temple construction (5:1-9:25). Bracketed by reports of forced labor required for the building (5:1-18; 9:10-25), the temple dedication reports the prayer of Solomon, the longest speech attributed to any character in Kings and significant in its anticipation of exile from the land and the temple (8:1-66). In 1 Kings 10 Solomon's economic engine is detailed, including accumulation of wealth and a report of Solomon's role as an arms dealer. Though the narrative can be read as pro-Solomonic propaganda describing a glorious monarch, the subtle and persistent use of the word justice (mišpat) linked with repeated reports of violation of Deuteronomic Torah suggest a more suspicious view of Solomon. Whether the condemnation of Solomon reveals what has been suggested from the start of his reign or is a surprising turn, God's rejection of Solomon is unequivocal (11:1-13).

The denouement reveals that Solomon has faced adversaries (Heb. śaṭan) throughout his reign (contra his claim to Hiram in 5:4) and reports the prophetic oracle anticipating most of the kingdom being ripped from the house of David with the secession of the northern tribes and the coronation of Jeroboam (11:14-43).

The narrative reports clashing value systems. The term mišpat can be a neutral descriptor of power structures. ANE monarchs accumulate wealth, wisdom, power, and alliances to their own advantage—royal mišpat. The Deuteronomistic History follows the values of Deuteronomic theology and Yahwistic justice, where true mišpat is care for marginalized people [Kings in the Hebrew Canon, p. 453; Mišpat, p. 461].

1 Kings 1:1–2:46

The Kingdom Established in the Hands of Solomon

PREVIEW

Though Solomon is regarded as a man of peace, the book of Kings opens with violence that rivals the final scene of *The Godfather*. The question that moves the plot is who will take over the family business. David's family business is the throne of Israel and Judah. Like *The Godfather*, the Succession Narrative (SN) involves interfamily rivalries and intrafamily plots and assassinations. While David asserts divine sanction for his royal claims, SN narrates the pursuit of the throne by the power-hungry Davidic house (2 Sam 9–20; 1 Kings 1–2). David avows to be free of "bloodguilt," but the narrator reveals that murder and intrigue are never far from the king. In the end David encourages Solomon to be strong and to avenge his enemies.

First Kings 1–2 reads like an ancient historical document, written as "history for history's sake," perhaps by an eyewitness to present the factual record. Scholars postulate that SN originally existed as an independent literary document later incorporated into Joshua–Kings (Rost). The entertaining storytelling style of 1 Kings 1–2 differs significantly from 1 Kings 3–11, with its many artistically characterized actors, creative structure, use of direct speech and dialogue, impressively graphic description of events, suspense, humor, and irony (Fritz: 10; Seow: 22). The omniscient narrator (who for example knows Adonijah's motives in 1:5) reports the events of

1 Kings 1–2 without extensive evaluative comment. David himself, the royal officials, and the people support the *wise* Solomon, who accepts their freely offered acclamation and takes necessary measures to free the court of divisive opposition, to establish the kingdom in Solomon's power (2:9, 46).

Recognizing its distinct issues and style, SN offers the propagandistic perspective of the imperial author, who defends Solomon's legitimacy. As pro-Davidic and pro-Solomonic (and pro-Judahite) material, SN demonstrates that Solomon's older brothers Amnon, Absalom, and Adonijah have disqualified themselves from the throne and establishes Solomon as the legitimate king by virtue of God's blessing and David's oath. A variation on this view is that, though the Lord's hand was not visible in the human affairs of court, God's promise prevails despite David's (and Solomon's) transgressions. Conversely, SN may be read as anti-Davidic and anti-Solomonic but pro-northern, pro-Israelite literature defending the secession of the northern tribes of Israel by showing that the violence and immorality of David and Solomon have disqualified them. Though likely written from a pro-Solomonic perspective, the violent excess undercuts the very legitimacy that the text asserts and raises the question about how God's purpose can be discerned in the human machinations and intrigue (Bodner 2019: 4).

OUTLINE

Enthronement of Solomon, 1:1-53
Consolidation of Solomon's Kingdom, 2:1-46

EXPLANATORY NOTES

Enthronement of Solomon 1:1-53

1:1-4 David's Weakened Condition

First Kings 1 concludes the David narrative and recounts Solomon's enthronement. The power struggle for David's throne brims with collusion and intrigue. When David last appeared in SN, he was ruling over a kingdom reunited after civil war and governed by powerful officials (2 Sam 20). Kings opens with a royal crisis—the aged, weakened king no longer *knows*, a term that not only describes his sexual impotence but also implies diminished capacity (in 1 Kings 1:11, 18, 27, David no longer *knows* kingdom events). The nationwide search discovers the very beautiful Abishag from a hill city in Issachar, anticipating the return of Bathsheba to the SN. Abishag is to *stand before the king* as Bathsheba will do shortly (1:2, 28). She will *lie in [his] bosom* (1:1-2) as did the lamb in Nathan's parable, a metaphor for Bathsheba (2 Sam 12:3). The once-powerful David, who took Uriah's wife and life from him, is subject to his servants' manipulations. The narrative treats the virgin Abishag as a pawn in a patriarchal, monarchic society, without rights, and living only for royal comfort.

1:5-10 Adonijah's Initiative to Become King

David's failing strength opens the door to succession politics. Though Adonijah's actions could be read innocently, the narrative views him with suspicion, depicting him as a second Absalom (David's son who led a rebellion against his father's kingship, 2 Sam 15–19). David's oldest surviving son, Adonijah *exalts himself, saying,* "I, even I, will be king" (1 Kings 1:5 AT). He imitates Absalom by assembling an intimidating loyal military guard, including horses, chariots, and fifty footmen, a force reminiscent of David's Cherethite and Pelethite mercenaries (2 Sam 15:1; see 8:18; 20:7). Though seemingly listing characteristics that explain Adonijah's formidability as a contender for the throne, the narrative subtly disqualifies Adonijah (whose name means "my LORD is Yah[weh]"). Adonijah is *a very handsome man*; as if to reinforce the link, he was *born next after Absalom* (1 Kings 1:6). Absalom, "praised so much for his beauty" (2 Sam 14:25-27), proved ill-suited as a Davidic heir. Though the narrator describes David himself as "ruddy," with "beautiful eyes," and "handsome," God discourages using appearance to judge leadership potential and chooses young David, not Jesse's oldest son, Eliab (1 Sam 16:6-13; also contrast with the physically attractive but tragically failed Saul, 1 Sam 9:2; 10:23-24; 15:35).

With the politically weighty endorsement of the traditional power bloc from David's years in Hebron, Adonijah seems to have gained the advantage. Joab is the wily military man who has survived David's attempt to replace him (2 Sam 20:4-10), and Abiathar is of the ancient priestly family from Shiloh. In the end the support of Joab and Abiathar also proves to be negative, Joab for his violence in peacetime (David warns Solomon not to *let his gray head go down to Sheol in peace*, 1 Kings 2:6) and Abiathar because he is of Eli's ill-fated house (2:27; 1 Sam 3:14). Characteristics that superficially qualify Adonijah prove to be his undoing.

Taking another page from Absalom's playbook (2 Sam 15:1, 7-12), Adonijah invites the royal household and the royal officials of Judah to a sacrificial festival at En-rogel. (Ironically, Samuel used sacrifice as a ruse when he anointed David: 1 Sam 16. Saul's impatient, unsanctioned sacrifice resulted in his rejection as king: 1 Sam 13:8-15. En-rogel is associated with Absalom's uprising, 2 Sam 17:17-21.) As Adonijah's royal claim gains strength, the narrative focuses on the exclusion of Solomon and his allies (1 Kings 1:8, 10). This rival power bloc from David's years in Jerusalem includes the rival priest Zadok, the general Benaiah, the prophet Nathan, and David's personal mercenaries. The narrative emphasizes Adonijah's unbridled and secretive aspirations, good looks, proximity to Absalom in lineage and actions, and discredited allies.

1:11-27 Nathan's Plot

Nathan moves to block Adonijah's power grab with audacious back-room political maneuvers. As court prophet of King David, Nathan has demonstrated a knack for creative rhetoric in bringing unwelcome news to a ruthless ruler without losing his life (cf. 2 Sam 1:14-16; 4:9-12). In doing this, he fulfills one of the major political roles of a prophet: speaking truth to power (Brueggemann 2001a). Nathan, a central prophet, had communicated divine disapproval for temple building (but promised David a dynastic "house" in 2 Sam 7) [Prophets, p. 465]. Later he condemned David's murderous, adulterous, rapacious abuse of power (2 Sam 12). Nathan again proves his acumen in court intrigue (and defends Bathsheba's interests, as he had in 2 Sam, e.g., 12:25). He enlists an ally in Bathsheba by sharing with her court intelligence of an exaggerated report that Adonijah has already become king (1 Kings 1:11). Underscoring Adonijah's heritage as a son of one of Bathsheba's rival wives, Haggith, Nathan warns Bathsheba that the outcome will mean life or death for herself and Solomon (1:12). He scripts a message for Bathsheba, couched as a pair of questions that communicate urgency without suggesting that David has lost his mental faculties (1:13). Nathan reassures Bathsheba that he will interrupt the conversation to confirm the news (1:14).

Without a word, Bathsheba exercises her prerogative to enter the king's private quarters. The narrator draws attention to Bathsheba's precarious situation: David is very old (and powerless), and Abishag is *attending the king* (1:15; she lies in his bed but is unable to rouse him). Bathsheba, bowing and doing obeisance (1:16, 31), prompts the king to invite her to make a request. Bathsheba follows Nathan's basic strategy but elaborates on his script. She turns Nathan's humble questions into bold assertions (1:17-18): David had sworn an oath promising that Solomon would succeed him on the throne. (The oath is unreported elsewhere, a suspicious omission for so significant an act.) *Behold! Adonijah has become king, though you, my lord the king, do not know it* (AT; the interjection *Behold!* calls David to a new perspective, awareness of the world outside his bedroom) [*Literary Criticism, p. 457*]. Bathsheba repeats Nathan's exaggeration that Adonijah's festivities are tantamount to coronation. She addresses David as *My lord the king*, a designation she repeats three more times in 1:20-21 (the phrase is a Hebrew wordplay on *Adonijah has become king*; J. T. Walsh 1996: 13). The king does not *know* of Adonijah's actions, implying that the king has lost power (1:4, 11, 18; cf. 2 Sam 14:20). Bathsheba elaborates, including information that the two disfavored royal officials, Abiathar and Joab, are supporting the coup, but *your servant Solomon* is not, implying that he remains loyal to David (1:19). Bathsheba outlines the plan for David to exert his power since *all Israel* is watching for David's succession orders, implying a threat to national unity (1:20). She concludes by reminding David what is at stake for herself and Solomon (1:21; cf. 1:12: *life*).

According to plan, Nathan interrupts Bathsheba, bowing his face to the ground in submission to David's sovereignty (1:22-23). Using the rhetorical reserve he had counseled for Bathsheba, Nathan addresses the king formally and politely. Nathan presents his intelligence report as a question, asking if David has appointed Adonijah king (1:24). His detailed message confirms Bathsheba's claims about Adonijah's actions, the guest list, and the recognition of Adonijah's kingship; he names some omitted from Adonijah's party: Nathan himself (*your servant*), Zadok, Benaiah, and *your servant Solomon* (1:25-26). Nathan concludes his speech with another question suggesting that nothing could happen in his court without David's knowledge and permission (1:27). Though Adonijah may simply be building support for eventual kingship, Nathan convinces David that Adonijah has been brazen (or foolish) enough to claim David's throne but that his officials remain loyal to David.

1:28-40 David's Initiative

The "act" of Solomon's enthronement unfolds in three "scenes." In scene 1, David summons Bathsheba and swears to her that he will fulfill his earlier oath to place Solomon on the throne, and Bathsheba responds with a prayer wish (1:28-31). In scene 2, David summons the three members of his inner court and instructs them to enthrone Solomon, and General Benaiah affirms the action with a prayer wish for Solomon's success (1:32-37). Scene 3 confirms the compliance of the royal court and the support of *all the people* (1:38-40).

David asserts control, conceding none of the weakness portrayed above (1:28-31). David summons Bathsheba (who *stands before the king* in a position of subservience) and swears by *the LORD, . . . who has saved my life from every adversity*, that on this very day Solomon will succeed him as king (1:28-30). Just as David's original promise may have been private pillow talk with Bathsheba, so David's oath is to Bathsheba alone (Provan 1995: 26). Left unsettled is the question whether years earlier David had made the oath that Bathsheba help him "remember," or whether he is the easily deceived senile old man (Seow: 19) who responds on cue, dissembling to avoid seeming out of touch with reality, as he had in 1:1-4. Bathsheba responds by bowing and prostrating herself and exclaiming, *May my lord King David live forever!*—a wish for David's eternal dynasty (1:31; cf. 1:16, 22).

David summons Zadok (opposing his rival priest, Abiathar), Nathan (the Lord's prophet and the king's adviser), and Benaiah (commander of the king's private mercenary force). The wily old king, cagey survivor of earlier court intrigue, imposes his will on the succession process (1:32). David's strategy is airtight, brimming with the confidence of an unchallenged sovereign (1:33-35). He orders a full entourage of the servants of the *lord* (king); the military power of the armed guard is primary to David's scheme. David can offer the symbols of power that Solomon's rival cannot access: the royal mule and the public assembly point outside the city walls in the Kidron Valley, at Gihon Springs (previously mentioned only as one of the rivers of Eden: Gen 2:13; 2 Chron 32:30). David's plan incorporates the pomp of royal coronation, with both priest and prophet anointing the king. David orders that they blow the trumpet; proclaim, *Long live King Solomon!*; and march in procession to the palace, where

Solomon is to be seated on the throne. David assumes authority to appoint the son of his own choosing as *prince* of both *Israel* and *Judah* (an ancient honorific, 1 Sam 9:16; 10:1).

The narrative attributes unexpected authoritative vigor to David, who can summon court officials, offer detailed plans for a coronation ceremony, and resolve questions regarding his successor with simple fiat. Whereas earlier Saul (1 Sam 10:20-25) and David himself (2 Sam 5:1-5) required negotiations with the people to secure the throne (as will Solomon's son Rehoboam, 1 Kings 12), David has unquestioned authority to determine succession. The fact that only the inner court witnesses David's authorizing speeches raises questions. Is this court memory consistent with the facts? Does the formerly feeble David rise to the occasion? Or does the inner power bloc of Jebusite priesthood (suggested as Zadok's background), personal prophet/adviser, and commander of the king's bodyguard fabricate David's speeches to promote their favorite?

Only the military officer Benaiah speaks (1:36-37). His support of David's plan is conveyed in two prayer wishes, that *the LORD, the God of my lord the king, so ordain [David's plans]* (1:36) and that *the LORD . . . be with Solomon and make his throne greater than the throne of . . . King David* (1:37). Benaiah's speech confirms that David's mercenaries will support Solomon in the succession struggle.

Scene 3 translates David's palace plans into public action (1:38-40). The procession, including Solomon on the king's mule, proceeds to Gihon for the anointing ceremony. The entourage involves the three primary coconspirators, but no mention is made of additional servants of the king, clarifying that the essential personnel are the military. Zadok the priest, not Nathan, anoints Solomon, foreshadowing the absence of the prophetic voice in Solomon's court. *All the people* proclaim, *Long live King Solomon!*, fulfilling the palace plan. The coronation narrative concludes with a people's parade accompanied by pipes, great rejoicing, and so much noise that the earth quakes with the glory of the event.

1:41-53 Adonijah's Reaction

Adonijah's guests at En-rogel, less than half a mile from Gihon, hear the tumult of Solomon's coronation (1:41). Battle-hardened Joab wonders aloud about the trumpet blast but is interrupted by the arrival of a messenger, Jonathan, son of the priest Abiathar (1:42; Joab's trumpet blasts had signaled failed coup attempts earlier, 2 Sam 18:16; 20:22). Adonijah seeks reassurance. *"You are a mighty man, and you bring good news."* *"On the contrary!"* (this rare negative interjection, a'bal, is used only eleven times in the Bible). *"Our lord the king, David, has made Solomon king!"* (1:42-43 AT). Jonathan's detailed repetition of the coronation events reinforces the hopelessness of Adonijah's position: the names of the conspirators (conspicuously including the mercenary guard; 1:44), the signs of coronation protocol (royal mule, anointing, ascension to the throne, popular acclamation; 1:44-47), and David's prayer of blessing (1:48). Reinforcing the increasingly desperate situation facing Adonijah, three times in his report Jonathan interjects the word translated *moreover (gam;* 1:46 NIV; 1:47 NRSV; untranslated in 1:48). Adonijah's guests *tremble* and dissipate (1:49). Adonijah seeks sanctuary at the altar (1:50). News of Adonijah's request for clemency is reported immediately with both reporter and Adonijah referring to *King Solomon* (1:51). Solomon's response, his first action in the narrative, is noncommittal, conditioned on Adonijah's actions (1:52). Solomon *sends* (a typical verb associated with royal power; cf. 1:44) *[Send, p. 476]* for Adonijah, who prostrates himself before *King Solomon* (1:53). Solomon's curt order putting Adonijah under house arrest concludes the chapter.

The story is a lesson in realpolitik. The skillful storytelling demonstrates the thoughtful planning, wisdom, and favor of Solomon's inner circle even as it reveals "cunning, vindictiveness, pettiness, insecurity, and sheer dishonesty" (Seow: 34). The historical narrative unfolds with little explicit reference to God's actions, raising the key question about God's involvement in Solomon's succession. Devious political machinations to establish absolute power have often been justified on religious grounds. Even in "the dark realities of power," Nelson concludes, "the good news is that God is in charge, even of political intrigue. The political structures of this world are not running wild, outside of God's control. They too are part of God's rulership . . . (Rom. 13:1-7; I Peter 2:13-17)" (1987: 22).

Consolidation of Solomon's Kingdom 2:1-46

First Kings 1 tells the dramatic plot masterminded by Solomon's allies to coax David into throwing his weight behind Solomon. Adonijah and his allies lack the political skill to gain the throne while Solomon and his allies succeed. Although no blood was shed, the high-stakes gamble for power is not fully resolved.

In 1 Kings 2 the aftershock of the temblor in the city of David is worked out. David's last will and testament call Solomon to Torah faithfulness (2:1-4), with specific instructions about eliminating enemies (2:5-9). The first closing royal formula records David's death, summarizes his reign, and reports his burial (2:10-12). The rest of 1 Kings 2 narrates three assassinations and one sentence to internal exile. The death of Adonijah resolves the threat to Solomon's throne from his older brother (2:13-25). Adonijah's dangerous allies, Abiathar and Joab, are exiled or executed (2:26-35). The chapter concludes with David's vengeance on Shimei from the grave (2:36-46).

2:1-12 David's Last Words and Death

The aged David, roused to engineer Solomon's coronation in 1 Kings 1, gives his two-part farewell address (2:1-9; cf. Joshua in Josh 23; Samuel in 1 Sam 12:1-25) before his death notice concludes the unit (2:10-12).

Alter posits that, to counter David's call for vengeance in part 2 of David's farewell speech, DtrH inserts part 1 to present Torah theology, using the chain of verbal formulas characteristic of Deuteronomy (441) [Kings in the Hebrew Canon: Kings and Deuteronomy, p. 453]. Echoing the Lord's imperative to Joshua (Be strong, be courageous, 2:2; cf. Josh 1:6-9), David urges devotion to Torah. The Deuteronomic style employs parallel verbs (walk, keep, heed, walk) and nouns (charge, ways, statutes, commandments, ordinances, testimonies, law) to emphasize his charge. Walking in the ways of the LORD is repeated seven more times in the Solomon narrative (1 Kings 3–11). Ordinances (mišpaṭ pl., frequently meaning "justice") is a key to interpreting the Solomon narrative [Mišpaṭ, p. 461]. The written . . . law [Torah] of Moses (2:3) sets the standard for evaluating kings (Deut 17:14-20). In keeping the law, David promises Solomon, You . . . prosper in all that you do and wherever you turn (cf. Deut 29:9; Josh 1:7-8; 1 Sam 18:5, 14, 15, 30). Part 1 concludes with the Lord's conditional promise that if David's heirs take heed . . . to walk before me in faithfulness, they will rule Israel forever. The Lord has promised David unconditionally to "establish the throne of his kingdom forever" (2 Sam 7:11-16; 1 Kings 11:36; 15:4; 2 Kings 8:19); the condition has been interpreted as applying narrowly to rule over all Israel (including the Northern Kingdom; Hens-Piazza 2006: 24), forfeited because of Solomon's failure to keep the law (1 Kings 11:31-39). Human experience of the Lord's covenant depends on their faithful response (9:3-9). The tension between God's unconditional covenant and human rejection of covenant characterizes the narrative of Solomon's reign and 1–2 Kings [Covenant in Kings, p. 443].

In part 2, David's instructions shift from Torah observance to political hardball (2:5-9). David's initial instruction is Be strong (2:2;

the word also describes Pharaoh's hardness of heart, Exod 7:13). The call to vengeance is consistent with David's earlier characterization and is worthy of "a dying mafia capo" (Alter: 441). His double reference to Solomon's wisdom reinforces the characterization of Solomon as an autocratic imperial ruler (1 Kings 2:6, 9).

David advises Solomon to eliminate Joab because he has tarnished David's honor by treacherously murdering Abner (2 Sam 2:18-23; 3:26-27) and Amasa (*the blood of war on the belt around his waist, and on the sandals on his feet* recalls Amasa's death; see 1 Kings 2:5-6; 2 Sam 20:4, 8-12). Likewise, David instructs Solomon to deal loyally with Barzillai's heirs by offering them a royal pension in return for their loyalty (1 Kings 2:7; see 2 Sam 17:27-29; 19:31-40; Konkel 2006: 57). David advises Solomon to eliminate Shimei the Benjaminite, who cursed and assaulted him as he fled from Absalom, but whom David pardoned with an oath of protection (1 Kings 2:8-9; 2 Sam 16:5-13; 19:16-23). The text does not clarify whether David's motivation is revenge, fear of Shimei's curse, or threat of Benjaminite rebellion (like the one after Absalom's aborted coup, 2 Sam 20).

Twice David connects his expectation that Solomon will execute Joab and Shimei with his confidence in Solomon's *wisdom* (2:6, 9) [*Wisdom in Kings, p. 484*]. Royal wisdom requires ruthless courage. Egyptian royal wisdom empowers the king to neutralize adversaries and reward allies (Seow: 28). David calls on Solomon to exercise wisdom—and to remove *shalom* (*peace*) from Joab (2:6; this *šalom* echoes Abner's peace mission in 2 Sam 3:21-23 and Joab's greeting of Amasa in 20:9). The divine gift of wisdom "is shadowed at its origin by the violence which David attaches to it" (J. T. Walsh 1996: 44). Wray Beal characterizes it as "chilling" because it "contextualizes politically expedient murder in torah obedience" (2014: 75).

David's aversion to bloodguilt (and the need to avenge innocent blood) is a primary theme in 1-2 Samuel. There David himself, other characters, and the narrator take great pains to insist on David's innocence when he is implicated in violent death. David magnanimously admits responsibility for Doeg's slaughter of Abiathar's family (1 Sam 22:20-23) and humbly confesses guilt in the death of Uriah the Hittite (2 Sam 12:13); but otherwise he is exonerated in the deaths of Nabal (1 Sam 25:26-34), Saul and Jonathan (1 Sam 24, 26, 29, 31; 2 Sam 1), Abner (2 Sam 3:28-39), Ishbaal (2 Sam 4), Absalom (18:5, 33), Amasa (20:9-10), and the sons of Saul (21:1-14)—all events that benefited David. Some scholars propose that the text is composed to exonerate David from the many deaths where he is not only implicated but also guilty (Halpern: xv, 76; Whitelam: 105). David's final speech exonerates Solomon's murderous policies and establishes precedent for Solomon to claim that the deaths of Adonijah, Joab, and Shimei are justifiable collateral damage and, ironically, make David the responsible party (2:6-9). Solomon's threat of an infant's violent death in the verdict demonstrating Solomon's wisdom is characteristic of his rule (2 Kings 3:16-28).

The closing royal formula reports David's peaceful death, burial, and summary of tenure (2:10-11). David was king for a full generation of forty years, united the kingdoms of Judah and Israel, and established the Davidic dynasty. This text concludes the story of David and introduces Solomon's reign, noting that *his kingdom was firmly established* (2:12).

2:13-25 The Death of Adonijah

The drama of Solomon's accession to the throne of Israel concludes with four acts narrating Solomon's elimination of his opponents by death or exile. Act 1, the death of Adonijah, consists of two dialogues, with ensuing action. In the first exchange Adonijah requests that Bathsheba ask Solomon's permission for him to take Abishag as wife (2:13-18). In the second act, Bathsheba passes the request to Solomon, who reacts angrily (2:19-22). The story concludes with the execution of Solomon's oath to kill Adonijah (2:23-25). Though the plot is clear, the narrative leaves motivation for and rectitude of actions unresolved.

What motivates Adonijah to approach Bathsheba and request Abishag? Bathsheba's inquiry, *Do you come peaceably?*, suggests suspicion (2:13). The transparency of the narrative characterization of Adonijah (1:5, 42, 50) suggests that Adonijah's request is innocent and naive, made with shalom (2:13), reflective of the surprising turn of events (*all Israel had their eye on me to be king*, 2:15 AT), acquiescent (the kingdom *was [Solomon's] from the LORD*, 2:15), deferential (*please ask King Solomon*, 2:16), and reflective of his undisciplined presumptiveness (1:6). Because Adonijah knows that *King Solomon* has power to *kill . . . with the sword* and has demanded that he *[prove] to be a worthy man* (1:51-52), his actions may reveal an unrealistic, self-centered, and spoiled attempt to restore honor or may be a brazen, risky, desperate ploy to gain political leverage.

Solomon's reaction confirms his characterization as a shrewd, suspicious monarch unlikely to consult, compromise, or clarify motivations (1:51-53; 2:2, 6, 9). Solomon interprets Adonijah's request as a claim for the royal harem and play for the throne by a dangerous rival (*He is my elder brother,* 2:22) in league with incumbent officials (Abiathar and Joab; see 2 Sam 3:7; 16:22). Solomon claims that he rules with divine sanction (*the LORD . . . established me and placed me on the throne,* 2:24; cf. 2:45). Read together, the suspicious interpretation of Adonijah's request with the claim that his rule is the result of divine intervention reveals Solomon's insecurity. Whether Solomon uses Adonijah's inquiry as an unjustified pretext to exterminate a rival or astutely detects a clever threat to his rule, his violent reflex demonstrates imperial wisdom (2:5-9), not Torah obedience (2:1-4; Whitelam: 150–53).

Bathsheba's characterization is open to divergent readings. Her power as queen mother is reflected in Adonijah's approach (2:13-14) and Solomon's deference (2:19). She may be, as she appears, a woman seeking to reconcile brothers by arranging a marriage, as evidenced by her positive response to Adonijah's request and her presentation of the request to Solomon (2:18, 20-21). Against this reading is her earlier characterization as a skilled rhetorician with shrewd political acumen (1 Kings 1:15-21, 28-31). She may present Adonijah's request to Solomon with full knowledge that she is providing him with an excuse for disposing of a dangerous rival (thus Bathsheba's act may be evidence of her wisdom; Vasholz: 49). The narrator does not resolve the question (J. T. Walsh 1996: 54).

Solomon shows himself to be strong, hard-hearted, ruthless, dispatching his only sibling rival. Benaiah proves himself to be a willing accomplice. The queen mother Bathsheba helps her son secure the throne.

2:26-27 Abiathar's Banishment

The dominoes begin to fall for Adonijah's party. Adonijah's death exposes his supporters. Solomon's characterization as the *strong* and *wise* imperial ruler is reinforced in act 2, the banishment of Abiathar.

Solomon announces the judgment on Abiathar—exile to Anathoth, a village three miles northeast of Jerusalem (Jer 1:1). Solomon offers banishment as a lesser punishment than the deserved death sentence (Solomon calls him *a man of death,* AT). Solomon does not bring formal charges against Abiathar, whose support of Adonijah is a capital crime in Solomon's court. Two extenuating circumstances save Abiathar's life. He had carried the ark of the Lord for David and *shared in all the hardships* of David. The brief report identifies Abiathar's exile as fulfillment of God's judgment of Eli (1 Sam 2:27-36) [*Prophets: Prophetic Word, p. 469*].

2:28-35 Death of Joab

Act 3, Joab's execution, unfolds in two scenes: Joab's appeal for sanctuary (2:28-30) and his execution (2:31-34), followed by a report of administrative changes (2:35). The consummate battle-tested insider, Joab receives news of Adonijah's death (and Abiathar's banishment; 2:28). Apparently Joab is warned by those who have supported Adonijah and seeks asylum, hoping to negotiate conditional clemency as Adonijah has done (1:51-53). King Solomon's intelligence network alerts the king to Joab's appeal (as it has with Adonijah, 1:51). Solomon *sends* Benaiah (*send* typically indicates royal control; also in 1:44, 53; 2:25, 36, 42) [Send, p. 476] to execute Joab (2:29).

The first scene ends in a stalemate after Benaiah, reluctant to violate sanctuary, orders Joab in the name of the king to abandon the altar; Joab refuses, forcing Solomon to choose between violation of sanctuary and negotiation (2:30). In scene 2, Solomon reissues the order for Joab's execution. Solomon's defense of his order to kill Joab at the altar is that Joab had shed blood *without cause* (2:31; Exod 21:12-14 denies sanctuary for willful attacks). Solomon convinces Benaiah that the execution is necessary to remove bloodguilt from David's house because Joab has unjustly killed Abner and Amasa (2:31-33; see 2:5). The king argues that the blood will be on Joab and his descendants, resulting in the Lord's shalom for the throne of David. As David had done during his lifetime, Solomon seeks to exonerate himself from guilt for killing rivals whose death benefits him politically (Whitelam: 107, 154).

Solomon makes two political appointments, replacing the supporters of Adonijah eliminated by exile and assassination with his allies (2:35). Benaiah is appointed to lead the army in place of Joab. Zadok, the priest associated with the Jerusalem cult, replaces Abiathar, the traditionalist with roots in Shiloh (1 Sam 1:3).

2:36-46 Death of Shimei

First Kings 2:36-46 explains that Solomon is innocent in the death of Shimei, the fourth enemy of the king eliminated after he takes power. Sympathetic readings exonerate *wise* Solomon, laying culpability for execution and exile on the king's adversaries. Suspicious readings condemn Solomon as a ruthless ANE monarch who transgresses Torah.

In act 4, scene 1 (2:36-38), the king, exercising royal prerogative, *sends and summons Shimei* (see EN on 2:8-9 for David's interactions with Shimei). Solomon limits Shimei's travels, warning him, *Your blood shall be on your own head* (2:36-37). The conditions forbid crossing the Wadi Kidron, restricting the Benjaminite from contact with tribal allies in rebellion against Solomon (J. T. Walsh 1996: 60–61). Shimei agrees and complies for *many days* (2:38). Three years later, in scene 2 (2:39-46a), Shimei leaves Jerusalem to pursue escaped slaves in Gath (west of Jerusalem, opposite the forbidden crossing of the Wadi Kidron, 2:39-40). Alerted by his intelligence network, Solomon *sends and summons Shimei* and questions him regarding his parole violation (2:42-43).

Because Solomon mentions a previously unreported oath and ignores the qualification that Shimei has not transgressed the forbidden crossing of the Wadi Kidron, justice would allow Shimei to respond to Solomon's interrogation. Rather than permit a defense, Solomon plunges ahead, implicates Shimei in a previously pardoned transgression (evil that you did to my father David), places responsibility for judgment on the Lord (the Lord will bring back your evil on your own head), calls down divine blessing on himself (King Solomon shall be blessed, . . . established before the Lord forever), and exonerates himself (2:44-45). Solomon orders Benaiah to kill Shimei (2:46a). In all three executions Solomon claims to act with the Lord's authority or in a manner that places bloodguilt on the guilty or both (2:24, 32-33, 44-45).

The chapter concludes with the narrator's comment that the *kingdom was established in the hand [power] of Solomon* (2:46b; in contrast to *firmly established* in 2:12, before the three executions). Twice Solomon has referenced the Lord's promise to *establish* him on David's throne (2:24, 45). The narrative characterizes Solomon's actions as *wise* (2:6, 9), blaming Adonijah for his own destruction (according to Solomon; 2:23), depicting Abiathar's banishment as merciful (in Solomon's words; 2:26), justifying Joab's execution as expiation of bloodguilt rather than retribution for supporting Solomon's adversary (Solomon's speech; 2:32-33), and depicting Shimei's fate as his own doing (Solomon's double justification; 2:42-45).

The reader is invited to consider whether Solomon's vicious brutality was misguided and unnecessary (Bodner 2019: 50). Solomon's emotional reaction to Adonijah implies that his execution is an act of fear, using Adonijah's request as a convenient excuse to eliminate a rival. The "merciful" clemency of Abiathar's capital offense (supporting a political rival) is a smokescreen for vindictiveness. His motive in eliminating Joab is a perceived threat (2:22, 28). Solomon fails to justly permit Shimei to defend his actions and neglects recommended generosity to the sons of Barzillai (2:7; J. T. Walsh 1996: 66–68; Whitelam: 155).

THE TEXT IN BIBLICAL CONTEXT
Joshua and Solomon

DtrH presents Joshua, the servant of the Lord, as the prototypical royal ideal even though he is not a king. He makes a copy of the Torah covenant and faithfully obeys it rather than claiming any personal absolute authority (Josh 8:30-35; 24:29). David's commissioning of Solomon echoes Deuteronomy's call to faithfulness, mirroring Joshua's commissioning and making Joshua the standard by which Solomon will be evaluated (Deut 4:29, 40; 6:5; 8:6; 31:7-8; Josh 1:1-9). Joshua's paradigmatic character as a faithful disciple of Moses underscores Solomon's failure to follow Torah; instead Solomon follows in the footsteps of David by escalating violence.

Joshua takes the path outlined in the Torah, but Solomon rejects Torah (Deut 17:14-20) [*Law of the King, p. 456*]. Joshua is commissioned by Moses and the people (Num 27:12-13; Josh 1:12-18); Solomon seizes power and is acclaimed king by a crowd of mercenaries. When Joshua defeats Jericho, he refuses to enrich himself with the spoils (Josh 6:24). Solomon extorts his empire (1 Kings 4:21; 9:20-22) and Israel (1 Kings 4:27-28) for personal advantage. When Joshua defeats a powerful foe, he hamstrings the horses and burns the chariots (Josh 11:9). Solomon accumulates war machinery (1 Kings 4:26-28; 10:26).

Solomon receives the charge given Joshua in Joshua 1:6: *Be strong, be courageous, and keep . . . the law* (1 Kings 2:2-3). Joshua reads the Torah to the people (Josh 8:34-35). There is no mention of Solomon's reading Torah. Solomon does not explicitly reject Joshua's example, but evidence is lacking that Solomon becomes a political leader who exercises power as Joshua does. Most of Solomon's successors will also fall short of this standard.

Peaceful and Violent Transitions of Leadership

Leadership transition unsettles the status quo. Joshua's peaceful succession is the exception. More typical is Abimelech's slaughter of his seventy brothers as he installs himself as king (Judg 9). Though the people reject Samuel's succession plan involving his sons, Saul takes power without shedding Israelite blood, extending mercy even to those *worthless fellows* who had questioned Saul's leadership (1 Sam 10:27; 11:12-13). Though David insists that he is innocent of bloodshed, many casualties precede David's kingship: Saul, Jonathan, and the messenger who reported their deaths (2 Sam 1); Abner (3:30); Ishbaal, son of Saul, and the men who claimed responsibility for his death (4:6-12); Saul's seven sons at Gibeon (21:1-14). Jeroboam becomes king of Israel without bloodshed, though Israel earlier assassinated the forced-labor official (1 Kings 12:18). Succession in Judah is typically a relatively peaceful transition from father to son, in contrast to Israel, where dynasties were rare and conspirators often assassinated the king's heir and eliminated his entire family, as Baasha did to Nadab and the *house of Jeroboam* (1 Kings 15:28-29). The contrast between succession in Judah and Israel is particularly remarkable with Jehu's massacre of the house of Ahab (2 Kings 9–10). This can be compared to Jehoiada's coup restoring Jehoash, with only the deaths of Ahab's daughter Athaliah (see comment on 2 Kings 8:26) and the priest of Baal (2 Kings 11:13-20). Violent transitions are typical in Israel but more exceptional in Judah.

THE TEXT IN THE LIFE OF THE CHURCH

Impugned Motives

Solomon's analysis of the motives for Adonijah's request of Abishag as wife may have been accurate, but it was fatal for his brother. Rarely is the result as dramatic as in the assassination of Adonijah, but impugning evil motives behind another's actions can lead to devastating results. Just as Solomon's assumption that he understood what motivated Adonijah led him to preemptive action, so too failure to explore others' aims can result in misunderstanding and fractured relationships. Clarifying what moves others to act can reduce the chances of falsely assigning bad motives to them. Simple communication exercises can reduce misunderstanding. A confessional approach can disarm and clarify. For example, I can explore things with my wife before assuming the worst. I might say, "When you take over a household chore that you had asked me to complete, I feel insecure because I am afraid I'm not meeting your expectations." Her response might reassure me that she had meant to lighten my load, not to correct my unsatisfactory performance; or it might lead me to better understand her expectations. This simple form helps avoid conflict when we take time to use it. Owning feelings and identifying concerns can reduce anxiety and create better communication. Perhaps Solomon's analysis of Adonijah's motives was accurate, but if Adonijah's intentions had been innocent, much bloodshed would have been avoided by testing assumptions before acting.

"Be Strong, Be Courageous"

David's last words give Solomon three direct commands: *Be strong, be courageous, and keep the charge of the LORD your God* (1 Kings 2:2-3). The term for *be strong* is also translated as "harden one's heart," as Pharaoh does. For leaders, the term could be a call to keep faith and move forward even when others are in despair. For disciples, the word fortifies those who grow weary of rejecting societal values in favor of kingdom values. When others insist that violence is necessary, the disciple is to be strong against temptation and in favor of peacemaking. When society pushes a lifestyle of selfish consumption, the disciple needs to be fortified to lead a simple life. *Be courageous* calls for one to live out one's humanity fully by rejecting worldly values and embracing Torah. *Keep the charge of the LORD your God* (1 Kings 2:3) refers to the *way of the LORD*. The Torah is not a set of rules for every situation but orientation to godly values. Keeping the law means practicing justice. Justice-keeping is a primary concern of the Solomon story. For leaders, justice has to do with an organizational structure that protects the powerless. For disciples, justice lives out God's egalitarian vision so that all community members have provision.

Gender Violence

The creation narrative offers an egalitarian worldview, rejecting hierarchies privileging patriarchal structures. God created humans in God's image without privileging a single gender. The word *helper* that describes Eve in Genesis 2 does not suggest inferiority; indeed, the term is most often used as a metaphor for God in the Hebrew Bible (Exod 18:4). Jesus includes women among his followers, giving them a prominent role in the Easter stories.

Tragically, patriarchal gender-exclusive hierarchy remains a powerful force in the church and in society. #MeToo is a contemporary liberation movement that confronts gender-based discrimination. It shares with Christians the repudiation of sexual violence in its many forms, including but not limited to date rape, inappropriate touching by those with power or privilege, and discrimination based on physical appearance. The Me Too movement decries the injustice of gender privilege that determines positions of leadership, responsibility, and creativity, a witness shared by faithful Christians. Such concerned people are particularly alert to injustice compounded when multiple forms of privilege increase vulnerability, as with the young, beautiful, and female peasant Shunammite from the hill country discovered when she was abducted and forced to *stand before* (1 Kings 1:2 AT) King David. The biblical text reports Abishag's story without comment, leaving it to the interpreter to identify and reject the patriarchal bias implicit in the tale.

1 Kings 3:1-28

Wise Beginnings

PREVIEW

In the English folktale "The Three Wishes," the woodsman foolishly uses his first wish for black pudding. Incensed, his wife wishes the pudding onto the end of his nose. When neither can remove the pudding from the nose, the woodsman ends up wishing the pudding from his nose and back to his plate. Young readers solve the problem by wishing for one thousand more wishes with their third wish. Solomon outdoes both the woodsman and our young reader friends by responding to God's offer to give anything he asks by requesting the skill to discern and do justice. God is so pleased with Solomon's choice that God does better than the folktale by offering Solomon—in addition to the requested wisdom—everything else he might have wanted, including wealth, long life, and honor, while instructing Solomon about what will bring him greatest success: Torah obedience.

OUTLINE

Foundations of Solomon's Reign, 3:1-15

    3:1-3 Introduction to the Reign of Solomon

    3:4-15 The Royal Dream

                First Report of Solomon's Sacrifices (3:4)

                God's Invitation to Solomon (3:5)

                Solomon's Prayer (3:6-9)

                God's Response (3:10-14)

                Second Report of Solomon's Sacrifices (3:15)

Solomon the Wise Judge, 3:16-28

EXPLANATORY NOTES
Foundations of Solomon's Reign 3:1-15

The dramatic narrative portrayal of the hard-nosed, bare-knuckle brawler who concludes that *the kingdom was established in the hand of Solomon* (1:1–2:46) gives way to the reports, lists, and accounting for the foundation of Solomon's reign that have little of the narrative tension and plot development of the first two chapters (J. T. Walsh 1996: 69). In 1 Kings 3, Solomon takes office humbly, deferentially, seeking the Lord's favor. Playing the part of an idealized Egyptian king (with the twist that loyalty to the Lord marks him as a true Israelite), Solomon seeks the way of his father, David. The foundation of Solomon's idealized reign consists of a series of brief introductory reports (3:1-3) and the story of the king's dream (3:4-15).

3:1-3 Introduction to the Reign of Solomon

The opening of the royal tale invites a double reading—reading with the grain in honoring the royal Solomon and reading against the grain in shaming Solomon for acting counter to the Deuteronomic ideal *[Reading Strategies, p. 473]*. Solomon's reign begins with the marriage alliance with Pharaoh (3:1), a report of popular cultic practices (3:2), and a summary of Solomon's relationship with the Lord (3:3).

Solomon's reign begins as it will end, with the report of a foreign marriage alliance, mentioned first as an indication of its importance to Solomon's standing (3:1a). Positively, Solomon claims equal status with Pharaoh and gains security by bringing Pharaoh's daughter into the city to prevent Pharaoh from causing trouble (Bodner 2019: 53). Negatively, becoming son-in-law to another makes one subservient and vulnerable to harmful influences (Deut 7:3-4 prohibits intermarriage because of ensuing compromises, as in 1 Kings 11:1-8). Solomon's architectural constructions project greatness and indicate commitment to the Lord and to the security of the people; but if the order of the building projects in 3:1b is indicative of Solomon's priorities, it indicates more concern for self-interest (*his own house* mentioned first) than for worshiping the Lord (in the *house of the LORD*) or protecting the people (*the wall around Jerusalem*; J. T. Walsh 1995: 486). Since the temple is not yet built, the people pursue the questionable practice of worship on the high places, permissible before cultic centralization in Jerusalem but condemned after temple dedication (Deut 12:2-7; 1 Sam 9:11-25; 10:5; 1 Kings 14:23-24; 15:14; etc.). In contrast, *Solomon loved the LORD, walking in the statutes of his father David* (3:3). Loving the Lord, the centerpiece of Deuteronomic piety, refers more to covenant loyalty than to emotional expression (Deut 5:9-10; 6:4-6; 10:12-22; 11:1). The phrase *David's statutes* (AT) is unparalleled in the Bible (elsewhere, *the LORD's statutes*, as in 1 Kings 2:3; 6:12). Since David constrains Solomon to walk in the Lord's statutes (2:3), it likely means to do what is right, but in the same context David's commands to Solomon were blood-thirsty and vindictive (2:5-9; cf. 15:5) *[Covenant in Kings, p. 443]*.

Solomon is an ideal successor to David, exercising unparalleled political power in international relations and embarking on an aggressive expansion of the capital and its temple. Despite the temporary difficulty of having to get along without a temple, Solomon lives in perfect accord with the statutes of David. The narrator emphasizes the interdependence of wisdom, prestige, and wealth, establishing Solomon's reign as magnificent (Knoppers 1993: 80). Reading against the grain alerts the reader to the possibility of Solomon's seduction to military and economic aggrandizement that affects social relations in a way contrary to Israel's covenant (Deut 17:14-20; Brueggemann 2000: 50) *[Egypt, p. 445]*.

3:4-15 The Royal Dream

The ostentatious demonstration of Solomon's love for the Lord—one *thousand burnt offerings!* (3:4)—is a magnificent display of Solomon's commitment to God. At the most important high place, the king himself sacrifices offerings burned to ashes (holocaust, keeping nothing for himself) a thousand times! How better to express one's love for the Lord?

God's appearance in a dream with promises (3:5) is similar in form to the ANE dream novella of royal inauguration typical of Egyptian coronations (*ANET* 449; Jones: 122). In the Bible, dreams are associated with God's promises to Abraham (Gen 15:12), Jacob (28:12), and Joseph (37:5, 9). This dream places Solomon on par with these great ancestors. God's offer is completely open: *Ask what I should give you* (1 Kings 3:5). Solomon's response is a model of faithful humility (3:6-9).

Solomon recalls the Lord's covenant loyalty to his father, David, acknowledging that David's obedient faithfulness to God was the proper human response (3:6). Solomon's place on the throne is a fit reward to his father and a gracious gift of God. Twice Solomon refers to God's *great and steadfast love*. David, says Solomon, walked *truly*, *righteously*, and *uprightly* in mutual covenant loyalty. Though appropriately humble, Solomon also appears in the text as a fitting royal figure. He continues in the line of the great David, emphasizing God's covenant relationship with the new king. Lest this be misread

as arrogance, Solomon emphasizes his own inexperience and dependence on God (3:7-8). His reference to himself as *only a little child* is
understood as polite deference. *Not know[ing] how to go out or come in*
refers to military inexperience (cf. Deut 28:6; 31:2; Josh 14:11; 1 Sam
18:13; 29:6; 2 Sam 5:2; 1 Kings 15:17) and possibly to Solomon's effective rule without recourse to war (Knoppers 1993: 82). Yet, reading
against the grain, perhaps this is disingenuous given his ruthless
slaughter in the previous chapter (J. T. Walsh 1996: 75, 77) and his
extensive chariot forces (4:26). Solomon humbly confesses that he is
in over his head as ruler of the great people chosen by God and
blessed by the covenant relationship that God has established.

After expressing his unworthiness, Solomon presents his
request, a petition that captures the essential qualities needed to
rule in a godly way (3:9). Rather than asking specifically for wisdom,
Solomon prays, *Give your servant a heart that listens* (AT, translating
šemaʿ; NEB: *a heart with skill to listen*; Cook: 40: *a hearing heart*; Bodner
2019: 57: *an obedient mind*). The heart—seat of virtue, reason, emotion, and will—is susceptible to being hardened (Exod 7:3, 13-14;
11:10) or made "fat" (Isa 6:10 RSV), dwelling on evil (Gen 6:5; 8:21),
or being "deceitful above all things" (Jer 17:9 RSV), but a hearing
heart is open and teachable (Isa 50:4; Rice: 34) [*All His Heart, p. 435*].
Solomon seeks the skills of a listening, attentive attitude. The first
to govern is the verbal form of *justice [Mišpaṭ, p. 461]*, to exercise
authority on behalf of the marginalized in the way that the Lord
governs (see Deut 10:17-19; the Hebrew verb *do justice* is used twice,
in 3:9 and in 3:28; the noun *justice*, used eighteen times in 1 Kings,
appears twice in 3:28 regarding Solomon's *justice* for two women).
As a humble child, Solomon requests a disposition oriented to doing
godly justice and discerning between good and evil (leaving no
room for compromise with evil).

God responds favorably to Solomon's prayer (3:10-14). After the
violence of 1 Kings 1–2, readers may wonder about God's approval.
David (1:48; 2:4), Solomon (2:24, 33, 45), and Adonijah (2:15) have
asserted that the Lord has established Solomon's reign, and Benaiah
(1:36-37) and the people (1:47) have blessed him in the Lord's name;
yet this is the first direct divine affirmation. God affirms Solomon's
prayer: *The word, this word that Solomon asked, was good in the LORD's
eyes* (3:10 AT; the opposite of God's evaluation of David's murder of
Uriah after committing adultery with his wife: "evil in his eyes,"
2 Sam 11:27 AT).

God promises to do what Solomon has requested—and more. The
Lord's response begins with rationale (3:11), makes a double promise

(3:12-13), and concludes with a conditional promise (3:14). While God's rationale focuses on Solomon's request, God also identifies three unspoken, unacceptable requests. An ANE sovereign, a king "like other nations" (1 Sam 8:5), would typically request long life, riches, and the death of his enemies, but Solomon's condensed request (just three words in Hebrew) is *discernment to hear justice* (3:11, in Cook: 41; NRSV: *understanding to discern what is right*). *Hearing justice* is the catchphrase that sums up God's mission statement for humanity at creation (McConville 2006: 33) and for Israel and its kings in 1–2 Kings. The great Shema calls on all God's people: "Hear, O Israel" (Deut 6:4-9). To hear is not only to understand but indeed to obey, to love, to walk with God. Covenant faithfulness is characterized by hearing, entering relationship with God, and keeping the law of God (Deut 6:4-6; 10:12-13). *Justice [Mišpaṭ, p. 461]* contrasts two alternative administrative value systems. Royal administrative justice develops an economic, political, and social system that funnels wealth to kings (1 Sam 8:9-18). Yahwistic, or Deuteronomic, justice protects the marginalized (Ps 72). God calls Solomon (and all kings and all Israel) to covenanted godly justice.

God continues with a double promise: *No one like you has been before you and no one like you shall arise after you* (3:12-13). First, God promises to do what Solomon asked: give him an open heart. In contrast to the innate wisdom (administrative skills) that David ascribes to Solomon (2:6, 9), the divine gift indicates divine presence (Provan 1995: 49; Hens-Piazza 2006: 39). Second, God promises Solomon even what he did not request: wealth and honor that exceed that of other kings during Solomon's lifetime. God's final promise of long life is conditioned on walking in the way of God and keeping (*guarding*) God's law and command (cf. Deut 30:15-20). This promise is hopeful, expecting that it will be fulfilled by both covenant partners. The conditional statement reminds the reader that king and people are bound together in the Torah covenant instituted through Moses and reiterated by DtrH in Samuel's retirement speech (1 Sam 12:14-15) *[Kings in the Hebrew Canon: Kings and Deuteronomy p. 453]*.

In response to God's gracious self-revelation, Solomon returns to Jerusalem to *stand before the ark of the covenant* (the posture of a loyal servant before his lord; see EN on 2 Kings 5), offering burnt offerings (indicative of total commitment), shalom offerings (celebrative of covenant relationship), and a feast for all his servants (3:15). In God's presence and in response to God's promises, Solomon's servants feast with the king, much like the elders of Israel and Moses celebrating the Sinai covenant (Exod 24:9-11). Though the Lord is pleased with Solomon's request, neither the Lord nor the narrator makes the claim that Solomon and Benaiah do, that Solomon's accession to the throne is because of the Lord's work. Solomon's return from formerly pagan high places to the ark of the covenant in Jerusalem is his first wise act (Hens-Piazza 2006: 40).

The positive reading of the dream is confirmed by God's approval of Solomon's request (3:10), but narrative gaps suggest a more negative evaluation [Reading Strategies: Reading against the Grain, p. 475]. The narrative opens with an extravagant cultic event on the chief high place. One thousand choice animals are burned to a crisp, ostensibly to indicate full allegiance to God. Because the text lacks any indication that Solomon shared David's reticence to offer anything without cost to himself (2 Sam 24:24), the sacrifices are plausibly the expropriated livestock of a needy populace. The second sacrifice suggests a preferred alternative to worship on the high places: Solomon offers sacrifices on the altar near the ark (3:15; Deut 12:2-7 specifies worship in the single place chosen by the Lord). Though the Lord offered Jacob a covenant in a dream (Gen 28), the dream-novella format is more reminiscent of a practice of the kings of "the nations" (1 Sam 8:5) than of God's communication with David (e.g., through the prophet in 2 Sam 7).

Although Solomon's humble prayer posture is highlighted above, his self-serving references to David's relationship with the Lord lead to the declaration You have made your servant king (1 Kings 3:7)—a claim made by Solomon yet never confirmed by the Lord or the narrator. The claim runs counter to Solomon's bloody, violent elimination of his rivals to secure kingship for himself. Since Solomon alone witnesses God's promises, God's offer of wealth and honor cannot be independently confirmed and may be interpreted as a self-serving apology for Solomon's vast wealth (10:23-27). More problematic, God offers Solomon wealth and honor, things prohibited by the law of the king (Deut 17:14-20). Because God gives good gifts, rather than interpreting the gift as a divine trap, the God-given wealth and honor could be divine provision meant to be shared with Solomon's needy constituents (15:10-8), obviating the need for Solomon's arms dealing (1 Kings 10:28-29), a violation of the prohibition against returning to Egypt (Deut 17:16). By substituting the gift of honor for the third unrequested gift, the death of his enemies (1 Kings 3:11), the narrator offers a subtle reminder of Solomon's bloody elimination of his enemies (1 Kings 2). Perhaps the offerings before the ark are an attempted corrective (3:15). Having been given the wisdom of God, Solomon offers sacrifices before God at the ark as a dutiful servant, or perhaps Solomon *stands before* the ark like a guilty person on trial. Having squandered the food resources of the people by burning one thousand animals whole, Solomon must account for his actions before God. *No one like [Solomon] has been before [him] and no one like [him] shall arise after [him]*—no one who so exploits wisdom to achieve wealth and power (3:12; 10:23-25) *[Wisdom in Kings, p. 484]*. Instead of learning his lesson, Solomon uses even more of the people's foodstuffs for a burnt offering and a feast for his retinue, the privileged few (3:15).

Solomon the Wise Judge 3:16-28

God has promised Solomon a heart of wisdom and discernment. The story about the judgment of the two women demonstrates Solomon's exercise of wisdom to do *justice* (*mišpaṭ*), fulfillment of God's mission by the king. The exquisitely told detective story/puzzle opens with two women standing before the throne (as Solomon *stood before the ark*, 3:15; Sternberg: 167). Readers share Solomon's perspective, informed of all that Solomon knows and facing the same gaps in information. The first woman presents her case, asserting that her living baby has been stolen and replaced by her rival's dead baby as she slept, then claiming the living child as her own (3:17-21). Her testimony seems valid until her rival gives testimony (3:22), creating an apparently insoluble riddle for both king and reader.

The reader shares the king's perspective as Solomon summarizes the issue (3:23; J. T. Walsh 2009: 49). When the king first demands a sword and orders the living baby to be divided, suspense builds because the reader no longer shares the king's perspective and does not understand his intent (3:24-25). Is the powerful king willing to butcher a baby before the throne? The mother of the living baby (the narrator informs the reader what the characters in the story do not know) cries out *because compassion for her son burned within her* (3:26; see also Gen 43:30; Lam 4:10; Hos 11:8) in contrast to her callous rival. *Compassion* shares the root of the word *womb* (indicative of mother love) and is characteristic of God's love for Israel (Hos 2:19; 11:8). Solomon's sword of judgment has produced its intended effect. He has solved the riddle. The king makes a clear proclamation, staying the sword (3:27). *All Israel hears the justice that the king judges, and they fear before the king because they see the wisdom of God is in him to do justice* (3:28 AT). By using the detective story genre, the narrator initially places the reader in Solomon's role, but Solomon's wise reversal of action places the reader, like Israel, in awe of Solomon (Sternberg: 169).

The narrative contains three riddles. Solomon solves the riddle of who is the mother of the living baby: the narrator reveals that the woman who burns with compassion is the mother, so Solomon says, *Give the baby to her and certainly do not kill him. She is the mother* (3:27 AT). The mystery of whether the first woman to present her case is the mother is unresolved (NRSV adds to the Hebrew by having the king say, *Give the first woman the living boy*). The report of justice produces a third mystery: left unresolved is whether the *fear of all Israel* (MT) is *awe* (wonder) at the king's wisdom (NRSV) or fear that the king practices justice at the edge of the sword.

The narrative makes the point that God has gifted the king with wisdom to do the most important task of a king: to do justice, accomplishing God's mission in Israel. The king provides justice for the least significant, the most vulnerable members of his kingdom. Long live the just and wise King Solomon! The third unresolved riddle is intensified by use of two words that sound almost the same in Hebrew, translated *stood in awe* and *perceived*. The words are commonly translated *fear* (*yareʾ*) and *see* (*raʾah*). Israel is well advised to be afraid and to keep watching to see whether the wisdom of God (an instrumental virtue) will be used to do kingly justice as practiced by the kings of the nations or to do godly justice to protect those on the margins *[Wisdom in Kings, p. 484]* (see also "Solomon and Wisdom" in TBC for 1 Kings 4).

THE TEXT IN BIBLICAL CONTEXT
Solomon and the Garden of Eden

The complex portrayal of Solomon presents him as an Adam figure who typifies fulfilled aspirations for a new Eden while also making him responsible for Israel's expulsion from the sanctuary-land (J. Davies 2011: 40). The temple itself will be an Eden-like sanctuary, with floral imagery from creation to highlight God's fecundity, a world re-created in the chaos of Israel's experience, a "creation story written in architecture" (Bodner 2019: 65; Fretheim 1999: 41; Mobley: 128). Solomon requests an understanding mind *to discern between good and evil* (1 Kings 3:9), echoing the description of the forbidden "tree of the knowledge of good and evil" (Gen 2:9, 17; 3:5). Like Adam and Eve, who are driven from the good garden after tasting of the tree, Solomon has his kingdom torn from him when he turns from the Lord's gifts of wisdom and long life by doing *evil in the sight of the LORD* (1 Kings 11:6, 9). Just as Adam blames Eve for his transgression and Eve blames the serpent (Gen 3:12-13), so the text places the blame for Solomon's unfaithfulness on his many wives

(1 Kings 11:1-8). Just as Adam and Eve are exiled from the garden, so Israel and Judah end in exile by following Solomon's rejection of the Lord's commands (11:32-33).

Created in the image of God to do justice, Solomon exercises imperial *dominion* (Heb. *radah*; 1 Kings 4:24; Gen 1:28). God warns that Eve's "desire" will be for her husband, and he will "rule" her. The narrator reports that Solomon's every "desire" (5:10; 9:11) was fulfilled as he *ruled* from the Euphrates to the border of Egypt (4:21). Like Adam, who names the animals (Gen 2:20), Solomon surpasses the world in his botanical and zoological wisdom (4:33). Like Adam (Gen 2:21) and even with his thousand wives, Solomon is without a suitable helper despite a God-directed deep sleep (1 Kings 3:5). Readers are left to wonder if God's gifts of wisdom and wealth and conditional promise of long life are tests like the forbidden Edenic tree (1 Kings 3:11-14).

Covenant: Conditional or Unconditional

Pleased with Solomon's request for a *hearing heart to do justice*, God promises Solomon *a discerning heart* and incomparable riches and honor, with no strings attached (3:13). God offers a conditional gift of *many days if* Solomon will *walk in my ways, keeping my statutes and my commandments* (3:14). Later, God makes commitments: *I will establish my promise with you . . . [and] will dwell among the children of Israel and will not forsake my people if [Solomon] will walk in my statutes, obey my ordinances, and keep all my commandments* (6:12-13, texts adapted) *[Covenant in Kings, p. 443]*.

After the temple dedication the Lord promises without condition to consecrate the temple (9:2-3), but conditional promises follow. God says, *As for you, if you will walk before me* (9:4), you will have an eternal dynasty (9:5). God warns of ruin and exile *if you do not keep my commandments and statutes* (9:6-9). The conditional (*if*) promises to Solomon (3:14; 6:12-13; 9:4-5) contrast with the unconditional covenant promises to make David's name great, to plant Israel in the land, and to give rest from enemies even when the son commits iniquity (2 Sam 7:14). This covenant is unconditional.

The conditional Mosaic covenant is often contrasted with the unconditional Davidic covenant. In the Mosaic covenant, God calls Israel to choose between life and death (Deut 30:15). "If you obey the commandments" (*mišpaṭ* pl.) *[Mišpaṭ, p. 461]*, I will "bless you in the land," God promises. "If your heart turns away," you (Israel) "will not live long in the land" (30:16-18). In the unconditional Abrahamic covenant, God promises to bless Abram, make him a great nation, bless all the earth through Abram, and give life in the land (Gen 12:2-3, 7). The promises are reiterated with a covenant ceremony (Gen 15, 17).

Some readers contrast the unconditional Abrahamic and Davidic covenants with the conditions given Moses and Solomon. Yet all God's promises are based on God's covenant faithfulness, independent of people's faithfulness. God will see to it that the promise is fulfilled despite human fickleness. At the same time, God's promises can be fully experienced only by faithful people. Rejecting covenant faithfulness removes people from the fullness of the promises. Ultimately it is true both that God is faithful and that human response matters. Covenants are both *conditional* and *unconditional*.

The human vocation to do justice within the creation and the Deuteronomic mandates inform our reading. First, God's call to live as God's image, to practice justice, remains unchanged by Adam and Eve's rebellion in the garden (Gen 1:27; 18:19). Second, God promises to restore a repentant people even if (after) they are exiled because of their failure to do justice (Deut 4:25-31; 30:1-5; 1 Kings 8:46-53). God calls humanity to practice justice, an invitation that extends to those who have failed to be covenant faithful.

No One like Him

The "no one like him" motif marks Solomon as a royal "type." God promises Solomon unparalleled wisdom (3:12), a gift that God intends for the practice of *justice* (3:28) but one that Solomon exploits to accumulate unparalleled wealth (10:20-25). Ahab, the second Solomon (Leithart: 119), uses his unparalleled military prowess and economic advantage to do more evil than any of his predecessors (16:30), worshiping Baal and subverting *justice* with his anti-Deuteronomic land practices (1 Kings 21). Hezekiah and Josiah are ideal royal types. Hezekiah, the first king to suppress the high places, *trusted the LORD so that there was no one like him among all the kings of Judah after him, or among those who were before him* (2 Kings 18:5). The greatest reforming king, Josiah, turned with all his heart to the Torah so that *before him there was no king like him, . . . nor did any like him arise after him* (23:25). Compared with Hezekiah, who is the exemplary king exhibiting trust, and Josiah, the exemplar in turning to the Torah, Solomon and his unparalleled wisdom without the requisite practice of justice fall short. He resembles Ahab, the most evil king in Kings.

THE TEXT IN THE LIFE OF THE CHURCH
Model Prayer Pattern

Solomon's prayer is a helpful model (3:6-9). He begins by reflecting on his heritage, centered on David, the servant of God, who walked in covenant faithfulness with God (3:6). The testimony to David's obedience is bracketed by the Lord's *steadfast love*. Prayer grows out of the intimacy of covenant faithfulness. Next, Solomon acknowledges his need as one who is insufficiently wise and experienced to govern, confessing his dependence on God (3:7-8). "The first requirement of leadership is to recognize the need for divine help and to seek it intentionally. It is important to face and acknowledge one's limitations and not to pretend to a competence that does not exist" (Rice: 36). Concluding with petition, Solomon prays to be equipped to practice justice (3:9). As God says of Israel's response on Sinai, if only Solomon "had such a mind as this to fear me and to keep all my commandments always" (Deut 5:29).

Prayer is enriched by a clear vision of our situation. Powerful prayer recognizes that God is able. Fervent prayer confesses dependence on God. Faithful prayer yields the heart to be changed, equipped, and used by God alone. See also Solomon's dedicatory prayer (1 Kings 8), Elijah's petitions (17:20-21; 18:36-37), and Hezekiah's request (2 Kings 19:14-19).

Petitionary Prayer Aims

Solomon's request is political—asking God to change national affairs by granting Israel a just king. Solomon's prayer recognizes that God's care for creation can be accomplished in the political realm and that God's people can participate with God in such a mission. In the 2015 Fuller Forum lectures, Walter Brueggemann admonished Christians to reject Solomonic royal justice in favor of Mosaic covenant justice. One respondent, John Goldingay, argued that it is very difficult for privileged Western Christians to pray for themselves. Goldingay's family prays each day for a different nation in the world where the cry for justice must go up. Prayer is effective political action, a powerful move, a faithful Christian discipline. Another respondent, Christena Cleveland, implored majority churches to practice solidarity with those of minority cultures who suffer social and political injustice in the U.S. At the forum, the audience responded favorably to issues of justice for the poor and marginalized and peace among nations (issues we associate with Anabaptism). Prayer is active obedience. Prayer works for justice. Petitionary prayer extends beyond immediate circles to appeal to God for needs worldwide.

Political Office and Involvement

The Bible instructs Christians to pray for imperial political leaders (1 Tim 2:1-2) but lacks specific instructions about participation in modern democracies. North American Mennonites have struggled to find consensus. Some do not participate in the political process of the kingdoms of this world, refusing to vote or run for political office. Others have been actively involved in partisan politics, served as elected officials, and engaged in political action. For sixteenth-century Anabaptists, the issue was clear. The sixth article of the Schleitheim Confession (1527) forbids serving as "magistrates." The prohibition is based on such rationale as Christ's example in refusing to be made king, the inevitable reliance on the sword to enforce policy, and allegiance to a Christian's heavenly citizenship. Contemporary Anabaptists do not forbid political involvement but are well advised to avoid the compromises anticipated by their religious forebears.

1 Kings 4:1-34

Solomon's Administration

PREVIEW

Babette's Feast narrates extravagant, generous love displayed with culinary artistry. A world-renowned Parisian chef living as a refugee and unpaid maid in rural Denmark spends a fortune on a meal for the last twelve members of a dying church. When Babette's hostess tearfully declares, "Now you will be poor the rest of your life," Babette replies, "An artist is never poor." The second hostess embraces Babette; her words conclude the story: "But this is not the end, Babette. In paradise you will be the great artist God meant you to be. Oh, how you will enchant the angels!"

In Scripture, food reveals much. From the fruit in the garden of Eden to the roasted lamb in Exodus, from the bread and cup of the upper room to the Lamb's banquet of the Apocalypse (Rev 19:9), eating habits give life or portend death. Solomon's menu displays the glories of his reign: abundance for the palace, but at what expense to the people?

In 1–2 Kings, God exercises sovereign control over the nations but remains hidden from view, invisible yet active in dreams, in the message of prophets, in events. With the literary device of promise and fulfillment, God's engagement is illustrated [*Prophets: Prophetic Word, p. 469*]. The lists and catalogs of 1 Kings 4 demonstrate that God's promises to Solomon of unparalleled wisdom, riches, and honor are being fulfilled (3:10-13). Ancient promises to Abraham of boundaries from Egypt to the Euphrates are fulfilled in Solomon's empire (Gen 15:18; 1 Kings 4:21, 24). Because God's hand remains hidden, events transpire in the realm of human history. Names and places lend the verisimilitude of contemporary court history. Read sympathetically, the report of Solomon's administrative structure celebrates a golden age, giving an inside view of Solomon's efficient bureaucracy. Solomon's unchallenged imperial grandeur impresses domestic and international audiences (J. T. Walsh 1996: 89). Careful reading suggests an alternative perspective. The double use of the word *justice* (*mišpaṭ*) brackets the description of Solomon's administration (*mišpaṭ* is the last word of 1 Kings 3:28 and of 4:28). *Mišpaṭ* contrasts the values of ANE royalty ("the ways of the king," 1 Sam 8:5, 9-18) with the justice of Yahweh (Deut 10:12-22; 17:14-20; Ps 72) [*Mišpaṭ, p. 461*]. What is apparently positive propaganda aggrandizing imperial power becomes an exposé of conspicuous consumption.

OUTLINE

Administrative Lists, 4:1-19
Catalog of Provisions, 4:20-28
Catalog of Solomon's Wisdom, 4:29-34

EXPLANATORY NOTES

Administrative Lists 4:1-19

Two lists, perhaps from royal archives or *the Book of the Acts of Solomon* (1 Kings 11:41), convey a well-organized, complex administrative structure. The social fabric of Israel is transformed from rural egalitarianism to society governed by an urban elite. *King Solomon* heads the two lists of officials, emphasizing his powerful position as *king over all Israel* (4:1). Both the *high officials* who make up the king's cabinet (4:2-6) and the *provincial officers* (4:7-19) are Solomon's, owing title and allegiance to their sovereign; they are in office to provide for the king and his household. Though the specific role of the officials is uncertain, the list suggests access to contemporary records of Solomon's court, situates Solomon positively among ANE imperial administrators, and indicates that the administrative justice of the king is handled efficiently (the lists suggest Egyptian administrative influence; Mettinger: 1).

If the order is a reliable guide, placing *the priest* (the definite article suggests *the high priest*, an overseer) at the head of the list indicates the significance of the office, importance fitting the central place of the temple. Azariah replaces his father, Zadok, who served with Abiathar until early in Solomon's reign (2:26-27, 35; 4:4). The exact roles of the secretaries and recorder are uncertain, though the need for royal correspondence and annalistic records would grow in an increasingly sophisticated administration (4:3). Benaiah, the army commander who was Solomon's "muscle" in the consolidation of his power, is not mentioned again, nor are any battles described during Solomon's reign, but the size of the chariot forces and extent of the empire suggest a central role for the military (1:36-37; 2:25, 29-34, 46; 4:21-28; 10:26). Nathan, prophet, friend, and counselor of David, has two sons in the list: Azariah, supervisor of the district officers; and Zabud, his father's successor as king's friend as well as priest (2 Sam 7:1-17; 12:1-14; 1 Kings 1:11-14, 22-27, 32-40, 45; 4:5, 7-19). The last name in the list is Adoniram, in charge of forced labor (2 Sam 20:24; 1 Kings 5:13-18; 9:15-22; 12:18). The list creates the impression that Solomon used his God-given wisdom to govern Israel with royal justice. From the Deuteronomic perspective the list suggests ruthless bureaucratic efficiency in exploitative military, taxation, and labor policies, punctuated by the last name, Adoniram, in charge of slave labor.

The second list names officers of administrative districts (4:7-19). To what extent the innovation replaces former tribal divisions is uncertain, but their purpose is clear: *provide provisions* (food) for the king's household (4:7 [twice], 27; Cogan 2001: 218–19). In 4:8-11, the names of the officials, rather than the districts, are primary, but the naming leaves gaps not evident in NIV and NRSV (e.g., *son of Hur* is *Ben-hur*, as if it were a name rather than a patronym or father's name). Two of the officials are Solomon's sons-in-law, raising suspicion of nepotism (4:11, 15). Also debated is the place of Judah (the official in charge of Judah is unnamed; the absence of the name of the land *Judah* in the MT [LXX supplies *Judah*] suggests that the tribe of David and Solomon was exempt from taxation; Wray Beal 2014: 96). The administrative structure is streamlined, efficient, reflective of royal wisdom (Davis 2002a: 46). The Deuteronomic justice perspective is suspicious of this wise efficiency. The officials are personal agents whose loyalty belongs to Solomon. *Officials* later act as overseers of forced labor (4:6-7, 27; 5:16; 9:23). What appears to be efficiency in the royal economy is imperial oppression when viewed from a Deuteronomic justice perspective. *Officials* are powerful agents who seize provisions from peasants as tithes and taxes, as Samuel foretold (1 Sam 8:9-18).

Catalog of Provisions 4:20-28

The description of Solomon's grandeur reaches its zenith in the hyperbolic, idyllic catalog summarizing life in Judah and Israel in the golden age of Solomon (4:20-28). The propagandistic value of this summary suggests its use during the reign of Solomon to show the glory of court life to his subjects, people in the hinterlands of Judah and Israel and beyond in Solomon's empire. The catalog opens in terms that match the fulfillment of the ancestral promises of progeny and land (4:20-21). The surfeit of the court is described (4:22-25). The defense system of horses and chariots rounds out the description (4:26-28).

Solomon's reign fulfills the Abrahamic promises (1 Kings 4:20-21; Gen 22:17; 32:12). *Judah and Israel* is inclusive, emphasizing unity, security, and absence of conflict. *Numerous as the sand by the sea* is linked to military might (Josh 11:4; Judg 7:12; 1 Sam 13:5; 2 Sam 17:11). To *eat and drink and be happy* celebrates prosperity in a land where the king's wisdom has devised an economic system ensuring provision that extends beyond the king's table. The boundaries of Solomon's domain, from the Euphrates River to the border of Egypt, match or exceed the grandest promises (Gen 15:18; Exod 23:31; Deut 11:24; Josh 1:4). The economic secret is that these nations bring Solomon *tribute* (contrast with Judg 3:15-18; 2 Kings 17:3-4, Israel's payment imposed by Assyria). As narrated, *tribute* payment appears to be given willingly, in recognition of Solomon's greatness (cf. 1 Kings 10:25).

The description of Solomon's abundance (4:22-25) begins with the king's daily table provision (4:22-23). Monthly, Solomon's court consumed 12,600 bushels of fine wheat flour and 25,200 bushels of coarse barley meal, four thousand cattle and sheep, as well as wild game and fowl. The list reemphasizes the source of the bounty: an imperial dominion peacefully supplies abundant stores (4:24). The first section of this description (4:20-25) concludes with a second reference to *Judah and Israel*, extending from northernmost Dan to southernmost Beer-sheba. The people live in shalom, each *under their own vines and fig trees.* This agricultural metaphor anticipates the blessings of the messianic era (Mic 4:4; Zech 3:10) though ominously more often a threat of judgment (Hos 2:12; Joel 1:7, 12; Amos 4:9; Hab 3:17; Brueggemann 1981: 195–98). The cosmic, eschatological language suggests that Solomon has introduced the shalom of the ultimate kingdom of God (or, alternatively, God's promise rather than Solomon's achievement, Bodner 2019: 62).

The final section itemizes horses and chariots, a measure of military might (4:26-28). Textual variants are reflected in the NIV (*four thousand stalls for* . . . *twelve thousand horses* follows LXX and 2 Chron 9:25) and NRSV (*forty thousand chariot stalls and twelve thousand horsemen* is from MT). The 3:1 ratio of horses to chariots holds in both counts, typical of the chariots drawn by two horses with a third in reserve. The report places Solomon among the greatest imperial rulers of the ancient world, emphasizing the efficiency of the district officers (Davis 2002a: 47) [*Archaeology: Solomon's Gates and Stables, p. 437*].

From the perspective of ANE royal administration, the catalog of provision for Solomon's court stakes the claim that Solomon is the greatest king of his era (1 Kings 4:20-28). His court consumes great quantities daily. His army is gigantic. From the Deuteronomic justice perspective, Solomon is indeed the greatest king among the nations and for this very reason is headed for judgment. Solomon's accumulation and consumption of resources at the expense of the people runs counter to the law of the king, a law prohibiting accumulation, particularly of horses (Deut 17:16).

The final word in the catalog anchors the issue regarding the two justice systems. Though camouflaged as *his charge* in NRSV and *quota* in NIV, the final word in the description is *mišpaṭ* (1 Kings 4:28). This catalog of court provisions ends with the term that concludes Solomon's verdict (3:28). Everything in this narrative reflects Solomonic *justice* [*Mišpaṭ, p. 461*].

Catalog of Solomon's Wisdom 4:29-34

Propaganda providing an accounting of Solomon's greatness is capped with praise for his wisdom. Solomon's wisdom is God's gift, fulfilling the promise of the dream (3:12-13) [*Prophets: Prophetic Word, p. 469*]. The lists demonstrate how God's promise of wisdom and riches is fulfilled (4:20-28); the fulfillment of God's promise for wisdom and honor concludes the chapter (4:29-34). Solomon is God's gift to Israel, the text declares.

As promised, *God gave Solomon very great wisdom, discernment, and breadth of understanding* (3:12; 4:29; 5:12). *Wisdom* generally is skill for living, used by Solomon for administration of a great empire (4:1-28) and as a world-renowned patron of learning, encyclopedic knowledge, literary art, and science (4:29-34) [*Wisdom in Kings, p. 484*]. Solomon's wisdom has been noted previously, in David's instructions to cut off enemies (2:6, 9), in the dream request and promise (3:9-13), and in Solomon's judicial verdict resolving a puzzling riddle (3:28). The terms used with *wisdom* further elucidate the gift (4:29). God gives Solomon *very great . . . discernment* (4:29). Solomon has asked for skill to *discern between good and evil*, and God has promised to give him ability *to hear justice* and *a heart that is wise and discerning* (3:9-12 AT). God also gives *breadth of understanding* (i.e., *wide heart* parallel to a *listening heart*, 3:9; *breadth*, used one hundred times for construction dimensions, indicates great capacity to be filled with large quantities of wisdom).

Like Israel's population, Solomon's wisdom is *as vast as the sand on the seashore* (4:20, 29). The greatness of Solomon's wisdom is measured by comparison, quantification, and reputation. The catalog compares Solomon favorably with the mysterious exemplary ancient sages (*east* is also translated *old*, perhaps referring to elders or to the Mesopotamian empires; *Ethan* is linked to Ps 89; *Heman* to Ps 88; named as a musician in 1 Chron 6:33; 15:17, 19; 16:41, 42; as the king's seer in 25:1-8; in 2:6, Ethan, Heman, Calcol, and Dada, a variation of Darda, are sons of Zerah) and to Egypt, the empire associated with Solomon (1 Kings 3:1). The rhetorical effect is that as Solomon's kingdom extends to surrounding nations, his wisdom is supreme in the world (4:24, 31). The catalog quantifies Solomon's proverbs and songs; a sample of these is found in the books of Proverbs and Song of Solomon and in Psalms 72 and 127 (1 Kings 4:32). Solomon also has an encyclopedic knowledge of nature, a seemingly unbounded range of biological learning (4:33). The superlative *all* summarizes Solomon's capacity (4:34). *People . . . from all the nations* and officials *from all the kings* come to hear wisdom from Solomon. His wisdom, wealth, and power are the wonder of the ancient world.

From a propagandistic, royal perspective, Solomon has God-given wisdom, which is further proof of his grandeur. From a Deuteronomic perspective, God gives wisdom to *discern justice* for the people, but Solomon turns it into a commodity to be used for royal advantage (3:9, 11). The lists of 1 Kings 4 aggrandize Solomon's splendor as God's gift but can serve as a warning about misappropriating God's good gifts. Lasine notes that Solomon is characterized by his skills, unlike his predecessors, for whom physical appearance is significant (2001: 130; Saul is handsome and tall, 1 Sam 9:2; David has beautiful eyes and is ruddy and handsome, 16:12).

THE TEXT IN BIBLICAL CONTEXT
Amos Criticizes Solomon

Granted that the law of the king prohibits the accumulation of silver, is it fair to argue that accumulation in and of itself is problematic (Deut 17:17)? Yes, laws of Jubilee return land to families, but isn't the issue land management rather than wealth redistribution (Lev

25:10, 13)? Isn't the key an attitude of generosity? Does God teach that wealth accumulation is outside God's will? After all, God did promise Solomon riches beyond comparison with other kings (1 Kings 3:13).

Reading Amos 6:1-8 with 1 Kings 4:20-28 reveals striking parallels. Amos 6 opens with a woe statement to those at ease and secure in the capital cities (6:1)—in contrast to the reported Pax Solomona, where all live under their own vines and fig trees (1 Kings 4:25). Amos challenges Israel to consider whether in fact they are more privileged than the surrounding nations (Amos 6:2); Solomon claims sovereignty (imperial authority) over kingdoms far and wide (1 Kings 4:21, 24). Amos accuses Israel of dependence on violence (Amos 6:3); Solomon boasts an army almost beyond calculations (1 Kings 4:26-28). Amos decries a luxury lifestyle with ivory furniture, rich fare, and musical improvisation (Amos 6:4-6); Solomon's furniture is ivory (1 Kings 10:18), his table overflows with the fatted calf (4:23), and he writes songs by the thousand (4:32). Amos warns his contemporaries that the self-indulgent, luxurious lifestyle (no mention of overt acts of injustice) will end in exile (Amos 6:7-8); God warns Solomon that failure to keep the law ends in exile (1 Kings 9:6-9).

Solomon and Wisdom

First Kings 4 addresses bureaucracy and wisdom. The chapter lists the technocrats with the wisdom skills to make the royal administrative justice system work efficiently (4:1-19). The chapter concludes with a catalog of the royal knowledge assembled by Solomon and recognized by the kings of the earth (4:29-34). As Brueggemann points out, "Knowledge is power," and "as the state seeks to have a monopoly on violence, so the state might also seek a monopoly on knowledge" (2005: 108). The prophet Jeremiah counters the Solomonic values of wisdom, might, and wealth with the covenantal triad of steadfast love, justice, and righteousness (Jer 9:23-24; Brueggemann 2013: 76). Jesus, the one greater than Solomon (Matt 12:42), grounds his wisdom in the greater righteousness that prioritizes blessing for the poor (5:3, 17-20) [Wisdom in Kings, p. 484]. "More than a sage, he is wisdom in person" (Gardner 206).

First Kings 4:29 uses the twin terms *wisdom* and *discernment* (3:9, 11-12). *Wisdom* and *discernment* appear together twice in Pharaoh's interaction with Joseph (Gen 41:33, 39). Joseph is the wise man whose knowledge qualifies him for highest office. With his special wisdom and strategic intelligence, Joseph saves Egypt and Israel at the price of citizens losing land ownership and entering slavery to the state of Egypt. Joseph, like Solomon, uses the morally neutral instrumental wisdom in concert with military might to exercise royal justice. Though wisdom is given by God to do justice, this reading of 1 Kings 4:29-34 shows how the gift can be distorted.

THE TEXT IN THE LIFE OF THE CHURCH
Wisdom of Solomon

Suderman deftly connects Old Testament wisdom with the challenge of the church's relations with secular knowledge. Pointing to the apparent dependence of Proverbs 22:17–24:22 on the Egyptian wisdom in the Instruction of Amenemope, Suderman invites readers to consider how church programs in world relief, justice work, and education influence and are informed by secular structures. Using case law regarding boundary stones, he shows that the biblical text enriches Egyptian wisdom by linking both Torah and wisdom to God the Redeemer (Exod 22:21; Deut 19:14, 27:17; Prov 22:28; 23:10-11). Unlike the trepidation of the church in its litigation with Galileo (early seventeenth century) and the 1925 Scopes Monkey Trial, biblical texts (e.g., Job 38–41; Prov 6:6-11; 30:24-31; 1 Kings 4:29-34) engage scientific observations about the physical world with robust confidence (Brueggemann 2005: 110, 118).

Although not without tension, the Renaissance development of the fine arts was led by artists and musicians who explored biblical themes in artful expressions to the glory of God. Rather than steeling the church against scientific discoveries that upset traditional views of the physical and biological universe, we do better to pursue learning with the boldness expressed with the inscription on the 1929 Mudd Hall of Philosophy at the University of Southern California: "Truth Shall Make You Free" (John 8:32).

Food Justice

Solomon's monopolization of available food resources in ancient Israel finds its parallel in the contemporary world. Though the world produces more than enough to feed the seven billion people on the planet, nearly one billion do not get the 1,800 or so daily calories required to avoid malnutrition. In the developing countries are more than 850 million hungry people. In the U.S. one in six face food insecurity, or about 50 million people, of whom 17 million are children. Nearly half the food produced is wasted. Roger Johnson, president of the National Farmers Union, an advocacy group for U.S. farmers, says, "In the undeveloped world, the waste happens before the food gets to people, from lack of roads and proper storage facilities, and the food rots. In the developed world, it's the staggering amount of food that's thrown out after it gets to our plates" (Koba). According to the Environmental Protection Agency, in 2017, almost forty-one million tons of food waste were generated in the U.S., with only 6.3 percent diverted from landfills and incinerators for composting.

Food distribution characterized early church life. Acts 2 describes distribution for those in need, going from house to house and breaking bread (2:43-47). An early church crisis was resolved when deacons were appointed to ensure that widows received food (6:1-6). Believers in Antioch gave relief to Judea (11:27-29). Paul quotes the Old Testament to encourage the church to feed enemies (Rom 12:20-21; quoting Prov 25:21-22; see also 2 Kings 6:20-23). Although not unique, one distinctive ministry of the believers church has been providing food for the hungry. Mennonite Central Committee was organized to provide food and food production equipment for starving sisters and brothers in Ukraine in 1920–25. MCC continues "to share God's love and compassion for all through relief, development, and peace in the name of Christ." In 2018 one hands-on project that involved more than thirty thousand volunteers provided nearly a million pounds of canned meat to needy persons, including people living in North Korea. Annually, MCC volunteers provide agricultural assistance and well-drilling expertise to help people feed themselves. MCC works in the national capitals of the U.S. and Canada to encourage government to redirect resources from weapons production to international aid. The contemporary church seeks to follow its first-century ancestors by providing for the hungry, rejecting the Solomonic system of accumulation, excess, and indulgence.

1 Kings 5:1-18

Solomon's Business with Hiram, King of Tyre

PREVIEW

International trade remains a vexing issue in the world economy. Low tariffs and free trade tend to benefit multinational corporations and wealthy consumers. Trade imbalances between nations are blamed for lost jobs and shrinking industries. Trade wars threaten financial markets. International trade deals like those described in 1 Kings 5 may have contributed to the impoverishment of Israelite peasants (Chaney 2014: 36–38). To provide Israelite oil and wheat in exchange for Phoenician lumber, the "command" economy required regionally specialized production, eliminating diversified production, which is best for hill-dwelling peasants farming small terraced plots. Trade made Solomon's building projects possible. The invisible result was increased risk for those most vulnerable. This text (5:1-18) and the concluding summary regarding trade with Hiram and forced labor (9:10-25) bracket the building reports at the center of the Solomonic narrative (6:1–9:9).

OUTLINE

Solomon's Proposal to Hiram, 5:1-6
Hiram's Response, 5:7-12
Solomon's Conscripted Labor, 5:13-18

EXPLANATORY NOTES

Solomon's Proposal to Hiram 5:1-6

King Hiram of Tyre, senior partner of an alliance with Israel, *sent his servants to Solomon* to renew diplomatic relations (5:1). Hiram was a *friend of David*, with economic relations, including Hiram's supply of cedar and labor for David's house, likely part of a mutually beneficial political alliance related to David's suppression of coastal Philistine power, giving Phoenician Tyre to the north freer access in international trade (2 Sam 5:11, 17-25). Hiram and Solomon renew the *treaty* (1 Kings 5:12).

Solomon *sent word to Hiram* (5:2; *send* is typical of royal prerogative) *[Send, p. 476]*. He explains his rationale for temple building and proposes a business transaction (5:3-6). Solomon's rationale *to build a house for the name of the* LORD *my God* includes that the Lord had put David's enemies *under . . . my feet* (AT; MT: *his feet*) and *given me rest on every side* (see Josh 21:43-45; 2 Sam 7:1, 11); and that the Lord had promised David, *Your son . . . shall build the house for my name* (1 Kings 5:3-5). Solomon proposes Israelite and Sidonian cooperation in felling cedars of Lebanon and that Hiram set his men's wages (5:6) *[House for the Name, p. 449]*.

Solomon's speech articulates deep piety, referring to *Yahweh* four times, the first identifying him as David's God (5:3) and the last two as *my* (Solomon's) God. *Rest on every side* is an ancient promise (Deut 25:19), fulfilled by Joshua (21:43-45) and David (2 Sam 7:1), but again promised to David (2 Sam 7:11) to be fulfilled with the peace and security of Solomon's imperial rule (*neither adversary nor misfortune*, 1 Kings 5:4, 12; cf. 4:21, 24). Solomon's temple is to honor *the name of the* LORD *my God*, fulfilling the mandate to create a place for the Lord's name to dwell. The expression *the name of the* LORD indicates Yahweh's ownership, support, or presence without limiting God's freedom to be present elsewhere (Deut 12:5, 11, 21; 14:23-24). Solomon interprets the Lord's statement to David (2 Sam 7:13) regarding a son who will *build the house* as a promise that his building project fulfills (1 Kings 5:5).

A Deuteronomic perspective on Solomon's proposal is more guarded. Though Moses calls for centralized worship, he makes no mention of a temple (Deut 12). Solomon reinterprets the rationale for the Lord's rejection of David's temple proposal. The Lord states a preference to be free to move among his people; Solomon refers to David's warfare (2 Sam 7:6-7; 1 Kings 5:3; cf. 1 Chron 22:8). Unlike David, who accepted his role as servant of the Lord, Solomon acts unilaterally without listening to the Lord's prophet. He acts as the Lord's patron by insisting on building a house for the Lord. The king who had asked for a heart skilled in listening has become the sovereign skilled in speaking (3:9). Solomon uses royal justice and wisdom rather than following the statutes of David. While kings of the ANE need temples to prove their muster, the Lord refuses this approach. By insisting on temple building, Solomon reverts to the royal wisdom rejected by the Lord in 2 Samuel 7.

Hiram's Response 5:7-12

Hiram *hears* Solomon's words, *rejoices greatly*, and *sends word* with details regarding terms of the transaction (5:7-9). Hiram's blessing fits the diplomatic context, reinforcing the characterization of Solomon as king of a great people, gifted by God with wisdom (5:7). Hiram *sends word* as a skilled negotiator, reiterating that he *has heard* the message Solomon *sent* (reinforcing Solomon's royal standing), repeating, and expertly revising Solomon's request, promising to fulfill *needs* in both *cedar* (as requested by Solomon) and *cypress* (or *fir*, a conifer used for flooring and doors as advised by Hiram; 6:15, 34). Hiram promises delivery service by Sidonians, who are excellent seafarers. Lastly, Hiram mentions payment by Solomon in general terms: provision of food for his *household*.

The negotiations follow ancient protocols characterized by diplomacy, politeness, and near obsequiousness (like Abraham's negotiations with the Hittites for a burial plot in Gen 23:10-16; Alter: 456; Master: 507). The report reveals final terms of negotiation (1 Kings 5:10-12). Hiram supplies Solomon's *every need* for lumber while Solomon *gives* (cf. Gen 23:11, 13) Hiram a twenty-year supply of wheat and oil (twice Solomon's annual wheat consumption, 1 Kings 4:22). The report concludes by lauding Solomon's negotiating skills, reasserting that *the LORD gave Solomon wisdom*, and by characterizing international relations with Tyre as peaceful (5:12).

Failing to recognize ANE negotiation protocols, interpreters argue either that Hiram cleverly renegotiates Solomon's original terms to his favor (J. T. Walsh 1996: 96–99) or that Solomon treats Hiram like a vassal and imposes favorable terms of his own (Provan 1995: 62–64; Wray Beal 2014: 104–8). While elsewhere Lebanon is treated like part of Solomon's dominion (implicitly in 4:21-24, explicitly in 9:19), the negotiations of 1 Kings 5:1-12 reveal that Solomon pays dearly for the lumber and labor of Lebanon but do not provide evidence that either Hiram or Solomon hoodwinked his trading partner. From a royal perspective, Solomon is an esteemed monarch who negotiates equitable terms for major construction that will allow him to project a powerful image in his empire. The Deuteronomic perspective raises provocative but unanswered questions about the wisdom and justice of Solomon's priorities in offering the produce of his people to procure luxurious lumber supplies. J. T. Walsh reads the statement regarding Solomon's wisdom after the negotiation with Hiram ironically: "Wisdom indeed!" (5:10-12) [*Wisdom in Kings*, p. 484]. Is Solomon acting wisely? What is the price of peace with Hiram? What is the cost of the trading agreement? Has the deal for luxury building materials benefited Israel, or is Tyre getting rich at Solomon's (Israel's) expense? Does Solomon's covenant with Tyre indicate shared values of autonomy, arrogance, self-indulgence, and indifference to Deuteronomic covenant values (Isa 23; Ezek 26–28; Bodner 2019: 64)? The text itself lets the reader address these unresolved questions, which resurface later in the story (9:10-14).

Solomon's Conscripted Labor 5:13-18

This paragraph reports on Solomon's conscripted labor force, the labor sent to Lebanon for lumber, the laborers in Israel quarrying stones, and a summary. Royal propaganda trumpets the efficiency of Solomon's labor force. The report maintains that *all* Israel cooperates under the leadership of Adoniram, first charged with forced labor by David (2 Sam 20:24; Israel rebels against Rehoboam's plan for forced labor, 1 Kings 12:18-19). In negotiation, Hiram had promised that his servants would deliver the timber to its Israelite destination (5:9), but in fact additional Israelite labor is required in Lebanon. The men work in shifts, one month in Lebanon and two months *at home*, either moving the timber from port to building site or *at home* on the land, producing foodstuffs necessary for the royal machinery in Lebanon and Jerusalem. The laborers and stonecutters in the Israelite hill country, with about one foreman for every fifty laborers, provide massive, costly stones, dressed for the temple (6:7). The work crew is the picture of efficiency, with international cooperation from Hiram and Gebal (a Phoenician port city later called Byblos) and the ready supply of Israelite labor (5:18). The report emphasizes Solomon's wisdom as negotiator and project manager. Solomon's wisdom (skill) and his piety (blessed by the Lord) are highly praiseworthy. The temple project, the centerpiece of his reign, is a monument to the glory of Solomon.

From a Deuteronomic perspective, the report offers a subtle but comprehensive critique of imperial Solomon. The project depends on *friendship* (5:2) or *treaty* (5:12) with Tyre. *Treaty* (*berit*) is translated *covenant* when applied to God's relationship of exclusive loyalty with Israel. As territory allocated to Asher but never conquered, Tyre is among the nations with whom Israel is forbidden to make a covenant (Exod 34:11-16; Josh 19:24-31). By entering the world of trade and commerce with Tyre, Solomon becomes susceptible to the autonomy, arrogance, and self-indulgence associated with indifference to covenant with the Lord (Isa 23; Ezek 26–28; Brueggemann 2000: 78). *Cedars of Lebanon* as emblems of pride, arrogance, and affluence point toward consumerism turned away from care for neighbors (Isa 2:13; 37:24; Jer 22:14-15; Zeph 2:14). Solomon's extensive reliance on *forced labor* intensifies the concern. Working in *forced labor* under *supervisors* is reminiscent of slavery under taskmasters and supervisors in Egypt (1 Kings 5:16; Exod 5:6). The combined loss of farm labor for those conscripted for work on the building projects and the enormous tax burden to provide for both royal houses are unsustainable and ruinous economically (Brueggemann 2000: 77–81) [*Covenant in Kings, p. 443*].

In claiming the Lord's gift of *rest on every side*, Solomon boasts that *there is neither adversary nor misfortune* (5:4). *Adversary* foreshadows the foes that the Lord raises against Solomon because of his illicit foreign alliances (11:1-4, 14, 23, 26). *Misfortune* (evil occurrence) translates two Hebrew words, also rendered *evil* [*Evil, p. 446*] and *blow* or *striking*; *blow* recalls Solomon's violent elimination of his adversaries as he assumed the throne, the only other occurrence of the term in 1–2 Kings (2:25, 29, 31, 32). First Kings 5 concludes with the phrase *to build the house*, leaving ambiguous whether the reference is to the temple or to Solomon's own house (J. Davies 2012: 118).

THE TEXT IN BIBLICAL CONTEXT
Forced Labor

"Forced labor" is the term describing Israel's slavery in the brickyards of Egypt (Exod 1:11). This forced labor was part of Egyptian government policy, thus imperial justice. Free labor made possible the supply cities and was Pharaoh's strategy to "deal shrewdly" with Israel and "to oppress them" (1:10-11).

Solomon's affinity with things Egyptian—from his wife, Pharaoh's daughter, to the chariots and horses imported from Egypt—extends to his economic system. The connection between Egyptian and Israelite slave labor may look wise to those with a royal lens, but to DtrH the parallel is sinister [*Kings in the Hebrew Canon: Kings in the*

Deuteronomistic History, p. 453]. Solomon fails to practice the justice laid out in Deuteronomy.

The report of Solomon's forced labor is revisited in 1 Kings 9:15-23. There the list of forced labor projects is more extensive. The second account corrects the impression left in 1 Kings 5 that all Israel was engaged in forced labor. According to 1 Kings 9, *all the people who were left* from the conquered-but-not-exterminated Canaanites, those *still left in the land, who were not of the people of Israel*—these were conscripted for slave labor. Of the Israelites, according to the "corrected edition" in 1 Kings 9, *Solomon made no slaves.* Joshua and Judges report putting the surviving Canaanites to forced labor, a merciful alternative to extermination (Josh 16:10; 17:13; Judg 1:28, 30, 33, 35; cf. Josh 9:27).

The second report presents a second problem. Not only does Solomon's economy depend on royal justice, but the narrator also reports an apparently acceptable division of the people between first-class citizens and others with questionable ancestry. Just as the tribute brought to feed Solomon's court appears to be justifiable if it comes from the surrounding nations, so slave labor appears to be acceptable if it doesn't touch first-class Israelites. Deuteronomy forbids moving aliens into second-class status (24:17). Like others on the margins, aliens are to be protected by those who wield administrative power (10:17-19).

THE TEXT IN THE LIFE OF THE CHURCH
Claiming the Lord's Endorsement

Solomon cites the words of the Lord to David to claim that the Lord has mandated temple building. He interprets the Lord's word to David as authorization to negotiate with Hiram for timber. Solomon reinterprets the Lord's prohibition of David building a house for God as a mandate for his own initiative.

We witness similar claims regarding God's will (though often unaware of our own tendencies to make such claims). When a transition is eased by quick house sales, we say, "The Lord is in it." On the other hand, difficulties may be attributed to opposition from the enemy. Recently a friend related that the message on a Nike T-shirt ("Just do it") was part of God's "mischievous" way of affirming a vocational change. Though perhaps innocent, these claims about following God's voice in pursuit of our own interests can become more sinister. Westerners, for example, often claim that a superior work ethic and a Christian culture have resulted in God's blessing. The late Rev. Fred Phelps of Topeka, Kansas, long blackened the eyes of Christians by protesting at military funerals with the message he claimed God had given: that Americans were dying in war because of U.S. policy favoring abortion and gay rights.

Some denominational leaders claim that their vision for the denomination is God's plan or God's leading. When those plans go awry, they claim that God is teaching them a lesson. Yet their mishandling of funds or resources and using those assets to fund their own plans created the problem in the first place. Not God.

We need, as Solomon did, a friend like the prophet Nathan. After initially encouraging David to do all that he had in his heart to do, Nathan returned to warn the king that the Lord had different priorities (2 Sam 7:4-17). Nathan communicated that God was David's patron, not the other way around. We treat God in a patronizing manner when we claim divine endorsement for human plans. The Ten Commandments forbid "taking the name of the LORD in vain" (Deut 5:11).

Human Trafficking

Solomon's empire depended on slave labor. Human trafficking as modern slavery continues to fuel the economy. Human trafficking accounts for an estimated $150 billion in annual profits worldwide. The International Labor Organization estimates that more than 20 million people are being trafficked, including 5.5 million children. Though human trafficking is thought to be a growth industry for criminal organizations, a complex set of cultural factors fuel the trade: these include poverty, unemployment, sexism, commercial demand for sex, and even globalization. Children, women, and men are subject to commercial sexual exploitation, slavery, organ removal, recruitment as soldiers, and begging. Although sex trade is a significant aspect of human trafficking, in 2010 the International Organization for Migration, the largest global provider of services to victims, reported assisting more victims of labor trafficking than those in the sex trade.

Local, national, and international agencies assist victims with safe havens, legal assistance, and policy advocacy. Mennonite Central Committee recognizes that while migration may be voluntary, it often is not. MCC partners with local churches and organizations to meet the needs of trafficking victims in relief, development, and advocating for justice while teaching trauma-healing skills. Awareness is the first step in moving toward solutions that help God's people avoid purchase of items manufactured by the forced labor of victims of human trafficking.

1 Kings 6:1–7:51

Solomon's Construction Projects

PREVIEW

Do you want to visit a castle or museum without leaving your living room? Virtual tours offer close-ups of ANE treasures now displayed in the British Museum in London and the Louvre in Paris. Every archaeological artifact mentioned in the commentary, even a virtual tour of the temple, is no further away than YouTube [*Archaeology*, *p. 436*]. And though the audiovisual dimension is missing, the detailed description in 1 Kings 6–7 provides a virtual tour of the temple, not an architectural plan.

First Kings 6–7 details the design, construction, and furnishings of the temple. The reader is overwhelmed by the building's exceptional size, glorious splendor (expensive materials and exquisite artistic designs), incomprehensible complexity, the fervor of the builder's piety, and the magnificent wealth and wisdom of the architect-builder. The textual tour makes grand claims about the glory of the builder and about his God.

At the center of the Solomon narrative (1 Kings 3–11), the report of the temple building (chs. 6–7) accounts for more than one-fifth of the Solomon story; if one includes related reports (5:1-18; 9:1-23) and the dedication (ch. 8), the total is half that story. Solomon's passion for the Lord as demonstrated in the temple-building account overshadows earlier questions and later criticism about Solomon's faithfulness (chs. 5–8; 9:10-23). Wisdom and wealth serve the greater purpose of the narrative, an exhibit of Solomon's love for the Lord.

The temple report is interrupted three times. Near the center of the report comes an excursus regarding the palace complex (7:1-12). Twice the Lord speaks to Solomon, once early in the building report (6:11-13) and again after the temple dedication (9:1-9), raising questions about temple building as an expression of faithfulness. The interruptions surface the defining tension between ethics and aesthetics, obedience and glory, Torah and temple, Israelite tradition and Canaanite practice, freedom and order. The interruptions remind the reader of the tension between royal administration featuring temple building and Deuteronomic justice emphasizing Torah faithfulness.

OUTLINE

Exterior Temple Structure, 6:1-10
Message of the Lord to Solomon, 6:11-13
Interior Temple Construction, 6:14-38
Palace Complex Construction, 7:1-12
Temple Furnishings, 7:13-51

EXPLANATORY NOTES

Exterior Temple Structure 6:1-10

The foundation of the temple narrative stands within the story of Israel in the land. The theological marker, *four hundred eightieth year after the Israelites came out of the land of Egypt*, places the temple construction at the midpoint between exodus and exile (6:1; Brueggemann 2000: 84). Because the exodus was to create a sanctuary of God's presence among God's people (Exod 15:17), the temple marks the completion of God's liberating act (J. Davies 2012: 120). After twelve generations of forty years each, the fullness of time for the twelve tribes and God's saving sovereignty over creation, history, and the nations is reflected in the temple construction (Wray Beal 2014: 119). If the temple marks the culmination of the exodus from slavery to Pharaoh, the report of forced labor for temple construction raises questions whether Solomon proves to be the new Moses or the new pharaoh (1 Kings 5:13-18; J. Davies 2012: 120).

The detailed description of the temple (and its construction), use of unfamiliar technical terms, and incomplete information from an architectural viewpoint—all these features suggest reading 1 Kings 6-7 as a tour, beginning as readers approach the temple. The textual guide points out the perfect symmetry of the building, ninety feet by thirty feet in area and forty-five feet high (6:2). From the east the guide leads to the outer court, or vestibule, fifteen feet deep running the width of the temple (6:3). The guide describes recessed windows (6:4), a three-storied supporting structure with stairwells and storage rooms that surround the temple (6:5-6), and the use of dressed stones precisely finished at the quarry so that the construction itself is done in hushed tones (6:7). The description of the building exterior concludes with reference to the use of cedar beams for roofing and the support structure (6:8-9). The guide ascribes grandeur to the temple by pointing out the symmetry, precision, complexity, solid structure, and exquisite aromatic wood of the *house that King Solomon built* (6:2). The theme, *he finished*, is introduced (6:9, 14, 38; 7:1, 40; 8:54; 9:1). The sevenfold use of the verb *finished* suggests a literary link with the seven days of creation (Gen 2:1-2; Exod 39:32; 40:33; see TBC).

Message of the Lord to Solomon 6:11-13

A word of the Lord to Solomon, *This house that you yourself are building*, interrupts the guided tour. The message springs a rhetorical trap. Reference to the house suggests that God will affirm the building. The divine word, a prophetic judgment speech in literary form, ignores the temple and focuses on Torah. Solomon intends temple construction to ensure the Lord's presence, but the Lord conditions his presence on three parallel, synonymous acts of covenant faithfulness: *If you will walk in my statutes, obey my ordinances, and keep all my commandments by walking in them* (cf. Deut 10:12-13) *[Covenant in Kings, p. 443]*. The human obligation is to keep the law of the Lord. The central term, *ordinances*, focuses God's message on doing justice *[Mišpaṭ, p. 461]*. The threefold condition is matched by a threefold promise. If Solomon does justice (*obeys . . . ordinances*), the Lord promises to *establish my promise with you, which I made to your father David* (a Davidic dynasty, the land for Israel, and long life for Solomon, 2 Sam 7:8-16; 1 Kings 3:11-14); to *dwell among the children of Israel* (cf. Exod 25:8; 29:45-46); *and not forsake my people Israel* (1 Kings 6:12-13). The promise is conditional (the Davidic promise in 2 Sam 7:15 is stated without conditions, but see 1 Kings 2:4; see also "Covenant: Conditional or Unconditional" in TBC for 1 Kings 3). This promise ties Israel's welfare to Solomon's obedience (1 Sam 12:14-15 links national fortunes to the king's actions). Ignoring the temple as a dwelling place, the Lord promises to *dwell among the children of Israel* (see 2 Sam 7:4-7, 10, where the Lord forbids temple building because the Lord has "moved about among all the people of Israel").

In sum, the Lord says, "This temple? Keep the law by doing justice, and I will dwell among you." The silence of the otherwise loquacious Solomon is conspicuous (Bodner 2019: 67).

Interior Temple Construction 6:14-38

The literary tour resumes with the reminder that *Solomon built the house, and finished it* (1 Kings 6:14; see EN on 6:9). The tour moves inside the temple to describe interior walls and floor (6:15-22). The stone is covered with cedar (walls and ceiling) and cypress (floor). The interior is divided between the *inner sanctuary*, or *most holy place* (thirty feet deep), and the rest of the building interior, the *nave* (NRSV) or *main hall* (NIV; forty-five feet). All interior wood is covered with *gold* (*gold* is repeated eighteen times in the temple tour, emphasizing its conspicuous extravagance). Gold chains separate the two inner chambers. *The most holy place* represents the theological viewpoint that the temple is the place where the divine realm intersects with earth. In the dark mystery of the most holy place, the Lord's holiness is most concentrated, most powerful, and most dangerous (Brueggemann 2000: 86). This is the first of seven times the temple construction-dedication uses the Hebrew term *holy* (6:16; 7:50, 51; 8:4, 6, 8, 10).

The tour describes the ornate interior of the temple (6:23-36). Two cherubim (mobile, powerful divine guardians) with wings spread across the inner sanctuary touch its outer walls. Elaborate wood carvings are overlaid with gold. Olivewood doors separate the inner sanctuary from the rest of the interior and the interior from the portico (6:31-32). The decoration, including carved gourds and flowers, creates the impression of a garden, styled as the restored garden of Eden, the perfect world where God meets restored humanity (J. Davies 2012: 127).

The temple tour is interrupted for the second time with a second chronological note (6:37–7:1), followed by a report of the palace complex construction (7:1-12). The temporal note reinforces the creation connection by pointing out that he *finished* (see 6:9; TBC) the house in *seven* years.

Palace Complex Construction 7:1-12

Although temple construction was finished in seven years, the additional building in the temple-palace complex was *finished* in thirteen more years (7:1). The chronological references provide a tour break. Outside the temple, the tour guide points to the five additional buildings of the palace complex. The House of the Forest of Lebanon, a building as tall as the temple but over four times the area, takes its name from the trunk-like cedar pillars supporting a branch-like roof (7:2-5; J. Davies 2012: 135). The Hall of Pillars is a quarter times larger than the temple area and has its own porch (7:6). In the Hall of Justice/Thrones the king is enthroned to do justice (7:7). Palaces house Solomon and Pharaoh's daughter (7:8). The description catalogs untold quantities of cedar, great costly stones for foundation and structure, and careful construction methods (7:9-12). The palace complex construction report is included without comment. The buildings showcase the regime's effective internal taxation systems and external tribute (4:1-28; Brueggemann 2000: 93).

A suspicious reading is critical of Solomon's construction [Reading Strategies, p. 473]. The verb finished is used for the fourth of seven times, suggesting that the palace is most important to Solomon, whose energies are divided, just as placing palace construction at the tour's midpoint divides the temple construction report. Though comparatively fewer details regarding the palace construction could suggest lesser importance, the size of the buildings and the nearly double length of time (thirteen years for the palace compared to seven years for the temple) suggest that the palace construction dwarfs that of the temple (Hens-Piazza 2006: 69–70). The temple construction is said to be finished (6:38), but the thirteen-year palace construction (7:1-12) interrupts the narrative report of the temple, suggesting that the temple furnishings and dedication (7:13–8:66) had to wait while Solomon tended to the palace. Pharaoh's daughter's palace, "an interruption within an interruption" (J. T. Walsh 1996: 68), points to Solomon's disastrous entanglements with foreign women (11:1-9). The third building of the palace complex (central in that it is the third of five buildings of the report) is the Hall of Justice, a reminder of the central priority of Israelite kings, to do justice (2:3; 3:9, 28, 6:12) [Mišpaṭ, p. 461].

Temple Furnishings 7:13-51

Solomon sends for Hiram of Tyre [Send, p. 476], not the previously mentioned king (5:1), but the son of a widow of Naphtali, trained by his father, an artisan from Tyre, and full of skill [wisdom, 4:29; 5:12], intelligence [discernment, 4:29], and knowledge in bronzework (7:13-14; Exod 35:31; Prov 1:5). Hiram makes two enormous bronze pillars (twenty-seven feet high and eighteen feet in circumference) to support the foyer roof (7:15-22). Crowned with capitals (adding more than seven feet to the pillars' height) adorned with lily latticework and two hundred pomegranates (representing the fruits of the restored Eden; J. Davies 2012: 140), the twin bronze pillars dominate the courtyard. Their names, *Jachin* ("he establishes") and *Boaz* ("in strength"), express hope that God will establish David's dynasty and Solomon's temple (Provan 1995: 72). Hiram casts additional bronze pieces for the *nave* (main hall): a bronze sea resting on twelve oxen, representing God's powerful control of chaos (7:23-26); ten elaborately decorated wheeled bronze stands, evidence of God's mobility (7:27-37); and ten bronze basins that rest on the stands and provide water for cultic functions (7:38-39). Hiram makes all the bronzework, including other bronze utensils necessary for cultic ritual. The bronze is so abundant that its weight was undetermined (7:40-47). Depicted as a sacred Edenic arbor, the temple interior offers worshipers a return to the garden to be renewed, re-created in pristine goodness (Mobley: 128).

Hiram does all the bronzework, while Solomon has someone else do the goldwork (7:48-50). When Solomon finishes the work (the Hebrew *šalam* echoes "shalom" and Solomon's name, *Shelomoh*), he places these items, along with the silver and gold that David had dedicated, in the temple treasuries (7:51).

The palace tour ends without commentary. Hiram's bicultural roots, intermingling of Canaanite statecraft and craftsmanship with Israelite covenantal tradition, may be an appropriate metaphor for the glory and dilemma presented by Solomon's temple (Brueggemann 2000: 96–97). The effect of the narratival tour is a sense of wonder at the extravagance of the description—precious stones, bronze beyond weighing, the oft-mentioned gold, and the overwhelming size and complexity of the project—all reflecting the glory of the builder. Solomon's wisdom is reflected in the glitter and glamor of this project. A suspicious reading of the extravagant glorification of imperial Solomon is suggested in several asides. The Lord's speech interrupts the tour with a promise of his presence conditioned on Solomon obeying *justice* (6:11-13). At the center of the tour, a report of the much larger and more numerous palatial structures is interjected (7:1-12). Identification of a Canaanite (Tyrian) artisan (and Canaanite building plans) and the palace for the harem introduce the foreign covenants with Pharaoh and others (7:8, 13-14). The extravagant expense in labor and materials is paid by imperial taxation. Holiness is not simply a theological construct but also sociological, controlling access to the *most holy place* in ways reflective of hierarchical social order (Brueggemann 2000: 85). Competing perspectives regarding the temple inform the temple dedication (1 Kings 8) and additional temple construction reports (1 Kings 9).

THE TEXT IN BIBLICAL CONTEXT
Finished the Work

Several literary motifs connect the temple building with strategic moments in the biblical story. Temple building begins in the 480th year after the exodus (= twelve generations, forty years each). The building takes seven years, suggesting the days of creation. The phrase *finished the work* occurs seven times in 1 Kings 3–11 (e.g., 9:1; cf. 8:54), another allusion to the seven days of creation.

Blenkinsopp refers to the phrase *finished the work* as the "conclusion formula," noting parallels with creation (Gen 2:2), tabernacle building (Exod 39:32, 43; 40:33), and land settlement (Josh 19:49, 51; Blenkinsopp: 280). For example, God "saw" what he had made, the heavens and the earth were "finished," and God "blessed" the seventh day (Gen 1:31; 2:1-3); in parallel, Moses "saw" the tabernacle construction, the tabernacle was "finished," and Moses "blessed" them (Exod 39:32, 43; 40:33). Blenkinsopp also notes parallels between creation (fill the "earth" and "subdue" it, Gen 1:28; God "finished" his work, 2:2) and Joshua's conquest (the "land lay subdued," Josh 18:1; they "finished" dividing the "land," 19:49, 51; Blenkinsopp: 290). We note that Moses "finished" writing the law (Deut 31:24), and he "finished" speaking all these words to all Israel (32:45). Blenkinsopp adds that the three-tiered structures in the design of Noah's ark, Solomon's temple, and the tabernacle (with its outer and inner courts and holiest place) correspond to creation of heavens, earth, and the waters under the earth (286).

The conclusion formula brackets significant epochs. "Finishing the work" of creation and "finishing the work" of the tabernacle frame covenants with Noah, Abraham, and Israel at Sinai. "Finishing the work" of writing Torah and "finishing the work" of the temple frame covenant renewal at Shechem and the Davidic covenant. Fretheim notes that the dedication of the tabernacle corresponds to the first day of creation (Exod 40:2, 17; as does the temple dedication, 1 Kings 8:2). Seven divine speeches in Exodus 25–31 correspond to the seven days of creation and to seven petitions in Solomon's temple prayer (1 Kings 8:31-53; Fretheim 1991: 269–71). *Finished the work* marks new stages in God's story with humanity: the earth, the tabernacle, the land, the temple. In each location God's human vocation to do justice supersedes human institutional limits.

The Temple in Old Testament Theology

While archaeologists seek evidence for Solomon's temple, the biblical text describes temple splendor. Ambivalent about the temple's role, the Old Testament's interest is not in archaeology but in how the temple fits God's relationship with Israel [Temple Theology, p. 477].

Prior to the tabernacle (Exod 25–40), the ancestors built altars as needed (Gen 12:7, 8; 13:4, 18; 26:25; 33:20; 35:1-7). Exodus records the Lord's instruction to build the tabernacle (Exod 25–31) and its construction (chs. 35–40). The tabernacle functions as a tent of meeting, as a tabernacle (dwelling place for God's glory), and as a sanctuary (holy place; Martens 2015: 105–7). Moses demands demolition of Canaanite high places, to be replaced by a single dwelling for the Lord's name (Deut 12) [House for the Name, p. 449]. Joshua prohibits offering sacrifice on a second altar (Josh 22:10-34) and leads covenant renewal at Shechem (24:25-26). After the chaos of Judges (21:25), the priest Eli tends the Lord's house with the ark of the covenant in Shiloh, a place for offering sacrifices and meeting God. When the Philistines capture the ark (1 Sam 4), the Shiloh shrine disappears.

David moves the ark of the covenant to Jerusalem (2 Sam 6:17-18; 1 Kings 3:15). The Lord rejects David's temple-building proposal because the Lord moves among Israel and the Lord will build a "house [dynasty]" for David (David is not the Lord's patron; 2 Sam 7:1-16; Eslinger: 18–19). The Lord predicts that David's son will "build a house for my name" (7:13; without clarifying whether this is a positive promise or a negative inevitability). David buys a threshing floor as a place for burnt offerings (24:18-25); the Chronicler takes this to be the location of the temple (1 Chron 22:1; chs. 22–29 recount David's extensive temple preparations) [Kings in the Hebrew Canon: Kings and Chronicles, p. 455].

Solomon reinterprets the Lord's prediction of a temple as a promise/mandate (1 Kings 5:5), but the Lord prioritizes Torah obedience over temple building (6:11-13; 9:1-9). The text of 1–2 Kings disapproves of the high places of Solomon (1 Kings 11:6-8), Jeroboam (13:1-3), and Judah (14:22-24) and approves of temple repair (2 Kings 12, 22–23) and centralization (2 Kings 18, 22–23), but the narrative ends with the temple in ruins (25:13-17).

Psalms praises temple worship (Ps 99 extols worship in Zion, God's footstool and holy mountain; Ps 100 encourages entering the temple gates and courts with praise). Ollenburger interprets the Jerusalem temple in the psalms of Zion as an expression of the Lord's kingship over creation, promising order and justice for the marginalized (156–58) [Temple Theology, p. 477].

In 1–2 Chronicles, Ezra, and Nehemiah, the theology of God as king drives the need for temple building (Konkel 2016: 477). Pro-temple prophets include Haggai, who rallies the people to support the temple, and Ezekiel, whose eschatological vision imagines life-giving rivers flowing from a rebuilt temple.

Jeremiah, whose perspective often overlaps with 2 Kings, warns against the deceptive words "The temple of the LORD, the temple of the LORD, the temple of the LORD" (Jer 7:1-15), echoing 1 Kings 6:11-13. Jeremiah preaches that the temple is insignificant in comparison with an ethical lifestyle, keeping the commandments, and protecting the marginalized. The Lord will not protect a shrine in the face of human rebellion. The Lord declares, "I will do to the house that is called by my name . . . just what I did to Shiloh" (Jer 7:14).

The royal temple, like royal wisdom, may be God's gift, but its value is determined by its contribution to Torah values, justice, peace, and covenant loyalty. When the temple, like wisdom, is used for royal aggrandizement, it endangers rather than enhances the Lord's purposes.

THE TEXT IN THE LIFE OF THE CHURCH
Discerning the Voice of God

Recognizing and interpreting the Lord's voice is a recurrent challenge in the Old Testament. Claims and counterclaims are made regarding the will of God. At times counsel from another person clarifies a claim. Some of the claims themselves appear to be far from what believers would recognize as God's will. Samuel needs to learn to recognize God's voice, but later, in the Lord's name, he proclaims devastating holy war against the children and livestock of Agag (1 Sam 3:1-14; 15:2-3). Jeremiah struggles against the prosperity gospel proclaimed by false prophets; he predicts that destruction is coming and urges the people to pray for Babylon's prosperity (Jer 28:5-9; 29:7). David benefits from having a prophet friend in Nathan who can give guidance regarding God's direction and confront sin (2 Sam 7, 12). The Lord directly addresses Solomon four times, but Solomon lacks a friend like Nathan. Solomon retains independence regarding the word of the Lord. This king experiences the voice in a dream or a vision (1 Kings 3:5, 11-14; 6:11-13; 9:3-9; 11:11-13). Solomon alone decides how to respond.

The book of Acts describes early church conflict resolution when leaders disagreed about God's direction. After hearing from Peter, Paul, and Barnabas, the Jerusalem Council sends word that "it has seemed good to the Holy Spirit and to us to impose on you no further burden" (i.e., not requiring circumcision; Acts 15:28-29). Paul and Barnabas had "disagreement . . . so sharp that they parted company" (15:39).

The church continues to struggle with interpreting God's voice. In the 2018 triennial meeting of the Mennonite World Conference (MWC) General Council in Kenya, the Faith and Life Commission guideline on consideration of controversial questions itself provoked controversy! According to a MWC news release, the General Council did not reach consensus on the guideline, but the proposed guidelines provided direction for the discernment process. Delegates discussed the proposal in open session, met as regional caucuses, considered amended drafts forwarded by the Executive Committee, and agreed to postpone action until all were ready to proceed. Biblical teaching about patience, suffering, forgiveness, and seeing the face of God in each other guided the efforts to walk in unity. The Executive Committee withdrew the proposal with recognition that MWC seeks to provide a safe space for learning from one another and to strengthen relationships in a diverse church.

1 Kings 8:1-66

Temple Dedication

PREVIEW

Church building dedications are grand events, requiring elaborate planning. Everyone involved in the building project and in use of the facility is invited. Processions into the new building engage all participants. Leaders of the construction address the assembly. Prayer dedicating the facility is a high point. Galas include festive foods. Similarly, each major element of the temple dedication, as well as the ark procession, the cloud of glory, the sacrificial offerings, Solomon's references to the Davidic promises and the Mosaic Torah, the celebration of the Festival of Booths, and Solomon's prayer all integrate the temple into Israel's life. This dedication report portrays "the temple as the culmination of Israelite history since the exodus and as the dawn of a new era" (Knoppers 1995: 233).

OUTLINE

The temple dedication report is introduced and concluded with narrative action (8:1-13, 62-66). Solomon's speech (8:14-61) forms the body of the dedication report. The speech is introduced and concluded with his blessing addressed to *all the assembly of Israel* (8:14-21, 54-61). Solomon's dedicatory prayer (8:22-53) includes appeals that the Lord keep his Davidic dynastic promise (8:22-26) and hear this prayer (8:27-30), with seven petitions that follow a general pattern: (1) situation, (2) appeal to hear, and (3) extended appeal or result of answered prayer (8:31-53). The broad outline can be construed as a *chiasm [Literary Criticism, p. 457]*.

A   Narrative Introduction, 8:1-13
  B   Solomon's Blessing of the Assembly, 8:14-21
    C   Solomon's Dedicatory Prayer, 8:22-53
  B^1 Solomon's Blessing of the Assembly, 8:54-61
A^1 Narrative Conclusion, 8:62-66

The dedication creates a climactic conclusion to Solomon's building activity. Though the building report characterizes Solomon as temple builder (1 Kings 5–7), the dedication narrative emphasizes that *all the people of Israel* joined to dedicate the building (8:2, 55, 62, 65). As he has throughout the construction, Solomon takes center stage, leaving bit roles for his fellow participants. Solomon's prayer outlines a (sometimes inconsistent) rationale for the temple's central role in Israel's worship. Solomon's speech and prayer claim that he serves the Lord and that the Lord endorses this project.

EXPLANATORY NOTES
Narrative Introduction 8:1-13

The narrative describes the ceremony ushering the ark of the covenant into the temple. The plot resolves two questions: Will Solomon and people transfer the ark without tragedy? Will the Lord approve of the cultic innovation? After assembling for temple dedication (8:1-3), the participants process with the ark from the tent of meeting, with the priests taking the ark into the most holy place of the temple (8:4-9), and the cloud of the Lord's glory fills the Lord's house (8:10-11). Solomon's brief poetic prayer completes the introduction (8:12-13). The narrative portrays the temple dedication as the culmination of Israel's story (6:1), incorporating the traditional elements of the exodus from Egypt (8:9), the Horeb covenant (8:9), the tabernacle (8:4), the ark of the covenant (8:3, 6-9), the priests and Levites (8:3-4), the elders and tribal leaders (8:1, 3), all Israel (8:2), and David's piety, including transfer of the ark and dedicated cultic vessels from *Zion* (= *city of David*, southeastern part of Jerusalem) northward to the temple (8:1, 4).

As temple patron, Solomon assembles Israel's elders, tribal heads, leaders of the ancestral houses, and priests, all traditionalists potentially resistant to cultic innovation, to witness the transfer of the oldest cultic artifact, *the ark of the covenant of the LORD*, from the city of David to *the inner sanctuary of the house* (8:1-3, 6). All Israel assembles in the festival of the seventh month, the Festival of Booths (Feast of Tabernacles; Lev 23:39-43; Deut 16:13-15). This harvest festival memorializes Israel's liberation from Egyptian slavery and commemorates God's provision during Israel's wilderness sojourn in tents. With invitations to slaves, Levites, strangers, and widows, the date coinciding with the festival assures maximum attendance (Deut 16:14). The traditional Torah reading underscores the priority of justice for the marginalized poor. Tabernacles symbolizes moving the ark from tent to house. After David's tragic mishap in moving the ark (2 Sam 6:6-7), Solomon has the priests carry the ark; priests and Levites transport the holy vessels from tent to temple (1 Kings 8:3-4). The festivity is marked by an uncounted number of animal sacrifices, repeated references to elders and priests, and an assembly of all Israel (8:5; cf. 2 Sam 6:13, 17).

Narrative slows with the detailed report, heightening suspense regarding the ark's transfer (8:6). Additional details mark the pageantry: the winged cherubim, the extended poles for carrying the ark (emphasizing the mobility of the ark and the Lord's freedom), and the contents of the ark itself (now lacking Aaron's budding rod and the jar of manna; see Num 17:10-11; Exod 16:32-34). In the ark, two tablets mark the covenant (1 Kings 8:7-9; cf. Deut 31:26). The first issue of tension in the plot is resolved with the ark resting safely inside the temple, and the answer to the second, God's acceptance of the transfer, follows as the glory of the Lord fills the house (cf. Exod 40:34-38). The cloud, the signal that the wilderness community was to move, fills the place that Solomon has built for the Lord's name, marking Solomon as in the tradition of Moses (1 Kings 8:10-11, 17, 20).

Solomon's poetic prayer interprets the divine presence and explains his own actions (8:12-13). The Lord *dwell[s] in thick darkness.* *Darkness* is associated with God's holy presence in giving the Torah (Exod 20:21; Deut 4:11; 5:22), with God's appearance (Ps 18:10-11), and with righteousness and justice (97:2). Impenetrable and mysterious, God's holy presence is symbolically conveyed in the darkness of the inner sanctuary. Solomon has *indeed built an exalted house* (God's heavenly abode, Isa 63:15), *a place for you to dwell forever* (1 Kings 8:13). Two different Hebrew verbs are translated *dwell*. *Dwell* (*šakan,* 8:12) is associated with the Lord's glory or presence in Israel (Exod 24:16; 25:8; Num 5:3). The covenant formula "I will be their God" is connected to the promise to "dwell" in Israel (Exod 29:45-46). The Lord promises to choose a place "for his name to dwell" (Deut 12:5, 11). As *dwell* (1 Kings 8:12) is associated with the tabernacle, Seow suggests the translation *The* LORD *has said he would tabernacle in thick darkness* to convey the Lord's free presence, avoiding language of an entrenched deity (Seow: 70). *Yašab* (8:13), the second word used

for *dwell*, often refers to permanent settlement, but it can also indicate "to sit," particularly to "sit enthroned" (Pharaoh on his throne,
Exod 11:5; the king on the throne, Deut 17:18; the Lord "enthroned
between the cherubim" of the ark, 1 Sam 4:4 NIV; Solomon enthroned,
1 Kings 1:30). While the latter term might be misinterpreted as
"residing," a preferred translation could be *established* (Seow: 70) or
seated (J. T. Walsh 1996: 111), indicating the Lord's sovereignty rather
than being bound to a location *[House for the Name, p. 449]*.

Reading the temple dedication narrative with the grain celebrates the apex of Solomon's glorious association with the Lord of
Israel and God's endorsement of Solomon's wisdom and piety
[Reading Strategies, p. 473]. Reading against the grain raises cautions.
Solomon assembles other participants (8:1), but he dominates the
scene, speaking without interruption in 1 Kings 8:12-61, the longest
speech in the books of Kings. The narrative emphasizes the ark of
the covenant of the Lord (*ark* is used eight times in 8:1-9), the
ancient mobile throne of the Lord, who "move[s] about among all
the people" (2 Sam 7:6-7). When the ark of the covenant containing
only the Torah tablets enters, the Lord's presence fills the house.
Solomon attempts to manage the traditions to support his royal
claims: the Lord sits enthroned on the ark, hidden except for the
poles that move God's throne on command. The God who resides in
heaven also dwells among those who obey the Torah, the marginalized who are hungry for Torah justice (Hens-Piazza 2006: 85;
Brueggemann 1988: 157).

Solomon's Blessing of the Assembly 8:14-21

Solomon's blessing *all the assembly of Israel* (1 Kings 8:14-21) parallels
the later blessing (8:54-61), bracketing the dedicatory prayer (8:22-
53). Three theological themes are developed. First, what God has
promised with his mouth his hand has fulfilled (8:15 AT) *[Prophets:
Prophetic Word, p. 469]*. Second, Solomon cites the Sinai covenant with
the Davidic covenant to show that the temple completes both covenants. Third, Solomon elaborates his temple theology, clarifying
that he has *built a house for the name of the LORD* (*name* appears in 8:16,
17, 18, 19, 20), correcting the possible misinterpretation that the
temple is God's actual dwelling place (8:13; Deut 12:5; Widmer: 237).
The reference to God's deliverance from Egypt brackets the speech,
rhetorically placing the temple within, not above, God's larger salvation story (1 Kings 8:16, 21) *[Covenant in Kings, p. 443]*.

Solomon's initial blessing of the people (8:14) shifts to praise of
God (8:15), rhetorically legitimizing Solomon's temple and reign.

The speech that praises God for fulfilling promises becomes praise for Solomon's accomplishment. The speech claims that Solomon's building project fulfills God's commitment to Israel through repeated references to *Israel* and the Lord's covenantal deliverance of Israel (8:16-17, 20-21). First, Solomon paraphrases the Lord's speech to David, reinterpreting it to make the election of David the culmination of God's purposes (rather than choosing a city for a house for his name; 8:16). Solomon interrupts the Lord's speech to insert that it was David's intention to build a house for *the name of the LORD, the God of Israel* (8:17). Again paraphrasing, Solomon reinterprets the Lord's rejection of David's plan to build the house as a promise that David's son is to *build the house for my name* (8:18-19). Interrupting his paraphrase of the Lord's speech again, Solomon uses a wordplay to assert that his building fulfills God's promise: The Lord *upheld [raised up]* his word, . . . and I *have risen* in my father's place (8:20). Solomon's refocus on himself is evident in his claims: *I have risen, I sit, I have built, I have provided* (8:20-21). The Lord's enthronement is overshadowed by the emphasis on Solomon, his building, and his reign. The blessing of the people is brilliant royal rhetoric. *All Israel* stands at attention to honor the king, who blesses them, reminding Israel repeatedly that Solomon's temple is the culmination of their salvation-covenant story and of the Lord's promises to David. Solomon's actions protect the covenant legacy by providing a place for the ark of the covenant of the Lord, made amid the exodus liberation from Egypt (Hens-Piazza 2006: 79–80).

Reading against the grain, Hens-Piazza raises questions about Solomon's self-centered claims, his ideology of legitimacy for kingship and the Davidic dynasty, and his manipulation of theology in service of his political aims. The last line of the speech undercuts Solomon's rhetoric by reasserting the central premise of covenant faith: the Lord delivers his people from imperial servitude (whether under Pharaoh or under Solomon; 2006: 80).

Solomon's Dedicatory Prayer 8:22-53

Solomon's dedicatory prayer (8:22-53) is the centerpiece of the temple dedication (8:1-66), itself the center of Solomon's reign, even arguably of the book of 1–2 Kings (Hens-Piazza: 2006: 80). The prayer develops several theological themes:

1. God's name is present at the temple; God attends to prayer directed to the temple, yet cannot be contained in earth and heaven, much less the temple.

2. God delivers and covenants with Israel yet demands covenant faithfulness.

3. God, whose covenant curses result in exile, is asked to forgive and restore.

4. God elected the house of David without conditions yet conditions future blessing on his heirs' Torah obedience.

Solomon as servant-mediator petitions for Israel yet seeks self-
serving covenant assurance as temple builder (turning temple theology into royal theology; Brueggemann 2000: 108). The prayer

1. addresses God's incomparable faithfulness with petitions
   that God confirm the Davidic dynasty (8:22-26);

2. petitions that God, who is greater than the temple, hear
   prayers directed to the temple (8:27-30);

3. lists seven petitions from a series of circumstances (8:31-51);
   and

4. petitions that God hear the pleas of Solomon and of Israel
   (8:52-53).

Solomon stands before the altar, assuming the posture of a servant
before his lord (*servant* is used three times of David, then four times of
Solomon in 8:23-30; Solomon arises from kneeling before the altar in
8:54). Solomon addresses the Lord as the unequaled *God in heaven above
or on earth beneath* (8:23), echoing Moses (Deut 4:39) and Rahab (Josh
2:11). The Lord *keep[s] covenant and steadfast love*, a phrase used only
here in 1–2 Kings (1 Kings 8:23; cf. Neh 1:5; 8:32; see TBC). Repeating an
earlier expression, Solomon addresses the Lord, who *promised with
your mouth* and has *this day fulfilled with your hand* (8:24; cf. 8:15).
Solomon twice petitions the Lord to confirm his promise to David that
there shall never fail you a successor before me to sit on the throne of Israel
(8:25-26). This pivotal paragraph presses the Lord for assurance
regarding the dynastic promise to David (8:22-26), linking the blessing
(regarding Solomon's temple as fulfillment of covenant relationship,
8:14-21) with the petitions for forgiveness (8:27-53). Though Solomon
seeks a guarantee of unbroken relationship, his petition twice introduces human covenant obligations: *Walk before you/me* (8:23, 25).

The rhetorical question in 8:27 (*Will God indeed dwell on the earth?
... Much less [in] this house that I have built*) balances and corrects possible misinterpretation of the earlier statement about God's dwelling in the house built by Solomon (8:12-13). The question introduces

the seven petitions (8:31-55) with clarification that the temple is a place of meeting, a place where God's people communicate with the Lord *in heaven your dwelling place* (8:30). Solomon seeks assurance that God hears prayers made *toward this house* (8:29). The paragraph (8:27-30) concludes with an intensified reiteration of the request that God *hear* (three times in 8:30) and introduces the petition *forgive* (five times in 8:30-50).

Solomon presents seven appeals (8:31-53), many corresponding to covenant curses (Deut 28:15-68). Structurally, each petition introduces a situation of need, the petitioner makes a request *in/toward this place*, Solomon requests that God *hear in heaven*, and he pleads that God *forgive* (four times) or fulfill the petition.

Prayer	Text	Situation	OT Citation	Human action	Extended appeal
1	8:31-32	Judge dispute	Exod 22:7-13	Petitioners swear an oath	God judges, declares innocence
2	8:33-34	Defeat/ exile	Deut 28:25-48	Repent, confess, pray	God forgives, restores
3	8:35-36	Drought	Deut 28:24	Pray, confess, repent	Hear, forgive, teach, send rain
4	8:37-40	Famine	Deut 28:21-62	Pray	Hear, forgive, act
5	8:41-43	Foreigner	Deut 4:34; Isa 2:2-3; 56:3, 6	Hear the Lord's name, pray	Hear, act, so that all may know the Lord
6	8:44-45	Battle	1 Kings 20, 22	Pray	Hear, uphold cause
7	8:46-51	Exile	Deut 28:63-68; 2 Kings 17:5-18; 24:2; 25:1-12	Repent, plead, turn back	Hear, forgive

Petition 1 envisions the sanctuary as a place of judgment where God will settle difficult cases. The petition focuses on God's commitment to justice and demand for righteousness among the people.

Petitions 2–4 concern consequences of the people's sin and correspond to Deuteronomic curses for Israel's covenant unfaithfulness. The expectation is that a defeated Israel will *turn* (*repent*; 1 Kings 8:33, 35, 47, 48), *confess* the Lord's name (Ezra 10:1; Neh 1:6; 9:2-3), *pray and plead with you in this house* (1 Kings 8:33). Solomon petitions that God will *hear in heaven, forgive the sin of your . . . people*, and restore them. Petitions 2–4 develop a theology of retribution, of cause and effect regarding human action and divine reaction [*Theology of Exile, p. 479*].

Petition 5 anticipates that *a foreigner* (used of Solomon's wives, 11:1, 8; the seductress, Prov 2:16), having heard of God's *great name*, will be prompted to pray. The prayer expects that God's answer will prompt the foreigner to *know . . . and fear you . . . so that they [all the peoples of the earth] may know that your name has been invoked* (1 Kings 8:43).

Petition 6, prayer by the Lord's people when they face an enemy in battle, asks that God *hear in heaven . . . and maintain their cause* (*justice*; 8:49, 58, 59 [twice]).

Petition 7, the most fully developed and climactic plea, anticipates exile caused by the people's sin and the Lord's judgment (2 Kings 17:5-18; 24:2; 25:1-12) and asks forgiveness so that their captors treat them with *compassion* (but does not ask restoration from captivity). Solomon includes all possible offenses (8:46), confessing *sin* (*missing the mark* [AT] used thirty-six times in 1–2 Kings), iniquity (AT; "twisting" or "perversion," 2 Sam 7:14), "evil" (Daniel's confession, Dan 9:5, 15). Solomon bases his prayer on the reminder that these, God's people and heritage, were delivered by the Lord from Egyptian captivity (Deut 4:20; Jer 11:4).

The coda brings closure by framing the prayer with the petition of the preamble (1 Kings 8:29-30), asking the Lord to hear *the plea of your servant and the plea of your people Israel* (8:29-30, 52). The appeal is based on the Lord's existing relationship with Israel, as the Lord's *heritage*, recipients of God's promise *through Moses, your servant*, through whom *you brought our ancestors out of Egypt, O Lord GOD* (8:53). Because the Lord delivers oppressed people in need of justice, the exiles can hope for God to act (Deut 4:25-31).

Solomon's confidence is rooted in the Lord's covenant established with the liberation of all Israel and personalized in the choice of David as king. Assuming that God has chosen this "place . . . out of all your tribes as his habitation to put his name" (Deut 12:9), Solomon issues seven pleas. He asks God to forgive and restore God's people, give heed to the foreigner so that all people on earth will know and fear God, and bring justice. The prayer begins with the perspective of the temple dedication and the hope that God will choose the temple for his name. The prayer ends with the perspective of exile, in the hope that God will hear their prayers and grant God's exiled people compassion from their captors.

Gillmayr-Bucher reads the prayer as transformation in the image of the king. Solomon, at the height of his power and wisdom, summarizes Israel's history and fulfilled promises, but also reinterprets Israel's religious tradition to serve future needs. Solomon recognizes that he cannot guarantee the people's identity, and thus transitions to a theology tying the future to prayer, as modeled by the praying king in 1 Kings 8 (Gillmayr-Bucker: 143).

Solomon's Blessing of the Assembly 8:54-61

Solomon *finished* (cf. 6:9) the prayer while kneeling before the altar, with arms outstretched (indicating fervent devotion; 8:54; cf. 19:18), and stood to *bless all the assembly of Israel* (8:55; blessings frame the dedicatory prayer, 8:14-21). The blessing urges God to keep past promises and the people to be faithful to the Lord's covenant so that all know that the Lord is God like no other (8:23, 60). The blessing opens by praising the Lord, who keeps promises (the promise of *rest* recalls the Sinai promise to Moses, Exod 33:14; fulfillment in the conquest of Canaan, Josh 21:43-45; 22:4; 23:1; rest from David's enemies, 2 Sam 7:1, 11; see "Joshua and Solomon" in TBC for 1 Kings 1–2; Solomon's rest, 1 Kings 5:4; the central place of worship associated with rest, Deut 12:10). Seeking assurance of the Lord's presence, Solomon presents four petitions: (1) *May he not leave us or abandon us*; (2) *Incline our hearts to him*; (3) *Let these words of mine . . . be near the* LORD *our God*; and (4) *Maintain the cause [justice] of his servant and the cause [justice] of his people Israel* (8:57-59). Solomon emphasizes the covenant obligations of the people in his petition (*May he . . . incline our hearts to him, to walk in all his ways, and to keep his commandments, his statutes, and his ordinances*, 8:57-58; cf. 6:11-13) and the concluding imperative (*Devote yourselves completely to the* LORD *our God* [*devote completely* is to have *hearts of shalom*; contrast 11:4], *walking in his statutes, and keeping his commandments*, 8:61 AT). Faithfulness motivated by the universalistic theme of petition 5 (8:41-43) is consistent with Israel's role articulated in relation to Abram (Gen 12:1-3), to Moses (Exod 19:5-6), and by the prophets (Isa 2:2-3; 49:6) [*Covenant in Kings, p. 443*].

Narrative Conclusion 8:62-66

The report of dedicatory sacrifices parallels the procession of the ark into the most holy place (8:1-13, 62-64). Recalling sacrifices beyond counting (8:5), the vast number (142,000) of oxen and sheep sacrificed as peace offerings (eaten as a feast *by the king and all Israel with him*) and burnt offerings with grain offerings overwhelms the bronze altar and leads to moving the festival into the temple court-yard. Following LXX, the NRSV reads that Solomon and all Israel celebrated the festival for seven days (NIV follows MT and reads *seven days and seven days more, fourteen days in all*; see 8:2). *All Israel*, from the northernmost Lebo-hamath to the southernmost *Wadi of Egypt*, had assembled (8:65). The temple dedication concludes with Solomon sending the people *to their tents, joyful and in good spirits* (8:66).

The temple dedication marks the culmination of the era of exodus from Egypt, settlement in the land, and institution of the monarchy as the high point of Israel's relationship with the Lord. Including elders, tribal leaders, priests, and Levites; making the people the beneficiary of Solomon's petitions; and involving *all Israel* in offering sacrifices (8:5, 62-63)—this inclusion emphasizes that all the people benefit from the temple (Knoppers 1995: 251-52). Theologically, the prayer balances royal temple theology (articulated in the phrase *a place for you to dwell forever*, 8:13) with temple name theology (reference to *the house for the name of the LORD, the God of Israel*, 8:20; and the hope that God will *hear in heaven your dwelling place*, 8:30). The dedication narrative highlights the benefits of the temple: this house of prayer

1. fosters the Lord's relationship with all Israel;

2. frees the people to focus on Torah obedience; and

3. serves to glorify the Lord's name among the nations.

Solomon is portrayed as an ideal monarch within royal temple theology, but the text includes warnings from the Torah perspective. Despite the inclusion of other leaders and *all Israel*, Solomon himself assumes the mediatorial role as priest and prophet. Solomon refers to himself with the honorific *your servant* in relationship to the Lord. In his final three petitions he insists that people will benefit from *the house that I have built* (8:43, 44, 48). Solomon's confession, *For there is no one who does not sin* (8:46), includes himself and foreshadows eventual judgment of his evil actions. The concluding image of the people joyfully returning to their tents foreshadows the next time the phrase is used, as the people reject Solomon's successor with the summons *To your tents, O Israel!* (1 Kings 12:16).

At the root of each of these literary signals is the contested sense of justice [*Mišpaṭ, p. 461*]. The Hebrew *mišpaṭ* (8:45, 49, 58, 59 [twice]) can refer to royal administrative policy (1 Sam 8:9-18) but is grounded in the Lord's passionate care for the marginalized (Deut 10:12-22).

Solomon concludes by asking that the Lord maintain *the cause [mišpaṭ] of his servant and the cause [mišpaṭ] of his people Israel.* Though Solomon has asked for the Lord's *justice* (3:9), in the end he pursues imperial *justice* through relations with Egypt (3:1; 9:16; 10:28-29) and the gods of the nations (11:1-13). This miscarriage of justice is evident in Solomon's obliviousness to his own responsibility for obedience (J. T. Walsh 1996:115) and the extravagance and commodification of animal sacrifices made possible by his efficient imperial systems of tax and tribute (Brueggemann 2000: 115–16, 120). Solomon's final words foreshadow his condemnation (8:61; 11:4).

From the perspective of exiles in need of shared identity, covenant obedience, not the king or the temple, becomes the unifying institution. Confession acknowledges the shame of disobedience to the Torah and neglect of the marginalized. Radical social nonconformity offers new identity. Confession is an act of hope. If Torah disobedience causes exile, obedience to the Torah can open the way to a better future (Smith-Christopher: 121).

THE TEXT IN BIBLICAL CONTEXT
Temple in the History of Israel

Several themes in the dedication narrative help integrate this text into Israelite history. *All Israel* (8:1-3, 5, 55, 62, 63, 65) and *my/your/ his people Israel* (8:16, 30, 33-34, 35-36, 38, 41, 43, 52, 56, 59) underscore not only the unified people but also the covenant relationship with the Lord (e.g., Deut 1:1; 5:1; 1 Sam 3:20; 2 Sam 5:5; 1 Kings 3:28; 4:1). *The house which bears the name* connects the dedication (1 Kings 8:16-20, 29, 43-44, 48; 2 Chron 2:1, 4) with David's house (2 Sam 7:13-16) and becomes part of the prophetic judgment (1 Kings 9:3, 7; 2 Kings 21:4, 7; Jer 7:4-15). By referring to himself as *your servant* (1 Kings 8:28-30; 3:6-9), Solomon seeks to place himself on par with Abraham (Gen 26:24), Moses (Num 12:7-8; Josh 1:2; 1 Kings 8:53; 2 Kings 21:8), Caleb (Num 14:24), and David (2 Sam 3:18; 1 Kings 8:24-26; 11:13; 2 Kings 19:34). The phrases used by Solomon reinforce Solomon's repeated reference in the prayer to the Lord's deliverance, past, present, and future.

Covenant Love—Ḥesed

The phrase *keeping covenant and steadfast love* (*ḥesed*) appears in 1–2 Kings only in Solomon's prayer (1 Kings 8:23; parallel in 2 Chron 6:14), referring to God's relationship with the servants of the Lord God of Israel. Elsewhere the phrase is used or adapted to motivate covenant faithfulness (Deut 7:9, 12) and in postexilic prayers (Neh

1:5; 9:32; Dan 9:4) [Covenant in Kings, p. 443]. In each case the Lord's favor is extended to those who obey God, reinforcing the Lord's invitation to reciprocal commitment while resisting unconditional divine obligation to the royal cult. In his dream Solomon thanks God for the steadfast love shown David by giving him a son upon the throne (3:6). Solomon refers to God's covenant with David (8:24). Later, God accuses Solomon of having broken covenant by failing to keep the Torah (11:11). Sakenfeld defines ḥesed as the obligation of the greater relationship partner to care for the weaker one (15). When Rahab "deal[s] kindly" with the spies, she calls for them to reciprocate with the same ḥesed that she has shown them (Josh 2).

The issue throughout 1–2 Kings is whether Israel and its kings will be faithful to covenant stipulations. Covenant faithfulness, steadfast love, is characteristic of God, repeated in the formula expressing the divine name (Exod 34:6-7; Num 14:18). Covenant disintegrates when Israel fails to practice steadfast love, which fulfills the covenant. Practicing covenant love is at the core of the people's relationship with God.

Blessings and Curses in a Theology of Retribution

DtrH [Kings in the Hebrew Canon: Kings in the Deuteronomistic History p. 453] and 1–2 Kings assume a theology of retribution: God rewards obedience with blessing and punishes disobedience with curses [Covenant in Kings, p. 443]. That is the basis for Solomon's petition (often attributed to DtrH) that prayer atone for the ill fortune that comes to disobedient Israel (1 Kings 8:33-40, 46). Covenant blessings (Deut 28:1-14) and curses (27:11-26; 28:15-68) depend on the people's behavior (Deut 30). Because Israel obeys Joshua and God's Torah, all the promises are fulfilled, and the people have rest (Josh 21:43-45). Cycles of apostasy are based on the theology of retribution: disobedience of a new generation results in God's judgment through enemy oppression; when the people cry for help, the Lord sends a deliverer (Judg 2:11-23). Samuel removes King Saul to punish him for his disobedience (1 Sam 15:23; 2 Sam 7:15). After David's adultery and murder, Nathan warns, "The sword shall never depart from your house" (2 Sam 12:10). Israel is exiled because the people reject the Lord (2 Kings 17:5-7). Judah is exiled because of Manasseh's sins (2 Kings 24:3) [Theology of Exile, p. 479].

This theology recognizes that sin brings consequences. The created order is designed such that we humans reap what we sow. The prophets confirm this view of cause and effect. Follow the law and thrive in the land, or disobey and hear the Lord say, "I will cast you out of my sight" (Jer 7:5-7, 12-15). Proverbs adds the perspective of wisdom (26:27).

Within Scripture, some voices question this theology. Job refuses to accept the conclusion that his troubles result from his own moral failure (27:1-6). If the innocent suffer, can the theology of retribution be accepted without qualification?

Solomon's prayer that God *not leave us or abandon us* (1 Kings 8:57) is based on the hope that even though judgment is a consequence of disobedience, judgment may not be the last word. Acknowledging that sin brings trouble, Solomon prays for God to relent, forgive, and restore broken people (8:49-50). This hope for grace challenges deterministic fate. Solomon appeals to God's knowledge that people will fear God when God acts graciously (8:40). Though the prophets warn that the people's sins will bring judgment, they also hold out hope (Jer 31:31-34; Hos 14; Joel 2:26-29; Amos 9:11-15). Grounded as 1-2 Kings is within Deuteronomic theology, the promise of return establishes the hopeful perspective that exile is not the end (Deut 4:25-31; 30:1-5). "Because the LORD your God is a merciful God, he will neither abandon you nor destroy you" (Deut 4:31).

Concern for the Foreigner

Solomon petitions God to hear the prayer of the foreigner that all the earth may know and fear God (1 Kings 8:41-43). The universal scope of God's concern for humanity is a recurrent Old Testament theme. Genesis 1-11 makes the case for God's sovereignty and governance of all nations. The call of Abram promises that through his offspring all nations will be blessed (12:3). A "mixed multitude" goes up from Egypt with the descendants of Jacob (Exod 12:38 KJV). At Sinai, God gives Israel a vocation as a "priestly kingdom . . . because all the earth is mine" (Exod 19:5-6 AT). Though demanding eradication of pagans (Deut 7:2) and rejecting marriage with other nations (23:2-6), God also calls for generosity to resident aliens (16:11; cf. Lev 19:33-34), including to Edom and Egypt (23:7-8). Joshua welcomes Rahab (Josh 2:1-21; 6:25). Ruth gains acceptance in Israel and extends the ancestry of David. David enjoys good relations with Nahash, king of the Ammonites (2 Sam 10:2). Elisha heals the enemy general Naaman (2 Kings 5) and feeds the army that comes to arrest him (2 Kings 6:22). Isaiah anticipates salvation that extends beyond Israel (19:23; 49:6; 56:1-8). Almost "over his dead body," Jonah evangelizes Nineveh.

The record is mixed. Israel is often hostile to the nations and attributes to God commands to destroy nations. On the other hand,

Solomon prays that foreigners will be heard at God's temple (1 Kings 8:41-43). The Old Testament extends God's salvation beyond Israel. In the New Testament, Jesus follows the Old Testament witness to include those outside Israel (Mark 7:24-30; John 4; Matt 28:18-20). Paul rejects compromise with Peter and others that threatens inclusion of the uncircumcised (Gal 2). To all who receive God, the Word gives power to become God's children (John 1:12).

THE TEXT IN THE LIFE OF THE CHURCH
Church Facilities

Although early Christians worshiped in the temple, persecution pushed them out into homes of believers (Acts 2:46; 3:1; 8:1; Col 4:15). As the church grew wealthier, they constructed buildings. Early Anabaptists driven from church buildings met in forest, caves, barns, homes, and even in a boat. Early Anabaptist meetinghouses were simple structures without the ornamentation that characterized Solomon's temple. Church building projects test community principles.

Buildings convey values. Multipurpose practicality fits the Anabaptist service mentality. Simplicity is a biblical and traditional value. A building with space and light moves the mind of creatures to the Creator. Rehabbing aging structures demonstrates thrift and prudence. Space devoted to fellowship, study, worship, and service indicates values. Structures not only serve the church by empowering ministry; their walls also limit a congregation, keeping others out or restricting the number participating in an activity. Worn, unkempt space can indicate unfaithful stewardship.

Culture also affects how space communicates. In ancient Israel, the temple description served the propaganda purposes of the king. The Lord initially resisted a *house*, which might communicate that God no longer moved among the people and was limited to a single earthly throne. In India, church meetinghouses can witness to the faithful stewardship of impoverished people. In the state of Andhra Pradesh, Christian believers who as indentured slaves roll small cigarette-like "smokes" called *beedis* (or *bidis*) had money withheld from their meager paychecks to build a church structure to the glory of God. Their sacrificial stewardship was a witness to their commitment. Such cooperation was a witness to the power of local community. They invited Western visitors to contribute for doors, roofs, and windows, showing that they recognize a larger worldwide communion. Their insistence that the cross atop the steeple reach a higher altitude than either the local mosque or the Hindu temple expressed their desire to demonstrate tangibly that Jesus is the only way. While one may question these expressions, this church building illustrates how culturally shaped values affect construction projects. A building communicates how the community understands itself and its relationship with God.

House of Prayer

Solomon appeals to God to recognize the temple as a house of prayer. In Jesus' criticism of temple business (Matt 21:13 and par.), he brings together Jeremiah's judgment that the house bearing the Lord's name has become a "den of robbers" (7:11) with Isaiah's promise of the day when the nations will come to the holy mountain of God, to the "house of prayer for all peoples" (56:7).

Though Jesus has harsh words for those who pray publicly in the temple with ostentatious, self-satisfied piety (Matt 6:5; Luke 18:9-12), the apostles frequented the temple at "the hour of prayer" (Acts 3:1). Congregational prayer remains a significant part of church liturgy. We enter worship with a prayer of invocation, asking God's blessing as we gather in God's presence. As Solomon did, we confess sin. We pray for the needs of the congregation (including afflictions we suffer, as in 1 Kings 8:37-38) and the world (8:41-43). As we part, a prayer of blessing (8:56-61) is often a scriptural benediction (e.g., Num 6:24-26).

Though we do not concern ourselves with praying *toward this house*, Solomon's dedicatory prayer assumes that petitionary prayer is vital for the Lord's people. Solomon's seven cases express prayer in a crisis. Piper, in *Desiring God*, suggests the metaphor of prayer as a walkie-talkie communication from a soldier behind enemy lines. In prayer, the believer directs divine power to spiritual conflict. Solomon models strategic prayer by appealing to God to intervene directly in conflict.

What is our theology of petitionary prayer? Is God expected to reverse exiles, eliminate epidemics, and transform social ills? Wells suggests one of three outcomes when we pray. In "the prayer of resurrection," God does all the work, transforming the situation with divine intervention. In "the prayer of incarnation," God transforms us as the character of Jesus, who experienced every weakness and temptation, is formed in us. "The prayer of transfiguration" stirs us to action, encouraging us to come alongside others, requesting prayer and offering them God's presence through ourselves (51).

The Church: Holy Temple in the Lord

Early Anabaptists followed Paul's metaphorical identification of the church, the people of God, with the Lord's holy temple (Eph 2:21-22). As people who no longer had access to consecrated buildings for worship, they reimagined themselves not only as the living temple but also as the true priests.

> The consecration of the symbolic temple of Solomon in Jerusalem shows us that the community of the Lord is consecrated by God through Jesus Christ with his Holy Spirit. It is a holy temple, the house of the living God, a pillar and foundation of truth. God wills to be worshiped in spirit and in truth in this temple [John 4:24]. . . . Here is the holy mystery of the signs of Sacrament, of baptism, of the Lord's Supper, which were given by Christ to all believers. We must come to this temple to celebrate spiritually unto the Lord. (Philips 1559, in Liechty: 236–37)

Dirk Philips explores the mystery of the incarnation: Jesus is the temple that lives on in the community of God's people. Ephesians describes the temple built on the apostles and prophets, with Christ Jesus the cornerstone. United in Christ, this building grows into a holy temple as people join God's community. God is present in the temple (Eph 2:20-22). Philips also explores the mystery of the sacraments, baptism, and the Lord's Supper. The building grows as disciples follow Christ in baptism. Christ nurtures the body through the bread and the cup. The spiritual temple, like the Jerusalem sanctuary, gives glory to God.

1 Kings 9:1-25

Temple Postscript

PREVIEW

Have you ever wished to hear God's audible voice? In the throes of difficult decisions, alone in the dark night of the soul, or caught on the horns of a dilemma, we want God to speak. In Samuel and Kings, God speaks to kings through prophets. David's dialogue with the Lord is mediated through Nathan (2 Sam 7). Solomon hears from God without a prophetic intermediary. Is direct divine communication a sign of God's love (2 Sam 12:25 NRSV footnote)? Is it a result of Solomon's stifling of the prophetic voice (1 Kings 11:29, 40)? The Lord's direct communication to Solomon reiterates his vocation to do justice (3:9-14; 6:11-13; 9:1-9). The notes that follow the Lord's communication recount the hidden price paid for temple construction, including lost territory (9:10-14) and forced labor (9:15-23).

OUTLINE

The Lord's Appearance to Solomon, 9:1-9
Narrative Report regarding Temple Building, 9:10-25
    9:10-14   Business with Hiram
    9:15-23   Account of Forced Labor
    9:24-25   Conclusion

EXPLANATORY NOTES

The Lord's Appearance to Solomon 9:1-9

After a transitional summary of Solomon's building activities (9:1; cf. 1 Kings 5-8), the Lord responds to Solomon's dedicatory prayer

(9:2-9; 8:22-53). Solomon has *finished* building the temple, the palace, and *all that Solomon desired to build* (seventh and last time this Hebrew verb *finished* is used in the temple report; cf. 1 Kings 6:9; see "Finished the Work" in TBC for 1 Kings 6–7).

The Lord's second appearance to Solomon forms a literary bracket with the Gibeon dream and echoes the Lord's conditional promise in the temple-building report (1 Kings 3:4-15; 6:11-13). God has granted more than Solomon's request in the inaugural dream by adding wealth and long life to wisdom (3:10-14). Here God exceeds Solomon's temple petitions by echoing Solomon's terms. God has paid close attention to the prayer! Solomon has asked God to *hear* (twelve times in 8:28-52) his *prayer* and *plea* (terms repeated nearly twenty times in 8:28-59). God responds, *I have heard your prayer and your plea. I have consecrated this house that you have built and put my name there forever* (9:3; echoing *house that I have built,* 8:13, 27, 43, 44, 48; nine references to the *house* for the Lord's *name*). The Lord promises, *My eyes and my heart will be there for all time* (superseding Solomon's request that the Lord's *eyes be open* toward the house, 8:29, 52) [*House for the Name, p. 449*].

A positive condition assures Solomon's dynasty if he walks, obeys, and keeps Torah (9:4-5; Deut 10:12-13; 1 Kings 2:3; 6:12; 8:58, 61). The series, typical of Deuteronomic rhetoric, concludes with *keep my ordinances* (*mišpaṭ*). Solomon had prayed to *hear justice* (3:9, 11); the Lord's promises reiterate the call for *justice* [*Mišpaṭ, p. 461*].

A negative condition, addressing Solomon *and his descendants,* warns of the consequences of *serving other gods* (9:6-9; cf. 16:31; 22:53; 2 Kings 17:12, 16, 33, 35, 41; 21:21) [*Idolatry, p. 449*]. Although this is the first time such an action is mentioned in Kings, it is strongly condemned in Deuteronomy (e.g., 5:7 [cf. Exod 20:3]; 6:14; 7:4; 8:19; 11:16, 28). Royal failure results in temple destruction and national exile (*cut off from the land,* 1 Kings 9:7-9; Deut 28:36; 29:24-28; 1 Sam 12:14-15). In contrast to the honor that the Lord promised Solomon (1 Kings 3:13), *Israel will become a proverb and a taunt,* and the house built by the king of proverbs will be destroyed (9:7; Deut 28:37; Jer 24:9; 1 Kings 4:32). When passersby ask about exile and destruction, the answer provides a causal connection between disobedience and suffering (9:9; Deut 28:20; 29:24-26) [*Evil, p. 446*]. Although the initial promise is stated with the assumption that Solomon will fulfill the conditions, the full message foreshadows Solomon's lost dynasty (1 Kings 11:26-40) and the exile (2 Kings 17:7-40; 24:20–25:21).

Solomon *desires* (1 Kings 9:1, 11, 19) honor in opposition to the Lord's *desire* for justice and *delight* in making Solomon king to do *justice* (Deut 7:7; 10:15; 1 Kings 10:9; Jer 9:24). The Lord's appearance lacks a narrative conclusion, leaving the threat of exile hanging over the rest of 1-2 Kings (Deut 4:25-31; 29:22-29; Nelson 1987: 61). Though the timing is unmentioned in 1 Kings, rabbinic scholars calculate that the Lord appears to Solomon in the tenth Jubilee after the exodus (five hundred years; 1 Kings 6:1 marks the start of temple construction as the 480th year after the exodus, and the Lord *appears* at the end of the twenty-year building process, 6:38–7:1; 9:1-2, 10). Leviticus 25 outlines Jubilee as a practice to protect the marginalized.

Narrative Report regarding Temple Building 9:10-25

9:10-14 Business with Hiram

This summary of construction business brackets the temple-building report (9:10-25; cf. 5:1-18). Commercial dealings with Hiram are resolved (5:1-12; 9:10-14). A revised account of forced labor amends the earlier report (9:15-22; cf. 5:13-18). An addendum concludes the building report (9:24-25).

At the end of the twenty-year temple-palace construction, the narrator reports that Solomon has traded land to Hiram for timber and gold (9:10-14; 5:7-12; *as much as he desired*, 9:1, 11, 19). When Hiram inspects the twenty Galilean cities, he is dissatisfied with the transaction (*Cabul* is obscure, perhaps the name of one of the cities; the meaning may be "fetter," reflecting Hiram's status as a junior trade partner; Provan 1995: 84–88; unlikely meaning "good for nothing," NRSV, NIV footnote). Read as royal propaganda, the last sentence is the punch line: Solomon wisely uses his power to trade worthless real estate for about sixteen tons of gold (9:19 confirms that Lebanon is part of Solomon's domain, posing Hiram as Solomon's vassal; see also 4:21, 24). Reading against the grain, Solomon's *desire* results in loss of a sizable portion of the land granted to Israel by the Lord [*Reading Strategies, p. 473*]. The land loss foreshadows exile and confirms that Israel is unable to meet the negotiated annual agricultural demands (Lev 25:23; Josh 1:6; 1 Kings 5:9, 11). The transaction raises the possibility that, contrary to the impression of the reports, Hiram bests Solomon in these trades (e.g., Hiram gains land, food supplies, positive trade advantages), indicating superior status and greater royal wisdom. Rather than sharing prosperity with the people of Israel (4:20, 25), by accumulating gold for royal luxuries, Solomon transgresses the law of the king (Deut 17:14-20) [*Law of the King, p. 456*].

9:15-23 Account of Forced Labor

Solomon conscripted forced labor from resident non-Israelites, indigenous peoples whom Israel subjugated but did not *destroy completely* (*ḥerem*; 9:16, 21-22) [*Violence in Kings: Devoted to Destruction, p. 482*], and appointed Israelite overseers (9:15-23). The *account of the forced labor* (9:15) lists Solomon's building projects:

1. the palace and the temple (1 Kings 6–7);

2. *Millo* ("filling") stone terraces supported by retaining walls to expand the footprint for buildings);

3. walls of Jerusalem (3:1), Hazor, Megiddo, Gezer, and other strategic approaches to Jerusalem;

4. storage cities;

5. cities for keeping horses and chariots; and

6. whatever else Solomon *desired* (9:1, 11, 19; J. T. Walsh 1996: 123).

The list is interrupted with the report of Pharaoh's conquest of Gezer (a *going-away* gift for his daughter, Solomon's wife). Pharaoh's army *destroyed completely* (9:21) a city just twenty miles from Jerusalem, an ironic reminder of Solomon's foreign alliances.

As evidence of Solomon's imperial dominance, the cities (1) stockpile Israel's agricultural production for trade or provision in time of war; (2) maintain overwhelming military power (horses and chariots) to enforce dominion within and outside Israel's borders (9:19); and (3) control trade routes (10:15; Wray Beal 2014: 150). First Kings 9:20-22 presents a revised explanation of the enslaved labor force. Unlike the force composed of Israelites (1 Kings 5:13-16), the second report identifies the slaves as non-Israelites (cf. Exod 3:7-8; Deut 7:1-2; Josh 16:10; 17:13; Judg 1:28, 30, 33, 35; 3:5-6), supervised by Solomon's *servants* (1 Kings 9:23; *five hundred fifty . . . officers*; cf. 4:7-19). One way to harmonize the accounts is to read 9:20-22 as clarification. Another is to interpret the temple builders as a temporary crew (5:13-16) and the city builders as permanently enslaved people (9:15-22).

From the imperial perspective, Solomon, the ideal monarch, rules an empire that benefits Israel, dominates others, and lives in peace and prosperity. Wisely, Solomon enslaves the indigenous people to provide inexpensive construction labor. The building projects allow Solomon to stockpile surplus gained in taxes and tribute to trade for luxury items from Tyre and to construct a military-industrial complex of buildings, chariots, and horses. Solomon builds what he desires in Jerusalem and in his empire.

From the Deuteronomic perspective, Solomon's accumulated wealth and power jeopardize his commitment to egalitarian justice (contrary to the law of the king, Deut 17:14-20). Solomon disobeys Torah by creating a slave class within Israel rather than through his failure to exterminate indigenous populations (Deut 7:1-6; Josh 16:10; Judg 1:28; contra J. T. Walsh 1996: 124; Wray Beal 2014: 151; J. Davies 2012: 197). The Deuteronomic command to *entirely destroy* (*ḥerem*) native populations is better understood as dramatic hyperbole to guard against assimilation of "Canaanite" religious and political values (see Deut 7:4-6; Judg 2:2-3; 3:5-6; Matties: 437–38). Israel's story begins with a "mixed crowd" (Exod 12:38), who are accepted as members of the "holy nation" (19:3-6). Deuteronomy insists on hospitality for the resident alien (along with other marginalized population, Deut 10:18-19). It is improbable that after five hundred years in Palestine, it would have been possible for Solomon to identify a non-Israelite ethnic population as a slave class. This perspective questions Solomon's insatiable *desire* for building projects instead of following Torah justice *[Mišpaṭ, p. 461]*. Solomon's policies deprive the enslaved people of human dignity and the overseers of human charity by requiring that they treat neighbors as slaves. Solomon acts like Pharaoh, having them build not only stables for horses and chariots but also *storage cities* (9:19), as Pharaoh's Hebrew slaves did (Exod 1:11; Leithart: 76).

9:24-25 Conclusion

The temple-palace construction conclusion reinforces the characterization of Solomon's imperial wisdom. Pharaoh's daughter moves into her house in the palace complex, completing the transition mentioned at the start of Solomon's reign (9:24; cf. 3:1; 7:8). Linking construction of the Millo to this transition suggests that other foreign dignitaries, additional wives of Solomon, and their foreign diplomats demanded extensive accommodations. Solomon's international prestige is reinforced by this reference. He himself officiates at the three annual temple festivals mandatory for all males in Israel (Deut 16:16), reinforcing the idea that religious observation is a function of the state (Hens-Piazza 2006: 92). While both references buttress the aura of Solomon's imperial power, both are susceptible to a more suspicious reading. The prominence of Pharaoh's daughter (at the beginning of Solomon's reign and at the end of the building report) raises caution about

Solomon's willingness to compromise traditional covenant allegiance, turning to Egypt not only in alliance but also for a pattern
for imperial administrative practice (cf. Exod 5:6-7; Deut 17:16-17
prohibits returning to Egypt and multiplying wives, code language
for international alliances). Though Solomon has been active in
offering sacrifices (3:4, 15; 8:5, 62-63), Solomon's priestly practices
indicate unbridled royal power. From the Deuteronomic perspective, Solomon usurps the priestly role. Solomon's self-aggrandiz-
ing is subtly criticized by the elaborate wordplay on the name
Solomon (*Shelomoh*) in the final verse (9:25), with the words *three*
(*shalosh*), *offerings of well-being* (*shelem*), and *completed* (*shalam*, a different Hebrew term from *finished*, 9:1). *So he [Solomon] completed the
house* (9:25).

THE TEXT IN BIBLICAL CONTEXT
The Shadow of Exile

The most important marker for understanding Old Testament faith
is Judah's Babylonian exile. Before exile in 586 BCE, Israel lives in the
land; covenant protects the people and demands their faithfulness.
Exile is the defining point in the identity of the people of God.

Moses warns that unfaithfulness results in exile (Deut 4:25-31;
28:36-37, 63-68). Though God offers life, Moses prophesies that disregarding Torah brings death. God's warning to Solomon renews the
threat of exile (1 Kings 9:1-9). Foreshadowing exile (2 Kings 17,
24–25), 1 Kings 9 tells Israel what is at stake. Read from the perspective of exile, 1–2 Kings explains the Lord's sovereignty while the
people of God suffer as aliens. While land is the place of blessing,
exile is purification for Israel (Jer 29). Deuteronomy promises God's
restoration of exiles despite human failure to live up to God's vocation (4:29-31; 30:1-5) [*Covenant in Kings, p. 443*].

Klein examines distinct canonical approaches to the issue of
exile in Lamentations and lament psalms, Jeremiah, Ezekiel, Second
Isaiah, and priestly sources; he reads DtrH as concluding that "exile
is a result of Israel's guilt" (26). Rooted in a peace church tradition,
Smith-Christopher notes that imperial oppression displaces God's
people and leaves them vulnerable (49–54); he claims that exile
gives rise to social and religious responses with contemporary theological significance for Christians (6) [*Theology of Exile, p. 479*].

The New Testament declares that aliens outside the common-
wealth are welcomed as community people (Eph 2:11-22). Former
aliens and strangers are God's people (1 Pet 2:9-11). Like Abraham
and the Old Testament heroes of faith, New Testament pilgrims

anticipate a heavenly city (Heb 11). Facing imperial oppression, Revelation anticipates the day when no temple will be needed, because the throne of God and of the Lamb will be in the city of God. Like the readers of 1–2 Kings, the worshipers in the heavenly city look forward to that day.

THE TEXT IN THE LIFE OF THE CHURCH
Sensitivity to Social Marginalization

The categories used to marginalize populations differ by culture. The marginalized might be identified by caste, religion, race, or origin. Canadians seek justice for First Nations while Americans address discrimination against people of color. The Pew Research Center reports that majority culture (white) evangelicals in the U.S. are twice as likely as evangelicals of color to believe that police actions are free of racial discrimination. Christena Cleveland, a social psychologist and public theologian, warns majority culture seminarians that their silence in the face of police violence against people of color is a breakdown in evangelical solidarity. Solomon reasoned that putting Canaanites to forced labor was acceptable because Israel was exempt. White evangelicals are tempted to rationalize that racial injustice is a personal issue. Solomon's discriminatory practice against the Canaanites was a failure to keep Torah justice [Mišpaṭ, p. 461]. By disregarding the perspective of believers in marginalized populations regarding institutional violence, majority evangelicals neglect biblical justice.

Racial intolerance threatens at multiple levels. Individually, we are tempted to regard difference as the deficiency of the other. Congregations are warned against discriminatory privileging based on wealth (James 2:1-13). In the U.S. a disproportionate number of people of color are on death row and more likely face death sentences when victims are white; this situation illustrates the difficulty of fair law enforcement and jurisprudence.

Analyzing the moral problem of slavery in the early church, Glancy concludes that Christians defended slavery because they accepted cultural norms regarding enslaved people as property. Abuse of power and privilege contributes to contemporary sexual exploitation. Glancy lauds the countercultural Christian witness of Gregory of Nyssa and his sister Macrina, who were profoundly shaped by the biblical account of humans being created in God's image and called to the human vocation of doing justice (97, 101-3).

Mixed-Up Worship

Solomon offered sacrifices three times a year on the altar he built for the Lord (9:25). Though made without evaluative comment, the report raises questions about Solomon's initiative. Worship protocol enforced on Saul (1 Sam 13:8-14) and Azariah (2 Chron 26:16-21) excluded kings from offering sacrifices; priests were assigned this task. Faithful worshipers defer to leaders designated by the community.

Anabaptist worship tradition, steeped in communitarian values, seeks to emulate New Testament practice. Paul's instruction suggests spontaneity within order: "When you come together each one has a hymn, a lesson, a revelation, a tongue, or an interpretation. Let all things be done for building up" (1 Cor 14:26). Stuart Murray and Sian Murray Williams capture this democratic, communitarian ideal in their book aptly titled *The Power of All*.

Solomon reminds us of the dangers of extremes. Ignoring the need for appropriate structure (or freedom), protocol (level of formality/informality), and right character may lead to excess. Discounting worship because of our suspicions is excessively critical. In faithful worship, people join the mission of God in the world, rejecting the gods of entertainment, power, and accumulation [*Idolatry, p. 449*].

Solomon's Commercial Enterprise

PREVIEW

"Events with celebrities" are popular at fundraising auctions. At a charity ball in Fresno, California, the city police chief offered helicopter rides in exchange for donations. In the 1990s, coffee, dinners, and overnight stays in the White House went to large campaign donors. According to reports, a donor of $10,000 would receive a reward of coffee with President Clinton; contributions of $100,000 garnered a seat at the president's table. Larger donations resulted in a night in the Lincoln Bedroom of the White House. Solomon took advantage of similar opportunities. To be in the audience of Solomon was in such high demand that he turned it into a major revenue source (1 Kings 10:1-2, 10, 24-25).

Twin themes are intertwined to impress readers with Solomon's grandeur: *gold* (9:28; 10:2, 10, 11, 14 [twice], 16 [twice], 17 [twice], 18, 21, 21, 22, 25) and *wisdom* (10:4, 6-8, 23-24). Bringing gold as tribute, nations come to *hear* Solomon's wisdom (10:2, 10, 24-25). First Kings 10 expands the report of Solomon's administrative policy with details about how his superlative wisdom prompts the nations' peaceful submission and tribute (4:1-19, 21, 24, 29-34); about how Solomon's court is extravagantly provisioned (4:22-23, 26-28; 10:4-5, 16-21); and about his chariot forces enforcing his policies (4:26-28; 10:26). The reports on Solomonic administration (chs. 4 and 10) frame the narrative centerpiece: Solomon's temple building (chs. 5–8). The earlier administrative report (ch. 4) and the three divine calls to *hear justice* by keeping Torah (3:10-14; 6:11-13; 9:4-9) provide context for the interpretation of 1 Kings 10 [*Reading Strategies, p. 473*]. God has given Solomon wisdom, riches, and honor (3:10-14). God expects Solomon to do justice (3:11; 6:12; 9:4). Solomon exploits the gifts (10:23) and neglects the Torah (Deut 17:14-20).

OUTLINE

Maritime Trade, 9:26-28
Visit of the Queen of Sheba, 10:1-13
Solomon's Accumulation of Wealth, 10:14-29
    10:14-22   Trade and Treasure
    10:23-25   Tribute Exchanged for Wisdom
    10:26-29   Import-Export of Horses and Chariots

EXPLANATORY NOTES
Maritime Trade 9:26-28

Solomon's commercial enterprise (9:26–10:29) depends on a complex economic engine with an active trading strategy (9:26-28; 10:11-15, 22, 26-29), efficient taxation (4:1-19, 26-28), forced labor (5:13-18; 9:15-23), and imperial tribute (4:21, 24; 10:10, 14, 23-25). The report of a single trade mission introduces Solomon's acquisition of wealth (9:26-28). Solomon builds ships at a seaport on the Red Sea, and Hiram supplies sailors for Solomon's crew. The mission to Ophir, the mythical source of gold, produces sixteen tons of gold for Solomon (Job 22:24; 28:16; Ps 45:9; Isa 13:12). The cooperative trading fleet is the cornerstone of a monopoly that includes not only ports on the Mediterranean Sea and the Indian Ocean but also overland connections (10:11-12, 22; J. T. Walsh 1996: 125).

Visit of the Queen of Sheba 10:1-13

The queen of Sheba takes center stage in her visit to Solomon; she *heard* (10:1), *came* (10:1-2), *told* (10:2), *observed* (10:4), *said* (10:6), and *gave* (10:10). Solomon's reply (10:3), his only action, splits the narrative reporting the queen's visit (10:1-2, 4-5). The queen's speech is the rhetorical highlight of her visit (10:6-9). The visit concludes with the queen giving a gift to Solomon (10:10), who, after a parenthetical interruption (10:11-12), reciprocates before she departs (10:13).

The queen hears about Solomon because of the fame of the Lord. Sheba's location is indefinite but traditionally in the southwestern part of the Arabian Peninsula (modern Yemen), connected to the trade route essential to Solomon's economic plan (Gen 10:7, 28; Job 6:19; Ps 72:10, 15; Jer 6:20; Ezek 27:22-23; 38:13). The queen tests Solomon with *riddles* (like Samson's wedding riddle, Judg 14:12-18; riddles are associated with the wise, Ps 49:4; Prov 1:6). The queen arrives in Jerusalem with a merchant *army* (AT; as the term is translated in 1 Kings 15:20; 20:1, 19, 25) of camels loaded with spices, gold, and precious stones. The queen speaks all that is in her heart to Solomon, who *told her all her words; not a word was hidden from the king that he didn't tell her* (AT; that is, he won the war of wits; Wray Beal 2014: 160). The queen *sees* all Solomon's *wisdom* (mentioned first) as well as the details of his court: palace (7:1-11), table (4:22-23), officials (4:1-19), servants and their vestments, and even offerings, a demonstration of the temple cult (8:62-64). The encounter leaves her breathless (10:5).

The queen's speech (10:6-9) opens with the flattery of international diplomacy, acknowledging that, though the *reports* (AT: *words*; 10:3 [twice], 6 [twice], 7) that she had heard about Solomon were beyond belief, they were inadequate to describe Solomon's *words* (AT; NRSV: *accomplishments*) and *wisdom* (10:4, 6, 7, 8). She expresses amazement at the happiness of Solomon's *wives* (according to the LXX; Heb. *men*) and servants, who hear his *wisdom* (10:8). She praises the Lord because of his *delight* in setting Solomon on the throne of Israel. The Lord's *desire* (*delight*, Jer 9:23-24) contrasts with royal *desires* (1 Kings 9:1, 11; 10:13; translated *needs* in 5:9, 10). The queen's speech reaches a climax in declaring that the Lord, motivated by his eternal love for Israel, has made Solomon *king to execute justice and righteousness* (10:9).

The gift exchange describes trade transactions (10:10-13). The queen *gives* (5:6-7, 9-11; 10:13 [twice]; diplomatic language for trade) Solomon more than four tons of gold (the amount of gold that Hiram paid for the twenty cities in Galilee, 9:14) and the largest shipment of spices ever (10:10). The parenthetical report of Hiram's commercial fleet contrasts him with the queen, a reminder that the queen's gifts are a relatively insignificant part of Solomon's income (9:28; 10:14; J. T. Walsh 1996: 128), and perhaps indicates that the queen appears in Solomon's court to protect her trade interests (J. T. Walton: 420; Wiseman: 129–31; Mulder: 507, 519–20). Solomon's gift to the queen matches all her *desire* in addition to what he gave her out of the hand of the king (10:13).

From the royal propaganda perspective, the queen's visit provides evidence of Solomon's unsurpassed grandeur, magnificence reported as far away as Sheba, yet greater than reported. The queen testifies to Solomon's unsurpassed wisdom, wealth, and fame (as the Lord had promised, 3:10-14). *Breathless* (10:5 AT) but not without words, the queen attributes Solomon's greatness to the Lord's desire and his love for Israel. A more suspicious reading, noting parallels with Hiram, raises questions about whether Solomon, distracted by flattery, gave more than he gained by meeting her *every desire* and giving *out of Solomon's royal bounty* (10:13).

From the Deuteronomic covenant perspective, the visit lays a rhetorical trap. Though overwhelmed by Solomon's words, wealth, and wisdom, the pagan queen's final words reiterate the Lord's mandate (3:10-14; 6:11-13; 9:4-9). Solomon's position and prosperity come with the vocation to *execute justice and righteousness* (10:9). Solomon's focus on his own wealth, wisdom, and fame has distracted him from providing justice for Israel. The contrast between the Lord's *delight* in making Solomon king *to execute justice and righteousness* and the queen's *every desire* recalls Solomon's *desires* (9:1, 11, 19; 10:9, 13).

Solomon's Accumulation of Wealth 10:14-29

First Kings 10:14-29 explains how Solomon accrued his wealth and stored the accumulation. The motifs of gold and wisdom are developed. Superlatives point to Solomon's incomparable greatness: *all* (10:15, 21 [twice], 23, 24, 29), *nothing like it ever* (10:20), *none* (10:21), *greater than* (10:23 AT), *every one* (10:25). Solomon's wealth results from commercial trade (10:14-22), wisdom-inspired tourism (10:23-25), and arms dealing (10:26-29). Readers detect propagandistic glorification and Deuteronomic criticism; these two perspectives collide.

10:14-22 Trade and Treasure

Solomon's wealth is produced by international trade (10:14-15, 22). Solomon gained twenty-five tons of gold in one year through tribute and trade, including income accruing through control of trade routes connecting Hittite, Syrian, Egyptian, and Mesopotamian traders with merchants from the Arabian Peninsula (10:14-15). In exchange for protected passage, traders paid tribute, transferring wealth to Solomon. The catalog of Solomon's luxury items includes accounting of gold shields, description of his unique ivory throne, and report of gold vessels (10:16-21). *Gold* (*beaten* in 10:16-17; *finest* in 10:18; *pure* in 10:21) was crafted into large shields for storage and display in the fortress-bank, the House of the Forest of Lebanon (7:2). Fitting the kingdom unequaled in wealth and power, the throne made of ivory and gilded with *pure gold* (as used in the most holy place, 6:20-21) is designed with steps that raise the monarch far above courtiers, guarded by twelve lions symbolizing royal power and equal to the tribes of Israel. Solomon's drinking vessels and all the table service in the House of the Forest of Lebanon are of gold since silver has no value—so great is the quantity of gold. The third report of the riches accumulated through maritime trade concludes this section (9:26-28; 10:11-12; 10:22).

10:23-25 Tribute Exchanged for Wisdom

Solomon's wealth is supplemented by wisdom tourists, kings who (like the queen of Sheba) seek audience with Solomon to *hear his wisdom*, bringing exotic gifts as tribute, admission to wisdom exhibitions (J. Davies 2012: 212). That God is the source of this wisdom can be a reminder of Solomon's unique royal status or that God's gift is for executing justice (3:10-14).

10:26-29 Import-Export of Horses and Chariots

Solomon's entrepreneurial skills extend to arms trading. Solomon's overwhelming chariot force affords him uncontested dominance (10:26; though the number appears to be smaller than in 4:27-28). The statement about the lack of value of silver is expanded to compare the valuable cedar with the more common sycamore as further proof of wealth (10:27). The commercial report concludes with an accounting of the military-industrial arms trade monopolized by Solomon as he acts as middleman between Egypt and the Hittites and Aram (10:28-29; *Kue* is in modern coastal Turkey, north of Cyprus; J. T. Walsh 1996: 130). Solomon's horse trading not only violates the Deuteronomic prohibition (Deut 17:16) but also arms Israel's enemies, the Hittites (2 Kings 7:6) and the Arameans (1 Kings 11:23-25; 20; 22; 2 Kings 5; 7; Leithart: 81) *[Egypt, p. 445]*.

The royal propaganda glorifies Solomon's wisdom, fame, wealth, and power, unrivaled among his ancient peers. The same text, read from the Deuteronomic covenant perspective, indicts Solomon for transgressing the accumulation prohibited in the law of the king (Deut 17:14-20). The law rules out the accumulation of horses and the horse trading with Egypt reported in 1 Kings 10:26-29, and the accumulation of large amounts of silver and gold (10:14-17, 22, 25, 27). The Lord, who grants Solomon's request for wisdom to *do justice*, to *govern* the Lord's people Israel, adds the gift of riches and honor (3:9, 12-13). The report indicts the king for failure to read the Deuteronomic law and learn from its primary concern for providing justice for the marginalized (1 Kings 9:26–10:29; Deut 10:12-22; 15:1-18; 17:18-20). The two competing visions for kingship come to a head. Solomon's unsurpassed wealth, wisdom, and glory, glittering from the perspective of royal propaganda, are an indictment of his failure to *execute justice [Mišpaṭ, p. 461]*. The next section of the Solomon story eliminates the tension by announcing God's judgment on Solomon (1 Kings 11:1-13). According to J. T. Walsh, "While the artistic impulse is served by a dramatic development from hopeful promise to tragic failure, the author's antecedent realization of the outcome has subtly shaped and colored the entire presentation" (1995: 493). Provan agrees with this perspective. "The reign is usually divided into an earlier period, in which Solomon was obedient and blessed by God; and a later period, in which he was disobedient, and God's judgment fell upon him. This popular reading represents an entirely shallow understanding of the Solomon story" (1999: 161–62). Two ways of doing justice have been vying for expression. Royal justice misuses God's gift of wisdom not only for selfish disputes but also for an imperial structure that distorts Deuteronomic justice.

THE TEXT IN BIBLICAL CONTEXT
Unexpected Wisdom

Sometimes God speaks through unexpected sources. In 1 Kings 3–11 two foreign monarchs, King Hiram of Tyre and the queen of Sheba, address Solomon. That king's conversation with Solomon is commercial trade. The queen has a more extensive conversation and concludes with the prophetic declaration that the Lord made Solomon king *to execute justice and righteousness*. Wisdom from the foreign queen must have been as unexpected as God's message coming to the prophet Balaam through a talking donkey (Num 22:22-35).

A surprising New Testament story involves a woman from outside Israel with advice to clarify the Lord's mission. A Canaanite woman from Tyre and Sidon asks the "Lord, Son of David," to help her daughter tormented by a demon (Matt 15:21-28; Mark 7:24-30). Basing his refusal on his own commission, Jesus demurs, "I was sent only to the lost sheep of the house of Israel." When the woman persists, Jesus refuses again, insisting that her non-Israelite status disqualifies her from his Israel-focused mission. The Canaanite woman replies with a word of wisdom to match Jesus' proverbial refusal. Jesus recognizes the woman's faith, articulates an expanded missional vision, and heals the daughter. The wise Canaanite woman helps clarify Jesus' mission. In the next story Jesus heals people and feeds four thousand people in a Gentile region (Matt 15:29-39). Mark follows the encounter with a healing of a deaf man from the Greek region of Decapolis and the feeding story (Mark 7:31–8:10). In the Gospels' story line, Jesus takes his ministry to more Gentiles after hearing the Canaanite woman's wisdom. One "greater than Solomon is here!" (Matt 12:42; Luke 11:31).

Both stories illustrate that God speaks through unexpected sources. Wise non-Israelite women guide the servant of the Lord. Counsel from the queen of Sheba warns a king who is not practicing justice. The Canaanite woman's repartee expands Jesus' ministry. God's voice is unexpected in both cases. (See TBC for 1 Kings 4.)

Accumulation and Hedonistic Lifestyles

In the context of the law of the king (Deut 17:14-20), the report of Solomon's extraordinary wealth reads less like propaganda celebrating royal power and more as a legal indictment. Solomon's accumulated wealth is stored in the royal palace, the House of the Forest of Lebanon: golden shields, fantastic furniture, and extravagant vessels and collections (1 Kings 10). Instead of using his wealth to relieve his subjects of heavy taxation (4:28; 12:4), Solomon accumulates more [Mišpaṭ, p. 461].

Torah restricts the accumulation of wealth. Jubilee protection of the marginalized is based on dual land ownership. Primarily, the land belongs to the Lord (Lev 25:23). Secondarily, land belongs to families and is to be returned to them in the fiftieth year. No conditions are placed on land return. Whether the original owner has lost the land because of unfortunate weather or lazy practices, the land is to be returned in Jubilee. The sabbatical year marks remission of debts (Deut 15:1). People forced into indentured service are to be treated fairly. Prosperous persons share generously rather than accumulating resources. The Lord blesses generosity (15:18).

Amos 6 pronounces woe on those who live at ease. The prophet condemns ostentatious living in a context of others' need—not simply unjust accumulation (cf. Amos 2:6-16). Calling Judah the sister of Sodom, Ezekiel identifies the guilt of Sodom as failure to "aid the poor and needy" though "she had pride, excess of food, and prosperous ease" (Ezek 16:48-49).

The rich fool tears down his barns to accumulate more (Luke 12:13-21). The rich man's wealth comes by way of abundant harvest rather than unjust action. He forfeits his life, however, because he retains ownership of the bumper crop rather than sharing with a community in need. Luke contrasts the rich ruler who wishes to inherit eternal life (18:18) with the greedy publican who extorted the wealth of others (19:1-10). The rich ruler claimed to have kept the Ten Commandments but went away sad because his wealth blocked the way into the kingdom. Zacchaeus, on the other hand, found salvation when he redistributed unjustly accumulated wealth—despite being a Roman collaborator.

When Paul solicits offerings for the needy poor in Jerusalem, he uses the example of Jesus, who become poor so that others could be enriched (2 Cor 8-9). Those who supply the needs of the saints are enriched; thanksgiving overflows to God. Paul teaches equality, a fair balance between giver and receiver.

THE TEXT IN THE LIFE OF THE CHURCH
For Such a Time as This

The queen of Sheba, who calls on Solomon to use his privileged position to do justice, addresses Christians today [Women in Kings, p. 485]. Privilege is not historical accident but God-given opportunity to join the mission of God. Doing right in personal relationships is important—and often more obvious. Changing unjust systems demands recognizing structural injustice and acting corporately to change powerful institutions.

Like Solomon, North American Christians are tempted to give primary attention to diets and fashions while neglecting the weightier matters of justice (Luke 11:42). Like Solomon, our privilege is a gift, not a reward for superior behavior. Like Solomon, we must choose between disproportionate accumulation and strategic engagement with a world that needs God's righteousness and justice.

Righteousness—that is, well-ordered personal relationships—is linked with justice, that is political systems conducive to righteous deeds. Privilege offers Christians from the Global North opportunities to do what is right personally. Pope Benedict has called Christians to address global warming by doing what each can do individually in daily life, reasoning that small signs of individual action can lead the church to engage large-scale systemic change. Race relations will improve in our neighborhoods as we treat those we meet with mutual respect. Systems that lead to profiling minority males for greater police scrutiny need to be changed for justice to prevail. While opposing South African apartheid, Christians needed to do more than avoid racial discrimination at home. Boycotting South African products was a powerful instrument in overthrowing unjust government.

Early Anabaptists lived from a spirituality that informed their lifestyles. They saw life through the "Jesus lens." Their words can inform our attitudes and practices.

Christ Jesus also spiritually restores the glory of Solomon's kingdom, the riches and plenty of gold and silver, the generous peace, the great wisdom and many other gifts, so that even the servants were blessed who could stand before him and hear the words of wisdom which came from his mouth. All of this is spiritually restored in Christ Jesus. . . . He is our wisdom, justice, holiness, and salvation. (Philips 1559, in Liechty: 238)

1 Kings 11:1-43

Solomon's Reign Assessed

PREVIEW

Written in the voice of the son of David, king of Jerusalem, Ecclesiastes corresponds to Solomon's life as told in 1 Kings 1–11. After reviewing the "vanity" (meaninglessness, vapor, noxious gas) of achievement, Ecclesiastes concludes with counsel to "remember your creator in the days of your youth" (12:1). With its retribution theology—"for God will bring every deed into judgment" (12:14)—Ecclesiastes confirms the verdict of 1 Kings 11: though God's grace mitigates judgment, Solomon gets what he has coming.

First Kings 11 breaks the celebrative tone of the royal propagandist's description of Solomon's glorious reign by announcing a negative theological verdict based on Deuteronomic criteria of justice [Mišpaṭ, p. 461]. The against-the-grain reading of 1 Kings 1–10 trumps the propagandistic portrayal by announcing the Lord's judgment: because Solomon fails to keep Torah, the kingdom will be torn from him and given to his servant [Reading Strategies, p. 473]. After the Lord's second appearance, warning Solomon to execute justice (9:4), and the queen's statement that the Lord chose Solomon to execute justice and righteousness (10:9), the understated Deuteronomic critique becomes more pointed. While the royal propagandistic report of Solomon's accumulation of gold and horses and chariots may be celebratory, the law's prohibition of such accumulation results in unstated negative theological judgment (10:21-29; Deut 17:15-16) [Law of the King, p. 456].

The subtle, ironic, implicit critique embedded in reports of forced labor (9:15-23), consorting with foreign powers (10:1-13, 23, 28-29), and accumulation of wealth and arms is made explicit in the theological verdict that opens 1 Kings 11 (Bodner 2019: 81).

After the announcement of judgment (11:1-13), the narrator introduces three adversaries raised up by the Lord to oppose Solomon (11:14-40). The narrative concludes with a royal formula that includes Solomon's death notice (11:41-43). First Kings 11 prepares for the separation of the Davidic united monarchy into the divided monarchy: the ten tribes of Israel, ruled initially by Jeroboam; and the kingdom of Judah, ruled by David's heirs.

OUTLINE

Judgment of King Solomon, 11:1-13
    11:1-8   Foreign Wives Turn Solomon's Heart to Other Gods
    11:9-13   The Lord's Judgment of Solomon
Solomon's Opponents, 11:14-40
    11:14-25 Hadad of Edom and Rezon of Aram
    11:26-40 Ahijah Appoints Jeroboam, Son of Nebat
Concluding Royal Formula for the Reign of Solomon, 11:41-43

EXPLANATORY NOTES

Judgment of King Solomon 11:1-13

11:1-8 Foreign Wives Turn Solomon's Heart to Other Gods

First Kings 11 opens with a dramatic shift in mood. Contrary to the Deuteronomic law of the king (Deut 17:17), Solomon *acquired many wives for himself.* The negative evaluation (11:1-3) forms a bracket with the introduction of the Solomon narrative (3:1-3). The statements that he *loved the* LORD (3:3) and that he *loved many foreign women along with the daughter of Pharaoh* and *clung to these in love* (11:1-2) stand in tension. The marriage with Pharaoh's daughter is reported without evaluation as Solomon's first royal act (3:1; cf. 7:8; 9:16, 24); the marriages reported in 11:1-3 are condemned as violation of the cited Deuteronomic law (Deut 7:3-4; Josh 23:12-13). Youthful Solomon and the people worship the Lord on the high places because the temple was unfinished (3:1-3); later, Solomon discredits the temple by building high places for foreign gods (11:7-8). In 1 Kings 3:3 Solomon is *walking in the statutes of his father David;* in 1 Kings 11:11 the Lord declares that Solomon has *not kept my covenant and my statutes.* Youthful Solomon asks for a *heart to hear justice* (3:9 AT), yet *when Solomon was old, his wives turned away his heart after other gods; and his heart was not true to the* LORD (11:4) *[Covenant in Kings, p. 443; Idolatry, p. 449].*

Solomon married women from Moab, Ammon, and Edom (kingdoms nearest Israel geographically and genealogically), Sidon (the region of Solomon's trading partner Tyre), and the Hittites (north of Israel; listed among the seven native nations with whom marriage is prohibited, Deut 7:1-6). In addition to citing laws forbidding intermarriage with Canaanites, the narrative underscores covenant violation with theologically loaded language: *Solomon clung* (NIV: *held fast*) *to these in love* (11:2). Deuteronomy commands that Israel *love the* LORD twelve times, including in the great Shema (6:5) and chapters 11 and 30 (three times each; linked to obeying Torah), and "hold fast to him" (Deut 10:20; 11:22; 13:4; 30:20; Josh 22:5; 23:8). The great quantity of wives and concubines accentuates Solomon's radical Torah violation (11:3). As the Torah citation warns (11:2), the wives *turned his heart away* (11:3, 4, 9; *turn* is also *bend* or *warp; heart* [or *mind*] is the seat of the will) *[All His Heart, p. 435].* Basing his request on David's *uprightness of heart* (3:6), youthful Solomon had asked for a *heart skilled in listening to do justice,* and God promised a *wise and discerning heart,* conditioning these promises on Solomon's *walking* as David had *walked* (3:9, 12, 14). The evaluation reports that Solomon's heart is warped, *not true to the* LORD *as was the heart of his father David;* this term *true* (*shalem*) *sounds like* Solomon (*Shelomoh*) in Hebrew (cf. 8:61). The Lord's promises to Solomon are given on the condition that Solomon *walk in my ways* (3:14), *walk in my statutes* (6:12), *walk before me . . . with integrity of heart* (9:4), but Solomon *walked after* (11:5 AT) *Astarte* (goddess; Heb. *Ashtoreth* substitutes the vowels for the word *shame*) and *Milcom* (meaning "king"; god consort of Astarte), Ammonite *abomination* (the term describes Chemosh of Moab and Molech of Ammon, for whom Solomon built high places, 11:5, 7, 10) *[Idolatry, p. 449].*

Solomon is indicted for marrying foreign women and following their gods (11:1-8). Until 1 Kings 11 the Explanatory Notes have contrasted a positive royal propagandistic reading of Solomon with a negative evaluation based on the Deuteronomic covenant. While Solomon's harem fits the grandiosity of his imperial overreach, 1 Kings 11:1-8 eliminates the narrative tension by explicitly charging Solomon with Torah violation and idolatry.

11:9-13 *The Lord's Judgment of Solomon*

The narrative shifts from indictment of Solomon (11:1-8) to the Lord's judgment (11:9-13): *the* LORD *was angry with Solomon* (11:9-10;

cf. Deut 1:37; 4:21, where the Lord was "angry" with Moses and did not let him enter the land; Deut 9:8, 20, where the Lord was "angry" with Israel and Aaron for worshiping the golden calf; the Lord's anger leads to exile, 1 Kings 8:46; 2 Kings 17:18) [*Provoke the Lord to Anger, p. 470*]. The Lord is angry because Solomon *turned away from the* LORD (see EN on 11:3-4) even though the Lord *had appeared to him twice, and he had commanded . . . that he should not follow other gods* (11:9). Three times the Lord's promise came with the condition that Solomon keep the commandments (3:14; 6:12; 9:4). The narrative indictment reads that *he did not observe what the* LORD *commanded* (11:10).

The Lord speaks to Solomon for the fourth time (11:11-13; the last time God addresses any king directly). In judgment speech form, the Lord indicts Solomon for his failure to *keep my covenant and my statutes that I have commanded you.* Deuteronomic covenant faithfulness makes justice for the marginalized and repudiates ANE royal administrative policy (i.e., following the nations' gods; 11:2, 5). Solomon's accumulation of wealth and weapons and his failure to execute justice have been recounted without evaluative comment (1 Kings 9–10); the Lord's judgment pronounces the verdict that Solomon has broken covenant. The terse announced sentence doubles the verb in Hebrew to emphasize the finality of the Lord's decision (*tearing, I will tear the kingdom from you*, 11:11 AT). The verb *tear* (used twice more in 11:12-13) foreshadows the prophetic action and announcement to Jeroboam (11:30-31; *tear* echoes Samuel's dismissal of Saul, from whom the kingdom was torn, 1 Sam 15:27-28; 28:17). The Lord limits the judgment in timing and scope. Judgment is postponed until after Solomon's death, honoring the promise to David by preserving his dynasty throughout his son's lifetime. The scope of the judgment is limited for the sake of *my servant David and for the sake of Jerusalem.* Note the contrast with *your father David*, reminding Solomon that faithful service matters more than natural descent (J. T. Walsh 1996: 137). *Servant* echoes the judgment that a *servant* of Solomon will replace him as king of Israel (11:11-12); it "foreshadows" the similarity of Solomon's servant Jeroboam with Saul's servant David (Bodner 2012: 35) [*Literary Criticism, p. 457*]. *One tribe* (Judah; implying rejection of Solomon's administrative redistricting, 4:7-19) is to be retained by Solomon's son (J. T. Walsh 1996: 136).

The verdict against Solomon is unanimous. The narrator charges Solomon with turning his heart from the Lord by following the gods of the nations (11:1-8). The Lord convicts Solomon for breaking covenant by disregarding Torah commands (11:11). Solomon's pursuit of royal administrative policies, glorified by the propagandistic presentation of Solomon's grandeur, makes him a "king . . . like other nations" (1 Sam 8:5). Solomon's accumulation of power, wealth, and political alliances is a repudiation of Torah and a failure to execute justice. The verdict announces the division of the kingdom, the focus of 1 Kings 11:14-40 and 1 Kings 12–2 Kings 17.

Solomon's Opponents 11:14-40

As the Lord rips the kingdom from Solomon, the narrative shifts from Solomon as leading character to the Lord's initiative. *The LORD raised up an adversary against Solomon* (1 Kings 11:14, 23), two non-Israelites *making trouble* for Solomon (11:14-25). The Lord commissions the prophet Ahijah to speak judgment against Solomon and designate Solomon's servant Jeroboam as the one for whom the Lord will build a house to rule Israel if he walks in the ways of David (11:26-40).

11:14-25 Hadad of Edom and Rezon of Aram

The Lord raises up the royal Edomite prince Hadad as an *adversary* against Solomon (11:14). *Adversary* here translates the Hebrew term *śaṭan*, as in 1 Chronicles 21:1, in Job (eleven times), and in Zechariah (three times), where Satan/satan is an agent of the Lord who brings charges against God's elect. Hadad's animosity is traced back to David's oppressive policies (summarized in 2 Sam 8:12-14). Joab is implicated in a six-month reign of terror that results in the slaughter of every male in Edom (1 Kings 11:15-16). Though Joab's brutality caught up with him when Solomon assassinated him upon the advice of David (2:6, 28-33), Joab's death did not atone for the damage done in Edom, and Solomon needs to deal with the consequences. With a group of royal servants, Hadad escaped to Egypt, where Pharaoh honored Hadad with a house, an allowance, land, a wife, and special treatment of his son (11:17-20). When Hadad learns that David and Joab are dead, he asks Pharaoh's permission to return to Edom (11:21). When Pharaoh resists the request, Hadad persists (11:22). The narrative report ends without resolution.

Like Hadad the Edomite, Rezon the Aramean was a survivor of David's devastating military attack on a neighboring state (11:23-24). Rezon was a fugitive from King Hadadezer of Zobah. After David eliminated Hadadezer (2 Sam 8:3-8), Rezon led his marauding band to Damascus, where he became king. Rezon *despised Israel and reigned over Aram* (11:25).

The abrupt, incomplete reports of Hadad and Rezon suggest a hidden purpose in the narrative. While Pharaoh's special treatment of Hadad can be attributed to Egyptian strategy to outflank Solomon, the text neither explains nor resolves the question about Hadad's request to return to Edom. Though Rezon is *an adversary of Israel all the days of Solomon* (contrary to Solomon's claim to Hiram that he had no *adversary*, 5:4), the sentence describing the actions of Rezon and Hadad is fragmentary. (NRSV supplies an additional verb to interpret 1 Kings 11:25, Rezon was *making trouble as Hadad did*, but J. T. Walsh translates more woodenly, *and the evil which Hadad . . .* ; 1996: 139.) Rather than seeking historical reconstruction of the original events, several scholars suggest reading these flashbacks with attention to parallels with Moses and David *[Literary Criticism, p. 457]*. Like Moses, Hadad escapes to Midian to avoid a murderous king (Exod 2:11–4:20); Hadad camps at Paran (Num 12:16–13:25); Hadad's son is adopted into Pharaoh's family; Hadad asks Pharaoh to let him go out of Egypt to his own land (Seow: 93). Like Joseph, he prospers, gains Pharaoh's attention, receives a house and a wife (Bodner 2012: 37). Like David, Rezon, the king's servant, leads a band of outlaws, captures a capital city, and becomes king (Hens-Piazza 2006: 112). The stories show how God is at work in raising up agents of judgment against Solomon (J. T. Walsh 1996: 140). The unfinished nature of the stories points ahead to the story of Jeroboam and enriches that narrative (Bodner 2012: 39).

11:26-40 Ahijah Appoints Jeroboam, Son of Nebat

The two foreign adversaries, Hadad and Rezon, prefigure the rise of Jeroboam, Solomon's replacement, profiling him as a new Moses and a new David (Bodner 2012: 40–41). The report of Jeroboam's rebellion begins with an introduction of Jeroboam (11:26-28). The main event, the prophet Ahijah's speech (11:31b-39), is introduced by symbolic action (11:29-31a) *[Prophets: Prophetic Word, p. 469]*. Jeroboam's flight to Egypt concludes the section (11:40).

Jeroboam son of Nebat (the quintessential sinner among Israelite kings is mentioned seventeen times after his death, always associated with sin) is an *Ephratite* (AT). Translated *Ephraimite* by NRSV and NIV, the term is both geographical, since Jeroboam is from the Ephraimite city of Zeredah, and associative. Jeroboam has affinities with Samuel (1 Sam 1:1) and David (1 Sam 17:12), both Ephratite (but David is from Judah not Ephraim), both *servants* who replaced their masters (Eli and Saul). The text emphasizes that he is the awaited *servant of Solomon* predicted by the Lord as Solomon's successor

(1 Kings 11:11), an introduction delayed by the tale of the two foreign adversaries (11:14-25). The naming of Jeroboam's mother
recalls the two previous royal rivals: Adonijah, whose mother is
Haggith, and Solomon, son of Bathsheba (1:5, 11); it anticipates the
other kings who succeed to David's throne (Jezebel is the only other
named mother of an Israelite king, 2 Kings 9:22). In contrast to
Rehoboam's Ammonite mother (14:21), Jeroboam's mother is an
Israelite, better fitting the Deuteronomic royal qualifications (Deut
17:15). *Jeroboam . . . rebelled [raised his hand] against the king* (11:26).

The introduction continues with a wordplay that is difficult to
translate. NIV interprets *word* as event or story: *Here is the account of
how [the word that] he rebelled against the king* (11:27); but *word* could
be understood as the *divine word*, the *prophetic oracle*, of Ahijah (as in
11:31-39 AT; J. T. Walsh 1996: 143); Saul's rejection and David's rise
were set in motion by a *divine word* (1 Sam 15:10; Seow: 94). The narrative flashback recalls construction of the Millo (9:15, 24; Solomon's
twenty-fourth year). The Millo (AT: *filling*), an earthwork foundation
of a new section of the city, was built after the completion of the
temple-palace complex and the divine warning to do justice (6:11-
13; 9:3-9; Bodner 2012: 46). In 11:28, Jeroboam is described as *very
able* (NIV: *a man of standing*), a Hebrew term used for the warrior
Jephthah (Judg 11:1), the wealthy landowners Boaz (Ruth 2:1) and
Saul's father, Kish (1 Sam 9:1), the military general Naaman (2 Kings
5:1), and the youthful David (1 Sam 16:18). Solomon, noting
Jeroboam's skill as a foreman, promoted him over all the forced
labor (AT: *burden*) of the house of Joseph, Jeroboam's own people
(11:28), foreshadowing the rebellion of the house of Joseph and the
other northern tribes and thrusting Jeroboam into leadership
(12:18-20).

About that time Jeroboam *goes out from Jerusalem* (AT). *Going out*
foreshadows Jeroboam's leading Israel from the control of the
Davidic kingdom in Jerusalem (11:29). Ahijah the Shilonite prophet
finds Jeroboam in the open country and performs a symbolic action
to unleash the prophetic oracle he is about to speak *[Prophets, p. 465]*.
Ahijah's hometown, Shiloh, was abandoned by the Lord in judgment
for its wickedness while Eli was priest (1 Sam 4; Jer 7:12-14). Just as
Samuel, the prophet from Shiloh, announced the end of Saul's kingship, so Ahijah of Shiloh announces Solomon's judgment. Ahijah
seizes and *tears* the new garment that *Jeroboam* (AT; cf. NRSV, NIV:
Ahijah) is wearing into twelve pieces (though the Hebrew is indefinite about whose garment is torn, the verb *seize* is not normally used
for one's own clothing). The verb *tear* connects the action to the

Lord's judgment speech, where the verb *tear* is used four times regarding Solomon's kingdom (11:11-13). The symbolic act resembles Samuel's interpretation of his own torn robe as a sign that Saul's kingdom is torn from him (1 Sam 15:27-28). *Garment* (*salmah*, a sign of wealth and social position in 1 Kings 10:25) is similar to *Solomon* (*Shelomoh*) in Hebrew. Like the new garment worn by Solomon's servant Jeroboam, Solomon's kingdom is about to be ripped to pieces and divided among the twelve tribes (Hens-Piazza 2006: 114).

Ahijah interprets the symbolic action with a speech that opens with his instruction to Jeroboam to take ten pieces of the robe, followed by an oracle introduced by a prophetic messenger formula, *Thus says the LORD, the God of Israel* (11:31-39) [*Literary Criticism, p. 457*]. The first half of the speech focuses on Solomon, with attention to the past and present (11:31-34); the second half focuses on Jeroboam and the future (11:35-39; J. T. Walsh 1996: 144–45). The Lord announces the sentence of judgment: he will *tear the kingdom from . . . Solomon* and give Jeroboam *ten tribes* (11:31; cf. 11:11-13, 30). Reference to *tribes* implicitly judges Solomon's administrative policies (the twelve districts, 4:7). The story is not concerned with the detail that the distribution does not account for the twelve tribes, a loose end tied up in 12:20-21, where the tribe of Benjamin assembles with the house of Judah against Israel. (The landless tribe of Levi, rejected by Jeroboam in favor of other priests, could also resolve the issue, 12:31; 13:33; Bodner 2012: 54.) Judgment is limited; David's house retains rule in Jerusalem because of the Lord's commitment to David (11:32; 2 Sam 7:10-16; 1 Kings 11:11-13) and his choice of Jerusalem (Deut 12:5-7; 1 Kings 9:3).

The indictment against Solomon and Israel (*they have*, 11:33 MT) brings together the narrative accusation of idolatry and the divine accusation of covenant breaking (11:5, 11-13). Idolatry is indicative not only of cultic unfaithfulness but also of unjust royal administrative policies [*Idolatry, p. 449*]. *Forsaking* the Lord (AT; forbidden but predicted, Deut 28:20; 29:25; 1 Kings 9:9) and failing to keep his *ordinances* (Heb. *mišpaṭ* pl.) is tantamount to breaking the Deuteronomic covenant, centered on doing justice (Deut 10:12-22; 17:14-20) [*Mišpaṭ, p. 461*]. Judgment is limited (*not take the whole kingdom away*) and delayed (*make him ruler all the days of his life*) because David responded to covenant election (*my servant . . . whom I have chosen*) with covenant faithfulness (1 Kings 11:34; cf. 11:32, 36, 39).

The second half of the divine oracle promises Jeroboam *the kingdom, . . . that is, the ten tribes* during the reign of Solomon's son

(11:35). The promise to Jeroboam is interrupted by the Lord's reiterated commitment that *my servant David may always have a lamp . . . in the city I have chosen* (11:36). *Lamp* has been interpreted *kingdom, deposit* (LXX), *remnant* (1 Kings 15:4 LXX), *dominion* (J. Davies 2012: 231); it is a *glimmer of hope* burning in the doom of judgment (J. T. Walsh 1996: 145). The focus shifts to Jeroboam with what "ranks as one of the most colossal promises" in Kings (Bodner 2012: 55): *You, even you, I will take* (11:31, 34-35 AT), *and you shall reign over whatever you desire* (11:37 AT). The second-person pronoun is emphatic. The verb *desire* echoes Abner's promise of the Northern Kingdom to David (2 Sam 3:21), reinforcing the theme that Jeroboam has a chance to become the new David (McConville 2006: 157). The Lord's promise uses covenantal terms (*I will be with you*, 1 Kings 11:38); it echoes the Lord's covenant with David (2 Sam 7:3, 9), commitment to the patriarchs (Gen 26:3), and promise to Moses (Exod 33:14). In contrast to the Lord's unconditional promises to David (2 Sam 7:16) but consistent with the conditions imposed on Solomon (1 Kings 2:4; 3:14; 6:11-13; 9:3-9), the Lord's promise to Jeroboam is conditioned on covenant faithfulness: *Listen . . . , walk in my ways, . . . keeping my statutes and my commandments* (11:38). Jeroboam's (and Israel's) future is filled with potential, but the context of judgment is foreboding. If David's fidelity, the model for faithfulness (11:33, 34, 38), is insufficient to preserve his son's reign, what are the chances for Jeroboam's house (J. T. Walsh 1996: 148; Bodner 2012: 55)? The oracle concludes with God's promise not to punish David's descendants *forever* (AT: *for all days*), a final note of hope of restoration (11:39; see Deut 4:29-31).

Solomon's final action recalls his executions of Adonijah, Joab, and Shimei while establishing the kingdom (1 Kings 2). Despite the secrecy of Ahijah's encounter with Jeroboam (*alone in the open country*, 11:29), Solomon's intelligence discovers the threat. Jeroboam's flight to Egypt echoes the story of Solomon's first adversary Hadad (11:17-22) and undercuts the narrative confidence that Solomon's relationship with Egypt is uniquely harmonious (despite the repeated references: 3:1; 7:8; 9:16, 24; 11:1). Solomon's attempt to kill Jeroboam parallels Saul's multiple attempts to kill David (Leithart: 88).

First Kings 11 introduces three adversaries (the Hebrew śaṭan is most often used for people) whom the Lord raises up against Solomon. Each of the first two is a foreign, non-Israelite śaṭan. The third is inspired by the divine oracle. The pivotal chapter explains the transition from the united monarchy to the division into rival kingdoms of Israel and Judah. In 1 Kings 11 the Lord intervenes directly to judge Solomon's idolatrous covenant failure and to introduce a new era in the Israelite monarchy, but within the narrative are hints pointing toward political factors that provoke rebellion against imperial oppression. Pagan idolatry supports imperial hegemony. Covenant failure violates justice. The foreign adversaries act on deep-seated alienation prompted by David's imperial policies. Jeroboam sees firsthand the injustice of forced labor and *leaves Jerusalem*. Ahijah the prophet hails from Shiloh, a city with covenant traditions that oppose centralized power in Jerusalem. Though implicit, the injustice of Solomon's violent and oppressive reign factors prominently in popular opposition recognized by the narrative long before Solomon's demise.

Concluding Royal Formula for the Reign of Solomon 11:41-43

The concluding royal formula typically references an annalistic source, a summary and evaluation of the reign, death and burial report, and the successor's name. Reference to the annals, lost to us, not only creates verisimilitude but also reminds the reader that the purpose of the narrative is theologically evaluative rather than comprehensive historical reconstruction. Unique to Solomon's concluding formula is reference to his wisdom, an ironic reminder that wisdom without obedience is insufficient, if it is wisdom at all (Wray Beal 2014: 174).

THE TEXT IN BIBLICAL CONTEXT

Prophets as Kingmakers

Old Testament prophets are political agents (Nathan in 1 Kings 1:11-14). Ahijah is the second prophet named in the royal narratives of Samuel and Kings who dethrones the reigning king and dynasty and crowns his replacement [Prophets, p. 465]. Samuel the seer anointed Saul (1 Sam 10:1, 24-25; 11:14-15), announced to him that he had forfeited the kingdom (13:13-14; 15:22-29), and anointed David in place of Saul (16:13). Through Nathan the prophet, the Lord promised David that his son would rule in his place (2 Sam 7:12-16). Nathan was in attendance when the priest Zadok anointed Solomon to be king (1 Kings 1:38-39, 44-45). After announcing to Jeroboam that the ten tribes of Israel will be torn from Solomon's heir and given to him (11:31-39), Ahijah disappears from the story until Jeroboam's wife inquires of Ahijah regarding her dying son (14:1-18). Ahijah announces not only that the Lord will cut off the house of Jeroboam but also that Israel will be exiled beyond the Euphrates because of Jeroboam's sin (14:14-16). Ahijah's prophecy is cited when Baasha assassinates Jeroboam's son, King Nadab, and destroys Jeroboam's house (15:27-30) [Prophets: Prophetic Word, p. 469]. The prophet Jehu announces to King Baasha that he too would be cut off because in evil he had led Israel to sin (16:1-4, 7).

Elijah announces judgment against Ahab and Jezebel, declaring that their dynasty would be cut off because Ahab had killed Naboth and taken his land and had sold himself to do evil (1 Kings 21:17-24). Elijah also announces the death of Ahab's heir, Ahaziah (2 Kings 1:15-17). Elisha has Jehu anointed to replace Ahab; Jehu executes Ahab's entire family (2 Kings 9–10). Elisha's young protégé announces that the judgment against Ahab is to be fulfilled and that Jehu will succeed him as king (9:6-10).

The report of Israel's exile cites the unheeded prophetic warnings (2 Kings 17:13-14). Isaiah supports Hezekiah's revolt against Assyria (19:2-7, 20-34). When Josiah discovers the Torah, he consults the prophetess Huldah, who confirms the inevitable judgment coming against Judah (22:14-20). Following Huldah, the prophetic voice is silenced in 2 Kings (though the book of Jeremiah narrates Jeremiah's interaction with Josiah's successors).

THE TEXT IN THE LIFE OF THE CHURCH
Passion, Love, and Marriage

Solomon's excessive accumulation in every area of life includes his many marriages, economic and political alliances to ensure political stability. His marriage practices, condemned as *evil in the sight of the LORD*, transgress Torah on multiple scales; marrying foreign women leads to idolatry (11:1-6). Solomon violates the law of the king prohibiting *acquiring many wives for himself*, excess made possible because of his monopoly on power (Deut 17:17). Solomon's multiple marriages were misogynistic and exploitative, an abuse of women seeking covenant marriage [Idolatry, p. 449].

Solomon's *love* for his foreign wives (11:1, 2) contrasts with his earlier *love* of the Lord (3:3); his *heart* is not true as David's *heart* had been (11:4). James Smith argues that humans are first and foremost lovers whose loves are shaped by rituals. Just as Solomon's love was shaped by participating in the rituals of idolatry, so modern humans become lovers of the lesser gods of malls, media, and electronic innovations. Longings and desires motivate passion, the quest to pursue the good life. Pursuing lesser gods—such as pleasure, wealth, power, and even family—is an idolatrous counterfeit of the purpose for which humans were created: to seek God and God's reign in the world (J. Smith: 19–25).

The title of the Old Testament's best-known love poem is "The Song of Songs, which is Solomon's" (Song of Sol 1:1). Though "King Solomon" is mentioned twice as the daughters of Jerusalem are called to see his palanquin (gold-and-silver-covered litter; 3:9-11), the poem itself glories in the romance of a young couple. The Song may be associated with Solomon because his many marriages suggest romantic love or because of his fame as a writer of songs (1 Kings 4:32), but perhaps the association is an ironic critique of Solomon's inability to enjoy romantic love (Brueggemann 2005: 206–10).

After warning against marrying those who have not been "born from above" and are thus "unequally yoked together with unbelievers," a seventeenth-century Swiss confession cites 1 Kings 11:1 in condemnation of "the transgressors of this and their punishment" (Twisck and Pieterisz 1617: art. 25). The citation is almost quaint in a day when previously forbidden living together before marriage and mixed-faith marriages have become commonplace. Though divorce is neither as scandalous nor as rare as it was in earlier generations when it disqualified those who had experienced it from church service, pastoral care for marital disharmony remains a priority. Solomon's story illustrates the obvious truth that comfortable ease is not a guarantee of fulfillment in marriage, home, or love.

Part 2

The Divided Kingdom

1 Kings 12-2 Kings 17

OVERVIEW

First Kings 1-11 explores Solomon's rule; the next major section of Kings spans the kingdom division through Israel's Assyrian exile in 722 BCE (1 Kings 12-2 Kings 17); the third major section of the narrative completes Judah's story through its Babylonian exile in 586 BCE (2 Kings 18-25).

The story of the divided kingdom opens with rebellion after the prophet Ahijah's announcement that Israel will be *ripped* from David's line. Solomon's former servant Jeroboam returns from Egyptian exile to lead Israel away from Davidic domination. The stories of Solomon's heir Rehoboam and the adversary Jeroboam are intertwined in 1 Kings 12-14.

Though both kingdoms are reported, the narrative focuses on Israel, the Northern Kingdom. First Kings 15-16 reports the unbroken line of David in Jerusalem and a series of brief, minor dynasties ending in rebellion and assassination in the north. Prophets Ahijah and Jehu announce that the royal houses of Jeroboam and Baasha are cut off because they reject Torah justice (1 Kings 12-16).

The situation is resolved with the rise of the Omride dynasty (1 Kings 16:21-2 Kings 9). Though extrabiblical evidence describes Ahab as a powerful and successful regional leader, his reign is overshadowed by prophets, principally Elijah and Elisha, whose stories are narrated in 1 Kings 17:1 (when Elijah bursts onto the scene unannounced) through 2 Kings 13:21 (when a corpse that touches Elisha's bones springs to life). Elijah condemns Ahab's Baal-dominated regime, exposing the powerlessness of the Baal myth on Mount Carmel (1 Kings 18) and announcing a death sentence for unjust royal accumulation in taking the vineyard of Naboth (1 Kings 21). The New Testament regards Elijah as the greatest prophet after

Moses and recognizes him within the eschatological hopes of first-century Israel. Elisha succeeds Elijah when he witnesses Elijah's assumption in a whirlwind (2 Kings 2). Elisha is allied with a company of prophets, apparently an anti-Omride community composed of disenfranchised northerners. Elisha is at home in corridors of power in both Israel and Aram and becomes a royal counselor, though as a peripheral figure. Anointed king by one of Elisha's disciples, Jehu rebels against the Omride dynasty and in a bloody coup eliminates both the royal house and the Baal apparatus (2 Kings 9–10). Like Omri, Jehu is followed by several generations, including Jeroboam II, whose success, like Ahab's, is given short shrift in the text (2 Kings 10:1–15:8). The prominence of the prophets in opposition to Ahab and Baal has led to the suggestion that these stories were collected by a prophetic school, preserved to legitimate Jehu's coup and dynasty, and later incorporated into 1–2 Kings (Wray Beal 2014: 231) [Prophets, p. 465].

Second Kings 15:9–17:6 focuses on Israel and reports frequent royal assassinations similar to the situation after Jeroboam's reign report (1 Kings 14–16). The encroaching kingdom of Assyria sends Israel into exile, an event explained as divine judgment for Israel's persistence in the sins of Jeroboam and rejection of prophetic calls for covenant justice (2 Kings 17:7–23). Assyria repopulates Israel with people who do not know the god of the land but quickly follow the pattern of Israel by mixing the justice (mišpaṭ) of their own gods with the justice of the Lord (17:24–41).

Israel pursues the sins of Jeroboam, anti-Deuteronomic covenant ideology that neglects divine justice and is linked with the cult of the golden calves, provoking the Lord to anger. The Judahite reformer King Joash pursues covenant justice under the tutelage of the priest Jehoiada, but it is a rare exception that fails when Joash trusts alliances rather than the Lord (2 Kings 11–12). Kings of Judah tolerate the proliferation of high places. Despite the Lord's intervention to save (13:4-5, 23; 14:25-27), both realms fail to practice Deuteronomic justice.

1 Kings 12:1–14:31

Rehoboam and Jeroboam

PREVIEW

Israel's revolt can be described as either rebellion or independence. The American Revolutionary War was for the British "the American Rebellion"; what for the Union was "the War of Rebellion," Confederate states called "the War for Southern Independence." In contrast to the heavy casualties of the U.S. Civil War, the Israelite secession of Israel from Judah cost the life of only one officer, the enforcer of the hated Solomonic practice of forced labor.

OUTLINE

EXPLANATORY NOTES
Israel's Rebellion against Rehoboam 1 Kings 12:1-24

Successful politicians excel at "reading the room." After assessing the mood of the audience, they adjust the message to the moment. "Overplaying one's hand," another political metaphor, miscalculates one's capacity to prevail in a political skirmish. Rehoboam loses control of Israel because he fails to listen to the elders, experts in reading a room, who warn him against overplaying his hand.

12:1-5 Israel's Ultimatum

Rehoboam goes to Shechem for his coronation (12:1). Meeting in Shechem portends well for the new king. As an ancient Ephraimite city of refuge (Josh 20:7) forty miles north of Jerusalem and lying on major trade routes, Shechem was the designated city for covenant renewal (Deut 27:4, 11-12; Josh 8:30-35; 24:1, 25). The designation *all Israel* suggests continued national unity (1 Kings 1:20; 4:1; 8:1-2, 65; 11:42). Rehoboam reaches Shechem seemingly confident in his coronation, a perfunctory covenant renewal, and continuation of the political status quo—the Solomonic administrative system with high taxes and forced labor. (Seow suggests Rehoboam's choice of Shechem is an assertion of his authority over the northern tribes, repeating Abimelech's foolish action in Judg 9-10; Seow: 100). Rehoboam is confident that *all Israel had come to Shechem to make him king.*

Several previous textual hints suggest that Rehoboam's confidence is ill-founded. For one, a more polemical reading of *all Israel* in 1 Kings 4-5 is suggested. Though the list of Solomon's officers is introduced by noting that Solomon ruled *all Israel* (4:1), the reference to the *twelve officials over all Israel* (4:7) is more problematic. Twelve districts (probably excluding Judah, the tribe of David and Solomon) supplied Solomon's provisions, so referring to *Judah and Israel* raises suspicion about the equity of the royal administrative policy (4:20, 25). *All Israel* designates Solomon's forced laborers (5:13; cf. 9:22). Rehoboam expects a unified people, but the ensuing narrative reveals the suspicious reticence of *all Israel* burdened by taxation and forced labor, since from here onward *all Israel* specifies the northern tribes (Wray Beal 2014: 180).

Locating the meeting in Shechem increases narrative tension. Shechem is the traditional place for covenant making, home of the Deuteronomic covenant with its restrictive law of the king and administrative policies (Deut 17:14-20) [*Mišpaṭ, p. 461*]. Abimelech's power grab ended in chaos in Shechem (Judg 9), a place where kingly power may be viewed with suspicion.

Jeroboam's summons and arrival raise tensions further (12:2-3). As a dangerous rival, exiled but not exterminated by Solomon, Jeroboam comes with firsthand management experience (11:28), prophetic approval (11:31), an alliance with Egypt (11:40), and the summons as representative of *all Israel* in the royal negotiations (12:3). Asserting sovereignty, the populace *sent and called* Jeroboam (12:20) *[Send, p. 476]*.

Jeroboam is a formidable challenger. Like Moses in Exodus 3-5, he returns from exile to confront the imperial powers and demand respite from forced labor (Simundson: 196-97). Jeroboam confronts Rehoboam regarding Israel's discontent with the status quo, a situation Rehoboam has assumed remains operative. *Lighten the hard service of your father and his heavy yoke . . . , and we will serve you,* declare Jeroboam and Israel (12:4). *Hard service* characterizes Israel's Egyptian enslavement (Exod 1:14; 6:9; Deut 26:6); the sole metaphorical use of *yoke* in 1-2 Kings is in this chapter, but elsewhere it describes oppression by the surrounding empires, thus characterizing Rehoboam as though a non-Israelite (Isa 9:4; Jer 27:8, 11-12; Deijl: 103). Jeroboam accuses Solomon's regime of imperial slavery (*yoke* is a metaphor for slavery; 1 Kings 12:4, 9, 10, 11, 14) and demands that Rehoboam adopt a new administrative structure, acting as their *brother* rather than a despot (12:4; Deut 17:15). Jeroboam offers to *serve* Rehoboam if he relieves the *hard service.* Jeroboam builds a trap by offering conditions that Rehoboam will reject, rejection that brings the judgment predicted by Ahijah (1 Kings 11:31).

Narrative tension builds as Rehoboam requests time (12:5), issuing the only order that *all Israel* will obey: *Go away . . . and then return.* (AT) Israel did so, but the next time Israel *goes away* it is to abandon Rehoboam (12:16).

12:6-15 Rehoboam's Response to Israel

Rehoboam *takes counsel* with two sets of royal advisers (12:6-11; cf. 2 Sam 14-17; 1 Kings 1:12), turning first to his father's advisers to ask how he should answer the people (12:6-7). Recognizing Rehoboam's tenuous political position, they counsel him to *speak good words,* promising that *today he will be a servant* and *serve them* (turning around Jeroboam's conditional promise that the people will *serve* Rehoboam if he responds favorably). The elders counsel that immediate caution will reap long-term rewards.

Rehoboam *disregards* (ʿazab) the elder's advice (as Israel *forsakes* the Lord's covenant, Deut 28:20; 29:25; 31:16) and *consults with* (yaʿaṣ) his contemporaries (1 Kings 12:8). By repeatedly quoting the people's request for a lighter yoke (12:9-10), Rehoboam and his advisers mock the people, reinforced by the similar sounds in Hebrew of *yoke* (*ʿol*) and *on us* (*ʿalenu*; J. Davies 2012: 240). The advisers counsel an inflammatory, vulgar response, advising him to increase the slavery (*yoke*) and intensify the discipline (from use of *whips* to use of *scorpions*, 12:11, 14), as well as boasting that his *little thing* (12:10 AT) is bigger than his father's loins (*little* is an apparent euphemism for penis; Seow: 102). When Jeroboam and the people *return* on the third day, Rehoboam uses the harsh language of his young contemporaries (without repeating the vulgarity; 12:12-14). Like Pharaoh (Exod 7:13), Rehoboam's failure to *listen to the people* not only results in loss of his kingdom but also facilitates fulfillment of the Lord's prophetic word (12:15. What happens on the plane of human history reveals that the Lord is the primary mover.

12:16-19 Israel's Departure and Rebellion

When they see that *the king would not listen to them* (unlike the Lord, who hears the groans of the Israelite slaves: Exod 2:23-25), *all Israel* rebels against the political alliance negotiated by the elders of Israel with David (2 Sam 5:3). Echoing the taunt song of Sheba's rebellion, when "all the people of Israel withdrew from David" (2 Sam 20:1-2), Israel repudiates its *share* and *inheritance* in David (terms evoking the conquest and settlement of Israel in the land; J. Davies 2012: 243). In contrast to their joyful departure from the temple dedication (1 Kings 8:66), Israel's return *to their tents* signals the end of Davidic rule. The people add to the earlier refrain: *Look now to your own house, O David* (12:16).

Rehoboam maintains control over only Judah, including the Israelites living in Judah's tribal towns (12:17). When *Rehoboam sent Adoram* (a variation of *Adoniram*, the official charged with forced labor, 1 Kings 4:6; 2 Sam 20:24), the implication may be that Rehoboam means to reduce the whole Israelite population to the more brutal form of labor imposed earlier on the Canaanites (1 Kings 9:15-22; Rainey: 202). Like Moab (2 Kings 3) and Edom (2 Kings 8), Israel acts *in rebellion* against foreign occupation by the house of David and *stones* Adoram *to death*. First Kings 12 describes this as rebellion from Judah's point of view, but it is revolution and freedom for Israel.

12:20 Jeroboam's Coronation

The coronation report of Jeroboam interrupts the focus on Rehoboam (1 Kings 12:20). In contrast with Solomon's investiture orchestrated by royal officials (1:28-39; acclamation by *all the people* is reported as an addendum, 1:40), *all Israel sends and calls* Jeroboam *to the assembly* (12:2) *[Send, p. 476]*. They make him *king over all Israel* as they had Saul and David. The assembly of "all Israel" had recognized Saul as king limited by "the rights and duties of kingship" (1 Sam 10:25). "All the tribes of Israel" made a "covenant" when they appointed David king "over all Israel and Judah" (2 Sam 5:1-5). Having repudiated Solomon's imperial order by rejecting Rehoboam's proposal to extend his father's administration, the people initiate, authorize, and establish the parameters of the reign of Jeroboam. The action fulfills the prophetic word (1 Kings 11:31-32; 12:15). Jeroboam is passive throughout. The note that only the tribe of Judah and some Benjaminites remain with the house of David reinforces the fulfillment of the word of the prophet (12:21, 23; Wray Beal 2014: 183) *[Prophets: Prophetic Word, p. 469]*.

12:21-24 *Judah's Army Assembled and Dispersed*

Israel's rebellion is completed successfully. First Kings 12:21-24 reports Rehoboam's acceptance of the new reality of Israelite independence. Rehoboam stands to lose not only agricultural production from most of Israel but also control of lucrative north-south trade routes, part of an extensive network of international highways in Canaan (Master: 509; Dorsey: 209). When Rehoboam assembles a large volunteer people's army (absent the mercenaries who protected David and Solomon, 2 Sam 20:7; 1 Kings 1:44), an otherwise unknown man of God, Shemaiah, warns Rehoboam and the troops to disband (see the parallel in 2 Chron 12). Rehoboam and the people *listen to the word of the LORD* and *return* home (AT). The secession of Israel from the empire of David and Solomon is complete.

The Kingship of Jeroboam 12:25–14:20

When a couple marries and has children, the question of holiday traditions (and countless other matters) must be resolved. Can the new family maintain the traditional commitments to their parents' homes? Will some of the traditions of the parents' homes be incorporated into the life of the newly forming family? Will the next generation revise or reject earlier traditions and move into patterns of their own? A great deal is at stake in these decisions. Relationships, independence, and power structures shape decisions. For a better analogy of the pressures faced by Jeroboam, imagine these decisions in a blended family, with additional extended families.

Jeroboam worked within multiple traditions. Prophetic voices had announced that the Lord was establishing Jeroboam and restricting Rehoboam. The prophet had demanded compliance with the Lord's commands (1 Kings 11:26-40; 12:21-24). First Kings 12:25-33 reflects Jeroboam's response to the powerful propaganda device of the Solomonic temple under the control of a foreign ruler, Rehoboam of Judah. Jeroboam feared that Israel's pilgrimages to the Jerusalem temple festivals, the priestly tradition, and the sacrificial cult would undermine Israelite loyalty. The Northern Kingdom would also suffer economically from lost tithes and tributes. In addition to regional rivalries, the question of compliance with the Deuteronomic law of the king informs our reading of Jeroboam's administrative innovations (Deut 17:14-20).

12:25-32 Jeroboam's Golden Calves

Jeroboam gained office in two ways: on the authority of the Lord's *prophet* (11:26-40) and by invitation of *all Israel* (12:20). The twin rationales of God's supervision and political factors might be named the "dual causality principle" (Amit 1987: 388, 400). Identifying theological development (prophetic promise; 1 Kings 11:26-40; 12:24) and political action (the Shechem assembly's rejection of Rehoboam's administrative plan, 12:1-24) informs our narrative interpretation. Jeroboam's throne is secured by divine promise. Jeroboam's political position is instituted by political assembly.

Jeroboam's administrative policy is laid out in 1 Kings 12:25-33 *[Mišpaṭ, p. 461]*. The unit can be divided into three subsections, each introduced by the name *Jeroboam* (12:25, 26, 32; Wray Beal 2014: 183). Jeroboam fortifies and resides in two cities (12:25), builds two cultic sanctuaries with furnishings (12:26-31), and institutes a cultic festival (12:32-33).

Given Jeroboam's experience in building fortifications (11:27-28), his first royal act to fortify Shechem comes as no surprise (12:25; NIV *fortified* is preferred to NRSV *built* since the city is already in existence, 12:1). Initially, Jeroboam resides in Shechem, the city associated with covenant justice (12:1; Josh 24:1). Jeroboam *goes out from there and fortifies Penuel* (AT). The reference to Jeroboam's *going out from [Shechem]* may indicate transfer of the capital to Penuel, east of Jordan near Jabbok (Doorly: 27-31). Neither Shechem nor Penuel is mentioned again in 1-2 Kings (Jeroboam's wife returns home to Tirzah, in the northern highlands about twenty miles northeast of Shechem, 14:17; Tirzah remains Israel's capital until Omri constructs Samaria, 16:24).

Jeroboam's building activities are reported without evaluation, though they necessitate continued reliance on forced labor (Coote:

68). Penuel and Shechem (and Bethel, where construction is reported, 12:29) are linked with the Israelite ancestor Jacob (Gen 32:30; 33:18-20; 28:19). Establishing the kingdom in ancestral cultic locations suggests attention to Israel's tribal interests and covenant traditions. Jeroboam's second phase of building projects is evaluated negatively (1 Kings 12:26-31). After fortifying the two capital cities, Jeroboam reforms cultic practices. He is motivated by fear that *the kingdom may well revert to the house of David* if Israelites return to Jerusalem for worship and *return to King Rehoboam* (repeated three times in 12:26-27, *return* is a theme alluding to the unsettled state in 1 Kings 12, where *return* [*šub*] is used twelve times). The speech revealing Jeroboam's fearful motivation for his building strategy is the longest of any royal soliloquy in 1–2 Kings (12:26-27). Jeroboam fears not that the unpopular Rehoboam threatens his throne but that, despite the prophetic promise of an enduring house (11:38), the people will *turn* away from him. By reducing traffic to Jerusalem, Jeroboam builds loyalty and averts loss of revenue in taxes, tithes, and expenditures. As Rehoboam did in 1 Kings 12:6-11, Jeroboam *takes counsel* (12:28). Unlike Rehoboam, who consulted two sets of counselors, no advisers are mentioned, suggesting that Jeroboam's strategy is his own (Bodner 2012: 85).

Jeroboam reforms virtually every part of the Solomonic cult. Solomon has dedicated the temple in Jerusalem. Jeroboam dedicates worship centers in cities conveniently within the boundaries of Israel. Stopping in Bethel, on the route to Jerusalem near the southern extreme of Israel, would shorten the journey. The cultic center in Dan was convenient for northern Israel. Bethel had cultic traditions linked to Abram (Gen 12:8) and Jacob (28:10-22; 35:3-16). Dan was linked to descendants of Moses (Judg 18:30).

In the most jarring innovation, Jeroboam places a golden calf in Bethel and one in Dan. Bulls were associated with the ancient Canaanite god El and with the storm god Baal. The text reports that Jeroboam was restoring the Canaanite bull cult that promised power and fertility. Some scholars argue that the calves were not idols but pedestals for the Lord, equivalent to Solomon's cherubim in the holy of holies (Hobbs: 162). Jeroboam's bulls represent village agriculture just as Solomon's lions symbolize war production (Coote: 68). Toews argues that the bulls are images of El-Yahweh, evidence of Jeroboam's commitment to Israelite traditional religion, and that the stories opposing the calves are anachronistic anti-Israelite polemics (106, 146, 149). Jeroboam himself refers to the calves as deities: *Here are your gods, O Israel, who brought* [pl. verb] *you up out of the land of Egypt*

(12:28). The parallels with the story of the golden calves fashioned by Aaron at Sinai (Exod 32) reinforce the evaluation in 1 Kings 12. Jeroboam, whom Israel may have envisioned as the Moses opposing Rehoboam's pharaoh in 12:3-4, is unmasked as the Aaron presenting golden calves as gods (Leithart: 96); Jeroboam and Aaron both declare that the calves are the gods (ʾelohim) that brought up Israel. Though the term ʾelohim can indicate the singular God, Elohim, by using a singular verb, the text reports that Jeroboam and Aaron use the plural verb brought to indicate their idolatrous intent.

Jeroboam's building initiatives are interrupted by an evaluation. The Hebrew text says simply, And this thing was sin (12:30a). Overt judgment has not been characteristic of the narrator (Bodner 2012: 93), and the text does not clarify how Jeroboam's initiatives are missing the mark or taking a wrong turn. Is it the idolatry of the golden calves (the most immediate reference to this thing)? Is it the rejection of Ahijah's requirement that Jeroboam keep the commandments (11:38)? Is it the return to the Solomonic construction practices requiring forced labor? Does it have to do with leading the people into sinful practices (so NRSV and NIV)?

With all these things in mind, the report of Jeroboam's actions as the "second Solomon" resumes. Matching Solomon's temple-building activity, Jeroboam builds houses on the high places (12:31). As Solomon exiled Abiathar from the traditional priestly family, Jeroboam replaces Levites with priests from among all the people (12:31; in violation of Deut 18:5, stipulating that the Lord has chosen Levi). Because Levitical priests are charged with reading the Torah before all Israel at the fall festival (Deut 31:9-13), Jeroboam's action raises suspicion that he is circumventing censure for violating covenant by embracing ancient Canaanite traditions (Doorly: 32). In contrast to Solomon's temple dedication at the Festival of Booths (Feast of Tabernacles), traditionally celebrated in the seventh month (1 Kings 8:2, 5, 62-64), Jeroboam inaugurates his cultic centers by appointing a festival in the eighth month (12:32). Though a later festival date may correspond to later harvest at the lower elevations in northern Israel, the explicit mention of the contrasting festival month, inconsistent with Torah stipulations, reminds the reader that Jeroboam's cultic reforms counter Solomon's institution (8:2; 12:32-33; Lev 23:39-43; Num 29:12-39).

Jeroboam's innovations may appear to be superficial cultic rearrangements. If the Lord was enthroned on cherubim in the Jerusalem temple, why not have the bull as his throne in Bethel and Dan? Why should the single place of worship in Israel prescribed in

Deuteronomy 12 be Jerusalem, a Jebusite stronghold until David's conquest, rather than Bethel, with traditions linking it to Abram and Jacob (Gen 12:8; 28:19)? Regarding an expanded priesthood, wasn't Samuel himself an approved priest with non-Levitical origins (1 Sam 1)? The festivals were associated with harvest, and perhaps one month was as good as another. Surely synchronizations necessitated by the Hebrew lunar-solar calendar coupled with the earlier Jerusalem harvest provided an innocent explanation for postponing the festival one month. Though the narrator evaluates high places negatively, they seem to have been an accepted part of Judah's worship until Hezekiah's reign (1 Kings 15:14; 22:43; 2 Kings 12:3; 14:4; 15:4, 35; 16:4; 17:9; 18:4). The reader may be tempted to disregard the innovations of Jeroboam as superficial.

Regarding the calf images as idols (not merely pedestals) links Jeroboam's cult with Canaanite royal ideology *[Idolatry, p. 449]*. Doorly interprets Jeroboam's transfer of the capital from Shechem (*he went out from there*, 12:25) and addition of non-Levitical priests as a break with the egalitarian economic, political, and social expectations of the Levitical centers of Shechem and nearby Shiloh (home of the prophet Ahijah and the earlier pre-monarchic temple of 1 Sam 1–4). Jeroboam broke with the Levitical administrative policies to pursue the imperial structures of ANE kings. He abandoned Shechem, rejected the Levitical priesthood, and demonstrated that he was unwilling to live under the Levitical social agenda endorsed in Shechem (Doorly: 32; Coote: 69; Boling and Campbell: 265).

The sins of Jeroboam were not only cultic innovations but also rejection of the Deuteronomic social agenda *[Sins of Jeroboam, p. 476]*. At Shechem *all Israel* blocked Rehoboam's royal administrative practices of high taxes and forced labor necessitated by a standing army, royal building projects, and opulent living standards. Shiloh, the home of the prophet Ahijah, was allied with Shechem. Levites, scribes, priests, and prophets loyal to Deuteronomy's social agenda insisted on limits of royal power. Jeroboam created a new social structure, a new priesthood, a new calendar, and a new capital to separate himself from the Deuteronomists.

12:33–13:10 *Man of God from Judah Confronts King Jeroboam*

First Kings 13 contains some of the most puzzling narrative in 1–2 Kings. A man of God from Judah prophesies against Jeroboam's altar, refuses Jeroboam's offer of hospitality on divine orders, but allows himself to be duped by the invitation of an old prophet in Bethel who claims to speak for the Lord. The man of God from Judah is killed because he disobeys the word of the Lord. The prophet from Bethel gives the man of God an honorable burial and orders that he be buried in the grave of the man of God because he had proclaimed the word of the Lord.

Made more mysterious by the anonymity of the principal characters (all but Jeroboam), the lengthy, convoluted story with miraculous elements confounds modern readers seeking a rational explanation. The story carries a parable-like message with various interpretations. The strange inscrutability of the Lord is entwined within the message of the story (Brueggemann 2000: 171). At least it is clear that the word of the Lord delivered by the man of God is fulfilled, that the Lord's commandment is authoritative, and that judgment against Jeroboam's sin is inevitable.

Having instituted an Israelite administrative and cultic structure, Jeroboam inaugurates the eighth-month festival in parallel to Solomon's temple dedication during the seventh-month festival (1 Kings 8:1-2; 12:32). Fearing that the people would turn against him (12:26-27), Jeroboam *alone . . . devised* the change (12:33; much as he takes his own counsel in 12:28). The primary verbs *went up* and *make* (each used twice in 12:33 AT) mark Jeroboam's enterprise. The first, *he went up to the altar*, brackets the actions of 12:33 and echoes Jeroboam's earlier concern that Israel would turn against him by *going up to offer sacrifices* in Jerusalem (12:27-28). The second, *he made*, reinforces the sense that Jeroboam, the expert builder, has seized the initiative. Jeroboam *made the altar* and *made [appointed] a festival for the people of Israel*. The verb *make* is used nine times in 12:25-33, eight times with Jeroboam as the subject (*built* Shechem and *built* Penuel, 12:25; *made* two calves, 12:28; *made* houses and *appointed* priests, 12:31; *appointed* a festival, *did* in Bethel, calves that he *had made*, *made* high places , 12:32). Jeroboam constructs a parallel administrative system to replace Solomon's. He acts both as a second Solomon (forcing his population to labor for state projects) and as a counterfeit (rejecting the Jerusalem temple system and thus the Lord's commands through the prophet, 11:38). As a royal builder employing forced labor, Jeroboam *misses the mark* (AT) of administrative justice [Mišpaṭ, p. 461]. As a cultic innovator rejecting the Lord's temple, he *makes a wrong turn* (AT), violating Levitical cultic expectations.

First Kings 13 opens at the climactic moment of Jeroboam's eighth-month festival (the narrative equivalent of a drumroll is the threefold report *he went up to the altar*, 12:32-33). Jeroboam *offers sacrifices* and *incense* on the altar (12:32; 13:1). Though these verbs are used to prescribe worship of the Lord in Torah and to describe Solomon's offerings at the temple dedication, their use in the Jeroboam narrative marks a shift. Excepting Elisha's sacrifice of his oxen (19:21), both terms, *offers sacrifice* and *offers incense*, describe only illicit cultic acts throughout the rest of 1–2 Kings. Like Solomon, Jeroboam presides over the festival from the altar of the temple (1 Kings 8:22). As Solomon presented his longest public speech at the altar during the festival (dedicatory prayer of 8:23-53, 56-61), Jeroboam appears primed to counter Solomon's rhetorical masterpiece.

An abrupt change in point of view swings the focus from Jeroboam's initiatives to prophetic judgment: *Behold, a man of God came from Judah with the word of the LORD* (AT) *[Literary Criticism: Elements of Narrative, p. 458]*. This dynamic shift signals a tension that runs throughout the story of Israel (1 Kings 13–2 Kings 17): the *man of God/prophet* characteristically confronts and limits royal power. The prominent prophetic role, most fully developed in Elijah's and Elisha's conflicts with kings, is foreshadowed by the story of the *man of God* and the *prophet* in 1 Kings 13. (The terms are used interchangeably in 1–2 Kings, but in this story, *man of God* distinguishes the character *coming out of Judah* from the *old prophet* of Bethel, introduced in 1 Kings 13:11.) The authoritative *word of the LORD* (13:1, 2) moves the prophet to confront Jeroboam. In this perplexing tale, the inscrutable *word* transcends rational locus and exercise of power (modern rationalists expect power to be connected to kings and armies, not to prophets and miracles) *[Prophets, p. 465]*.

The man of God from Judah dramatically *cries out against the altar* (AT) with a prophetic judgment oracle, *Thus says the LORD* (13:2, 4, 21, 32) *[Literary Criticism: Poetry, p. 460]*. Citation of the prophetic word asserts the Lord's sovereignty, not prophetic inerrancy. No other prophetic proclamation is more important to the narrative than this pronouncement at Bethel *[Prophets: Prophetic Word, p. 469]*. At the dedication of Jeroboam's rival cultic shrine (920 BCE), the *word of the LORD* anticipates Josiah's reform (620 BCE; 2 Kings 22–23). The prophecy anticipates what Jeroboam most feared: that the Davidic dynasty would prevail over his kingdom (12:26). It also explicitly names Josiah (13:2) and announces that the priests who *offer incense* (the term used for Jeroboam's illicit fire) will be *sacrificed* (12:32; the verb describes Jeroboam's actions) and the altar itself desecrated by human bones (unclean objects, particularly corpses, make things unclean; to touch what is holy with anything dead is offensive, Num 6:6-7). Josiah fulfills this prophecy (preserving the monument to the man of God; 2 Kings 23:15-18). The prophecy of the man of God from Judah concludes with a *sign*: the altar will be *ripped apart* and its ashes spilled out (1 Kings 13:3; failure to properly dispose of sacrificial ashes and fat invalidates and desecrates the holy place, Lev 6:10-11).

The miraculous *signs* reinforce the power of the *word* (1 Kings 13:3, 5). The *signs* and the *word of the* LORD overpowering Jeroboam's imperial design recall the *signs* of the man of God Moses while liberating Israel from imperial Egypt (Exod 4:21; 7:3, 9; 11:9-10; Deut 4:34; 6:22; 13:1-2). The *sign* of the altar being *ripped apart* (AT) by the *word of the* LORD echoes the Lord's *word* to Solomon (whose kingdom was to be *ripped* from him, 1 Kings 11:11-13) and the *word* and *sign* of Ahijah *ripping* Jeroboam's new garment as meaning that the Lord was about to *rip* the kingdom from Solomon (11:30-31).

The conflict rages between *the king*, with his imperial power, and the *man of God*, empowered by the *word of the* LORD (13:2, 4). Stretching out his *hand*, the king orders, *Seize him!* Jeroboam's *hand* has been raised in rebellion against Solomon (11:26-27 AT); *hand* describes such power as Solomon's control of the kingdom (11:12, 31, 34 AT) or as the power of God (18:46).

A series of *signs* demonstrate the power shift. First, the powerful royal *hand* is frozen in the extended position, ironically locking Jeroboam's show of force. Second, the altar is *ripped apart* and the ashes poured out (13:5 AT). Third, Jeroboam is humbled to requesting that the man of God *pray* for him (in contrast to his rival Solomon, who himself *prays* for Israel in cultic pageantry, 8:28, 29, 54). The king requests that the *hand* he could not *draw back to* himself be *restored* (13:4, 6). Fourth, the man of God prays, and the hand is *restored* (13:6; the verb *turn* is used sixteen times in 1 Kings 13). *Turning, drawing back, returning,* and *restoring* (Eng. translations of Heb. *šub*), whether by king or man of God, are here done only *by the word of the* LORD.

The king attempts to reassert power with his own word, inviting (ordering) the man of God to come to his home to eat (13:7). Rejecting the king's gift protects the man of God from the king's attempt to exercise control over him and to function as his patron (13:8-10; cf. 2 Kings 5:16, 26). In obedience to the command *by the word of the* LORD, the man of God is not to *eat* or *drink* or *return by the way* that he came (1 Kings 13:9-10). Like both Solomon (3:14) and Jeroboam (11:33, 38), the success of the *man of God* depends on his walking in the *way* determined by the *word of the* LORD (*way* in 13:9, 10, 12, 17, 24, 25, 26, 28, 33).

The speech and signs of judgment via the man of God interrupt Jeroboam's inaugural festival. The king of Israel is powerless to oppose the *word of the* LORD spoken by a man of God from Judah. With words, signs, and events, God judges Jeroboam's sin, the disobedient idolatrous cultic activity with its rejection of the justice championed by the Levites of Shechem.

13:11-19 *Prophet of Bethel Entices Man of God from Judah*

A new, puzzling character, the old prophet of Bethel, takes center stage. The prophet's son reports in detail the *deeds and the words* of the man of God (13:11 AT). At the prophet's request, the sons *saddle a donkey* (13:13; cf. 13:23, 24, 27, 28, 28, 29) and help the prophet pursue the man of God (13:12-14). The prophet finds the man of God sitting under *an oak tree* (resting but not eating or drinking; see EN on 13:20) and invites him to his home for a meal (13:15). The man of God refuses the invitation, twice rehearsing the command *by the word of the* LORD prohibiting him from eating, drinking, or returning by the way he had come (13:16-17).

Here the plot twists. Claiming a *word from the* LORD via *an angel* countermanding the earlier orders, the prophet instructs the man of God to *return*. The readers are told what is hidden from the man of God: the prophet speaks deceptively. No further explanation is given (13:18). Is the deception part of the inscrutable plan of the Lord (see 1 Kings 22 for the prophet Micaiah's explanation of a lying spirit from the Lord's throne)? Is the prophet engaging in sabotage, perhaps motivated by regional or national rivalries? Or does the narrative raise suspicions about prophecy itself? (Kissling argues that the presentation of Elijah in 1 Kings 19 raises doubts regarding prophetic reliability in Kings generally [15, 97].) The old prophet's lie tests the faithfulness of the man of God to the *word of the* LORD (Torah anticipates false prophets speaking in the Lord's name, Deut 18:20). The man of God who had received the *command* of God fails to walk in the way of the *word of the* LORD. He accepts the old prophet's hospitality, *returns* with him, and eats and drinks in violation of the Lord's command (13:19 AT). The man of God falls for the ruse and disobeys the Lord.

13:20-25 *Announcement and Fulfillment of Judgment*

As they sit at the table (cf. innocently sitting under the oak in 13:14), the *word of the* LORD comes to the old prophet who has *made him return* (13:20 AT). The prophetic messenger formula (*Thus says the* LORD) identifies what follows as a formal judgment oracle. The old prophet *cries out* (13:2, 4, 21, 32), accusing the man of God of returning, eating bread, and drinking water (see 13:8), and announcing that he would not be buried in the family plot (indicating a dishonorable death). The man of God, like Jeroboam, has failed to obey the word of the Lord. Just as the man of God gave Jeroboam a sign (the ripped altar) to authenticate the word of judgment, so the old prophet gives the man of God a sign of authentication [*Literary Criticism: Poetry, p. 460*].

The immediate completion of the sign authenticates the sovereign word of the Lord, the word from the man of God to Jeroboam as well as that of the old prophet to the man of God. The old prophet has them *saddle for him a donkey*, linking man of God and prophet. A lion meets the man of God *on the way* (doubling back and then proceeding is a route forbidden by the Lord) and kills him, leaving his body *on the way*, the donkey standing beside it, and the lion standing beside the body (13:23-24). Once more the narrative signals a new perspective: *Behold, people passing witnessed the body thrown* in the way *and the lion standing beside it* (13:25 AT).

13:26-32 Prophet Honors the Man of God

When the people report the odd event in the city, the old prophet who *made him return* (AT) recognizes that the events confirm the judgment against Jeroboam. The prophet sees that the Lord has acted against the man of God who disobeyed his *command*, fulfilling *the word of the LORD* spoken by the man of God (13:26). The narrative reports in detail the old prophet's saddling a donkey, finding the body *on the way*, with the donkey standing by the body, and the lion standing beside both body and donkey but harming neither (12:27-28). The man of God *returns* with the body, mourns, and buries the body *in his own grave* (13:29-30 AT). The story concludes with a final speech by the old prophet to his sons (13:31-32). After ordering that he himself be buried in the grave with the man of God, the old prophet confirms fulfillment of the *word* that the man of God *cried out* by the *word of the LORD* against the altar (13:2, 4, 21, 32; 2 Kings 23:17). The old prophet adds that the judgment includes the houses of the high places in the cities of Samaria (constructed generations later by Omri), detail that parallels naming Josiah as the one who will desecrate the altar (13:2).

Repetition of key words identifies primary themes, including *the word of the LORD* (*word* is used thirteen times, ten of them *of the LORD*); *command* (once as a noun, twice as a verb), *the way* (eleven times), *return* (fourteen times), *cry out* (four times), *man of God* (fifteen times), *prophet* (eight times), and even *donkey* (eight times) and *lion* (six times). The double story addresses Jeroboam's exercise of power (his politics). Authority rests with the Lord, who communicates his word through his prophetic agents. Humans are to obey the word of the Lord, walk in the way of the Lord, and return to that way when addressed by God's messengers. The word of the Lord against Jeroboam's politics is a primary theme against the northern kingdom of Israel. The judgment speech announces the demolition of the altar, the central symbol of Jeroboam's administration, and a series of symbolic actions reinforce prophetic veracity [*Prophets: Prophetic Word, p. 469*].

Although the man of God pronounces judgment against Jeroboam at the altar, the story involving the man of God with the old prophet reinforces the message and invites additional reflection. In one reading the man of God represents Jeroboam (Bodner 2012: 112–13). Despite receiving the Lord's command to walk in his way, the man of God turns to the forbidden way in Bethel, resulting in death. Another reading suggests that the messengers' anonymity associates them with their country of origin (Leithart: 101). The man of God (Judah) speaks against the sins of Israel, but the old prophet (Israel) deceives him (Judah) by the ways of the northern tribes, resulting in the wrong way, leading to death. The old prophet (Israel) is united with the man of God (Judah) in death (exile), a sign of restored hope. Reis, noting a small but significant variation in the man of God's repetition of the divine prohibition (13:9, 17), suggests that the greedy man of God returned to enrich himself and better his circumstances (379–83).

Another approach identifies the donkey with Israel. The father of Shechem is *Hamor* (Heb. *ḥamor*, "donkey"; Gen 34). Israel walks in the way of the Canaanites, worshiping calves and practicing deceit. Josiah, the "lion" of Judah (Gen 49:9), will attack the altar of Jeroboam. *Lions* attack a false prophet (1 Kings 20:36) and the people living in Israel after the Assyrian deportation (2 Kings 17:24-26). Sweeney suggests that Shechem is the place of deception and lies and that Judah will act against corruption (2007a: 181–82). Jeroboam himself points beyond this story to authenticate the prophetic word regarding Solomon and the kings of Judah (Wray Beal 2013: 123–24).

In sum, the Lord opposes and will destroy the sins of Jeroboam. Like the man of God, Israel and its kings know the Lord's commandments but fail to keep them. They, like the man of God, are easily deceived by a transparent ruse. The word of God is so powerful that it rings true even when spoken by an unfaithful man of God from

Judah or an old prophet of Bethel, perhaps not even a loyal Yahwist himself. Having been deceived is no excuse. Disobedience leads to the Lord's judgment.

13:33-34 Summary of Jeroboam's Apostasy

The chapter concludes with a summary of Jeroboam's *evil way* and *sin*: making non-Levitical priests for the high places. The editorial comment unequivocally announces complete destruction of the house of Jeroboam. Several terms reinforce the message. The Hebrew *dabar*, translated in NRSV as *event* (1 Kings 13:33) and *matter* (13:34), also frequently translates as *word* (the term used thirteen times in 13:1-32). Even after this *word* from the man of God substantiated by the story of the old prophet, Jeroboam is unmoved, refusing to *turn from his evil way*. The Hebrew *šub* (NRSV: *change*; NIV: *again*) is frequently associated with repentance (summarizing the message of the prophets calling on Israel and Judah: *Turn from your evil ways*, 2 Kings 17:13). Of the 107 times *šub* appears in 1-2 Kings, 29 are found in 1 Kings 12-13. The term is often used nontheologically. *Turn* does reinforce the basic issue of how the nation will *turn*— whether away from the appeal for just treatment of the labor force, as Rehoboam does, or away from the Levitical covenant of Shechem, as Jeroboam does. Bodner notes that *sin* may indicate a "wrong turn" or a "burden" (2012: 93, 118-19). Jeroboam leads the people onto the evil way, with a wrong turn toward Bethel and Dan, but away from Jerusalem. He burdens the people with building projects that replace the yoke of Rehoboam with onerous religious policies. The failure to *return* from their false *turns* leads the people and their leaders to *evil ways* that become *sin*. Characteristically, the judgment on the kings of Israel is that they did evil by following the *ways* or the *sins* of Jeroboam (twenty times) *[Evil, p. 446]*.

The focus on the non-Levitical priests reinforces Doorly's thesis that the sin of Jeroboam was rejection of the Levitical values of Deuteronomic covenant justice, symbolically reinforced by the cultic innovations (32) *[Mišpaṭ, p. 461]*. Jeroboam rejected the law of the king (Deut 17:14-20) and *all Israel's* demand for just administration. This *word* (NRSV: *matter*) became *sin*, and the king failed to *turn from his evil way*. Like Jeroboam, Israel and Judah were cut off from the land.

14:1-20 Judgment on Jeroboam

Fulfillment of the judgment announced in 1 Kings 13 begins in 1 Kings 14. Like the acted signs of the shriveled hand, the broken altar, and the death of the disobedient man of God, the death of

Jeroboam's son from illness becomes a sign of coming judgment. The immediacy of these events authenticates the Lord's word delivered by the man of God and the old prophet.

Ahijah's speeches (1 Kings 11:31-39; 14:6-16) frame Jeroboam's actions (12:25–13:33), reinforcing the authority of the word of the Lord over kings. First, Ahijah declares to Jeroboam that the Lord is tearing the kingdom from Solomon and giving it to him and will build him an enduring house if he will keep the Lord's commands as David did (11:31, 38). After the report of Jeroboam's *evil way* and *sin* (13:33-34), Ahijah's judgment announces that the Lord will cut off Jeroboam's house (14:6-16).

The judgment scene opens with the report that *at about that time* (see 11:29) the son of Jeroboam falls sick (14:1). The name of Jeroboam's son, Abijah, meaning "my father is Yah(weh)," indicates that Jeroboam considers himself a worshiper of Yahweh at the time his son is born. The death of Abijah may portend the death of the relationship with the Lord (Hens-Piazza 2006: 141).

As he did when he pled with the man of God to restore his hand (13:6), Jeroboam must acknowledge that the prophet of the Lord, not the priests that he has put in place, has access to divine power. Jeroboam orders his wife to go in disguise to Shiloh (ten miles north of Bethel, nearly twenty miles south of Tirzah) to the prophet Ahijah. Jeroboam's wife, like the prophets in 1 Kings 13, is unnamed, perhaps implying parabolic significance (Bodner 2012: 133). As directed by Jeroboam, she visits the prophet. After hearing the prophet's message, she carries the death of her son in her footstep when she returns to Tirzah.

The purpose of the disguise is not clear. Perhaps Jeroboam seeks to hide his identity from the prophet to avoid a negative outcome (cf. Saul's disguise before meeting the prophet Samuel, 1 Sam 28:8; Ahab's attempt to avoid death predicted by the prophet Micaiah, 1 Kings 22:30). Bodner suggests that the disguise is camouflage meant to deceive the people, arguing that Jeroboam is motivated by the same fear of rejection by Israel that led to the golden calves in Bethel and Dan (12:26-28; Bodner 2012: 127); Jeroboam acts in fear that revealing this dependence on the prophet of the Lord would undermine his own cultic establishments (14:2). This disguise, like those of Saul and Ahab, ends in disaster and death. The word of God cannot be thwarted by human, even royal, schemes. The simple gift of bread may be part of the disguise, a humble gift appropriate for a peasant but inadequate for the king (14:3). The word for *cakes* is used elsewhere only for the crumbly bread the disguised Gibeonites used to deceive Joshua (Josh 9:5, 12). Bringing a gift may also be designed to placate the prophet and result in a more favorable message (especially as it is sweetened by honey). Perhaps Jeroboam's wife plans to sit at table and to break bread with the prophet, a prominent theme in the deception described in 1 Kings 13, explaining why she *got up* (from a seated position in 14:17) before leaving the house of Ahijah. If so, Ahijah resists the temptation to fraternize with royal power and dismisses the queen without sharing a meal.

The wife of Jeroboam follows her husband's orders as outlined (14:4). She, like the nation of Israel, silently complies with the king's wishes. The people follow the king's administrative policy without reported complaint despite its cost (see EN on 12:25-33 regarding the public expense of Jeroboam's building programs); Jeroboam's wife obeys without a word, though the result will be the death of her son.

Like the prophets of 1 Kings 13, Ahijah is empowered by the word of the Lord (14:4-6). Weakened by old age, his eyes are failing, perhaps eliminating the need for the disguise. Though the seer (another designation for prophets; cf. 2 Kings 17:13) cannot see, his ability to hear the word of the Lord is undiminished. Detecting the queen's footsteps at his door, Ahijah addresses the wife of Jeroboam directly, verbally tears away her disguise as he had ripped the new garment in 1 Kings 11:30, announces that he is *sent* (by the Lord) *[Send, p. 476]* with devastating judgment (AT: *heaviness*), and instructs her to deliver the message to Jeroboam.

Ahijah's judgment speech (14:7-16) follows the typical format, opening with the messenger formula *Thus says the* LORD (used thirty-three times in 1–2 Kings; eight times with the additional phrase *the God of Israel*) *[Literary Criticism, p. 457]*. Ahijah's accusation regarding the *sin . . . of Jeroboam* (1 Kings 13:34) begins with a review of the gracious opportunity the Lord has given the king, using terms reminiscent of Ahijah's first encounter with Jeroboam. The Lord has *raised* him (Jeroboam *raised his hand* against Solomon in 11:26-27) and *ripped the kingdom* from David (14:7-8a AT; see 11:31) with the promise of an enduring kingdom if Jeroboam would obey as David had (see 11:38). The indictment against Jeroboam is fivefold: the Lord accuses him of doing more *evil* than his predecessors (including Solomon, from whom the kingdom has been torn), making *other gods*, casting *images*, *provoking the* LORD *to anger*, and *thrust[ing God] behind [his] back* (14:9, 15-16).

The accusation, that Jeroboam *has done evil, provoking the* LORD *to anger by making other gods*, is followed by announcement of judgment:

*Therefore the LORD will bring evil upon the house of Jeroboam and cut off . . .
every male* (14:9-10 AT) *[Provoke the Lord to Anger, p. 470]*. The use of two
vulgarities signals emotional intensity: *males* are those who *piss
against the wall* (KJV), and the house of Jeroboam will be consumed
like *one burns up dung*. The vulgar, debasing, and humorous form of
the idiom expresses derision and scorn (Jemielity: 100–101; cf. 1 Kings
16:11; 21:21; 2 Kings 9:8). Shameful foul smells underscore Ahijah's
announcement that no one will receive a proper burial (save Abijah,
the only one pleasing to God yet who is about to die of his illness,
1 Kings 14:11-13). In a text filled with signs of prophecy and fulfillment (1 Kings 13–14), Abijah's death is yet another. *Both bond and free
in Israel* (14:10; or *even the sick and the feeble*, Cogan and Tadmor: 107)
indicates no exemption from judgment (Deut 32:36; 1 Kings 21:21).
Failure to receive a popular burial is probably borrowed from treaty
curses (McKenzie 1991: 79). Abijah's death is the immediate evidence
that the prophecy will be fulfilled. Ahijah announces that the judgment against the house of Jeroboam will be executed by a new king
whom *the LORD will raise up* (cf. 11:14, 23) to *cut off the house of Jeroboam*
without delay (14:14) *[Prophets: Prophetic Word, p. 469]*.

Coming almost before the nation is founded, the announcement
of Israel's exile from *this good land* is stunning (14:15-16; echoing the
Deuteronomic promise of *good land* emphasizes the tragic loss; see
Deut 4:40; 7:13; 30:9, 18)! As if to underline its unexpected nature,
the announcement of judgment (fulfilled in 2 Kings 17:23) comes
before the accusation of sin: The people have made Asherah poles
(related to the Canaanite fertility goddess; 14:15; 16:33; 18:19;
2 Kings 13:6; 17:10, 16; 21:3), thus *provoking the LORD to anger* (1 Kings
14:9). Jeroboam led Israel to commit the *sins of Jeroboam* (the phrase
appears twenty-one times in 1–2 Kings, notably in 2 Kings 17:22)
[Sins of Jeroboam, p. 476]. Idolatry, linked with Canaanite royal ideology, violates Deuteronomic justice. The people silently follow the
king's revolution against Deuteronomic values and lose the land of
promise *[Idolatry, p. 449]*.

The prophetic judgment is emotionally intense, evidenced by
(1) a review of the Lord's expectation that Jeroboam would obey the
Lord's commandments and that his house would be established;
(2) the length of Ahijah's speech; (3) the scatological language (urine
and dung in 14:10-11); and (4) the accusation that Jeroboam and the
people are *provoking the LORD to anger* (14:9, 15). The structure of the
speech conveys intense feeling.

Jeroboam's wife returns to Tirzah (a new capital introduced
without explanation; cf. 1 Kings 16:23-24). Her footstep at the

prophet's house had announced her arrival, and her stepping on the threshold of her own house portends her son's death (14:17). *All Israel mourns Abijah, according to the word of the LORD spoken by his servant the prophet* (14:18). This is the only time in 1–2 Kings when *all Israel* behaves in accord with the word of the Lord, foreshadowing the judgment two hundred years in the future. Abijah's death is yet another sign that the Lord's prophetic word is authoritative *[Prophets: Prophetic Word, p. 469]*.

A concluding royal formula "closes the file" on Jeroboam (1 Kings 14:19-20) *[Chronology, p. 439]*. The *acts* (*words*) of Jeroboam are written in the Book of the Annals (AT: *the words of the days*) of the Kings of Israel. Jeroboam has fought wars and ruled as king, just as the elders of Israel had requested of Samuel (1 Sam 8:4-5). As Jeroboam's accession to power is out of the ordinary (like Jehu in 2 Kings 9–10), the concluding formula includes the length of reign typically placed in the opening royal formula. His burial with his ancestors gives him a more honorable end than is predicted of his male offspring. Nadab's succession is the first in a series where the king's heir reigns only until a rival assassinates and replaces him. Unlike the Davidic house with its divine promise of an enduring dynasty, Israelite dynasties are rare and brief. Unable (or unwilling) to thwart Jeroboam's anti-Deuteronomic administrative policy, Israel retains the means to limit dynastic power.

Summary of the Reign of Rehoboam in Judah 14:21-31

The opening royal formula provides the summary of Rehoboam's age at ascension to the throne (forty-one years), term of office (seventeen years), mother's name and nationality (14:21, 31), and capital *[Chronology, p. 439]*. Solomon's thousand wives included the Ammonite mother of Rehoboam, Naamah (Solomon had built high places for two Ammonite gods, Milcom and Molech, 11:4-7).

Rehoboam's rejection of the restricted covenant with Israel proposed at Shechem ended Davidic rule over the northern tribes. No additional reference is made to Rehoboam's policies, and he is not accused of any evil act. Rather, the tribe of Judah is indicted for doing what was *evil, provok[ing the LORD] to jealousy with their sins* exceeding those of their ancestors (14:22). Judah built cultic facilities that rivaled the temple and appointed *holy ones* for the cult *[Idolatry: Holy Ones/Cult Prostitutes, p. 451]*. Just as the golden calves reveal Jeroboam's anxiety of rejection despite the Lord's promise, so Judah's idolatry reveals anxiety about life in the land. The *pillars, poles*, and *green trees* are part of the forbidden Canaanite fertility cult

(Deut 12 not only stipulates that Israel worship the Lord in the place to be chosen by the Lord but also requires that Israel demolish the high places on the hills and under trees and break down the altars, pillars, Asherah) *[Idolatry, p. 449]*. Though it is unlikely that the male and female *holy ones* (AT) were *temple prostitutes* (1 Kings 14:24; cf. Deut 23:18-19; 1 Kings 15:12; 22:46; 2 Kings 23:7; DeVries: 185; Wray Beal 2014: 204–5; Cogan 2001: 387), the cultic personnel promised fertility—an affront to the Lord's covenant promises (Deut 7:12-16). The Lord had chosen to place his name in Jerusalem and had driven out the nations before the people of Israel, but Judah rejected the Lord and adopted *all the abominations of the nations* that had been removed for their evil ways (1 Kings 14:21, 24).

This king is characterized by weakness and war. Rehoboam's bronze shields are replicas of the golden shields Solomon had made (10:17) but that were lost in the invasion of the Egyptian pharaoh Shishak (Shoshenq in extrabiblical sources), a campaign reported on an inscription in the temple of Amon at Karnak (1 Kings 14:25-28; the inscription mentions 150 sites in the Negev and Israel but does not list Jerusalem; Cogan 2001: 390). Rehoboam is reduced to employing *runners* (mercenary bodyguards) to move the bronze replicas into the temple when the king visits and back into safe storage in the guardhouse when he leaves (14:27-28). Though Rehoboam had obediently withdrawn his armies deployed against Israel (12:21-24), he has constant war with Jeroboam (cf. 1 Kings 15:6; *hostility* but not armed conflict, says DeVries: 185). The concluding royal formula is typical except for the repeated reference to the queen mother, a reminder that Rehoboam continues Solomonic policies (14:29-31). His successor, his son Abijam (a variation of Abijah, the name of Jeroboam's firstborn), preserves the Davidic line.

THE TEXT IN BIBLICAL CONTEXT
Women on the Threshold

In a book about kings, women play an understated but significant role *[Women, p. 485]*. Women often find themselves in liminal spaces, positions on either side of a boundary or threshold. Abijah's mother is the character in the story with whom Abijah, the house of Jeroboam, and the nation of Israel move from life to death as she crosses the threshold of the house (14:17). Caught in no-man's-land between tribes of Israel, the Levite threw his concubine into the street to protect himself, only to confront her violated body thrust upon the threshold (Judg 19:27). Jephthah's daughter was sacrificed in accord with the vow her father had taken regarding "whoever comes out of the doors of my house to meet me" after victory in battle (Judg 11:30-31, 34). The death of the powerful queen Jezebel involves another opening in the wall, a window (2 Kings 9:30-33). David's wife Michal, a liminal character in the royal households of both her father and his rival, helps David escape Saul through a window (1 Sam 19:12), but later she finds herself in limbo in the palace after looking through a window to see David dancing before the ark (2 Sam 6:16). Rahab reverses the negative association of liminal openings with women when she helps the spies escape through a window and keeps the cord there to signal her loyalty to Israel and the Lord (Josh 2:15). Not so fortunate is the mother of Sisera, who looks out the window hoping in vain for the return of her son in victory over Israel (Judg 5:28).

The biblical text itself might be regarded as a threshold for women. The patriarchal perspective of biblical narrative and injunctions has been used to restrict women in leadership. The biblical trajectory also frees women from their limited, liminal status. From the egalitarian creation story to the leadership roles of Phoebe (Rom 16:1), Junia (16:7), Prisca (Acts 18:2; Rom 16:3), Mary Magdalene (Luke 8:1-3; John 20:11-8), and others in biblical narrative and in church life, women are freed in egalitarian leadership. Threshold imagery might be regarded as bittersweet, associated with violence against women but also offering vistas of hope.

Donkeys and Prophets

Animals act as God's agents in several stories in 1–2 Kings. In addition to the donkey and the lion in 1 Kings 13, ravens feed Elijah according to the word of the Lord (17:2-6). When Elisha curses the boys of Bethel, two she-bears maul forty-two boys (2 Kings 2:23-24). The Lord sends lions among the pagans who resettle Samaria but fail to worship the Lord, and they kill some of them (2 Kings 17:25; cf. 1 Kings 20:36).

The donkey and the lion act as divine agents when the man of God disobeys the word of the Lord (1 Kings 13:23-29). Way develops a series of parallels between 1 Kings 13 and the story of Balaam (Num 22:21-35). In both, God uses the unusual behavior of a donkey to bring judgment on a prophet who disobeys the word of the Lord (22:18, 20, 28-30; 1 Kings 13:1, 2, 5). Role reversals are featured in both stories. Balaam's donkey sees and speaks for the Lord; the man of God becomes a sign of God's judgment while the lion abstains from eating as the man of God was to have done. Way notes the prominence of the words *way* (twelve times in 1 Kings 13 and eight

times in Num 22) and *return* (sixteen times/once). The stories function similarly, with the focus on the word of the Lord, the animals
acting as divine agents of judgment against prophets, and the role
reversals (Way: 59).

THE TEXT IN THE LIFE OF THE CHURCH
Politics, Polarities, and Bluster

Rehoboam's political strategies read like a playbook of some contemporary politicians. The crass trash talk of his advisers is at home
in today's tweetstorms. Beyond the bluster of profane communication, modern politicians also operate in a polarized social climate.
"Trickle-down" economic strategies enrich the top echelon at the
expense of day laborers. Ethnicity, political perspective, and economic status determine insider and outsider standing. The lost
middle ground of shared interests makes attempts to compromise
and seek the common good increasingly unlikely—just as it was in
ancient Israel.

False Religious Forms

In his bid to establish religious legitimacy, Jeroboam created rival
objects of worship, artifacts of gold, objects of royal pretense (Deut
17:17). The calves are idols, borrowing from the Canaanite fertility
religion the belief that "the gift of life is within our power"
(Brueggemann 1982a: 62–63). This religious syncretism is specifically
banned (Exod 20:4-5; Deut 5:8-9). Jeroboam attempts to domesticate
the Lord, reducing him "to administrable size." Domesticating God to
make worship safer remains tempting (Brueggemann 1982a: 62–63).

Early Anabaptists rejected the safer worship they had left
behind. They referenced Jeroboam's apostasy as the idolatry to be
avoided. "Because of Jeroboam, there was also a falling away from
the kingdom of Solomon. He left behind the true worship of God and
chose a false kind of worship. . . . Likewise, because of the Antichrist,
there was a spiritual falling away from true doctrine in the kingdom
of Christ." For the Anabaptists, the "false, hypocritical" state church
with its "priests, altars, offerings, church services and pomp and its
terrible defilement of the sacraments of Christ" amounted to "a
Babylonian captivity [with] the Antichrist" (Philips 1559, in Liechty:
240). The Anabaptist vision expressed hope that "God now won-
drously delivers his people, . . . with steadfast admonition from the
holy Scriptures and his messengers, . . . to go with joy to Jerusalem,
there to rebuild the temple and the city. This is the church of Christ,
as can be clearly seen" (242).

Syncretism today marries Christianity to political parties and civil religion (particularly in the U.S.). Such affiliations are temptingly self-serving and "safe" from critique of militarism, misogyny, and racism. True religion cares for orphans and widows and seeks peace (James 1:27; Deut 10:17-19).

Idolatry

The Creator made humans in the image of God, as God's true representatives, mandated to exercise stewardship—in community—as male and female (Gen 1:1, 26-28). God limited human dominion by prohibiting human image-bearers from shaping counterfeit images of God, thus making idols (Exod 20:2-4). In *Playing God: Redeeming the Gift of Power*, Crouch describes an idol as "a cultural artifact that embodies a false claim about the world's ultimate meaning" (55). Idols "offer transcendent benefits and demand ultimate allegiance" (56; Bates: 153-55). Idols deceptively promise fulfilling life apart from God (Crouch: 64-66). Injustice is idolatry, a false image, destroying the true image of God; idolatry is the exercise of violent domination that eradicates the image-bearing capacities of the poor (71-72). ANE idolatry is ensconced in the myth of the powerful human (king) who represents the false cultural image (idol) promising life (fertility) while violently demanding absolute control (imperial sovereignty) [Idolatry, p. 449].

Jesus warns against the idolatry of mammon (wealth; Matt 6:24). Paul calls the Colossians to "put to death . . . fornication, impurity, passion, evil desire, and greed (which is idolatry)" (3:5). In the list of the works of the flesh, idolatry stands alongside fornication, strife, and carousing (Gal 5:19-21). Idolatry may be anything that replaces worship of God; yet materialism, militarism, violence, injustice, and sexual impurity are particularly linked to false worship (Rev 18:4-20; 21:27). When Christians attribute their wealth to the markets, economic policies, rugged individualism, or superior work ethics, they may be susceptible to false worship of lesser gods (cf. EN on 1 Kings 17–18). The prophets decry false worship, including temple sacrifices, when such fails to produce justice for the oppressed, orphan, and widow (Isa 1:10-23; Jer 7:3-15; Amos 5:21-24).

Today, "principalities" and "powers" (using NT imagery, Eph 3:12 KJV; 6:12-13) are "our collective cultural moods or mass consciousness or institutions . . . that we take as normative and absolutely needed . . . but are collective evil that doesn't look like evil" (Rohr: 106). Jesus leads the revolt against counterfeit and deceptive powers of economics (generosity defeats the greed of conspicuous consumerism), of racism and sexism (building egalitarian, inclusive communities), and politics (overcoming military violence by non-violent love for enemies at the cost of his own life; Boyd 2012: 152–54). While individuals are virtually powerless in their stand against the system, Christian communities live with an alternative imagination to form alternative systems for serving, living simply, sharing, and loving enemies (Rohr: 106).

1 Kings 15:1–16:34

Kings in Turmoil

PREVIEW

Sociologists have structured North American culture by naming "generations" according to characteristic patterns. Born in the years 1920–45, builders value dedication, sacrifice, and hard work. Baby boomers, born 1946–64, seek personal gratification. Gen X (busters), born 1965–83 or so, are practical and value diversity. Gen Y (millennials), born approximately 1980–2000, are optimistic, confident achievers. The children of Gen X, called Gen Z (the snowflake generation), born 1997–2012, are insecure as they face the growing income gap. Gen Z is to be succeeded by the children of millennials, the alpha generation, the first generation of the twenty-first century.

First Kings 1:1–16:20 describes three generations of leaders. Solomon, king of Israel and Judah, governed the first generation (chs. 1–11). The second generation established two politically independent realms (11:26–14:31). Instability, chaos, and confusion characterized the third generation (15:1–16:20). The narrative pace accelerates from Solomon's forty-year reign, recounted in eleven chapters, to Jeroboam and Rehoboam's twenty years, presented in three chapters; then eight kings appear in forty years and just two chapters. In Israel, short-lived dynasties produce few noteworthy events or persons. The unbroken Davidic dynasty in Judah is overshadowed by the powerful kingdom of Israel. Overlapping royal reports introduce, evaluate, and situate the kings with his rival of the other kingdom [Chronology, p. 439]. The reports cite the Annals (*the book of the words of the days*; e.g., 15:7 AT) of the Kings of Judah or Israel as sources for additional information. The brief reports (a "dry chronicle," J. T. Walsh 1996: 206) describe the continuing slide into political and religious decay.

Israel, with its disjointed dynastic interruptions, descends into increasing instability and shorter royal tenures. After Zimri rules for a week (16:15), half the divided Northern Kingdom follows one ruler and the other half another (16:21-22), resulting in two kings labeled more wicked than their predecessors (Omri and Ahab; 16:25, 33). In Judah, Asa introduces reforms to recover from the sins of Rehoboam and Abijam (15:12-15). Literature imitates life as the tedium of the repetitious royal formulas corresponds to the repetitious reports of idolatry, high places, and the sins of the fathers (aptly described by Wray Beal as "the tedium of warfare and cultic sins"; "Israel's sin is anything but inventive," 2014: 215–16; Leithart: 110–13). "Godlessness is dull" (Davis 2002a: 180). There is no narrative, only the soporific memo-like summaries and statistics that refuse the subversive particularity of specific persons (Brueggemann 2018a: 5).

The chronological, alternating royal reports begin with the reigns of Abijam and his son Asa (15:1-24). The technique of "resumptive repetition" creates "an impression of simultaneous periodization" (e.g., Baasha's story of 15:33–16:9, elaborated in the Asa report in 15:16-22; Hens-Piazza 2006: 149). Though they remain one people of God, by God's will they live with political division under the rule of two kings (J. T. Walsh 1996: 208).

OUTLINE

Abijam King of Judah, 15:1-8
Asa King of Judah, 15:9-24
Nadab King of Israel, 15:25-32
Baasha King of Israel, 15:33–16:7
Elah King of Israel, 16:8-14
Zimri King of Israel, 16:15-20
Omri King of Israel, 16:21-28
Ahab King of Israel, 16:29-34

EXPLANATORY NOTES
Abijam King of Judah 15:1-8

The report of Abijam sets the pattern of brief summaries followed in 1 Kings 15–16. The opening royal formula names *Abijam* (meaning "my father is Yam," Canaanite god of the sea, in NRSV and most Hebrew manuscripts; the more orthodox form of the name, *Abijah*, "my father is Yah[weh]," in NIV and other ancient versions), syn-chronizing his reign with Jeroboam (15:1). Abijam's mother, Maacah, is Abishalom's daughter (a variant spelling of Absalom). If this Absalom is David's son and Solomon's half-brother, we see evidence of endogamy, marriage within the royal class. Maacah is the name of Abijam's mother as well as the mother of Abijam's son Asa (see EN on 1 Kings 15:10, 13; see 2 Sam 10:6, 8; 1 Kings 2:39).

Abijam *walked in all the sins of his father* (15:3 NASB). A similar phrase, *walking in the sins of Jeroboam*, is used repeatedly in 1 Kings 15–16 to evaluate the kings of Israel (15:26, 34; 16:19, 26, 31). Rehoboam's sins are not reported, allowing several possibilities: the cultic sins of Judah listed within the report of Rehoboam's reign (14:22-24); Rehoboam's unjust social policy, countered by the Shechemite appeals for justice (12:2, 13-14); dependence on military weapons (contrary to Deut 17:16), based on the report of war between Jeroboam and Rehoboam (and Abijam; 1 Kings 15:6-7). Abijam's heart (seat of decision-making) was not *true*, as David's had been, as evidenced in his final charge to Solomon to walk in the ways of the Lord (2:3). Abijam falls short of the Davidic ideal and walks in the sins of his father by failing to practice Torah *[All His Heart, p. 435]*.

Reference to David's heart shifts attention to the Lord's commit-ment to David (15:3). The Davidic dynasty continues unbroken in Jerusalem (in contrast to the short-lived dynasties in Israel) because of the Lord's gift to David, *a lamp in Jerusalem*, defined as *setting up his son after him* and establishing Jerusalem (15:3-4). The first reference to a *lamp in Jerusalem* is Ahijah's promise that David's line will rule over Judah (11:36); the promise is confirmed despite Jehoram's behavior (2 Kings 8:16-19).

The Lord's promise to protect the Davidic dynasty is related to David's commitment to doing *what was right . . . all the days of his life* (1 Kings 15:5). The reward-retribution theology often attributed to 1-2 Kings would fit neatly with the promise-obedience equation set out above, but for the clause *except in the matter of Uriah the Hittite* (1 Kings 15:5), the only reference in 1-2 Kings to David's sin (2 Sam 11). Perhaps the point is that David's sin is exceptional, not charac-teristic of David (J. Davies 2012: 292). If so, the reference to Uriah illustrates that though sin is inevitable, repentance and return are possible (Hens-Piazza 2006: 151; J. T. Walsh 1996: 211). The reference may demonstrate God's graciousness despite human failure (Leithart: 121). Or perhaps David's obedience is significant, but the Uriah-Bathsheba episode cannot be overlooked. Brueggemann con-cludes that the *nevertheless* of the Lord's faithfulness overcomes the *except* of David's failure, illustrating the tension between the demand for human obedience and the Lord's promise (2000: 188–89). The addition, *except in the matter of Uriah the Hittite*, can also be read as deconstructing the praise given to David. Like David, his heirs Solomon, Rehoboam, and now Abijam have fallen to the temptation to manipulate power in unjust, self-serving ways. *The matter of Uriah the Hittite* is far more than an exception: it is typical royal policy. Kings maintain their position by using power to defend their own interests [Mišpaṭ, p. 461].

Other than reference to Abijam's sins, we learn only of the continual warfare between Judah and Jeroboam (reported twice in 15:6-7). The concluding royal formula includes typical reference to the *Annals* and the burial of Abijam. Asa, son of Abijam, succeeds his father as king.

Asa King of Judah 15:9-24

Asa's reign stands out for his positive evaluation and the more detailed explanation of his foreign relations and military strategies. The opening royal formula includes the chronology with Jeroboam, his tenure, and identification of his mother (NIV: *grandmother*) as Maacah (15:9-10). The problem of father (Abijam: 15:2) and son (Asa) having mothers of the same name is usually resolved by surmising that Maacah was Abijam's mother and continued in the role of queen mother during the time of Asa (NIV; J. T. Walsh 1996: 211). Another alternative is that Abijam and Asa were brothers (given the short three-year tenure of Abijam), though it is possible that two different women named Maacah were mothers of successive kings. A more shocking alternative is that Asa is the son of an incestuous union of the wicked Abijam with his own mother (Provan 1995: 126). Asa ruled forty-one years, longer than any Davidic king other than Azariah (2 Kings 15:2) and the wicked Manasseh (21:1).

The report evaluates Asa's cultic reforms (15:11-15) and compares him favorably with David, doing *right in the eyes of the LORD* (15:11 NIV; Asa's son Jehoshaphat also *walked in all the way of his father*, doing *right in the sight of the LORD*, 22:43). Doing what is *right* is a condition for the Lord's blessing (Exod 15:26; Deut 6:18) and the opposite of doing what is right in their own eyes (Deut 12:8). To do *right* is to keep the Lord's commandments (Deut 12:28).

The report highlights Asa's cultic reforms, including the removal of the cult officials [Idolatry: Holy Ones/Cult Prostitutes, p. 451], the idols (a derisive term reminiscent of the word *dung* in 1 Kings 14:10) [Idolatry, p. 449], the queen mother, and her Asherah image

(15:12-15). The term *queen mother* (*gebirah*, in Kings only in 1 Kings 11:19; 15:13; 2 Kings 10:13; related terms appear in 2 Kings 24:15; Jer 29:2) refers to what was apparently a position of some power and influence. This text suggests that Maacah used her influence to support the Asherah cult (1 Kings 15:13; Ben-Barak; Ackerman) [*Queen Mother, p. 472*].

Asa's failure to destroy the high places is characteristic of the reports of limited reform by the kings of Judah who precede Hezekiah and are otherwise evaluated favorably (15:14; 22:43; 2 Kings 12:3; 14:4; 15:4, 35) [*Idolatry: High Places, p. 450*]. Despite this failure, the evaluation is that *the heart of Asa was true to the LORD all his days* [*All His Heart, p. 435*]. After three kings whose hearts were not true to the Lord as David's had been (Solomon, Rehoboam, and Abijam), Asa breaks the sin cycle, demonstrating that one need not be bound by an evil pattern (Wray Beal 2014: 216). Absence of any reference to a positive influence from priest or prophet suggests that the Lord directly influenced Asa (Leithart: 116). His renewed commitment will be followed by his son Jehoshaphat (1 Kings 22:43). Asa's piety extended to his gift of dedicated offerings to the temple (15:14; cf. David's gifts, 7:51).

Although Asa's reign is evaluated almost completely positively, his military and political maneuvering demands scrutiny (15:16-22). Asa's military actions are presented as those of a faithful king who faces real political situations (Brueggemann 1982a: 72). Is Asa's good evaluation qualified by his turning from God to trust in foreign military power (Hens-Piazza 2006: 153)? No evaluative statements are recorded. When Asa suffers disease, the expected explanation connecting it with unfaithful behavior may be implied but is unstated (15:23). The reader is left to fill the gaps left by the evaluative silence of the narrative.

The war that had marked relations between Israel and Judah since Rehoboam and Jeroboam continues unabated (15:16). Baasha, king of Israel and nemesis of Asa, escalates tensions with his fortifications at Ramah of Benjamin, encroaching on the environs of Jerusalem (just five miles south of Ramah; 15:17). Baasha's tactics create a permanent siege, strategically cutting off the main access to Jerusalem from the north as well as access to the coastal plain and blocking Asa from retaliating against Israel. Faced with this desperate geopolitical situation and militarily impotent to overcome it, Asa ups the ante by proposing a covenant with Aram, Israel's northern neighbor, at the cost of *all* the recently devoted treasures of the temple and the palace.

The alliance upsets the balance of power between Israel and Judah, complicating future international relations for both kingdoms (1 Kings 22 reports Asa's son Jehoshaphat as an ally of Israel in battle against Aram). Asa compromises the exclusive covenant between the Lord and the people of God by proposing an alliance with Ben-hadad of Aram, in Damascus. Later prophetic action condemns the king of Israel (apparently Ahab) for forming a covenant with Ben-hadad (20:34-42). Other references to *covenant* in 1–2 Kings are to the exclusive relationships between the Lord, the kings, and the people (1 Kings 8:23; 11:11; 19:10, 14; 2 Kings 17:15, 35, 38; 23:3); or to the *ark of the covenant* (1 Kings 3:15; 8:1, 6, 21). Asa declares that his proposed alliance with Aram renews the covenant that had been in place between their fathers. Given Abijam's brief tenure and the existing covenant between Aram and Israel, it seems more likely that Asa's reference is to the covenant between David and Aram (2 Sam 8:3-12; 10:6-19) than to a pact between Ben-hadad and Abijam.

Asa *sends* all the gold and silver in the royal treasury to Ben-hadad (1 Kings 15:15, 18), underscoring the royal politics of Asa's moves. *Send* is frequently the action of kings as they exercise royal control *[Send, p. 476]*. Asa, the faithful king with a true heart, acts like his ancestors who took things into their own *hands* (power) and *sent* servants to achieve their own ends. The *present* (*bribe*, 15:19 AT; cf. Exod 23:8; Deut 16:19) persuades Ben-hadad to break the alliance with Israel and *conquer* extensive territory in northern Israel (15:20). Forced to take defensive actions, Baasha withdraws from Ramah (15:21).

Asa issues a proclamation requiring the people of Judah without exception to reposition the defense bulwark against Israel (15:22). The national labor force is conscripted in the interest of "national defense" (Brueggemann 2000: 191). This is the first explicit reference to *forced labor* (AT) in *Judah* in 1 Kings (though the term itself is not used). When *King Solomon conscripted forced labor out of all Israel* (5:13; 9:20-22), he apparently exempted the tribe of Judah (4:7-19; cf. 12:14). The lack of exceptions to Asa's forced-labor program suggests that an ongoing practice is universalized in this emergency (Hens-Piazza 2006: 160). Using the materials of the fortifications abandoned in Ramah, Asa builds up two fortified cities. Geba of Benjamin, on the main road to Jerusalem and having control of access to Jericho, was next door to Ramah and the home of Levitical priests who were no longer favored in Israel. Mizpah, four miles northeast of Ramah, is the location of Saul's investiture as king in 1 Samuel 10, where Samuel drew up the rights and duties of the king

[Mišpaṭ, p. 461]. Mizpah was also the assembly place for the anti-Benjaminite alliance convened in defense of the Levite whose concubine had been murdered in Benjamin (Judg 20:1). The favorable association with Levites suggests internal political motives involving powerful tribal blocs.

Though Asa's military victories may be counted as a success of his policies (Adam: 65), they come at a high cost identified without evaluative comment. Commended for his wholehearted devotion to the Lord evidenced by the devoted gifts for the temple, Asa sacrifices the entire treasury to buy the Aram alliance. Though interpreters characterize the management of temple and palace funds as a litmus test (Wray Beal 2007: 213), the narrative silence in evaluation of this action intriguingly draws the reader into the story without settling the issue. Alliances with pagan kings have proved to be dangerous even to the wise Solomon, whose marriages to foreign princesses turned his heart to other gods (1 Kings 11:1-8). The reformer kings Jehoash (2 Kings 12:18) and Hezekiah (18:15; 20:13-15), like Asa, seek to avoid military devastation by giving temple treasures to invading powers. Though the loss is of little concern to Asa, his initiative results in loss of the Israelite land annexed by Ben-hadad (parallel with Solomon, 9:11). Lowery argues that Asa's cult reform is an exercise of royal power and that the use of forced labor demonstrates greater control over economics, politics, and society. His use of the temple treasury further demonstrates his exercise of royal administration (Lowery: 94–99, 211) [Mišpaṭ, p. 461].

Asa's closing royal formula includes several details that set him apart (1 Kings 15:23-24). He is the first of ten kings of Israel and Judah whose *power/might* is mentioned in the summary (16:5, 27; 22:45; 2 Kings 10:34; 13:8, 12; 14:15, 28; 20:20). Asa was among a small group of kings who built cities (Solomon, 1 Kings 9:15-19; Jeroboam built Shechem and Penuel, 12:25; Omri built Samaria, 16:24; Ahab built cities, 22:39; and Amaziah rebuilt Elath, 2 Kings 14:22). Though the narrative continues its practice of nonevaluative comment, the penultimate detail of his reign regards Asa's illness in old age (J. Davies 2012: 293). The cause-and-effect assumptions suggest that Asa's reign ended poorly as the consequence of his foreign alliance and strategy of forced labor and high taxes. The report of lost temple treasures and of Asa's ill health leaves the Lord's positive review a question and open for later theological speculation (2 Chron 16:7-12; Hens-Piazza 2006: 153; Brueggemann 2000: 192). Asa is buried with honor and succeeded by his son Jehoshaphat (1 Kings 15:24).

Nadab King of Israel 15:25-32

The typical Israelite opening royal formula identifies Nadab's father, Jeroboam, places him in Asa's second year, and reports his two-year tenure (15:25). Because the narrative has been following Asa and his conflict with Baasha, Nadab's successor, the file system moves back in time to resume the story of the kings of Israel, creating the impression of simultaneous periodization (Hens-Piazza 2006: 149).

Two primary phrases characterize Nadab. Earlier in 1 Kings, *evil in the sight of the LORD* first describes Solomon and Judah (11:6; 14:22) [*Evil, p. 446*]. For the rest of the kings of Israel, it is the standard characterization (15:34; 16:7, 19, 25, 30; 21:20, 25; 22:52; 2 Kings 3:2; 8:18, 27; 13:2, 11; 14:24; 15:9, 18, 24, 28; 17:2). The phrase is used in the judgment leading to Israel's exile (2 Kings 17:11, 13, 17). The phrase describes the most wicked of Judah's kings, Manasseh, (21:2, 6, 9, 12, 15, 16, 20) and the descendants of Josiah (23:32, 37; 24:9, 19). Nadab also *walks in the way of* Jeroboam and *in the sin that he caused Israel to commit*, a description of most of the kings that precede Ahab (Baasha, 1 Kings 15:34; 16:2; Zimri, 16:19; Omri, 16:25). The formulaic language produces the rhetorical effect of merging the reports of these kings with brief reigns, horrible evaluations, and dynasties lasting at most two generations. First Kings 15–16 depicts the relentlessly evil kings of Israel deteriorating into the rule of Omri and Ahab, who exceed all their predecessors in doing evil.

Baasha's *conspiracy* against Nadab fulfills the prophecy of Ahijah of Shiloh (15:27-30; *conspire/conspiracy* is used nine times more to describe the politics of Israel: 16:9, 16, 20; 2 Kings 9:14; 10:9; 15:10, 15, 25, 30; and four times regarding the kings of Judah: 12:20; 14:19; 21:23-24). Nadab leads the army in a siege of the Philistine city of Gibbethon (1 Kings 15:27), near Israel's western boundary, indicating that northern Israel was not threatened by any of its neighbors (Aram, the most likely threat, was as yet allied with Israel, 15:19). Possession of Gibbethon would extend Israel's power to the coastal plain (Sweeney 2007a: 196). Baasha attacks Nadab at the battlefield, then eliminates the house of Jeroboam.

The principle of dual causality (introduced in EN on 12:25-32) guides our reading of Baasha's conspiracy. Baasha acts *according to the word of the LORD spoken by his servant Ahijah of Shiloh* (15:29-30 AT) [*Prophets: Prophetic Word, p. 469*]. The elimination of the house of Jeroboam results from the Lord's judgment because of Jeroboam's sins and the sins that he caused Israel to commit, which *provoked the*

LORD *to anger* (characteristic also of Baasha himself, 16:2, 7, 13; Omri and Ahab, 16:26, 33; 21:22; 22:53; the summary of Israel's sins, 2 Kings 17:11, 17; and Manasseh, 21:6, 15; 23:26) *[Provoke the Lord to Anger, p. 470]*. The *sins of Jeroboam* (1 Kings 12:25-32; 13:33-34) take Israel on a wrong turn, burden Israel unnecessarily, and ultimately cause Israel to fail to reach its objective of achieving justice (Bodner 2012: 93, 118, 136) *[Sins of Jeroboam, p. 476]*. The *wrong turn* is away from faithful worship of the Lord in the Jerusalem temple and toward graven images (golden calves, at Bethel and Dan) that are counterfeit to Israel's vocation in the image of God. The unnecessary *burden* includes the weight of royal administrative projects that demand forced labor and heavy taxes (the concerns of the Shechem congregation, 12:4). Israel fails to love the Lord by practicing the Lord's justice for marginalized persons (Deut 10:12-22) *[Mišpaṭ, p. 461]*. Israel, like its kings, walks in the ways of Jeroboam and suffers the resulting instability of regime change (15:30).

Less overt in the narrative is the dimension of causality linked with human political aspirations. The narrative identifies Baasha as the son of Ahijah of Issachar (15:27), suggesting power battles between tribal groups (Hens-Piazza 2006: 154). Nadab and his father, Jeroboam, were descendants of Rachel's grandson Ephraim (1 Kings 11:26); Baasha is of the tribe of Leah's son Issachar. Baasha's revolt tips the balance of power from the tribes of the central hill country (Ephraim and Manasseh) toward the Galilean-based tribes (including Issachar; Sweeney links Baasha's political motivation as a quest for commercial advantages through access to the Jezreel valley and the coastal plain [2007a: 196]). Noting that the narrative places theological rationale alongside political actions, Brueggemann warns his readers against either fideism, which attributes everything to God, or a "cynicism that takes the public process to be void of meaning" (2000: 194).

Nadab's closing royal formula references the *Annals of the Kings of Israel* but omits notice of his death, burial, and successor, omissions standard in cases of assassination (15:31; cf. 16:8-10; 2 Kings 9:21-26). Between the concluding royal formula of Nadab (1 Kings 15:31) and the opening of Baasha's reign (15:33), the narrative link (15:32) repeats the war report of 1 Kings 15:16, an example of "resumptive repetition," creating the impression of contemporaneous events (Hens-Piazza 2006: 150). This literary device is also used in 16:7, where the narrator's citation of Jehu's prophecy follows the concluding royal formula of Baasha, underscoring the validity of the prophetic word (J. T. Walsh 1996: 214) *[Prophets, p. 465]*.

Baasha King of Israel 15:33–16:7

The structure and content for the reports of Baasha and his son Elah parallel the reports of Jeroboam and his son Nadab. The parallel material includes prophetic denunciations of the father (Jeroboam by Ahijah, 14:7-16; Baasha by Jehu, 16:1-4) predicting the demise of both houses, rehearsing the provision of God to each, condemning them for their bad responses, using horrific images of judgment. The structure and content point to the continuity of the sins of the two houses, with Baasha perpetuating the sins of Jeroboam (Konkel 2006: 271; Seow: 121).

The Baasha opening royal formula provides the same information and evaluation as that of Nadab (15:33-34), reinforcing the rhetorical blending of these brief, evil dynasties into a single blurred image. One addition is the reminder that Baasha rules in Tirzah (Jeroboam's capital, seven miles northeast of Shechem, on a rocky ridge controlling east-west routes between the Jordan Valley and the western mountain district and also the north-south route to Shechem), setting up the contrast with Omri's moving the capital to Samaria (16:24). Baasha's reign of twenty-four years exceeds that of Jeroboam by two years.

As with Nadab, Baasha's reign is reported without detail excepting the judgment against it. Also like Jeroboam, Baasha is confronted with a prophetic word of judgment, by Jehu son of Hanani (16:1-4; a character of the same name prophesies about forty years later, during the reign of Jehoshaphat, 2 Chron 19:2). The message closely parallels Ahijah's word against Jeroboam (1 Kings 14:7-14). The accusation opens with a declaration of the Lord's sovereign authority over historical events: *I exalted you out of the dust* [lowly position or coronation like the miracle of creation as a divine gift: Brueggemann 2000: 197] *and made you leader over my people Israel* (16:2). Baasha *walked in the way of Jeroboam, provoking* the Lord *to anger [Provoke the Lord to Anger, p. 470].* Jehu announces the same punishment suffered by the house of Jeroboam.

The closing royal formula (16:5-6; 15:31) reports that Baasha was buried in the capital, Tirzah and includes the additional charge that Baasha is judged *because he destroyed* the house of Jeroboam (16:2-4, 7)! The narrative distinguishes between the judgment that the Lord would bring evil upon the house of Jeroboam (14:10) and the human action that puts judgment into effect (Baasha's violence). The announcement reveals not only that God will judge unbridled evil but also that the Lord does not excuse human violence even when it fulfills prophecy. The prophecy extends guilt to all future royal assassins (Zimri, 1 Kings 16:10; Jehu, 2 Kings 9:14-26; Shallum, 15:10; Menahem, 15:14; Pekah, 15:25; and Hoshea, 15:30; Sweeney 2007a: 198) [*Violence in Kings, p. 480*].

Elah King of Israel 16:8-14

The report of Elah son of Baasha follows the pattern established by the report of Nadab son of Jeroboam (15:25-31). The opening royal formula is routine (16:8). Elah's military commander Zimri *conspires* (see note on 15:27) against the king who has abandoned his duties (he was *drinking himself drunk* in the capital city) and kills him (16:9-10). As Baasha had done, Zimri exterminates the house of Baasha, extending the violence to include not only his male heirs but also his male friends (16:11; the narrator uses the vulgarity that the prophet Ahijah had used, 14:10). The narrative describes Zimri's destructive violence, repeating the report of Baasha's violence against the house of Jeroboam. This happened *according to the word of the* LORD, *which he spoke . . . by the prophet Jehu* (16:12) [*Prophets: Prophetic Word, p. 469*]. The reason given for the Lord's judgment is also virtually identical, naming both Baasha and his son Elah. The additional phrase translated *with their idols* (16:13) underscores the ineffectualness of their brief dynasty. *Idols* renders a word more frequently translated *breath* ("vanity," Eccl 1:2). Are we to read that Baasha and Elah breathe the air of idolatry or that even their breath provokes the Lord's anger? Perhaps the idols are less substantial than air. The concluding royal formula cites the royal annals (16:14). As is standard when a king is assassinated, reference to death, burial, and successors is omitted. The nearly identical reporting reinforces the narrative perspective that the kings of Israel are evil yet ultimately insignificant in their exercise of royal power.

Zimri King of Israel 16:15-20

Zimri's reign stands out as the shortest of the kings of Israel. His one-week tenure becomes proverbial in Jezebel's insult of the conspirator Jehu when she addresses him, *Zimri, murderer of your master* (2 Kings 9:31). The abbreviated opening royal formula makes no mention of Zimri's father (1 Kings 16:15). Word of Zimri's conspiracy against Elah spreads to the battlefront Philistine city of Gibbethon (15:20-21, 27). There *all Israel* makes the army commander Omri king (16:15-16). Omri marches on Zimri in Tirzah and the army enters the city as Zimri locks himself inside the palace citadel and commits suicide by burning the building over himself (16:18). The brief indictment of Zimri matches his brief reign: Zimri committed sin, did evil in the eyes of the Lord, walked in the way of Jeroboam, and caused Israel to sin (16:19). Despite the brevity of his reign, Zimri incurs the same indictment as his predecessors in the concluding royal formula (16:20), though no mention is made of the death of his heirs.

Omri King of Israel 16:21-28

The reports of ever briefer and less significant dynasties end in chaos. Though twice the narrative reports that *all Israel* was with Omri (12:20; suggesting the first popular support of a king since Jeroboam; J. T. Walsh 1996: 216), an interim period opens between Zimri's reign and that of Omri (16:21-22). Half of Israel follows Tibni son of Ginath while half follows Omri. Based in part on the fact that Tibni's father is named while Omri's is not, speculation suggests that Tibni represented popular Israelite tradition and legitimacy while Omni was Canaanite and the favorite of the troops (Jones: 225). The text is silent on the issue; whether the conflict reflected tribal, ethnic, or social boundaries cannot be determined (Wray Beal 2014: 224). After an unspecified time of conflict and the death of Tibni, Omri prevails and becomes king. Omri, absent theological legitimacy, is the winner and holds the power (Brueggemann 2000: 200).

The opening royal formula places Omri on the throne of Israel in the thirty-first year of Asa, with a twelve-year tenure (including the four years of civil war), half of that time with the capital in Tirzah and half in Samaria (16:23). Though Omri establishes one of the most powerful dynasties of Israel, the only event reported about Omri is his purchase, fortification, and construction of Samaria (16:24). It may be that the hill of Samaria bought in a commercial transaction is neutral, not part of any tribe, affording greater royal flexibility and power (Sweeney 2007a: 204; Wray Beal 2014: 224). Its central location and neutrality make Samaria an ideal capital for the north until the exile. Commanding the central trade routes, Samaria (about seven miles west of Shechem and Tirzah) increases access to the coastal plain and to trade with Phoenicia. Its location on a higher hill (than Tirzah), with western access, makes the site eminently defensible above the surrounding valley (the name *Samaria* means "lookout mountain"; though see also 16:24, which links the name with its former owner).

The concluding royal formula reports that Omri *did what was evil in the sight of the LORD; he did more evil* than all his predecessors, referencing the sins of Jeroboam, causing Israel to commit sin, and *provoking the LORD, the God of Israel, to anger* (16:25-26) [*Provoke the Lord to Anger, p. 470]*. Like Baasha and Jeroboam before him, the record of Omri mentions both his deeds and his power. Omri consolidates power through domestic building projects that inevitably depend on forced labor of the king's subjects (16:24). These typical royal administrative policies follow the pattern set by Solomon, running roughshod over the appeals of the Israelite assembly for *a lighter yoke* (12:4). Omri is the first king buried in Samaria.

Ahab King of Israel 16:29-34

The opening royal formula places Ahab in the thirty-eighth year of Asa. Ahab rules twenty-two years in the capital city, Samaria (16:29). Yet the Ahab file remains open through 1 Kings 22:40, though frequently submerged beneath the prophetic narrative of Elijah and Elisha.

In contrast to the opening royal formulas of his predecessors and successors, *Ahab son of Omri* is mentioned three times in two verses, indicating his importance for the narrative as the head of the dynasty and for the significance of his religious policies (Wray Beal 2014: 224). The brief evaluative comment states that Ahab was more evil than any of his predecessors (16:30; cf. 16:25). The itemization of Ahab's sins (16:31-33) is framed by reference to doing *evil in the sight of the LORD* (16:30) and *provoking the anger of the LORD, the God of Israel* (16:33). The framing statements highlight divine displeasure but provide a subtle reminder that the Lord is keeping watch over his people. God looks for Israel's faithful response to the covenant of Deuteronomy (Hens-Piazza 2006: 161).

Ahab's sins are identified in the opening royal formula. Like his predecessors, Ahab walks in the sins of Jeroboam, including the employment of forced labor to build cities (16:31, 34; 22:39; cf. 12:25-33). The sins of Jeroboam are compounded by Ahab's marriage of alliance with the foreign queen Jezebel (her name is from *noble*, or means "where is the prince?," an epithet for the Canaanite god Baal, corrupted in the narrative with a play on the word *dung*; J. Davies 2012: 313; Deut 7:1-6 prohibits intermarriage with Canaanites because it leads to idolatry). Ahab worships Jezebel's god Baal, the god of rain and fertility and constructs a Baal temple for Baal with a sacred pole for *Asherah*, the consort of Baal (1 Kings 16:33 NIV). The sins of Jeroboam are rejection of the Deuteronomic justice of the Levitical priests *[Sins of Jeroboam, p. 476]*; now the sins of Ahab, under the influence of Jezebel and in service of Baal, compound the problem in that they involve political and economic structures in addition to the requisite cultic innovations *[Idolatry, p. 449]*. Like Solomon, who married Sidonian foreign women (11:1), Ahab married for political alliances, yet was influenced by social, political, and religious value systems. Jezebel, through her prominent role in the narrative, embodies the social ideology of Canaan (Brueggemann 2000: 202). Such becomes evident in the story of Naboth's vineyard: in lands where Baal is worshiped, the king controls all real estate (1 Kings 21). Such insolent behavior provokes the Lord's anger more than *all the kings of Israel who were before* Ahab (16:33).

Omri is a David-like king who initiates a counterfeit Davidic dynasty (Leithart: 119). Ahab follows the pattern of Solomon, extending the Omri-David/Ahab-Solomon pattern another generation. Like Solomon, Ahab marries an idolatrous, foreign princess who leads him into apostasy (11:1-3; 16:31). Jezebel comes from Sidon, twin city of Tyre, home of Solomon's ally Hiram (1 Kings 5). Ahab, like Solomon, builds places of worship for his foreign wives (11:7-8; 16:32-33; cf. 20:3-7). The closing royal formula reports that Ahab, like Solomon, uses ivory in his palace and builds cities, undoubtedly employing forced labor, another parallel with Solomon (22:39; Leithart: 119).

Appended to the summary of Ahab's reign is a notice that Hiel of Bethel rebuilds Jericho. Hiel's association with Bethel points to the cultic sanctuary as a corrupting influence on Israelite life. The death of Hiel's sons confirms the authority of the word of the Lord (see also 16:7, 12, where the word of the Lord thwarts royal power) *[Prophets: Prophetic Word, p. 469]*. Though scholars are no longer in agreement that the deaths are the result of child sacrifice, the reign of Ahab begins under the cloud of death (J. T. Walsh 1996: 219).

Placing this story *in the days of Ahab* points to the growing influence of Canaanite idolatry and to the king's failure to keep the word of the Lord. Ahab, like Hiel, is engaged in building projects that are contrary to the word of the Lord. Just as the actions of the one man, Achan, in taking devoted things from Jericho on the day of conquest results in military defeat for Israel at Ai (Josh 7), so Ahab's leadership brings devastating results to Israel (Wray Beal 2014: 225). Rebuilding Jericho, the place destroyed in the first battle led by Joshua in taking Canaan, points toward a reversal of Israel's control of the land, anticipating exile (Sweeney 2007a: 206-7). The concluding formula for the reign of Ahab is delayed until 1 Kings 22:39-40 by the insertion of a series of stories relating the conflict between Ahab and Elijah.

THE TEXT IN BIBLICAL CONTEXT
What's the Real Story about Asa?

The relationship between 1–2 Kings and 1–2 Chronicles is a matter of much conversation but little agreement [Kings in the Hebrew Canon: Kings and Chronicles, p. 455]. One popular theory is that Kings predates Chronicles and is a major source for the latter. First Kings 15 reports that Asa completed a sweeping but incomplete cultic reform, leaving the high places untouched (15:12-14). Asa strategically makes a treaty with Ben-hadad of Aram against Baasha of Israel. Asa's long reign ends without condemnation but with a report that Asa's feet were diseased. After the primary theological presuppositions of DtrH [Kings in the Hebrew Canon: Kings in the Deuteronomistic History, p. 453] (and the Chronicler), is the disease a sign of divine disfavor and judgment? If so, why does the text fail to explain the disease? Is it simply a medical report without any explanation other than that even the good may suffer?

The Chronicler answers those questions (2 Chron 14–16). In 2 Chronicles 15, Asa's record is even more positive than in Kings, including removal of the high places of Judah and parts of Israel. Asa's large army repulses an Ethiopian army twice its size through miraculous answer to prayer (14:9-15). Asa follows the direction of the prophets. However, near the end of Asa's reign, Chronicles reports Asa's alliance with Ben-hadad. The prophet condemns this alliance and reports further injustice by Asa (16:7-10). Asa's backsliding results in disease; his reliance on physicians is further evidence of Asa's loss of faith (16:12). So 2 Chronicles resolves the gaps in 1 Kings 15, clarifying that while failure does not necessarily indicate lost spirituality, it has present and future consequences (Konkel 2016: 328–30) [Kings in the Hebrew Canon: Kings and Chronicles, p. 455].

Idols or Vanities?

Israel provokes the LORD God of Israel to anger with their idols (1 Kings 16:13, 26; Deut 32:21). The word translated idols (hebel) is used thirty times in Ecclesiastes (rendered as "vanity"). Hebel is breath or vapor, with a valence of meanings ranging from the transitory nature of steam to the noxious odor of gas; it may be transparent; it is nothing; there is no substance (D. Miller: 27–30). In the chapter analyzing Israel's exile, we read that Israel went after hebel and they became hebel (They went after false idols and became false, 2 Kings 17:15). Jeremiah uses hebel eight times. NRSV interprets hebel as follows: "The customs of the people are false" (Jer 10:3); "idols" (10:8); "They are worthless, a work of delusion" (10:15); "Our ancestors have inherited nothing but lies, worthless things in which there is no profit" (16:19); "[Their idols] are worthless, a work of delusion" (51:18). The delusional power of idolatry lies in deceit, creating false reliance on what does not exist.

THE TEXT IN THE LIFE OF THE CHURCH

Old Testament Violence

One of the problems of the Old Testament for the church, particularly for Anabaptist Christians, is divinely sanctioned violence. How can the God of Jesus Christ order the people of God to wreak violence on other human beings (Deut 7:1-6)?

Prophecy on eliminating the houses of Jeroboam and Baasha introduces the issue of divine violence (1 Kings 15–16). Ahijah prophesies that Jeroboam's family is to be wiped out (14:10-11). Jehu announces that the house of Baasha is to be consumed like Jeroboam's (16:1-4). If these prophecies are fulfilled, surely the destroyer acts in the Lord's name. The prophet Elisha commands another prophet to anoint Jehu king (2 Kings 9:3). When the young prophet carries out that command, he exceeds Elisha's mandate, saying, *You shall strike down the house of your master Ahab*, adding detail of how the Lord will avenge the blood of his servants and cut off Ahab's house (9:6-10).

Two biblical statements call into question the assumption that there is a direct correlation between the Lord's intent to judge and the divine mandate of a human agent to do violence. First, the prophet Jehu spoke the word of the Lord against Baasha *in being like the house of Jeroboam, and also because he destroyed it* (1 Kings 16:7). Though Baasha's elimination of Jeroboam fulfilled the Lord's prophetic word, Baasha's violence violated God's order. God may judge, but divine judgment does not authorize human violence. Second, Hosea, writing after Jehu assassinated Ahab's family, declares, "I will punish the house of Jehu for the blood of Jezreel" (Hos 1:4; Jezreel was location of the massacre, 2 Kings 9:30–10:11). Though the prophet who goes beyond Elisha's orders is not condemned, the house of Jehu is culpable for the Jezreel bloodshed [*Violence in Kings*, p. 480].

The prophetic condemnation of the violent deaths of two royal families suggests a distinction between divinely instituted judgment and divinely sanctioned execution. Baasha's and Jehu's violence fulfill prophecy but violate divine order. The ruthless murder of the innocent members of the extended royal family is condemned.

Rohr offers a positive alternative to state-sanctioned violence: "alternative communities for sharing resources, living simply, and imagining sustainable and nonviolent future" (105–6). He argues that corporate evil can only be overcome by corporate good. Such communities of cooperation oppose the societal values of individuality, greed, and competition of the "powers" and "principalities" (Eph 6:12 KJV). Building such communities, Rohr asserts, is the strategy we learn from Paul's missionary communities.

Urbanus Rhegius

In a tract against Anabaptists, the Lutheran "conciliator" (unifier) Urbanus Rhegius cites the violent reforms of the pious "Christian" kings Asa, Jehu, and Josiah approvingly, as examples of the kind of state action needed to restrain the Anabaptist heresy (Snyder and Klaassen: 223).

An Anabaptist confession of faith written in Holland in 1618 has a statement in tune with 1 Kings 15, concluding that "those . . . who make themselves unworthy of salvation through their own perversity . . . are justly rejected by God because of their own evil" (de Ries 1618, in C. Dyck: 12).

Two early Radical Reformers, Jan Matthys and John of Leiden, used violence to overthrow and rule Münster (1534–35). Their Peasants' Rebellion ended with much loss of life. Motivated by these events, Menno Simons led the Dutch Anabaptists to eschew violence even against violent threats like those of Rhegius.

Elijah against Baal Worship

PREVIEW

Historians have recorded the story of Western civilization by giving primary attention to powerful political leaders. The story features Julius Caesar, Constantine, Charlemagne, Napoleon. From time to time the political story is interrupted by prophets who have such an impact that the storytellers must include their voices. The influence of Martin Luther and Martin Luther King Jr. equals that of presidents, kings, and generals. In the Old Testament, the prophet Elijah breaks into the narrative as dramatically as modern prophets. Elijah, his disciple Elisha, and the sons of the prophets play major roles in 1 Kings 17–2 Kings 9 [*Prophets: Sons of the Prophets, p. 467*].

King Ahab and Queen Jezebel pursue political-religious policies that compound the errors of their predecessors [*Sins of Jeroboam, p. 476*] with commitment to Baal ideology [*Idolatry, p. 449*]. The ancient Baal myth ascribes the annual rainy season to Asherah's awaking the sleeping Baal, the god of fertility, who defeats the deities responsible for drought death (Mot, the god of the dry season). The reemergent Baal brings life-sustaining rainstorms. In this system politics and cult are one. Canaanite deities delegate earthly powers to the king. At the top of the hierarchical political structure as the gods' representative, the king owns the land, brings rain essential for the agricultural cycle, and exercises power over the people through heavy taxation and forced labor to monopolize resources for accumulated wealth, trade, building projects, and military. Elijah, Yahweh's champion of those oppressed by the Baal-Ahab hierarchy, confronts royal power, giving voice to those silenced in the narrative: the peasants and the poor (Hens-Piazza 2006: 162). Because of the vicious power of their opponents, heavyweight boxers often appear quite cautious in the early rounds of a prize-fight. In a battle no less vicious, for Elijah in three opening "rounds" (1 Kings 17:1-7, 8-16, 17-24) two issues are primary: The word of the Lord is the source of power, and the God of life overcomes the power of death. The word of the Lord reveals that the power for life lies outside the royal administration (Brueggemann 2000: 218).

OUTLINE

Elijah in Exile, 17:1-24
    17:1-7   Scene 1: Fed by Ravens at the Wadi
    17:8-16   Scene 2: Fed by a Widow in Zarephath
    17:17-24   Scene 3: Restoring Life to the Widow's Son
Elijah Confronts Ahab, 18:1-46
    18:1-16   Presentation to Obadiah
    18:17-40   Contest on Carmel
    18:41-46   Prayer for Rain

EXPLANATORY NOTES

Elijah in Exile 17:1-24

17:1-7 Scene 1: Fed by Ravens at the Wadi

Abruptly, Elijah interrupts the narrative with an announcement of judgment against Ahab (17:1). Elijah ("my God is Yah[weh]") comes without credentials from the otherwise unknown place of Tishbe in Gilead, east of the Jordan. Confronting Ahab directly, Elijah's terse speech begins with an oath in the name of the living Lord God of Israel. The prophet addresses Ahab but he *stands before* (serves) the Lord. Elijah's loyalty to the Lord places him in opposition to Ahab and his god Baal. The living God announces judgment, a death sentence: there will be a drought contingent on the prophet's *word* (tantamount to God's word). A significant theme in 1 Kings 17, *word* is used ten times, seven with reference to the word of God or his prophet Elijah (17:1, 2, 5, 8, 15 MT, 16, 24; J. Davies 2012: 318). The truncated judgment speech announces a sentence without the expected indictment for wrongdoing [Literary Criticism, p. 457]. Ahab's introduction (16:29-34) has established the king's loyalty to Baal as such an affront to the Lord that no spoken accusation is needed.

The human political dispute between prophet and king corresponds to the cosmic theological conflict between Yahweh, the God of Israel, and Baal, from the Canaanite pantheon. Yahweh takes the fight directly to the nature god Baal, claiming authority over life and death. Because King Ahab as patron of Baal claims to exercise political authority and provide fertility (J. Davies 2012: 317–18), Elijah, prophet of Yahweh, directly challenges that authority. Yahweh is the God who lives; Baal is absent, impotent to provide rain necessary for fertility (life).

The word of the Lord instructs the prophet to hide from Ahab in familiar territory east of the Jordan, *by the Wadi Cherith* (17:2-4; a wadi is a rain-fed gully that dries up quickly). The word of the Lord not only directs Elijah but also promises water from the wadi and ravens bringing *provision* (AT; cf. 4:7, 27; 17:9; 18:4, 13). Elijah follows the word of the Lord and lives (17:5). Ravens provide bread and meat twice daily (17:6). After *the end of days* (AT), the wadi dries up. *The land* has been negatively affected by the judgment brought on by Ahab's behavior (17:7). The opening round establishes the power of the word of the Lord, the fierce loyalty of Elijah to the Lord, and the living Lord as provider and judge. Ahab is powerless. The Lord cares for his loyal servant. The land is devastated.

17:8-16 Scene 2: Fed by a Widow in Zarephath

The word of the Lord activates Elijah, directing a move to the Sidonian city of Zarephath (17:8-9), where an unexpected agent will provide (see 17:4). *Provision* comes from a poor widow from the non-Israelite territory of Jezebel. The Lord's directive provides for the prophet. As before, Elijah obeys the word of the Lord (17:9-10). No sooner has Elijah approached the gate of the city than, to the amazement of the storyteller (*behold!* 17:10 AT), the widow herself appears on the scene [*Literary Criticism: Elements of Narrative, p. 458*]!

The human provider is Sidonian and a widow, hardly a promising combination. Elijah first asks for a little water. As she goes, Elijah calls out, asking for *bread in your hand* (17:11; *hand* indicates agency or power; Elijah's word empowers the powerless widow; see 17:16). For the first time the woman speaks (17:12), using an oath like the one Elijah used in addressing Ahab (17:1). With death seemingly imminent, the Sidonian widow swears by the living God of Elijah (not the Baal of Jezebel and Sidon). Elijah had asked for a *little water* and a *morsel of bread*, but she informs him that she has only a handful of flour and a *little* (a word used only these two times in 1 Kings) oil to make into bread for their last meal before she and her son die.

Elijah's audacious, demanding reply begins with words of assurance: *Do not be afraid* (17:13-14). The word is typical in salvation oracles spoken to those without resources, promising the Lord's intervention to alter life circumstances (Brueggemann 2000: 211; Gen 21:17; 26:24; Exod 14:13; Isa 41:10, 13, 14; 43:1) *[Literary Criticism: Poetry, p. 460]*. Elijah asks her to make him a little bread first and, only after he has been fed, to make food for herself and her son. Citing the Lord's word, Elijah promises a supply of flour and oil until the Lord sends rain. As surprising as Elijah's word is, no less surprising is the woman's faithful compliance with that word. Using Elijah's words to the woman, the narrator reports that the meal did not *come to an end* (AT), nor did the oil *fail* (used three times in Deut: 2:7; 8:9; 15:8). This happened according to the *word of the LORD* as it was spoken through *the hand of* Elijah (17:16 AT; see 17:11) *[Prophets: Prophetic Word, p. 469]*.

The second preliminary round goes to the word of the Lord, the source of life. Not only Elijah but also the Sidonian widow and her son live by the word of the living Lord of Israel, who provides.

17:17-24 Scene 3: Restoring Life to the Widow's Son

Scene 2 has more complexity than scene 1. Then scene 3 presents an increased urgency in the battle of life and death. The problem is presented as an illness so powerful that the breath of the son of the *mistress* (feminine for Baal or lord) of the house is not left in him (17:17). The lad's mother lodges an urgent and accusatory complaint. In anguish she reasons that the man of God came not to relieve suffering but to identify her sin and bring death to her son (17:18). The woman shares the worldview that many readers find in the text itself: life can be understood as a simple equation of reward and punishment. In her magical twist on this view, her sin has been unnoticed until the man of God comes into proximity and brings the woman and her sin to God's attention. By asking *What have you against me?*, the woman reminds Elijah that, far from being a sinner, she is a generous woman who has taken great risk to show hospitality to the prophet from Israel. Her complaint humbly declares an injustice.

Elijah moves into immediate action. He physically removes the boy from his mother and transports his lifeless body to the prophet's upper room (17:19). That Elijah has an upper room, a prophet's chamber (2 Kings 4:10), is a new revelation, increasing the sense of the widow's generous hospitality and supplying a retreat for intense prayer. The narrative conveys the high intensity by reporting verbatim two separate prayers sandwiching the report of an acted prayer as the prophet lies upon the body of the child three times. This detail signals an intense, prolonged struggle between the power of death and the prophet, an agent of life. Elijah's first prayer is a complaint: the prophet repeats the widow's accusation (that God is responsible for the child's death) as a question. By directly addressing the Lord (*"O LORD my God"*), Elijah claims intimacy (17:20). The question form is typical of lament accusation [*Literary Criticism: Poetry, p. 460*]. There is no petition in this prayer. The acted prayer of repeatedly lying on the dead body as a way of transferring life to a corpse further increases intensity (17:21; in 2 Kings 4:34, Elisha uses the same prayer strategy; cf. 13:21). The second quoted prayer addresses God in the same way, with the request that the Lord return the boy's *life force* to *his innermost parts* (17:21 AT).

The miracle is assured when the Lord *hears* Elijah's voice (17:22 AT). The Lord characteristically *listens* to the cries of his oppressed people (Exod 2:24; 6:5) and to the prayers of kings (1 Kings 9:3; 2 Kings 13:4; 20:5; 22:19). The Lord *hears* his prophet and responds for the benefit of a Sidonian widow and her son. Elijah *takes the child, brings him down, out of the [roof] chamber and into the house, gives him to his mother*, and speaks a word of life (17:23 AT). The explicit detail highlights the wonder of the story.

The mother responds to the miracle. *"Now this I know,"* the woman says to Elijah, *"that you are a man of God and the word of the LORD in your mouth is truth"* (17:24 AT). *Truth* in Kings indicates reliability in relationship (in prayer, Hezekiah uses *truth* to claim his *faithfulness with a whole heart*, 2 Kings 20:3). The Sidonian widow, in contrast to her countrywoman Jezebel and to most Israelites, confesses trust. She recognizes the word of the Lord in the prophetic voice. This widow has risked life itself in providing hospitality and receives life back, confirming the faithfulness of the Lord's word.

Three early rounds establish the word of the Lord as central. Elijah hears and heeds God's word. God provides life in the face of death. The early rounds of this conflict end in *truth*.

Elijah Confronts Ahab 18:1-46

18:1-16 Presentation to Obadiah

A new word from the Lord to Elijah opens 1 Kings 18. Elijah will engage in a toe-to-toe confrontation with Ahab in challenge of the king's idolatrous practices. The Lord commands Elijah to show himself to Ahab and promises that the Lord will send a rainstorm upon the ground. Elijah obeys the Lord's word by going to Ahab to demonstrate that it is Yahweh, not Baal, who provides fertility and prosperity in the land (18:2).

Absent mention of fear, we deduce that Elijah, guided by the word of the Lord, has no concerns for safety. More surprising, the Lord has given the promise of rain but no instructions about what to communicate to Ahab. No more is said of the Sidonian widow (17:8-24), who disappears as abruptly as she has appeared.

Tension is raised by an interlude, delaying Elijah's confrontation of Ahab. In 1 Kings 17 the attention of the story line has shifted from the powerful, privileged royal houses (characteristic of 1 Kings 1–16) to Elijah and the powerless, nameless foreign widow. First Kings 18:1-16 reinforces that shift. The primary plot of 1 Kings 18 simply requires that Elijah address Ahab to convene the Carmel confrontation. Obadiah's cameo with its complex characterization adds narrative depth.

Though King Ahab summons Obadiah (18:2b-6), the narrative focuses on Obadiah through 18:16, when he disappears from the story. Obadiah ("servant of Yah[weh]") serves Ahab by overseeing his house, a contradiction present throughout the presentation of Obadiah. Positively, the narrator notes that Obadiah *greatly fears the* LORD (18:3 AT), a claim repeated by Obadiah himself (18:12). When Ahab orders Obadiah to join him in seeking grass for the animals, we note that when Ahab goes one *way*, Obadiah takes a different *way* (18:5; cf. the *ways* of Jeroboam and his successors, 1 Kings 13:33; 15:26, 34). When Obadiah meets Elijah, he treats the prophet with respect, falling on his face in greeting and addressing him as *my lord* (18:7). In seeking to establish his faithfulness to the Lord, Obadiah describes how he secretly yet courageously *has hidden* one hundred prophets of the Lord from the murderous Jezebel and *provides* them bread and water (18:13 AT; cf. 17:9). This characterization portrays Obadiah as faithful to his name, "servant of the LORD." Obadiah, servant of Elijah, anticipates Elisha, successor of Elijah, in his provision for this group of prophets (2 Kings 4:38-44) [*Prophets: Sons of the Prophets, p. 467*].

But Elijah's response to Obadiah's humble greeting, *Is that you, my lord, Elijah?* (18:7 AT), unmasks Obadiah's hopelessly divided loyalty (parallel to the people of Israel). Elijah undercuts Obadiah's address of Elijah as *my lord*, saying, *Go, tell your lord, behold! Elijah is here* (18:8 AT; *your lord* refers to Ahab). Obadiah admits as much when he himself refers to Ahab as *my lord* (18:10; and in his quotation of Elijah's words in 18:11, 14) but claims loyalty to Elijah when he asserts, *I your servant have revered the* LORD *from my youth*, and again refers to Elijah as *my lord* (18:12-13). The Obadiah-Elijah dialogue shows Obadiah's resistance to the word of the prophet because of his fear of Ahab's royal authority. Yet in the end, Obadiah obeys Elijah's mandate, *Go, tell your lord, "Behold, Elijah"* (18:8 AT, 16). The confession of Obadiah (*"Behold, Elijah"* is equivalent to "Behold, my God is Yahweh") will be echoed by the people (*"The* LORD *indeed is God; the* LORD *indeed is God,"* 18:39). Obadiah, the servant of the Lord who serves Ahab, enriches the narrative by foreshadowing the confession of the people of Israel.

Though the focus is on Obadiah, Ahab's (and Jezebel's) presence lurks ominously in the background. The story mocks the impotence of Ahab, the wannabe Canaanite king supposedly responsible for the land's fertility. Ahab is dependent on Obadiah, the servant of Yahweh. The king, reduced to the work of a low-level farmhand, hopes to *find* grass (18:5; having been unable to *find* Elijah even by using the power of his statecraft and military intelligence apparatus, 18:10, 12). Failing this desperate effort, Ahab's military apparatus, horses and mules, will be *cut off* (18:5 AT), further undercutting Ahab's power. Jezebel's efforts to *cut off* the prophets of the Lord are thwarted by a house official (18:4).

Not only are Ahab and Jezebel involved in life-and-death, cat-after-mice strategies, but Elijah's reply to Obadiah also reiterates the life-and-death nature of these encounters of power. Elijah swears by *YHWH Sabaoth, who lives* (18:15 AT). Ahab is trying to save his military machine by looking for some grass, but Elijah serves the Lord of heaven's armies (in 1–2 Kings, *hosts* or *Sabaoth*, pl. in Hebrew, most often refers to human armies; Elijah uses it here and on Mount Horeb, 19:14; 22:19; 2 Kings 3:14; the term also refers to gods of the idolatrous, 17:16; 21:3, 5; 23:4-5; here the hosts that serve the Lord might include natural bodies, sun, moon, stars, and the deities associated with them, including Baal, who rides on the storm clouds). Ahab, servant of Baal, the god of rainstorms and fertility, is powerless before Yahweh, the creator and sovereign of the land. Ahab obeys Elijah's summons through Obadiah and goes to meet Elijah, setting up the drama to follow (18:16).

18:17-40 Contest on Carmel

Ahab reinforces the hostility between them by addressing Elijah as a *troubler of Israel* (18:17; used of Achan, Josh 6:18; 7:25; one who consorts with dark supernatural forces to do harm, to hex; DeVries: 217). Elijah gives as good as he gets, replying that he has not troubled Israel, but Ahab and his house have rejected the Lord's commandments and followed Baal, falsely attributing prosperity to the idol (18:18). They have disobeyed the commandments of the Lord and invoked the anti-Deuteronomic system of idols, priests, economics, exploitation of the marginalized, and the king's monopolization of wealth and power (Hens-Piazza: 2006: 176) *[Mišpaṭ, p. 461]*. It is a matter of life and death (Deut 30:15). Elijah quickly moves on with his plan for a showdown on Mount Carmel with the 850 prophets who support the cultic and administrative apparatus imported with Jezebel from Sidon; Baal's prophets are to show up for a showdown to be witnessed by *all Israel* (1 Kings 18:19). Ahab complies with Elijah's demand (18:20).

The narrative mocks the forces of Ahab and Baal by pointing out that they are given every advantage. Baal is the storm god, depicted in a stele (stela) from Ugarit with a spear that looks like a lightning bolt, so fire from heaven should be his forte (J. Davies 2012: 341). Elijah is outnumbered 850 to 1 (Elijah twice mentions being outnumbered: 18:19, 22). The sacrifice is assembled on Mount *Carmel* ("vineyard of God"), a Baal sanctuary, one of the wettest and lushest places in Canaan, a place where the Baal prophets presume that they have a home-field advantage (Beck: 299). Elijah allows the Baal prophets choice of the bull and the first opportunity to win the contest.

After assembling the people and the prophets, Ahab disappears from the narrative until after the fire falls from heaven (18:20, 41). Elijah works directly with the overlooked populace. Though the narrative most frequently faults kings for Israel's apostasy, king and nation (linked initially in Samuel's speech, 1 Sam 12:14-15) are together responsible for Israel's ultimate demise (2 Kings 17:21-23; Hens-Piazza 2006: 182). When the people assemble, Elijah addresses them twice. First, he challenges them with a question about how long they will *limp* between *two different opinions* (1 Kings 18:21 uses the verb *limp*; in 18:26 NIV, the Baal priests are *dancing*; the term *opinions* in 18:21 interprets the Hebrew word *branches*, which here may suggest crutches for the people who limp or limbs for birds hopping from one place to the next). The people do not *answer* (*answer* is a theme in this story: 18:24, 26, 29, 37 [twice]), substantiating Elijah's charge that they are sitting on the fence. Elijah is making demands: Israel must reject the false claims that Baal provides food and prosperity by confessing that the Lord is their provider. In Elijah's call for decision, he scrupulously sets up the condition by completing the logic of the sentence in the first case, *If the LORD is God*, but not in the second case, *If Baal* (18:21), a subtlety better represented in NRSV than in NIV. The people remain silent, the narrator emphasizes.

Elijah's second speech lays out the conditions of the challenge (18:22-24). He emphasizes that he has given his opponents every advantage, including the numerical advantage that the Baal prophets have over the lone prophet of the Lord. Elijah sets up the contest: both the prophets of Baal and Elijah will prepare a bull for sacrifice without lighting the fire, then call for their gods to answer by fire. The people respond, "*Good word*" (18:24 AT).

Elijah continues with the initiative, offering the Baal prophets the "advantage" of going first (18:25). Elijah again points out their numerical superiority. The contest should be to Baal's advantage. As the storm god who has been defeated by drought, Baal is challenged to produce a single lightning bolt to ignite the sacrifice. The narrator playfully reports the failure of the Baal prophets' attempts to entice Baal to act (18:26-29): They cry from morning till noon. There is *no voice* (or sound; the implicit taunt is that the god of lightning should be able to rumble with thunder if not strike fire to the bull). There is *no answer* (cf. 18:21). The prophets *dance* (*limp*) about the altar (cf. 18:21). Elijah ridicules the Baal prophets: *Call with a great voice. He is (after all) a god. He's distracted with other thoughts* [occupied in the bathroom, Jemielity: 22]. *He's wandered off or away on a trip or taking a nap and needs to wake up* (18:27 AT). The narrative picks up the taunt, reporting that they did call out in a *great voice* (18:28 AT; in contrast to their silent, deaf god). *As was their custom, they cut themselves with swords and lances until the blood flowed* [*Idolatry, p. 449*]. The self-mutilation may be part of a homeopathic ritual related to the Baal myth as the goddess Anat tries to awaken Baal to bring life-giving, seasonal rain (Moore: 105). The word translated *custom* is the Hebrew *mišpaṭ* [*Mišpaṭ, p. 461*]. Having rejected the justice system of the Lord (the Levitical Torah), the prophet-priests of the Baal system have mixed cultic and political blood until life seeps out of the whole thing. Midday passes, evening nears, and still *no voice, no answer, and no response* (18:29). The priests may dance, limp, and cry out, but as the day ends, they are bleeding. Baal shows no signs of life.

The narratival vocabulary shifts from mocking to sacramental (18:30). Painstaking detail, reporting each of Elijah's actions, slows the narrative pace. Elijah invites the people to *come near* (18:30 AT), using the language of the sacrificial system, commanding people and priest to approach the altar (Exod 28:43; 30:20; Elijah *comes near* in 1 Kings 18:36). The people comply with Elijah's imperative invitation (18:30). Elijah *repairs* (a term usually translated "heals") the altar that had been *thrown down* (elsewhere a term for destruction in time of war, as in 3:25). The narrator links the number of twelve stones to the tribes of Jacob with an intriguing intertextual connection (in 18:31 Elijah quotes God's speech to Jacob at Bethel, *Israel shall be your name*, Gen 35:10; similarly, after wrestling all night, the man tells Jacob, "You shall no longer be called Jacob, but Israel," 32:28; 35:10-12). The intertextual allusions focus on the covenant relationship and the related promises that Yahweh, not Baal, had made to all Israel. The emphasis on the Lord opposed to Baal is reiterated by observing that Elijah *built an altar in the name of the LORD* (18:32).

The narrative slows further as Elijah digs a large trench around the rebuilt altar. Step by step, Elijah *arranges* (AT) the wood, cuts up the bull, and arranges it on the wood (arranging the wood is typical in Levitical cultic instruction, Lev 1:7, 8, 12; Abraham's offering of Isaac, Gen 22:9). The suspense builds as Elijah three times orders that four jars filled with water be spilled out on top of the altar and the wood and fill the trench (water is a scarce commodity that Ahab was scouting for as Elijah appeared to him, 1 Kings 18:5, 33-35; the promise of rain in 18:4 is yet unfulfilled, 18:41-45).

Finally, at the time of the evening sacrifice, Elijah *approaches* (cf. 18:30) and addresses God as *Yahweh, God of Abraham, Isaac, and Israel* (18:36 AT), a variation of his earlier prayer for the widow's son ("*O Yahweh, my God,*" 17:20-21 AT). Though the Lord is addressed, the audience includes the people limping between two opinions. One opinion is represented by Israel's king, who has transferred his loyalties to prophets and a *custom* (*mišpaṭ*; 18:28) whose lord is Baal. The other way is represented by Elijah ("my God is Yah"), who addresses Yahweh, the God of covenant promises made to Israel. Elijah issues two pleas: *Let it be known* and *Answer me, . . . answer me* (18:36-37). Both petitions are answered when fire falls from heaven. The first petition, *Let it be known*, has three objectives: that the people will know that the Lord is God, that Elijah is the Lord's prophet, and that Elijah's strategy has been prompted by direction from the Lord. The primary thing is knowing that the Lord is God; everything rises and falls on this reality. If the Lord is God, he is God in Israel, and full loyalty to the covenant is Israel's reasonable response. Second, people will experience Elijah as prophet, as the authoritative voice to be heeded (Deut 18:15-22). Third, the audience (both the characters in the story and the readers) learns for the first time that, according to Elijah's words to the Lord, the contest with fire from heaven is not Elijah's idea but is inspired by the Lord, the *God in Israel*. The second petition, *Answer me*, has two purpose clauses. The first reiterates the petition that Israel would experience the Lord as

God. The second purpose clause results in a previously unspoken event: the Lord has *turned their hearts back* (1 Kings 18:37).

As narrative tension reaches its apex, the fire of the Lord falls, consuming the offering, the wood, the twelve stones, the dust, and even the water in the trench (18:38). Having witnessed this colossal event, the people fall on their faces, confessing, *Yahweh, he is God; Yahweh, he is God* (the confession implicit in the name *Elijah*; 18:39 AT).

Elijah orders seizure and execution of the false prophets at the wadi near Mount Carmel (18:40). Is the reader to approve of Elijah as one who keeps the Torah mandate to execute false prophets (Deut 13:5; 18:20) and utterly destroy (*herem*) those who worship other gods as *a whole burnt offering to the LORD your God* (13:12-18)? If so, the bull consumed by fire is not the only whole offering of the day.

The narrative reports the violence without evaluation. While Elijah's actions may be defensible within Torah, his actions raise questions. Has Elijah overreached? On what basis does he act as if there is no alternative but to execute 450 (or perhaps 850) humans with the sword? Is this an act of justice, or does this violence violate Yahwistic justice and shalom? Elijah confuses the objective of the event by making it a contest between prophets rather than between deities. The Lord's victory on the mountaintop ends with the murderous act of the Lord's prophet in the valley (Hens-Piazza 2006: 180) [*Violence in Kings, p. 480*]. (See "Critique of Elijah's Violence" in TBC below.)

18:41-46 Prayer for Rain

Elijah's victory on Mount Carmel puts him in position not only to eliminate rival prophets but also to give orders to Ahab, who reappears (he was last seen in 18:20). Elijah commands Ahab to arise, eat, and drink because he can hear the roar of rain! (Prophets are seers who can foresee the future; Elijah, attuned to the Lord's word, can "fore-hear" God's actions.) While Ahab dines, Elijah resumes his prayer with intensity matching his earlier prayers, crouching to the ground, with his face between his knees (18:42; earlier prayers, 17:20-22; 18:36-37; cf. 2 Kings 4:34-35). Six times Elijah prays, sends his servant to search for a cloud, receives the disappointing answer, *There is nothing* (18:43). After the seventh prayer, the servant returns with good news: *Behold, a small cloud the size of a man's hand is rising from the sea!* (18:44 AT).

Foreshadowing Elisha's gesture of superiority (sending his servant to communicate with Naaman instead of addressing him directly, 2 Kings 5:10), Elijah sends his servant to tell Ahab, *Saddle up and head down lest the rain shower tie you up* (18:44 AT). A wooden translation of the unique Hebrew phrase rendered *In a little while* (18:45 NRSV) or *Meanwhile* (NIV) would read something like *And it was until thus and until so* (AT), emphasizing the staggering nature of this incident: *the heavens grew black with clouds and wind; there was a heavy rain* (18:45). Following Elijah's orders, Ahab mounts his chariot and goes down to Jezreel.

In a story filled with reminders that the Lord's power is with Elijah in opposition to Ahab, even the trip down the mountain reveals that the *hand* (*power*) of the Lord is on Elijah's side. Elijah *girded up his loins* (AT: *mustered his strength*) and *darted in the face of Ahab to the approach to Jezreel* (18:46 AT). Elijah either leads Ahab or outraces him.

THE TEXT IN BIBLICAL CONTEXT
Elijah, Elisha, and Jesus

In his Nazareth synagogue sermon, Jesus announces the fulfillment of Isaiah's good-news prophecy and cites the examples of Elijah and Elisha as precedent for his own priorities (Luke 4:16-30). Jesus marvels that though there were many widows in Israel, Elijah was sent to the widow in Sidon (4:25-26). His message is not popular in his hometown (4:28-29). Jesus learns from the two prophets to extend the focus of his mission beyond his hometown and eventually to "the ends of the earth" (Acts 1:8).

Foreign Women

The widow of Zarephath is an intriguing character. Anonymous, powerless, without support from an extended family, she is an innocent sufferer in the drought-induced famine. Responsible for a dependent child, the widow is industrious, gathering fuel for a final meal, but resigned to the fate of premature death. When the strange prophet demands that she feed him before feeding her own child, she acts in faith. Her theology is akin to that of 1–2 Kings; she reckons that her son's death is divine judgment for overlooked, unintentional, and unrecognized sin brought to the attention of the gods by the prophet's proximity. When her son revives, the woman confesses her faith that the word of Elijah is the word of the Lord of Israel [*Women in Kings, p. 485*].

The anonymous widow is by no means the only "foreign woman" who proves to be virtuous rather than dangerous (contra Num 25; Ezra 10). Hagar, the Egyptian slave girl of Sarai, calls the Lord by the new name "El-roi," the God who sees (Gen 16:13). Judah recognizes that the Canaanite widow Tamar, who tricked him into an incestuous liaison, was more righteous than he (38:26). Pharaoh's daughter preserves Moses' life (Exod 2:5-10). Jael, wife of Heber the Kenite, assassinates the enemy general Sisera to save Israel (Judg 4:18-22). Ruth of Moab protects Naomi and gives birth to David's grandfather (Ruth 4:21-22).

The widow of Zarephath has few positive counterparts among the foreign women in Kings. The most striking contrast is with her countrywoman Jezebel. The widow feeds the prophet of the Lord; Jezebel kills the Lord's prophets and feeds the prophets of Baal and Asherah (1 Kings 18:4, 13, 19). The widow saves Elijah's life; Jezebel tries to take it (19:1-2). Powerful Jezebel influences Israel to reject Yahweh for Baal, while the powerless widow confesses faith in Yahweh and his prophet. Elijah protects the life of the widow's son but proclaims the death of Jezebel's house (21:20-26; 2 Kings 9:7-10).

Though love for foreign women results in Solomon's downfall (11:1-8), another exception to the negative characterization of foreign women is the queen of Sheba (10:1-13). Like the widow, the queen remains anonymous. The queen is like Jezebel in wealth, power, and royal influence but is like the widow in confessing God's purposes for God's leader (10:9). Unlike Solomon's wives, who entice him to worship foreign gods, the queen of Sheba encourages Solomon to fulfill the Lord's purpose (Matt 12:42; Luke 11:31). (See also TBC for 1 Kings 9-10.)

Contested Deity

Elijah forces a confrontation between two competing cultic systems. He sets up the contest to force the people straddling two options to choose. He shows that Baal is lifeless, without voice, and without power. The Lord is reclaiming territory usurped by Baal, demanding that Israel attribute prosperity to their God rather than to an idol (cf. Hos 2:8-9, 16).

The prophet Isaiah also creates a contested reality between the Lord of Israel and the idols of Babylon, taunting them to state their case (Isa 41:21; 45:21). Isaiah demonstrates that the Lord alone is the creator who founded the earth and sits high above it as sovereign (40:12-26). The Lord alone opens rivers for the thirsty poor and needy (41:17-20). So the Lord challenges the other deities to a contest: Has anyone foretold past events or is any able to tell what is about to happen (41:21-29; 42:9; 44:7; 45:21; 46:8-11; 48:3-8, 14-16)? Babylon's gods are fraudulent idols made by human craftsmen from created objects (41:7; 44:9-20; 46:5-7). The Lord is sending Bel and Nebo, the gods of Babylon, and their people into captivity (46:1-2; 48:14). The Lord brings salvation and justice to the peoples (51:4-5). Using Old Testament imagery, Revelation also mocks the blasphemous imperial powers (12:13–13:18). The great whore, Babylon, is burned in fiery judgment (Rev 17). The word of God defeats the enemy (19:13, 15).

These texts claim the Lord's sovereignty. The gods are silent because they do not exist. Israel suffers defeat not because the gods of the conquering nations are superior but because the Lord is at work.

Sin and Punishment

The widow of Zarephath raises a fundamental problem underlying 1–2 Kings. "What is the relationship between sin and punishment? What happens when obedience does not bring about life, but rather ushers in death?" (S. Wyatt: 453). First and Second Kings clearly explains that exile is God's judgment on faithless Israel. Though blessed with the Torah, Israel rejects God's ways and practices idolatry and injustice worse than their predecessors in the land. For exiles struggling with the question of God's fairness, the text makes the case that the sins of Jeroboam, Ahab, and Manasseh outweigh even the renewal of Joash, Hezekiah, and Josiah.

Though the overarching story makes the case that judgment is not only fair but also inevitable, the issue of theodicy, why bad things happen to good people, resists a single, simple answer. The widow's suggestion that Elijah's presence has called attention to her unresolved sin reflects both the pervasiveness of the theology of retribution and its absurdity. The widow is without recourse and risks all to save the Lord's prophet, yet her son dies. Elijah's lament, with complaint, *O LORD . . . , have you brought calamity even upon the widow by killing her son?*, and plea, *O LORD my God, let this child's life come into him again* (1 Kings 17:20), is the genre characteristic of the psalmist who cries out for God's deliverance in times of undeserved suffering (e.g., Pss 3–7, 11–13). Yet 1–2 Kings not only defends the fairness of God's judgment in Israel's exile but also illustrates God's merciful deliverance and protection for God's chosen ones (2 Kings 4:1-7, 8-37, 38-42; 13:4-5, 23).

When the disciples ask Jesus whether the man born blind suffers because of his own sins or those of his parents, Jesus rejects those alternatives (John 9:2-3). Jesus heals the man, who then believes in Jesus. The healing becomes a sign that leads to faith.

Critique of Elijah's Violence

First Kings 18 narrates Elijah's slaughter of 450 prophets of Baal. Typical of 1-2 Kings, no evaluative comment guides the reader in assessing Elijah's action. The absence of evaluative comment may suggest an implicit critique of the violence. Hens-Piazza faults Elijah for making the event about his superiority over other prophets (2006: 180) [*Violence in Kings, p. 480*].

Kissling interprets both Elijah and Elisha as "unreliable characters." Flannery develops the interpretation, reading Elijah's actions as partial obedience, half-hearted allegiance to the Lord's ways: when the Lord commanded Elijah to appear to Ahab, he instead went to Obadiah (18:1-3; Flannery: 165). Flannery also reads with suspicion Elijah's claim to be alone among the prophets of Yahweh since we know that Obadiah has rescued one hundred prophets (18:3-4, 13; 166). He also points out Elijah's partial obedience to the Lord's instruction to go out and stand on the mountain (19:11, 13) and his repeated complaint that he is the lone remaining prophet (169). Kissling argues that Elijah, not the Lord, initiates the contest with fire (99).

Flannery concludes that Elijah's slaughter of the Baal prophets should be read in the context of the failed violent reforms of Jehu (2 Kings 9-11) and Josiah (2 Kings 23:20). He suggests that Obadiah is the faithful *servant of Yah[weh]*, who pursues an alternative, nonviolent resistance to Baal worship that not only saves lives but also avoids bloodshed [*Kings in the Hebrew Canon: Kings in the Deuteronomistic History, p. 453*] (Flannery 172-73; Olley 1998: 37).

THE TEXT IN THE LIFE OF THE CHURCH

Extreme Poverty

The story of the widow of Zarephath invites reflection on the church's response to those separated by distance, ideology, or religion. Ana Revenga, director of the Poverty and Equity Group at the World Bank, is optimistic that a generation-long trajectory of reduced numbers of persons living in extreme poverty will continue. Extreme poverty, defined by income needed to meet basic needs in the poorest nations of the world, is quantified at two dollars per person per day. The percentage of those living in such extreme need declined from 44 percent in 1981 and 37 percent in 1990 to below 10 percent in 2018.

For continued progress the World Bank deems necessary the safety-net programs that provide minimum income in exchange for a commitment to keep children in school and current with vaccinations. Richer nations play their important role in reducing poverty more successfully when they reduce demands on the poorer nations and give them ownership of programs, policies, and strategies. Key factors to maximize the impact of wealthier nations in alleviating extreme poverty include open markets to give agriculturalists a fair price for commodities, gender equality, and keeping a focus on extreme poverty in the world during uncertain economic times at home. Revenga deems these factors essential to addressing the needs of the one billion people living on less than two dollars a day (Frykholm: 32–34).

A Troubler of Israel

Early Anabaptists reference Elijah's conflict with political and religious opponents. Balthasar Hubmaier (in *A Brief Apologia*) defends himself against charges that he is an agitator by citing Ahab's charge that Elijah was the troubler of Israel (1 Kings 18:17-18): "Note that if Ahab had not attached himself to Baalish bishops, monks, and priests, there would have been lasting peace in the land" (1526, in Pipkin and Yoder: 303). Dirk Philips contends with those he considers false teachers when he defends himself against those who question his spiritual credentials:

> There are many who contradict us here. Many say that no one can teach and restore the fallen worship again except they be called of the Lord by a living voice from heaven. Just as Elijah [they say] did not punish the priest of Baal nor restore the fallen worship of Israel before he had received a command from the Lord and was sent to Ahab. (Philips 1564: 217)

Philips argues that faithfulness to Scripture and to community discernment are adequate credentials in contending for biblical values.

The church's witness for peace and justice often makes it the troubler of government. As conscientious objectors to military service, Joseph Hofer and Michael Hofer, Hutterite brothers from South Dakota, were imprisoned, tortured, and killed in American prisons during World War I. In summer 2017, four women with No More Deaths were arrested and sentenced to prison for leaving water for migrants in the Arizona desert. Convicted in U.S. federal court, they asked, "If giving water to someone dying of thirst is illegal, what humanity is left in the law of this country?"

1 Kings 19:1-21

Elijah after Mount Carmel

PREVIEW

Catherine of Siena (1347–80) balanced contemplative and active life. She spent three years alone in a room, where she fasted, prayed, and experienced daily visitations from Jesus. One day Jesus appeared in Catherine's doorway, inviting her into an active life of prison visitation and nursing those sick with the plague. She pursued conflict resolution among church leaders. At times her public ministry was interrupted by a vision of Jesus.

Elijah, too, was an activist who practiced solitude and pursued a vision of the Holy One. In 1 Kings 19, Elijah is fresh off one of the most dramatic events in 1–2 Kings. Threatened with death, Elijah flees to the mount of God. Textual clues suggest that Elijah expects an experience of the divine presence akin to Moses' on Sinai (Exod 34:5-8). A voice promises that the Lord will pass by, but God is not present in three successive powerful acts. Finally, Elijah hears a silent voice. The trip to the mountain ends with a new commission to ministry. The reader is left to puzzle how, if at all, Elijah has experienced God.

OUTLINE

Jezebel's Threat, 19:1-3
Elijah at Horeb, 19:4-18
   19:4-9a   Elijah's Flight

19:9b-18   Dialogue: The Lord and Elijah
Elijah and Elisha, 19:19-21

EXPLANATORY NOTES

The Lord's climactic victory over Baal confirms Elijah's perspective, but Jezebel does not concede defeat. The story resumes "the morning after" (1 Kings 19:1).

Jezebel's Threat 19:1-3

Jezebel's threat to kill Elijah energizes the plot of 1 Kings 19. Indeed, Jezebel represents unmitigated evil. The Baal system introduced by the alliance with Sidon assumes the royal prerogative to override Deuteronomic covenant priorities [Idolatry, p. 449]. Jezebel's opposition to Yahweh has been established (killing the Lord's prophets while providing for the Baal and Asherah prophets, 18:4, 13, 19), but she speaks for the first time, setting up the narrative conflict (19:2).

Ahab gives Jezebel a thorough account of the events on Carmel, reporting all that Elijah had done, having killed all the prophets (19:1; the quotations in this chapter are mostly a free mixture of NRSV and AT). Jezebel reacts immediately and fiercely, sending a messenger to frighten Elijah (19:2; send signals Jezebel's royal authority, absent action by Ahab) [Send, p. 476]. With an oath in the name of the gods, Jezebel's message, threatening to make Elijah's life like the life of the slaughtered prophets, recenters the earlier theme of life and death (17:1, 12, 18, 20-23; 18:4, 9, 10, 12, 13-15, 40). Life is used seven times in 1 Kings 19:2-17 (19:2 [twice], 3, 4 [twice in MT], 10, 14); kill, die, or death appears six times (19:1, 4, 10, 14, 17 [twice]). Jezebel's death threat by a messenger may be a ruse to induce Elijah to flee on his own initiative. If Jezebel had intended Elijah's death, she would have sent troops rather than a threat. Lacking the political clout to withstand the popular outcry if she resorted to deadly violence, Jezebel's threat is effective. At the apex of his influence, Elijah flees for his life (19:3; Konkel 2006: 302; J. T. Walsh 1996: 267; Kissling: 101–2).

The prophet—who has spoken prophetic judgment against King Ahab (17:1), leveraged the drought to advantage over Ahab, called fire from heaven, slaughtered prophets, and prayed rain from a cloudless sky—is afraid (18:3; see "Fear" in TBC). Elijah is the only servant of the Lord in 1–2 Kings who acts out of fear. Readers speculate about the psychological factors that moved Elijah to fear. Has the adrenaline rush of the energy-demanding confrontation on Carmel exhausted Elijah's reserves? Is the efficiency of the regime's security forces something Elijah has overlooked in his actions on Carmel? Does Elijah fear Jezebel's power to retaliate for killing her prophets? Is Elijah overly dependent on supernatural reinforcement from the Lord? The report includes feelings characteristic of post-traumatic stress disorder, or PTSD, particularly acute for those who have participated in brutally violent atrocities (like the mass killing of the prophets in 1 Kings 18:40): paranoia, hopelessness, lack of eating, excessive sleep (Smith-Christopher: 91–93).

Uninterested in Elijah's psychological state, the text simply says that Elijah *was afraid; he got up and fled for his life* to Beer-sheba (19:3), the southernmost point of Solomon's territories (1 Kings 4:25; Gen 21:31-33). Leaving his servant, Elijah goes another day's journey into the wilderness. The series of action verbs in 1 Kings 19:3-4 (*fears, arises, flees, comes, leaves, flees, comes, sits, requests*) leaves the reader breathless. The prophet has traveled almost the length of Judah and Israel and is spent (J. T. Walsh 1996: 267).

To this point the story is about Elijah's conflict with Jezebel, her reaction to his victory at Carmel, and his fearful escape. This situation sets up the story, but the narrative shifts. With the dismissal of the servant, the last of the supporting cast disappears. Neither Ahab nor Jezebel is heard from again in 1 Kings 19.

Elijah at Horeb 19:4-18

Elijah's encounter with God has often been interpreted as a pilgrimage renewing his prophetic commitment (a *re-call*, Sandoval: 12). J. T. Walsh argues that Elijah intends to renounce his prophetic calling, suggesting that the question shifts to what happens when a prophet wants to leave office. "How will Yahweh respond? And what will happen to the prophet?" (1996: 265). Elijah is in full crisis—whether suffering PTSD or a midlife faith collapse.

Elijah travels to Horeb (the name used in Exod 3:1; Deut 1; 1 Kings 8:9 for the mountain known as Sinai in Exod 19, 34; Lev 25–27). The narrative surfaces parallels between Elijah's visit to Horeb and Moses' experience on Sinai (Exod 19–34). There Moses, after crossing the wilderness, fasts forty days and nights, receives the Lord's covenant, and experiences the Lord's presence passing by the cleft in the rock. Perhaps the implication is that Elijah demands of the Lord a confirmation equal to that of Moses and consistent with the fire from heaven on Carmel. The narrator may be creating a contrast between the unequaled prophet Moses and the lesser Elijah (Deut 18:18; 34:10). A fuller discussion of the parallels between Moses on Sinai and Elijah on Horeb appears in the TBC below.

19:4-9a Elijah's Flight

In fear Elijah *flees* (or *went*; 19:3-4) another day's journey into the *wilderness* (the isolated liminal territory where Israel wandered for forty years, Deut 2:7). Exhausted, he collapses under a *broom tree* (flora more shrub than a tree); the *solitary broom tree* reflects Elijah's isolation. In despair Elijah *pleads that his life [soul] might die* (AT here and below in most of the remainder of this chapter; an expression as awkward in Hebrew as in English, J. Davies 2012: 354), asking in effect that the Lord take his life, the very thing that Elijah had feared of Jezebel and that had motivated his flight. Elijah's request is abrupt and brusque (without the polite form he used in 17:21): *Enough! Now, O LORD, take my life! I am no better than my ancestors* (19:4; J. T. Walsh 1996: 267). Elijah's request echoes Moses' experience (Num 11:11-15). Perhaps *ancestors (fathers)* refers to the prophets who preceded him, indicating that Elijah senses that, like his predecessors, he has been ineffective at bringing reform to Israel (Seow: 140; Leithart: 141). Elijah lies down and falls asleep under the *one broom tree* (MT; the repetition underlines the isolation). Elijah falls asleep, perhaps hoping never to awaken.

The immediacy of the vivid narrative report is hard to convey in translation. The word *behold* signals surprise (and new perspective) in both verses 5 and 6 (MT) *[Literary Criticism: Elements of Narrative, p. 458]*. As Elijah sleeps, *Surprise! A messenger touches him* (*angel* in NRSV and NIV is based on the identification in 19:7, but the same word describes Jezebel's *messenger* in 19:2). The text invites the reader to the shocking uncertainty that the sleeping Elijah experiences. The messenger/angel *surprisingly touches* Elijah to awaken him. Is this messenger's *touch* the kiss of death or of new life? (The corpse that *touches* Elisha's bones is revivified, 2 Kings 13:21; the Lord's *touch strikes* the king with leprosy, 15:5.) The messenger issues a two-word command: *Rise! Eat!* (1 Kings 19:5). Countering Jezebel's messenger threatening death, this messenger offers provisions for life.

Elijah awakens and looks around. *Surprise! Bread baked on a hot coal with a jar of water!* (19:6). This word for *bread* is used only six other times in the Old Testament (e.g., Passover in Egypt, Exod 12:39; wilderness manna, Num 11:8; widow's provision for Elijah, 1 Kings 17:13). *Jar* is used only six other times (three times referring to the *jug of oil* that is never exhausted, 17:12-16). The Lord, who has provided bread and water for Elijah during the drought, provides for Elijah's needs as he did for the people in the wilderness (J. Davies 2012: 355). Four one-word sentences tersely describe Elijah's actions—he *eats, drinks, returns, lies down. Return* (NRSV translates the Hebrew idiom as *[he] lay down again*) indicates the prophet's stubborn *repeated* withdrawal (J. T. Walsh 1996: 269).

The messenger of the LORD (explicitly identifying him as the Lord's *messenger*) *returns a second time and touches him* (19:7). The angel's action, *return*, matches Elijah's (19:6); the Lord's messenger is as persistent as the prophet. *Return* is a theme in the prophetic call to Elijah and Elisha (19:15, 20, 21). The angel's message begins with the same double imperative as before: *Arise! Eat!* (19:5, 7). The message adds a purpose clause: *For more than enough for you [is] the way* (19:7). The repeated *enough* matches Elijah's *"Enough!"* when he arrives at the broom tree and requests that his life be taken (19:4, 7). *Way* is not defined in the text but marks the contrast between the *way* of Obadiah and the *way* of Ahab (18:6-7). Elijah obeys the angel's command. The narrative moves the action quickly: *He arose, ate, drank, and went in the strength of that food forty days and forty nights to the mount of God, Horeb* (19:8). The trip to Horeb recalls both Moses' Sinai experience and Israel's meeting with God on the mountain as they escape from slavery in Egypt (Exod 19–34).

Upon Elijah's arrival at Mount Horeb, the narrative slows again. *He comes there to the cave, and he spends the night there* (19:9). The repeated *there* and the definite article (*the*) call attention to location. Though Moses meets God in "a cleft in the rock" (Exod 33:22), we note the allusion to Moses' Sinai encounter. The reference to *the cave* also contrasts Elijah with Obadiah, who hides one hundred prophets in two caves to protect them from Jezebel (18:13), while Elijah hides in the cave after fleeing in fear of Jezebel.

19:9b-18 Dialogue: The Lord and Elijah

The narrative marks surprise (and a change in perspective) with the word that NRSV translates *then* (19:9). *Behold, the word of the LORD says to him, Why are you here, Elijah?* The angelic messenger has provided food and drink and sent Elijah on *the way* (19:7). After their exchange on Horeb, the Lord will commission Elijah to *return on your way* (19:15). The brief question is ambiguous. Perhaps Elijah is there "to exercise the privilege of the prophet" to *stand before the LORD* in the Lord's council (19:11; Leithart: 142). After the emphasis on location in the first half of 19:7, the question rather focuses on what Elijah is doing *here*, rebuking Elijah for journeying to the mountain, far from the place for which he had been called as a prophet (Wray Beal 2014: 253; J. T. Walsh 1996: 272). God's challenge invites Elijah to examine his reluctance to perform his prophetic duties. If Elijah is seeking to replay the scene of Moses communing with God, the question may confront that motivation. In that case the Lord is asking, "Elijah, do you think that you can re-create the intimacy that Moses had with the Lord? Do you seek to place yourself on equal footing with Moses?" The Lord's question is not a clear indictment and shows openness to further dialogue. The prophet's reply indicates lack of clarity and a desire to be taken into the Lord's confidence (J. Davies 2012: 357).

Elijah's response conveys intensity: *I have been zealous with zeal for YHWH of the armies* (19:10; Phineas and Saul express zeal for the Lord and for Israel, Num 25:11, 13; 2 Sam 21:2). Elijah identifies the Lord as *Yahweh of the armies*, reflecting the Lord's powerful intervention in this conflict (1 Kings 18:15; 19:10, 14; 2 Kings 3:14). Israel itself, Elijah contends, has rejected the Lord in three ways. First, the comprehensive, essential accusation is that they *have forsaken your covenant* (forsaking the Lord results in covenant curses, Deut 28:20; 31:16; in the cycles of apostasy, Judg 2:12-13; 10:6-13; in the warning of temple destruction, 1 Kings 9:9; 11:33; in Israel's exile, 2 Kings 17:16; in Manasseh's apostasy, 21:22) *[Covenant in Kings, p. 443]*. To *forsake* the Lord is to reject Deuteronomic covenant values *[Mišpaṭ, p. 461]*. Elijah is *here* (on Horeb) because Israel has *forsaken* the Lord. Second, they have destroyed the Lord's *altars* (including the altar on Carmel, 18:30). Third, they have killed the Lord's prophets (Jezebel's actions, 1 Kings 18:13; 19:2). Elijah is convinced that he stands *alone* against the enemy (18:22; 19:10, 14; cf. Gen 2:18, where the Lord says that "it is not good that the man should be alone"). Elijah is *here* because he opposes Israel's rejection of covenant values, cultic impropriety, and violence against the prophets. Elijah threatens Ahab's royal system; Jezebel reacts with the threat against his life—and her track record of killing prophets is impressive (18:5, 13).

Elijah accuses the people of infidelity without much detail. Leithart argues that Elijah is fully justified. Rejection of renewed covenant, Leithart contends, demands judgment, and the Lord concurs with Elijah's indictment by sending him back to destroy the house of Ahab (19:15-18; Leithart: 142). Despite the efforts of prophets and reforming kings, the people are destined for exile (1 Kings 14:15-16; 2 Kings 17:35-40).

Leithart's conclusion is contested by most commentators. A few recent scholars have evaluated Elijah's character negatively. Kimelman argues that the Lord relieves Elijah of his prophetic duties because he has failed to perform the prophetic task of defending the people before the Lord (as Abraham in Gen 18 and Moses in Exod 32 had done; Kimelman: 25-26). Others fault Elijah for misplaced egotistical priorities. His actions are governed by zeal for his own life enmeshed in his zeal for the Lord as reflected by his inaccurate conclusion that he alone remains faithful (Hens-Piazza 2006: 189–90; J. T. Walsh 1996: 273). Elijah's overzealousness has placed him at risk and caused him to overlook a better interpretation of the facts (Brueggemann 2000: 235; Seow: 142). Overcome by misplaced fear, Elijah is reacting to Jezebel's threat when in fact Israel, far from having forsaken the covenant, has renewed the covenant by confessing that Yahweh is God (1 Kings 18:39; Wray Beal 2014: 253). By this confession, far from having torn down the Lord's altars, the people have supported Elijah in rebuilding an altar of the Lord. Not only has Obadiah preserved one hundred prophets against the threats of Jezebel, but also the Lord is about to correct Elijah's complaint that he is alone (19:18). Elijah complains that the people have killed the prophets even though the text reports only that *Jezebel* is killing the Lord's prophets and threatening his life. (Elijah himself is the greatest killer of prophets, 18:40.) Perhaps Elijah discounts the worthiness of prophets who hide from Jezebel in caves, though that is what he himself is doing. Perhaps Elijah has dismissed his servant, left the territory of Israel and Judah, and arrived at Horeb to renounce his calling (J. T. Walsh 1996: 273). The response of the Lord indicates great persistence in extending the call to Elijah (in the face of Elijah's resistance) and great patience in continuing to invite communication (despite Elijah's speech apparently designed to cut off dialogue).

The Lord's command to *stand before the* LORD requires that Elijah assume a posture of loyal service and readiness for the Lord's command (19:11; cf. 17:1). The Lord explains the surprising significance of what is about to follow (and calls for a new perspective): *Attention! Yahweh passing!* (At Passover the Lord "passes through" Egypt, Exod 12:12, 23; the Lord "passes by" Moses on Sinai, 33:19, 22; 34:6.) Three powerful events ensue. First, a mighty wind, an earthquake, and fire (1 Kings 19:11-12). These natural phenomena accompany the Lord's appearance on Sinai (the Lord descends in fire and the mountain shakes violently, Exod 19:18). On Mount Carmel, Elijah has witnessed the power of the Lord in fire and wind (1 Kings 18:38, 45). Here each mighty event is followed by the same refrain: *not in the wind Yahweh, not in the earthquake Yahweh, not in the fire Yahweh* (19:11-12). The sequence continues, but without the refrain. *And after the fire a voice of finely ground [razor-thin] silence* (19:12; this term is translated as "fine" dust in Isa 29:5; 40:15; "silence and voice I hear" in Job 4:16). If the Lord is not in the wind, earthquake, or fire, does the Lord pass by in the strange silence? The text does not clarify. The silent voice contrasts the Lord's presence with the absence of Baal, where the loud voice of the prophets of Baal is met by the absence of any voice of Baal (*no voice, no answer, and no attention*, 1 Kings 18:27-29 AT). The silent voice of the Lord also contrasts with the fire of the Lord demanded by Elijah's prayer on Carmel (18:36-38), a silent rebuke for Elijah's dependence on fiery drama to communicate the Lord's authority (DeVries: 237). The *voice of razor-thin silence* is not explained. The divine is beyond the mighty natural events and beyond human comprehension (J. T. Walsh 1996: 276).

Though the voice and the Lord's *passing by* remain unexplained, *when Elijah hears he wraps his face in his mantle and goes out and stands in the cave entrance* (19:13) The text does not interpret Elijah's actions or define what he hears. Some interpreters fault Elijah for a slow, incomplete response to the command to *stand . . . before the Lord* (19:11; Flannery: 169; Provan 1995: 146), seeing evidence of Elijah's preoccupation with self-preservation in his covering himself with his mantle (Hens-Piazza 2006: 190) and exhibition of fear in his stopping at the cave entrance (Wray Beal 2014: 253).

As Elijah stands at the cave entrance with his face covered by his mantle (see also 19:19), the text reads, *Surprise [Behold]! And to him a voice said, "Why are you here, Elijah?"* (19:13; repeating verbatim the earlier question in 19:9). Elijah responds exactly as he did previously (19:14; cf. 9:10). How is the reader to understand this? Is this voice also the word of the Lord? Does the question (repeated without variation) imply that Elijah has in some way been unfaithful in his trip to Horeb? Is it a different question, demanding an explanation of Elijah's slow and incomplete response to the command to stand before the Lord, even at the cave entrance? How will we read Elijah's identical reply? Is Elijah's response appropriate? Is it faithful? Does it indicate incomplete insight? Is Elijah stuck in a rut?

In interpreting Elijah's response in 19:10, Roi acknowledges that it could reveal the persistent prophet's zeal for the Lord in contrast to the people's rejection of the Lord (*I alone am left, and they are seeking my life*; Roi: 39). He concludes, however, that Elijah is so concerned for his own survival that it preempts his commitment to his prophetic office; the Lord's response (*Anoint Elisha . . . in your place*, 19:16) informs him that he has been removed and that his prophetic ministry is terminated (Roi: 44). Kissling agrees that Elijah's response indicates his unreliability as a prophet (120–21).

We, however, interpret Elijah's response as indication of his overly zealous and radical prophetic stance. The verbatim repetition is consistent with his combative confrontation of Ahab and violent judgment of the Baal prophets on Carmel. Elijah operates without filters in his radical rejection of the royal ideology of the Baal cult. With driving passion for Yahweh alone against other gods and unjust practices, Elijah confronts the royal system, using over-the-top rhetoric, drama, and violence. His repeated response to the Lord employs a similar rhetoric of exaggeration, much like the methods that brought him to the brink of war in 1 Kings 18. The narrative neither endorses nor condemns Elijah's methods but serves notice that Elijah's violent way resembles the *way* of the king, not the servant of Yahweh (18:6). The Lord himself responds quietly, explicitly not present in wind, earthquake, or fire (19:11-12). Obadiah's quiet and risky behavior in Ahab's court is a legitimate alternative to Elijah's combative approach (Roi: 47).

The Lord does not respond directly but addresses Elijah with a series of commands, an explanation, and a rebuke (19:15-18). If Elijah has intended to resign his prophetic calling, the Lord rejects that attempt and recommissions him: *Go, return . . . , arrive, . . . anoint.* Elijah's *way into the wilderness* has been an escape from Jezebel and from his duties as a prophet (19:4), but now the Lord commands, *Return on your way . . .* In reporting Elijah's flight from his prophetic calling, the verb *return* indicates the prophet's stubborn resistance (19:6), a resolve met by the angel's persistent *return* to rouse the prophet (19:7). The Lord's command to *return* resolves the prophet's vocational crisis (19:15). The angel has warned the fleeing prophet, *The way is more than enough for you* (19:7).

The Lord's new commission reroutes Elijah on his *way to the wilderness of Damascus,* north of Israel. The Lord instructs Elijah to *anoint* three individuals (Samuel the seer anointed Saul and David, 1 Sam 10:1; 16:13; Zadok with Nathan the prophet anointed Solomon, 1 Kings 1:39, 45). *The LORD, the God of* the *hosts* of heaven (19:10, 14), orders Elijah to move beyond Israelite territory to *anoint* Hazael as king of Aram, through whom the Lord will judge his people (2 Kings 10:32; 13:3). More conventionally, Elijah is to *anoint* Jehu as king of Israel. While anointing a prophetic successor is unprecedented, the Lord also commands Elijah to *anoint* Elisha as prophet in his place. With this command, death returns to the story: Jehu will kill those who escape the sword of Hazael, and Elisha will put to death those who escape Jehu. Jehu does indeed kill two kings who escape the sword of Hazael (2 Kings 9:24-28). The reference to Elisha killing those who escape Jehu's sword is not clear, since the incident is not mentioned later in Kings. All three of the anointed leaders join

Elijah in opposition to the house of Omri, to eliminate the dynasty. The Lord corrects Elijah's assertion that he is alone: seven thousand Israelites have not worshiped Baal (1 Kings 19:18; the number is auspicious: seven is a complete number, and thousand is the largest Hebrew number). This final comment is a rebuke of Elijah's complaint that he alone is faithful to the Lord (19:10, 14).

Elijah and Elisha 19:19-21

With the Lord's mandate, Elijah departs *from there* (his retreat from his prophetic call, 19:9-11), travels along the Jordan River valley, and finds Elisha ("my God saves") plowing, in command of a team of field hands with twelve pairs of oxen, including the pair that he himself drives. Shaphat, father of Elisha, is evidently a wealthy farmer in Abel-meholah (a boundary town just west of the Jordan and south of Beth-shean, 1 Kings 4:12); Elisha is a capable, industrious overseer. Without a word Elijah *passes by* Elisha (on the verb *passes by*, see 19:11), throwing the prophet's mantle on Elisha, continuing on his way (with this mantle Elijah has protected his face on Horeb, 19:13; with the mantle Elijah and Elisha *pass by* the Jordan, 2 Kings 2:8, 13, 14).

Recognizing the mantle as a symbolic call to follow Elijah, Elisha requests permission to say his goodbyes before joining Elijah. Elijah replies, *Go, return. What have I done to you?* Elisha *returns* (complying with Elijah's command; the verb is associated with prophetic mission in 1 Kings 19:6-7, 15); slaughters one yoke of oxen, using the plowing equipment as cooking fuel; and feeds the people. With this sacrifice, Elisha leaves father, mother, his people, vocation, and possessions and follows Elijah. Just as Joshua was the servant of Moses (Exod 24:13; 33:11; Num 11:28), so Elisha becomes the *servant* of Elijah (2 Kings 3:11).

Without explanation, the text reports the actions of Elijah and Elisha, leaving open the question of whether Elijah obeys the commission given by the Lord on Horeb (J. T. Walsh 1996: 280). Suspicious readers doubt the conversion of Elijah, finding fault with his failure to anoint Elisha or, indeed, even to say a word to the person who becomes his servant (Provan 1995: 147–48). Elijah is criticized for limiting Elisha's role to that of servant rather than accepting him in the role assigned by the Lord, as his successor (19:16). Others interpret Elijah's call of Elisha as faithful return to ministry, not unfaithful half-heartedness (Epp-Tiessen: 40). Elisha's response is faithful, abandoning family and fortune and foreshadowing his concern for orphans and widows by feeding the people (19:21; 2 Kings 4:1-7).

THE TEXT IN BIBLICAL CONTEXT
Fear

Fear is an infrequent topic in 1–2 Kings, making Elijah's fear of Jezebel all the more striking (19:3). Frequently *fear* is reverence to the Lord or other gods (four of nine times in 1 Kings; thirteen of nineteen times in 2 Kings). Adonijah and all Israel *fear* Solomon (1 Kings 1:50, 51; 3:28). Prophets reassure those in frightening circumstances, *Do not be afraid* (1 Kings 17:13; 2 Kings 6:16; 19:6). Elijah, the only servant of the Lord to act from fear in 1–2 Kings, flees for his life in a crisis of faith (1 Kings 19:3; cf. 2 Kings 1:15).

Fear is a primary theme in the story of Gideon (Judg 6–8). Gideon hides in a wine press while winnowing wheat. The Lord assures the timid Gideon, "Do not fear, because the LORD is your shalom" (6:23 AT), thus identifying Gideon's problem as fear. In fear, Gideon removes the Baal shrine at night. Two-thirds of Gideon's army leaves in fear. With Gideon paralyzed by fear, the Lord offers an additional sign before battle (7:10-15). It is as if all the fear of the Bible is concentrated in the Gideon story (Jeter: 71–72). Like Gideon, Nicodemus comes to Jesus at night to avoid the Jews (John 3). In fear, the disciples demand signs (Mark 13:4). Like Gideon, who is called a "mighty warrior" but pales when called to action (Judg 6:12), Elijah confronts hundreds of false prophets but quails before Jezebel.

Though fear can paralyze great warriors and great prophets, God repeatedly frees Israel from fear. The Lord's words of assurance, "Do not fear," come to Abram (Gen 15:1), Hagar (21:17), Isaac (26:24), Moses (Num 21:34), Joshua (Josh 8:1; 10:8), dwellers in Jerusalem (Isa 8:12), the Babylonian exiles (Isa 40:9; 41:10, 13, 14; 43:1, 5; 44:2; 51:7; Jer 46:27-28). Gabriel reassures Mary (Luke 1:30). An angel comforts the shepherds (Luke 2:10). Angels calm terrified women at the empty tomb, "Fear not!" (Matt 28:5; Mark 16:6). The risen Jesus reassures startled disciples, "Peace be with you" (Luke 24:36; John 19:19, 21, 26). Freed from fear, the people of God experience God's salvation (Exod 14:13-14). God's deliverance frees even soil and animals from fear (Joel 2:21-22)!

Questions

God asks Elijah, *What are you doing here?* The question probes Elijah's purposes in fleeing to Horeb. God's questions strategically set the agenda in other pivotal texts. In the garden the Lord God addresses Adam: "Where are you?" When Adam admits that he is hiding in shame, God asks, "Who told you that you were naked? Have you eaten from the tree of which I commanded you not to eat?" (Gen 3:9-11). These questions set the agenda for God's judgment on the serpent, the woman, and the man. The Lord questions Cain, "Why are you angry, and why has your countenance fallen? If you do well, will you not be accepted? . . . Where is your brother Abel? . . . What have you done?" (4:6-7, 9-10). When Hagar flees Sarai's abuse, the Lord asks, "Hagar, where have you come from and where are you going?" (16:8). The Lord asks Abraham and Sarah, "Why did Sarah laugh? . . . Is anything too wonderful for the LORD?" (18:13-14). The Lord is self-reflective, asking, "Shall I hide from Abraham what I am about to do?" (18:17). When he wrestles with Jacob, he asks, "What is your name?" (32:27). Jacob's sense of identity changes as he recognizes that he strives with God and others.

God's questions invite reflection and offer a different perspective. They probe such issues as purpose, aim, identity, and motivation. Why is Elijah afraid? Why has he fled to Horeb? Elijah's answer reveals limited perspective. God's question seems to move Elijah back to his task of confronting royal justice (= injustice). The next time he appears on the scene, it is with the Lord's question for Ahab, *Have you killed and also taken possession?* (1 Kings 21:19). Elijah's intervention produces amazing results, eventuating in yet another divine question, this one apparently reflecting the Lord's wonder: *Have you seen how Ahab has humbled himself before me?* (21:29). The Lord's question produces results in an unexpected way.

Jesus responds to questions with questions. When tested about taxes, he asks, "Whose face is on your coin?" (Luke 20:24 AT). When no one dares question Jesus further, he asks the riddle about how "the Messiah is David's son" (20:41). Jesus enjoins service among his disciples with the rhetorical question, "Who is greater, the one who is at table or the one who serves?" He answers that question, "I am . . . one who serves" (22:27). The risen Jesus introduces his interpretation of Moses and the prophets by asking, "What are you discussing? . . . What things?" (24:17-19, 25-26).

THE TEXT IN THE LIFE OF THE CHURCH
Effectual Fervent Prayer

Elijah's prayer encourages Christians to pray, particularly in times of suffering and sickness (James 5:13-18). Elijah's example encourages prayer for forgiveness and healing.

Elijah's prayer life takes a turn in 1 Kings 19. Elijah is in intense dialogue with God. Though Elijah requests that his life end, his prayer shifts from petition to discernment. The dialogue helps the disheartened Elijah identify how he has become misguided. Recognizing that he is in the wrong place, Elijah returns to his mission.

Elijah's prayer is effective not simply because his emotional fervor obligates God to act. In prayer, Elijah works with God. In noting that the prayer of Elijah closed the windows of heaven, James reveals that Elijah works in sync with God's plans (James 5:13-18). Before Elijah prays for rain, he knows that the drought is over. The Lord has told him that rain is on the way before he meets Ahab. Yet Elijah prays fervently for rain—even with this assurance. The prayer on Horeb also challenges the idea that prayer is simply talking God into something that might not otherwise be possible. Elijah enters dialogue with God to discern future direction and to regain his equilibrium.

Like Elijah, Christians are to be people of prayer. The model prayer of Jesus also joins heaven to earth (Matt 6:9-13). The three "you" petitions invite God to introduce the reign of God into the world. The three "we" petitions invite partnership in the working out of that reign on earth. A reconciling community is a praying community. Though we express our fight with principalities and powers differently than Elijah's story does, we too are engaged in a fervent battle for justice in a world where the systems oppose God's reign of justice.

Avoiding Persecution and Martyrdom

Early Anabaptists knew that "the blood of the martyrs is the seed of the church," but they avoided persecution when possible (Tertullian, *Apology* 13). Menno Simons cites the example of Elijah fleeing Jezebel (1 Kings 19:3) to defend his actions. "No Scripture directs us to go where we know beforehand that we shall die or be put in prison for life, but we are admonished in plain words to flee from tyrants" (Menno: 573). Dirk Philips agrees and uses the same example for his defense:

> Elijah also knew that God is almighty. He also trusted his Lord and God that he could protect him well. Nevertheless, he feared for himself before Jezebel and fled into the wilderness. . . . If Elijah hid himself from Jezebel and Christ from Herod, why should the true teacher not do the same? (Philips 1564: 229)

For Philips, the Elijah story is a wealth of support for the holy remnant, the tiny band of faithful believers opposed by the mainstream state church:

Why have the false prophets, and priests, and shepherds always been so many in the world and the pious ones so few? Against so many hundred false prophets and priests of Baal, it is scarcely possible to find one Elijah. Against so many lying prophets of Ahab it is scarcely possible to forget one Micaiah. True teachers must be tested by the cross. (1564: 212)

Philips also refers to the example of Elijah, Obadiah, the hidden prophets, and the faithful seven thousand to encourage confidence in times of opposition:

The prophets, the children of the prophets, and many God-fearing people in Israel (when they already lived among the godless and the servants of idols, at the time when Baal and other idols of the heathen were honored in Israel) bowed neither their heart, nor their knees, nor their bodies before any idols in Israel, but they worshiped the God of Israel, the Lord of heaven and earth, they hid themselves before tyrants and kings, and God guarded them marvelously by his grace [1 Kings 18:13, 19] (1564: 186)

The Sounds of Silence

In the *Jewish Bible Quarterly*, Waldman engages the paradoxical image of the silent sound that Elijah heard on Horeb. Waldman invites the reader to consider the otherness and strangeness of God's communication. The silence is not absence or void, but it communicates the ineffable word of God (Rabbi Abraham Heschel). Waldman cites rabbinic midrash (commentary) that describes total silence in earth and heaven where God speaks with a sound that has no echo. The text drives home that God's otherness and mystery is neither isolation nor indifference. God is *not in* the word, just as God is *not in* wind, earthquake, or fire. Rather, these are instruments that God uses. As such, the word does not belong to prophets, who must remember that the message of God is beyond their grasp. The story warns against an overfamiliarity with "the word of the Lord" that can plague preachers and teachers. Just as Elijah's spiritual energies are renewed by the voice of soft silence, so the preacher is rejuvenated through immersion in the nonverbal mystery to return to hear, proclaim, and act on God's word (Waldman).

The title of Terrien's Old Testament theology, *The Elusive Presence*, recognizes the otherness of God's communication. The very name of God, "I AM WHO I AM" (Exod 3:14), reflects the divine mystery, always beyond human grasp and control but at the same time inviting. Jesus speaks of the Spirit as wind known by its effects though never seen. As Emily Dickinson's poem title "Tell All the Truth but

Tell It Slant" advises, God speaks the truth by speaking *slant*. God's voice is now in the rippling brook, now in the hubbub of community voices awaiting worship, now in the silent stillness of a wintry evening just before dusk. Elijah, who demands to be in control, finds himself meeting God in the sheer silence beyond the world that he can manage.

Elijah's long pilgrimage to the mount of God is a quest to hear God speak afresh. Having lived by the power of the word of the Lord (1 Kings 17:2, 8; 18:1), Elijah experiences God's silence at a lonely time of ministry. In the 2019 Believers Church Lectures at Fresno Pacific Biblical Seminary, Foursquare Church pastor A. J. Swoboda encouraged attentiveness to the Spirit's voice, but he also recalled Mother Teresa's testimony of having moved to Calcutta (now Kolkata) to serve the dying poor on the strength of God's word to her as a teen. Later, as she wrote about her long dark night of the soul, she confessed that she had never again heard God speak so clearly. The story of Elijah on Horeb reminds us that we are to be obedient to God's voice and to recognize God's presence within the sheer silence of our experience.

1 Kings 20:1-43

Ben-hadad of Aram
against the Lord of Israel

PREVIEW

Apologetics uses reasoned argument to defend Christian faith. Isaiah argues that Yahweh, not Marduk, is God because Yahweh alone has declared future events in advance (Isa 44:7). On the Areopagus, Paul seeks to persuade the Athenians regarding the identity of "an unknown god" (Acts 17:22-31). The aim of the exodus is that everyone (including the pharaoh) would know "that I am ... God" (Exod 6:7; 8:22; 9:16; 10:2).

Through an unnamed prophet, the Lord promises Ahab that he will deliver Israel from the enemy so *you shall know that I am the LORD* (1 Kings 20:13, 28). The Lord challenges Ahab to reorient his administrative strategy from dependence on political, economic, and military powers to dependence upon God (Hens-Piazza 2006: 201). Just as the Carmel confrontation with the Baal prophets inspires Israel to confess, *The LORD! He is God* (18:39 AT), so deliverance from overwhelming military foes is supposed to lead Ahab to covenant faithfulness. *Know[ing] that I am the LORD* should radically restructure Ahab's politics.

First Kings 20 is complicated by the rare use of the name *Ahab* (three times compared to seventeen times in 1 Kings 18 and fifteen times in 1 Kings 21). Though Ahab is rarely identified as *king of Israel* elsewhere, in 1 Kings 20 he is identified as *king of Israel* thirteen times; in two of the three times his name is used, he is called *King*

Ahab of Israel (20:2, 13). In 1 Kings 22, Ahab is named only once but is referred to as *king of Israel* seventeen times (22:20). Since the king in 1 Kings 20 is weak militarily but archaeological artifacts attribute numerous chariots to Ahab, Gray and Seow argue against identifying the king in 1 Kings 20 and 22 with Ahab (Gray: 414–18; Seow: 146) *[Archaeology: Mesha Stele, p. 438]*; others contend that Ahab is king (Cogan 2001: 471–72; Sweeney 2007a: 239–40). We will focus on the textual narrative, not historical questions; the primary narrative issue is the assessment of Ahab's kingship (Hens-Piazza 2006: 197).

OUTLINE

Battle of the Mountains, 20:1-21
Battle of the Plains, 20:22-34
Judgment against the King of Israel, 20:35-43

EXPLANATORY NOTES
Battle of the Mountains 20:1-21

First Kings 20:1-2 turns the focus from Elijah the prophet (the central character in 1 Kings 17–19) to international conflict between Israel and its northern neighbor, Aram (Syria). Ben-hadad, king of Aram, has the upper hand. Ahab, king of Israel, is a vassal responding to the threats of his overlord. In the opening scene, Aram's power over Israel sets up the narrative's primary interest: Ahab's failure to depend on the Lord (20:1-12).

Shock and awe (the technical modern military term is "rapid dominance") is a military strategy that employs overwhelming power to paralyze the enemy and destroy its will to fight. With thirty-two kings, their horses, and chariots, Ben-hadad inspires terror as he leads his army against Samaria (20:1 AT). Aram *lays siege*, a typical means of forcing tribute payment, treaty obligations, and participation in military alliances (Sweeney 2007a: 241; cf. 2 Kings 6:24-25). Prebattle communication between Ben-hadad and Ahab is related in three rounds of exchanges (20:2-4, 5-9, 10-11). In Ben-hadad's opening gambit, he sends messengers into Samaria to lay claim to the silver and gold and the best of the wives and children of the king of Israel (20:2-3). The message underscores Ben-hadad's dominance in the overlord-vassal relationship with Israel, a sovereignty that rivals what is normally attributed to the Lord. *Thus says Ben-hadad* mimics the prophetic messenger formula (11:31) *[Literary Criticism, p. 457]*.

The king's initial response is conciliatory, conceding more than Ben-hadad demands. As vassal, Ahab addresses Ben-hadad, *My lord, O king.* Ahab concedes that he and all that he has belong to

Ben-hadad (20:4). The king's willingness to surrender raises questions about whether Ben-hadad and the king of Israel understand ownership (*mine, yours*) in the same way. For Ahab, this seems to be a formality, conceding vassal status and willingness to enter a treaty with Aram. Ahab is not inviting Aram to invade the palace and help themselves to the contents (DeVries: 248).

Ben-hadad's messengers return to clarify Aram's demands (20:5-6). The message begins, *I sent to you* (*send*, typically the action of kings, is used seven times in 1 Kings 20, emphasizing Ben-hadad's overwhelming power: 20:2, 5, 6, 7, 9 MT, 10, 17) *[Send, p. 476]*. The message clarifies that he is not simply claiming hypothetical ownership. Ben-hadad restates the unequivocal demand, *"Deliver [give me]* your wealth and family" (20:5 summarized). He adds that he is *sending* his minions into Samaria to *take . . . away* all the king's and the city's valuables, whatever he chooses (cf. exile, 2 Kings 23:34; 25:19-20; ransack, 24:7; 25:14-15, 18-19). Ben-hadad's preliminary negotiations are a pretense to set up inevitable hostilities.

The king of Israel responds with alarm (1 Kings 20:7). After consultation, the elders and all the people counsel the king not to do as demanded (20:8). Apparently looking for middle ground, the king sends back a polite message, saying, in effect, "I am willing to surrender, but resist opening my capital to be ransacked." The third exchange is pure prebattle propaganda (20:10-11). Ben-hadad swears by the gods that his troops are so numerous that there won't be enough dust left for each soldier to carry away a handful (1 Sam 17:43). He concludes with the prepositional phrase *in my feet* that is translated *follow me* but could be a vulgarity (1 Kings 20:10; cf. 1 Sam. 24:3; alternatively, Ben-hadad says there isn't space enough in Samaria for his soldiers to stand; Alter: 515). In his greatest display of resistance, the king of Israel responds with caustic wit (= "Don't count your chickens before they hatch," 20:11 equivalent). Ben-hadad, drunk with wine as well as arrogance, orders his army to prepare for battle while he remains in his battle tent, unconcerned, rash, and overconfident (20:12).

The battle report is interrupted by a surprise (*Behold!* [MT] often signals a change of perspective) *[Literary Criticism: Elements of Narrative, p. 458]*. The story of thirty-two kings with countless soldiers, horses, and chariots is interrupted by *one prophet* (1 Kings 20:13 AT), who breaks into a closed, hopeless situation with the Lord's word. (The balance of power is controlled by the word of the Lord in the mouth of the prophet, the word of life and death: used fifteen times in 1 Kings 17–19, e.g., 17:2; 18:1, 36-37; 19:9.)

The prophet's ironic question draws attention to Aram's over-whelming military superiority. Though Ahab can see the enemy's awesome power and is paralyzed by it, the Lord upends the military equation with the promise of divine deliverance. The repeated inter-jection offers a surprising, new perspective: *Behold! Today is the day of salvation!* (paraphrase). The Lord promises, *I will give the army into your hand* (or *power*, 20:13 AT), reversing Aram's demand (that Israel *give* wealth and hostages; 20:5). The Lord aims to transform Ahab from dependence on pagan militaristic ideology to Deuteronomic covenant commitment (*You shall know that I am the LORD*; singular verb forms address Ahab directly).

Ahab's question is skeptical if not incredulous: *By whom?* (could Israel possibly have victory? 20:14). This third and final reference to *Ahab* by name in 1 Kings 20 recalls his reliance on Baal (16:31-32) and his military (18:5). Rather than engage the Lord's prophet, Ahab simply asks how the battle is to be engaged. The repeated prophetic messenger formula (*Thus says the LORD*) contrasts with Aram's mes-sengers, and the strategy counters military shock-and-awe threats. The prophet commands, *Muster all the servant boys of the district gov-ernors* (AT; *boy* may refer to infants like Moses, Exod 2:6; even to fourteen-year-olds like Ishmael, Gen 21:14; or Abram's military, 14:24). The small band of untrained fighters demonstrates that vic-tory belongs to the Lord (recalling Gideon's three hundred against countless Midianites, Judg 6–7; Cogan 2001: 465).

The king again asks about tactics: *Who will bind the action?* (20:14 AT). The prophet answers simply, *You.* NRSV and NIV read *bind* in the sense of "initiate." Gray reads *bind* as *clinch* or *wrap up the battle*, explaining the prophetic judgment against the king of Israel when he makes a covenant with Ben-hadad (20:34-43; Gray: 425). Against 32 kings with their armies, horses, and chariots, the king musters 232 youngsters, followed by all the rest of the people, 7,000 in all (the number of those who have not kneeled to Baal, 19:18). A boys' army musters against a great multitude, a fierce fighting machine (20:15). (Another interpretation is that the Israelite troops are com-mandos, a mobile, light brigade that seizes the initiative and defeats an overconfident, drunken foe; Gray: 425; Sweeney 2007a: 242.)

The troops join the battle at high noon (20:16). The overconfi-dent Ben-hadad and allied kings are drinking themselves drunk. The boys who serve Israel's district governors lead Ahab's army (20:17). Ben-hadad receives regular military intelligence reports. As soon as the Israelites leave walled, besieged Samaria, Ben-hadad orders that the entire Israelite army be taken prisoner, whether they come for a peaceful parley or to do battle (20:18). What does an army do when they meet a group of children? Whether they come in peace or in war, there is no need for a slaughter; taking them alive will mean greater spoil, more slaves for the allies. The narrative repeats the unconventional strategy: 232 youngsters are marching out from the city, followed by the rest of the people (20:19). As the Arameans approach to arrest the youngsters in the vanguard, each Israelite *strikes* one man (20:20 AT; *strike* is used eleven times in 1 Kings 20). Startled, the army of Aram retreats in disorder. The half-drunken Ben-hadad flees on horseback. With the battle won, the king of Israel himself goes out (*to wrap up the battle* as predicted in 20:14 AT), *strikes* Aram's military horses and chariots, and *strikes* Aram with a great slaughter (cf. Josh 10:10). The Lord's promise has been fulfilled, but there is no indication of a change in the king of Israel.

Battle of the Plains 20:22-34

The Lord has saved Samaria from prolonged suffering and almost certain destruction. The prophet who spoke the word of salvation and provided the winning strategy approaches the king of Israel with commonsense counsel. Though the prophet instructs the king to prepare and *to know and see* (20:22 AT), the narrative reports no preparations.

Simultaneously, as anticipated by the prophet, the Arameans evaluate their failed strategy and plan for a better outcome. The Aramean strategists operate on two levels. Militarily, they reorganize the structure of the army, replacing the thirty-two kings with *other officers* (NIV preferred; the term is more likely political than military; J. T. Walsh 1996: 303), and they rearm, replacing horses and chariots lost in the previous battle (20:23-25). Strategically, they have learned, as did Sisera against Deborah and Barak (Judg 4–5), that chariots can be a disadvantage in the mountains. They plan to stage the new battle on the plains. The military strategy is sound, but unfortunately for these advisers, they attribute Israel's victory to Israelite gods of the mountains, a fatal mistake; the Lord takes their assumption as an affront (20:28).

As predicted by the prophet, Ben-hadad again invades Israel. As planned, the Arameans deploy in the plains, attacking Aphek. The mention of Aphek raises the stakes for Israel. Aphek, located near Jezreel, has been an ignominious battlefield for Israel twice in its history. At Aphek the Philistines captured the ark of the Lord when they slaughtered Israel's armies (1 Sam 4:1-10). Again, the Philistines mustered for battle at Aphek, defeated Israel, and killed Saul and his sons (1 Sam 29:1; 31:1-7). Ben-hadad *musters the Arameans and goes up to Aphek to fight Israel* (1 Kings 20:26 AT) The verbs are the same ones used in 20:1, portending that the second battle will end as the first one did. The fate of Israel is in the balance (J. T. Walsh 1996: 304).

Israel marches to battle, *mustered and provisioned* (20:27; see also 4:7, 27; 17:4, 9; 18:4, 13). The comparison of the tiny Israelite army, *like two little flocks of goats*, with the superior forces of the Arameans, who *fill the earth* (AT), demonstrates that the king has failed to heed the advice to prepare for battle; it may also contrast horses and chariots with guerrilla warfare (Deijl: 128). Militarily, Israel is hopelessly outnumbered, out-prepared, and out-strategized. They are at Aram's mercy.

As before, a man of God approaches the king of Israel with a word from God (20:28). The salvation speech opens with the messenger formula, *Thus says the* LORD. Though the Arameans have referred to Israel's "mountain" gods generically, not using the personal name *Yahweh*, the Lord has taken their claim that Israel's deity is without power in the valley as an insult. Because of this, the man of God tells Israel's king again, *I will give all this great multitude into your hand.* The statement reiterates the aim of the previous miracle, this time with a plural verb form: *You [all] shall know that I am the* LORD. Ahab has failed to acknowledge the Lord's victory; now all Israel is invited to confess and commit to the Lord.

After a seven-day standoff, the battle is joined (20:29). Israel slaughters one hundred thousand foot soldiers; the twenty-seven thousand survivors flee into Aphek, where a wall collapses on them and kills the rest (20:30). Ben-hadad flees and enters the city to *hide* in an inner room.

Ben-hadad is cornered in Aphek; his army is destroyed, and the city wall is in ruins. His servants politely request that the defeated king allow them to dress in contrition, wearing tokens of penitence (sackcloth) and submissiveness (ropes for those led away into slavery), and throw themselves on the mercy of the king of Israel, asserting that Israel's kings are characterized by covenant loyalty (*ḥesed*; the term raises the question whether the king's loyalty is to the Lord or to his treaty partner from Aram; 20:31-34). Defeated, Ben-hadad is silent, so his servants approach the king of Israel. The ensuing three exchanges between Aram and Israel match in number the prebattle communications (20:2-11). First, Ben-hadad's servants use the polite language of vassal to overlord and request that Ahab's *servant*, Ben-hadad, be allowed to live (18:32). The roles are reversed; now Ben-hadad is the supplicant, with the king of Israel in control of the relationship. The king responds to the opening communication by referring to Ben-hadad as his *brother*, changing the terms of negotiation from vassal-overlord to trading partners. In the second exchange Ben-hadad's men take the king's reply as a good omen, repeat the words *your brother*, and hurry to respond to Ahab's invitation by bringing Ben-hadad to him (18:33). The king of Israel welcomes Ben-hadad into his chariot. In the third exchange, with its negotiations for peace, Ben-hadad offers to restore territory lost to Aram in an earlier war and more favorable trading relations (18:34). Israel's king accepts the offer, saves Ben-hadad's life, and makes a covenant (*treaty*) that appears politically and economically advantageous for Israel. The narrative concludes with the king of Israel exercising sovereignty. He makes the covenant and *sends him* away (*send* is used twice in 20:34 MT) [*Send, p. 476*].

In purely political terms, Israel is successful. Reversing status in the covenant relationship with Aram from vassal to overlord, the treaty with Ben-hadad is politically sagacious; it regains lost territory and gains trading privileges in Damascus, an important ANE business center. In practical terms the king has handled this foreign policy crisis well. He consults elders to gain popular backing for resistance. He keeps diplomatic solutions alive as long as possible. He is judicious, pragmatic, and strategic in contrast to the arrogant, impulsive, pompous, drunken Ben-hadad, who fritters away his enormous advantage. Looking ahead, the king of Israel resists the impulse to annihilate the enemy, making a deal that produces material advantages for his nation (Seow: 151).

Unfortunately for the king, pragmatism counts for little in the values of the Lord in 1–2 Kings. Ahab's failure to know the Lord is addressed in the exchange of prophet and king in 1 Kings 20:35-43 (see below). Ahab's frame of reference is distorted, limited to exchanges between political powers and unaware that dependence on other powers renders impossible a relationship of dependence on God (Hens-Piazza 2006: 201). The narrative develops the case that covenant agreements with pagan nations are inevitably corrupting. When one is the vassal, everything in one's house belongs to the overlord (see 20:3-6). Even in a position of strength, human alliances are value statements. Covenants with Aram are at odds with the covenant of the Lord.

Judgment against the King of Israel 20:35-43

The sons of the prophets oppose the treaty between Israel and Aram (this is the first mention of this prophetic guild prominent in the stories of Elisha; see 2 Kings 2:3; 4:1, 38; 6:1) [*Prophets: Sons of the Prophets, p. 467*]. The Lord has brought a miraculous defeat to Aram, but the king of Israel squanders his advantage by allowing the king of Aram to escape. Judgment is about to fall.

Before he addresses the king, the prophet sets up an acted juridical parable. The unidentified prophet, speaking the *word of the* LORD (AT; see EN on 20:13), politely orders another prophet to *strike* him (20:35). When the second prophet refuses, the first announces judgment, using the form of a prophetic judgment speech (accusation and announcement) [*Literary Criticism: Poetry, p. 460*]. The accusation is that the second prophet has failed to listen to the voice of the Lord. The announcement is that a lion will kill (*strike*) him as soon as he leaves. The word is fulfilled (20:36). The prophet commands another to *strike* him. This man *strikes* and wounds the prophet.

This strange interlude shares features with 1 Kings 13, as noted in the TBC below. The commands appear to be nonsensical, the judgment unfairly harsh. Yet the outcome confirms the reliability of the prophetic word of God.

Disguised by a bandage over the wound and covering his eyes, the prophet waits for the king along the way (20:38). When the king appears, the prophet tells a self-incriminating fiction about losing a prisoner of war (20:39). The king accepts the story at face value and agrees with the terms: *Your life . . . for his*. The prophet declares, *You yourself have decided your judgment* (*mišpaṭ*; 20:40 AT). The prophet removes the disguise, revealing his identity as a recognizable member of the prophetic guild (20:41). The prophet's judgment against the king follows the judgment form (messenger formula, accusation of sin, and announcement of penalty; 20:42). The accusation is that the king has *sent out* the man that was in his *hand* (power). This action is grievous because the king of Aram has been placed under the ban (*ḥerem*), devoted for destruction (Ahab is placed in the same category as Saul, 1 Sam 15; Deijl: 129). Sweeney reads the story as a missed opportunity to rid Israel of a dangerous foe who eventually has Ahab killed in battle (2007a: 241, 244); Philip Stern argues that Ahab's responsibility to *bind* the battle in 20:14 entails death for Ben-hadad (46) [*Violence in Kings: Devoted to Destruction, p. 482*]. The announced judgment corresponds neatly to the penalty that the king has declared for the prophet's hypothetical tale about losing a prisoner. The decree, *You yourself have decided it*, seals Ahab's fate. The prophet extends the judgment from the life of the king to the life of the people (20:42), foreshadowing the exile

(Brueggemann 2001b: 121). As Nathan had trapped David into pronouncing judgment against himself with a parable (2 Sam 12), the unnamed prophet traps Ahab into pronouncing his own sentence. Unlike David, who repented, the king goes home *resentful* (obstinate against the call to repent) *and sullen* (stormily indignant, 20:43). The two terms appear a few verses later to describe Ahab's resentment at Naboth's refusal to sell his vineyard (21:4-5) but are used nowhere else in the MT [*Violence in Kings: Violence Involving Elijah and Elisha, p. 481*].

THE TEXT IN BIBLICAL CONTEXT
Prophets, Lions, and Acted-Out Parables

First Kings 20:35-43, like 13:11-32, has disturbing literary features that challenge interpreters. Both stories concern an unnamed prophet who receives immediate divine judgment and is killed by a lion, though the prophet seems unaware of his guilt (13:24; 20:36). Both prophets are called to incarnate the message, to give their lives to communicate the intensity of divine judgment. What appears to be capricious mirrors the inscrutability of God's judgment. The prophet's death is a sign for the king. Both prophets disobey a divine order that seems somewhat arbitrary, even nonsensical (in 13:9-18 the story is complicated by a contradictory message from the old prophet; in 20:35 the prophet refuses to wound his fellow prophet with a sword; though the order comes by the word of the LORD, the second prophet appears unaware of its source; the phrase by the word of the LORD is used seven times in 1 Kings 13 but nowhere else in 1 Kings except in this chapter).

Human obedience does not always require understanding. Though forbidden fruit is illogical from the human perspective, God sets the standard (Gen 2–3). When God gives a direct command, the prophet must not transgress it—even when another prophet speaks.

Both Jeroboam and Ahab fail to do the will of the Lord (13:1-10; 20:34, 42). Both kings make political initiatives that seem wise (Jeroboam builds cities and shrines, 12:25-30; Ahab makes a beneficial treaty, 20:34). Both decisions are condemned by prophets. The kings react obstinately (13:33-34; 20:43). Jeroboam and Ahab set standards for evil behavior (13:34-35; 16:30; 21:20-24). The parallels underscore the depth of evil associated with Jeroboam and Ahab, particularly their administrative bias against Deuteronomic values [*Mišpaṭ, p. 461*]. The acted parables end in the deaths of prophets, foreshadowing inevitable impending judgment (14:15-16; 21:29b).

"Know That I Am the LORD"

Twice the Lord explains his purpose for intervening in the battle against Aram. He declares to Ahab, *You shall know that I am the LORD* (20:13, 28). God's purpose echoes the exodus (Exod 6:7; 7:5; 10:2; 14:4; 16:12). The narrative "reminds Israel that the Lord is still the same God and Israel the same people" (Provan 1995: 152). Knowing the Lord is linked to the covenant formula, "I will be your God, and you will be my people" (cf. Ezek 11:20; 14:11; 34:24, 30-31). In covenant, Israel experiences benefits and responsibilities. The God of covenant saves, intervenes to cause victories and invert situations (as happens in 1 Kings 20). Human responsibilities include covenant faithfulness. "To 'know Yahweh' is to acknowledge Yahweh's governance and to respond obediently to that governance. Israel's endless theological work is to come to terms with the distinctive, uncompromising character of Yahweh" (Brueggemann 2000: 248). Knowing the Lord recognizes not only his victory but also his sovereignty. Knowing the Lord goes "against accommodating, compromising political perspective that is willing to deal in the real world" (253).

THE TEXT IN THE LIFE OF THE CHURCH
Knowing the Lord

God delivers so that all Israel will *know the LORD* (1 Kings 20:13, 28). God's salvation is an invitation to know God. People of God aim to know Christ, to be in Christ. Jesus says, "I am the good shepherd. I know my own and my own know me" (John 10:14). Later in the discourse, Jesus links knowing himself to knowing God, loving God, and obeying the commandments of Jesus (14:20-21), a close parallel to loving God, serving God, and walking in God's ways (Deut 10:12-13). The prayer for the Ephesians is that God "may give you a spirit of wisdom and revelation as you come to know him" (1:17). Paul prays, "I want to know Christ and the power of his resurrection and the sharing of his sufferings" (Phil 3:10).

Root argues that in a world that doesn't pay attention to God, prayer is the primary pastoral responsibility. Recalling Daniel Simons's "invisible gorilla" experiment (a YouTube fixture; participants in the experiment instructed to count the number of passes of a basketball never notice the person in a gorilla suit who walks through the game), Root says that God is active even though people's diverted attention fails to recognize God at work. Prayer broadens our attention on the world to enable us to look for God's arrival. God is at work and doing ministry among us; God is free to come to whomever God wishes (Root).

Ahab's failure to recognize the Lord as deliverer corrupts his ethics. We are shaped to know the Lord in worship so that we may live in pursuit of God's values. To know God is to commit to justice and covenant love by caring for the poor and the needy. Jeremiah says of Josiah, "He judged the cause of the poor and needy. . . . Is not this to know me?" (Jer 22:16). Jeremiah calls Israel to boast "that they understand and know me, that I am the LORD; I act with steadfast love, justice, and righteousness in the earth, for in these things I delight" (9:24). To know God is to commit to justice and covenant love by caring for the poor and the needy.

1 Kings 21:1-29

Naboth's Vineyard

PREVIEW

Eminent domain, the right of government to expropriate property for public use (e.g., Iowa farmland for an interstate pipeline), can force real estate sales that promote powerful private interests. In contrast, fundamental to Israelite justice was the inviolability of family land rights: patrimonial land distributed by tribes was protected (Num 26:52-56; 27:1-11; 36:1-12; Josh 13-19). Jubilee, based on the premise that the land belongs to Yahweh, legislates land redemption for patrimonial land lost in foreclosure (Lev 25:23). Torah protects land rights against fraudulent actions (Deut 19:14; 27:17). In 1 Kings 21, Yahwistic land laws come into conflict with royal Baal ideology, which places land under royal control.

OUTLINE

Act 1: Possession of the Vineyard, 21:1-16
- 21:1-4   Scene 1: Ahab's Proposal to Naboth
- 21:5-7   Scene 2: Jezebel's Interview of Ahab
- 21:8-14   Scene 3: Jezebel's Initiative against Naboth
- 21:15-16 Denouement: Ahab's Possession of the Vineyard

Act 2: Judgment against Ahab, 21:17-29
- 21:17-19 Scene 1: Judgment of the Lord
- 21:20-26 Scene 2: Elijah's Encounter with Ahab
- 21:27-29 Scene 3: Ahab's Repentance

EXPLANATORY NOTES

Elijah and Ahab return to center stage, with Jezebel playing a major role. The issue of royal justice versus Deuteronomic justice involves a land dispute. Justice defined as "Who has the say?" is the problem presented in the plot [Mišpaṭ, p. 461].

Act 1: Possession of the Vineyard 21:1-16
21:1-4 Scene 1: Ahab's Proposal to Naboth

Act 1 narrates how Ahab comes to take possession of Naboth's vineyard (21:1-16). In scene 1 Ahab seeks possession with a direct proposal to Naboth (21:1-4). The chapter opens by locating Naboth's family land (inheritance), a vineyard next to Ahab's palace (21:1). The resumptive phrase And it was after these words (things; AT) transitions from the battle report involving the king of Israel with unnamed prophets. Although the phrase is likely interpreted well by the NIV (Some time later), this phrase recalls the prophetic judgment that by releasing an enemy devoted to destruction, Ahab will pay life for life and people for people (20:42). The reference to the prophet's words foreshadows Elijah's judgment (21:20-24) and the Lord's speech reinforcing judgment against Ahab's family (21:28-29) [Violence in Kings: Devoted to Destruction, p. 482].

The text does not explain why King Ahab of Samaria (the unusual designation may imply that Ahab should be content with his current holdings; cf. links with 1 Kings 20:2, 13) has a palace in Jezreel. Though Samaria is Ahab's capital, Ahab returns to Jezreel from Carmel (18:46). In 1 Kings 20, Aram attacks Ahab in Samaria. Some speculate that Ahab had shifted the palace from Samaria or that he had a seasonal palace in Jezreel. Recent excavation indicates that Jezreel (nine miles east of Megiddo) was the crossroads of two trade routes with strategic military and economic significance for defense fortifications (a base for cavalry and chariotry with a moat, tower, and guarded gate) and tax revenue (Franklin). Whatever historical rationale there might be, 1 Kings does not clarify why Ahab has a palace in Jezreel.

The action opens with Ahab's blunt demand (lacking the customary polite phrase, 20:7) that Naboth sell him the vineyard (21:2). Yet Ahab's real estate proposal is a rejection of Deuteronomic egalitarian agrarian policy, this in favor of royal domination that in effect returns the people to Egypt (Deut 11:10; 17:16) [Egypt, p. 445].

Naboth rejects Ahab's proposal out of hand (1 Kings 21:3). His oath (The LORD forbid) communicates the vehemence of his rejection. Naboth's reason is clear to him and to Ahab. While for Ahab the property is a vineyard, for Naboth it is inheritance. Torah requires that the *inheritance* remain within the family (Lev 25:23). *Vineyard* describes not only the horticulture typical of Israel's *inheritance* (Exod 23:11; Lev 25:3-4; Num 16:14; Deut 6:11) but also Israel itself (Deut 4:20-21; Isa 5:1-7; Jer 12:10). Exclusive commitment to the Lord is linked to land and to care for needy persons in the land (Deut 15). When Ahab proposes to buy Naboth's land to turn it into a garden (a typical royal Egyptian practice, Deut 11:10), he encroaches on the basic rights of Naboth in Israel and threatens the Deuteronomic justice system.

Ahab's actions indicate that he accepts Naboth's word as definitive, leaving him without recourse. The king does not insist that Naboth knuckle under to his pressure (21:4). Ahab goes home *resentful and sullen* (as he has after the prophet's rebuke, 1 Kings 20:43). Ahab's refusal to eat renews the theme of eating/fasting (significant in 1 Kings 17–19). At the outset of the story, Ahab's "fast" is a form of sullen protest (see 21:7, 9, 12, 19, 23-24, 27). Ahab is communicating to his royal household that life is not worth living if the king doesn't get his way. His refusal to eat gets the attention of Jezebel, the first step in manipulating her to act as Ahab dare not.

21:5-7 *Scene 2: Jezebel's Interview of Ahab*

Noticing Ahab's withdrawal, Jezebel questions the king (21:5). Knowing that Jezebel will not tolerate the niceties of Israel's egalitarian land tradition, Ahab presents the basic facts of his negotiations with Naboth, yet with minor changes to present himself in better light (21:6). First, he presents his offer of favorable terms to Naboth. Second, Ahab reports Naboth's retort without mention of the ancestral inheritance, inserting in Naboth's rejection the word *vineyard*, making the proposed exchange a straight business deal. Ahab's manipulation of Jezebel allows him *deniability*, shifting responsibility to the queen, who may not understand Israelite values.

Jezebel is incredulous. From a Sidonian perspective of royal power, Jezebel asks Ahab, *Is this how you act as king over Israel?* (21:7 NIV). Yet this is precisely the way a king of Israel is supposed to rule: respecting ancestral inheritance as an inalienable right. Jezebel, promising Ahab a prosperous and pleasing outcome, tells him to get up and eat. She will *give* what Nathan has refused to *sell* (NIV; the two English words translate a single Hebrew term used seven times previously in 21:2-6). Jezebel will *give* Ahab the *vineyard*.

21:8-14 *Scene 3: Jezebel's Initiative against Naboth*

Acting in proxy for Ahab, Jezebel flies into action, writing letters to the leading men of Jezreel and requiring that they initiate cooked-up legal proceedings against the innocent Naboth that will result in false charges, wrongful verdict, and his precipitous death (21:8-10). Jezebel creates the impression of legal proceedings by using the king's seal (Neh 9:38; Jer 32:10-14). To *fast* is to seek God's favor in the face of sin (2 Sam 12:16), but it is often viewed by the Lord with suspicion (Isa 58:3; Joel 1:14; eat/fast is a primary theme in the narrative, 1 Kings 21:4, 7, 9, 12, 19, 23-24, 27). Jezebel calls for *scoundrels* (scoundrels entice Israel to follow false gods, Deut 13:13; Judg 19:22) to bear false witness that Naboth has *cursed* God and the king. Jezebel writes that the elders and nobles are to *stone* Naboth to death (the penalty for scoundrels, Deut 13:10).

The *elders* (12:6-13; 20:7-8) acquiesce without resistance, following Jezebel's plot precisely (21:11-14). They stone Naboth *with stones and he dies* (21:13 AT). Jezebel has seized the initiative, as indicated by her action to *send* letters (21:8, 11); the elders are implicated when they *send* (21:14) their report of Naboth's death to Jezebel *[Send, p. 476]*. Naboth is *dead* (*dead* refers to Naboth six times in 21:10-16; 2 Kings 9:26). The land reverted to the crown on the principle that Naboth had failed to live up to his social responsibilities (1 Sam 8:14; then 2 Sam 9:1-13; 16:1-4; and 19:24-30 assume David's right to reassign land; Russell: 468).

21:15-16 Denouement: Ahab's Possession of the Vineyard

With her mission accomplished and Naboth *dead*, Jezebel turns back to Ahab with final instructions and report. *Get up!* she repeats (21:7 AT), *take possession of the vineyard. . . . Naboth is not alive, but dead* (21:15). Israel *dispossesses* the pagan nations and *takes possession* of the inheritance (mentioned over sixty times in Deuteronomy; the Lord *dispossess [drives out]* the pagan nations, 1 Kings 14:24; 21:26). Ahab *takes possession* of Naboth's vineyard (21:16, 18, 19).

The narrative uses identical construction of the two sentences describing the action of Jezebel (21:15) and Ahab (21:16). *As soon as Jezebel heard that Naboth . . . was dead*, she speaks to Ahab (21:15). *As soon Ahab heard that Naboth was dead*, he follows the word of Jezebel (21:16). *He got up and went down to take possession of Naboth's vineyard* (NIV). Ahab's actions parallel Jezebel's actions. Ahab bears an equal responsibility for the death of Naboth because Jezebel has acted in his name.

Act 2: Judgment against Ahab 21:17-29

21:17-19 Scene 1: Judgment of the Lord

In act 1 the primary action is initiated by Jezebel in the name of Ahab, doing what kings do in the Sidonian-Baal system, manipulating local officials to acquire the property Ahab desires. Act 2 opens with a power shift as the Lord seizes the initiative and upends Jezebel's actions. The conflict, set up as Sidonian royal justice over Yahwistic Torah in the first half of the chapter, shifts to king versus prophet. *The word of the LORD* addresses Elijah (21:17; see EN on the power of the *word of the LORD* in 20:13) *[Prophets: Prophetic Word, p. 469]*. Using Jezebel's word to Ahab, the Lord commands Elijah, *Get up!* (21:18 AT). The Lord's speech describes a scene that is incongruous from the Deuteronomic perspective: a king of Israel has *dispossessed* the *inheritance* of a faithful Israelite. Parallel construction of the two parts of the judgment speech communicates urgency and judicial deliberation. The indictment, including initial instruction, *You shall say to him,* and messenger formula, *Thus says the LORD,* together present the accusation in the form of a question: *Have you killed, and also taken possession?* This identifies two offenses: murder and stealing property *[Literary Criticism: Poetry, p. 460]*. The verb *kill* is different from the word (*die*) used consistently in 21:10-15; *kill* is the term for murder as prohibited in the Ten Commandments (Exod 20:13; Deut 5:17). The announcement of judgment (sentence) follows the form used for the accusation: an initial instruction, *You shall say to him;* the messenger formula, *Thus says the LORD;* and the announcement, *In the place . . . , dogs will also lick up your blood* (21:19). The Lord's speech points out the incongruity of the situation. King Ahab of Israel (and from Samaria) is in the vineyard of Naboth (in Jezreel) to *take possession.*

21:20-26 Scene 2: Elijah's Encounter with Ahab

Scene 2 opens with Ahab and Elijah in Naboth's vineyard. Ahab's greeting, *Have you found me, O my enemy?* (21:20), recalls his greeting in their prior meeting (*Is it you, you troubler of Israel?,* 18:17; Hens-Piazza 2006: 208). Unlike the elusive Elijah, whom Ahab was unable to *find* (18:10, 12), Ahab is easily found at the place he has unjustly acquired. Elijah responds with the judgment speech prompted by the Lord, supplemented by the prophet with a more unflinching statement (Brueggemann 2000: 260). Foregoing both the messenger formula and the details of the Lord's indictment (killing and taking possession of the ancestral inheritance), Elijah simply accuses Ahab, *You have sold yourself to do what is evil in the sight of the LORD* (21:20). *Evil* is the standard characterization of Ahab (16:30). The Hebrew term for *evil* is used four more times in this chapter (21:21, 25, 29 [twice]). Elijah himself threatens to bring *evil* (*disaster*) on Ahab (21:21). The summary judgment repeats that he *sold* himself *to do evil* (21:25, cf. 21:20). In 21:29, the final sentence of the chapter, the Lord uses the word *evil* twice (the Lord will bring *evil* [*disaster*] on Ahab's family but not *evil* on Ahab himself) [*Evil, p. 446*].

In his direct speech to Ahab (21:20b-22), Elijah speaks in his own authority without attributing the judgment to the Lord as the Lord had instructed (21:19a, 19b). Elijah's announcement of judgment (21:20b-22) is more complex than the Lord's original and parallels previous judgment of Jeroboam and Baasha (21:19; 14:10, 14; 16:3, 11). After the threat to bring evil, Elijah says the Lord will *consume* Ahab. He will *cut off* Ahab's heirs (Jezebel *cut off* the prophets, 18:4). Ahab's male heirs are identified by using the conventional vulgarity (14:10; 16:11). Like the first two threats, the third threat echoes the judgment against Jeroboam and Baasha: *I will make your house like the house of Jeroboam . . . , and like the house of Baasha* (21:22). Elijah returns to the accusation: *provoking the LORD* (15:30) and *causing Israel to sin* (15:26, 30, 34; 16:2, 13, 19; 16:26; 22:52), an accusation made against Jeroboam and his successors, including Omri. Ahab not only leads the people into the sins of Jeroboam, but also incites them to worship Baal and acts treacherously by enabling Jezebel in the death of Naboth and taking his land [*Provoke the Lord to Anger, p. 470*].

The word of the Lord addresses Jezebel (21:23-24 MT: *and to Jezebel the LORD said*). Though modern versions attribute the judgment of Jezebel to Elijah, the original is ambiguous, inviting the reader to hear both Elijah's voice and the narrator's; the Naboth narrative is emblematic of the evil policies of Jezebel and Ahab (J. T. Walsh 1996: 201). Jezebel's offense requires no indictment, because it is so heinous. Thus Jezebel, who has encouraged Ahab to eat while she proclaims a fast in eliminating Naboth, will herself die in Jezreel and become food for dogs (21:23). The prophecy concerning Jezebel is fulfilled through Jehu (2 Kings 9:10, 36). The judgment against the house of Ahab is repeated, with the details regarding predators' consumption of their dead bodies. Ahab, his evil wife, and his descendants will disappear (1 Kings 21:24; as had Jeroboam and Baasha, 14:11; 16:4).

After Elijah's judgment speech, the narrator summarizes the negative evaluation of Ahab (21:25-26; 2 Kings 17:17; J. T. Walsh 1992: 200). Jezebel, who epitomizes royal injustice, is the source of this evil. Somewhat surprisingly, Ahab is condemned for idolatry, not murder (1992: 209), an indictment that demonstrates the link between idolatry and injustice [*Idolatry, p. 449*]. Not satisfied with Elijah's comparison of Ahab to Jeroboam and Baasha, the narrator links Ahab with Israel's idolatrous enemies who have been eliminated from the land (Deut 7:1; Hens-Piazza 2006: 209). The idolatry of the Amorites, Ahab, and Jezebel (like the golden calves of Jeroboam) represents a political structure where the king, linked with the gods, manipulates power to royal advantage. The Lord will not tolerate systemic injustice in the land. Like the Amorites, Israel faces exile.

21:27-29 Scene 3: Ahab's Repentance

In 1 Kings 21:27-29, the narrative makes a most unexpected turn. Ahab, who has just been called the most evil of all kings, *listens to these words* of Elijah (21:27 AT). The story of Naboth's vineyard opens with Ahab humiliated and sullen because of the preceding prophetic rebuke (20:42-43) and Naboth's refusal to sell his ancestral inheritance (21:4). Ahab's resentment led him to curl up in bed and refuse to eat. At the end of the story and after prophetic judgment, Ahab repents, leading to parallel actions, but the opposite disposition. Tearing his clothes, wearing sackcloth, fasting, and lying in sackcloth, Ahab goes about *dejectedly* (translated *gentle* in three of its other five uses in the OT). By *tearing his clothes* in dejection, Ahab avoids having the kingdom *torn* from him in his lifetime (1 Kings 11:11-13, 30-31 AT). The food theme, opened by Ahab's manipulative and pouting fast (21:4), is resolved by Ahab's fasting in remorse and repentance (21:27). In her confidence in royal power, Jezebel implores Ahab to eat; now Ahab receives a reprieve in true fasting. Jezebel, who declares a fast to scapegoat Naboth, is to be consumed as food for the dogs. The Lord describes Ahab as *humbled* (twice in 21:29; in Judges and 1-2 Samuel, enemies are humbled in battle; Lev 26:41 associates *humble* with repentance). In response to Ahab's repentance, the word of the Lord to Elijah postpones Ahab's day of judgment (21:28-29). Despite his unsurpassed evil, Ahab's humble repentance activates the Lord's mercy, a word of hope for exiles.

Ahab with Jezebel pursues royal policy that reverses Deuteronomic values. The Lord, having freed Israel from imperial tyranny and given them liberated land, has instituted egalitarian justice to protect the marginalized. Ahab, in embracing the royal system characterized as "the sins of Jeroboam" and the worship of Baal, forces the re-Canaanization of Israel (Leithart: 154). First Kings 21 "must not be read as a simple one-on-one confrontation but as a decisive clash of systems" (Brueggemann 2000: 265).

THE TEXT IN BIBLICAL CONTEXT
The Land Is the Lord's

The Naboth story narrates unjust land practices that undermine economic justice with violence. While Psalm 24:1 praises the Creator, "The earth [ʾereṣ is also translated "land"] is the LORD's and all that is in it," the psalm describes social justice (24:3-6) under God's rule (24:7-10). Yahweh proclaims, "The land [ʾereṣ] is mine" (Lev 25:23) in the context of Jubilee, the return of ancestral land to the family on the Sabbath of Sabbath years. Jubilee (on the fiftieth year) offers Torah justice. Whether family land was lost to drought and unjust taxes or through poor management, the new generation begins anew with the ancestral land, ANE economic capital. Isaiah condemns the unjust economic practices of eminent domain (family land being added to the large estates of royalty and urbanites; Isa 5:8-10) [Economics in Ancient Israel, p. 444].

Though Jesus is landless, his teaching is shaped by his Old Testament values. Jesus talks about sowing and harvest as kingdom values (Matt 13; John 4:35). When the disciples eat grain gleaned from fields, they benefit from Old Testament gleaning laws (Matt 12:1). Jesus tells the parable of the rich fool who loses his soul by failing to recognize that the rich harvest of his land is meant to feed his community, not his storehouse (Luke 12:20).

Ahab, Ezra, and Nehemiah

Rofé develops the parallel between the story of Naboth's vineyard and the postexilic situation in Ezra-Nehemiah. Nehemiah condemns usury among the Jewish population, linked not only to land foreclosure but also to child enslavement (2 Kings 4:1-7). Rofé points out that just as Jezebel, the foreign wife of Ahab, is portrayed as sinner and seducer, so in postexilic Jerusalem the foreign women are accused of leading the Jews astray (Ezra 9:1-4; 10:6-44; Neh 13:23-31). Rofé demonstrates that the Naboth story can be read alongside the Ezra-Nehemiah narrative (102-3). Both situations warn against unbiblical values that privilege wealthy classes and threaten community life.

The Sins of the Fathers

How are we to understand the final act of the Lord in 1 Kings 21 in responding to Ahab's repentance? Is the final word a salvation oracle since judgment is postponed until after the day of Ahab? How does this square with the rest of 1-2 Kings and other Scripture?

First, corporate identity means that individuals are members of socially coherent groups. If one person is guilty (or shamed), the whole group shares the guilt (shame; e.g., Achan's theft implicates the whole family, Josh 6-7; Kaminsky: 54; Latvus: 90). Ahab's heirs benefit or suffer from Ahab's actions and share his culpability. Ahab's shame in his family's misfortune is personal and corporate.

Second, the Lord tilts toward mercy when extending mercy or judgment. When the Lord passes by Moses, he declares that steadfast love extends to the thousandth generation, but iniquity to the third or fourth generation (Exod 34:6-7). The last phrase may indicate that when a father or grandfather commits sin, there are implications for children and grandchildren, but the next generation may choose to break the cycle by repenting from "generational sin."

Third, later prophets reject the notion that the Lord punishes children for their parents' sins. Ezekiel sets aside the proverb "The parents have eaten sour grapes, and the children's teeth are set on edge" with the promise "Only the person who sins . . . shall die" (18:2-4). While consequences of sin may bring national disaster without distinguishing between righteous and evil (Hab 1:5-11), punishment of evil is directed at the sinner, not the sinner's family. Deuteronomic law forbids punishing the family of the criminal for another's violation (Deut 24:16). In answer to the disciples' question, Jesus declares that a man's blindness is not the result of the sin of the man or his parents (John 9:1-3).

The postponement of Ahab's judgment is a story of grace, not undeserved judgment. Evil Ahab repents and judgment is postponed. Ahab is succeeded by not one descendant but two (brothers Ahaziah and Joram), an extension of God's grace beyond what might have been expected. God postpones judgment even in the most wicked of families. When neither Ahaziah nor Joram follows Ahab's repentant humility, both are judged for their own culpability (2 Kings 1:16-17; 3:1-3). Their evil is not unrelated to Ahab: both are influenced by Jezebel and reject the way of the Lord. The opportunity of third- or fourth-generation mercy is missed. The prophecy against Ahab is fulfilled when his family is wiped out, but his sons' judgment is because of their own sins. On the other hand, their families are "collateral damage" when the new oppressors mercilessly and shockingly create a reign of terror (2 Kings 9–10; an action condemned in Hos 1:4-5).

THE TEXT IN THE LIFE OF THE CHURCH
Latifundialization

As participants in Days of Prayer and Action for Peace in Colombia, a delegation of North American Mennonites flew from Bogotá to the Río Magdalena for a two-hour riverboat trip. In a farming community of resistance, El Guayabo, they met families who had gained land rights after homesteading open land for thirty years. The landowner of a vast tract of land had hired violent gangs to force out the campesinos. The delegation transported two village elders back to Bogotá to meet U.S. Embassy staff and press their claims.

Issues of land rights are not uncommon in Latin America. The Panamanian Anabaptist church has gained expertise through experience with multinational lumber companies and lent that know-how to Colombian churches facing similar problems. By joining marginalized folks facing unjust land exploitation, the church is behaving like Elijah confronting Ahab. Like Elijah, the church provides prayer and action to support the weak against the powers whose action threatens life.

Closer to home for North Americans, Indigenous land claims are contested in Canada and the U.S., and U.S. factory farming and urban development encroach on family farms. Gentrification in cities threatens traditional neighborhoods. When individuals are evicted from homes for missed rent payments or power is interrupted during cold winter months, local church action is required.

Palestinian Christian Reading of 1 Kings 21

Like all Scripture readers, Palestinian Christians read the Bible from their own context, as an ancient Christian community reduced to a tiny minority, seeking to live peaceably with Palestinian Muslims and Israelis. While Zionist Christians celebrate the restoration of the state of Israel, Palestinian Christians feel disenfranchised by annexation separating them from land that their families have owned for generations. Naim Ateek, founder of the Sabeel ("The Way") Center and an Episcopal priest and Israeli citizen, says he seeks to learn from Jesus' "life under occupation and his response to injustice" to bring meaning to "all those who suffer under occupation, violence, discrimination, and human rights violations." Ateek reads 1 Kings 21 as the story of every Palestinian Christian. Each awaits a day when justice will prevail for those who have suffered loss of life and land. He "encourages Christians from around the world to work for justice and to stand in solidarity with the Palestinian people" (quoted in Katulka).

Not all Christians will find this Palestinian Christian reading of 1 Kings 21 congenial. Christians can agree that God condemns the violent expression of royal power that cost Naboth life and land. The Naboth story continues to call believers to seek justice by speaking out for those who have been harmed by unjust power.

1 Kings 22:1-53

Ahab's Last Battle

PREVIEW

Modern heads of state rely on military intelligence for information about enemy advances. American presidents have a checkered history of trusting inaccurate information, demanding that the evidence be revised to support their policies, and rejecting irrefutable proof. Although Jehoshaphat insists on consulting a prophet of Yahweh, Ahab falls prey to these misguided approaches.

First Kings 22 shows the results of failure to heed the word of God, an attitude epitomized by Ahab, Israel's most *evil* king (16:30; 21:25). After featuring Elijah the prophet (chs. 17–19), the text returns its focus to Ahab in three related stories (chs. 20–22). In the first story the prophet warns that Ahab's life is to be forfeited for releasing the captured enemy Ben-hadad (20:42). In the second story Elijah announces that dogs will lick up Ahab's blood as judgment for killing Naboth and taking his vineyard (21:19). Literary devices tie 1 Kings 20–22 together. Paired stories of war between Israel and Aram (20:1, 16, 24; 22:31; both reference thirty-two military commanders) frame the prophetic condemnation of Ahab for unjust disregard of Deuteronomic land laws (1 Kings 21). The war stories feature enacted prophetic messages (20:35-42; 22:11), blows struck against prophets (20:37; 22:24), and disguises (20:41; 22:30). The stories call the characters to heed the Lord's word (20:13, 14, 28, 42; 21:17-29; 22:5, 7, 19, 28, 38). In the final story, Ahab's name appears only in Micaiah's citation of the Lord's statement (22:20; in contrast to Jehoshaphat, named thirteen times), in parallel with

1 Kings 20, where Ahab is named but three times (20:2, 13-14). Historical critics have raised questions about the identity of the king of Israel in both chapters (Sweeney 2007a: 238–40, 254–57). Our literary reading asks why the narrator avoids the king's name. Are narrators so exasperated with Ahab that they cannot bring themselves to form the proper name (Brueggemann 2000: 268)? Is the *disguise* of Ahab not only part of the narrative but also in the telling of the story (22:30; J. Davies 2012: 401)? After the battle account, 1 Kings closes the reign of Ahab (22:39-40), reports Jehoshaphat's reign (22:41-50), and opens Ahaziah's reign (22:51-53).

This exquisitely told royal narrative affords a range of presentation strategies. Like Shakespeare plays, often humorously presented in contemporary costume, 1 Kings 22 can be read like a farce with sitcom-like suspense. Though the reading below takes a serious approach, notes are offered where seeing humor might be appropriate.

OUTLINE

Ahab Consults with Jehoshaphat and the Prophets, 22:1-28
    22:1-4   Ahab's Proposal to Jehoshaphat
    22:5-28   Consultation with the Prophets
Battle Narrative, 22:29-38
Closing Royal File of Ahab, 22:39-40
The Reigns of Jehoshaphat and Ahaziah, 22:41-53
    22:41-50 The Reign of Jehoshaphat
    22:51-53 The Reign of Ahaziah

EXPLANATORY NOTES

Ahab Consults with Jehoshaphat and the Prophets 22:1-28

The focus in this war narrative is on the courtroom consultation, not the battlefield (akin to recording an orchestra's warm-up with brief excerpts from the performance itself). Nearly three-fourths of the text is devoted to the consultation. Suspense is more heightened in the court scene than in the battle.

22:1-4 Ahab's Proposal to Jehoshaphat

After the annual warfare between Aram and Israel in 1 Kings 20, there has been a three-year interlude without conflict (22:1). First Kings 18:1 introduces the end of a three-year drought; 22:1 introduces the end of a three-year cease-fire with Aram. From Jeroboam until Omri, Israel and Judah are at war. The Omride dynasty, allied with Sidon through Ahab's marriage to Jezebel (16:31), seals an alliance with Judah through the marriage of Jehoshaphat's son Jehoram to Ahab's daughter (2 Kings 8:18; Athaliah, 2 Kings 11). Though Jehoshaphat succeeds Asa in 1 Kings 15:24, he is not mentioned again until he appears without further introduction as the junior partner in a military alliance with Israel (22:2).

The three-year peaceful interlude has come after the Lord's intervention for Israel so that, as the Lord says, Ahab will *know that I am the LORD* (20:13, 28). Emboldened by his victory over Ben-hadad and motivated by quest for economic and military power, Ahab disrupts the God-given respite from war. Israel's king addresses his servants (possibly including Jehoshaphat), observing that Ramoth-gilead is controlled by Aram (22:3). Ramoth-gilead—a city of refuge (Deut 4:43; Josh 20:8) in Gad, east of the Jordan River, and one of Solomon's district centers (1 Kings 4:13)—is strategic to securing the Transjordan of the Northern Kingdom and the King's Highway, with its access to the Gulf of Aqaba, the Red Sea, and the Arabian Peninsula (Sweeney 2007a: 255; Master: 505, 509). If the king is to expand his influence, Ramoth-gilead is the next logical prize. The king of Israel asks Jehoshaphat to go into battle with him (22:4). Jehoshaphat vows that his armed forces are available to Ahab, possibly indicating that he is in a position of servitude (cf. 2 Kings 3:4-27).

22:5-28 Consultation with the Prophets

Jehoshaphat's polite request that the king of Israel *inquire first for the word of the LORD* introduces narrative tension (22:5; cf. 14:5; 2 Kings 1:2-16; 3:11). In response the king of Israel *gather[s] the prophets together, about four hundred of them* (1 Kings 22:6), recalling the Asherah prophets of Jezebel (18:19, 40). The king asks, *Shall I go to battle . . . , or shall I refrain?* (22:6a). The prophets' response is ambiguous—perhaps a promise, perhaps a prayer: *The LORD will* [AT: *May the LORD*] *give it into the hand of the king.* Also uncertain is the name of the deity cited in prophecy. While NRSV follows an ancient version reading *LORD* as *Yahweh*, NIV follows the Hebrew, where the prophets refer to *Lord* (*Adonai*), leaving undetermined whether they speak for Yahweh or for Baal (22:6b). Nor do the prophets specify what will be given into the king's hand, nor to which king! Although the entire episode is deadly serious, it contains elements of humor, as here when Jehoshaphat requests *real* prophets (of Yahweh) now that they have heard from Ahab's tame mouthpieces (22:7). The king is reluctant to inquire of the otherwise unknown Micaiah because his messages invariably bring the king *trouble/evil* (22:8 AT; vv. 16-18 suggest earlier conversations; Zucker: 157–59; note the irony in Ahab admitting that he is associated with *evil*; see 16:30; 21:20-21, 25, 29) [*Evil*, p. 446].

Narrative tension builds through an extended delay underscored by the king's summons: Micaiah is to *hurry* (22:9 AT). In the first interlude the narrator describes the royal court, convened on the threshing floor in the city gates, where justice is rendered (22:10-12). In prophetic judgment, wheat is separated from chaff on the *threshing floor* (Exod 15:7; Ps 1:4; Isa 29:5; 41:2; Hos 13:3; Bodner 2019: 126). The kings, dressed in royal robes, occupy the seats of power on center stage, surrounded by the cacophony of prophets who *prophesy* (1 Kings 22:10, 12; the Baal prophets *prophesy* while dancing around the altar, 18:26, 29). An otherwise unknown prophet Zedekiah appears. Though *Zedekiah* connotes "Yah[weh] is righteous," the epithet *ben Chenaanah* (son of Canaan) suggests anti-Yahwistic connections with the Amorites, with whom Ahab is associated (21:26). Zedekiah performs an acted salvation oracle, using horns that he has made for himself. Employing the messenger formula *Thus says the* LORD [*Yahweh*], Zedekiah promises, *You shall gore the Arameans until they are destroyed* (22:11) [*Literary Criticism: Poetry, p. 460*]. The prophets amend and clarify the initial word, adding, *Go up . . . and triumph; the* LORD [*Yahweh*] *will give it in to the hand of the king* (22:12; cf. Josh 1:9). The setting, designed to convey immense royal power at the center of the kingdom, is a scene of chaos, noise, and disorder (ridiculous and humorous to some readers).

Building tension, *the messenger* sent to *summon Micaiah* urges him to toe the party line: *Look! [Behold!] Pay attention, please. All the other prophets have colluded to present a united favorable message. Please* [again] *let your words be like their words; say something favorable* (22:13 AT; *favorable*, used twice in 22:13, is the word spoken by the king in 22:8, 18). The exchange epitomizes the ideological battle between Yahweh and Baal for the future of Israel (on the human level the battle is between the prophet and the king; Brueggemann 2000: 269).

Micaiah introduces an opposing perspective, declaring, *As the* LORD *lives* (22:14). This is the fifth time this oath has been spoken since 1 Kings 17:1 (17:12; 18:10, 15; Elisha uses the oath in 2 Kings 2:2, 4, 6). The oath pledges confidence in the Lord's greater power (echoing the people's confession after fire falls from heaven, *The* LORD *indeed is God*, 1 Kings 18:39). Micaiah will not go along with the other prophets but will speak whatever the Lord Yahweh says to him.

Postponing the conflict no longer, Micaiah and king square off in the chaotic throne room. The king (of Israel) modifies his inquiry

from *Should I go up to Ramoth-gilead to battle?* to *Should we go up?*
(22:15 AT; perhaps he hopes that Micaiah will be more favorable to
a coalition that includes the righteous Jehoshaphat). Micaiah mocks
the king by parroting the prophets, *Go up and triumph; the* LORD *will
give it into the hand of the king.* The king ironically insists that Micaiah
swear to tell me nothing but the truth in the name of Yahweh (22:16 AT;
Bodner 2019: 126). Micaiah has induced the king to invite Yahweh's
word, making him tacitly admit that his prophets lack credibility. So
Micaiah warns the king to withdraw from his evil, self-centered
battle plans at Ramoth-gilead (22:15-18). Rather than setting a fatal
trap, Micaiah offers *favorable* (good) strategy, attempting to cre-
atively persuade the resistant king to reconsider plans (Moberly
2003: 7–14).

Micaiah reports a vision of *all Israel scattered . . . like sheep [with]
no shepherd* (the term *scatter* foreshadows exile, Deut 4:27; 28:64;
30:3). Micaiah conveys the Lord's concern for the people left without a leader (*lord*) and without hope for their safe return (22:17).
Failing to grasp that the Lord's word prioritizes the people's safety
(shalom), the king complains to Jehoshaphat that this *disaster* (MT:
evil) was what he expected because this prophet never prophesies
favorably (22:18; cf. 22:8). Though the prophecy anticipates the king's
death, the thrust concerns *evil* consequences for the people. After
failing to persuade the king by using irony (22:15-16) and a vision
(22:17-18), Micaiah turns to a report of the heavenly throne scene.
The heavenly court corresponds directly to the royal court in
Samaria (Moberly 2003: 9). Micaiah's report of the heavenly throne,
with the powers in the council standing at attention, unveils the
deceit in the royal court in Samaria—not a previous decision made
by the Lord to bring *evil* on the hapless king. The court of the Lord
interprets (and parallels) events in the king's court. The Lord seeks
someone who will *entice Ahab, so that he may go up and fall at Ramoth-
gilead* (22:20-22; cf. Deut 11:16). Ahab is being duped by the proceedings in the court scene (the Hebrew term for *duped* is also translated
"silly," Hos 7:11). The *lying spirit* works among the false prophets,
offering a self-serving message to a king in self-seeking pursuit of
Ramoth-gilead. Micaiah's heavenly vision reveals self-deception and
false prophecy. *The* LORD [not Micaiah] *has decreed disaster for you*
(22:23). The tough message aims to persuade Ahab to repent, as he
has previously (21:21, 27). Though Ahab misinterprets Micaiah's
intentions as antagonistic, the prophet offers Ahab life.

The scene concludes with controversy. First, Zedekiah slaps
Micaiah, derisively accusing him of being duped by a lying spirit

(22:24; *slap* is rendered *strike* in the assassinations of the houses of Jeroboam and Baasha, 15:27, 29; 16:7, 10-11, 16; in prophetic action, 20:35, 37; and in Ahab's death, 22:34). Uncowed by violence, Micaiah retorts that Zedekiah will need to hide *in the inner chamber of the inner chamber* (22:25 AT; cf. 20:30; perhaps the term means "toilet," Judg 3:23-24).

The king places Micaiah in the custody of the city governor and the king's son (22:26-27), confined on reduced rations of bread and water (the diet Obadiah provided for the prophets hidden from Jezebel, 18:4, 13) until the king comes in *peace* (*shalom*). Micaiah ripostes that if the king *returns in shalom*, it will be evidence that the Lord has not spoken through him (22: 28). *Return* (*šub*) can be translated *turn from sin* (8:35), *repent* (8:47), or return from exile (Jer 16:15). The king's failure to *turn* from evil precludes his *return* from battle. Micaiah exits, warning, *Listen up, all you people!* (1 Kings 22:28 AT).

Both the evil Ahab and the otherwise pious Jehoshaphat trust the fake news of royal power. Jehoshaphat has persisted in hearing from a Yahwistic prophet. Ahab has insisted that Micaiah tell the truth. Jehoshaphat's political loyalty outweighs the word he hears from the Lord.

Battle Narrative 22:29-38

Ignoring the prophetic word, Jehoshaphat accompanies his ally, the king of Israel, to Ramoth-gilead (22:29). When the king announces that he will go into battle disguised as a regular soldier, attempting to thwart Micaiah's prophecy (see Saul in 1 Sam 28:8; Jeroboam's wife in 1 Kings 14:2), Jehoshaphat alone is dressed as royalty, making him the target of Aram's strategy to pursue only the king of Israel (22:30-31). As the battle opens, the commanders (mis)identify Jehoshaphat as king of Israel, pursue him, and, as they are closing in for the kill, realize that they have the wrong king. Though his actions do nothing to distinguish him as a brave soldier, Jehoshaphat avoids death by crying out (22:32). The soldiers of Aram withdraw (22:33).

In 22:34-46, the battle transpires as Micaiah foretold. A random arrow *strikes* Israel's king in a gap in his armor, and he is fatally wounded (the *striking* of the prophets is a sign of the Lord's judgment, 20:35; 22:24). Propped up to watch the battle, the king witnesses the total defeat of his army. The scattered army retreats, fulfilling prophecy *[Prophets: Prophetic Word, p. 469]*.

The king is buried in Samaria (22:37). The conflict between the king who sold himself to the evil of Canaanite royal ideology and the powerful word of the Lord through the prophets Elijah and Micaiah is spotlighted in a note on the washing of the king's chariot (21:38; see 21:19-20; 22:17, 28). *According to the word of the LORD*, dogs lick up the blood of Ahab (21:19—though in Samaria rather than Jezreel). Reference to prostitutes at the pool of Samaria reminds the reader of the king's infidelity (Hens-Piazza 2006: 219) *[Prophets, p. 465]*.

Closing Royal File of Ahab 22:39-40

The Ahab file closure reports that Ahab had built cities (22:39-40; extensive building—discovered by archaeological excavations at Samaria, Dan, Hazor, Megiddo, and Tirzah—is attributed to Ahab's rule: Greenwood: 302–4; Cogan 2001: 498) and a palace of *ivory* (cf. 10:18; Mazar: 406–15) *[Archaeology: Ahab the Builder, p. 437]*. Characterized as the most evil of all the kings, Ahab has provoked the Lord and caused Israel to sin by perpetuating the sins of Jeroboam (16:31; 21:22) *[Sins of Jeroboam, p. 476]*, serving Baal (16:31-33; cultic apostasy including royal ideology) *[Idolatry, p. 449]*, rejecting egalitarian land practices (1 Kings 21), and developing royal building projects that burden Israel as had Solomon (11:33) *[Mišpaṭ, p. 461]*. Though Ahab's chariots are mentioned only briefly (22:35, 38), the archaeological record indicates that Ahab developed an unequaled military machine (the Assyrian Monolith Inscription references a large force of chariots and infantry in the coalition against Shalmaneser III *[Archaeology: Black Obelisk of Shalmaneser III, p. 438; Archaeology: Solomon's Gates and Stables, p. 437]*. Ahab, the first king of Israel who is both the son of a king and the father of a king, is succeeded by his son Ahaziah (22:40).

In summary, Hamilton suggests three insights from 1 Kings 22. One, the story is one of human tragedy. Ahab meets his just fate, not simply because he gets the punishment that is his due but also because he rejects God's mercy extended through prophetic warnings of the consequences of going to battle. Two, God's mercy to Ahab is limited by human rebellion and rejection. Three, the narrator chooses to portray God as a narrative character with normal character development (not as a "philosophical construct"). This presupposes that God will also interact with relational qualities rather than as a theological abstraction (662–63).

The Reigns of Jehoshaphat and Ahaziah 22:41-53

22:41-50 The Reign of Jehoshaphat

The orderly (and monotonous) opening and closing of royal files that characterizes 1 Kings 15–16 is interrupted by the stories of Elijah and Ahab. After Ahab's royal file closes, the Jehoshaphat file opens (22:41). The closing royal file of Asa (15:24) mentions that his son Jehoshaphat succeeds him. Without further introduction, Jehoshaphat reappears in the battle report of 1 Kings 22. Jehoshaphat follows the way of his righteous father, Asa, but like Asa and the other righteous kings preceding Hezekiah, Jehoshaphat fails to remove the high places (15:11; 22:43). Jehoshaphat makes peace with Israel, though apparently as junior partner of Ahab (22:44). Jehoshaphat distinguishes himself in seeking the word of the Lord's prophet on the way to battle (22:5, 7; 2 Kings 3:11). The standard formula regarding the Annals of the Kings of Judah typically concludes the narrative of a king, but here it seems to come in the middle of the story. Jehoshaphat continues the policy of Asa by eliminating *the remnant of the holy ones* (1 Kings 22:46 AT) *[Idolatry: Holy Ones/Cult Prostitutes, p. 451]*.

Taking advantage of the weakened position of Edom, Jehoshaphat seeks to use the southern port of Ezion-geber on the Gulf of Aqaba for a commercial shipping expedition, but shipwreck disrupts the venture before they can acquire the gold of Ophir (22:47-48). Jehoshaphat rejects Ahaziah's proposal that the shipping expedition be a joint enterprise, indicating that Jehoshaphat has stronger standing than he did with Ahab and no longer is obligated to follow the wishes of the king of Israel (22:49; J. T. Walsh 1996: 366). The Jehoshaphat file closes with the report of his death and burial and the succession of his son Jehoram as king of Judah, though the opening royal formula for Jehoram is postponed (22:50; 2 Kings 8:16-19). Although the Jehoshaphat file is closed, 2 Kings 3:4-27 reports another battle east of Jordan involving Jehoshaphat allied with Israel.

22:51-53 The Reign of Ahaziah

The opening of the Ahaziah file introduces him as the son of Ahab, ruling in Samaria beginning in the seventeenth year of Jehoshaphat and with a reign of two years (22:51). Ahaziah is condemned both for doing evil in the sight of the Lord and for walking *in the way of Jeroboam*, who made Israel sin; thus he follows the way of his father and mother, worshiping Baal as influenced by Jezebel. Ahaziah *provoked the LORD, the God of Israel, to anger, just as his father had done* (22:53; see 16:33; 21:22; the judgment parallels that of Jeroboam, Israel, Baasha, and Omri, 14:9, 15; 15:30; 16:2, 7, 13, 26) *[Provoke the Lord to Anger, p. 470]*.

First Kings ends on a discordant note. Though the occasional king of Judah does right, Israel does evil without exception. Even in

Judah, evil kings are common; under the best of kings, the high places continue to create problems for the people. Second Kings opens with a final story about Ahaziah of Israel.

THE TEXT IN BIBLICAL CONTEXT
Divine Deception

Three stories about otherwise unknown prophets (1 Kings 13, 20, 22) are joined by the motifs of deception, disguise, and anonymity; by death; by the word of the Lord; and by violence (*strike* is a violent term most often translated *kill*: 15:29; 20:20, 21, 29; 22:24, 34). The man of God from Judah is killed by a lion when he disobeys the word of God (1 Kings 13). When a prophet refuses to obey a prophetic divine word that he wound a fellow prophet, the disobedient prophet is killed by a lion (1 Kings 20). Micaiah warns Ahab that God has sent false spirits to deceive him with false confidence; Ahab is deceived and killed (1 Kings 22).

The stories puzzle over divine deception as a prophetic device. Several interpretations are possible. First, what appears to be divine deception is not. The man of God was deceived by a false prophet, not God (1 Kings 13). The son of the prophet who refused to wound his colleague was disobedient, not deceived (1 Kings 20). The lying spirit in heaven parallels the lying false prophets in Samaria. When Micaiah repeats their lies, he reveals the deception. Second, the narrative reports human experience of God. God's ways are inscrutable, appearing deceptive to finite humans.

Third, some might dare question God's reliability. Under what circumstances might God use deception? Might God use lies to test humans? Is God's control of the future limited (Ezek 26; 29:17-20)? Fourth, what appears to be divine deceit reveals the unreliability of prophecy. The real problem is not that God deceives but that prophets can be deceived (Kissling). Fifth, the stories reveal the complexity of God's ways. Ultimately, God through Micaiah reveals the deception (see the first option above). The story of Micaiah and Ahab reveals not only that God acts in obscure ways and brings retributive judgment on the guilty, but also that God's ways are trustworthy, faithful, patient, transparent (revealing the deception all around Ahab), and merciful (warning Ahab so that he can avoid death; G. Miller: 46-57).

The third option, that God deceives, accepts the witness of this biblical text at face value. Seow comments that this confounding theological message does not fit our preconceived notions of God's unimpeachable goodness, a notion that "ironically, is too limiting for God" (167). This passage, he says, forces us to deal with God's sovereignty, divine freedom to use any means, even those contrary to human reason or morality. As sovereign, God oversees all that goes on, light as well as darkness (Isa 45:7). God may harden hearts (Exod 4:21; 9:12), incite people to do wrong and condemn them (2 Sam 24:1), or deceive people (Jer 4:10). These views challenge readers to consider the mysterious and inscrutable nature of God.

False Prophets

Moses anticipates the problem of false prophets (Deut 18:22). False prophets may deceive by having their omens fulfilled, but their idolatrous rejection of the Lord God reveals their apostasy (13:1-3). The Baal and Asherah prophets are false because they reject the Lord (1 Kings 18). Ahab's prophets are false, as revealed by their unreliable prophecy (1 Kings 22). Though Elijah and Elisha are ardent Yahwists whose words come true, their penchant for violence raises questions about their reliability as well (1 Kings 18; 2 Kings 2:24; Kissling). The Mosaic Torah values covenant faithfulness, justice, and peacemaking in the community of God's people.

Basing her work on the Jerusalem Talmud, Suzanne Stone asks whether the authoritative solution regarding authoritative prophecy is to be found in the truth of the spoken words or in the integrity of the prophet's character. In 1 Kings 22, Micaiah's message is the same as that of the false prophets: *Go up . . . ; the LORD will give it into the hand of the king* (22:15; cf. vv. 6, 12). Since neither prophecy identifies the victorious king, the words are true. Maimonides approaches the question from the Deuteronomic instruction regarding prophets (Deut 18), prioritizing character (18:15) over true messages (18:18; S. Stone: 363–66).

Jesus condemns the devil as "the father of lies" (John 8:44). The devil seeks to deceive God's people with "foul spirits" coming from the mouth of the false prophet, who perform signs (Rev 16:13). The destiny of the beast and the false prophet is the lake of fire (19:20).

THE TEXT IN THE LIFE OF THE CHURCH
Peacemakers and "Manly Men"

In *Borderline: Reflections on War, Sex, and Church*, Goff writes, "This book is about what it means to be manly. . . . War is about domination, and 'manly' men extend that domination over women." Christians, men and women, "are called to live into a particular story that is dramatically different from the rest of 'the world.' The story of man conquering his enemies or conquering women—that is, the man-story that counts vulnerability as a vice—is not the story of Christ" (Goff: xv–xvi).

Jehoshaphat is caught between these stories. A man of peace, Jehoshaphat insists on hearing from the Lord before battle (1 Kings 22:5, 7). In battle, instead of resisting, *Jehoshaphat cried out,* and the captains turned back from pursuing him (22:32-33). *Jehoshaphat also made peace with the king of Israel* (22:44). When Jehoshaphat marches for battle, musicians praise the Lord while the enemy self-destructs (2 Chron 20). Jehoshaphat also acts as a man of war. When the king of Israel proposes war, Jehoshaphat joins without hesitation (1 Kings 22:1-4; 2 Kings 3:7). Jehoshaphat fights as Jehoram's ally against Moab (2 Kings 3). The annals link the *power that he showed* with *how he waged war* (1 Kings 22:45).

Christians have been torn between the stories of Jehoshaphat, man of peace, and Jehoshaphat, man of war. Early Anabaptists confessed that the use of the sword was the way of the world, not the way of Christ. Contemporary Anabaptists claim reconciliation as the center of our mission. Mennonite World Conference's Shared Convictions confess, "The Spirit of Jesus empowers us to trust God in all areas of life so we become peacemakers who renounce violence, love our enemies, seek justice, and share our possessions with those in need." Like Jehoshaphat, we struggle to live faithfully with our history and convictions. Early twentieth-century German Mennonites, enamored with the Kaiser and his pious wife, dropped their guard and their confessional statement against military service. In World War II, German Mennonites were caught up in the story of war. In that war and in the Selective Service draft, North America Mennonites struggled. Many chose conscientious objection to war; others participated in military service.

Jesus consistently chose the way of peace. Peter testifies, "Christ also suffered for you, leaving you an example, so that you should follow in his steps. . . . When he was abused, he did not return abuse . . . but he entrusted himself to the one who judges justly" (1 Pet 2:21-23). God's people follow the Prince of Peace to avoid being swept up into the story of "manly men."

Early Anabaptists and False Prophecy

Menno Simons encourages disciples to stand true despite their small numbers. Contrasting Micaiah, "who spoke the real truth and predicted calamity in the name of the Lord," to "four hundred false prophets in the days of Ahab, king of Israel, who with one voice predicted good fortune and prosperity," Menno calls the church to remain faithful against overwhelming odds (Menno: 90). Dirk Philips warns against people who, like Ahab, "love lies and hate the truth and do not endure it that one like Micaiah should come and tell them the truth" (1564: 200). Menno calls the church to testify to the truth, unlike the false teachers who "play the hypocrite, flatter lords and princes and humor the world. . . . There is nobody who opposes ungodliness with the Word of the Lord nor reproves the wickedness of the world" (Menno: 91). Pilgram Marpeck similarly contends that "against all ahabic prophets who to please Ahab (we mean all the authorities and rulers of the world), have united against the Lord" (161).

American evangelicals of the twenty-first century have identified increasingly with political candidates, parties, and policies that support military expenditures, international weapons sales, private gun ownership, and reduced medical services for the poor. In *Beating Guns: Hope for People Who Are Weary of Violence*, Claiborne and Martin seek to rally followers of Jesus to act to reduce gun violence. Sider, in *Just Politics: A Guide for Christian Engagement*, encourages Christians who defend the life of the unborn also to support medical care for pregnant people and young children and thus be more consistently "pro-life."

The Prophet Elijah and King Ahaziah

PREVIEW

The problem of Old Testament violence is exemplified in the prophetic judgment of 2 Kings 1. When the Israelite king attempts to use overwhelming military force to compel his surrender, Elijah, the prophet of God, counterattacks by calling down fire from heaven to consume one hundred men who are simply following the king's orders. Modern readers resist the strangeness of a story with an out-of-this-world miraculous (some might say "magical") event narrated as front-page news. A God who arbitrarily wipes out people who have no personal grievance against Elijah offends modern sensitivities. The prophet's violent actions in the name of the Lord raise questions about Elijah's character. Did the prophet simply lose control of his emotions and wipe out all these people? This story seems so far from the gracious God we recognize in Jesus that readers are tempted to discard the story, if not the whole Old Testament, as counter to the gospel [Violence in Kings, p. 480].

OUTLINE

Opening Royal Formula for Ahaziah (22:51-53)
    Narrative Report: Moab's Rebellion; Ahaziah is ill (1:1-2)
        Divine Messenger to Elijah: "Get Up!" (1:3)
        Judgment Speech: ". . . you shall surely die." (1:4-8)
          Narrative Report of Three Military Cohorts (1:9-14)

Divine Messenger & Elijah's Compliance: Elijah got up (1:15)
Judgment Speech: ". . . you shall surely die." (1:16)
Narrative Report: Ahaziah died (1:17)
Closing Royal Formula for Ahaziah (1:18)

EXPLANATORY NOTES

Narrative Report: Ahaziah Faces Moab's Rebellion 1:1

Exploiting weakness during royal transition, Moab rebels against
Israel (2 Kings 1:1). Before the issue is resolved (3:1-27), the narrative
explains the absence of Ahab's heir, Ahaziah (1:2-18), and reports
the transition from Elijah to Elisha (2:1-18).

Ahaziah Is Ill and Inquires about His Future 1:2-17a

Ahaziah follows Jezebel and Ahab in Baal worship *[Idolatry, p. 449]*, the
way of Jeroboam [Sins of Jeroboam, p. 476], and provoking the LORD, the
God of Israel, to anger [Provoke the Lord to Anger, p. 470] through unjust
policies (1 Kings 22:51-53). Ahaziah's inquiry of Baal will result in his
immediate death (2 Kings 1:2-16). The themes of Baal cult and death
characterize the conflict between royal policies and prophetic
Yahwism.

Incapacitated by an unelaborated household accident (possibly
misfortune in the toilet chamber, Judg 3:20, 23-25), Ahaziah's physical *fall* anticipates his fall from power. Otherwise identified as *the
king*, his name appears again only in the closing royal formula
(2 Kings 1:17-18; cf. 1 Kings 20 and 22 for infrequent use of the king's
name). Ahaziah *inquires* of the gods (*inquires* is a technical term for
seeking an oracle: 2 Kings 1:2, 3, 6, 16 [twice]; 3:11; 8:8; 16:15; 22:13,
18; 1 Kings 22:5, 7, 8). Ahaziah's *inquiry* challenges the Lord's sovereignty (as did Jeroboam in disguising his wife to *inquire* of Ahijah,
1 Kings 14:2). Both inquiries end in death (14:17; 2 Kings 1:17).
Ahaziah's choice of Baal-zebub may relate to the Ekron conjurer's
reputation for healing or otherwise positively influencing the
future. The narrator expresses hostility to Baal worship by referring
to Baal-zebul ("exalted lord") by the corrupted form *Baal-zebub*
("Lord of the flies").

Ahaziah *sent messengers* (*send* emphasizes royal authority) *[Send,
p. 476]*. The Lord's *messenger* directs Elijah *to meet the messengers of the
king* (1:3; NRSV translates the Heb. *messenger* as *angel*). Elijah learns
the judgment of Ahaziah, but his delivery to the king is delayed (1:3-
4, 16) *[Literary Criticism: Poetry, p. 460]*. Accusation of judgment
charges the king with apostasy: *Is there no God in Israel?* (AT).
Faithfulness to the Lord excludes contact with other deities (Deut

5:7). The messenger formula (*thus says the* LORD) precedes the announcement of judgment: certain death (Hebrew expresses certainty by repeating the verb *die*, 1:4, 6, 16; death of Ahab's descendants is prophesied in 1 Kings 21:24) [*Prophets: Prophetic Word, p. 469*]. The king receives a death sentence because he seeks Baal-zebub rather than the Lord.

The command-compliance structure (*so Elijah went*, 2 Kings 1:4) echoes Elijah's response to the word of the Lord in 1 Kings 17:5, 10. The narrative builds immediacy and suspense by relaying Elijah's message through the messengers (2 Kings 1:5-6). The king's messengers become messengers of the Lord! Two "innocent" changes to the original judgment emphasize the king's responsibility: The messengers move the messenger formula to the beginning of the speech. They change the source of the inquiry from the plural *you all* (1:3 AT) to the singular *you yourself are sending to inquire* (1:6 AT). The judgment is unchanged: the king will *certainly die* (1:4, 6 AT).

The king demands a description of the man who declares judgment. The English *What kind of man was it?* (NIV) translates the Hebrew *What was the mišpaṭ of this man?* (1:7). The messengers interpret the question to be about his physical appearance, but readers sensitized to Torah *justice* may recognize the issue related to the question, Who has the say? (Where does power lie?) [*Mišpaṭ, p. 461*]. The messengers answer that the man is a *baal [lord] of hair* (AT). Sent to communicate with Baal-zebub, the messengers return with word from a different *lord*. Upon hearing that *a hairy man, with a leather belt around his waist*, had intercepted the messengers, the king identifies him immediately: it must be *Elijah the Tishbite* (1:7-8). Like his father, the king regards Elijah as the enemy (1 Kings 21:20). Unlike his father (21:27), Ahaziah never considers repentance and through royal power seeks to silence Elijah's word.

As indicated by the section outline, the parallel narrative reports of three captains with fifty men is in the center of this story (2 Kings 1:9-14). Aware of his parents' encounters with Elijah, the king uses surprise and superior numbers. When the first captain approaches Elijah, the narrative signals that the surprise will be a reversal of power: *Look out! [Behold!] He [Elijah] sits on top of the hill* (AT) [*Literary Criticism: Elements of Narrative, p. 458*]. The overconfident captain boldly demands, *Man of God, the king says, "Come down"* (1:9). Echoing the power encounter on Carmel (1 Kings 18:20-39), yet without consulting the Lord, Elijah calls fire down from heaven, consuming his foes. Scene 2 (2 Kings 1:11-12) replays scene 1 (1:9-10; the absence of "Behold!" in scene 2 signals that what happens is no surprise).

The third captain's approach (1:13-14) opens like a replay of the previous two. The king—blind to the reality that he can *send* but is unable to *bring down* the prophet—insists that royal power trumps prophetic word. His refusal to recognize his limitations leads the king to risk innocent lives in a delusional abuse of power (Hens-Piazza 2006: 231). The third captain is under no such illusion! Like the others, the third captain was *sent* with his fifty and *went up*, but he issues no command. Though he addresses Elijah as "*man of God*," the tone is not derision but respect. The third captain throws himself down on his knees, uses the polite Hebrew form (translated *please* in NRSV), and twice begs mercy on his *life*. The captain's use of the narrator's literary warning of upcoming surprise marks the reversal. *Behold!* [NRSV: *Look*; NIV: *See*] *Fire came down from heaven!* (AT). He repeats his plea for mercy to preserve his life.

The repeated verb *come down* focuses the question of power. Marked by the interjection *Behold!*, the captain's perspective shifts when fire *comes down* (1:10 [twice], 12 [twice], 14). The prophet *comes down* only on orders from the Lord, not the king (1:9, 11, 15 [twice]). When the angel reappears to reassure, *Fear not* (AT), and to command, *Go down*, Elijah *comes down* in compliance with the command (1:15). Elijah finally delivers the judgment: *The bed that you have gone up to there? You will not come down. You will die! Die!* (1:4, 16 AT). The death threat is fulfilled. *He died according to the word of the LORD that Elijah spoke* (1:17a AT).

The judgment of Ahaziah is set apart from the fire-from-heaven miracles. Royal formulas form the outer pair of statements (1 Kings 22:51-53; 2 Kings 1:18) The second pair opens with a sick king (1:2) and closes with a dead king (1:17). The third pair is a doublet: it includes both the angel's command (and human compliance) and the judgment speech (1:3-8, 15-16). The first statement of the judgment speech is doubled by the report of the king's messengers complying with Elijah's command (1:3-4, 5-8). At the center comes the triple report of the captains and their fifties (1:9-14). Within the inner triplet we see both the miracles and the climax: royal acquiescence to the prophet. Inquiring of Baal instead of Yahweh exposes Ahaziah's religious, political, and social policy as idolatrous and unjust.

Ahaziah's Closing Royal Formula 1:17b-18

The closing royal formula uses standard language that references the Annals of the Kings of Israel. No mention is made of Ahaziah's burial (in line with Elijah's prediction regarding the bodies of Ahab's descendants, 1 Kings 21:24). The historian mentions that Ahaziah dies without heirs and is succeeded by his brother Jehoram in the second year of Jehoram son of Jehoshaphat of Judah. Yet Jehoram's, or Joram's (2 Kings 8:16), opening royal formula is delayed (3:1-3), interrupting the story of kings with the narrative of the prophetic mantle passing from Elijah to Elisha [Chronology: Kings Ahaziah and Jehoram, p. 441].

This story raises a troubling issue—how can God be implicated in the death of more than one hundred soldiers who seem culpable of nothing other than being in the wrong place at the wrong time? Does the God of justice send fire on bystanders, creating his own "collateral damage"? Where is justice?

Two notes are necessary before addressing this question. First, we will not be able to satisfy contemporary standards of justice in our reading of this story. This should not surprise us. We are reading literature twenty-five hundred years old, produced with different cultural presuppositions. Second, to create the best reading possible, we need to define the genre of this material. What kind of literature is this, and how does its logic work?

Written in narrative historiographical style, 2 Kings 1 is a controversy story addressing the issue of power (indicated by the word mišpaṭ, 1:7). Yahweh, through his prophet, has the say; the king does not (a point reinforced by the rare use of Ahaziah's name, 1:2, 17-18). Though the king acts as if he is powerful (sending messengers and military, 1:2, 6, 9, 11, 13, 16), the Lord's messenger blocks the king with orders to Elijah, a judgment speech ironically conveyed to the king by his own messengers (1:6), though dramatically delayed until enacted by Elijah (1:16). The suspense and repetition reinforce the inevitability of the Lord's judgment. The historical narrative reporting the king's death (1:2-8, 15-17) brackets the miracle story of fire from heaven (1:9-14), a story offensive to readers troubled by the loss of innocent lives.

Reading the miracle as rhetorical device does not resolve the objectionable prophetic action but does offer a different perspective. Because power lies with the Lord and his prophet, the third captain, who pleads for mercy and bows to prophetic authority, models royal submission to the Lord. The integration of the controversy story with a miracle story establishes a claim. The outer portions provide historical data (1:2-8, 15-16). The literary structure separates history from the divine message in the acted parables of miracle stories (1:9-14). The miracles convey the message: royal officials who are just will recognize and submit to divine authority.

Olley suggests that the absence of the person of YHWH from the narrative indicates that Elijah acts in his idiosyncratic dramatic and violent confrontational manner out of fear (*Do not fear*, 1:15; 1998: 44). The message for an exilic audience might be that God's ways are gracious—and not always confrontational (51). No definitive resolution of these questions is offered here. Rather, we invite the reader to engage the text despite its distance historically and ethically. Humans struggle to convey God's authority over royal power and God's commitment to peace. The storytelling in 2 Kings 1 reflects that struggle.

THE TEXT IN BIBLICAL CONTEXT
Whose Kingdom Will Prevail?

With its counter-system of justice, 1–2 Kings pits Deuteronomic Torah against ANE royal values [*Mišpaṭ, p. 461*]. The key question is this: Who has the say? Does power lie with the prophet or the king? What happens when kings and people reject Yahweh for the royal system identified with the sins of Jeroboam or with Baal? The prophet Ahijah dethrones the dynasties of Solomon and Jeroboam (1 Kings 11:31-39; 14:6-14) and foretells exile, the ultimate disaster for both houses (14:15-16; 2 Kings 17; 25). Jehu eliminates Baasha's house (1 Kings 16:1-4). Elijah and Elisha condemn Ahab's dynasty because those kings pursue royal power instead of Yahwistic justice (1 Kings 17–2 Kings 10).

The Lord's sovereignty is the foundation of Israel's salvation. The Song of Victory (Exod 15:1-21) celebrates the Lord's victory over Pharaoh and the gods of Egypt; the Lord is sovereign "for he has triumphed gloriously," Miriam sings (15:21). God's royal authority is central to Psalms. Enthronement psalms (47, 93, 96–99) confess that the Lord is "King" (Brueggemann 2014a: 49–53). The sovereign Lord has overcome all rivals. The Lord rules the gods of the peoples (Pss 96:4-5; 97:7). The Lord's governance produces shalom, order in the face of chaos. Chaos, represented by such powers as the Rahab monster (Ps 89:10-11), is defeated so that order and peace, righteousness, justice, and steadfast love prevail (89:14). While the Lord has a special connection with Israel (Pss 97:8; 99:6), the Lord's realm is cosmic (97:7; 99:2). The Lord's rule establishes and protects the Deuteronomic covenant values:

Mighty King, lover of justice,
    you have established equity;
you have executed justice
    and righteousness in Jacob.
(Ps 99:4; cf. 96:1, 13; 97:2)

These values reverberate throughout Scripture. The Lord's sovereignty is the basis for the Lord's paradigmatic claim for justice to be given to the oppressed (Deut 10:17-18). The poet envisions God's sovereign triumph as good news of peace in Zion (Isa 52:7). When Jesus proclaims the inbreaking reign of God, healing comes to the marginalized (Mark 1:14-15). Jesus' reign is superior to that of Rome, as Jesus testifies before Pilate (John 18:33-38). The book of Revelation anticipates divine rule (11:15).

When the Lord rules, peace prevails, justice is done, truth is ascendant. The Lord who rules is Israel's covenant God. Covenant people live for justice, but when they oppose these values, they oppose God's rule and suffer accordingly. While experienced as judgment (like the death of a hundred innocent soldiers), the Lord defeats chaos as a saving act for those without a defender.

Slow to Judge and Quick to Save?

The Bible witnesses to the God who is slow to anger but quick to save. As the Lord passes by Moses, he proclaims, "Yahweh, Yahweh, a God merciful and gracious, slow to anger" (Exod 34:6-7 AT). God judges kings who *followed the sins of Jeroboam* (2 Kings 13:2-3), yet this is the God of mercy who *saw the oppression of Israel* (13:4) and *gave Israel a savior* (13:5).

If such texts reflect the testimony of Israel, how are we to read the counter-testimony (Brueggemann's terminology in *Theology of the Old Testament* [1997])? Ahaziah is judged after a brief two-year reign. The judgment falls indiscriminately, apparently, on one hundred unsuspecting soldiers. Zimri dies in political chaos as judgment for sin after just one week in office (1 Kings 16:15-20)! Speedy justice indeed! Achan takes booty, and his whole household is executed on the day his sin is detected (Josh 7). The story of Ananias and Sapphira offers a New Testament parallel (Acts 5:1-11). One lie regarding their offering, and both die in a moment at the feet of the apostle; then "great fear seized the whole church" (5:11). Where is mercy?

These texts reflect testimony and counter-testimony, a scriptural dialogue pondering how to interpret evil, divine judgment, and sin. Judgment can be viewed as merciful warning to covenant people. Is Achan's violent death justifiable as a deterrent against additional acts of covenant breaking in Joshua? When the church witnesses the death of two who "lie to the Holy Spirit," the result is fear—and holiness. The judgment of Ahaziah and his troops is brutal, a warning for others, an act of mercy for those who heed the Lord's message. The enacted parable-miracle story reaches its climax with the third captain, who recognizes the Lord's authority and pleads for mercy.

THE TEXT IN THE LIFE OF THE CHURCH
Cruciform Hermeneutic

Christian interpreters struggle with Elijah's calling fire from heaven to devour one hundred human beings. Brueggemann reads the text not as a "healing narrative" but as "political discourse on power realities" (1982b: 9). The point of the story is that Yahweh alone, not the royal administrators, has power for life and death, power that is exercised in inscrutable ways. Gray discounts the historicity of the tale, relegating it to legend (along with Elisha's curse on the rude boys of Bethel in 2 Kings 2:23-25) because of its "moral pointlessness" (459). Jones posits that 1:9-16 is a later (sub-Christian) appendix to the original Elijah narrative (376). Refuting the suggestion that Elijah is acting contrary to God's will, Davis says, "Blame Yahweh—he did it" to protect his prophet and to prove that Yahweh, not Baal, is God (2002b: 20–22). Davis rejects Wallace's characterization of Elijah as "mistaken, self-centered, and stupid." Wallace suggests that God took the side of "the foolish and unworthy prophet," who "made a callous and dramatic fool of himself" (77–78). This reading casts Elijah as "an unreliable character" (Kissling: 114) [Literary Criticism: Narrative Subgenres, p. 460].

Boyd proposes "cruciform hermeneutics." He argues that Christ on the cross demonstrates God's ethic, but that humans who act in God's name do not consistently follow this nonviolent approach. Boyd posits that when God gifts Elijah with supernatural power to call fire from heaven, the prophet is free to use the divine energy wisely, as he does when he outduels the prophets of Baal (1 Kings 18:38); or foolishly, in immolating the captains and their men (2 Kings 1:10, 12). Like the judges who make foolish choices after the spirit of the Lord has fallen upon them (Jephthah's oath, Judg 11:29-31; Samson's violence, 14:19; 15:14-15), Elijah has freedom to use divine power foolishly or well. According to Boyd's reading, Elijah's indefensible violence runs counter to God's purposes (2017: 1218–27).

Shaped by Old Testament justice and peacemaking, Jesus refuses to misuse God-given power. The devil's temptations anticipate self-serving reliance on violence (Luke 4:1-13). Jesus references Elijah's care for a foreign widow, not his violent judgment (4:25-26). He rejects the disciples' inclination to call fire on the Samaritan village (9:54-55). When he is arrested, Jesus stops the use of the sword and heals his opponent (22:50-51). God vindicates Jesus, who disarms the powers and triumphs over them on the cross (Col 2:11-14).

2 Kings 2:1-25

Elisha Invested with Elijah's Spirit

PREVIEW

The 2005 film *Joyeux Noël* depicts a 1914 Christmas truce during the First World War. After German, French, and Scottish combatants sing Christmas carols, enemy officers meet in no-man's-land to call a cease-fire. Soldiers emerge, wishing each other "Merry Christmas." They exchange chocolate, champagne, and photographs of loved ones and play soccer. After the truce, both sides refuse to resume fighting, so these frontline battalions are retired and reassigned. No-man's-land became a liminal space, a boundary marker.

Second Kings 2 is a boundary text outside "royal time," between Ahaziah's closing and Joram's opening royal formulas (1:17-18; 3:1-3; Brueggemann 2000: 293). The Jordan River is a boundary place, between wilderness and land of promise. In this generational transition, the Lord's spirit, power, and guidance pass from Elijah to Elisha. In this numinous, mysteriously supernatural narrative, a most perplexing issue is what it will mean for Elijah's spirit to pass to Elisha. Unresolved narrative puzzles reinforce the mystery, including Elijah's resistance to Elisha's company (2:2, 4, 6); the trek from Gilgal in the hills a few miles north of Bethel, *down* through Bethel, on down to Jericho, then to the Jordan; Elisha's responses to the repeated messages from the sons of the prophets (2:3, 5); Elijah's conditions for Elisha's inheritance of his prophetic mantle (2:10); whether Elisha meets the conditions (2:11-12); and the prophets' insistence on searching for Elijah (2:16-17) [*Prophets: Sons of the Prophets, p. 467*].

In Israel, power is held by prophets more than by kings; the dramatic prophetic transition contrasts with the routinized royal formulas (this is the only OT story dealing with prophetic succession; O'Brien 1998: 1). Prophets order dynastic change (Elijah brings judgment on Ahab, 1 Kings 21:20-24; Elisha initiates Jehu's revolution, 2 Kings 9:1-10); the text narrates judgment on the evil of kings (1 Kings 16:19). The most significant transition occurs when Elisha inherits the spirit of Elijah. He parts the water (2 Kings 2:14), knows inside information (2:3, 5, 18), and sends powerful agents (2:17). Elisha inherits a double portion of Elijah's spirit, which is powerful, intriguing, inscrutable.

OUTLINE

Elijah Ascends in a Whirlwind, 2:1-18

2:1-8	Down from Gilgal, Past Bethel, to the Jordan
2:9-12	The Chariot of Fire
2:13-14	The Return Trip
2:15-18	The Search for Elijah

Miracle of the Water Supply, 2:19-22

Boys and Bears, 2:23-25

EXPLANATORY NOTES

Elijah Ascends in a Whirlwind 2:1-18

2:1-8 Down from Gilgal, Past Bethel, to the Jordan

The opening phrase summarizes 2 Kings 2:1-18 thus: *When the LORD was taking up Elijah in a whirlwind to heaven* (AT). This announcement of the mysterious event deflates narratival suspense (the reader knows the outcome before it is narrated) but raises curiosity about a report that defies rational explanation. The two prophets appear together for the first time since Elijah's "calling" of Elisha (1 Kings 19:19-21). To the end of his ministry, Elijah is obedient to the word of the Lord, making a final pass through Israel's central territory from Gilgal (2 Kings 2:1), down to Bethel (2:2-3), to Jericho (2:4-5), and through the Jordan River (2:6-8) because, he says, *the LORD has sent me* (2:2; *sent* is an act of royal power) [*Send, p. 476*]. In the first of three exchanges, Elijah politely orders Elisha to remain in Gilgal. At each point in the journey, Elisha responds to Elijah's order that he stay with an oath on the authority of the Lord and of Elijah that he will not leave Elijah. The narrative does not explain Elijah's "deeply enigmatic" resistance to Elisha's company (Brueggemann 2000: 295) but confirms Elisha's resolve and loyalty and provides a way for Elisha to follow on his return from the Jordan (Fretheim 1999: 137).

As the two arrive at Bethel and then at Jericho, the sons of the prophets ask Elisha whether he knows that the Lord will take his master that day [Prophets: Sons of the Prophets, p. 467]. Elisha's terse reply, I know; be silent (2:3 AT), adds to the narrative puzzle (see EN on 2:18). The narrative employs identical language for the second leg of the journey from Bethel to Jericho (2:4-5). At the Jordan, fifty sons of the prophets stand at a distance opposite the two (2:7). The interrupted routine of the journey signals the story's high point.

At the Jordan, the boundary marker for Israel's entry into the land of promise, Elijah strikes the water with the mantle he has used to cover his face on Mount Horeb and to call Elisha (2:8; 1 Kings 19:13, 19). When the water parts, they cross [over] on dry ground (cf. Exod 14:22).

2:9-12 The Chariot of Fire

After the crossing, Elijah invites Elisha to ask what he can do before he is taken (2 Kings 2:9). Elisha requests a double portion of Elijah's spirit (the inheritance of the oldest son, making Elisha successor of Elijah; see Deut 21:17). Elijah's puzzling answer is It will be hard for you what you ask; if you see me being taken from you, it is yours; and if not, it will not (2 Kings 2:10 AT). This puzzling response reinforces our sense of the inscrutability of the spirit. Lost in conversation as they walk along (distracted from the anticipated departure), the term Behold! shifts the narrative perspective to Elisha as a chariot of fire and horses of fire surprise and separate them [Literary Criticism: Elements of Narrative p. 458]. Elijah goes up in a whirlwind to heaven.

The narrative employs verbal forms to slow the action to frame-by-frame movement. Frame 1 is Elisha seeing (2:12 AT). Though undefined, Elisha is seeing Elijah's departure. Frame 2 quotes Elisha as he is crying out, "My father, my father, the chariots of Israel and its horsemen!" (AT). As Elisha witnesses the power of God demonstrated in the chariots of the Lord of hosts (cf. 1 Kings 22:19), the spirit of Elijah empowers Elisha. Horses and chariots mark raw, royal (and illicit) power (1 Kings 4:26; 9:19, 22; 10:26; cf. Deut 17:16) [Horses and Chariots, p. 447]. Greater than royal power are the Lord's horses and chariots (2 Kings 6:14-17; 13:14).

The freeze-action narrative demonstrates that Elisha meets Elijah's condition for the double portion of the spirit: Elisha witnesses Elijah's departure along with the powerful heavenly forces escorting Elijah in the whirlwind. The story pauses at the boundary between two Jordan crossings. The delivering God of Elijah is present and active. Elisha describes what he sees: the powerful forces of heaven linked to the person of Elijah. Elisha meets the condition set by Elijah and inherits his spirit-power. Frame 3 in the still-action narrative is not seeing Elijah anymore. With this phrase, the narrative returns to live action. Elisha tears his clothes in two pieces, grieving for the departed Elijah.

2:13-14 The Return Trip

Elisha moves back into action. Elijah is gone, but his mantle has fallen back to earth, so Elisha picks it up, returns to the Jordan, stands on its banks, and imitates his master by striking the water with the cloak. Elisha's question, Where is the LORD, the God of Elijah?, may indicate some combination of doubt and confidence. Has he truly inherited a double portion of Elijah's spirit? Will Elijah's God now work through him? Does Elisha represent the Lord in Israel? When he strikes the water as Elijah had, the river divides (the description uses the same idiom as in 2:8) and he crosses back into Israel and the land of his company of prophets. Like Joshua the servant of Moses, who imitated his predecessor's parting the waters of the sea by crossing the Jordan River on dry ground (Josh 3–4), Elisha, servant of Elijah, crosses the boundary marked by the Jordan and reenters Israel proper (see TBC on parallels with Moses and Joshua).

2:15-18 The Search for Elijah

The sons of the prophets standing on the opposite bank perceive that the spirit of Elijah is with Elisha when they witness the power demonstration of the parted river, and they commit themselves to the new leader (2 Kings 2:15).

Like grieving friends, the sons of the prophets are eager to do what they can in this moment of loss. They insist on sending a search party of fifty valiant men on the chance that the spirit of the Lord has dropped Elijah in a remote location (2:16). Elisha recognizes that this is a fool's mission, which will turn up empty. Undeterred, the prophets persist until, out of shame, Elisha issues the orders, Send them (2:17). When they return empty-handed, Elisha cannot resist saying, I told you so! (2:18 AT). With the double portion of Elijah's spirit, Elisha knows, perceives (6:17), foretells (6:9-10), heals (2:21; 4:35, 41). Elisha takes pride in knowing (see 2:3, 5) and offense when the Lord hides information from him (4:27). Though we interpret the "double" portion to be the oldest son's inheritance,

Elisha works twice as many signs as Elijah did, including provision of food, raising a dead boy, and parting the Jordan.

Miracle of the Water Supply 2:19-22

In a series of miracle stories, Elisha provides for the needy people of the land related to the company of the prophets. As with Elijah, Elisha's first miracle involves water and the word of the Lord. Unlike Elijah, whose opening word announces drought to the land (1 Kings 17:1), Elisha ("my God saves") provides relief for the earth. Elisha mirrors Elijah's opposition to the unjust exercise of royal power, but his approach often contrasts with that of his fiercely isolated predecessor.

In 2:18, Elisha returns to Jericho (the city associated with the curse of Joshua; see EN on 1 Kings 16:34). The city's inhabitants present their problem to Elisha (2:19) *[Literary Criticism: Narrative Subgenres, p. 460]*. The city's location is *good*, but the water is *evil* (MT). Bad water has resulted in lack of productivity (it is a land of miscarriage). The city's prosperity depends on having a good water supply, and they ask the prophet for help. The solution is typical of the miracles of Elisha. He involves the people in the resolution of the problem by asking them to provide a new vial of salt (2:20). The prophet himself takes the salt to the water spring and speaks in the name of the Lord: *I have healed these waters; there will not be from them any more death or miscarriage* (2:21 AT; when Moses sweetened the water, the Lord declared, "I am the LORD your healer," Exod 15:26 AT). We note the contrast between the power of Elijah and the miracles of Elisha. Elisha promises no more *death* in 2 Kings 2, while the Elijah story is marked by the pervasiveness of *death* in the drought and confrontation with the prophets of Baal (1 Kings 17–18) and in the report of 102 soldiers killed by fire from heaven (2 Kings 1). The evidence of the miracle persists to the time this narrative is recorded (*to this day*, 2:22). Elisha is a prophet whose God is a savior. His God brings prosperity to the earth (2:19).

Boys and Bears 2:23-25

The next vignette is jarring. Elisha, the mild, people-oriented, healing prophet of the previous story, turns into a vengeful old man, provoked by *small boys* shouting a childish insult about the prophet's appearance: *baldhead* (2:23). The healer is associated with terrorism: the story ends with forty-two little boys mauled by bears! Elisha, like Elijah, exercises prophetic power to judge with violence that appears to be inexcusably harsh (see EN on 2 Kings 1). Early rabbis were so scandalized by the story that they rejected the event as narrated. For them, the phrase "neither she-bears nor forest" became an idiomatic expression for "it never happened" (Alter: 534) [Literary Criticism: Narrative Subgenres, p. 460]. Another reading suggests that Elisha "learns through painful experience that the charism [gift] is not for oneself but for the service of others" (O'Brien 1998: 16). On the other hand, Brueggemann takes the story as a call to fearlessness because God has taken sides with those who "walk the walk" (2013: 110). Other readers seek to exonerate the prophet by noticing that the venue, Bethel, is the home of Jeroboam's golden calf cult and is hostile to Deuteronomic values, arguing that while the term young boys (MT: naʿar) may refer to a newborn (1 Sam 4:21), it can describe warriors in an army (Gen 14:24; 1 Sam 14:6; 2 Sam 2:14; 18:15; 1 Kings 20:14, 19); Joshua at the time he commanded the Israelite army in the wilderness (Exod 33:11); and the overseer Jeroboam (1 Kings 11:28). The verb cursed means to "make light of them" (AT), to treat them as inconsequential. Mauled is not the word typically used to denote killing (the worn-out wineskins of the Gibeonites used to deceive Joshua were "torn," Josh 9:4; the earth shook because of the jubilation of the crowd, 1 Kings 1:40 AT). Perhaps another rabbinical explanation (the source of this popular justification is uncertain) suggests that a gang of young toughs from the anti-Yahwist city of Bethel accosted Elisha with violent insults. When Elisha treated their insults lightly, they became violently riotous, possibly toying with bear cubs. Enraged, the cubs' mothers gave the boys a good licking. This troubling narrative raises questions about prophetic reliability (see "False Prophets" in TBC for 1 Kings 22).

The juxtaposition of the story of healing (2:19-22) with the story of judgment (2:23-25) demonstrates that God blesses with life or curses with death, depending on human response to God's prophets (Seow: 178). The story witnesses to Elisha's succession as he retraces Elijah's exit route—from the wilderness, across the Jordan, to Jericho, to Bethel, to Carmel, and settling in Samaria (2:25), where Elisha's style of opposition to royal power contrasts with Elijah's confrontational ways.

THE TEXT IN BIBLICAL CONTEXT
Leadership Transition
Elisha is Elijah's successor just as Joshua follows Moses. Elijah's rolled mantle calls on God to open the waters for dry-land crossing of the Jordan, as did Moses' rod at the sea (Exod 14:16). Across the Jordan, Elijah is mysteriously taken to heaven, near the location

where Moses is mysteriously buried by the Lord (Deut 34:5-6). The servant Elisha imitates his master Elijah when he goes back across the Jordan, much as the Jordan crossing of the servant Joshua parallels how his master, Moses, led Israel across the sea (Josh 3–4; Exod 14–15). Both Elisha ("my God saves") and Joshua ("Yahweh saves") bring God's saving power first to Jericho (Josh 6; 2 Kings 2:19-22). Just as Joshua sought to eradicate the gods of Canaan, so Elisha directs a young prophet in anointing Jehu to eliminate Ahab's Baal worship (Josh 24:14-15; 2 Kings 9–10).

Leithart develops similar parallels with Jesus in the Gospels (his name is the Greek parallel of Joshua, Matt 1:21). First, he compares Elijah with John the Baptist, the lone voice in the wilderness; and Elisha with Jesus, who is surrounded by disciples, cleanses lepers (Mark 1:40-45; cf. 2 Kings 5), and restores dead sons (Luke 7:11-17; cf. 2 Kings 4:18-37). Then he turns the analogy to Elisha following his master, Elijah, just as the disciples follow their master, Jesus— leaving home and family (1 Kings 19:19-21) just as the disciples leave business and family (Mark 1:16-20) and continue the ministry of the master after his ascension to heaven (Leithart: 171).

THE TEXT IN THE LIFE OF THE CHURCH
Life, Death, New Life

Life and death are primary themes in the stories of Elijah and Elisha. Though the Old Testament rarely reflects about life after death, both stories offer some intriguing hints. Elijah ascends to heaven without passing through the pale of death. Both prophets "live on" after death by offering life to others. Elijah's mantle becomes Elisha's sign of Elijah's spirit, through which Elisha offers life to Jericho and the company of the prophets. Elisha's dead bones revivify a corpse (2 Kings 13:20-21). In the New Testament, Jesus raises the dead (Mark 5:35-43; Luke 7:11-17; John 11). More significantly, Jesus is the resurrection and the life (11:25), the firstborn from the dead (Col 1:18), who offers life to all who believe in him (John 3:16). Christian hope anticipates life forever with the Lord. More than that, Jesus' resurrection offers hope for those on earth caught in lifeless despair. The one who is the way, the truth, and the life opens a new direction for people caught in dead ends (14:6). Foreshadowed by Elijah and Elisha, Jesus brings saving power to individuals, families, churches, and societies locked in mortal combat. Elijah appears with Moses when Jesus is transfigured, and he talks with Jesus (Mark 9:2-13). Elijah, Elisha, and Jesus empower contemporary believers to seek new beginnings from the midst of despair.

Mystery and the Numinous

The EN identify curious elements in 2 Kings 2 and label the story as numinous. Like a hall of mirrors, the tale of Elijah's departure leads readers to puzzle about distorted reflections. How can we learn from this journey into the looking glass? The mysterious inscrutability of whirlwinds to heaven and disjointed conversations points toward unexplainable elements of life. Elijah leaves the earth and ministry. The tale teases us with questions about mortality and life after death. The prophets try to warn Elisha that Elijah's departure nears, only to be silenced. Is the issue too opaque for words, or is Elisha dealing with denial? Elisha appears to fulfill the conditions Elijah sets on inheriting his spirit, but explicit confirmation is missing. Leadership transitions can be equally puzzling—both in choosing good leaders and in making clean breaks. Horses and chariots of fire defy rational explanation. The figure of speech *the chariots of Israel and its horsemen* (2 Kings 2:12; cf. 13:14) invites the reader to choose prophetic rather than military power.

The mystery of the text suggests contemplation of the mystery of life. Scripture raises questions. Answers are not always evident.

2 Kings 3:1-27

War with Moab

PREVIEW

War seldom achieves its objectives as advertised. In the American Civil War, both sides expected to vanquish the other in a matter of weeks or months, but the bloodiest American war lasted four years, devastated most of the southern U.S., failed to end racial inequality, exacerbated divisions for generations, with conflict that festers to this day. World War I, "the war to end all wars," made possible Hitler's rise to power, leading to World War II. The 1992 U.S.-led, United Nations–sanctioned Operation Restore Hope aimed to disarm rival Somali factions. The Battle of Mogadishu, expected to be a humanitarian incursion, resulted in what Americans called "horrific footage" of desecrated American corpses and hundreds or thousands of Somalian causalities. Fighting resumed when foreign forces withdrew.

A three-kingdom coalition squashed Moabite rebellion after Ahab's death. The twists and turns in the expedition make for dramatic but confusing narrative. First, the three kings are stranded without water. Then Moab misreads the situation and initiates an attack, expecting easy plunder. The Israel-led force devastates the land of Moab. But with the sacrifice of the Moabite king's heir apparent, *great wrath came upon Israel, so they withdrew* (2 Kings 3:27). The war fails to achieve its objectives.

OUTLINE

The File on King Jehoram of Israel, 3:1-3
War against Moab, 3:4-27
    3:4-8   Expedition of the Three-King Alliance
    3:9-20   The Lord's Miracle of Water
    3:21-27   The Defeat in Moab

EXPLANATORY NOTES

The File on King Jehoram of Israel 3:1-3

The overlapping filing system of kings of Israel and Judah presents a confusing chronology of Jehoshaphat and his Israelite contemporaries. In sequence with Ahab of Israel, Jehoshaphat's reign is reported in 1 Kings 22:41-50. The evaluation formula and death notice are uncharacteristically separated by a few verses, but the Jehoshaphat file appears complete.

Ahab's son Ahaziah rules for only two years before his premature death. Another son of Ahab, Jehoram, succeeds Ahaziah as king of Israel in the second year of King Jehoram son of Jehoshaphat in Judah (2 Kings 1:17). The royal narrative is interrupted by the Elijah-Elisha transition (2 Kings 2).

In 2 Kings 3 the royal narrative resumes, with King Jehoshaphat of Judah reigning contemporaneously with King Jehoram of Israel (in apparent conflict with the report in 1:17) [Chronology: Kings Ahaziah and Jehoram, p. 441]. In 2 Kings 3:1 the royal formula places the ascension of Israel's Jehoram in the eighteenth year of Jehoshaphat of Judah and reports a twelve-year reign (roughly 850-840 BCE). Like all the kings of Israel, Jehoram does evil, following the sins of Jeroboam (3:2-3), but compares favorably with the rest of the Omride dynasty and is credited with removing the Baal pillar placed by Ahab and Jezebel.

If Jehoram removes the Baal pillar, two questions surface. First, why does Jehu need to get rid of Baal worship in the Northern Kingdom (2 Kings 10)? Second, why is Jehoram still condemned as evil? Apparently Jehoram's reforms are incomplete. Removing one pillar, perhaps from a place where Yahweh was also worshiped, did not eliminate the Baal cult. Furthermore Jezebel, the queen mother, remains in power, supporting the Baal cult. By pursuing the sins of Jeroboam, Jehoram's policies disrupt the Deuteronomic economy and justice system [Sins of Jeroboam, p. 476]. Jehoram, if a reformer at all, does not produce the necessary results to win Elisha's favor (3:13-14).

War against Moab 3:4-27

3:4-8 Expedition of the Three-King Alliance

Israel had a long relationship with its eastern neighbor Moab (Gen 19:30-38; Num 21-25; 31:8, 16; Judg 3, 11; Ruth 1-4; 1 Sam 22:3-4; 2 Sam 8:2; 1 Kings 11:7-8, 33). How Ahab came to exact tribute from Moab is not explained. Apparently Moabite subservience had continued since David (2 Sam 8:2).

The transition from Ahab to his heirs opens the door for Mesha, shepherd-king of Moab, to revolt against Israel to avoid tribute (2 Kings 3:4-5). Jehoram musters all Israel to quash the rebellion (3:6). This is the last time the narrative names Jehoram son of Ahab as king of Israel until it refers to him as Joram son of Ahab in 2 Kings 8:16-29; 9:14-29.

Jehoram's message to Jehoshaphat matches Ahab's (3:7; 1 Kings 22:4). Likely a weaker covenant partner, Jehoshaphat responds as he had earlier: I am with you, my people are your people, my horses are your horses (2 Kings 3:7; 1 Kings 22:4). Although the Hebrew (cf. NIV) does not identify the speakers in the further exchange between the kings (3:8), the NRSV reasonably interprets that Jehoram determines the route to Moab.

3:9-20 The Lord's Miracle of Water

Jehoram, the king of Israel, accompanied by his apparently junior partner Jehoshaphat with Judah's vassal, the unnamed king of Edom (1 Kings 22:47-48), chooses the much longer route through the wilderness of Edom and around the Dead Sea (on its west and south), avoiding Moab's northern fortifications (the Mesha Stele claims military victories over Israel in northern Moab; ANET 209-10) [Archaeology: Mesha Stele, p. 438]. When the armies are stranded by lack of water in the wilderness of Edom, Jehoram, the king of Israel, issues a cry of woe, accusing the Lord of summoning them to be handed over to Moab (3:9, 10, 13, 27).

Jehoshaphat asks that the king of Israel consult the prophet of Yahweh (3:11; see identical wording in 1 Kings 22:5, 7). As in 1 Kings 22, the king of Israel has made war plans without prophetic consultation. Though Jehoshaphat's request in 1 Kings 22 may have been a ploy to delay battle, in 2 Kings 3 a word from Yahweh is their only hope. A servant of Israel's king knows of Elisha's presence, identifying him by his family ties and as the one who used to pour water on the hands of Elijah (3:11; indicating Elisha was Elijah's servant, but under the circumstances an ironic allusion to his role in supplying life-giving water, 2:19-21). The three kings go to meet Elisha. (In 2 Kings

5:11 Naaman complains that he thought the prophet would come out to meet him. Here three kings seek Elisha's presence, reflecting their powerlessness.)

The hostility between Elijah and the house of Ahab extends to Elisha and the last king of Ahab's dynasty. Elisha charges that he has no relationship with the king of Israel, who should instead consult the prophets of his parents (3:13). The king of Israel responds, falsely blaming the Lord for having summoned the three kings. Elisha swears by the powerful living Yahweh of the armies, in whose presence he stands—emphasizing that his loyalty to the Lord is in tension with his ongoing conversation with the king (3:14), and that the only reason for the conversation is his regard for Jehoshaphat; he considers the king of Israel a nonentity. The narrator matches the opinion of Elisha, not mentioning the kings again in the chapter (except to report Moabite speech about them in 3:21, 23). The kings disappear; the narrative is dominated by Elisha, his prophetic speech, and the fulfillment of his words.

Inspired by a musician (3:15; reminiscent of Balaam's inspiration and Saul's prophecy, Num 23:2-3, 14-15, 29; 24:1-2; 1 Sam 10:5-6, 10-13), Elisha promises salvation from the Lord. The double messenger formula (*Thus says the LORD*, 2 Kings 3:16-17) introduces the promise of water *[Literary Criticism, p. 457]*. First, the Lord promises that the ravines will be filled with water for humans and animals without storms or rainfall (ruling out Baal the god of storms as the source). Elisha himself adds a message to the divine oracle: the water miracle will be a *trifle* (2:24: *curse*) because the Lord will also give Moab into their *hand* (*power*) and they will *strike* all the fortified cities and all the choice cities (3:18-19 AT; Elijah and Elisha *strike* the Jordan, 2:8, 14; the Lord *strikes* Aram with blindness, 6:18; *strike* is used four times more in 3:23-25, including three times to report the fulfillment of the prophecy). Elisha predicts that the coalition armies will fell all good trees, plug every spring, and ruin every piece of land with stones (3:19). Without endorsing the devastation, Elisha announces human actions resulting in environmental disaster for Moab. The next day the divine promise is fulfilled as water flows from Edom and fills the land (3:20).

3:21-27 *The Defeat in Moab*

Phase 1 of the battle report explains that Moab, having mobilized every able warrior regardless of age, misinterprets the water covering the earth for the blood of the armies and, deceived by its faulty military intelligence, rushes for plunder, exposing themselves to

Israel's attack (3:21-23). In phase 2 Israel rises in the camp to *attack Moab* (AT) and, as they pursue the fleeing Moabites, they continue to *attack* (3:24). In phase 3 the armies fulfill Elisha's prediction of devastation, but several anomalies alert the reader to an unexpected conclusion. Elisha predicts that Israel will *strike* all the cities, but the narrator reports that Israel *overturns* the cities. The report of the devastation of the land reverses the order of the prediction, covering every good piece of land with stones, stopping up all the water springs, and felling all the good trees (typical practice in the ANE to endanger the enemy's economy). The slingers surround and *strike* Kir-hareseth, fulfilling the prophecy literally but not defeating the enemy.

Phase 4 reports the actions of the king of Moab, who when he realizes that he is overwhelmed, tries to escape through the weakest part of the enemy lines, the front defended by Edom, but the line holds (3:26). When that desperate strategy fails, the king sacrifices his oldest son on the top of the wall (3:27). The last sentence of the battle report seems to turn all the prior action on its head. Instead of reading that Israel forced Moab to submit and pay annual tribute, the narrative concludes that *great wrath came upon Israel, so they withdrew from him and returned to their own land.*

Commentators struggle to interpret the odd, unexpected ending. The battle report in 2 Kings 3 parallels 1 Kings 22. Both identify the king of Israel just once (Ahab in 1 Kings 22:20; Jehoram in 2 Kings 3:6). Both kings ask Jehoshaphat to join them in battle, and he agrees (1 Kings 22:4; 2 Kings 3:7). Jehoshaphat suggests that they inquire of the Lord through a prophet. Animosity marks the relationships between the kings and the prophet/Yahweh (1 Kings 22:8; 2 Kings 3:13-14). Both prophets swear by Yahweh who lives (1 Kings 22:14; 2 Kings 3:14) and refer to the Lord as Yahweh of hosts (1 Kings 22:19; 2 Kings 3:14). The parallels suggest a similar rhetorical strategy, particularly since this conclusion is so baffling. Though not conclusive, the suggestion that Israel is self-deceived in 2 Kings 3 (as Ahab is self-deceived; see EN on 2 Kings 22) seems plausible (Wray Beal 2014: 314; Leithart: 181; Westbrook: 532). Judgment falls on these kings who make war for personal advantage (in 1 Kings 22, to control the lucrative trade route through Ramoth-gilead; in 2 Kings 3, for annual tribute). Ahab pays for his overreaching strategy with his life. In 2 Kings 3 *great wrath comes upon Israel*, and they withdraw (v. 27). The prophecy of Elisha is not false: Israel is deceived by their interpretation of the prediction that they will *strike* Moab and faces *great wrath* because they overreach. This reading does not associate the wrath against

Israel with the child sacrifice (reported in 3:27). The sacrifice along with the unsuccessful escape attempt indicates Moab's desperation, making the Israelite withdrawal from Moab without exacting tribute more noteworthy (House: 264). Despite the miracle of water supply, the attacks by Moab, and the military superiority and success of the coalition of kings, *great wrath* (attributed to the Lord; cf. Deut 29:28) thwarts the selfish military initiatives of the Omride dynasty.

THE TEXT IN BIBLICAL CONTEXT
Sacred Pillars

The sole redeeming feature of Jehoram of Israel is his removal of *the pillar of Baal* (3:2). Uninscribed stone pillars, standing alone or in clusters, were common in Canaanite worship as symbols for the gods (Wray Beal 2014: 312). They were originally seen as neutral memorial stones in Israel, as when Jacob erects pillars to mark his meeting with the Lord; God responds positively to these monuments (Gen 28:18, 22; 31:45; 35:14). In the covenant ceremony, Moses sets up twelve pillars on the mountain (Exod 24:4). As pillars become associated with Canaanite non-Yahwistic cults, Torah demands that Israel break up pillars devoted to the gods (23:24; 34:13). Setting up cultic pillars is prohibited in Palestine (Lev 26:1). Deuteronomic law requires that Israel smash the pillars of the nations in the land and prohibits setting up pillars for the Lord (Deut 7:5; 12:3; 16:22). Under Rehoboam, Judah sets up pillars, apparently influenced by the queen mother from Ammon (1 Kings 14:21-23).

Jehoram eliminates the pillar of Baal, but apparently his effort either is half-hearted or is thwarted by Jezebel. In his anti-Baal initiative, Jehu's reformers smash the pillars, burn them, and destroy the temple of Baal, making it a latrine (2 Kings 10:26-27). The accusation against Israel in the exilic summary is that Israel has set up pillars on every high hill and under every green tree (17:10). When Hezekiah removes the high places, he smashes pillars (18:4). Josiah's reform includes smashing the pillars that remain from the idolatrous pantheon of Solomon (23:14). Hosea condemns the pillars as an affront to the Lord (Hos 3:4; 10:1-2; Mic 5:13). While most of the condemned pillars are erected for Baal or other idols, the approving attitude toward Jacob's pillars in Genesis seems to have changed in Deuteronomy and in Kings.

Both customs and legal codes change over time in the Old Testament. Far from one set of ethics for all time, different circumstances allow for different standards. The law and the customs are adapted to fit the times.

Fighting Moab

The Jehoshaphat-Moab war report in 2 Chronicles 20 differs substantially from the report in 2 Kings 3. Before the battle with Moab, the prophet Jehu son of Hanani (1 Kings 16:1) has condemned Jehoshaphat's alliance with Ahab and willingness to "help the wicked and love those who hate the LORD" (2 Chron 19:2). In 2 Chronicles the prophet Jahaziel, a Levite, declares, "The battle is not for you to fight; take your position, stand still, and see the victory of the LORD on your behalf" (20:17). Although Moab mistakenly believes that Israel and Judah have destroyed each other (2 Kings 3:23), in Chronicles the Lord ambushes Moab and its allies (Ammon and Edom), who kill each other. Judah sings praise to the Lord but does no violence to the enemy (2 Chron 20:19-22). Rather than wrath breaking out against them, Jehoshaphat has rest, and the enemy kingdoms fear God (20:29-30; cf. 2 Kings 3:27).

Though it is conceivable that Chronicles reports a different battle, both report Moab's destruction. If, as scholars believe, Chronicles is literarily dependent on Kings (Konkel 2016: 24–25), what is the reader to make of the contrasting narratives of what appears to be a single battle? Konkel describes 1–2 Chronicles as midrash on earlier traditions (ancient commentary: "the study of a text to make it relevant to the needs of a community, an attempt to make a biblical text contemporary and relevant," 29). If so, the Chronicles narrative can be read as implicit judgment on the self-serving, scorched-earth destruction of the environment described in 2 Kings 3. Israel's soldiers themselves suffer. Moab's king loses his firstborn son. Second Chronicles 20, on the other hand, follows classic Yahweh war protocol. The enemy initiates violent conflict. Jehoshaphat confesses absolute dependence on the Lord. The Levitical prophet promises deliverance. The army of Judah sings praise to the Lord. When Judah arrives at the battlefront, the enemy lies dead before them. Judah rejoices, the nations fear the Lord, and the land has rest. Thus 2 Chronicles 20 appears to be another voice in the conversation regarding war (Matties: 19–20). Both 2 Kings 3 and 2 Chronicles 20 warn the reader about the consequences of reliance on violence.

Isaiah laments Moab's destruction in an oracle of both judgment and salvation (Isa 15–16). The prophet weeps for human pain (15:1-5), environmental destruction (15:6-9), and children's distress (16:1-4a). Recalling Isaiah 16:11, "Therefore my heart throbs like a harp for Moab," Parker studies the horrors of war suffered by children. The oldest son of the Moabite king, the most privileged in the realm, is not immune from the violence of war that effects collateral damage on the most vulnerable: children. Like Jephthah sacrificing his daughter (Judg 11:34-40), the royal father sacrifices his firstborn son for success of his military ventures. Children (and other vulnerable members of society) suffer from war's violence. When drones destroy vehicles, youthful passengers are "collateral damage." Disproportionately, they suffer famine and disease. Armies recruit child soldiers. Children raised in a society that glorifies military superiority are conditioned to reject peacemaking. Great wrath comes upon the aggressors in war because of the suffering of the children (Parker: 116–18).

THE TEXT IN THE LIFE OF THE CHURCH
Environment and War

In an article titled "The Effects of War on the Environment," Lallanilla describes "the most famous" environmental disaster related to war, the deforestation of 4.5 million acres of Vietnam resulting from U.S. use of twenty million tons of Agent Orange and other herbicides. "Widespread deforestation, unchecked hunting, soil erosion, and contamination of land and water by human waste occur when thousands of humans are forced to settle in a new area." When Hutus fled Rwanda in 1994, national parks in that country and nearby Congo were devastated. Some thirteen million displaced Syrians have deforested the most productive sections of their country, resulting in soil erosion and an international dust storm. Lallanilla recognizes that potential for much greater disaster has been averted or postponed by the inactivity of nuclear arsenals. The U.S., Canadian, and European forces leave a disproportionately large carbon footprint in their production of military equipment and jet fuel consumption.

As was true of the environmental devastation created by the armies of Israel and Judah in Moab, the uncritical assumption that military objectives trump environmental concerns works against reversal of these practices. As evidenced by Lallanilla's citation of Deuteronomy 20:19 in the introduction to his article, giving voice to the biblical witness is one faithful response to environmental devastation in war. Disarmament, nuclear and conventional, is also consistent with biblical shalom. The Christian call to peacemaking and creation stewardship is anticipated by the report of the Moabite war in 2 Kings 3.

2 Kings 4:1-44

Elisha's Miracles

PREVIEW

Mama O opened the Tree of Life restaurant in downtown Fresno, California, in gratitude for the rescue-mission program that helped her son overcome addiction. She exclusively employs graduates of the mission recovery program. Her employees, who would find it difficult to get work elsewhere, belong to a community of faith that understands the rich meaning of the neon sign "Jesus Saves." Like Elisha ("my God saves"), Mama O provides vision and opportunity to help the helpless help themselves.

In 2 Kings 4, Elisha brings life in the face of debt slavery (4:1-7), death (4:8-37), poisoned food (4:38-41), and famine (4:42-44). Three of the stories involve the *company of the prophets*. Rentería gives evidence that members of this community committed to Yahweh justice have been impoverished by royal economic injustice *[Prophets: Sons of the Prophets, p. 467]*. The miracle stories illustrate that without the hope inspired by the prophet's imagination of what the Lord can do, the people would sink into hopeless despair; and without the cooperative engagement of the community in need, the prophetic imagination would remain inert *[Literary Criticism: Narrative Subgenres, p. 460]*.

OUTLINE

4:11-17   Miracle Birth
4:18-37   Death and Life
Miracle Stories: Death in the Pot and Leftover Bread, 4:38-44

EXPLANATORY NOTES
Miracle Story: A Widow Facing Bankruptcy 4:1-7

Elisha intervenes to save marginalized persons in the prophets'
community. Like a typical miracle story, this narrative opens with
the problem: a creditor threatens to enslave the two children of an
unnamed widow to settle her unpayable debt (4:1). The desperate
widow *cries out* (AT) to Elisha. Laws protecting aliens, widows,
orphans, and victims of creditors who "cry out to me" anticipate
such a situation (Exod 22:21-27). When overwhelmed by imperial
injustice, Israel cries out to the Lord for deliverance (Exod 14:10, 15;
Deut 26:7; Josh 24:7). Elisha intervenes for those who cry out for help
(2 Kings 4:40; 6:5, 26).
The widow reminds the prophet that he *knows* that her husband
was loyal to the Lord (4:1). *Servant* underscores the man's relationships with the Lord and with the prophet (Solomon is the Lord's
servant, 1 Kings 8; Obadiah is Elijah's *servant*, 1 Kings 18:9, 12). The
widow emphasizes that the creditor comes to take her children as
slaves (the same term is translated *servant*). The widow strategically
acknowledges that Elisha already *knows* this case, having observed
that Elisha has reacted to earlier communication from the prophetic guild by insisting, perhaps defensively, that he *knows*
(2 Kings 2:3, 5, 18).
Although the law permits a limited term of slavery for indebted
adults, seizing children as collateral for a dead man's debts violates
protection offered the marginalized (protection of widows and
orphans is among the legal rights of the indebted, Exod 21:2-6;
22:21-27; Deut 15:1-2, 12). Indebtedness results not from regular
business dealing (modern capitalism) but rather from the inability
of the poor to pay for daily needs. The protection of the marginalized reminds Israel of the Lord's compassion in delivering them as
aliens. Treatment of the poor is to be generous, liberal, and ungrudg-
ing (Deut 15:7, 10). Creditors are prohibited from entering the house
of a neighbor to take a pledge (24:10-11). The widow presses Elisha
to defend social, legal, and economic justice.
Elisha characteristically puts the responsibility for action back
on the widow: *What shall I do for you? . . . What do you have in the house?*
(2 Kings 4:2). This call to appreciative inquiry moves her from powerlessness (*Your servant has nothing in the house*) to identification of

resources (*except a jar of oil*). Seizing the opportunity, Elisha orders the woman to enlist the cooperation of her community, asking *all* her neighbors for *not just a few* flasks (4:3-4). Inspired by prophetic imagination, she asks for empty vessels, not a handout. As instructed, the widow shuts the door behind her; as the children bring her the jars, she pours oil (4:5). When they have filled the last jar, the oil stops (4:6). She reports to the man of God, who instructs her to *sell the oil*, pay the debt, and *live on the rest* (4:7; cf. 4:43-44: *have some left*). Like Elijah, who provided oil for the widow of Zarephath and her son (1 Kings 17:16), Elisha provides for the Israelite widow and her children.

Short Story about the Woman of Shunem 4:8-37

The unnamed woman in the next story is wealthy and married to an aging landowner. Evidently without relationship to the prophetic guild, she lives in northern Israel, provides resources for Elisha, and takes initiative to resolve the crisis she faces. The phrase *one day* marks the three scenes of the story (4:8, 11, 18).

4:8-10 Woman's Hospitality

Scene 1 establishes the initiative of the woman, who offers Elisha hospitality. Elisha *passes over to Shunem* (4:8 AT; Shunem is about fifteen miles southeast of Elisha's residence at Mount Carmel; cf. 1 Kings 1:3). The *great woman prevails upon* Elisha to eat at her house and persuades her husband to build a guest room on the roof for the one she *knows to be a holy man of God* (2 Kings 4:8-10 AT).

4:11-17 Miracle Birth

In scene 2, Elisha seizes the initiative, sending *his servant Gehazi* to summon the woman. Though she *stands before him* (as Elisha *stands before the LORD*, 5:16 AT), Elisha directs his questions to Gehazi, seeking to repay all her *trouble* (4:11-13). The woman responds directly to Elisha that his help is unnecessary. After consulting with Gehazi, Elisha summons the woman and announces that she will *embrace a son* in the new year (4:14-16). The woman replies, *No, my lord! Man of God, do not lie to your maidservant* (AT). The woman gives birth as Elisha has said (4:17).

The annunciation type-scene is unique in that Elisha, not the Lord, offers the son; the child is unnamed and otherwise not a significant character; and the expected report that the husband *knew* his wife is missing (Amit 2003: 283.). The narrative suggests that neither Elisha nor the *great woman* wishes to be indebted to the other's generosity. Elisha appears to seek to establish prophetic authority by addressing Gehazi (not the woman directly) and offering to use his influence with powerful people.

4:18-37 Death and Life

One day (scene 3) the grownup boy (great, as describes his mother, 4:8 AT) becomes ill, is carried to his mother's embrace, and dies (4:18-20). Carrying the boy to the bed of the man of God, the woman politely requests a servant and a donkey for a fast trip to the man of God (4:22-25). The narrative reports the woman's initiative and the apparent relational distance of the father without explanation. When the woman is asked for information about her situation by her husband and by Gehazi (and Elisha; 4:23, 25, 26), she opaquely answers, *Shalom: All is well* (4:23, 26 [four times] AT). The Shunammite woman—who is in control of her life, her marriage, and her household—is overwhelmed by an issue of life and death. She who would keep a firm grip on life *seizes* (AT; the term translated as *urge/prevail* in 4:8) the feet of the man of God. Elisha, who seems preoccupied with having prophetic insight (2:3, 5, 18; 4:1) or insider information (4:14), is nonplussed by the Lord's withholding news of the woman's distress (4:27). In facing the death of the boy, the powerful woman has lost control of her life, and the insightful man of God finds himself in the dark.

The woman's lament, a pair of rhetorical questions accusing the man of God of imposing his gift upon her against her will, breaks the impasse (4:28). Interrupting the woman's lament, the man of God sends Gehazi back to the woman's house at full speed (4:29). Unsatisfied by his actions, the mother insists that the man of God return with her (4:30). Gehazi races ahead and follows the instructions regarding the staff of the man of God (laying the staff on the face of the child), but death prevails: there is *no sound* (cf. 1 Kings 18:26, 29) *or sign of life* (2 Kings 4:31). Gehazi returns to meet the man of God with the brief message: *The child hasn't arisen* (4:31 AT).

Elisha comes to the house (4:32; his name is used in the narrative for the first time since 4:17). The situation is urgent: *Behold! The lad dead, lying on his bed!* (AT). The series of terse actions continues: *He came, and he shut the door behind them, and he prayed to the LORD* (4:33 AT). The narrative slows to describe the high point of the action. *He got up and lay down upon the lad, and he put his mouth upon his mouth and his eyes upon his eyes and his hand upon his hand and crouched upon the lad* (4:34 AT; *crouched*, also in 4:35, is used elsewhere only for Elijah's posture in praying on Carmel, 1 Kings 18:42). *And the flesh of the lad grew warm.* Step by painstaking step, the narrative conveys the tension. Each verb elongates the moment. *And he returned and he walked in the house this way [!] and that way [!] and he went up [again] and he stretched himself out upon him [again]! The lad sneezed seven times. The lad opened his eyes!* (4:35 AT).

Narrative style matches content in intensity. Action verbs dominate scene 3. Breathless, the narrative races from action to action. Elisha engages in a prayer ritual like Elijah's. Alone with the boy in his upper room, Elisha repeatedly stretches his body upon the lad and calls to the Lord (cf. 1 Kings 17:21). Like Elijah, Elisha receives the boy of his hostess restored to life.

The man of God (named in 2 Kings 4:32, but unnamed again in MT for the rest of this story) reverts to communicating through an impersonal messenger as earlier (4:11-16, 36). He instructs Gehazi to call *this Shunammite woman and he calls her and she comes to him and he says, "Raise up your son." And she comes and she falls on his feet and she bows to the ground and she picks up her son and she exits* (4:37 AT).

The narrative places Elisha in relationship with a powerful woman, a dynamic that tests the willpower of each. The woman directs the story, prevailing upon Elisha to stay in her house, proposing to her husband to build the roof chamber, commandeering transportation during harvest for a fast trip up Mount Carmel, refusing to leave the prophet until he returns to her home—and her dead child. Elisha is *the man of God,* but the unnamed Shunammite woman wields power to gain her objectives. Elisha's indirect communication style through a servant creates distance and may be his deliberate attempt to establish authority. Though Elisha dominates the action in providing birth of the child and in restoring the boy, the prophet learns that his powers are limited and that he is dependent on God (Amit 2003: 292). The story is about well-being (shalom), a word used ironically. The God of Israel gives life to the son of an extraordinary woman who extends hospitality to the man of God.

Miracle Stories: Death in the Pot and Leftover Bread 4:38-44

The chapter concludes with two miracle stories. Elisha provides food in famine for the prophetic guild *[Prophets: Sons of the Prophets, p. 467].* Famine, linked to covenant transgression, especially the failure to provide for the marginalized, affects the prophetic community (1 Kings 17:1). Their daily life is threatened by food insecurity, the prophet intervenes to help the individuals involved to imagine a

different result, and a miracle resolves a complication [Literary
Criticism: Narrative Subgenres, p. 460].

Elisha returns to Gilgal to host the prophetic guild (2 Kings 4:38).
Elisha instructs his servant to get a pot boiling for stew. Someone
gathers unrecognized poisonous wild cucumbers from field vines
and slices them into the stew (4:39; on gathers, cf. collecting manna
in the wilderness, Exod 16:4-5; gleaning by the poor, Lev 19:9-10;
Ruth 2:2-3). They pour out (serve; the woman poured out oil, 2 Kings
4:4-5) the stew for the men, who begin to eat it. As they eat, they cry
out (as the widow cried, 4:1), Death in the pot, man of God! (4:40 AT).
Elisha asks for meal, throws it in the pot, then orders that it be
poured out (4:41 AT). There was not an evil thing [word] in the pot (AT).

In the second story a man from Baal-shalishah presents bread of
the firstfruits to Elisha (4:42; the place name related to Baal suggests
danger). The man brings twenty barley loaves plus ears of corn.
Elisha, again acting as host, orders that the food be served to the
men. Elisha's attendant (AT) protests that the food will not be enough
for a hundred people (4:43; cf. 1 Kings 18:4; 19:21; 2 Kings 6:22-23).
Elisha insists that he serve the food, declaring that the Lord promises leftovers (AT; cf. the rest in 4:7). The attendant obeys, and the
word of the Lord is fulfilled (4:44).

The twin stories demonstrate that, through Elisha, the Lord
saves the prophetic guild from death. Human cooperation (cucum-
ber gathering; offering firstfruits) is an essential but inadequate
resource. Elisha intervenes to produce a miracle (associated with
the declaration that there is no evil word [thing] in the pot, 4:41 AT;
associated with the word of the LORD, 4:44). The vocabulary of these
two miracles stories underscores the Deuteronomic values of the
prophetic community. Jesus and the Christian community extend
the tradition of sharing the supply of bread in compassion to those
in need (Mark 6:30-44; Acts 2:45-46; 6:1-6).

THE TEXT IN BIBLICAL CONTEXT
Women Characters in Kings

Two female characters play primary roles in 2 Kings 4. A prophet's
widow appeals to Elisha for assistance with a creditor (4:1-7). A
wealthy woman persuades Elisha to eat her food, her husband to
build a roof chamber for the prophet, and the prophet to save her
dead son (4:8-37). These two women, like most women in 1–2 Kings,
are unnamed.

Women associated with Elijah and Elisha are distant from the
corridors of power. The widow of Zarephath—in contrast to Jezebel,

the queen from the same region—offers hospitality to Elijah and later confesses that the word of the Lord is with the prophet (1 Kings 17:9-24). Like the widow of Zarephath, the Shunammite woman provides hospitality by offering a prophet's "chamber," has a son who lives because of the prophet's intervention, later loses him to death, then receives the revived son back to life after the prophet's appeal to the Lord. Distant from royal power, both mothers accuse the prophets of responsibility for the deaths of their sons, demanding justice.

Outside the royal narrative, likely unaware of royal power plays and the Deuteronomic covenant, these female characters initiate action to influence the prophet. The widow of Zarephath has experienced the drought and famine that are judgment on Ahab. The widow of the prophetic guild suffers poverty because of royal policy. The Shunammite woman ignores royal power in 2 Kings 4, though later famine affects her land and she depends on royal action to restore her land and earnings (8:1-6). In a male-dominated narrative, these female characters initiate action independently. Their stories depict domestic life outside the corridors of power [Women in Kings, p. 485].

Bread of the Firstfruits

The Feast of Firstfruits (Festival of Weeks) is one of three major festivals requiring attendance of all Israel (Exod 23:14-19). This harvest festival brings first of the wheat harvest to the Lord (34:22; Lev 2:14; the first of the barley is offered at Passover time, seven weeks earlier, Num 28:16). Grain offerings benefit the Levitical priests (Lev 23:17, 20). The presentation of the firstfruits bread to the prophetic guild suggests a relationship with the Levitical priests (Exod 23, 34; Lev 2, 23; Num 18). Both groups depend on offerings for their physical needs. Neither has real estate. Their share of the land is the tithe presented to the Lord (Num 18:20-26).

Both Levitical priests and prophets champion the Deuteronomic covenant. When Jeroboam rejects the covenant stipulations, he replaces the Levites. When Jezebel usurps the property of Naboth, a prophet speaks out against her actions. When the Omride dynasty rules in Israel, a prophetic guild gathers as a community to protect individuals, providing resources for the marginalized who are adversely affected by royal policy. Royal power opposes instruction regarding Deuteronomic covenant values by marginalizing prophet and priest. The prophetic guild tells tales of resistance to counter the hegemony of the Omride power structure (Rentería: 113,

125–26). In postexilic Israel the Torah was associated with the Feast of Firstfruits (Exod 20; 23:16-17).

In first-century Judaism the day of Pentecost climaxes the Feast of Firstfruits. The Spirit unites believers from every nation, empowers the church for mission and fellowship, and teaches disciples the way of Jesus. Learning from Torah, the church shares with those in need.

THE TEXT IN THE LIFE OF THE CHURCH
Powers for Death and Life

Like the stories of Elijah (1 Kings 17–19), the stories of Elisha (2 Kings 4–7) contrast the death associated with royal power and the life associated with the prophetic community (Seow: 191; Wray Beal 2014: 326–28; Brueggemann 2000: 326–29). Ahab's family falsely credits Baal as life-giver. Baal gives only death; Yahweh alone gives life. In contrast to the sterile, closed royal system, prophetic imagination offers miraculous, death-defying, egalitarian community. Political structures, economics, debt slavery, health, food distribution, and ecology are disordered under the Baal-royal realm but abundant under Yahwistic covenant. "The man of God acts on more than just a grand political scale" but addresses as well "the mundane, personal needs of people living life day to day" (Seow: 191).

In his sermon proclaiming "the year of the Lord's favor," Jesus appeals to both Elijah and Elisha to express his vision to extend God's Jubilee beyond Israel (Luke 4:18-27). Like the prophets, Jesus raises a dead girl (Mark 5:40-42) and the widow's son (Luke 7:11-17), feeds the hungry crowds (Mark 6:30-44), and heals lepers (1:40-45; Luke 17:11-19). The church structures itself as an egalitarian community that meets economic and social needs, with concern for widows (Acts 2:43-47; 4:32-37; 6:1-7). Followers of Jesus in Anabaptist communities seek to live with countercultural, life-giving values. Ron Sider, an ordained Mennonite and Brethren in Christ minister, has called Christians to recognize the spiritual, social, and political implications of the Bible that lead to a consistently pro-life strategy, seeking economic wholeness as well as eternal life.

Elisha's local strategy empowers economic initiatives. In 2 Kings 4, Elisha's miraculous interventions include initiative and participation by those in need. The social enterprise initiative of the Center for Community Transformation at Fresno [Calif.] Pacific Biblical Seminary helps start small businesses that create jobs. Rock Pile Yard Services is a landscaping business of FACE (Fresno Area Community Enterprises), the community outreach organization of

North Fresno Mennonite Brethren Church designed to meet the economic, social, and spiritual needs of its immediate neighborhood. Rock Pile Yard Services employs those who face nearly insurmountable obstacles to employment. Church-based initiatives such as Rock Pile and FACE do locally what Mennonite Central Committee and Brethren Disaster Ministries have done globally to free those trapped in unjust structures.

2 Kings 5:1-27

Naaman the Leper, Elisha, and Gehazi

PREVIEW

When a family member suffered a serious infection while on holidays in London, we were astonished to receive immediate free access to a skilled physician, who wrote a prescription that was filled by the chemist for less than a British pound. Canadians and Americans love to debate who has better access to universal healthcare. The politicization of healthcare is much older than liberal democracy, as evidenced by the healing of Naaman.

In the story of Naaman, Elisha's struggle with life over death shifts from domestic life to international politics. In 2 Kings 4, Elisha depends on the Lord to provide life to marginalized households. In 2 Kings 5, Elisha's dependence on the Lord extends life to a foreign political power but exposes grasping exploitation in his own household. The enemy Naaman arrives in Samaria with an ostentatious display of military power, demanding a miraculous cure. The loyal Israelite Elisha offers help. The following chapter describes further Aramean military exercises disarmed by Elisha (6:8-23).

This story demonstrates that power lies not with political, economic, or military forces but with the word of the Lord. The temptation to use religious position for personal advantage seems greatest for those with great spiritual gifts—not only in the biblical story but also in contemporary life. The characters in 2 Kings 5 demonstrate a range of possibilities for dealing with the temptation—from a slave girl's selfless testimony to God's power to the unassuming authority of the prophet, and even to the grasping greed of one who takes advantage of his proximity to power.

OUTLINE

Act 1: The Cure, 5:1-14
    5:1-7   Scene 1: Naaman's Quest
    5:8-10   Scene 2: Elisha's Offer
    5:11-14   Scene 3: Naaman's Response
Act 2: The Conversion, 5:15-19a
Act 3: The Contamination, 5:19b-27
    5:19b-24 Scene 1: Gehazi's Initiative
    5:25-27   Scene 2: Elisha's Judgment

EXPLANATORY NOTES

The healing of Naaman, a miracle story, is related in three acts; each act resolves the conflict and could end the story. Yet acts 2 and 3 extend the story, further demonstrating the storyteller's skill. Repeated terms and contrasts artfully communicate the tale. The little girl from Israel who stands in the presence of the wife of the great man of Aram offers a word of hope to her captors. After his skin is restored (returned) to that of a little boy, the great man returns to stand in the presence of the Israelite man of God. When the man of God refuses the great man's gifts, the man makes additional requests. The story ends when the servant who stands in the presence of the man of God attempts to profit from the healing; then he must leave the presence of Elisha because the great man's illness now clings to that servant and his family.

Act 1: The Cure 5:1-14

5:1-7 *Scene 1: Naaman's Quest*

Naaman, commander of the Aramean king's army, is *great* (cf. 4:8) in the presence of (*before*) his master, a valiant warrior through whom the Lord granted victory to Aram (5:1; anticipating the Lord's use of empires as his instruments of judgment). These positive attributes pale in insignificance compared to the last descriptor: Naaman has leprosy, a socially debilitating skin disease, whatever its precise medical diagnosis (most consider it unlikely that ancient leprosy is Hansen's disease, modern leprosy; perhaps it is disfiguring absence of skin pigmentation; Alter: 543). Naaman's great reputation is the more ironic (and galling to Naaman), given the disabling disease.

A *little girl* enslaved during an Aramean raid of Israel *stands before* (NRSV: *serves*) the wife of the *great man* Naaman (5:2-3). To *stand before* someone is a recurring idiom in this story, indicating a subservient relationship (Alter: 543). Though exiled, the maid speaks to her *mistress* (the feminine of *warrior* in 5:1): *If only my lord were before [in the presence of] the prophet in Samaria; then he would cure him of his leprosy* (5:3 AT; cf. 5:6, 7, 11). In the chain of command the small girl *stands before* the valiant woman, wife of the great commander, who *stands before* his master, the king. The small girl wishes for the lord to *stand before [as petitioner of]* the prophet as he currently *stands before [in service to]* his king (MT). The story subverts the royal power structure (for analysis of the narrative contrasts, see Cohn 1983).

When Naaman reports the girl's words to the king, he orders Naaman to go, *sending* with him a letter of authorization to the king of Israel (5:4-5) *[Send, p. 476]*. Naaman departs, taking a king's ransom in silver, gold, and clothing. The king assumes that healthcare is the prerogative of the state, that it is very costly, that it is for sale to those with sufficient wealth; he is unable to hear the little girl's statement that healing comes to one who *stands before* (*petitions*) the prophet.

The commander brings the Aramean king's letter to the unnamed king of Israel (5:6; anonymity emphasizes his unimportance). King-to-king, the letter demands a cure. *With this letter, attention [Surprise!], I send my servant Naaman so you will cure him of his leprosy* (AT) *[Literary Criticism: Elements of Narrative, p. 458]*. This is a state matter. The king of Aram flexes his superior muscles over the king of Israel, demanding access to his healthcare system.

Upon reading the letter, in an act of distress or grief (cf. 6:30), the ignorant, powerless, unnamed king tears his own garments (contrast the new clothing sent as payment for the cure). *Am I a god, to control life and death?* (5:7 AT). The question is ironic because royal Baal ideology attributes divine authority over life, land, and the justice system to the king. The distressed king imagines a conspiracy and calls on his courtiers to see the obvious: not that Yahweh through his prophet has power of life and death but that the Arameans are picking a quarrel.

Scene 1 sets the action. The powerful Aramean king, having received intelligence from a small captive Israelite girl, sends a letter with his powerful but diseased army commander, offering extravagant payment for the cure from leprosy. Chain-of-command power politics are in play. In this narrative world, however, power is upside down. The little captive girl, with her knowledge of the prophet, is at the top. To his dismay the desperate king of Israel finds himself outside the corridors of power.

5:8-10 Scene 2: Elisha's Offer

Scene 2 opens when Elisha the man of God, who has eyes and ears in the palace, learns that the king has torn his clothes in despair (5:8). He *sends* to the king, asking why he has torn his clothes, implying that his distress results from his false perception that as king he is the powerful one in Israel. Using the term of deference, perhaps ironically, the prophet offers, *Please, have him come to me* (AT). As the result, the powerful commander of the empire will learn what only the little captive girl in Aram knows: there is a prophet in Israel empowered by God. The entourage of horses and chariots arrives at the prophet's gate (5:9). In deference, Naaman *stands* at the doorway (see 5:11, 15-16; a variation on *before* in 5:1), recognizing that power lies with God's prophet. Elisha *sends a messenger* to the waiting commander, who tells him, *Go* (the third time this verb is used; the king of Aram had also ordered Naaman, *Go!*, and he *went* in 5:5), *wash in the Jordan seven times.* That Elisha does not even come out and stand before the mighty warrior reinforces his rejection of the royal view of power. The prophet promises Naaman that his flesh will be *restored* (*return*; MT: *šub*) to him and he will be *clean* (being ceremonially clean is referenced fifty-seven times in Leviticus; e.g., clean from leprosy, Lev 13:6). The name *Elisha* disappears from the text after 5:10; he is not named as a character again until he confronts Gehazi (5:25).

5:11-14 Scene 3: Naaman's Response

The unspoken demonstration of power is not lost on Naaman, who is furious (5:11)! As he has done when ordered to go by the king (5:5), he obeys Elisha's command to leave, but now he goes off to talk to himself. "*Attention!*" [the word indicates a shift in perspective; see the essay *Literary Criticism: Elements of Narrative, p. 458*]. "*I thought to me he will definitely come out, and stand, and call in the name of Yahweh his God, and wave his hand* [the term used of the cultic "wave offering," Lev 7:30; 8:29 NIV], *and cure the leprosy.*" *He did an about-face and stormed off* (AT; *about-face*, from the root for *before*, indicates subservience; cf. 2 Kings 5:1). Naaman's charged rhetoric exposes his fury that Elisha has refused to treat him with the expected honor.

Naaman's servants face a delicate task. Having made this arduous trek, Naaman's furious rejection of Elisha's perceived slight will end in greater humiliation, as the servants recognize. The servants *approach* Naaman (5:13; the verb is used to describe Moses' unique proximity to the Lord, Exod 20:21; 24:2; the cautious *approach* of the prophetic guild to Elisha, 2 Kings 2:5). Like the *little* girl who is powerless aside from what she knows about the prophet, the servants have little power beyond their wisdom; but both the girl and the servants are effective agents in the healing (contrast the supposedly self-assured powerful king of Israel; Ngan: 591; W. Smith: 208–11).

Addressing Naaman with respect and endearment, *My father,* they use irrefutable logic to point out that if the commander would have been willing to perform a great feat, a muddy bath in the Jordan is worth the risk. Listening to his servants' coaxing, Naaman acts *according to the word of the man of God,* dipping *seven times* (5:14).

Reciting Elisha's words exactly, the story reports that *his flesh was restored like that of a little boy, and he was clean*—as promised by the *little girl.*

The cleansing of Naaman is the great reversal of the story. The man *great before his master* follows the advice of the little girl who stands before his wife; he stands before the Israelite man of God, who humiliates Naaman by refusing to stand before him, sending a messenger as he would to an inconsequential visitor. The cure is effected without the expected ritual, but through a muddy bath repeated seven times, a sign of total humiliation. With the reversal complete, Naaman's skin is *restored* (*šub,* the word for *return* from exile or *repent*) like that of a little boy. The contrast in power is not primarily between Aram and Israel, but between the Lord's prophet and the royal military establishment of Aram and Israel.

Act 2: The Conversion 5:15-19a

Naaman's *restored* skin results in a converted mindset. As promised, Naaman's flesh is *restored* (5:10, 14). This *commander* himself *returns to (restored or transformed)* the man of God (5:15).

Naaman has come *with his horses and chariots;* now *he and all his company* [cf. 6:24: *entire army*] *come and stand before him* (5:9, 15). Naaman's speech indicates transformation as he dramatically declares his new perspective: *Behold! The God of Israel is the only God in the earth* (5:15 AT). Naaman's monotheistic confession of Yahweh's exclusivity expresses the Deuteronomic perspective, in positive contrast to Israel (Deut 6:4; 32:21, 39) [*Kings in the Hebrew Canon: Kings and Deuteronomy, p. 453*].

Naaman begs, *Please accept a present [blessing] from your servant* (2 Kings 5:15b). Because he (Elisha) *stands before* the living Lord (5:16 AT), he refuses to *take (grasp)* goods from Naaman (the Hebrew term

for *grasp* is used in 5:5, 15, 16 [twice], 20 [twice], 23, 24, 26 [twice];
Achan grasps the banned goods, Josh 6:18; 7:1). Naaman *urges* him to
grasp it (5:23), but the man of God refuses in an oath to the Lord, who
saves and provides (as demonstrated in the four stories of 2 Kings 4).

Elisha's posture as a servant of the Lord prohibits his acceptance
of the gift. Naaman reconsiders, then confesses that the Lord, not his
servant the prophet, has the authoritative healing power (Ngan: 592).

Naaman, politely (saying *"your servant"* twice) requests that he be
given *two mule-loads of earth* so that he can worship the Lord on
Israelite soil (5:17). He will, he adjures, worship no other God but
Yahweh. With his next breath, however, Naaman begs for an indulgence: *On one count* [or *in this word/thing*], *may the* LORD *pardon your
servant* (the word *pardon* is used frequently in Leviticus and Numbers
for forgiveness associated with the cultic sacrifice and in Solomon's
dedicatory prayer in 1 Kings 8). Naaman realizes that his position will
compromise his vow, forcing yet another *turn*. He will be obligated to
give his hand (*power*) to his master and to bow in homage to the
Aramean god Rimmon. The opening request is repeated to conclude
this speech: *May the* LORD *please pardon your servant in this one count*
(AT). Elisha's reply, *Shalom*, is ambiguous, leaving in doubt whether
forgiveness has been granted because he and the Lord understand
that political realities sometimes demand compromises, or whether
it is a final (resigned or ironic) greeting, *Farewell!* (5:19a AT; Fritz: 260).
In the end Naaman behaves much like Israel, confessing that the Lord
is God (1 Kings 18:39) while accepting the existence of other gods.

The second act, the shortest, is narrated primarily as dialogue.
Having retained freedom and integrity by refusing Naaman's gift,
the prophet bids him farewell. While the story might well end there,
a final act opens in 5:19b.

Act 3: The Contamination 5:19b-27

5:19b-24 Scene 1: Gehazi's Initiative

The royal perspective trades in power, wealth, and violence.

Gehazi introduces another perspective. Though Gehazi is the
young man of Elisha (AT), he does not live within the imaginative freedom of his master (5:20). Gehazi's self-talk lays out his strategy.
Behold! (untranslated in NIV and NRSV) could be rendered "This calls
for a different perspective!" His master had spared *that Aramean
Naaman* (the language is disparaging) by failing to *grasp* the spoils
from his *power* (hand). Elisha had sworn by Yahweh to take nothing
(5:16), but Gehazi swears, *By Yahweh, I will race after him* to *seize something from him* (AT; Gehazi has *raced* to bring life to the Shunammite's

son, 4:24, 26). Gehazi *pursues* Naaman (5:21; Pharaoh's army pursues
Israel, Exod 14:4, 8, 9, 23). Naaman alights from his chariot of war
with the conventional but ironic, *Shalom?* Gehazi answers, *Shalom!*,
as he violates shalom. *My master sends me with this word.* "*Surprisingly,
at this very moment, two young boys from the prophetic guild have arrived*"
(5:21-22 AT; cf. 5:14, 20, 23). Gehazi plunges on, asking politely for
silver and clothing. Back in the world of patronage, Naaman *urges*
Gehazi as he had Elisha, *Grasp double,* and orders two of his *young
boys* to *go before* Gehazi (AT). The delicious irony of a miniature
reversal of Naaman's caravan with Aramean spoils becomes awkward as Gehazi approaches *the citadel* (5:24). Gehazi *grasps* from their
power (*their hands*), *stores* their gifts, and *sends the men* on their way
(AT; Gehazi is giving orders like royalty).

5:25-27 Scene 2: Elisha's Judgment

In the final scene, Gehazi *stands to his lord* (not *before;* perhaps indicating opposition rather than submission). Elisha (named for the
first time since 5:10) asks succinctly, *From where, Gehazi?* He responds
deferentially, *Your servant didn't go out and about* (5:25 AT).

Elisha's judgment speech accuses, *Didn't my heart go with you when
a man turned from up in his chariot to meet you? Is now the time to grasp
silver and to grasp clothing?* (5:26 AT). Gehazi received the first two
items mentioned from Naaman. The rest of the items listed in
Elisha's accusation are luxury items that Gehazi might purchase
with his double silver jackpot. *Olive orchards and vineyards* are prototypical Israelite uses of the land. *Sheep and oxen* usually refer to sacrificial animals in 1–2 Kings. *Slaves* are the marginalized who suffer
injustice. The list reads like Samuel's warning regarding the administrative policies of the king (1 Sam 8:10-17) [*Mišpaṭ, p. 461*].

Elisha announces judgment: *Therefore the leprosy of Naaman shall
cling to you, and to your descendants forever* (2 Kings 5:27; Deut 13:17
warns against allowing consecrated items to "cling to their hand";
28:21 threatens that pestilence and disease will "cling" to disobedient Israel). Like Gehazi, servant of Elisha, Israel, servant of the Lord,
has chosen to allow injustice to cling to them. Like Gehazi going out
from *the face of* Elisha (AT), Israel will go out from the presence of the
Lord into exile.

THE TEXT IN BIBLICAL CONTEXT
Leprosy as Punishment

In isolated cases leprosy is part of a curse, a brief punishment, or a
lifelong banishment. More typical is the apparent problem of a skin

disease that requires priestly attention, teaching, and adjudication. Diagnosing leprosy is detailed in Leviticus 13–14. Being unclean is not necessarily related to sin. The Bible first mentions leprosy as one of the signs for Moses (Exod 4:6). Leprosy is punishment for sin in the rebellion of Miriam and Aaron (Num 12). David curses the family of Joab with ongoing leprosy when Joab assassinates Abner (2 Sam 3:29). King Uzziah's proud usurpation of priestly duties in the temple results in leprosy (2 Kings 15:5; 2 Chron 26:19-23). Lepers play a key role in breaking the Syrian siege (2 Kings 7).

There is no indication that Naaman's leprosy is punishment for sin even though Naaman may be guilty of war crimes against Israel, including abduction of the young girl serving Naaman's wife. So Naaman's leprosy is an unexplained circumstance; yet without doubt Gehazi contracts the disease as judgment. Leprosy fits the offense since Gehazi benefits from Naaman's healing when the Lord is to be reverenced as provider. Naaman has arrived with arrogance but leaves humbled by the simple cleansing procedure, by the prophet's rejection of payment, and by being reduced to begging for Israelite dirt. Gehazi arrogates profit to himself from Naaman's misfortune despite the prophet's example to the contrary.

The disease of Miriam and of King Uzziah is like that of Gehazi in two regards. One, the disease is punishment for sin. Two, the sin is one of seeking prestige. After reporting that Miriam, with Aaron, is agitating against Moses' leadership role, the narrative describes Moses as the most humble man ever (Num 12:1-3). Though 2 Kings 15 reports only that Uzziah becomes leprous, Chronicles clarifies that when the king becomes proud, the Lord strikes him with leprosy, the priests exclude him from the house of the Lord, and his son replaces him as ruler (2 Chron 26:21). Like Uzziah and Miriam, Gehazi's arrogance results in shameful exclusion from the people of God.

Healing for the Nations

The violent exclusion of non-Israelites from the covenant with Yahweh troubles contemporary readers. Deuteronomy 7:1-6 promises that the Lord will "clear away" the occupying nations; it commands that Israel must "defeat them" and "utterly destroy them." Postexilic Ezra sends away wives and children who are identified as "peoples of the lands with their abominations" (Ezra 9). Faithfulness precludes association with those who cannot show Israelite pedigree—more so, demands destruction of such persons when they are in the land of Israel.

The treatment of Naaman contrasts sharply with that perspective. Other texts also take a more positive view of nonbiological Israel. When Israel exits Egypt, the text reports that "a mixed crowd also went up with them" (Exod 12:38). When Israel enters Canaan, Rahab and her family are included because Rahab deals "kindly and faithfully" with the spies (Josh 2). David is descended from Ruth of Moab (Ruth 4:13-22). Isaiah promises that the nations will stream to the Lord's mountain (Isa 2:2) and that nations will come to their light (60:3). Jonah shows that the Lord forgives those who repent, even wicked Nineveh. Deuteronomy emphasizes that strangers are to be welcomed into the father's house, strangers who include unrelated homeless people from within or outside Israel (Deut 10:19; 14:28-29; 16:13-14; 31:12; Ruth 1-4).

Kings is generally suspicious of foreigners (e.g., Solomon's foreign wives are regarded as the source of his trouble), but several texts picture non-Israelites more positively. The queen of Sheba implores Solomon to practice justice (1 Kings 10:1-11). Elijah's stay with the widow of Zarephath extends life to her and her son (17:8-24). The raiding party from Aram is given a feast when they are captured (2 Kings 6:20-23).

These stories anticipate the gospel of Jesus. Particularly apt is the healing of the demon-possessed daughter of the Syrophoenician woman in Mark 7:24-30 (called a Canaanite in Matt 15:21-28). Jesus applauds the faith of the foreign leper who returns to give thanks (Luke 17:11-19). The gospel is radically inclusive, prompting believers to "struggle for the breadth of love and acceptance that more nearly approximates the breadth of God's love. The paradox of the gospel is that its unlimited grace so scandalizes us that we are unable to receive it" (Culpepper: 108).

THE TEXT IN THE LIFE OF THE CHURCH
Pursue the Lord: Seek First the Kingdom

Two worldviews clash. The autonomous royal view values physical prowess, military might, political hierarchy, gender exclusivity, and economic wealth. This mindset offers both haves and have-nots a set of values that determines place. The prophetic worldview imagines life shaped by righteousness and justice.

Two worldviews clash in the contemporary world as well. While different elements of the imperial worldview may receive more emphasis, militaristic consumerism and entertainment have given advantage to the *haves*. Privilege is tied to race, gender, nationality, and age. Sexism and misogyny not only create glass ceilings but also result in exploitative focus on sexuality—and a thriving pornography industry.

Elisha exposes the world powers and shuns the advantages he might reap from them. He offers health to the powerful enemy, knocking down walls of exclusion. Yet he challenges these very powers by refusing to approve of Naaman's compromises or to receive what the imperial system values. Gehazi's pursuit of these commodities pollutes his family.

Jesus teaches disciples to pursue first God's rule in this world and God's commitment to righteous justice for the marginalized. He guides that pursuit by warning against worry and the accumulation of treasures on earth (Matt 6:19-34). Anabaptist Christians have long struggled with how to encourage one another to pursue righteousness. Binding and loosing has proved particularly challenging (18:15-20). In article 4, the 1527 Schleitheim Confession calls for separation "from the evil and from the wickedness the devil planted in the world. . . . The command of the Lord is clear when He calls upon us to be separate from the evil." Things highly regarded by the world are suspect and require the believing community to withdraw from Babylon and earthly Egypt. Before long, separation becomes linked to simplicity and simplicity linked to restrictive dress. When coupled with the ban (art. 2, also part of the original confession and demanding separation from believers who refuse to receive discipline), legalism seems to be inevitable.

Contemporary disciples pursue God's rule while eschewing worldly pursuits. How easily legalism distorts these values when a community seeks to put them into practice. Elisha's warning that now is not the time for accumulation guides the discerning community.

Menno's Example

Menno Simons lived by the values of Elisha, who provides healing for the Arameans returning to arrest Elisha in the following chapter (2 Kings 6:14). In 1545, Menno Simons was evicted from his haven in East Friesland (in Germany) by Empress Anna on the recommendation of the Reformed leader John à Lasco, who judged Menno to be a heretic. In the winter of 1554, a ship bearing members of John à Lasco's exiled congregation arrived as refugees at the Lutheran city of Wismar. That city refused to rescue the Reformed congregation when their ship froze in harbor. Knowing the former hostility and the present risk, the congregation led by Menno (resettled in Wismar) rescued the refugees, provided them refuge, and engaged in disputation about matters of faith. In a bid to win favor in the Lutheran region, these Reformed church members published a list of Mennonites, leading to their expulsion from this haven. For the Mennonites, providing help for those in need was a higher value than their own safety.

Anonymous Christians

Contemporary missiologists struggle with an issue akin to Naaman's request for pardon when he bows to Rimmon (2 Kings 5:18-19). Though Jesuit theologian Karl Rahner coined the phrase "anonymous Christian" to describe a person who lives in the grace of God and attains salvation outside of explicitly constituted Christianity, the descriptor might be extended to Jesus-followers who do not leave the Hindu or Muslim communities where they are converted. Proponents of the Hindu Krista Bhakta movement argue that Hindus who turn to Christ should not be forced to abandon their culture and identity, but rather should be Jesus-followers while serving God as Hindus. Rather than being baptized and joining a Christian church, these converts participate in a water ceremony and attend house churches. Though Islam presents a different situation, Christian missionaries explore evangelistic methods that allow converts to remain in Islam. Does Elisha's response to Naaman's request inform contemporary consideration of the question? Lasine suggests that readers are free to choose from three interpretive options (2011: 24-25). First, Elisha's word of "Shalom" may reflect his indifference to the question (5:19). Lasine contrasts Elisha's theological focus (e.g., his failure to make a Yahweh-only argument to the Arameans, 6:15-23) with Elijah's anti-Baal polemic (2011: 9-15). Second, the reader may read shalom as blessing, the recognition that real-life faith demands compromises. Third, the reader may read shalom as dismissively ironic, evidence that Elisha rejects Naaman's confession as insincere. Earlier Christians allowed little room for compromise. When a Christian inquirer protested that he could not leave the military position he held when converted, "because I must live!" Tertullian is said to have replied, "Must you?" As Christians we seek to serve the one who became flesh to reveal God, the one who is "full of grace and truth" (John 1:14).

2 Kings 6:1–7:20

Elisha's Final Three Acts of Deliverance

PREVIEW

When the apartheid South African government tried to silence opposition in 1989, worshipers filled Saint George's Cathedral in Cape Town. As Archbishop Desmond Tutu was preaching, hundreds of police entered the cathedral in a show of force intended to intimidate. Armed with automatic weapons, they lined the walls, took out notebooks, and recorded Tutu's words. Not to be intimidated, Tutu addressed the police directly. "You are powerful, very powerful, but you are not gods, and I serve a God who cannot be mocked. So, since you've already lost, I invite you today to join the winning side!" The congregation erupted in dance and song and spilled into the streets. The police's armed intimidation had failed, overcome by the archbishop's confidence that God would triumph over evil (Wallis: 347–48).

Elisha, the man of God, has proved to be equally at ease with kings and generals (2 Kings 3, 5) and with people far from the corridors of power (4:1-44). Elisha is a leading character in three miracle stories in 2 Kings 6–7. The first involves a day in the life of the prophetic guild (6:1-7). In the next story—involving kings, armies, chariots, and horses—Elisha gives courage to his servant and peace to his land (6:8-23). The third story relates a miracle including vulnerable women and the king's court, the Aramean army, and four lepers (6:24–7:20). God brings justice to marginalized persons.

The stories read like comedies. Though without a laugh track to help contemporary readers catch ancient humor, these stories feature not only comic elements but also comedy in classical definition, as in the positive ending of Shakespearean comedy. Though each has a positive outcome in an otherwise dark narrative, the issues are serious, pointing Israel to the salvation found in Deuteronomic values rather than the royal systems of power.

OUTLINE

Miracle of the Ax Head, 6:1-7
Seeing Horses and Chariots, 6:8-23
The Siege of Samaria, 6:24–7:20
    6:24-31   Siege and Famine
    6:32–7:2   Elisha's Prediction of Relief
    7:3-15   The Lepers' Discovery of Deliverance
    7:16-20   Fulfillment of Two Prophecies

EXPLANATORY NOTES
Miracle of the Ax Head 6:1-7

This story is the quintessential test of credulity regarding the historicity of biblical miracles. The combined unlikelihood of the event and insignificance of the loss work together to create skepticism among readers otherwise willing to accept miracle stories as lived events. As one wit asked, "If the question is whether God *could* do such a miracle, I have no doubt that the Creator of the universe could do so. My question is why the Creator of the universe would *want* to do so." This juxtaposition of questions suggests the need to better understand what is at stake in the prophetic community, what the text says about the reported event, and the possibility of reading the story as laugh-out-loud humor [*Literary Criticism: Narrative Subgenres, p. 460*].

The report is straightforward. The prophetic community's living quarters have become too *tight* (6:1 AT). The housing shortage may result from growth in the prophetic guild as marginalized persons are squeezed off the land by economic disparities exacerbated by royal political policies, all this coupled with the attraction of the charismatic Elisha (Rentería: 115). Community members propose a do-it-yourself building project to their leader Elisha, who accompanies them in their work—a day in the woods chopping trees (6:2-4).

When the ax head of one of the prophets falls into the Jordan (6:5), his exclamation of woe seems an overreaction. Why does the loss of a borrowed iron ax head provoke such consternation, let alone a place in the story of miraculous intervention? Iron was a highly valued commodity in ancient Israel. Though Israel was no longer dependent on Philistia for ironsmiths (1 Sam 13:19-22), the metal was relatively rare, essential for agricultural and military tools, and valued like gold for ornamental use. The loss of a large iron tool would be economically devastating for the impoverished community. Elisha characteristically involves the community in the solution, asking the man to point out the location of the loss and throwing a stick in the spot. NIV and NRSV report that he *made the iron float* (2 Kings 6:6). Both of the other uses of the verb can be translated "the water flowed" (Deut 11:4; Lam 3:54 AT). Whether the miracle is floating iron or some long-forgotten change in river current, the missing ax head is located. Elisha again engages the worker by having him *throw out his hand* to retrieve the valued tool (6:7 AT).

The storytelling is exquisite. Having healed the most-feared enemy general of leprosy, a prophet in the woods with his disciples is unflappable when a valued tool is lost. A man who can save a soldier from leprosy can make iron float. *God saves* (the meaning of the name *Elisha*) the prophetic community. When read in context after the healing of Naaman, the story demonstrates Elisha's concern not only for international politics but also for ordinary persons, the sons of the prophets, whom Elisha honors with his presence (Gilmour: 161, 213) *[Prophets: Sons of the Prophets, p. 467]*.

Seeing Horses and Chariots 6:8-23

The focus returns to the stage of international politics, kings, and horses and chariots. Though affairs of nations are in play, the story centers on the attendant of the man of God receiving vision that reorients his perception of power. By subverting the overwhelming first-strike, shock-and-awe firepower and the state-of-the-art spyware of the king of Aram, Elisha playfully reimagines how power works (Wray Beal 2014: 345). The narrative continues to highlight Elisha's prescient vision (2:3, 5; 4:16, 27; 5:26; 6:9, 12, 16-17; 7:2). Human-generated war ends with God-given peace—and possibly a chuckle about how an unarmed man defeats the entire Aramean army.

The scene opens in the secret councils of the unnamed king of Aram who was warring against Israel (6:8). In consultation with his military advisers, the king sets ambushes to trap Israel. The *man of God* counters Aram's military action by *sending [Send, p. 476]* to the king of Israel, calling on him to be on guard in passing the specific location of the Aramean ambush (6:9). The king in turn repeatedly passes on the warning (6:10), thus thwarting the Aramean strategy.

In the councils of Aram, the king's heart *storms* (AT; cf. Jon 1:11, 13) with rage. Summoning his servants, he interrogates them to discover the leak (2 Kings 6:11). One of the king's spymasters fingers Elisha, whose intelligence penetrates the secret chambers of the Aramean palace itself (6:12). The king activates his spy network to find Israel's secret agent (6:13). They report that Elisha is in Dothan, the strategic outpost guarding the rich Jezreel valley and Samaria, the capital city, and twelve miles to the north of Samaria (cf. Gen 37:17). The king of Aram *sends* an overwhelming military force of horses and chariots and his large army to surround the city and arrest the prophet (2 Kings 6:14; cf. 1 Kings 20:1, 26-27). A story told to mock the national power of a militarized state would be hard-pressed to set up a better situation: the king with the greatest stealth strategies in the region is being grounded by a low-tech prophet who simply sends a message to the king of Israel to avoid suspicious places.

The attendant of the man of God rises early the next day, startled *[Literary Criticism: Elements of Narrative, p. 458]* to see the city surrounded by horses and chariots (2 Kings 6:15). Echoing the words of the junior prophet who had lost the ax head (6:5), the servant cries out in terror, *Alas, my lord! What will we do?* (AT). Elisha responds to the distress of isolation, abandonment, and helplessness with a prophetic word of salvation and reorientation grounded in the presence of the Lord (Brueggemann 2000: 347). *Don't be afraid,* he says, *our forces outnumber the enemy* (6:16 AT). In the first of three prayers that affect vision, Elisha asks that God open the servant's eyes so that he can see (Heb. *see* [*yirʾeh*] and *fear* [*tiraʾ*] sound similar, though spelled differently; vision from the Lord will replace fright). The Lord responds as Elisha has prayed, opens the man's eyes, and empowers him to see what is not visible to the ordinary eye. To the servant's surprise (and perhaps glee: *Behold!*), *the mountain is full of horses and chariots of fire all around Elisha* (6:17). If horses and chariots measure power, horses and chariots of fire evidence the Lord's superior power (cf. 2:11).

The enemy came down toward him (6:18 AT; cf. Naaman *going down* into the Jordan, 5:14). Elisha interrupts the Aramean army just as it is poised to strike, praying the Lord to *smite this gentile nation with blindness* (AT; or *bedazzled*; this word is used elsewhere only when the men of Sodom were blinded by the angels, Gen 19:11; Hobbs: 78). The Lord acts according to Elisha's word.

Elisha continues to toy with the army, offering what he claims to be superior military intelligence but leading the blinded men into Samaria (6:19). A blinded army follows an unknown guide, the person they have been sent to capture. Instead, this little underdog captures the huge army.

Inside Samaria's walls, Elisha prays the third time for a change in vision (6:20). The Lord responds as requested, again opening blind eyes so that they can see their unexpected (behold!) situation: they are inside the enemy capital. The Arameans' predicament is the comic punch line.

Now the king of Israel *sees* the unexpected: the enemy at his mercy in his capital! In his excitement the king turns to the prophet for counsel. Addressing Elisha as *My father*, his excitement is conveyed in the repeated question, *Shall I strike them? Shall I strike them?* (6:21 AT; *strike* with blindness, 6:18; cf. *strike* Moab, 3:23-25).

Elisha's reply is emphatic: *No, you shall not strike them* (6:22 AT). His reasoning, *Would you kill those you have captured with your own sword or bow?* (NIV), counters the prophet's confrontation of the king in 1 Kings 20 when the captured King Ben-hadad of Aram is released rather than executed (*strike* occurs eleven times in 1 Kings 20). Where some see implicit criticism of the earlier failure to *strike* Ben-hadad, other readers see criticism of violent military strategy. Elisha instructs the king to serve the enemy bread and water (Obadiah's food for prophets, 1 Kings 18:4, 13) and let them go. The king exceeds the prophet's instruction, preparing a *great feast* (2 Kings 6:23). The king of Israel *sends* them to their master (a royal sending in peace). Feeding the helpless enemy results in the end of the Aramean raids.

In a story with exaggerated proportions, Elisha reads the mind of Aram's king, who sends horses and chariots to capture this unarmed man. Fortified by fiery chariots, Elisha asks the Lord to open and close eyes until the enemy is captured in Israel's capital. The king of Israel follows Elisha's orders, and peace breaks out! Is this comic relief? An underdog story? Satire on the powerlessness of the ruling elite (LaBarbera: 637)? A factual military report? The story is filled with wonder.

The story concludes that *marauding bands* stopped *raiding* (6:23 AT). Rezon of Damascus first organizes *marauding bands* (1 Kings 11:24-25). One of these bands kidnaps the girl who will become Naaman's servant (2 Kings 5:2). Later, when a Moabite *marauding band* surprises them, a burial party tosses the corpse into Elisha's tomb; the dead man is revived (13:20-21). Marauding bands take an outsized role in the story of Kings even though the term is used only once more (24:2). Living in constant fear of terrorism, kidnapping, violence, and destruction keeps a people on edge. Relief from marauding bands brings shalom to Israel.

The Siege of Samaria 6:24–7:20

6:24-31 Siege and Famine

King Ben-hadad of Aram mobilizes his entire army to lay siege to Samaria (6:24). Historians are unable to definitively place Ben-hadad. Perhaps Ben-hadad is best understood as a literary punch line in the Elijah-Elisha stories (1 Kings 17–2 Kings 13), a comedic character used to glorify Yahweh over imperial power (see 1 Kings 20). Aram's siege is so successful that people are subjected to overwhelming food insecurity, evidenced by exorbitant prices for the head of a donkey and a small portion of dove dung (possibly with grain for nutrition, but more likely fuel; 6:25). This is the crude language of a peasant tale: ass's head and pigeon poop for sale in the food market (Sweeney 2007a: 305)!

More striking than the commodity prices is the vignette reporting the woman's plea to the king: *Save me, my lord king!* (6:26 AT). The king's response is desperate: *Save you? Let the* LORD *save! How could I save? Do you want me to go down to the corner market and get you a bag of groceries?* (6:27 AT and paraphrase; threshing floor and wine press would provide unprocessed basics but are outside the besieged city). The exchange, marked by the woman's deference yet desperation, highlights the king's responsibility to provide for the people. The king sidesteps responsibility, confessing that the Lord alone saves. The king's hopelessness contrasts ironically with the name *Elisha*, meaning "my God saves."

Realizing that the woman wants to lodge a plea for justice, the king continues with a single Hebrew word: *What?* (6:28-29). Without guilt or shame, the cannibalistic mother addresses the king on the question of justice (Fretheim 1999: 159). Her plea focuses more on the unfair duplicitous ruse of the mother who refuses her own son than on the barbarity of eating her child. The cannibalism underscores the price that Israel pays for royal injustice and foreshadows the sieges that precede exile (Jer 19:9; Lam 4:10; 2 Kings 17:5-6; 25:1-7). When the king tears his clothes, revealing that he is wearing sackcloth next to his skin (6:30), his actions may indicate sadness, compassion, helplessness, or anger against Elisha and the Lord. His oath, calling down a curse upon himself if Elisha escapes death, lends most credence to the last suggested motive and highlights the king's failure (6:31). He does not take responsibility by asking himself, "What kind of royal policy leads to war?" Instead, he blames Elisha and the Lord: "Where is the salvation that we have come to expect when death threatens?" The devastation of war ends in chaos, a sign of covenant curse (Deut 28:53-57).

Hens-Piazza wrestles with the conundrums presented by the dialogue between the king and the mother (1998: 93–102; 2006: 274–76). The unfinished story of the conniving mothers pits women against each other in service of issues of power, violence, and blame; their lives are swallowed up in power games between nations and among leaders. The story gives expression to oft-neglected voices (1998: 92). A marginalized woman gives witness against the price of famine and conflict, royal exercise of power without sensitivity to the costs of war (Brueggemann 2000: 356–57). The story demonstrates that every member of the community, including a child, has intrinsic value to the Lord.

6:32–7:2 Elisha's Prediction of Relief

At home with the elders of Samaria, Elisha is characteristically prescient, anticipating the messenger sent to enforce the king's oath and the arrival of the king himself (6:32). Elisha calls Jehoram a *son of a murderer*, an apt characterization—and a reminder of Jezebel and Ahab's violent policies (6:32 AT). The prophet locks out of his house the king trapped inside Samaria. The messenger delivers the king's accusation that Yahweh has brought this *evil* on the city (6:33 AT), continuing his pattern of refusing to take responsibility [Evil, p. 446]. The king complains, *Why should I hope in the LORD any longer?* (6:33). Laments typically indicate trust, but the king rejects the Lord rather than requesting salvation [Literary Criticism: Poetry, p. 460].

In contrast to the king's hopelessness, Elisha proclaims a salvation oracle, announcing bargain prices for flour and barley *tomorrow* (7:1). When the king's attendant objects that such a thing is impossible even if the Lord makes *windows* in heaven, Elisha's speech turns to judgment: *You shall see it with your eyes, but you shall not eat from it* (7:2). A happy day for Samaria will bring disaster to the king's court [Literary Criticism: Poetry, p. 460].

7:3–15 The Lepers' Discovery of Deliverance

The scene shifts to four men locked out of the city because of their leprosy (cf. Num 5:1-3). The narrator reports their deliberations as gallows logic (if not gallows humor): We have three options. Two of them, going into the city or staying here, result in starvation. *We might as well try entering the Aramean camp, where the enemy will either spare us or kill us. Since we are going to die anyway, what's the risk?* (2 Kings 7:3-4 paraphrase).

The empty camp catches the men by surprise (7:5 AT: *Behold!*). The narrator explains that the Lord caused the Aramean army to hear *noise* and flee (the word *sound* or *voice* is used three times in 7:6; cf. the *sound* of the king's footsteps, 6:32; no *sound/voice* from Baal, 1 Kings 18:26, 29; the silent *voice* of the Lord, 19:12). The army panics at the *rumor/noise* of horses and chariots, presumably Hittites or Egyptians (2 Kings 7:6; a Hebrew wordplay; fearing *Egyptians* [*miṣrayim*], the Aramean camp is invaded by *lepers* [*meṣoraʿim*]). The Arameans flee, forgetting horses and donkeys and everything in their tents (everything except what they throw away as they abandon camp in disorganized retreat, 7:15). Again the army of Benhadad is defeated by the Lord (1 Kings 20:21; 2 Kings 6:14-18). The Arameans flee, but the starving city of Samaria remains locked inside, besieged by empty tents. The narrator knows what has happened; the lepers know; Elisha knows deliverance approaches; Israelite royal military intelligence remains in the dark.

Moving from tent to tent, looting, feasting, and hoarding valuables, the lepers again huddle to consider options: *Today we have a good battle report* [the term reports Joab's victory over Absalom, 2 Sam 18], *but if we keep still, guilt will find us* [Heb. ʿawon for *guilt* is used only twice in Kings but about one hundred times in the prophets to indicate both iniquity and its consequences; cf. 1 Kings 17:18]. *We need to report this to the king's house* (7:8-9 AT). When the gatekeepers pass the lepers' report to the king, more gallows logic (or is it humor?) ensues (7:10). First, the suspicious king conjures that the empty camp is another Aramean ambush, a ruse to get the unsuspecting but starving citizens of Samaria to open their gates (7:11-12). The king fears an imaginary Syria just as Syria acted in fear of an imaginary Egypt (Brueggemann 2001b: 78). One of the starving servants, following the line of logic employed by the lepers, proposes sending out five mounted men to assess the situation since the worst thing that can happen is that the starving men will be killed (7:13). When the king agrees, the investigators discover that *sure enough* (behold!), all the way to the Jordan River is littered with materials discarded in panic (7:14-15 AT).

7:16-20 Fulfillment of Two Prophecies

Following the miracle story form [*Literary Criticism: Narrative Subgenres, p. 460*], 2 Kings 7:16-20 reports the reaction to and evidence of God's intervention. First, the people loot the spoil; flour and barley are sold for the bargain prices predicted (7:16). Second, the judgment against the king's attendant (7:2) is fulfilled. Though he sees the evidence of the miracle, the people trample him to death in the gate, the place of justice (7:17; Bodner 2019: 153). The verbatim repetition of the exchange between the captain and the man of God and the repeated death report underscore Elisha's capacity to see and proclaim God's saving action (7:18-20). The narrative points to the failure of the Omride dynasty (Sweeney 2007a: 314; Hobbs: 93).

Second Kings 6:24–7:20 recounts the third in a series of Elisha's miracles that result in the salvation of Israel (6:1-7, 8-23). In each potentially devastating situation, God's agent Elisha ("my God saves") delivers the threatened party. Elisha is characterized by his capacity to see what is about to happen, speak a word of salvation, and mediate God's deliverance. Each story can be interpreted at face value. A young prophet is saved from heavy financial loss of a valuable iron tool (6:1-7). Attempted Aramean ambushes are miraculously thwarted, and the raiding stops (6:8-23). God miraculously frightens the Aramean army that has Samaria locked in a death-siege (6:24–7:20). The Lord has the power to save individuals and cities from apparently hopeless situations.

These stories can also be read as underdog tales designed to foster a sense of identity among a decimated, discouraged population. The characters in these stories look squarely at disaster and laugh in the face of death and the imperial powers. One heroic prophet who is loyal to the Torah can overcome an army. Empowered by clear self-identity, trust in God, and clever wit, these hardy people survive despite overwhelming odds. With the ingenuity to overcome bankrupting loss, and empowered by an army of horses and chariots invisible to the naked eye, they are clever enough to outwit the military intelligence of a powerful king. LaBarbera suggests that Elisha the peacekeeping prophet overcomes horses and chariots by leading marginalized people; he is the servant who sees horses and chariots of fire, the lepers, and the people of the city, who trample the powerful military commander to death (651). When faced with starvation, loss of home, and death, people attuned to the voice of God and the hope of the prophet outlive the skeptical realism of the king and his captain. Neither hunger nor fear is at home in the world ruled by the Lord (Brueggemann 2001b: 84). "My God saves" is more than a name or a slogan. This is a way of life! For an exilic audience, these stories support the Deuteronomic promise (Deut 4:225-31).

THE TEXT IN BIBLICAL CONTEXT
Opened Eyes, Seers, and Apocalyptic Visions

God empowers Elisha with miraculous insight into the royal council and of fiery horses and chariots (2 Kings 2:11-12; 6:17). Elisha's prayer opens eyes, those of his servant and of the blinded army.

Prophets and seers foresee exilic judgment (17:13). Elisha anticipates bargain prices despite famine (7:1). The prophet Micaiah sees
Israel scattered, without a leader, as well as the Lord enthroned with
the heavenly host (1 Kings 22:17, 19).

Classic writing prophets had extraordinary vision. Jeremiah
sees Jerusalem's future in baskets of figs (Jer 24:1-10). Though he
can foresee the future, Jeremiah warns that the prophets' visions
come from their own minds (23:16-40). Ezekiel's surreal visions
anticipate apocalyptic prophecy (Ezek 1:4-28). Daniel's visions
describe the rise and fall of empires (Dan 7–12). The book of
Revelation refers to itself as the "revelation [apocalypse]" of Jesus
Christ, a testimony, a prophecy (1:1-3). Using Old Testament prophetic imagery, John describes visions of Jesus, the throne of heav-
en, and the heavenly city.

Though saying that apocalyptic vision is not about the future is
an overstatement (Revelation shows readers "what must soon take
place," 1:1), the visions uncover divine perspective of the present
reality. Imperial power totters and falls—now. The Lamb comforts
martyrs in their suffering. Elisha opens eyes to the present balance
of power. The injunction classically translated *Behold!* is an imperative to see from a new perspective [*Literary Criticism: Elements of
Narrative, p. 458*].

Feeding Enemies

In the long-festering antagonistic relations between Aram and
Israel, the lonely word of hope is the report that the raids of Aram
stop after the king of Israel serves a feast to a captured army (2 Kings
6:23). God loves strangers and feeds them and calls on Israel to follow
suit (Deut 10:18-19). The book of Proverbs turns the wisdom of that
encounter into instruction. The way to overcome an enemy is to give
food and drink (25:21-22). Paul quotes the proverb in his instruction
not to return evil for evil (Rom 12:20-21). Jesus extends bread and
cup to his disciples, even those about to betray and deny him. Ever
since Abraham extended hospitality to three strangers (Gen 18),
God's people have been entertaining angels "unawares" (Heb 13:2).

THE TEXT IN THE LIFE OF THE CHURCH
Underdog Churches

Sociologists studying American religious practices report that
despite prominent headlines describing decreasing church attendance among younger adults, church attendance in fact is no worse
than steady. Millennials seek churches that eschew megachurch

models and practice countercultural community life. Christians who had given up on the institutional church appreciate freedom to express skepticism, discuss doubts, and raise questions about American evangelical culture. Research indicates that younger generations tend to see Christian culture as simplistic, judgmental, moralistic, and lacking the sophistication needed to address contemporary questions. Countercultural, authentic, and justice-seeking churches that reach the next generation resist institutional power-broking for underdog status (Kinnaman: 235–38).

Radical Reformation stories in the *Martyrs Mirror* witness to "underdog" Christianity. Among them is Maeyken Wens, who was arrested in April 1573 and imprisoned in the Steen castle of Antwerp, Belgium. On the eve of her execution, she wrote a farewell letter to her fifteen-year-old son, the oldest of her five children: "Adieu once more, my dear son Adriaen; ever be kind, I pray you, to your afflicted father all the days of your life, and do not grieve him. . . . I have written this since I was sentenced to die for the testimony of Jesus Christ." Maeyken was executed on October 6, 1573, with a tongue screw to prevent her from testifying to the crowd. Adriaen attended the execution, but when his mother was tied to the stake, he fainted. When he regained consciousness, he found the tongue screw in his mother's ashes, and ever afterward he treasured the memento of her faithfulness (Van Bracht 1950: 980).

Member churches of Mennonite World Conference relate stories reflecting their underdog status. Phone Kao, a Mennonite Brethren missionary among the Khmu people on the Laos-Thai border, leads a church of more than forty thousand believers who have committed themselves to Jesus. One of the most effective evangelists fearlessly enters unreached villages to proclaim the good news despite torture by government agents who have smashed his face with the butt of a machine gun and imprisoned him in a crowded cage with brutal criminals for six months at a time. When he and his colleagues are released from detention, they return to their evangelistic ministry.

Like Elisha, these prophetic voices are at home in their underdog status. Whether contemporary North Americans, fifteenth-century martyrs, or southeast Asian missionaries, they see reality differently from the cultures they serve. They pay a price for choosing the way of Jesus and Elisha.

2 Kings 8:1-29

Interlude

PREVIEW

Leadership transitions challenge churches, businesses, nonprofits, and governments. According to Collins in *Built to Last*, succession plans that safeguard institutional values can help organizations flourish through multiple generations. In 1–2 Kings is a story of changing leaders. Second Kings 8 transitions from the Elisha story to political history in Israel and Judah. As the chapter opens, Elisha's positive influence with the unnamed king protects the Shunammite woman (8:1-6). On the international stage, Elisha provokes regime change in Damascus (8:7-15). The narrative shifts from Elisha to reports of Jehoram of Judah (8:16-24) and his heir Ahaziah (8:25-29), allies of the Israelite king Joram (or Jehoram). This transitional chapter sets up the fall of the Omride dynasty. After Elisha commissions a young prophet to anoint Jehu as the next king of Israel (9:1-3), Elisha is silent until his final appearance (13:14-21).

OUTLINE

Protecting the Shunammite Woman, 8:1-6
Anointing Hazael as King of Aram, 8:7-15
Royal Transition in Judah, 8:16-29

EXPLANATORY NOTES
Protecting the Shunammite Woman 8:1-6

The opening vignette of 2 Kings 8 is no less a miracle story than others where Elisha intervenes to help the marginalized (4:1-7,

38-44; 6:1-7). Though introduced as a great woman (4:8), living among her own people and not in need of Elisha's support with the king (4:13), married to a man with lands and servants (4:18-24), and persuasive enough to convince both Elisha and her husband that she should offer the prophet hospitality (4:9-10), the Shunammite woman is caught in the life-death vortex of the Elisha narratives (pitting the prophet of Yahweh against the idolatrous king). After restoring her son to life (4:32-37), Elisha warns her to flee a seven-year famine in Israel by sojourning elsewhere (8:1). With her husband absent from the story, the woman takes *her household* to settle in the land of the Philistines (8:2). In her absence the Omride land policies swallow up her house, her fields, and her livelihood (8:3; see 1 Kings 21 for an example of royal Baal land practices).

In 2 Kings 8:4 we meet Gehazi, Elisha's servant, who has contracted Naaman's leprosy because of his avarice for land and wealth (5:26-27). Gehazi's presence in the king's court suggests that this story circulated independently before it was gathered into the narratives involving Elisha and may follow Elisha's death chronologically (Alter: 554). Gehazi is regaling the king about Elisha's *great things* (restoring the Shunammite woman's son to life is at the top of the list, 8:5; cf. 4:35). Providentially *[Literary Criticism: Elements of Narrative, p. 458]*, at this moment the woman herself appears in court and *appeals* to the king (8:3, 5; a technical term to describe a plea for true royal justice; Alter: 554; Israel *appeals* to the Lord for justice, Exod 5:15; 22:23, 27). What is perhaps Elisha's greatest miracle follows. When the king catches a vision of *great things* done under the Lord's direction, he is freed to step outside self-serving royal *mišpaṭ* to *restore* the fields expropriated as part of his royal land management—including lost income during the woman's absence (2 Kings 8:6; *restore* [*šub*] describes *return* from exile, Isa 49:5-6; 51:11; *restoration* of fortunes, Jer 15:19; Brueggemann 2001b: 102–4). The scene is an enacted parable. As the boy returns to life, eventually to inherit the land after the family's return from Philistine exile, the reader may envision the return of Israel from the death of Mesopotamian exile (4:35; Bodner 2016: 209–12).

Elisha's prophetic career has ping-ponged back and forth between political intervention in the royal court and protection of marginalized people. In this transitional story (absent the prophet himself), these two spheres overlap. Elisha's values protect an old friend and effect justice in public policy.

Anointing Hazael as King of Aram 8:7-15

Second Kings 8:7-15 completes Elijah's mandate to anoint Hazael king over Aram (1 Kings 19:15-17). Though he passes his mantle to Elisha (19:16, 19-21; 2 Kings 2), Elijah anoints neither Hazael nor Jehu. Elisha's disciple anoints Jehu in 2 Kings 9. This text reports Elisha designating Hazael king of Aram.

Though Elisha had been Aram's public enemy number one, outsmarting Aramean royal intelligence (6:8-23), healing the Aramean commander Naaman (5:14) and sparing the Aramean army (6:22-23) apparently provide Elisha diplomatic immunity in Damascus, where he is received with honor as *the man of God* (5:1-19; 6:20-23; 8:7-8). As a model patron of the prophet, Ben-hadad sends Hazael to inquire about his recovery from illness (8:7-8). In contrast to the deceitful Jeroboam (1 Kings 14) and the apostate Ahaziah, king of Israel (2 Kings 1), Ben-hadad sends forty camels loaded with the best of Damascus. Hazael deferentially *stands before* Elisha and uses the humble self-designation *your son* to inquire on Ben-hadad's behalf (8:9). Elisha instructs Hazael to tell Ben-hadad that he will *surely live* even though Elisha declares that Ben-hadad will *certainly die*, setting in motion Hazael's coup by anticipating the treachery of the king's servant (8:10; prophetic deceit recalls 1 Kings 22:15-23; 2 Kings 3:13-19, 27b). A high-drama stare-down between Elisha and Hazael (who shamefully averts his gaze) ends with the man of God weeping that he is powerless to change destiny (8:11). The emotional exchange sets the stage for Elisha to confront Hazael with his tyrannical legacy: *You will do evil to Israel, you will set their fortresses on fire, you will kill their young soldiers, you will dash their little ones in pieces, you will rip open their pregnant women* (8:12 AT; code for violent, demeaning atrocities to be committed as judgment against Israel; cf. Amos 1:13; Ps 137). Still a submissive subordinate, Hazael demurs, dismissing his capacity to do such a *great thing* because he *is a mere dog* (8:13). Elisha's prophecy activates Hazael's royal pretensions, prompting the deception and assassination of Ben-hadad and seizure of the throne (8:14-15). Elisha acts as a kingmaker in the name of Yahweh, the God who controls life and death and superintends international politics.

Royal Transition in Judah 8:16-29

The narrative shifts to Judah's royal house. The chronology is confusing *[Chronology: Kings Ahaziah and Jehoram, p. 441].* First, a variation of the name Jehoram is Joram. Second, Jehoram's Judean royal contemporary, also named Jehoram (Joram), is first reported king after the death of his father, Jehoshaphat (1 Kings 22:50). Second Kings 1:17 reports that the Israelite Jehoram becomes king in the second year of the Judean Jehoram; 3:1 names the Israelite Jehoram as king in Jehoshaphat's eighteenth year, seven years before Jehoshaphat's death. One explanation for the report in 8:15 is that Jehoram (Joram) of Judah comes to the throne in the fifth (rather than seventh) year of Jehoram of Israel in a (two-year) coregency with Jehoshaphat in Judah. An additional confusion is that the king of Israel is not named in 3:7–8:15.

Despite these complications, the report of royal transition in Judah closes the gap between Jehoshaphat and his heirs and introduces the characters of the Jehu coup in Israel (2 Kings 9–10) and the rise of Joash (= Jehoash, 11:21) in Judah (2 Kings 11–12). Perhaps the jumbled report is an additional signal that royal succession after the Omride dynasty is chaotic. "Israel and Judah are becoming indistinguishable, so much so that even the names of the kings are the same" (Leithart: 216). (Hayes and Hooker postulate that Jehoram of Judah and Jehoram of Israel are one and the same individual; 35.)

The opening royal formula of King Jehoram of Judah places him chronologically (8:16), notes his age and length of reign (8:17), and links his royal administrative policy to the kings of Israel because he married Ahab's daughter (8:18). Though the narrative reports that Jehoram of Israel follows the sins of Jeroboam but not the ways of Ahab and Jezebel (3:2-3), no such clarification is given regarding Jehoram of Judah and his wife (Athaliah, daughter of Ahab and thus granddaughter of Omri, 8:26). The formula concludes, noting that the Lord preserves Judah because of his promise to give David *a lamp forever* (8:19 AT; 2 Sam 21:17; 1 Kings 11:36; 15:4).

Joram of Judah is unable to quash the successful revolts of Libnah (in western Judah near Philistine territory) and Edom (in revolt *to this day*, presumably the date this event is recorded; 2 Kings 8:20-22). Judah's military alliance with Israel does not produce desirable results. Joram's closing royal formula refers to the Annals of the Kings of Judah and his burial (8:23-24). His son Ahaziah succeeds Joram. The opening royal formula of King Ahaziah son of Jehoram of Judah (Ahaziah of Israel was the Israelite Jehoram's older brother) gives standard information (8:25-27). NRSV resolves the identification of the queen mother Athaliah as daughter of Ahab (8:18) and granddaughter of Omri (8:26 MT: daughter) by clarifying that she is *granddaughter of King Omri*. Like his father, Jehoram, Ahaziah of Judah walks in the sins of the house of Ahab (Ahaziah's grandfather). His identification as *son-in-law* indicates either that he also married a

relative or that he is truly an Omride (8:27). Like his grandfather
Jehoshaphat, Ahaziah of Judah joins Israel in battle against Aram at
Ramoth-gilead (8:28; strategic battle to control the trade route
known as the King's Highway; Master: 505). After King Joram of
Israel has been wounded in the battle and has returned to recuper-
ate in Jezreel, Ahaziah of Judah comes to visit Joram (8:29). The
pieces are set for Jehu's revolt.

The disrupted genealogy parallels the chaos of the royal house(s).
At the height of royal power in the Omride dynasty, Elijah, Elisha,
and other prophets take center stage. Not only does Elijah best
Ahab, Jezebel, and Ahaziah (1 Kings 17–2 Kings 1), but the king also
goes unnamed for more than five chapters (2 Kings 3:8–8:15). The
story suggests that, next to prophets, kings are insignificant trou-
blemakers. Though ancient battle records credit Ahab with thousands of chariots [Archaeology: Mesha Stele, p. 438], in the biblical story
Ahab and his descendants are virtually defenseless, dependent on
prophets supported by horses and chariots of fire (2 Kings 2:11-12;
6:17; 13:14). After the jumbled royal chronology of 1 Kings 22–2 Kings
8, the opening and closing royal formulas of 8:16-27 temporarily
impose order on the narratival structure. Real chaos breaks loose in
the royal palaces when Jehu assassinates Joram and Ahaziah; no
closing royal formula is included for Ahaziah (9:27-29).

THE TEXT IN BIBLICAL CONTEXT
Divine Agency through the Prophetic Word
The prophetic word brings about the Lord's will in 1–2 Kings
[Prophets: Prophetic Word, p. 469]. The Lord refuses to destroy Judah
because he has promised to give David a lamp . . . forever (2 Kings 8:19).
Amit labels the combining of the twin rationales of God's supervision
and political factors the "dual causality principle" (1987: 388, 400; see
EN on 1 Kings 12). Matties identifies the "agency of the prophetic
word" (402-3). Events occur not simply because of human agency,
but because the Lord's word orders events. Matties traces the motif
to Deuteronomy 8:3 and identifies twelve additional "moments" that
the narrator evaluates as having occurred by the agency of the prophetic word (1 Kings 11:29-40 and 12:15b; 1 Kings 13:3 and 2 Kings
23:16-18; 1 Kings 14:6-16 and 15:29; 1 Kings 14:12 and 14:17-18;
1 Kings 16:1, 3, 7 and 16:12; Josh 6:26 and 1 Kings 16:34; 1 Kings 21:21-
29 and 2 Kings 9:36; 2 Kings 1:2, 16 and 1:17; 2 Kings 7:1-3 and 7:16-18;
2 Kings 10:30 and 15:12; 2 Kings 21:10-16 and 24:2; 2 Kings 22:15-20
and 23:30). Matties notes the tension between the prophetic word
and human behavior. The Lord preserves Jehoram because of the

promise to David, but the people end up in exile. Though the Lord has warned Israel and Judah by every prophet and every seer, Israel has failed to heed the word of the Lord (17:13-14; Matties: 402).

Family Feud

A strange thing happens to the royal Judean bloodline in 2 Kings 8. David's line merges with the line of Ahab; from this point onward, the Davidic kingdom is also the Omride kingdom. This union foreshadows the final judgment of Jerusalem and Judah.

The Lord's covenant commitment to David continues even if David's son commits iniquity (2 Sam 7:8-16). David's grandson Rehoboam and his son Abijam had hearts that were not true as David's heart had been, but the Lord still gave David a lamp in Jerusalem (1 Kings 15:3-5). The promise of a lamp for David and his descendants forever is repeated when Jehoram son of Jehoshaphat walks in the way of the kings of Israel because he is Ahab's son-in-law, married to Ahab's daughter Athaliah (2 Kings 8:16-19, 26).

The Lord's judgment on Ahab is irreconcilable with the Davidic promise. God announces judgment on Ahab and his house, cutting off every male (1 Kings 21:21-24, 29; 2 Kings 9:7-10). The threat is fulfilled when Jehu wipes out the heirs of Ahab in Israel, including Ahaziah son of Jehoram of the Davidic line and Athaliah daughter of Ahab (9:27-28), and Athaliah kills the rest of Ahaziah's family (11:1). Only Joash son of Ahaziah escapes, hidden by Ahaziah's sister Jehosheba, who reveals the lone male heir (of Ahab as well as David) just before Athaliah is assassinated (2 Kings 11). The divine promise of an everlasting throne for David is merged with divine threat of extermination for Ahab. Both dynasties pursue policies incompatible with their covenant commitments (Brueggemann 2000: 379).

The gospel of Matthew opens with "the genealogy of Jesus the Messiah, the son of David, the son of Abraham" (1:1). Uncharacteristically, the genealogy includes four mothers (Tamar, Rahab, Ruth, and the wife of Uriah), all non-Israelites (or the wife of a non-Israelite). Unnamed but also among the matriarchs of Jesus' line are the wicked foreign queens Jezebel and Athaliah. Jesus comes to save his people from their sins (1:21).

THE TEXT IN THE LIFE OF THE CHURCH
Single Bloodlines and Shadow Selves

Living with a divided self results in disintegration. Solomon loves the Lord and loves his foreign wives (1 Kings 3:1; 11:1-3). The divided value system eventuated in civil war, with Israel dividing from Judah

(1 Kings 12). The later kings of Judah struggled with the "mixed bloodlines" of Ahab and David. According to Carl Jung, the human unconscious is a "shadow" self, a creative reservoir of the unknown person, potentially positive but often negative because of the human tendency to suppress what is not favorable. Jungian psychological therapy helps the client encounter the shadow side and experience assimilation of the unknown into the individuated (whole) person. Therapists advise clients to acknowledge and unleash strong feelings rather than try to suppress them and then be overcome by dangerous emotions in crises.

Jesus warned against the division of serving two masters, especially God and mammon (Matt 6:19-21, 24 KJV). He brings unity to divided individuals, communities, and society (Eph 2:11-22). Jesus is our peace, breaking down the dividing walls that separate Jew from Gentile. He prays that his disciples may be one, as he and the Father are one (John 17). Nonetheless, when the division is sharp, Paul and Barnabas part ways to accomplish mission (Acts 15:39). The Spirit helps believers discern when unity, forbearance, or division is the best way to follow Jesus.

2 Kings 9:1–12:21

Royal Transitions

PREVIEW

Sensitive to public opinion, modern generals seek to limit collateral damage (civilian casualties) through precision strikes, drone aircraft, and strictures against chemical weapons. "Grunts on the ground" prefer overwhelming firepower that breaches these safeguards to protect their "siblings" in the trenches. The regime change reports of 2 Kings 9–12 reveal similar tensions. In both Israel and Judah, the Omride ruler is assassinated and the Omride dynasty terminated. Baal worship in the central shrine of the capital cities is extinguished. Subsequent Israelite and Judean rulers, though ardent Yahwists, do not always act according to Torah. Despite their similar aims, the two nations pursue diametrically different strategies.

In Israel, Jehu seizes power in a bloody coup, assassinating Ahaziah of Israel and Joram of Judah, executing the queen mother Jezebel, wiping out the sons of Ahab, and assembling Baal loyalists for slaughter (2 Kings 9–10). The Lord commends Jehu's dealing with the house of Ahab, but the narrator condemns him for pursuing the sins of Jeroboam (10:29-31).

In Judah, the priest Jehoiada removes the queen mother Athaliah, daughter of Ahab, who seizes power by destroying nearly all the royal family (2 Kings 11–12). The high priest stages a coup with two fatalities, Queen Athaliah and Mattan, the high priest of Baal, and crowns the Davidic heir. Guided by the priest, King Jehoash (Joash) restores Yahweh worship and repairs the temple (12:1-16).

Jehu's bloodbath is contrasted with the minimal violence of the Jerusalem coup (Fretheim 1999: 173; Barré: 42–46). Though scholars suggest either that the text supports Jehu's dynasty (Sweeney 2007a: 330–31) or, alternatively, that the story is an apology for the rule of Joash (and later Josiah; Barré: 140–41), our focus is on the themes of *shalom* (used ten times in 2 Kings 9–10) and *mišpaṭ* (Yahwistic justice opposing the Baal's royal administrative policies) *[Mišpaṭ, p. 461]*.

OUTLINE

Coup in Israel, 9:1–10:36
9:1-14a	Anointing Jehu as King
9:14b-29	Assassination of Two Kings
9:30-37	Execution of Jezebel
10:1-17	Slaughter of the House of Ahab
10:18-28	Baal Worship Destroyed
10:29-36	Closing Royal Formula

Coup in Jerusalem, 11:1–12:21
11:1-17	Queen Athaliah Assassinated; New Royal Covenant
11:18-21	Baal Worship Destroyed
12:1-3	Opening Royal Formula
12:4-16	Temple Restoration
12:17-18	Hazael's Invasion
12:19-21	Concluding Royal Formula

EXPLANATORY NOTES

Elisha, the leading character in 2 Kings 2–8, opposes the violent, oppressive Omride dynasty. Promoting justice for the marginalized, Elisha and his predecessor, Elijah, have battled royal political ideology, centralized economic policies, and internationalized military alliances. Elisha triggers revolt by anointing Jehu (9:1-3) and reappears in a final vignette (13:14-21), but the story line returns to the kings of Israel and Judah.

Coup in Israel 9:1–10:36

9:1-14a Anointing Jehu as King

The anointing of Jehu fulfills the final piece of God's mandate that Elijah anoint Hazael, Jehu, and Elisha the prophet, foreshadowing Jehu's violent revolt by predicting that Jehu will kill *whoever escapes from the sword of Hazael* (1 Kings 19:17-21; see 2 Kings 8:7-15). Elisha sends one of the sons of the prophets to the battlefront in Ramoth-gilead on an urgent mission, to anoint Jehu as king of Israel (9:1-3; urgency is conveyed in the phrase *Gird up your loins*; see also 4:29)

[Prophets: Sons of the Prophets, p. 467]. The unusual inclusion of a third
name (Nimshi may be a clan name) clarifies that Jehu's father is not
King Jehoshaphat son of Asa (1 Kings 22:41; the Assyrian Black
Obelisk refers to Jehu as son of Omri, indicating the dominance of
the Omride dynasty; Cogan and Tadmor: 106) *[Archaeology: Black
Obelisk of Shalmaneser III, p. 438].* This dangerous task is to be accomplished in secret. The young prophet is to take Jehu into *the inner
room of the inner room* (2 Kings 9:2 AT), to declare that Jehu is king
over Israel, and to flee without delay (9:3, 6b; 1 Kings 20:30; 22:25).
Anointing kings is rarely reported, each marking a significant transition: Israel's first king, Saul (1 Sam 10:1 is the only other reference
to a flask or vial); David to replace Saul (16:13); Solomon as David's
successor (1 Kings 1:34, 39); Joash in restoring the Davidic dynasty
(2 Kings 11:12); Jehoahaz (23:30).

The *young man, the young prophet* (Hebrew uses *youth* twice) goes
to Ramoth-gilead, anoints Jehu, and invokes the prophetic messenger formula, *Thus says the LORD the God of Israel. I anoint you king over . . .
Israel,* following Elisha's script (9:4-6). Emphasizing that Yahweh, not
Baal, is the God of Israel, the young prophet elaborates that Jehu is
anointed *over the people of the LORD* (9:6b). The young prophet expands
the divine oracle to declare that Jehu is to *strike down the house of your
master Ahab, . . . [to] avenge on Jezebel the blood of my servants the prophets, and the blood of all the servants of the LORD* (9:7). The house of Ahab
is the focus of divine judgment and the target of Jehu's violence (of
the eleven references to *the house of Ahab* in 1–2 Kings, six are found
in 2 Kings 9:7-9; 10:10-11, 30). Using the vulgar language to identify
males as employed in earlier judgment oracles (1 Kings 14:10; 16:11;
21:21), the young prophet adds to Elisha's instructions by quoting
Elijah (21:21), *I will cut off from Ahab every male, bond or free, in Israel*
(2 Kings 9:8; the phrase *bond or free* indicates that there are no survivors). The young prophet continues, still quoting Elijah (1 Kings
21:22-23), adding, *No one shall bury her* (2 Kings 9:9-10a; this is the first
prophecy explicitly denying Jezebel burial; not receiving a proper
burial was a matter of great shame; Trafton: 78; Isa 14:18-20; Jer 16:4).
Returning to the script given him by Elisha, the young man opens the
door and flees (9:10b) *[Literary Criticism: Poetry, p. 460].*

The young prophet's elaboration uses more inflammatory, violent rhetoric than Elisha's original instruction. Elisha deescalates
Israel's reliance on military violence in relations with Naaman
(2 Kings 5), the blind Arameans (6:8-23), and the siege of Samaria
(6:24–7:20). The sons of the prophets promote royal violence, not
only in Jehu's anointing but also in faulting the king for showing

mercy to the king of Aram (1 Kings 20:35-43) *[Prophets: Sons of the Prophets, p. 467]*.

When Jehu returns to the *servants of his lord* (9:11 AT; the description underlines the treasonous nature of the coup), one of them asks, *Is it shalom?* This term *shalom* indicates harmony and well-being politically and religiously, prosperity, health, wholeness, stability, order, and good community relations, all conditions that the Omride dynasty has placed in short supply (Fretheim 1999: 169; Konkel 2006: 483) *[Mišpaṭ, p. 461]*. Throughout 2 Kings 9–10, *shalom* is used in an ironic sense (nine times in 2 Kings 9 and 10:13; a verbal form of *shalom* is used in 9:26). Joram's royal house repeatedly asks Jehu if he is coming with *shalom*; Jehu repeats, in essence, "What do you know about *shalom?*" (9:18, 19, 22). Jehu's first round of violent action against Ahab's house concludes with Jezebel's sarcastic question regarding *shalom* (9:31). While the order imposed by the Pax Omride disrupts Deuteronomic justice and is a mockery of *shalom*, Jehu's violent actions fail to produce *shalom*. The questions regarding *shalom* can be read not only as Jehu's criticism of Ahab but also as critique of Jehu's violent strategies.

The army commander pursues his question about the prophet, *Did he come in peace? Why did this madman come to you?* (AT; *madman* is a dismissive, offensive insult of the prophet; cf. David in 1 Sam 21:14-15; Jer 29:26; *madness* relates to impending judgment against Israel, Deut 28:34; Hos 9:7). The question anticipates the breakdown of order, the loss of peace, and the chaotic *madness* that Jehu triggers (Jehu drives like a *madman*, 9:20 AT). Jehu in his *madness* (behavior outside conventional social order, powerful, but threatening) desires to overthrow legitimate, established authority (Brueggemann 2000: 383, 385). When Jehu tries to dismiss the prophet's actions, the officers will have none of it. *"Lies!" they respond. "Please tell us"* (9:12 AT). Whether bewildered or simply buying time, Jehu sputters, *"This and this"* (AT). Then, regaining composure, Jehu admits that the prophet has anointed him king.

The military officers join the rebellion, placing their robes under the feet of Jehu, pledging fealty to their new lord (cf. Mark 11:7-8). They blow the trumpet to announce a new king, the first trumpet blast reported since Solomon's coronation (1 Kings 1:38-40). They declare, *King Jehu!* (9:13 AT). Like the coronation of Solomon, the coronation of Jehu includes both divine anointing and human acclamation with military support (Brueggemann 2000: 384).

The opening narrative is summarized: *Jehu son of Jehoshaphat son of Nimshi conspired against Joram* (2 Kings 9:14a; cf. conspiracy against Baasha, 1 Kings 15:27; and Zimri, 16:9; Jehu's descendants rule until Shallum *conspires* against Zechariah, 2 Kings 15:10). The conspiracy among the military officers is fueled by impatience with Joram's ineffective leadership, costly failures in war with Moab and Aram, and the difficulty in defending Ramoth-gilead (Cogan and Tadmor: 120). Second Kings 9 links the prophets to Jehu and the military council, suggesting that the people are seeking redress from the royal order, which pursues the sins of Jeroboam (3:3) [*Sins of Jeroboam, p. 476*]. The Omride dynasty has outdone Jeroboam with its costly building projects and extravagant lifestyle (1 Kings 22:39), its disregard for Israelite land laws (Naboth's vineyard, 1 Kings 21), and Jezebel as a constant reminder of these injustices (Konkel 2006: 482). Announcing that the Lord will make the house of Ahab like that of Jeroboam reinforces the link with Jeroboam (9:9). The conspiracy involves more than a private word spoken in Jehu's barracks. The military, inspired by the populace weary of the royal system, unites in a plot to overthrow the existing regime.

9:14b-29 Assassination of Two Kings

Jehu executes the first phase of his coup with nearly surgical precision, decapitating the royal house without collateral damage (9:14b-29). He races *madly* from Ramoth-gilead to Jezreel, where he discovers both Omride kings, Joram of Israel and Ahaziah of Judah, and eliminates both in a single barrage. From there he rides into the city of Jezreel, discovers Jezebel, and after quick but brutal repartee, has her executed. Jehu ends the disruptive Omride rule and returns Israel to Yahweh. Yet what begins with execution of the offending monarchs quickly devolves into violence of epic proportions.

This coup account opens with the report that King Joram of Israel has been leading the Israelite troops in the defense of their border city Ramoth-gilead against Hazael (2 Kings 9:14b-16; cf. 8:28-29). The city, though claimed by Israel (1 Kings 22:3), has been contested since the time of Ahab, who lost his life in battle there (22:1-36). Israel is *guarding* the city, suggesting that Israel has wrested control of the city from Aram (2 Kings 9:14b). After the anointing of Jehu, the narrative resumes, reminding the reader that Joram has returned to Jezreel to recover (9:15; see 8:28). Jehu calls on his coconspirators to seal the camp. *If you are in this with your life,* he says, *don't let anybody get away to report our coup in Jezreel* (9:15 AT). Jehu rides his chariot to confront the wounded Joram and King Ahaziah of Judah, who is visiting his uncle (9:16).

As Jehu arrives, Jezreel is on alert. A tower sentinel reports that a *large company* (9:17 AT; the term refers to floodwater or to a mass troop movement) approaches. Joram orders a horseman to meet the company to ascertain their intentions by repeating a one-word message: *Peace?* The word echoes ironically throughout the report. The horseman carries out his orders, using the messenger formula (*"Thus says the king"*) before asking Joram's one-word question, *Shalom? Peace? Is everything in order?* Jehu barks back sarcastically, *What is to you and to shalom? Turn in behind me* (9:18 AT). The watchman reports the scene to Joram.

Joram sends a second horseman with the same assignment (9:19). Joram's reaction is reminiscent of that of his brother Ahaziah, also suffering from mortal injuries, when Ahaziah sent three successive companies of soldiers to bring Elijah into royal custody (2 Kings 1:1-17). Ahaziah's first two companies failed to return because Elijah called down fire against them. When Elijah accompanied the third company, he delivered the prophetic judgment announcing Ahaziah's death. Now the second horseman-messenger's exchange with Jehu is identical to the first. The watchman reports to the royals below, adding, *The charioteer drives like Jehu, like a madman!* (9:20 AT; cf. 9:11). Meanwhile, the unexpected military horde continues to bear down on Jezreel.

The fast-paced narrative of Jehu rushing from the battlefront to Jezreel is slowed by detailed, deliberate reporting of Joram's response to Jehu (9:15-20). Joram, now recovered, orders that his chariot be readied and his horses harnessed (9:21). Joram's last order is a command meant to tie things down and place them in order, but things have spun out of royal control, disrupted by a madman. The two kings ride out in royal splendor to meet Jehu, each in his own chariot. Unable to match Jehu's fiery approach, they exude confidence with royal authority.

Jehu accosts the royal relatives in front of Naboth's vineyard, where Elijah declared the Lord's judgment against Ahab (1 Kings 21:20-24), quoted by the prophet at Jehu's anointing (9:6-10). For this third time, Joram addresses his one-word query directly to Jehu, *Shalom?* (9:22). Jehu snaps back for the third time, *Shalom?* Like Ahaziah, Joram meets death with the third query. Jehu ascribes the breakdown of justice and order to the *whoredoms and sorceries of . . . Jezebel.* The twin terms reference religious infidelity (idolatry and allegiance to the cult of Baal, Asherah, and Anat pervert not only religious observance but also social policy; they are paired similarly regarding Nineveh, Nah 3:4). *Whoredom* (used for the prostitutes washing in the blood of Ahab, 1 Kings 22:38) is the biblical metaphor for covenant betrayal, abandoning the Lord for foreign gods (Exod 34:16; Lev 17:7; Deut 31:16). *Sorceries* are associated with the imperial practices of Pharaoh (Exod 7:11) and of Babylon (Dan 2:2) and the pagan practice of improper sex and magic (Lev 18). The twin words *whoredoms and sorceries* match the double-edged sword of Jezebel's royal orders opposed to Yahweh's justice. First, Jezebel, the champion of Baal, attempts to murder the prophets of the Lord (1 Kings 18:4; 19:2; 2 Kings 9:7), prophets aligned with the poverty-stricken commoners (e.g., 2 Kings 4:1-7). Second, Jezebel rejects Israelite land justice in declaring Naboth's vineyard the eminent domain of the royal house (1 Kings 21). The indictment against Jezebel concerns "a regime that deliberately and continually acted in ways contrary to Yahwism and in defiance of Yahweh" (Brueggemann 2000: 385).

Jolted by Jehu's confrontation, Joram flies into action, *turns his hand*, wheels about his chariot (9:23 AT; *turn* [*hapak*] describes Ahab's withdrawal from battle after being mortally wounded, 1 Kings 22:34; it is used of the judgment on Jerusalem, where it parallels the judgment on the house of Ahab, *turning* over the dish to wipe it clean, 2 Kings 21:13). Calling to Ahaziah, Joram only has time for one last exclamation: *Treason, Ahaziah!*

In contrast to Joram, who *turns his hand* to flee, Jehu uses his *full hand* (*strength*) to draw the bow, striking down Joram (9:24 AT). Seizing the moment, Jehu orders Bidkar (the only reference to Jehu's cohort) to toss the corpse into the field of Naboth (9:25). In his firefight with the royal cousins, Jehu pauses to recall the Lord's oracle against Ahab (1 Kings 21:19). Jehu's citation alters and intensifies the Lord's message. The accusation of judgment adds reference to the blood of Naboth's sons (2 Kings 9:26). The report in 1 Kings 21 mentions only the death of Naboth, leaving unresolved the possible complication that Naboth's heirs could present a case against Ahab's seizure of the inheritance. Jehu adds to the Lord's original words a divine oath (*I swear*) and the verbal form of *shalom* (translated *repay*). Just as Jezebel's plot included the collateral damage of deaths of Naboth's entire family (mentioned here for the first time), so the judgment on Ahab extends to the next generation. Royal justice is served. The prophecy-fulfillment schema is explicit *[Prophets: Prophetic Word, p. 469]*. Jehu orders that the body of Joram be discarded on the plot of ground that belonged to Naboth, claiming that all of this happens *in accordance with the word of the LORD* (9:26). The narrative does not resolve the question of whether Jehu fabricates the oracle to support his violent coup or if it is a free recollection of 1 Kings 21:19. (Fulfillment of divine prophecy does not excuse excessive violence, 16:7.) After citing the prophecy against Ahab, the narrative returns to action. Jehu's pursuit of Ahaziah clues the reader in on the excessive violence of Jehu's reform. Is Ahaziah a target because he is allied with Joram, because he is of the house of Omri (son of Athaliah, 2 Kings 8:26), or because he is implicated in the sins of the kings of Israel (Hens-Piazza 2006: 292)? Though Jehu does not cite prophecy to justify Ahaziah's death, from his viewpoint purging demands elimination of all those associated with Omri. King Ahaziah escapes in the direction of the *garden house* (AT), a development consistent with Ahab's intent for Naboth's vineyard (1 Kings 21:2). Jehu's retinue strikes Ahaziah with a mortal wound (9:27). Though death is imminent, he flees to Megiddo, avoids the ignominy of being carrion of the birds of prey, and is honored with a royal burial (9:28).

Jehu's actions disrupt the royal court, signaled by the absence of the closing royal formulas for both Joram and Ahaziah. An abbreviated opening royal formula for Ahaziah appears *after* his death and burial (his doom is so sure that his death is reported before the narrator states that he has become king, 9:21-29; Leithart: 221). The synchronization of the reign of Ahaziah with Joram is also irregular (reports alternately place Ahaziah on the throne in the twelfth or eleventh year of Joram, 8:25; 9:29). The chronological note disrupts the flow of the narrative as the double assassination disrupts the Omride dynasty.

9:30-37 *Execution of Jezebel*

Jezebel reappears for the first time since Elijah prophesied that she would be eaten by dogs (1 Kings 21:15, 23). The narrator has attributed the evil of Ahab's reign to Jezebel, who has incited him to do evil (21:25). The long-anticipated death of Jezebel closes the file on the worst period for the kings of Israel (16:30-33).

She plays her role as wicked queen to the hilt (2 Kings 9:30). As Jehu enters Jezreel, Jezebel, with her eyes painted and her head adorned, looks out the window, unbowed, calling down an insult recalling the last non-Omride king, Zimri, whose reign lasted only seven days before he took his own life when overwhelmed by Omri (1 Kings 16:15-20). Her last words are sarcastic and derogatory. *Shalom?* she asks, the fourth time Jehu is greeted with that word (9:31). Linked with the address *Zimri, murderer of your master*, the question rings with insulting irony. Jehu is not bringing peace! Ignoring the insult, Jehu orders the attending eunuchs to throw her down (9:32-33). Jezebel's blood splatters against the wall (feminine counterpart to males identified as those who *piss against the wall* in 9:8 AT) and on the horses. The woman who has shed the blood of the Lord's prophets and the innocent Naboth has met her just end. As the Lord has judged Jezebel deserving of death, the fact that she dies in the city gates, where judges gather to mete out justice, is ironically appropriate (Quine: 411).

Callously, Jehu enters the palace to feast on the food and drink of the royals, establishing his credentials as king, then orders the burial of *that cursed woman* (9:34). When he learns that only her skull, feet, and the palms of her hands remain, Jehu again quotes Elijah, claiming that the prophet's words have been fulfilled (9:35-37). He again expands the prophecy (1 Kings 21), declaring, *The corpse of Jezebel shall be like dung on the field in the territory of Jezreel, so that no one can say, "This is Jezebel."* Jezebel's violence is matched by Jehu's vengeance. Jehu's shalom is founded on violence. With unbridled ambition for power, Jehu defends his violent overreach by citing the word of God, repeatedly exaggerating the original oracle, and sounding increasingly like someone covering his own tracks (Hens-Piazza 2006: 293, 297).

Jehu has successfully fulfilled the judgment prophesied by Elijah against Ahab. Ahab, Jezebel, and Joram are dead. The military is firmly in Jehu's control. No one in the royal establishment has the stomach for a fight against the commander of the army who has snuffed out the three royals without opposition.

The question "Is there shalom, Jehu?" rings throughout this chapter. The story opens with Elisha's limited orders that Jehu be anointed king. The mad young prophet, with only Jehu as witness, embellishes the mandate by adding, *Strike down the house of your master Ahab* (9:7). Presumably the assassination of Joram and Jezebel would accomplish that command. Appropriating the Lord's promise that *the whole house of Ahab shall perish . . . [and] dogs shall eat Jezebel* (9:8, 10), Jehu justifies his violent excess.

The report juxtaposes royal order with Yahwistic shalom. Ahab's royal "justice" has been grasping, greedy, and violent, leaving the people without economic recourse. Border war is evidence of a breakdown in international relations, creating further loss of life. The mad prophet and the mad general violently disrupt the status quo (the "shalom" of the house of Ahab). When the family of Ahab asks repeatedly, *Is this shalom?*, Jehu never answers directly. There can be no shalom under Ahab's injustice. Though a new monarch replaces the old, the question regarding shalom persists. Will

Elisha's limited mandate prevail, or will excessive violence make peace unattainable? The question about whether Jehu might bring shalom is to be answered shortly.

10:1-17 Slaughter of the House of Ahab

The massacre of the royal house reported in 2 Kings 10 is among the great bloodlettings in the biblical story. Jehu slaughters everyone connected to Ahab. After each report of killing, the narrative pauses to take measure of the loss of human life and to consider whether shalom has come. The movement from one killing field to the next produces a haunting rhetorical effect. No Israelite royal is safe from Jehu's sword.

Second Kings 10:1-10 reports the death of Ahab's seventy sons in Samaria (the number seventy recalls Abimelech's slaughter of his half-brothers, Gideon's seventy sons, as he become king of Shechem, Judg 9). Jehu sends a written message to people with responsibility for Ahab's descendants (2 Kings 10:1). The list of addressees matches the chaotic overkill of the narrative. He *sends* (characteristic of royal power) the letter to Samaria, to the princes of Jezreel, to the elders, and to the guardians of Ahab (NRSV: *the sons of Ahab*). Jehu provocatively proposes that former allies and subordinates of the king appoint a champion (*the best*) of the royal princes to take the throne of Ahab and to engage in battle against the army of Israel under Jehu's command (10:2-3).

Those who receive the letter are absolutely *terrified* (10:4). They take counsel, agreeing that opposition to Jehu is hopeless. The respondents to Jehu are listed: the palace chief, the mayor of the city, the ruling elders, and the guardians of Ahab (10:5). They offer unconditional surrender to Jehu, identifying themselves as *servants* of Jehu, agreeing to whatever Jehu demands (*the best*), a series of actions that dissolve their covenant with the house of Omri and Ahab and enact new covenant obligations with Jehu (Wray Beal 2014: 378). Jehu writes back, demanding the heads of the men of their master (the wording is ambiguous enough to require the recipients to interpret whether Jehu is demanding the leaders or the physical heads of Ahab's family). He demands that these *heads* be brought to him in Jezreel by the next day (10:6). The instructions are as explicit as they are dastardly. Ahab's descendants are in the custody of Samaria's city leaders, *their guardians* (10:6 AT). The city leaders obey Jehu: they kill the seventy sons, place their heads in baskets, and *send* them to Jehu in Jezreel (10:7; the verb characterizes royal action; here it describes obedience to a direct royal order) [*Send, p. 476*].

To Jehu, the messenger reports the city officials' compliance with his orders (10:8). Jehu maximizes the propaganda potential of the city officials' obeisance, ordering two stacks of heads to be piled at the entrance to the city gate, where they are to remain on public display until morning. The next morning, as merchants and city elders assemble for official business and judicial proceedings, Jehu interrupts with a speech calling attention to the ghastly spectacle of seventy royal heads piled up at the gates of justice (10:9-10). Jehu confesses that he conspired to kill the king but asks who killed these (bodiless heads rolling around at the gate). Perhaps he feigns innocence, but more likely he makes the point that the city officials of Samaria are too frightened to oppose him and are now complicit in the coup. Employing a standard judicial formula used in a court of law, Jehu declares the leaders of Jezreel *righteous* (KJV; Sweeney 2007a: 337).

The term *righteous* can be interpreted from several perspectives. Jehu may be cynically implicating others in the deaths of the princes whose heads are stacked in the gates. Alternatively, Jehu's words may be an appeal to the judges gathered in the gates to make impartial judgment about the *rightness* of the violent acts they are witnessing, particularly based on his citation of Elijah's prophecy (10:10). The term may be ironic in that these *righteous* ones are heirs of the elders of Jezreel who murdered Naboth, one of their own, in conspiracy with Queen Jezebel (1 Kings 21). Another perspective on the term *righteous* relates it to the dominant narrative theme of *shalom* (political and religious well-being). The use of the term *righteous* ironically implicates (and condemns) all the characters: Ahab, who is the most evil (least righteous); Jehu, who fails to achieve well-being through his violence; and Israel as a whole, implicated in their silent complicity with both Ahab and Jehu. Jehu concludes the speech at the gate with another allusion to the prophetic oracle against the house of Ahab: *Know then that there shall fall to the earth nothing of the word of the LORD* (10:10).

Jehu appropriates the mad prophet's promise that the Lord *will cut off from Ahab every male* (9:8) as a mandate to slaughter Ahab's descendants and associates, claiming that violent strategy is not freely chosen but rather is action required to faithfully accomplish God's will (Fretheim 1999: 171). What at first appears to be a summary statement of Jehu's victory in fact reveals the stunning scope of his massacre (10:11). Not only does the narrative present Jehu as fulfilling the judgment that all Ahab's descendants will die but it also specifies that the slaughter includes *all* Ahab's *great ones, acquaintances* (those who *knew* him), and his Baal priests (see 2 Kings 10:18-28), leaving no *survivors* (used seven times in Josh 10 to describe Canaanite conquest).

Having eliminated any possible opposition in Jezreel, Jehu turns to Samaria (2 Kings 10:12). Two vignettes chronicle Jehu's activities on his way to Samaria. First, Jehu meets an apparently unsuspecting contingent from the Judean royal house on its way, by their own admission, to greet (*to shalom*, the last time the word is used in the chapter) *the royal princes of Israel and the sons of the queen mother*, the people Jehu has just massacred (10:13) *[Queen Mother, p. 472]*. They profess peace, but Jehu responds with violence. Rejecting the possibility of peace while potential supporters of Ahab survive, Jehu orders them taken into custody and executed. Forty-two more victims are thrown into the pit at Beth Eked ("Shearing House of the Shepherds" 10:14).

Second, Jehu encounters Jehonadab son of Rechab and interviews him; upon learning that the heart of Jehonadab is as true as the heart of Jehu, he welcomes Jehonadab into the chariot to accompany him and witness his *zeal for the* LORD (10:15-16; *zeal for the [honor of the]* LORD is used elsewhere only of Phinehas in Num 25:11 and Elijah in 1 Kings 19:10, 14) *[All His Heart, p. 435]*. Jehu's enthusiasm for an alliance with Jehonadab indicates his need for support from ardent Yahwists (Hens-Piazza 2006: 301). Later, Jehonadab accompanies Jehu as he goes into the Baal temple to slaughter the Baal worshipers (10:23; Jer 35 relates the story of the nomadic descendants of the similarly named "Jonadab son of Rechab," who flee as refugees into Jerusalem during the Babylonian invasion of the land. Those Rechabites are commended for their faithfulness to the ancestral tradition of avoiding contamination by the corrupt culture that surrounds them; their relationship to this Jehonadab is uncertain; perhaps "rechab" is not a personal name but a reference to a guild of chariot builders, explaining why Jehu allies himself with a potential military supplier; Wray Beal 2014: 380). When Jehu arrives in Samaria, he continues the slaughter of the descendants of Ahab, killing *all who were left to Ahab in Samaria, . . . according to the word of the* LORD *that he spoke to Elijah* (10:17).

10:18-28 Baal Worship Destroyed

Jehu has established himself as king in Samaria by using brute force. Subtlety is not part of his approach. Jehu destroys everything attached to Ahab.

The final part of Jehu's takeover, the elimination of the Baal cult associated with Ahab and Jezebel, demands a new strategy. Though

Baal worship is widespread, it will hardly do to annihilate the entire population. Even in the heyday of the Baal cult, seven thousand had refused to bow to Baal (1 Kings 19:18). Later, Jehoram had limited the influence of the Baal cult further (2 Kings 3:1-3). Jehu needs a clever ploy to flush out the remaining true believers among the Baal worshipers.

Jehu *assembles* all the people (10:18; Ahab *assembles* all Israel at Mount Carmel under Elijah, 1 Kings 18:19). Then Jehu claims that he will outdo Ahab in his *service* of Baal. Jehu's mission is to eliminate Baal, named eleven times; *serve* (*worshipers*) appears eight times (2 Kings 10:18-28). Jehu invites the Baal devotees, prophets, priests, and *worshipers* to a great Baal *sacrifice*, warning that any Baal worshiper who fails to assemble will die (10:19; 1 Kings 13:2 predicts *slaughter/sacrifice* of the priests of the high places). The narrative explains that the *sacrifice/slaughter* is a *cunning trick* (Gen 27:36) to separate Baal worshipers from the rest of the population, then *wipe them out* (AT; NRSV: *destroy*; used over twenty times in Deuteronomy and Joshua for the annihilation of the idolatrous people in the land before Israel). *Destroy* (*'abad*) is a play on a word pronounced with a similar sound, *'abad* (*serve*). Jehu claims he will *serve* Baal, but in fact he will *destroy* Baal.

On Jehu's orders, all Baal worshipers gather in sanctified assembly; the Baal temple is filled to the gills (*mouth to mouth*, 2 Kings 10:21 AT). To mark Baal worshipers, all are garbed in the festal garments of Baal (10:22). Jehu enters the temple with Jehonadab and instructs those present to expose any Yahweh worshipers among them (10:15-16, 23). Then Jehu plays out the charade, offering burnt offerings to Baal, while ordering the eighty guards to be vigilant, warning that anyone who allows an escape will pay with his own life (10:24). After the burnt offering, the guards carry out Jehu's orders, slaughtering (*nakah*, smiting) every Baal worshiper (10:25). In the inner room of the house of Baal, the guards remove and burn the pillars of Baal, *destroy* (*nataṣ*) the temple, and turn it into a latrine (10:26-27; *nataṣ* is used in anticipating Israel's invasion and destruction of Canaan, Deut 7:5; 12:3). Jehu *wipes out* Baal (*shamad; the third* verb translated *destroy*; used over thirty times in Deut; Josh 9:24; 11:20; 2 Kings 21:9). Jehu's aim is annihilation of the Baal cult.

10:29-36 Closing Royal Formula

The narrative evaluation affords Jehu a mixed legacy (10:29-31). The Lord commends Jehu for having *done well* in applying to Ahab's house all that was in the Lord's heart and promises that Jehu will be rewarded with a dynasty exceeding Ahab's, to the fourth generation (10:30). This commendation is the most positive given any king of Israel (Konkel 2006: 486). Sandwiched around this endorsement, the analysis accuses Jehu of focusing his reforms too narrowly (10:29, 31). Retaining the golden calves in Bethel and in Dan, Jehu does not "guard to walk" in the law of the Lord (Deut 10:12 AT). He fails to *turn from the sins of Jeroboam* (10:29, 31; *turn* is used thirty-one times in 2 Kings, more than in any other OT book) [*All His Heart, p. 435*].

Although no causal link is stated, the text reports that the Lord begins to *trim away* Israelite territory (10:32-33 AT). With Israel's military preparedness, international alliances, and social fabric weakened by the brutal revolt, Hazael fulfills Elisha's prophecy with conquests throughout the area east of the Jordan (8:12). Jehu not only loses territory and control of trade routes but also is forced to pay tribute of gold, silver, precious vessels, a royal scepter, and javelins to Shalmaneser III of Assyria, as recorded on the Black Obelisk (Cogan and Tadmor: 120; Konkel 2006: 475-76, 482; *ANET* 280) [*Archaeology: Black Obelisk of Shalmaneser III, p. 438*]. The concluding royal formula reports that Jehu's *acts* (AT: *words*) are recorded in the Book of the Days of the Kings of Israel, that he is buried in Samaria, that he ruled twenty-eight years, and that his son Jehoahaz succeeds him (10:34-36).

This two-chapter report focuses on Jehu's coup to the exclusion of any report on his kingship. The narrative reports a mad prophet who anoints a mad general who disrupts the order of Ahab's descendant King Joram with a bloody coup. While the violent coup fulfills Elijah's prophetic judgment against Ahab's house, it institutionalizes bloodshed without fundamentally altering the political order. Jehu's violence defeats a dynasty that defended Baal political and religious values, but his reign fails to establish Deuteronomic values of peace and justice [*Sins of Jeroboam, p. 476*].

Coup in Jerusalem 11:1–12:21

11:1-17 Queen Athaliah Assassinated; New Royal Covenant

Meanwhile in Judah, dramatic events also occur. Athaliah, the daughter of Ahab and mother of Ahaziah, moves to take advantage of the political vacuum created by the assassination of her son Ahaziah, king of Judah (9:27-28; 11:1). With violence that outdoes Jehu (she *destroys* her own grandchildren), Athaliah nearly eliminates the house of David, setting herself up as the sole Omride survivor and heiress to the political dynasty. Her takeover is reported succinctly: Athaliah *destroyed* the royal *seed* (11:1 AT; the Lord will *destroy* Ahab, 9:8; Jehu *destroys* the servants of Baal, 10:19). The word *seed* makes explicit the threat to the promised Davidic line (David's *seed/descendants*, 2 Sam 7:12; 1 Kings 2:33; 11:39). Athaliah's usurpation interrupts but does not undo God's earlier promise of a continuing Davidic line (1 Kings 2:4). A champion of the Baal cult, Athaliah extends the unjust, violent governance of the Omride dynasty to Jerusalem (2 Kings 11:3, 18). The introduction of Athaliah sets up the conflict between Canaanite royal policy and Deuteronomic covenant values (11:1-3) *[Mišpaṭ, p. 461]*. That the name Athaliah means "Yah[weh] is great [exalted]" may be read ironically: even her name warns against devotion to Baal (K. Stone: 244).

Princess Jehosheba rescues one royal heir, Joash, son of Ahaziah, as Athaliah kills his brothers (11:2; association of Athaliah with Jehoram and Ahaziah, who did evil because they were of the house of Ahab, is a "flashback" device; Dutcher-Walls 1996: 28). A daughter of King Joram/Jehoram of Judah (son of Jehoshaphat; 8:16, 24), Jehosheba is a member of the Davidic royal house. The mother of Jehosheba is not identified, suggesting that Jehosheba's mother was not Athaliah but another wife of Joram. (Later, 2 Chron 22:11 identifies Jehosheba as the wife of the priest Jehoiada, named in 2 Kings 11:4.) Jehosheba *hides* Joash and his nurse from Athaliah *in a bedroom* so that he is not killed, risking her life to safeguard the innocent from an Omride queen as Obadiah did when he *hid* the prophets from Jezebel (11:2; 1 Kings 18:4, 13; cf. Exod 2:2-3). Joash remains *hidden in the house of the LORD* for six years while Athaliah reigns over Judah (11:3). The narrative pits Athaliah the Omride in the royal palace against Jehosheba, who protects the Davidic heir in the house of the Lord.

The priest Jehoiada, who also functions as commander-in-chief, initiates the coup against Athaliah and the coronation of Joash (11:4-17; Cohn 2000: 79). Though Jehoiada is not identified as priest until 11:9, his power to command the military officers, to make covenants, and to control the king's movements reveals his primary role in reestablishing a covenant community. Jehoiada *sends [Send, p. 476]* for the captains of the military guard, identified as the *Carites* (perhaps a variation of *Cherethites*, David's mercenary force, 2 Sam 8:18; 15:18; 20:7, 33; 1 Kings 1:38, 44) and the *guards* (*runners*, so called because they run before the king's chariot, as in 2 Kings 10:25). Although their relationship with Athaliah is unclear, as mercenaries the commanders provide protection for the occupant of the palace. Working surreptitiously, Jehoiada secures or perhaps usurps the loyalty of the military leadership by summoning *them to him in the house of the* LORD, *making a covenant [berit] with them, putting them under oath in the house of the* LORD, *and showing them the king's son* (11:4 AT). In the house of the Lord, Jehoiada *commands the captains* with details about protecting *the king* (11:5-8; he refers to Joash as *king* three times in his speech to the captains). Jehoiada positions the mercenaries strategically, mustering both the divisions going off duty and those coming on duty to guard the king's house, the Lord's house, and the king (clarity on details of the protective shield of men surrounding Joash eludes modern readers; Long 1991: 148). The officers are to arm their troops, protecting *the king* as *he comes in and goes out* (11:8 AT; see EN on 1 Kings 3:7 for the military connotations of this phrase). Following the detailed plan of *the priest Jehoiada*, the captains position their troops, armed by Jehoiada with the weapons of David (2 Kings 11:9-11; another reminder of the conflict between the houses of David and Omri). Ordered to use deadly force as necessary, the armed guard establishes a protective corridor around the king. The ceremony of investiture proceeds without a violent threat to the king.

Jehoiada's plan to engage people and king in covenant renewal unfolds as outlined. Jehoiada brings out the king's son, places the crown on him, and gives him a *covenant* (11:12; ʿ*edut = treaty or testimony*, NRSV footnote; *copy of the covenant*, NIV). The troops and the people (first mentioned in 11:13) make Jehoash king, anointing him, clapping their hands, and shouting, *Long live the king!* The priestly anointing (indicating divine approval) and popular acclamation (including priest, military, and people) echo Solomon's coronation (1 Kings 1:39) but contrast with Jehu's secret anointing by the prophet's assistant with acclamation by the military elite (2 Kings 9:6, 13) *[Covenant in Kings, p. 443]*.

Hearing the noise, Athaliah enters the house of the Lord and is startled by the scene (11:13; *behold!* signals that what follows is from Athaliah's perspective, heightening the dramatic effect; Cohn 2000: 79). Her appearance focuses the conflict between Omride practices and covenant values. She sees the king standing next to *the pillar, according to custom, with the captains and the trumpeters . . . , and all the people of the land* (11:14; "all the enfranchised citizenry of Judah," Wray Beal 2014: 391) *[People of the Land, p. 464]*. Custom (*mišpaṭ*) stresses both Joash's legitimacy (Provan 1995: 222) and Deuteronomic justice (1 Sam 10:25) *[Mišpaṭ, p. 461]*. Athaliah *tears* her clothes and *cries* out, "*Treason! Treason!*" *Tears* (*qaraʿ*) and *cries* (*qaraʾ*) are homonyms, the similar sounds of the words reinforcing Athaliah's shock. *Treason* describes rebellion or conspiracy (cf. 2 Sam 15:12; 1 Kings

16:20; 2 Kings 12:20; 15:10, 15; 17:4). Jehoiada orders that Athaliah be removed from the temple precincts (11:15). The captains arrest Athaliah, escort her out, and execute her at *the horses' entrance to the king's house* (11:16; Jezebel was trampled to death by horses, 9:33; Cohn 2000: 80).

Jehoiada makes a three-party covenant (*berit*) with the Lord, the king, and the people (11:17), the high point of 2 Kings 11. After the relationship between people and king is disrupted by Athaliah (as well as the century-long Omride alliance with Judah, 1 Kings 15:24; 22:2), the covenant between the Lord and David and his descendants is renewed (2 Sam 5:3; 7:11-6; 1 Kings 8:15-16, 25-26; 12:1), committing them to be "the people of the LORD" (Deut 27:9). The absence of an explanation of the two terms translated *covenant* (*berit*, 11:4, 17; *ʿedut*, 11:12) suggests that the terms are familiar and nearly interchangeable. *Covenant* (*berit*) is the more common term, used twenty-six times in 1–2 Kings. Jehoiada gives Joash the physical *covenant* (*ʿedut* in 11:12; 1 Kings 2:3; 2 Kings 17:15; 23:3 KJV: *testimony/ies*; *ʿedut* as object placed in the ark of the covenant, Exod 40:20; the stone tablets of the Ten Commandments, 32:15; 34:29). Beyond the immediate context, the covenant-making offers hope for resolution to the *ripped* covenants that have marked the Kings narrative (Ahijah condemns Solomon's covenant failure, 1 Kings 11:31-36; Rehoboam rejects covenant renewal in Shechem, 12:1-19; Jehoshaphat's alliance and Joram's marriage to Ahab's daughter formalize submission to Ahab's values, 22:42; 2 Kings 8:18). This covenant ceremony anticipates Josiah's covenant renewal (23:1-3).

11:18-21 Baal Worship Destroyed

Covenant faithfulness motivates the people to eliminate the symbols of the Baal cult, the representation of the anti-covenant imperial policies of Athaliah and the Omrides (11:18; Brueggemann 2000: 412–13). They *tear down* Baal's temple (10:27; 23:7), *destroy* altars and images (18:4; 23:14-15), and kill Mattan, the priest of Baal. The priest Jehoiada posts guards over the house of the Lord and orchestrates the coronation parade, having the military and the people escort the king through the guards' gate into the royal palace and to the throne (11:19; cf. Solomon's coronation parade, 1 Kings 1:38-40). The people of the land rejoice, and the city is *quiet* after Athaliah's death (2 Kings 11:20). The *quiet* city of Jerusalem, in contrast to the violence associated with Jehu's coup in Jezreel and Samaria, parallels the peace after Joshua's conquest ("the land had rest from war," Josh 11:23; 14:15; Judg 3:11, 30; 5:31; 8:28). Jehoash (a variation of Joash) becomes king at the age of seven (2 Kings 11:21). The atypical report of the king's age outside the opening royal formula calls attention to Jehoash's youth, suggesting that the positive turn toward covenant renewal is more central to success than royal leadership. Covenant renewal resets relations between king and people and between Yahweh and Judah.

Long posits that the twin aspects of political and theological restoration are captured in a metaphor of space; a profaned Jerusalem and royal palace are purified for Davidic Yahwism through the actions of the priest within the temple (1991: 147; the centrality of the temple is marked by the references to the *house of the LORD*, used twenty-two times in 2 Kings 11–12). Under the priest's tutelage, Jehoram's primary act is temple restoration (2 Kings 12).

12:1-3 *Opening Royal Formula*

The opening royal formula varies from the established pattern by placing the age of the king at ascension first, apparently for emphasis *[Chronology, p. 439]*. Jehoash's reign is synchronized with that of Jehu, king of Israel (12:1). Silence about the usurper Athaliah creates a seven-year gap in the chronology. The queen mother Zibiah is from Beer-sheba and thus native to Judah, unlike Athaliah from Israel. Jehoash is characterized positively because of the teaching of Jehoiada (12:2). The secondary assessment faults Jehoash for failing to remove the high places where the people continue to offer sacrifices (12:3), perhaps indicating reservations about Jehoash.

12:4-16 *Temple Restoration*

The report of Jehoash's reign centers on funds for temple renewal. Temple renovation often signals national restoration (Sweeney 2007a: 351). Jehoash's initiative indicates commitment to Yahwistic values and demonstrates royal authority over cultic institutions. The king directs the priests regarding the temple receipts and authorizes them to distribute funds for building repairs (12:4-5). Jehoash orders them to take the temple proceeds from assessments or voluntary offerings to repair damage to the temple. An assessment may be the payment of a vow (Lev 27:2-8) or a head tax (Exod 30:11-16; 2 Kings 23:35). Sometime after the original order, in the twenty-third year of his reign, Jehoash discovers that the priests have failed to keep up with temple repairs. The apparent administrative failure may indicate priestly resistance or incompetence (though perhaps the reference to the timing of Jehoash's intervention reflects royal negligence). Jehoash summons Jehoiada for an accounting (12:6-7). The king uses a lawsuit form to move the priests to action. The accusation of failure to sustain the temple repair comes as a question (12:7). The judgment is that the priests are no longer to use the funds for their own purposes and are to devote them to temple repair. Apparently the issue has eroded public confidence in the integrity of the priests. After Jehoash's intervention, the priests surrender access to the funds for personal use and lose control of the temple repairs. The money goes directly to the workers doing repairs (12:11-12).

The priests devise a system to restore public trust. Jehoiada places a chest in the temple under the care of the priestly doorkeepers; these guardians place all the money earmarked for temple repair in the chest (12:9). When the chest fills, accountability is ensured by having two people, the secretary of the king and the high priest, count the sacred coin and place it in safekeeping (12:10). Using careful accounting, they pay the overseers of the repairs, who in turn pay the craftsmen and purchase materials, wood and stone (12:11-12). No *accounting* is required of the overseers because they are trustworthy (12:15). Two additional notes regarding the use of offerings close the account of temple offerings and repairs. First, money designated for temple repair is used exclusively for that purpose, not for gold or silver temple furnishings (12:13-14). Second, the priests continue to receive income from guilt and sin offerings (12:16).

The detailed report of the fundraising and temple repairs highlights its importance. The specialized technical terminology, lacking drama or emotion (the matter-of-fact narration is "bland," Hobbs: 149), confounds clear interpretation of the details by modern readers (e.g., *donors* mentioned in 12:5 and 7 signifies *purchaser* but may refer to those presenting dues or offerings, Sweeney 2007a: 352; alternatively, they are *assessors* who fix costs of sacrifices and invest temple funds, Gray: 586). Although no explicit evaluation of the temple renovation is given, the report may be read as an affirmation of Jehoash's commitment to do *what was right in the sight of the* LORD (12:2). His restoration of Yahweh temple worship reinforces rejection of Baal. The renewal indicates his commitment to justice, extending not only to his fair payment of workers but also to their trustworthy accounting (Hens-Piazza 2006: 317). The priests receive correction and cooperate with the project. The report of temple renewal implies Jehoash's commitment to covenant fidelity, but the extensive detail without evaluation leaves uncertain whether the king's focus on the repair of the temple is to be evaluated positively or negatively.

12:17-18 Hazael's Invasion

Hazael's invasion of Judah is the second major reported event of Jehoash's reign. Hazael has been hazing Israel for some time, *trimming off parts of Israel* east of the Jordan (10:32-33). The king of Aram marches westward across the territories of Israel and Judah to Philistia, to take the city of Gath, strategic for control of military and trade routes (12:17; Wray Beal 2014: 401). When Hazael moves against Jerusalem, Jehoash empties the temple treasuries to give tribute to Hazael, bribing him to withdraw from the military campaign. The narrator does not explicitly evaluate Jehoash's action. At the price of bankrupting the national treasury built up for four generations, Jehoash avoids a siege of Jerusalem and possibly disastrous military defeat by Hazael. The text does not indicate whether Jehoash is to be commended for avoiding bloodshed or condemned for failing to trust the Lord for deliverance (Hens-Piazza 2006: 317). Contrasted with the positive report on temple reform and coupled with the rebellion that results in Jehoash's assassination, the narrator leaves the reader with a balanced or ambiguous view of this king, who is evaluated as commendable but with significant reservations (Brueggemann 2000: 422).

12:19-21 Concluding Royal Formula

The concluding royal formula closes the file on Joash (Jehoash), referring to *the Book of the Annals of the Kings of Judah*, an indication that the report is based on historical records (12:19). Instability continues in the royal succession process as two servants of Joash conspire to assassinate him (12:20-21). The motive for their conspiracy is not identified, but perhaps not all royal counselors agreed with the king's tribute payment. The book of Chronicles reports that Joash had killed the son of the priest Jehoiada, suggesting conflict between royal and priestly houses (2 Chron 24:25). This conspiracy is the third of four consecutive royal transitions in Judah related to violence, preceded as it is by the assassination of Joash's father, Ahaziah (9:27-28), the conspiracy of Athaliah, and her death (11:1-16). Joash's son Amaziah takes vengeance on Joash's assassins (14:5), but the instability continues when Amaziah, too, is assassinated by conspirators (14:19).

THE TEXT IN BIBLICAL CONTEXT
Comparing Regime Change in Israel and Judah

Fretheim notes, "The violence of Jehu may be explicitly contrasted with the minimal violence perpetrated by Jehoiada on Joash's behalf in a comparable move to power in chapters 11–12" (1999: 173). Considered in tandem, the regime changes in Israel and Judah recorded in 2 Kings 9–12 are a study in contrasts (Barré: 42–45). Jehu's coup is led by a military man who attributes his violent seizure of power to the prophets. Jehu emerges from the secret meeting with the young prophet, stating initially that the prophet's message had simply been *I anoint you king over Israel* (9:12). As the coup unfolds, Jehu himself is described as a *madman* (9:20 AT), repeatedly quoting (and exaggerating) the prophetic oracles as mandate for violence. In contrast, the seven-year-old child Joash (Jehoash) is publicly anointed king by a priest, confirmed by popular acclamation, and placed in a covenant relationship with the Lord and the people. The narrative makes no claim of divine support. The priest enlists military cooperation to deter violence, limiting it to two deaths, those of the usurper queen and the Baal priest. Humans assume responsibility for their actions by making covenants with the Lord and among themselves.

In Israel, the coup upsets shalom; in Jerusalem, covenant renewal brings *quiet* to the land. In both cases the Omride ruler is removed and Baal worship extinguished. In Israel, the narrator affirms Jehu's opposition to Ahab as a fulfillment of the Lord's mandate, but in the same breath he negatively assesses Jehu's failure to carefully follow the Lord's Torah. Jehoash is commended for doing right in the sight of the Lord by following the Torah of the priest (12:2). Ultimately the narrative evaluates Jehoash by covenant criteria, assessing him as doing right as taught by the priest but failing in not removing the high places and in compromising with the enemy (Dutcher-Walls 1996: 185). Second Kings 9–12 narrates the two regime changes without comment on the contrasts (see TBC for 2 Kings 13–14 for reference to Hosea's condemnation of Jehu's violence, Hos 1:4-5). Imposing right religion through violence contrasts negatively with the story of shalom-filled faithfulness.

Jehoash, a Second Solomon

Second Kings 11–12 presents Jehoash as a second Solomon (1 Kings 1–11). Their coronations include these parallels: Jehoash is the first king since Solomon said to be anointed by a priest. Both assassinate rival family members and their allies (Adonijah and Joab; Athaliah and Mattan) with assistance from mercenaries (Cherethites, Carites). Noisy crowds are assembled to acclaim the king. *Mišpaṭ* is associated with both (1 Kings 2:3; 2 Kings 11:14). Their youth and inexperience are highlighted (1 Kings 3:7; 2 Kings 11:21).

Their devotion to the Lord is demonstrated by the central place of the temple built by Solomon and first repaired by Jehoash. Jehoash, who *did what was right in the sight of the* LORD *all his days* (12:2), is evaluated more positively than Solomon, whose *heart was not true to the* LORD (1 Kings 11:4). Solomon built temples to the gods of the nations while Judah under Jehoash destroyed the temple of Baal. Solomon conscripted forced labor for his buildings, but Jehoash paid the workers fairly (1 Kings 5:13-18; 2 Kings 12:15). Both tolerated high places.

In the end both die under threat. Condemned by the Lord and the prophet Ahijah, Solomon faces external and internal adversaries (1 Kings 11). Jehoram is assassinated by his servants after bribing an enemy to avoid war (2 Kings 12:17-21). Though the condemnation of Solomon is explicit and that of Jehoram is implicit, neither realizes the potential expected by their righteous mentors, David and Jehoiada (for parallels between Jehoash and Josiah, see TBC for 2 Kings 22–23).

THE TEXT IN THE LIFE OF THE CHURCH

Shalom with Justice, Not Violence

Enns, a German Mennonite church representative to the World Council of Churches, writes that peace comes not by violence but by justice. In *The Peace Church and the Ecumenical Community: Ecclesiology and the Ethics of Nonviolence*, Enns defends justice and peace as a true expression of the gospel (2007). He emphasizes the importance of prayer as part of this movement; he agrees that shalom eschews violence but requires justice in social structures.

Christian scholars demonstrate that violence against injustice fails to bring peace. Hens-Piazza contends that Elijah's violence against the prophets and Jehu's fury against Jezebel are contagious. Jezebel, the foreign woman, is the scapegoat for the same offenses that Elijah and Jehu themselves commit (2006: 294-96). The frequent association of the term *shalom* with Jehu in 2 Kings 9–10 ironically shows that peace cannot be achieved through violence (Seow: 226). "Violence finally does not bring true peace. The *shalom* of Ahab, Jezebel, and Baal is no real peace and needs to be subverted and undone; but Jehu falls short of establishing a *shalom* that is genuine" (Fretheim 1999: 173). The issue is not simply idolatrous apostasy but also injustice in royal policies that ruin Naboth's vineyard (175).

James Cone, speaking from a Christian community that has experienced centuries of racialized oppression, warns that "nonviolence" can be used as a weapon to silence protest. White writes that

Cone "focused attention on divine justice in which divine wrath and divine love are not at odds with each other. He captured the subversive element in Christian thought that perceives love as violence against the status quo of white supremacy. Cone sees what he calls 'the terrible beauty of the cross'" (White: 10). While Anabaptist Christians eschew violent means, Cone shows that nonviolence without justice is insufficient.

Early Anabaptist Commentary

For Menno Simons, the deaths of Ahab and Jezebel as well as Jehoash show that human sinners "must bear [God's] punishment eternally and be subject to His judgment and wrath." Informed by 2 Chronicles 24:20-22 and Matthew 23:35, Menno refers to Jehoash as one "who was slain by his own servants to avenge the innocent blood of pious Zachariah, whom he slew between the temple and the altar" (Menno: 202). In his context, Menno writes to encourage marginalized disciples to depend on God, not human violence, to bring justice (Rom 12:19).

Dirk Philips comments on the incompleteness of Jehu's revival:

> Some may well hate the harlotry and sorcery of Jezebel and have a zeal against the priests and prophets of Baal. Nevertheless they themselves walk in the sins of Jeroboam and allow the golden calves (erected in the place of divine worship by the godless king) to stand and remain as judgment against themselves but a stumbling-block and destruction for others. (1564: 208–9)

The comment reminds contemporary followers of Christ that personal piety without commitment to social justice is half-hearted discipleship.

Kings of Israel and Judah during Jehu's Dynasty

PREVIEW

Anabaptists debate whether "two-kingdom theology" precludes participation in a liberal democracy. Does voting or holding office implicate Christians in an anti-Christ system? The ancient prophets seem to have had a similar debate. Elijah opposes Ahab unequivocally. Elisha is an insider who anoints Jehu and supports his dynasty. Amos, Hosea, and Micah, as outsiders with little access to the palace, condemn royal injustice.

Jehu's revolt is a watershed event, ending the dynasty of Israel's most evil kings (2 Kings 9–10; 1 Kings 16:29-33). Jehu rejected unjust royal appropriation of ancestral land (2 Kings 9:25-26, 36) and eliminated the Baal cult. Weakened by the violent coup and the loss of the Sidonian ally, Israel lost control of trade routes and the associated revenues (Master: 509–10), paid tribute to Assyria *[Archaeology: Black Obelisk of Shalmaneser III, p. 438]*, and lost Israelite territory to Aram (10:32-33; 13:3). Although Jehu is commended for doing right concerning the house of Ahab (10:30), his regime is ineffective politically and religiously. Ridding the land of Baal worship is an advance, but it is not enough. Jehu and his sons do not turn from the sins of Jeroboam (10:31; 13:2, 11; 14:24) *[Sins of Jeroboam, p. 476]*. The Jehu dynasty failed to return Israel to Deuteronomic justice *[Mišpaṭ, p. 461]*.

Second Kings 13:1–14:29 reports the reigns of Jehu's first three successors—Jehoahaz (13:1-9, 22), Jehoash (13:10-19, 23-25; 14:8-16), and Jeroboam (14:23-29)—and the reign of their contemporary in Judah, Amaziah son of Joash (14:1-22). The narrative of wars and successions in Israel and Judah is interrupted by the report of Elisha's final actions, death, and a related post-death miracle (13:14-21). At three points during the Jehu dynasty, the narrative describes the Lord's deliverance despite Israel's apostasy (13:5, 23; 14:27). Though Israel dominates Judah, Aram threatens Israel. Roughly equal space is devoted to Israel and Judah, but the narrative focuses primarily on Israel. God's freedom is apparent as the righteous kings of Judah suffer calamity while the wicked kings of Israel prevail (Hobbs: 177–78; Wray Beal 2014: 422).

OUTLINE

Jehoahaz of Israel, 13:1-9
Jehoash of Israel, 13:10-13
Death of Elisha, 13:14-21
Relief from Hazael of Aram, 13:22-25
Amaziah of Judah, 14:1-22
Jeroboam II of Israel, 14:23-29

EXPLANATORY NOTES
Jehoahaz of Israel 13:1-9

The structure of 2 Kings 13–14 includes overlaps, resumptions, premature and repetitive closing royal formulas, and the interruption of "royal time" for the Elisha burial story (13:14-21). Jehoash/Joash of Israel continues as an active character after the first report of his burial; the closing royal formula is repeated (13:13; 14:15-16). Though characterized as "loosely connected and haphazardly placed" (Seow: 234), "arranged in partial disarray," with "connections that violate the literary borders between reigns" (Long 1991: 164), the unexpected structure points toward a surprising message. The text juxtaposes the Lord's provision of a savior with Israel's continued practice of the sins of Jeroboam. This unexpected, undeserved deliverance contradicts the overarching theme that evil results in judgment.

The opening royal formula characterizes Jehoahaz as one who does evil (13:1-2) *[Chronology, p. 439; Sins of Jeroboam, p. 476]*. The Lord's anger kindled, the Lord repeatedly hands Israel into the power of the kings of Aram, Hazael and his son Ben-hadad (13:3).

The exchange between Jehoahaz and the Lord (13:4-6) recalls both the exodus and the cycles of apostasy in Judges (Exod 2:23-25; Judg 2:11-23; 3:7-15). When the unfaithful people provoke the Lord to anger, the Lord gives Israel into the hand of Aram (2 Kings 13:3) *[Provoke the Lord to Anger, p. 470]*. Defeat moves a desperate Jehoahaz to *entreat the* LORD (13:4; 1 Kings 13:6; Judges 3:9). *The Lord hears and sees the oppression of Israel* (cf. 2 Kings 13:4 NIV) and gives Israel a savior so that they *go out from the hand* of Aram (13:4-5 AT), echoing the exodus (Exod 2:23-25; 3:9; Deut 26:7; *go out* from Egypt is used five times in Exod 6 MT). The sequence of apostasy-oppression-crying out-deliverance partially parallels the Judges cycle (Judg 2:18; 4:3; 6:9; 10:12). Like the cycles of apostasy in Judges, in Kings "negative spirals . . . result in ever-worsening consequences" (Morgenstern: liv).

The puzzling reference to an unidentified *savior* underscores God's willingness to save in the future (13:5; Bodner 2019: 170). Among the candidates for the role of *savior* are (1) the Assyrian king Adad-nirari III, whose conflict with Aram provided Israel respite from Aramean oppression; (2) Jehoash (13:24-25); (3) Jeroboam II (14:27); and (4) the temporary relief afforded by the shifting political environment (Cogan and Tadmor: 143; Wray Beal 2014: 408). Several textual features suggest linking the God-sent *savior* with the prophetic word (Elisha in 2 Kings 13:14-21; Jonah son of Amittai in 14:25). First, the apparently disjointed textual structure employs the closing royal formulas to bracket out Jehoahaz (13:9) and Jehoash/ Joash (13:13) before the final appearance of Elisha, though both kings reappear in 2 Kings 13—after reports of their burial. Second, the name Elisha ("my God saves") associates Elisha with God's salvation. Third, the textual logic hinges on the word *nevertheless* (13:6). Despite the *savior* from the Lord, Israel *does not depart from the sins of Jeroboam* and worships the Asherah *[Idolatry, p. 449]*. The textual devices point to an important, unexpected theological claim: God sends a *savior* despite the sin of Israel.

The Israelite military is not among the candidates for savior of Israel. Conflict with Aram has *destroyed* Jehoahaz's army and chariot force and made them like *dust* (13:7; 9:8; 10:19; 24:2). Ben-hadad's threat to reduce Samaria to *dust* in 1 Kings 20:10 finds an ironic fulfillment. The standard closing royal formula concludes the report on the reign of Jehoahaz (2 Kings 13:8-9; reference to *his might* can be read ironically).

Jehoash of Israel 13:10-13

Opening and closing royal formulas summarize the reign of Jehoash (13:10-13). The reign begins in the thirty-seventh year of the reign of the king of Judah with the same name (and the same variation of the name: Joash) *[Chronology, p. 439]*. Like his predecessors, Jehoash of Israel does evil in the sight of the Lord and is buried in Samaria with the kings of Israel. Though the files open and close on Jehoash in 2 Kings 13:10-13, he plays a role in the death of Elisha in the next unit (13:14-21). He reappears again with the report of the victories in battle with Aram prophesied by Elisha (13:24-25). Jehoash battles Amaziah of Israel (14:8-14), followed by a nearly verbatim repeat of the closing royal formula (14:15-16). Closing the royal file on Jehoash before the report of Elisha's death highlights the primary role of the prophet.

Death of Elisha 13:14-21

The mind-numbing succession of evil kings in Israel is interrupted by a final story of the prophet Elisha—and a story involving his corpse. Having closed the royal file without opening another, the narrative returns to transitional space, where the story of Elijah and Elisha takes precedence. Like 2 Kings 2, this story narrates the passing of one of the two dominant prophets in 1 Kings 17–2 Kings 13 (after a fifty-year absence since Elisha sent the young prophet to anoint Jehu, 2 Kings 9:1-3). The textual interlude highlights that the power of the Lord in the prophets is independent of and superior to royal authority (Cohn: 87). The gap between royal files supports the rhetorical logic that the God-sent *savior* is the prophet.

Joash of Israel *goes down* to meet Elisha on his deathbed (13:14). Joash laments Elisha's fatal illness, crying out, *My father, my father! The chariots of Israel and its horsemen!* (quoting Elisha's cry at Elijah's departure, 2 Kings 2:12 NIV). Joash's exclamation acknowledges the superiority of prophetic authority (Bodner 2019: 171). True power in Israel resides not with the monarchy in pursuit of the ways of Jeroboam but with the prophets committed to the justice of the Lord [*Mišpaṭ, p. 461; Sins of Jeroboam, p. 476*]. The king confesses that power and authority belong to Yahweh and his servants the prophets. Ellul calls Elisha "the visible and active presence of God himself," with consolation for the afflicted (90).

Elisha responds to Joash's confession with an enacted symbolic prophecy ("ritual drama," Sweeney 2007a: 359; "sign-act" akin to Ahijah's tearing the garment, 1 Kings 11:29-32, Seow: 237). Elisha commands, Joash complies, and Elisha explains the symbolic action: *The LORD's arrow of victory, the arrow of victory over Aram! For you shall fight the Arameans in Aphek until you have made an end of them* (2 Kings 13:15-17). By striking only three times, Joash fails the prophetic test, angering Elisha, who exclaims that partial obedience to the command will result in only partial victory over Aram (13:18-19).

This symbolic action scene, though mystifying for the contemporary reader, extends the rhetorical logic of 2 Kings 13–14, condemning the king's failure to use all the arrows as incomplete obedience, much like Ahab's failure to pursue victory over Aram at Aphek (1 Kings 20:26-43; "disregard for the will of God in holy war," Seow: 238). Elisha's ministry ends with angry judgment of the dynasty of Jehu, instituted by Elisha (parallel to Samuel's grief at Saul's failure as king, 1 Sam 15:35–16:1).

The final Elisha stories demonstrate that Elisha ("my God saves") is a conduit for the Lord's salvation (13:5; Weingart: 266). The final miracle story may be read as a dramatic parable. Just as Elisha's bones brought life after death to the man *thrown into the grave of Elisha*, so the reader can find hope despite the death of the nation *thrown* into exile (13:21; 24:20; Bodner 2016: 209–12). Just as the report of Elisha's death interrupts the report of the Jehu dynasty, so the Lord breaks into the story with the promise of salvation, of life after death. The Lord overcomes the *nevertheless* of Israel's pursuit of the ways of Jeroboam with the *nevertheless* of life from dead bones (Ezek 37). Though the story of the Lord's power over life and death exercised by Elijah and Elisha is complete (Hens-Piazza 2006: 323), the voice of the prophets resonates in Jonah son of Amittai (2 Kings 14:25), the prophecy of Huldah (22:14-20), and the writing prophets (Isaiah, Jeremiah, Ezekiel, and the minor prophets).

Relief from Hazael of Aram 13:22-25

The disrupted narrative form, the report of Elisha's death (13:14-21) inserted between two reports of the closure of the royal file of Jehoash (13:12-13; 14:15-16), points to the surprising saving mercy of the Lord despite Israel's sinful ways. The "pausal moment" of 2 Kings 13:22-25 ("analepsis"—narrative interruption with new background information) extends the disrupting interlude with the claim that the Lord delivers Israel (Long 1991: 165). The royal reality is despair. King Hazael of Aram, fully the scourge that Elisha anticipated (8:7-15), *oppressed* Israel throughout the reign of Jehoahaz (13:22; see 13:4). Divine mercy interrupts royal despair. The Lord's gracious covenant compassion (Exod 33:19; 34:6-7; 1 Kings 8:33-34, 47-50, 59; 9:3; 18:36) keeps the Lord from *destroying* and *sending* Israel away (see also 2 Kings 8:19, where the Lord would not *destroy* Jehoram of Judah because of his promise to David to keep a lamp burning in his name). Though the Lord's covenant mercy explains why Israel is not yet destroyed by the powerful enemy, the text warns that exile has not happened *until now*, reminding the reader of the inevitable fate awaiting the rebellious nation (13:23) [*Covenant in Kings, p. 443*]. Though the deliverance is less complete than it might have been (13:17-19), nonetheless God delivers Israel as Jehoash *defeats* Ben-hadad and restores cities that Jehoahaz lost to Hazael (13:25; *defeat* used forty-three times in 2 Kings).

Amaziah of Judah 14:1-22

Shifting the perspective back to Judah, the standard opening royal formula [*Chronology, p. 439*] introduces Amaziah with reservations, citing his failure to live up to the model of David (14:3; cf. 16:2; 18:3; 22:2) and to remove the high places for sacrifice (14:4). Though the long-lasting Davidic dynasty contrasts with the situation in Israel (1 Kings 2:4; 8:25; 9:5; 11:36; 15:4; 2 Kings 8:19), tables have been reversed with Jehu's dynasty (10:30). Ahaziah (9:28), the usurper Athaliah (11:16), Joash (12:20), and Amaziah (14:19) are assassinated, evidence of instability in Jerusalem.

Amaziah's reign is dominated by violence (Brueggemann 2000: 439). Amaziah's reprisal against his father's assassins (14:5) is the first of three acts attributed to him as king, all violent but none fully successful. Execution of his father's killers fails to protect Amaziah from the same fate (14:19). The narrator quotes Deuteronomy 24:16 in commending Amaziah for sparing the families of the assassins (14:6; see TBC).

Second Kings 14:7-14 reports Amaziah's military ventures. Amaziah takes *Sela* ("the rock"; the Nabatean rock-city of Petra; Fanwar: 1074) and reestablishes Judean control over Edom (14:7; Edom is a barometer of the status of the kings of Judah, Seow: 241; see 1 Kings 22:47; 2 Kings 8:20-22). The victory is bloody but incomplete; it remains for his son to rebuild the important Red Sea port Elath (14:22).

Amaziah overreaches by challenging Jehoash to *look one another in the face* (14:8). Amaziah refuses to listen to the wisdom of Jehoash warning against battle (14:9-11). The battle location in Bethshemesh, a border town in northwest Judah (Brandfon: 696), indicates that the military advantage is with Israel. When Israel prevails, Judah's men scatter, and Jehoash captures Amaziah, destroys the city wall of Jerusalem between two primary gates, takes hostages, and loots gold and silver (14:12-14), foreshadowing the destruction of Jerusalem and the exile of Judah in 2 Kings 25 (Provan 1995: 236–37).

The repeated closing royal formula on the reign of Jehoash of Israel marks the unexpected favor of God despite Israel's sins

(14:15-16; see also 13:12-13). Though Elisha condemns Jehoash's failure to trust fully in the prophetic word (cf. 13:14-19), the Lord uses him to restore Israel's fortunes. Amaziah's trust in military power results in humiliation.

Though Amaziah survives Jehoash by fifteen years, the closing royal formula for Amaziah reports a conspiracy against him without specifying what motivated the opposition (14:17-21). Amaziah flees to the military post of Lachish, thirty miles southwest of Jerusalem, but Amaziah's pursuers assassinate him. Amaziah is buried with honors in the royal cemetery of Jerusalem [*Archaeology: Lachish, p. 439*].

The people of Judah make Amaziah's sixteen-year-old son Azariah king (14:21). The motivations of the various groups involved in supporting kings are not clear. Amaziah's father, Joash, is installed with the support of *the people of the land* (11:17-20); on Amaziah's investiture, the text reports only that his mother's hometown was Jerusalem, perhaps indicating the source of his support (14:2). *The people of Judah* supporting Azariah may represent another faction. The narrative footnote that it was after Amaziah's death that *the king* (Azariah) rebuilds Elath (14:22), the port city on the Red Sea (1 Kings 9:26-28; 10:11-12), is further indication of the limits of Amaziah's royal capacity.

Jeroboam II of Israel 14:23-29

The narrative shifts back to Israel with the accession of Jeroboam II, son of Joash of Israel (14:23). The longest reign of a king of Israel merits one of the briefest reports (less than Zimri, with a reign of just seven days, 1 Kings 16:9-20); though Jeroboam is credited with restoring Israel's control over lost territory, the report emphasizes the saving act of the Lord. The report of Jeroboam's reign includes an opening royal formula (14:23-24), an account of the Lord's salvation (14:25-27), and a closing royal formula (14:28-29). The opening royal formula synchronizes with Amaziah, reports the length of tenure (forty-one years, exceeded only by Judah's Amaziah with fifty-two years and Manasseh with fifty-five years), and characterizes Jeroboam II as doing *evil in the sight of the LORD* by failing to *depart from the sins of Jeroboam son of Nebat* (14:24) [*Chronology, p. 439; Sins of Jeroboam, p. 476*]. Nothing in the typical opening formula prepares the reader for the dramatic reversal of fortunes in Israel during the reign of Jeroboam II.

The account avoids mentioning the king by name and attributing Israel's prosperity to his actions (*He himself restored the border of*

Israel, 14:25 AT; the Hebrew *he himself* is emphatic, but the personal name is absent). The gains re-establish the territorial limits of Solomon's reign, from Lebo-hamath in northern Lebanon to *the Sea of the Arabah*, the Dead Sea [*Archaeology: Solomon's Gates and Stables, p. 437*]. The text directs attention toward the surprising message that the Lord is giving a *savior* to Israel (and away from confidence in Israel's king and its military) according to Jonah, one of only two latter prophets named in 1–2 Kings (Isaiah is the other, 2 Kings 19–20). Jonah also proclaims that the Lord is merciful even to pagan Nineveh (Jon 4:2) [*Prophets: Prophetic Word, p. 469*]. Yahweh, *God of Israel* (2 Kings 9:6; 10:31)—who was moved to save Israel by the entreaty of Jehoahaz (13:4), by his gracious compassion, and by the covenant with the ancestors (13:23)—is moved again by the bitter distress and helplessness of Israel (14:26). *Distress* (*oppression*) echoes the situation of Israel in Egypt (Exod 3:7), as does the root of the word *bitter* (1:14). The phrase *bond or free* is another unexpected reference in this message of hope since the other uses of the phrase are connected to announcements of complete destruction of northern dynasties (1 Kings 14:10; 21:21; 2 Kings 9:8; Olley 2011: 212).

The report concludes, *The LORD . . . saved them by the hand of Jeroboam son of Joash* (14:27), finally resolving the identity of the *savior* that *the LORD gave Israel* (13:5). The Lord, who *saved Israel* from the hand of the Egyptians and from their enemies, uses the *hand* (*power*) of Israel's greatest king to *deliver* (Exod 14:30; Judg 2:18; *deliver*, used twenty times in Judges, characteristic of the Judges cycle). The concluding royal formula adds to the standard language the report that Jeroboam has successfully *recovered* [*turn*; see 2 Kings 14:25] *for Israel Damascus and Hamath for Judah* (AT 14:28; a puzzling identification resolved by NRSV and NIV as *had belonged to Judah*). Jeroboam's son Zechariah succeeds him (14:29).

Just seven verses report the forty-one-year reign of Jeroboam II, the high point of Israelite power and wealth. The narrator's struggle to understand Jeroboam's success within the story of divine judgment against Israel's unremitting failure to serve the Lord (2 Kings 17) is evident in the statement that opens 14:27. The twin summary statements *He has not banished them until now* (13:23 AT) and *The LORD had not said that he would blot out . . . Israel* (14:27) strikingly underscore the Lord's freedom. Divine grace is not bound by human unrighteousness (Wray Beal 2014: 422).

The disjointed literary structure underscores the surprising theological message (Nelson 1987: 126). The ascendance of Israel despite its apostasy and the reduced fortunes of Judah despite a relatively positive report of Amaziah's piety run counter to expectations. The word of the Lord through Elisha (13:14-21) and Jonah (14:25) assures the kings that the Lord will give them victory. The Lord's saving acts of compassion outweigh his anger (13:3, 5, 23; 14:25-27; Fretheim 1999: 187-88). The reports of 2 Kings 13–14 effectively debunk the rigidly formulaic view that God rewards good and punishes failure by showing that sinful Israel is saved by God through sinful Jeroboam (Hens-Piazza 2006: 322-33). The Lord moves outside the stereotypical condemnation of the kings of Israel to affirm the Lord's concern for Israel (10:30; 13:4-5; 14:25-27; Brueggemann 2008: 27).

The literary fault lines open fissures for God's gracious acts of salvation, offering hope for despairing exilic readers of the story (Olley 2011: 214-16). The prophetic messages point beyond this text to other prophets, including the book of Jonah with its emphasis that the grace of God extends beyond Israel to the feared imperial enemy in Nineveh. These fissures also open the reader to the messages of Hosea and Amos condemning the violence and economic oppression associated with Jeroboam II (see TBC below).

THE TEXT IN BIBLICAL CONTEXT
Deuteronomic Torah

The full quotation of the Torah of Moses limiting punishment to the guilty (and not their descendants) is unique in 1–2 Kings (2 Kings 14:6; Deut 24:16). Deuteronomic Torah limits royal power in Judah and Israel. Primary Torah values are righteousness and justice (Vogt: 216-20, 229-30).

Scholars agree that Deuteronomic values are the standard of evaluation for Joshua through Kings. In the Deuteronomic worldview the sovereign Lord is present with God's people through Torah and Torah obedience, the practice of egalitarian righteousness (Vogt: 229). The central place of Torah limits the powers of kings, as is evident in the limited retribution of Amaziah (14:6; Vogt: 225). Kaminsky argues that the legislation in Deuteronomy 24:16 was generated by the story of Amaziah and included to limit the monarch's power by prohibiting the king from inflicting capital punishment (129).

Vogt also addresses the issue of centralization of worship in the place that the Lord will choose (Deut 12). He contends that two issues are primary. First, all competing loyalties are to be rejected. Second, the Lord's sovereignty is emphasized by worshiping at the place the Lord chooses. According to Vogt, the issue is not that worship should be limited to one place, but that Torah obedience is the experience of God's presence. The high places are a problem when they erode loyalty to the Lord.

Prophetic Voices: Hosea, Amos, Isaiah

Hosea and Amos prophesy judgment against Israel during Jeroboam's reign [*Prophets, p. 465*]. Hosea uses the metaphor of adultery to accuse Israel of covenant unfaithfulness. Though the Lord has provided for Israel, Israel has lavished its wealth on the false gods of violence, oppression, and opulence.

Unlike the unevaluated report of Jehu's coup (2 Kings 9–10), Hosea announces judgment against "the house of Jehu for the blood of Jezreel," declaring that the Lord "will break the bow of Israel in the valley of Jezreel" (1:4-5). Hosea decries oppression, rebellion, pride, and the lack of faithfulness, loyalty, and covenant "knowledge of God" (4:1). Addressing priests and prophets for their failure to teach the Torah, Hosea accuses Israel of having broken the Ten Commandments and having lost themselves in violence ("bloodshed follows bloodshed," 4:2; 3-10; 5:1). Instead of righteousness and covenant love, the people have practiced wickedness and injustice (10:12-13). The Lord agonizes over the fickleness of his people, yearning to love as a husband loves a wife and as a parent loves children. The prophet expresses hope for Israel's renewed faithfulness, walking in the righteous ways of the Lord (14:1-7).

Hosea and 1–2 Kings condemn Israel's idolatry. The covenant people have forsaken Torah ethics. Kings and Hosea agree that royal justice is to be shaped by Deuteronomic values, and the marginalized are to be protected by the powerful; both agree that Israel has failed to live up to this ideal.

Amos announces judgment against Israel's rebellion, concluding with a comprehensive indictment for having afflicted the poor, hazed the religious, rejected the prophets, and relied on violence; military defeat is predicted (Amos 2:6-16). He warns that the anticipated "day of the LORD" will not bring the expected deliverance but will result in judgment (5:18-20). Justice and righteousness, not sweet-flowing worship melodies, are the antidote to injustice (5:21-24). Amos indicts the wealthy for their luxurious, complacent lifestyle (6:1-8). Even with such a blistering condemnation, Amos concludes with a word of hope (9:11-15).

The theme of justice is prominent in Amos. The sins of Jeroboam son of Nebat (1 Kings 12–2 Kings 23) involve not only idolatry but also injustice. Amos focuses more on unjust economic practices of his own contemporary, Jeroboam II, than on improper worship.

Isaiah, a contemporary of Hosea and Amos, addresses Judah; he links violence to oppression of the poor. "Your hands are full of blood. Wash yourselves; . . . cease to do evil, learn to do good; seek justice, rescue the oppressed, defend the orphan, plead for the widow." (Isa 1:15-17). Isaiah declares that shedding blood, scarlet and crimson, is unjust (1:18).

The three prophets agree. The urban royal elite disregard the rural peasant and the marginalized. Unfair courts, loans, and taxes violate Torah and bring destruction.

THE TEXT IN THE LIFE OF THE CHURCH
Remembering Fallen Heroes

Elisha is remembered as the man of God who preserved a marginal community under threat from internal economic pressures and external military foes. In addition to Elisha's powerful intervention during his lifetime, two stories are told about how he reaches back from the grave to give salvation. On his deathbed he promises victory to Jehoash of Israel. From his grave, Elisha resuscitates a man being buried. These fantastic stories are the things of legend.

Anabaptists have ambivalent appreciation for past heroes. Mennists, now called Mennonites, were nicknamed after Menno Simons, the sixteenth-century Dutch reformer. We remember church leaders from the Radical Reformation as well as more recent leaders of note. We often lament that gone are the days when a great leader could speak for all and create consensus in critical moments. Where have the great leaders gone?

We live in an age when superheroes are limited to action movies. We tend toward a less hierarchical and more egalitarian view of leadership. We recognize great leaders after we have gained the perspective of time. Perhaps in the future we will, with nostalgia, remember some current leaders made great with the passing of time. Perhaps we live in a world where our more egalitarian perspective is God's gift, which allows us to find strength within the community of the saints.

Mercy Triumphs over Judgment

One of the puzzles of 2 Kings 13–14 is that God's salvation comes despite the anger of the Lord kindled against Israel for its persistence in sin. God saves Israel by the hand of Jeroboam despite the report that the king has done what was evil in the Lord's sight.

The epistle of James calls readers to care for the poor and practice egalitarian economics [Mišpaṭ, p. 461]. Concluding that "mercy triumphs over judgment," James prescribes the "royal law": loving one's neighbor as oneself (2:8-13). Loving the neighbor eliminates partiality and judgmental attitudes. Christians are called to extend mercy, not judgment. For mercy to triumph, the practice of "wisdom from above" is needed, characterized by gentleness, willingness to yield, and peacemaking (3:13-18).

2 Kings 15:1–17:41

The Fall of Samaria

PREVIEW

"Let the good times roll"; with confetti and strobe lights, this meme celebrates a hedonistic culture. The phrase articulates a bull-market investment strategy on Wall Street. Though market collapses devastate many for decades (e.g., the Great Depression), big governments bail out big banks with big tax breaks justified by trickle-down economic theories. The "good times" economic strategy of Jeroboam II and Uzziah created an urban elite with an agrarian revolution that promoted cash crops at the expense of subsistence diversification needed to feed the farmers (Chaney 2014: 38) [*Economics in Ancient Israel, p. 444*]. When Assyrian imperial power reasserted itself in the third quarter of the eighth century (746–722 BCE), peasants bore the brunt of the economic burden while the urban elite "let the good times roll."

Second Kings 15:1–17:41 reports the final kings of Israel; Judah's kings Azariah (= Uzziah), Jotham, and Ahaz; and the fall of Samaria with Israelite exile from the land. Because of the brief tenure of the post-Jehuide kings, this summary of the six last kings of Israel has been dubbed "king-of-the-month club." The reigns of the Israelite kings reported here primarily as royal formulas and coup stories total about thirty years. In contrast, two kings of Judah, Jotham and Ahaz, rule for thirty-two years. Though the dynasty is stable, Judah is even weaker than disintegrating Israel. This sad tale collapses into a judgment summarizing Israel's failure and explaining repopulation of the land by the Assyrian Empire.

The precipitous decline of Israel's fortunes from its prosperous heyday under Jeroboam II to its ultimate collapse in the Assyrian exile (722 BCE), a series of mostly forgettable and insignificant rulers, includes explicit verdicts rendered on the individual kings (Brueggemann 2000: 459). The brief details of each ruler are insufficient to set apart the summaries, yet together they build to a climax of a harsh, negative verdict upon the royal history of Israel and Judah (Hens-Piazza 2006: 334). The fortunes of Judah relative to Israel appear to be brighter in 2 Kings 15 than in the previous chapter, but Israel's exile foreshadows that of its southern neighbor.

OUTLINE

EXPLANATORY NOTES

Azariah of Judah 15:1-7

After focusing on the Lord's deliverance of Israel under Jeroboam II (2 Kings 13–14), the spotlight shifts to Judah. The standard opening royal formula and evaluation (doing what is right in the eyes of the Lord but failing to remove the high places) recall Azariah's father, Amaziah (15:1-4) [*Chronology, p. 439*]. The only reported detail of Azariah's fifty-two-year reign (second only to the fifty-five-year tenure of Manasseh) is that the Lord struck him with leprosy so that he lived in a separate house while his son Jotham ruled in his stead (15:5). The narrative reports that Jotham ("Yahweh is perfect"; Gray: 619; 15:32-38) *executed justice over the people of the land* (AT 15:5b). In the otherwise unremarkable litany of successive kings, the reference to *doing justice* (AT) reminds the reader of its significance in this story [*Mišpaṭ, p. 461*].

The report of Azariah's reign (15:1-7) and that of his son Jotham (15:32-38) bracket the reports of the five kings of Israel in the chapter. Details of Azariah's reign baffle contemporary interpreters. Are Azariah and Uzziah variations of the same name, or is Uzziah the throne name (15:13, 30-34; both mean "victory of Yahweh"; Wray Beal 2014: 427)? Does his long term include coregencies with his father or his son or both? The Chronicler's lengthy account of Uzziah explains the length, success, and failure of Uzziah's reign as well as the cause of his leprosy (2 Chron 26). In 2 Kings 15 the reign of Azariah in Judah complements the central focus on the decline of Israel, concluding with the typical closing royal formula (15:6-7). Azariah is the first king of Judah to die a natural death since Joram (8:24) [Kings in the Hebrew Canon: Kings and Chronicles, p. 455].

Zechariah of Israel 15:8-12

In Israel, Zechariah succeeds his father, Jeroboam II, with the evaluation that he *did not depart from the sins of Jeroboam son of Nebat* (15:9). After the opulence and military success of Jeroboam's forty-one-year reign, Zechariah, the final ruler of the Jehu dynasty, is king for only six months (15:8, 10). The Lord's promise to Jehu of ruling descendants to the fourth generation has been fulfilled (15:11-12) [Prophets: Prophetic Word, p. 469]. A period of instability follows Shallum's assassination of Zechariah.

In contrast to Omri and Ahab, the epitome of evil, Jehu's dynasty is viewed more favorably than any other period of the Northern Kingdom (10:30; 13:4, 14-24; 14:27). Zechariah's death severs the last explicit link to divine intervention to save Israel, and the direct influence of Elijah and Elisha ends. Second Kings 15 recounts the last five transitions to the throne of Israel, its decline, and its disintegration. Reference to fulfilling the word of the Lord is absent until the exile report (17:12-13), though evil is done in the *sight of the* LORD (15:18, 24, 28; 16:2; Jotham does *right in the sight of the* LORD, 15:34).

Shallum of Israel 15:13-16

Shallum, *son of Jabesh* (perhaps a patronym identifying his father's name but more likely connecting him to the region of Jabesh-Gilead, east of the Jordan River, Jones: 521) strikes down Zechariah in public, an indication of popular support for his action (15:10). According to the NIV footnote, some Septuagint manuscripts read that Shallum struck *in Ibleam*, ironically placing the assassination at the place where Zechariah's great-grandfather Jehu struck Ahaziah of Judah in his coup against the Omride dynasty (9:27). The standard opening royal formula synchronizes Shallum's brief one-month reign with that of King Uzziah (= Azariah; 15:13) [*Chronology, p. 439*]. Menahem conspires against Shallum and rules in his place (15:14). The closing royal formula mentions Shallum's conspiracy and the Book of the Annals without including any evaluation of Shallum, an oversight that makes him uniquely free of a negative assessment among all the kings of Israel (15:15). Rather than creating a sense of something more positive, the absence may reflect disinterest in Shallum as well as a chaotic downward spiral within Israel itself.

The conspirator Menahem, son of Gadi (likely a personal name, though some associate Gadi with the region of Gad in the Transjordan; Gray: 622), from the rival power center of Tirzah, Israel's capital under Baasha (1 Kings 15:33) attacks Shallum in the capital city of Samaria. Because Tiphsah refuses to *open* to him, Menahem sacks its territory, *ripping open* their pregnant women, an act of extreme brutality against life itself, a war atrocity that Amos condemns in Ammon (2 Kings 15:16; Amos 1:13; cf. 2 Kings 8:12).

Menahem of Israel 15:17-22

Like Shallum, Menahem (incongruously meaning "comforting") has been introduced before the standard opening royal formula commences the file on his reign, reflecting the chaos prevailing in both narrative structure and content. The narrator evaluates Menahem as another king of Israel who continues in the sins of Jeroboam (15:17-18) [*Sins of Jeroboam, p. 476*]. The single episode reported of Menahem is the tribute paid to King Pul (Tiglath-pileser III; 15:29; 16:10; *ANET* 283) to gain support for his hold on the kingdom and to entice the withdrawal of the Assyrian army, tribute financed by a fifty-shekel tax on the wealthy of Israel (15:19-20). Menahem is the agent of these actions (Menahem *gives* Pul the funds and *exacts the money from Israel*). The amount, commensurate with other tributes, is sufficient to pay for an entire army (18:14; Hobbs: 200). The Assyrian army financed through Menahem's tribute returns to attack Pekah (15:29; Dubovský 2014: 340). The concluding royal formula of Menahem reports that his son Pekahiah ("Yah[weh] illumines") succeeds him (15:21-22).

Dubovský points out that the account of Menahem is centrally located in the chapter, is the longest of the accounts, and is the most revealing in content. Menahem is guilty of war atrocities; his extreme violence denies covenant justice. His extraction of wealth from Israel to pay Assyria reverses flow of tribute from other peoples paid to Solomon (1 Kings 4), making him the foolish anti-Solomon. Though Menahem buys time for himself and his heir, his payments support the Assyrian army, which will desolate Israel (Dubovský 2014: 338–40).

Pekahiah of Israel 15:23-26

Sandwiched between the introductory and concluding royal formulas of the reign of Pekahiah is the report that his trusted captain Pekah conspires against Pekahiah in the citadel of the palace, the most secure place in Samaria (2 Kings 15:25). His conspiracy involves a company of fifty men (cf. 2 Kings 1:9; 2:7; 13:7), hailing from Gilead, a region in the Transjordan, indicating regional rivalries. The growing complexity of the conspiratorial acts and division signals increasing instability (Dubovský 2014: 324–32).

Pekah of Israel 15:27-31

The report of Pekah's reign begins with the opening royal formula (15:27-28). The twenty-year tenure does not fit within the chronology, giving rise to speculation that Pekah led a rival regime east of the Jordan allied with Aram to form the anti-Assyrian Syro-Ephraimite coalition (Hobbs: 201). The alliance (see 15:37) threatens Assyrian control of the lucrative trade routes near Samaria, including the King's Highway south of Gilead, the coastal route between Tyre and Philistia (Way of the Sea), and the overland route through the central highlands The narrative reports that Tiglath-pileser captures much Israelite territory and takes its *people captive to Assyria* (15:29). In contrast to the earlier Assyrian advance where Menahem took the initiative (15:19-20), Tiglath-pileser controls the action. The progressive Assyrian dominance is consistent with Assyrian strategy to reduce independence of nations blocking its aims (control of trade routes between Assyria and the Great Sea, the Mediterranean), a strategy which includes exiling the wealthy (Dubovský 2006: 155–57, 163). Conquest of the cities named in the text strategically opens the territory of Samaria to Assyrian aims (Konkel 2006: 553; Sweeney 2007a: 376).

The coup of Hoshea against Pekah is the last of the conspiracies reported in 2 Kings 15. The report itself (15:30) is even more concise than that of Shallum against Zechariah (15:10); but in contrast with the others, this report is distinguished by linking it with Assyria's conquest and deportation of captive people (15:29), underlining the deteriorating plight of Israel (Dubovský 2014: 329–31). The anti-Assyrian strategy of Pekah is disastrous for Samaria; Hoshea conspires against Pekah and assassinates him (15:30). The concluding royal formula includes no burial notice (15:31).

Jotham of Judah 15:32-38

The focus on the downward spiral in Israel is interrupted by reports of the reigns of Judah's kings, Jotham and his son Ahaz. Readers have met Jotham as the coregent of Azariah/Uzziah, who rules with justice (15:3). The standard opening royal formula offers a positive if qualified evaluation of Jotham's reign (15:32-35) [Chronology, p. 439]. One indication of the difficulty in using the years supplied in the royal formulas to reconstruct a timeline is the contradiction between dating an event in Israel to the twentieth year of Jotham's reign and the report of Jotham's sixteen-year reign (15:30, 33). While coregency is a plausible explanation, the complications are more involved than the discrepancy identified here. The king's mother, Jerusha, is a daughter of Zadok, a priestly name, possibly indicating priestly association and explaining the report of Jotham's only royal act, a temple-building project. The closing royal formula is interrupted by the threat of Rezin of Aram and Pekah son of Remaliah against Judah (15:36-38). The threat is attributed to the Lord without explanation, perhaps anticipating judgment on Jotham's successor, the evil king Ahaz. Jotham dies and is buried without responding to the Syro-Ephraimite coalition.

Ahaz of Judah 16:1-20

The king-of-the-month club is interrupted by a full report of the reign of Ahaz of Judah. Second Kings 16 begins with an extended opening royal formula (16:1-4), followed by the report of international conflict involving Aram, Israel, Edom, and Assyria (16:5-9), a report of Ahaz's anti-Yahwistic temple reforms (16:10-18), and the closing royal formula (16:19-20). Ahaz's reign is a total disaster religiously, economically, and politically. Unlike his father and his son and most of the kings of Judah who precede Ahaz, this king rejects the ways of the Lord. Not only does he fail to continue their current policies; Ahaz also initiates changes that oppose Deuteronomic values.

The opening royal formula includes the standard data (16:1-2) [Chronology, p. 439]. Among the chronological problems presented with these years is that Ahaz's reign begins when he is twenty years old, lasts sixteen years, and is succeeded by his twenty-five-year-old son Hezekiah, making Ahaz eleven years old at Hezekiah's birth. Though solutions involving a coregency with Jotham are plausible, nothing in the text supports such theories. Perhaps it is better to attribute the disruption in dates to the political turbulence caused by the invasion of Tiglath-pileser III (Konkel 2006: 564).

The extended negative evaluation indicts Ahaz for failure to *do what was right in the sight of the* LORD *his God, as his ancestor David had done* (16:2-4). Unlike the four immediately preceding kings of Judah, for whom positive assessment (*he did what was right in the sight of the* LORD) is followed by negative exceptions (12:3; 14:4; 15:4, 35), Ahaz is an unqualified failure. Like Jehoram (8:18), the only other king of Judah introduced without mention of the name of his mother, Ahaz *walked in the way of the kings of Israel* (16:3), imitating them by following the sins of Jeroboam and the evil Ahab. The Ahab-like behavior of Jehoram and his son Ahaziah is attributed to their family connections (8:18, 27), but Ahaz, who like all Judah's kings after Jehoram, is descended not only from David but also from Ahab, is worse for having no immediate negative role models as an excuse (Wray Beal 2014: 437). Like Ahab, who *acted most abominably in going after idols, as the Amorites had done, whom the* LORD *drove out before the Israelites* (1 Kings 21:26), Ahaz follows *the abominable practices of the nations whom the* LORD *drove out before the people of Israel* (16:3; this phrase is also used of Rehoboam, 1 Kings 14:24) *[Idolatry, p. 449]*. The most serious cultic offense, *he even made his son pass through fire* (2 Kings 16:3, likely a reference to child sacrifice), is listed first. The Deuteronomic covenant prohibits the "abominable practices" of Canaan, which "the LORD hates," such as "burning their sons and their daughters in the fire to their gods" (Deut 12:31; 18:10). Child sacrifice, such as to Molech, is prohibited (Lev 18:21; 20:1-5) but practiced in Israel by the people who replace the exiles (2 Kings 17:31), by Manasseh (21:6), and by the people of Judah who worship at the high place of Hinnom (Jer 7:31). Ahaz's anti-Deuteronomic, anti-Yahwistic practice includes sacrifice *on the high places, on the hills, and under every green tree* (2 Kings 16:4). Whereas his predecessors are sanctioned for allowing worship on the high places (1 Kings 22:43; 2 Kings 12:3; 14:4; 15:4, 35), Ahaz is condemned not only for worshiping on the high places himself but also for extending that worship to the hills and to every green tree, a reference to Canaanite fertility cults with the associated illicit sexual rites (Ackerman: 152–63), activity also expressly forbidden by the Deuteronomic covenant code (Deut 12:2; Judah also worshiped *on every high hill and under every green tree* during Rehoboam's reign, 1 Kings 14:23; Israel worshiped *under every green tree* before exile, 2 Kings 17:10). The transgressions mark Ahaz as the nadir of evil among the kings of Judah preceding Manasseh, who outdoes them all. This catalog of sins indicates Ahaz's complete rejection of the Lord.

The Ahaz report proceeds without further evaluation. The body deals first with Ahaz's reaction to the apparently irresolvable political threat posed by being caught between two greater powers, the Syro-Ephraimite coalition and the Assyrian Empire (16:5-9). This is followed by details of Ahaz's cultic reforms, developing his earlier decisions (16:10-18). By setting the stage with the negative evaluation of Ahaz's theological orientation, reporting the political situation and decisions, and detailing the cultic reforms without comment, the account leaves narrative gaps. The Chronicler's reinterpretation of the narrative and the perspective of the prophet Isaiah, a contemporary of Ahaz who offers an alternative solution for Ahaz's predicament, help fill those gaps (see TBC) [Kings in the Hebrew Canon: Kings and Chronicles, p. 455].

The narrative returns to the threat of Aram and Israel attributed to the Lord (15:37; the Lord's actions may be interpreted as consequence of Ahaz's rejection of the Lord's ways, 16:1-4). With the goal of forcing Ahaz to join their Syro-Ephraimite coalition against Assyria (15:29), Aram and Israel march on Jerusalem and besiege it, but they are unable to conquer Ahaz (16:5). With Ahaz and his army shut up in Jerusalem, Judah loses control of the Edomite port of Elath, rebuilt by Ahaz's grandfather, King Azariah of Judah (see EN for 2 Kings 14:22 on Edom as a barometer of the fortunes of the kings of Judah). The Hebrew text recounts that Aram claimed Elath, but the NRSV follows other ancient versions to say that Edom regained Elath (16:6). With the subsequent defeat of Aram by Assyria, coupled with the report that the status quo had prevailed to this day, Edom appears more likely. Ahaz's rejection of the Lord leaves him in a desperate situation, overpowered by the immediate Syro-Ephraimite threat and in the shadow of the aggressively destructive Assyrian Empire.

Walking in the way of the kings of Israel (16:4), Ahaz is unable to imagine trust in the LORD the God of Israel (as his son Hezekiah does in 18:5; see Isa 7), so he must choose between the opposing military threats. By opting for an alliance with Assyria, he avoids the most immediate threat for a much bigger, longer-term, and more dangerous foe. The besieged king sends messengers to Tiglath-pileser of Assyria (16:7). Though reported without evaluation, the message repudiates allegiance to Yahweh in return for an alliance with Assyria. Ahaz pledges his subservience to Tiglath-pileser, referring to himself as his servant and his son, self-designations that are used by the Davidic king to express his loyalty to Yahweh (2 Sam 7:14; Pss 2:7; 89:20, 26). Ahaz begs Tiglath-pileser to come save him (the Lord saves Israel from Egypt and Aram, Exod 14:30; Deut 20:4; 33:29; Brueggemann 2000: 468). Bereft of a relationship with Israel's savior Yahweh, Ahaz risks aligning with Assyria for immediate relief from the siege of Aram and Israel, without regard for the implications that submission to Assyria entails for future generations (2 Kings 18:7, 13). With the message Ahaz *sends* Tiglath-pileser a *bribe* from the temple and palace treasuries, silver and gold devoted to the service of the Lord (16:8 AT; Deut 27:25 pronounces a curse against anyone who takes a *bribe*; see also Exod 23:8; Deut 10:17; 16:19). Much as King Asa of Judah did when he sent a bribe to Ben-hadad in Damascus under threat from Baasha of Israel (1 Kings 15:18-19), Ahaz seeks relief from a superior power (Ahaz, like Asa, seeks a treaty with a northern power against a northern power and cleans out the temple treasury; Hezekiah follows this pattern, 2 Kings 18:14-15; Lowery: 95). Ahaz invites Assyrian intervention, paying the Assyrian army to invade and destroy Aram and Israel, actions that have been initiated and reported above (15:29). While the language *your servant and your son* (16:7) is indicative of a formal relationship and Judah becomes subservient to Assyria, the text is silent regarding a covenant treaty binding the two. What is clear is that Ahaz has rejected the Lord as savior, pledged loyalty to Assyria, and sent funds from the Lord's temple to the empire.

King Ahaz travels to Damascus to meet the victorious *King Tiglath-pileser* (16:10). The formal titles indicate a state visit. Throughout the reported cultic reform (16:10-18), *King Ahaz* takes initiative. He *goes*, *meets*, *sees* an altar in Damascus, *sends to the priest Uriah a model of the altar, and its pattern, exact in all its details* (16:10; the Hebrew term for *model* is translated as God's "image" in Gen 1:26; 5:1; cf. tabernacle "pattern" in Exod 25; the term for *details* is translated "workmanship" twenty-five times in Exod). Although the text does not indicate the provenance of the altar and Assyria apparently was tolerant of the religious practices of conquered nations, Ahaz likely would have imitated Assyrian religious forms rather than an Aramean novelty. When *King Ahaz* arrives back in Jerusalem, *Priest Uriah* has the new altar ready for use (16:11). Still the initiator, Ahaz *comes, sees* the altar, *draws near* the altar, *goes up* on the altar, *offers* offerings, *pours out* the drink offering, *dashes* the blood, *brings the altar*, and *commands the priest* that the new altar is to replace the old bronze altar dedicated by Solomon (16:12-15 AT). The old altar is moved to the side but retained to *inquire by* (16:13-15).

Priest Uriah complies with the commands of *King Ahaz* (16:16). The titles point throughout to the official capacity of *King Ahaz* as the chief cultic officer giving orders to his servant, *Priest Uriah* (like Solomon, 1 Kings 8:5, 62-64; Jeroboam, 1 Kings 12:33–13:1). Ahaz orders more extensive renovations to the temple, including removal of brass fixtures (16:17-18). The motivation of the cultic reforms is undefined. Whether the renovations provide bronze to pay a never-satisfied demand for tribute or indicate submission to Assyria is uncertain. Assyria does not demand that its vassals worship the Assyrian gods, but the cultic reforms imply deference to the Assyrian overlords. Even though Jerusalem temple worship of Yahweh likely continues, Ahaz's reforms indicate submission to Assyria, demoting both Ahaz and Yahweh to serving Assyria and its gods, the starry host of heaven (Wray Beal 2014: 439). Use of the terms *model, pattern,* and *details* (16:10) implies a wholesale rejection of the Torah in acquiescence to the Assyrian Empire. These conclusions are consistent with the ambiguous conclusion of the report: *He did this because of the king of Assyria* (16:18). The closing royal formula (16:19-20) reports that Ahaz dies in peace, succeeded by his son Hezekiah. Though only the opening royal formula explicitly condemns him, Ahaz is characterized as evil. Dependent on the ways of the nations with other gods, Ahaz is a powerless pawn under the influence of the foreign empire. Judah does not offer a clear alternative to the nation of Israel, a people about to be carried into exile because of their moral bankruptcy.

Hoshea of Israel 17:1-6

The opening royal formula introduces Hoshea as king of Israel in Samaria, synchronizing his years with the reign of Ahaz of Judah and evaluating him as evil in the eyes of the Lord, but somewhat less negatively than his predecessors (17:1-2) *[Chronology, p. 439]*. Israel is hanging by a thread, desperately in need of a *savior* (Hoshea, like Joshua, means "salvation"). Hoshea is powerless to resist the Assyrian Empire and, at first, surrenders to King Shalmaneser V, becomes his vassal, and pays tribute (17:3). After paying annual tribute, Hoshea succumbs to the constant temptation of returning to Egypt (the law of the king warns against returning to Egypt for military aid, Deut 17:16), withholds the annual tribute, and makes overtures to King So of Egypt (17:4).

The strategy is suicidal. Egypt is not a reliable ally, and the king of Assyria eventually arrests and exiles Hoshea. Hoshea withstands the invasion and siege of Samaria for three years, but he surrenders in his ninth year (17:5-6; the biblical narrative likely telescopes two Assyrian campaigns, including the second led by Sargon II, into one; Dubovský 2008: 3). The Israelites are exiled to distant parts of Assyria and even farther east. The story of an independent Israel ends with Hoshea. No closing royal formula is needed for the deposed Hoshea. Instead, the rest of 2 Kings 17 provides a theological explanation of the exile and the subsequent resettling of the land by migrants from Mesopotamia.

Summary: Israel's Final Kings

The conspiracy of Shallum is the first of four coups reported in 2 Kings 15 after Jeroboam's long reign, an intensity of upheaval that exceeds even that of the narrative after the reign of the first Jeroboam (1 Kings 15:27–16:20; three kings are assassinated prior to Omri). While each conspiracy report has the common elements of a "fixed formula" (e.g., name of conspirator, name of conspirator's father, name of the assassinated king, location of conspiracy, common verbs that narrate conspiracy, attack, death, and resulting reign), the free variables in the four reports indicate an intensifying and destabilizing trajectory, reaching its peak in the period leading toward the exile (Dubovský 2014: 322–26). The regime changes may be associated with changes made in international alliances, with Shallum countering the pro-Assyrian Jehuide policy with an intent to affiliate with Aram, countered by Menahem's pro-Assyrian policy (Pul supports Menahem's coup, 15:19-20), in turn countered by the pro-Aramean, anti-Assyrian policy of Pekah (15:37), who is attacked by Assyria (15:29) and unseated by Hoshea (15:30); Hoshea breaks his treaty with Assyria for an alliance with Egypt (17:3-4) [*Egypt, p. 445*]. The fading fortunes of Israel correspond to the Assyrian strategy of encroachment, reducing the independence of the vassal state, extracting payment as they set their allies in office (15:19-20), reducing territory and exiling their elite class (15:29), and finally subsuming them into the Assyrian Empire (17:5-6).

Israel Exiled to Assyria 17:7–23

Interpretation of Israel's deportation to exile (17:7-23) and explanation of the new occupants of the land (17:24-41) interrupt the historical narrative. Without extensive commentary, 1–2 Kings reports events through speeches and prayers, miracle stories, battle reports, and the royal formulas, with evaluation of each king. Never has the narrator drawn back the curtain from events unfolding onstage to interpret their meaning for Israel and Judah. The Israelite exile is so cataclysmic that the narrative is interrupted with "a chapter of reflection." Ostensibly describing Israel's exile, the interpretation applies to Judah as well, foreshadowing an exile without a parallel evaluation (2 Kings 24–25; see 17:13, 18-19 for reference to Judah).

Second Kings 17:7-23 explains the disaster of 722 BCE, Israel's exile to Assyria, not as a geopolitical event brought about by Assyrian military power but as the judgment of the Lord God of Israel against a disobedient people (Bloch-Smith). The interpretation accuses the people (not just their kings) of having sinned against the Lord their God by *worshiping* other gods, following the ways of the dispossessed nations and the ways of Israel's kings, and offering illicit worship on the high places (17:7-12; "democratization of sin," Rösel: 87–88). The accusation addresses their failure to listen to the prophets whom God sent to warn Israel and Judah regarding their rejection of God's covenant law by illicit cultic acts (7:13-17a). The interpretation of the exile concludes with the announcement of judgment: the Lord has been provoked to anger, rejects Israel, removes them from his sight, and exiles them from their land (17:17b-23) [*Provoke the Lord to Anger, p. 470*].

Primary attention is given to cultic violations—idols, false gods, high places, divination. The issues of idolatry and false worship cannot be ignored, but these cultic symbols signify anti-Deuteronomic, anti-Yahwistic forms of sexuality, economics, and social welfare affecting social, economic, political, military, and moral community life (Brueggemann 2000: 478) [*Idolatry, p. 449*].

The opening summary sentence encapsulates the exile report: Israel *sinned against the LORD their God* (17:7). Through Moses, the Lord has warned Israel that the Canaanites will "make you sin" if you covenant with them (Exod 23:33). On Mount Sinai, Moses declares that the people who worship the golden calf have "sinned a great sin" (Exod 32:30-31; Deut 9:16, 18). In the temple prayer, Solomon asks the Lord to forgive those who pray after having *sinned* (1 Kings 8:31, 33, 35, 46, 47, 50). When the prophet Ahijah addresses Jeroboam's wife, he accuses the king of having *sinned* and having caused Israel to *sin* (14:16; Rehoboam and Judah are accused of *sin*, 14:22). The narrative develops a refrain in evaluating the kings of Israel who lead Israel in the *sins of Jeroboam* (1 Kings 15:26, 30, 34; 16:2-3, 7, 19, 26; 21:22; 22:52; 2 Kings 3:3; 10:29, 31; 13:2, 6, 11; 14:24; 15:9, 18, 24, 28) [*Sins of Jeroboam, p. 476*].

The sin of Israel is an affront to *the LORD their God, who had brought them up out of the land of Egypt from under the hand of Pharaoh king of Egypt* (17:7). God liberates Israel from slavery to an imperial power, to free them from unjust economic policies that exploit the weaker for the benefit of the stronger. Rejecting the God "who brought you out of the land of Egypt, out of the house of slavery" (Exod 20:2), violates the first commandment, "You shall have no other gods before me" (20:3). Second Kings 17 elaborates the consequences of that violation. The opening sentence of the Deuteronomistic explanation of Israel's exile (17:7) provides the framework to read 2 Kings 17. Israel's sin against the Lord results in exile. The sin is associated with the unjust economic practices of Jeroboam and his successors, the return to Egypt-like imperial exploitation.

The indictment includes two accusations: Israel feared other gods and *walked in the customs* of the dispossessed nations and its own kings (17:7-8). The gods of the nations are a constant threat. In the covenant renewal ceremony, Joshua offers the people some gods that are alternative to the Lord, the gods "beyond the River" in Mesopotamia, the Egyptian gods, and the gods of the land (Josh 24:15). The gods signify the values of these nations. To *fear the gods* is to commit to false values. To *fear Yahweh* is to *know the justice* (*mišpaṭ*) of the Lord (2 Kings 17:26 [twice], 27, 34 [twice], 37, AT) and keep the Lord's commandments and statutes (Deut 5:29; 6:2). The covenant's rejection of other gods (Exod 20:3) results in a lifestyle that eschews the craving of things (20:17), violence (20:13), lies (20:16), and misappropriation of others' property (20:15) [*Covenant in Kings, p. 443*].

The *customs of the nations whom the LORD drove out* and *the customs that the kings of Israel had introduced* represent the same threat (2 Kings 17:8): exchanging the fear of the Lord for fearing other gods. The word here translated *customs* is frequently translated *statutes* and used in series with other terms designating Torah (Deut 6:2; 8:11; 10:13), such as *commandments* and Torah (2 Kings 17:13), or *ordinances* (*mišpaṭ*, 17:37). Imitation of *the nations whom the LORD drove out* (17:8, 11) leads the Lord to *remove Israel from his sight* (17:18, 23).

Second Kings 17:9-12 lists cultic offenses. Israel imitated the practices of the nations, engaging in a *cover-up* (AT) of the *things that were not right* (17:9). They have built high places, set up Asherah poles, consecrated hills and green trees (17:10; violating Deut 12:2-3; 1 Kings 14:23; 2 Kings 16:4). In these illicit cultic locations, they made sacrifices and served idols. By imitating *the nations whom the LORD carried away before them* and doing *wicked things*, Israel was *provoking the LORD to anger* (17:11, 17; cf. Deut 4:25). The exile fulfills Ahijah's prophecy that the Lord would *scatter them beyond the Euphrates because they have made their sacred poles, provoking the LORD to anger* (1 Kings 14:15) [*Prophets: Prophetic Word, p. 469*].

Second Kings 17:13-17 focuses on the prophetic warnings to Israel and Judah. The Lord's speech aligns two primary biblical traditions: *Torah* is the content of the message of *every prophet and every seer* (17:13). The Lord has *warned Israel and Judah* through the prophets and seers to *turn* (*repent*) from evil and pursue *Torah*. In the earliest such warning, Moses the prophet calls heaven and earth to *witness* the warning that Israel will not endure long in the land (Deut 4:26). The Lord instructs the seer Samuel to "warn" Israel about "the ways of the king" (royal *mišpaṭ*; 1 Sam 8:9). Ahijah anticipates that the Lord will *root up Israel . . . , and scatter them beyond the Euphrates . . . because of the sins of Jeroboam, . . . which he caused Israel to commit* (1 Kings 14:15-16). The Lord sends saviors like Elisha ("my God saves") and Jeroboam II (by whose hand he *saved* Israel in 2 Kings 14:27), who delay judgment; but Israel's decline continues unabated, leading to the nadir narrated in 2 Kings 15:8-31, a deteriorating situation anticipating the exile (15:29). "Stiff-necked [stubborn] like their ancestors" (Exod 32:9; 33:3, 5), Israel has failed to *hear* (2 Kings 17:14, 40; Deut 5:1; 6:4: "Hear, O Israel") or to *act loyally* (2 Kings 17:14, 40 AT; see Gen 15:6). Israel has *rejected* the law, the ancestral *covenant* (2 Kings 17:15, 35, 38; last referenced in 13:23), and the warnings (17:15, 20). The *false idols* they worshiped have made them *become false* (17:15; *false* is translated "vanity" in Ecclesiastes, "mere vapor"). Israel has gone the way of the *nations that were around them* (a variation on *nations whom the LORD drove out*, 17:8). They have worshiped images and false gods (Asherah, *all the host of heaven*, Baal, 17:16). Worship of golden calves characterizes Jeroboam (1 Kings 12:28); the cult of Asherah and Baal is attributed to Ahab of Israel (16:32-33; 18:19; see also 2 Kings 13:6). The focus on prophetic warnings concludes that these practices *provoked the LORD to anger* (17:17 AT).

The catalog in 2 Kings 17:10, 17 addresses violations reported only of Judah in 1–2 Kings. Child sacrifice (condemned in Deut 12:31) is attributed to Ahaz (2 Kings 16:3) and Manasseh (21:6, 16). Divination and augury (Deut 18:9-14) are practiced by Manasseh (2 Kings 21:3-6; cf. 16:15). Manasseh worships the *host of heaven* (21:3). Worship *on every high hill and under every green tree* (17:10) is a practice attributed only to Judah (1 Kings 14:23-24; 2 Kings 16:4). Second Kings 17:18b-19 introduces an aside with direct reference to *the tribe of Judah*. With Israel exiled, 2 Kings 18–25 focuses on Judah, a nation headed for disaster through failure to keep the commandments of the Lord, walking in the *customs* of Israel (17:8, 13). This evaluative summary foreshadows Judah's exile more than a century later (2 Kings 24–25).

Second Kings 17:18-23 announces the sentence of judgment (*therefore* marks the transition from accusation to announcement)

[Literary Criticism, p. 457]. The judgment matches the offense: the Lord *removes* (17:18), *rejects* (17:20), and *removes* (17:23) the people of Israel, all verbs that describe Israel's sins against the Lord. Provoked to anger (17:18; cf. 17:11, 17) by Israel's failure to *turn away* from the sins of Jeroboam (3:3), the Lord *turns them away* (NRSV: *removed them) from his face* (17:18 AT). The Lord has *rejected all the descendants of Israel* because Israel has *rejected* the statutes of the Lord (17:20; cf. 17:15 AT). The Lord has *punished* Israel (the word also describes rape, Deut 22:24, 29; Judg 19–20) *[Provoke the Lord to Anger, p. 470]*. Israel and Judah are *thrown* from the Lord's presence (2 Kings 17:20; not to be resuscitated like the corpse *thrown* [*šalak*] onto Elisha's bones, 13:21).

The people of Israel have continued in *the sins of Jeroboam*, reference to Israel's violation of covenant through improper cultic actions and unjust practices (17:21-23; *the kings*, typically judged for leading Israel to sin, are mentioned only in 17:8). The text references the separation (*torn*, 1 Kings 11:31) of Israel from the house of David and the accession of Jeroboam as a critical event leading to exile. Jeroboam *drove* Israel from the Lord and *made [Israel] commit great sin* (2 Kings 17:21) *[Sins of Jeroboam, p. 476]*. The nation *walked in the sins of Jeroboam* and did not *turn* from them, so the Lord *turned* Israel away from his presence (17:22 AT; cf. *remove/turn* in 17:18). The exile fulfills the word of the prophets. Israel is exiled to Assyria *until this day* (17:23, 34, 41).

Others Settled in the Land of Israel 17:24-41

Israel is exiled from their land to Assyria (17:7-23). Second Kings 17:24-41 explains how imported people who *fear Yahweh but also serve their carved images* (17:41 AT) continue in the land, as well as the corrupt nature of these inhabitants. The new occupants in cities of Samaria and Bethel are immigrants exiled from their own territory in the eastern part of the Assyrian Empire. If they intermarry with any survivors in the land, the text explains the mixing of not only the ethnicity but also the religious practices of the people of Samaria. The new people *fear Yahweh* while they *serve the gods* they brought with them from their native lands (17:33, 41). The tone is ironic, setting up a point of view (that it is possible to *fear Yahweh* while *serving the gods*; 17:27-33, 41 AT), only to demolish it with the perspective that such syncretism (fusion of Yahweh-and-idol worship) is illicit (17:34). The Lord's covenant speech (17:35-39) after the reported syncretistic practices (17:24-33) makes the point that the resulting situation is parallel to Israel's historic behavior

(17:40). Syncretistic practice continues to be the way of Israel (Fretheim 1999: 193). The descriptors indicate that *fearing the* LORD (17:25, 28, 32, 33, 34, 36, 39, 41 AT) and doing his *justice* (17:34, 37 AT) are antithetical to *worshiping/fearing the gods* (17:7, 35, 37, 38), doing the *mišpaṭ* (*customs*) of the gods (17:33, 34, 40), or *serving the gods* (17:33, 35, 41).

The account opens with a general report of the Assyrian resettlement policy in Samaria (17:24). The king of Assyria orders that the immigrants *take possession* of Samaria (the verb used more than eight times in Deuteronomy and Josh, describing Israel's possession of the land; the Lord *dispossessed* the nations, 1 Kings 14:24; 2 Kings 16:3; 17:8; 21:2; Ahab *took possession* of Naboth's vineyard, 1 Kings 21:15). To *take possession* of Samaria is to enter the Lord's covenant territory. Just as Israel *settled* in the lands of the east (2 Kings 17:6), so also Israelite territory was *settled.*

Demonstrating that removal of Israel in no way indicated that he had abandoned the land, Yahweh *sent lions* to kill some of the people because they did *not worship [fear] the* LORD (17:25). The first reference to a lion attack in Kings involves the man of God from Judah mauled by a lion after violating the Lord's word (1 Kings 13:24-28). Later, a lion kills a prophet in divine judgment (20:35-36). The lion attacks give evidence of the Lord's demand that those living in the land worship Yahweh as sovereign.

The people report the lion attacks to the king of Assyria, admitting that the new occupants do not know the *law of the god of the land* (17:26; *law* translates *mišpaṭ*, "justice policies"). *Mišpaṭ* is more than customary behavior or ritual practices [*Mišpaṭ, p. 461*]. The king commands that an Israelite priest be sent back to teach the *mišpaṭ of the god of the land* (17:27). An exiled priest resettles in Bethel to teach the people how *to fear the* LORD (17:28 AT).

Instead of the exclusive devotion to Yahweh involved in *fearing the* LORD and *doing mišpaṭ*, the teaching (*torah*) of the resettled priest results in widespread syncretism, an outcome developed with four rhetorical moves in 2 Kings 17:29-41. First, 17:29-31 details the way every resettled nation makes its own gods, places them in the shrines the people have made for their gods on the high places, and, nation by nation, practices its own religious and administrative policies (*mišpaṭ*).

Second, 1 Kings 17:32-34 points out the incompatibility of *fearing* and doing the *mišpaṭ of the* LORD while continuing to *serve their own gods* and *practice their former mišpaṭ.* Evidence includes (1) continued worship at the high places with priests appointed from *all*

sorts of people (17:32; like Jeroboam, 1 Kings 12:31; 13:33); and
(2) misguided attempts to *fear the* LORD while they *serve their own
gods* (2 Kings 17:33). This incongruity is restated at the end of the
subsection: *To this day they continue to practice their former customs
[mišpaṭ]* but *do not serve the* LORD *and . . . do not follow his mišpaṭ*
(17:34 AT).

Third, the Lord's covenant speech (17:35-39) interrupts the
report *[Covenant in Kings, p. 443]*. The covenant with Jacob prohibits
fearing the gods (17:34, 37, 38 AT) and demands *fearing the* LORD
(17:36, 39 AT) and keeping his *mišpaṭ* (four different terms for "law"
are used in 17:34, 37). The seven prohibitions (*not fear, bow, serve,*
and *sacrifice* to the gods and *not fear, forget, fear*) and five imperatives (*him fear, bow, sacrifice, observe, fear*) are preceded by either *not
(loʾ)* or *him (lo)*; in Hebrew the words for *no (loʾ)* and *him (lo)* sound
the same when read aloud, creating an ironic rhetorical effect
(17:35-39). The imperatives and prohibitions address human covenant partners, but the focus is on the covenant LORD, *who brought
you out* of slavery in Egypt *with great power and with an outstretched
arm* and who promises to *deliver you out of the hand of all your enemies*
(17:36, 39).

Fourth, a double indictment follows (17:40-41): One, Israel and
the recent settlers are indicted for failing to *listen* (*obey*), rejecting
the primary Deuteronomic command: "Listen, O Israel, the LORD is
one LORD" (17:14, 40; Deut 6:4 AT). This failure results in the anti-
mišpaṭ of the foreign imperial oppressors Egypt and Assyria and
their own kings, notably Solomon, Jeroboam, and Ahab. Two, the
summary indicts new settlers and *their ancestors* (Israel) for claiming
to *fear Yahweh* while *serving their carved images* (17:41).

Second Kings 17 overwhelms the reader with a sense of pathos
not unlike the book of Lamentations. The people are exiled because
they sinned. They did the *mišpaṭ* of the nations and worshiped their
gods. Repeated prophetic warnings were ineffective, provoking the
Lord to great anger. The exiles are charged with the sins of Jeroboam,
with rejection of Deuteronomic values. The new immigrants are like
the original native population that preceded Israel: ignorant of the
Lord, who rescues slaves. Their information about the Lord comes
from a discredited priest who gives them enough instruction to
engage in syncretistic mockery of covenant faithfulness, *fearing* the
Lord while *serving* their native gods. The Lord's final covenant
speech addresses the contemporary audience. The God who delivers
slaves from Egypt calls for covenant loyalty, doing justice, and worshiping the Lord alone.

THE TEXT IN BIBLICAL CONTEXT
Exile and Return: Deuteronomy 30 and Isaiah 40–55

The literary relationship between Deuteronomy and 1–2 Kings guides our reading. Deuteronomy is the valedictory of Moses before Israel enters Canaan. Second Kings 22–23 describes a reform based on a rediscovered book of the law, often postulated to be proto-Deuteronomy, the initial law code of biblical Deuteronomy. Kings reads as if its values are determined by Deuteronomy. Some scholars suggest that the influence flows the other direction, that Deuteronomy is written to encode the values assumed in Kings. Whatever is concluded about the textual history, the relationship between Deuteronomy 30 and 2 Kings 17 is one of correspondence. While 2 Kings 17 ends with Israel in exile, Deuteronomy anticipates return from exile (30:1-3). Moses calls exiled Israel to repent with the expectation that God will "restore" and gather them "back . . . into the land" (30:3, 4-5; cf. 4:25-31). "Moreover," Moses says, the Lord initiates renewal. "The LORD your God will circumcise your heart and the heart of your descendants" so that the people obey, and thus God will bless (30:6-10).

The hope-filled rhetoric declares that the command is well within reach (30:11-14). The life-shaping choice is positive and possible. It is a life-and-death choice; Moses anticipates that his audience will choose life filled with blessing in the land. Loving and obeying God is the way of life.

Isaiah 40–55 encourages exiled Israel to ready themselves for a new exodus. The Lord as sovereign leads the return of Israel to the land, comforting and carrying them (40:1-11). The return from exile will overshadow the exodus from Egypt, long counted as God's greatest act of deliverance (43:14-21). God calls Israel to the mission of being "a light to the nations" (49:6).

Lamentations

The book of Lamentations deals with the exile of the chosen people in a tenor that resembles 2 Kings 17. Five poems wrestle with the hopeless chaos facing Jerusalem after 586 BCE. Though the lamenter is Jerusalem, the situation is that of exiled Israel. In contrast to the detached third-person perspective of 2 Kings 17, written to justify the Lord's judgment, Lamentations expresses the experiential dimension of the sufferer who has lost everything. Yes, the opening poem admits, the people "sinned grievously" (1:8), but the focus is on the overwhelming loss. The book opens with the words "How lonely sits the city / that once was full of people." Near the end of the first poem, the exiled person laments:

See, O LORD, how distressed I am;
    my stomach churns,
my heart is wrung within me,
    because I have been very rebellious. . . .
for my groans are many
    and my heart is faint.
(1:20, 22)

The message is articulated in its form as well as its words. The first three poems are sixty-six-line acrostics, carefully ordered cries of lament. The third poem attempts to speak positive and good theology (3:22: "The steadfast love of the LORD never ceases") but ultimately returns to the ashes. With the fourth poem (a reduced forty-four-line acrostic), the lament moves toward exhaustion. The final poem (Lam 5) of just twenty-two lines expresses despair by the collapse of the acrostic form. A furtive prayer for restoration breaks down into expression of despair:

Renew our days as of old—
unless you have utterly rejected us,
    and are angry with us beyond measure.
(5:21-22)

Lamentations and 2 Kings 17 suggest little hope. Second Kings grieves that the chaos continues *to this day* (17:41). Like Lamentations, 2 Kings 17 focuses on the loss, the collapse of life, the inescapability of an unacceptable situation.

THE TEXT IN THE LIFE OF THE CHURCH
Solidarity in Suffering

The contemporary church struggles to express lament. Churches with positive messages are associated with growth. Joel Osteen has succeeded Norman Vincent Peale and Robert Schuller. Popularity is measured in worship attendance, book sales, and the number of people who try to duplicate their success.

This message sounds hollow to many thoughtful (often former) churchgoers. Soong-Chan Rah found a ready audience when he launched a church plant in Cambridge, Massachusetts, using a series of sermons from Lamentations as his text. In a 2016 interview in *Preaching Today* titled "The Power and Beauty of Lament," Rah explains his context:

Our community was already made up of overachievers to begin with—that's how they got into schools like Harvard and MIT—so what they needed was the balancing of that kind of triumphalism, success-driven narrative with a dose of lament that is oftentimes underrepresented. . . . When you are ministering in the city, especially a community with overachievers, the reality of lament is necessary.

Lament speaks to those struggling to hear God in the dark night of the soul, inviting them to find a community of fellow travelers. Indeed, lament must be available for people going through unexpected loss, suffering, and grief. Lament empowers churches that live in relative ease to connect with the needs of people and churches around the world suffering the effects of pandemic, climate change, and economic disruption.

Indeed, 1–2 Kings narrates exile and loss. Lamentations expresses pain through poetry. The community of faith uses media that best communicate deep loss.

Refugees

On UN Refugee Day 2016, more than sixty million refugees, internally displaced persons, and asylum seekers lived on the planet, over half of them under age eighteen. More than half the refugees were from Syria, Afghanistan, and South Sudan. Forty percent of the displaced persons were hosted in the Middle East and North Africa, and 30 percent more in the rest of Africa. Europe and the Americas hosted less than 20 percent. The UN Sub-Commission on the Protection and Promotion of Human Rights adopted the Pinheiro Principles (named after their Brazilian author) in 2005. The principles include the rights to housing and property restitution and to voluntary safe return.

A major Mennonite story of displacement and resettlement is narrated in various forms. The 1955 juvenile historical fiction of Barbara Smucker, *Henry's Red Sea*, relates the story of refugees from Russia, a tale populated with American soldiers, Russian officers, and a midnight train ride in darkened boxcars based on events in Berlin in 1946. *And When They Shall Ask* (written and directed by John Morrow) is a 1983 feature-length movie about the Russian Mennonite experience from 1788 to the mid-twentieth century. It reenacts historic events, interviews witnesses to these events, airs archival film footage, and culminates with scenes of Mennonite life in the former Soviet Union. The film addresses the question, Can faith triumph in the face of great adversity?

In *Up from the Rubble*, Peter Dyck and Elfrieda Dyck describe Mennonite refugees escaping war-torn Europe to find new homes in South America and Canada. The traveling exhibit *Along the Road to*

Freedom (a Mennonite Heritage Centre project curated by Ray Dirks) tells of Russian Mennonite women displaced to Canada in the 1920s and to Canada and Paraguay in the 1940s. The exhibit pictures loss, persecution, and suffering that often end in love, kindness, selflessness, faith, and forgiveness. In her afterword to Rudy Wiebe's 1970 novel *Blue Mountains of China* about the same migrations, Kröller describes the Mennonite epic as an "odyssey that describes *all* human beings who struggle to overcome personal . . . and collective hardship and attain redemption" (Kröller: 305). Mennonite congregations work together to support refugee families. In a February 2017 article in the *Washington Post*, reporter Colby Itkowitz describes the reception given the Almahasnehs, a family of six Syrian refugees who arrived in Lancaster County, Pennsylvania, after three and a half years in a Jordanian refugee camp. When Church World Service asked East Chestnut Street Mennonite Church about sponsoring refugees, two dozen people signed up. The church grew close to the Syrian family, sharing resources and supporting their language learning. Harley Kooker, who first worked with refugees in Vietnam, said, "When I see refugees now being shut off like that, I think, 'How on earth can we be so hardhearted?' I was always taught that we love whoever, regardless of ethnicity, race, religion, you know, that's who my Jesus is, that's what my Jesus taught." Group coordinator Laura Kanagy added, "There are many different messages flying around right now about borders and walls and terrorism and bans. But here is *our* message to you: You are very welcome here, and you are loved."

Part 3

The Southern Kingdom to Judah's Exile

2 Kings 18–25

OVERVIEW

After Israel's exile in 722 BCE (2 Kings 17), 2 Kings 18–25 narrates Judah's demise nearly 150 years later. A pattern of bad king/good king characterizes the Judah-alone era (722–586 BCE). King Ahaz of Judah, who has behaved like the kings of Israel (16:2-3), is succeeded by the righteous Hezekiah (18:1–20:21). Hezekiah is followed by Manasseh, a king so evil that exile becomes inevitable (21:14-15); then succeeded by Josiah, who turns to the Lord with his whole heart (23:25). Despite the accolades paid Hezekiah and Josiah for unsurpassed faithfulness (18:3, 5; 22:23; 23:25), the Ahab-like wickedness of Ahaz and Manasseh makes exile inevitable (16:2-4; 21:10-15). After the reigns of Josiah's ineffectual heirs (23:31–25:7), the book of Kings ends in destruction, deportation, and exile (25:8-30). Despite the sorry ending, 2 Kings 18–25 offers hope to those who emulate Hezekiah and Josiah.

The theological themes of 1–2 Kings are elaborated in this final section of the book. Sovereign God uses the nations to test and judge the covenant people. Hezekiah's superlative trust is tested when the Assyrian imperial army throttles Jerusalem in siege warfare. After initially failing the test of trusting the Lord by seeking to avert destruction through tribute, Hezekiah's growing trust is rewarded with divine intervention and elimination of the threat (2 Kings 18–19). Though lauded for his trust, Hezekiah's apparent negotiation for an alliance with Babylon reveals his short-sighted and self-centered policies (2 Kings 20). Ahaz, Manasseh, and Amon reject the Lord, provoking the Lord's anger and making exile inevitable. According to DtrH, Manasseh's record-long fifty-five-year reign makes exile inevitable because he sheds innocent blood in his idolatrous pursuit of royal justice (= injustice). Josiah's temple restoration leads to a Torah-focused revival and the elimination of cultic abominations.

Though scholars have debated whether 1–2 Kings ends in hope or despair, reading the text in the context of Deuteronomy provides clarity. Deuteronomy assumes not only exile but also repentance, renewal, and return (Deut 30). Covenant faithfulness requires God's people to live out their vocation given in creation, managing the earth as people created in the image of God. Deuteronomy defines covenant love for God as care for the marginalized (10:12-21), just as the Lord declares the human purpose to be righteousness and justice (Gen 1:28-29; 18:19).

2 Kings 18:1–20:21

The Reign of Hezekiah

PREVIEW

The king's heart is a stream of water in the hand of the LORD;
    he turns it wherever he will.
All deeds are right in the sight of the doer,
    but the LORD weighs the heart.
(Prov 21:1-2)

Ours is a cynical age. When we witness pious rituals, we suspect false motives, perhaps because we know our own fickle hearts. By taunting Hezekiah's religious reforms, the Assyrians try to agitate Judean skeptics who regard Hezekiah's revival as a power grab, not authentic faithfulness (18:22). Hezekiah's relief that Babylonian exile will occur only after his death increases suspicion that Hezekiah's temple renewal is self-serving (20:19).

In 2 Kings 18–19, apparently conflicting or overlapping reports of Assyrian invasion and Judean responses challenge interpreters. The outline below depends on Fewell's identification of narrative technique, including both summary report (18:13-16; 19:8-9) and scenic presentation (18:17–19:7; 19:10-34). Summary report accelerates time, telescopes events, and produces an overview. Scenic presentation slows the pace, reports detail, and develops themes (Fewell: 80). Parallel accounts of Hezekiah's reign in Isaiah 36–39 (largely identical to 2 Kings 18–20) and in 2 Chronicles 29–32 (primarily focused on Hezekiah's religious reforms) present additional puzzles for the reader.

OUTLINE

Opening Royal Formula, 18:1-8
Reprise: Report of Israel's Exile, 18:9-12
Sennacherib's Invasion of Judah, 18:13–19:37
   18:13-16   Summary Report of Assyrian Invasion
   18:17–19:7 Dramatic Assyrian Taunt; Hezekiah Consulting Isaiah
   19:8-9   Summary Report of Assyrian Military Action
   19:10-34   Sennacherib's Boast, Hezekiah's Prayer, Isaiah's
                Response
   19:35-37   Summary Report of Sennacherib's Withdrawal
Hezekiah's Prayer for Healing, 20:1-11
Envoys from Babylon, 20:12-19
Closing Royal Formula, 20:20-21

EXPLANATORY NOTES

Opening Royal Formula 18:1-8

Threatened by the Assyrian superpower, trapped in idolatrous abandonment of the Lord, Judah inaugurates a new king. The opening royal formula synchronizes Hezekiah's reign with Hoshea of Israel, provides chronologies, and identifies Hezekiah's mother (18:1-3) *[Chronology, p. 439]*. Hezekiah is a righteous king whose trust in the Lord is superlative. Hezekiah, the sixth of seven kings of Judah to do *right in the eyes of the* LORD (1 Kings 14:8; 15:11; 22:43; 2 Kings 12:2; 14:3; 15:3, 34; 22:2), does *as his ancestor David had done* (18:3; the seven include Asa, 1 Kings 15:11; Josiah, 2 Kings 22:3; unlike his father, Ahaz, 16:2-4). Hezekiah's reforms fulfill cultic law in four powerful acts (18:4; Deut 12:2-7). First, Hezekiah *eliminates* (AT) the high places that have compromised Judah's worship since Solomon and Rehoboam (1 Kings 11:7; 14:23), tolerated by kings who otherwise did right (15:14; 22:43; 2 Kings 12:3; 14:4; 15:4, 35), through the reign of his predecessor Ahaz (16:4). Second, Hezekiah *smashes* (AT) the pillars often associated with Baal worship (2 Kings 3:2; 10:26-27; 17:10; as ordered in Deut 7:5; 10:2; like Asa in 1 Kings 15:13 and Josiah in 2 Kings 23:14). Third, he *cuts down* the Asherah pole (like Moses, Exod 34:13; Gideon, Judg 6:25-30; Asa, 1 Kings 15:13; Josiah, 2 Kings 23:14). Fourth, he *crushes* Nehushtan (Moses "crushed" the golden calf, Deut 9:21), the bronze serpent Moses crafted as a means of salvation (Num 21:4-9; a serpent is associated with Canaanite fertility cults and Asherah; Jones: 562) *[Idolatry, p. 449]*.

Hezekiah's reforms are motivated by his unique trust in God (*There was no one like him among all the kings of Judah*, 2 Kings 18:5). Hezekiah's *trust* (*baṭaḥ*; 18:19 [twice], 20, 21 [twice], 22, 24, 28; 19:10) is tested, particularly in facing the mocking insults of the Rabshakeh's speeches. (*Trust* is used only of Hezekiah in 1–2 Kings, but seventy-eight times in Psalms, Isaiah, and Jeremiah NRSV.) Hezekiah *held fast* to the Lord (18:6; as a man "clings" to his wife, Gen 2:24; the verb *cling* is used in synonymous parallel with the terms *serve, swear by, love, walk, follow, fear, listen*; cf. Deut 10:20; 11:22; 13:4; 30:20). Israel has refused to *turn away from* the sins of Jeroboam (2 Kings 17:22 AT); Hezekiah *did not turn away* from the Lord but *kept the commandments* of Moses (18:6 AT). *The* LORD *was with* Hezekiah (18:7) as with David so that whenever he *went out* to war, he had *success* (AT; Deut 29:9; Josh 1:7-8; 1 Sam 16:18; 18:5, 12, 14-15; 2 Sam 5:10; 11:1; 1 Kings 2:3). In contrast to Ahaz, Hezekiah *rebels* against the king of Assyria and does not *serve* him (2 Kings 16:7; 18:20; cf. Josh 22:16, 18, 19, 29; 2 Kings 24:1, 20; Israel *served* the gods, 2 Kings 17:12, 16, 33, 35, 41). Hezekiah's success involves reclaiming Philistine territory *as far as Gaza* (18:8). His success *from watchtower to fortified city* reverses Israel's cultic apostasy (17:9). Hezekiah's trust, contrasted with Israel (18:9-12), is tested and grows (18:13–20:19).

Reprise: Report of Israel's Exile 18:9-12

The report of Israel's exile in these verses repeats 2 Kings 17:5-6. Israel has transgressed the Lord's covenant (17:15, 35-39; 18:12), failed to *obey the voice of the* LORD, and has not *listened* to the covenant (*šamaʿ* used twice in 18:12), a sharp contrast with Hezekiah, who *kept the commandments that the* LORD *commanded Moses* (18:6; Moses commands Israel to "hear the statutes and ordinances," Deut 4:1; 5:1; 6:4). Though dating the Assyrian siege of Jerusalem at the time of Assyria's removal of Israel in 722 BCE presents an impossible chronology, the parallel references contrast Hezekiah's trust with Hoshea's faithlessness (Hens-Piazza 2006: 360). Apostate Israel is carried into exile; Judah remains in the land because Hezekiah trusts the Lord [*Archaeology: Sennacherib's Prism, p. 438*].

Sennacherib's Invasion of Judah 18:13–19:37

The commendation of Hezekiah (18:1-12) sets up the test of his trust in the Lord (the events of 18:13–20:19 are dated to his fourteenth year). Scene by scene, Hezekiah demonstrates growing capacity to trust—and the Lord delivers. First, Hezekiah acts like a helpless vassal by using temple treasure to pay tribute (18:15), trusting the ways of a king "like other nations" (1 Sam 8:5, 9) [*Mišpaṭ, p. 461*]. Next, when Assyria presses for further concessions, Hezekiah in distress appeals to the prophet Isaiah, hoping that *the* LORD *your God* may have *heard all the words of the Rabshakeh*, the official speaking for the Assyrians (18:17-35; 19:3-4). When Assyria presses yet again, Hezekiah himself prays directly to God (19:9-19): *Save us, . . . that all the earth may know that you, O LORD, are God alone* (19:19 AT). Still in Hezekiah's fourteenth year, when confronted with news of his impending death to illness, Hezekiah asks the Lord to *remember . . . how I have walked before you in faithfulness* and receives a reprieve— and assurance of deliverance (20:1-3, 5-6). The final scene reports both what appears to be an illicit alliance with Babylon (20:12-13) and Hezekiah's submission to the prophetic message (20:19). Hezekiah's story is a study in growing trust within a larger historical trajectory ending in exile. The narrative contrasts the conflicting claims of supremacy by Sennacherib, whose presence and power create the conflict, and of Yahweh, whose presence and power resolve the conflict. Though both Sennacherib and Yahweh are unseen, Hezekiah personifies the shift from Sennacherib's imperial dominance to Yahweh's sovereign liberation. The speeches of the Rabshakeh and the letter of Sennacherib claim sovereignty that the narrator considers a blasphemous affront to Yahweh (18:19-25, 28-35). As Hezekiah moves from impotence to effectiveness, Sennacherib is reduced from autonomy to subjection to Yahweh (Fewell: 82–83).

18:13-16 Summary Report of Assyrian Invasion

After eight years of successful Judean rebellion, Sennacherib, the new king of Assyria, seizes *all the fortified cities of Judah* (18:13). The contemporary Assyrian annals boast the conquest of Phoenicia, Philistia, and forty-six eastern Judean cities and brag that Hezekiah is shut up in Jerusalem "like a bird in a cage" (*ANET* 287–88). Without military resources to repulse Sennacherib, Hezekiah *sends* his surrender to the king of Assyria (18:14). "*I have sinned*" (AT; used throughout 1–2 Kings of the *sins* of Jeroboam), Hezekiah says "*Give me anything*" (AT; in other words, Hezekiah requests that the Assyrian king impose conditions of surrender).Sennacherib demands three hundred talents of silver and thirty talents of gold (the Assyrian annals confirm the demand, recording a larger amount, *ANET* 287–88). When looting the temple and palace treasuries leaves Hezekiah short, he strips temple doors and doorposts to pay tribute (18:15-16). Thus Hezekiah responds like a typical ANE vassal facing overwhelming military power. Lacking military resources, Hezekiah uses wealth accumulated in more prosperous days to placate imperial power.

18:17-19:7 Dramatic Assyrian Taunt; Hezekiah Consulting Isaiah

The tribute payment fails to placate the voracious imperial appetite. Sennacherib *sends [Send, p. 476]* a large army with three high officials from the Assyrian siege of Lachish in western Judah to Hezekiah at Jerusalem (18:17) *[Archaeology: Lachish, p. 439]*. The Assyrian *Tartan* (highest ranking general), the *Rabsaris* ("chief eunuch," another high-ranking military office), and the *Rabshakeh* ("chief butler," a chief officer who acts as spokesman, perhaps because of his command of Hebrew, 18:26) summon Hezekiah. Three high officials of Jerusalem (*Eliakim*, the royal steward; *Shebnah*, the scribe; and *Joah*, the recorder) come out to the diplomatic summit (18:18; Cogan and Tadmor: 229-30). Using typical Assyrian diplomatic disputation, the Rabshakeh aims to undermine the confidence of those addressed (J. T. Walsh 1996: 272-76). The derisive, taunting, intimidating propaganda addresses Hezekiah, a second test of Hezekiah's trust (a retake of the first failed exam).

The Rabshakeh sends a message to Hezekiah through his envoys (18:19-25). The polite diplomatic form of the opening words is ironic: *Please send Hezekiah this message* (18:19 AT). The standard messenger formula, *Thus says the great king, the king of Assyria [Literary Criticism, p. 457]*, intensifies the intimidation factor (the Rabshakeh reduces Hezekiah's status by referring to him by name without title while reinforcing the Assyrian's superiority by using title but no name; Hyman: 215). The use of the messenger formula, typical of prophets who speak for Yahweh, reveals a conflict between Sennacherib, who makes divine claims of autonomy, and Yahweh, who will eventually demonstrate his supremacy over the Assyrian Empire (1 Kings 11:31; 14:7; 21:19; 2 Kings 3:16; 7:19; 9:6; 18:19, 29, 31; Fewell: 82-83). The rhetorical question *On what do you base this confidence of yours?* not only conveys the Assyrian's propagandistic message (Sennacherib alone is trustworthy) but also addresses Hezekiah's need to reorient his *trust* from royal strategies (18:13-16) to Yahweh (the question of *trust* [AT: *rely on*] will be addressed to Hezekiah and Jerusalem seven more times: 18:20, 21 [twice], 22, 24, 30; 19:10). Sennacherib's claims of divine autonomy are reflected in the two insults of 18:20. The Rabshakeh accuses Hezekiah of making empty claims that he has strategy and power for war. Because strategy and power are given by Yahweh, the Rabshakeh's insult makes an implicit claim that Sennacherib, not Yahweh, has ultimate power (Job 12:13; Isa 11:2; Rudman: 104). The Rabshakeh's rhetorical question *On whom do you now rely, that you have rebelled against me?* (2 Kings 18:20) again implicitly claims divine sovereignty for Sennacherib.

Rebel may be action against king (18:7) or against God (Josh 22:16, 18, 19, 29). Hezekiah has *rebelled* against Sennacherib by giving allegiance to Yahweh (2 Kings 18:7; Rudman: 104). Sennacherib's blasphemous challenge tempts Hezekiah to trust imperial power rather than Yahweh alone.

The Rabshakeh continues, hypothetically offering the two alternatives open to Hezekiah and scornfully dismissing both. First, the Rabshakeh discounts Egypt as a reliable ally against Assyria (18:21). Relying on Egypt, he says, is like using a crushed reed as a staff. It will shatter and pierce your hand, but it won't support you. (Perhaps the Rabshakeh is alluding to an unreported attempt by Hezekiah to gain support from Egypt rather than trusting the Lord to deliver, Isa 30:1-5; 31:1-3) [*Egypt, p. 445*]. In an aside the Rabshakeh speaks for himself directly to Hezekiah's officials (18:22-24), suggesting another alternative: trust in the Lord. Perhaps playing on the unpopularity of Hezekiah's elimination of the high places, the Rabshakeh asks whether Hezekiah's reforms have undermined Israel's faith (18:22). He challenges with a wager, asking, *If the king of Assyria were to give you military armaments in the form of two thousand horses, would you have enough troops to take advantage of them?* (18:23 AT). The Rabshakeh pokes fun at Judah's *might* (18:20 AT), so reduced that Judah cannot muster even such a small number of troops. The taunt continues, *If you cannot find the manpower for the military weaponry that I alone can supply, how do you think you will succeed by relying on unreliable Egypt?* (18:24 AT). Speaking again for Sennacherib to Hezekiah, the Rabshakeh blusters, *How can you rely on the LORD? I'm threatening Jerusalem on orders from the LORD* (18:25 AT; not implausible based on the judgment on Samaria in 2 Kings 17, but more likely another propagandistic ploy, playing to internal opposition; the Lord confronts the Rabshakeh's misplaced confidence in 19:21-34).

Hezekiah's messengers interrupt, requesting that the Rabshakeh switch to diplomatic Aramaic rather than the Judean Hebrew dialect to avoid demoralizing the people listening from the walls of Jerusalem. *We, your servants, are official government diplomats,* they humbly plead. *Please* [a Hebrew word indicating respect], *speak to us in the official diplomatic language* (18:26 AT). Addressing the officials directly, the Rabshakeh asks, *Whom do you think my master sent me to address? Don't you know that I'm speaking to the people so desperate for food and water that they are doomed to eat and drink their own body wastes?* (18:27 AT). The Rabshakeh uses vulgarities to emphasize the insult.

To persuade the people on the wall that Sennacherib and not Hezekiah (nor Yahweh) is trustworthy and sovereign, the Rabshakeh uses prophetic speech forms (messenger formula, 18:28, 31), themes (*trust* in 18:30 AT and *deliver* in 18:29, 30, 32, 33, 34, 35 [twice]; cf. 19:11-12), and language (e.g., inverting the Deuteronomic promises of blessing, vine, fig tree, Deut 8:8) to demand their surrender (18:28-35). The Rabshakeh claims to be the true prophet sent to protect the people from Hezekiah's deception. The messenger formula (*Hear the word of the great king. . . . Thus says the king*) stresses the claim that Sennacherib, not Yahweh, exercises divine authority (18:28-29). Four prohibitions follow, contesting Yahweh's promise of deliverance and covenant blessings. With the first, the Rabshakeh argues that Hezekiah is *deceiving* them by urging trust in the Lord to *deliver* (Eve is "deceived" by the serpent, Gen 3:13 NIV; the Lord "delivers" Israel from Egypt, Exod 3:8; 6:6; 18:9-10; none can "deliver" out of the Lord's hand, Deut 32:39; the Lord promises to *deliver* his people, 2 Kings 17:39). The second prohibition reiterates both themes, *trust* and *deliver* (18:30). After the third prohibition (18:31a), a reiteration of the messenger formula introduces the king's invitation to *bless* (*make . . . peace*), making a counterfeit offer of the original Deuteronomic covenant blessings of life in a land of abundance (18:31b-32a; parallel to Deut 8:7-9; 30:15). The Assyrian Empire offers good life under imperial rule, prosperity that Israel has not experienced since Solomon (1 Kings 4:25) and that neither Hezekiah nor the Lord can provide, he claims. The fourth prohibition (2 Kings 18:32b) develops the primary theme of deliverance by using rhetorical questions to make the claim that the gods of the nations have been powerless against the king (not the gods) of Assyria (18:33-35; 19:12). The list of nations is geographical, leading from the Euphrates to Samaria (Zvi: 89). The inclusion of three nations resettled in Samaria delivers the message that Assyria intends to repeat the treatment of Samaria, deporting Judah also (17:30-31). The propaganda of the imperial messenger concludes by raising doubts that the Lord can deliver Jerusalem from the *hand* (power) of the invading empire. Many of the major elements of the speech have parallels in Neo-Assyrian annals (Cohen: 46–47). Sennacherib claims to be God's rival for Judah's trust, the one who can give security, land, life. Like Pharaoh and God in Exodus, or Baal and God in 1 Kings, the choice is between trusting God or imperial power (Nelson 1987: 239).

After Hezekiah's orders, the people are *silent* (18:36; cf. Exod 14:14). The people's refusal to acquiesce is a rejection of Sennacherib's blasphemous imperial challenge to every facet of Judah's worldview and theology (Park: 45). The officials report the Rabshakeh's message to Hezekiah (18:37). Hezekiah and his officials tear their clothes in distress and cover themselves in penitential sackcloth (19:1-2). Facing the Assyrian imperial threat is the second test of Hezekiah's resolve to trust the Lord. As he has done when he stripped the temple of its gold to pay tribute to Assyria (18:15-16), Hezekiah again proceeds to the *house of the* LORD (19:1). Though earlier his reliance on accumulated wealth mimics the kings of the nations, in his second test King Hezekiah *sends* his officials (*senior priests*, 19:2, replace Joah in the delegation, 18:37) from the temple to the prophet Isaiah (an unusual appearance of a canonical prophet in 1–2 Kings). The messenger formula, *Thus says Hezekiah,* contrasts Hezekiah's deferent dependence on the Lord with Sennacherib's arrogant defiance (19:3). Hezekiah's request to Isaiah conveys equal parts despair and trust. The king characterizes the situation as *a day of distress, of rebuke, and of disgrace. Day of distress* can refer to a day of "terrible troubles," when God judges Israel for breaking covenant (Deut 31:17, 21; Judg 10:14), or can be linked to hope for deliverance (1 Sam 10:19; 26:24; 2 Sam 4:9; 1 Kings 1:29). The *day of rebuke* refers to judgment (Ezek 5:15; 25:17; Hos 5:9). *Disgrace* is linked to breaking covenant (Deut 31:20) and to blasphemy (2 Sam 12:14; Neh 9:18, 26; Isa 52:5). Using a proverbial metaphor of childbirth, Hezekiah recognizes the formidable threat presented by Sennacherib. His message pivots to greater hopefulness with the word translated *It may be* (also rendered *perhaps* or *unless*). Hezekiah's hope rides on the possibility that there is another audience to the Rabshakeh's words. *Perhaps* the Lord has also heard the words that *mock the living God* (2 Kings 19:16, 22, 23; Goliath "mocked" the Lord and his armies, 1 Sam 17:10 AT). From the temple dedicated for prayer (1 Kings 8:28-54; 9:3), Hezekiah asks Isaiah to *lift up . . . prayer for the remnant* (2 Kings 19:4, 31; 21:14).

The narrative turns on Isaiah's response to Hezekiah (19:6-7). With a double messenger formula that counters the Assyrian imperial messages, Isaiah offers Hezekiah the classic words of assurance: *Do not be afraid* (see also 1 Kings 17:13; 2 Kings 1:15; 6:16). Hezekiah has become fearful by *hearing words* of the Rabshakeh that *reviled* the Lord (19:22 NIV: *blasphemed*). The Lord will cause the king of Assyria to *hear a hearing* (AT; a rumor), *return to his land, and fall by the sword* (19:7).

19:8-9 Summary Report of Assyrian Military Action

The detailed "scenic presentation" (18:17–19:7) shifts to a report of Assyrian military action (19:8-9). The Rabshakeh returns to find the king of Assyria fighting Libnah, a fortified city of Judah east of

Lachish, and thus pressing toward Jerusalem (19:8) [*Archaeology: Lachish, p. 439*]. Isaiah has promised that the Lord will cause the Assyrians to *hear a hearing* (19:7 AT). When the Rabshakeh *hears* about Sennacherib's movements, and *he* (likely Sennacherib) *hears* about Cush's (*Ethiopia*'s) military advance, hopes for Jerusalem's deliverance rise. Yet the verbs (*hear* [twice]) perhaps foreshadow future deliverance; for the moment nothing comes of the rumors. The Assyrians continue their assault on Judah.

19:10-34 *Sennacherib's Boast, Hezekiah's Prayer, Isaiah's Response*

From Libnah, the Assyrian sends another threatening message to Hezekiah, challenging Isaiah's reassurance and warning Hezekiah not to be deceived by false reliance on the Lord (19:10-13). The Rabshakeh had warned the people of Hezekiah's deception (18:29); now Sennacherib warns Hezekiah against God's deception, demanding that Hezekiah examine the evidence supporting Assyria's claim of irresistible power (19:10-11). Assyrian armies have *utterly destroyed* all their enemies (in Deuteronomy–Samuel, the Lord "utterly destroys" Israel's enemies; this is the only place in the OT where enemies threaten to *utterly destroy* Israel). Citing a list of conquered peoples, the king mocks Hezekiah by asking why he should *rely* on the Lord to *deliver* (19:1013) [*Violence in Kings: Devoted to Destruction, p. 482*].

Hezekiah returns to the temple and spreads out the Assyrian letter *before the* Lord (19:14-15; the phrase indicates loyal service to a master; see EN on 2 Kings 5). Hezekiah offers petitionary prayer (19:15-19): (1) The address expresses confidence in the Lord's sovereignty against Sennacherib's claims, confessing that Yahweh is God of Israel, sovereign over the nations (19:15; cf. Exod 9:14-16; Deut 4:35, 39; Ps 86:10; Isa 44:6), creator of heaven and earth. (2) The first petition calls on the Lord to *hear* and to *see* (Exod 2:23-25) Sennacherib's words, *sent to mock the living God* (2 Kings 19:16; *mock* in 19:4, 22). (3) The complaint acknowledges Assyria's conquest of the nations but contrasts the nations' gods made by human hands with the sovereign Lord (19:17-18). (4) The primary petition evokes exodus deliverance: *Save us from his power that all the kingdoms of earth may know that you, O Yahweh, are God alone* (19:19 AT; cf. Exod 5:2; 7:5; 14:18, 30; Elijah's plea for the Lord's vindication, 1 Kings 18:36-37; counter to Ahaz's petition that Assyria *deliver*, 2 Kings 16:7). The confident Hezekiah has answered the taunts not only of the king's letter (19:10-13) but also the Rabshakeh's taunts to the people

(18:33-35; Park: 125). Hezekiah's bold prayer expresses the trust that marks him (18:5).

Isaiah sends the Lord's message as a three-part prophecy: an oracle directed to Sennacherib (19:21-28), a sign of deliverance (19:29-31), and an oracle of salvation (19:32-34). The Lord's response to Hezekiah's plea is a response to Sennacherib's arrogance, using the Assyrian's rhetorical devices to reproach their mockery and reassure Hezekiah that the Lord hears: messenger formula (19:20-21a; counters 18:19, 28, 31) and a taunt song that addresses Sennacherib with three voices: by the virgin daughter Jerusalem (19:21b-22), a quotation of Sennacherib's own boasts (19:23-24), and the Lord's voice (19:25-28; Fewell: 84–86).

First, virgin daughter Jerusalem responds derisively to Sennacherib. He has presented himself to Jerusalem as a military victor and abundant provider (18:31-35), but she reduces him to a jilted suitor, mocking, scorning, and throwing her head back at the idea of accepting his advances (19:21; Peckham: 86). The rhetorical question *Whom have you mocked and reviled?* matches in form, tone, and content the Rabshakeh's opening challenge: *On whom do you now rely, that you have rebelled against me?* (18:20). By *mocking* and *reviling* Jerusalem, Sennacherib has *mocked* and *reviled* the Lord (19:4, 6, 16, 22, 23). Second, the Lord quotes Sennacherib in mocking mimicry of his ridiculously hyperbolic claims of military success (19:23-24); the Lord mimics the Rabshakeh's mocking quotation of the Lord (*Go up against this land, and destroy it*, 18:25). Ironically, Sennacherib's quotations of Hezekiah (18:29-30, 32) and God (19:10) reveal his own self-deception (Fewell: 85). The Lord, the third voice of the taunt song (19:25-28), is given the last word. The opening rhetorical question, *Have you not heard that I determined . . . ?*, echoes the claims of Sennacherib's letter (*You have heard what the kings of Assyria have done*, 19:11) and confronts the Rabshakeh's rhetorical ploy (*The LORD said to me, Go up against this land*, 18:25). Sennacherib may be uninformed about the Lord's plans (19:25-26), but the Lord *knows* Sennacherib's comings and goings (19:27; *sitting* may be a reference to his reign; *going out and coming in* refers to military action). The taunt song concludes with the Lord threatening to tame the Assyrian like a wild animal, with *hook* and *bit* (19:28), imagery used in Assyrian victory reliefs depicting deportation to exile, matching the Assyrian's usurpation of the biblical image of *utter destruction* (19:11 AT). The Lord will *turn* him around and send him home (*turn*, often meaning "repent": 17:13; 18:14, 24; 19:7, 8, 9, 28, 33, 36). The taunt song affirms the reliability of Hezekiah's trust in the Lord's deliverance. Sennacherib's rhetoric reviles, mocks, and blasphemes the Lord. The Lord will turn Sennacherib around and lead him back on the way he came.

The second part of the prophecy, the sign of deliverance (19:29-31), matches Sennacherib's promise of a land of life, not death (18:31-32). The contrast gives the lie to the imperial boasts, asserting the Lord's autonomy over life and death (Deut 30:15). The Lord offers Hezekiah a *sign* (2 Kings 19:29; a sign marks the covenants with Noah and Abraham, Gen 9:12; 17:11; Hezekiah's father, Ahaz, rejects a sign: Isa 7:11-14). Much as God provides in Jubilee (Lev 25:19-22), for two years Judah shall eat whatever grows of itself. The sign of renewed agriculture points to the fecundity of the surviving *remnant* of Judah, taking root and bearing fruit (2 Kings 19:4, 29-31).

The third part of the message, an oracle of salvation, is introduced by a prophetic messenger formula (19:32-34). The message has three elements: (1) Sennacherib will never lay siege to Jerusalem, despite his bluster (19:32); (2) he will *return* by the way that he came (19:28, 33, 36); and (3) the Lord will *save* the city (19:34; answering Hezekiah's petition in 19:19). The Lord's salvation is motivated by the Lord's reputation (see Hezekiah's appeal in 19:19; cf. Exod 9:16) and by his covenant promises to David (1 Kings 11:13, 32; 2 Kings 8:19).

19:35-37 *Summary Report of Sennacherib's Withdrawal*

The denouement summarizes the resolution of the crisis, reporting the destruction of the Assyrian army and the death of Sennacherib (19:35-37; the summary telescopes events occurring over a span of about twenty years; Fewell: 80). First, the Lord's messenger strikes down many Assyrians (19:35). Second, Sennacherib *returns* to Nineveh (19:36). Third, two of Sennacherib's sons assassinate their father, and a third son, Esar-haddon, succeeds him as ruler of Assyria (19:37). The king who mocks the gods of the nations dies in the temple of his god, unprotected from the violence that has characterized his rule. His trust in a powerless god is contrasted with Judah's trust in the true God (Uehlinger). Wilson sees in the Hezekiah narratives a major theme in Kings, the question of foreign policy, with the narrator supporting a policy of non-alliance with imperial powers (1995: 94).

Hezekiah's Prayer for Healing 20:1-11

The temporal references (*in those days*, 20:1; *at that time*, 20:12), the time marker in the Lord's message (20:6 adds fifteen years to

Hezekiah's life), and the surrounding context suggest that the story of Hezekiah's healing (20:1-11) and the subsequent story of the Babylonian visitors (20:12-19) are flashbacks located amid the Assyrian invasion report (18:13-19:37). The Lord delivers Jerusalem and Judah on a national scale (2 Kings 18-19) while also lengthening Hezekiah's life (2 Kings 20). The events explore the Lord's *deliverance* (20:6) while extending the test of Hezekiah's *trust*, primary themes in 2 Kings 18-20. The narrative analyzes the efficacy of human prayer within divine freedom (Bodner 2019: 194).

Hezekiah's illness is the fourth type-scene of a king receiving an oracle from a prophet predicting death (Jeroboam, 1 Kings 14; Ahaziah, 2 Kings 1; Ben-hadad, 2 Kings 8:7-15) *[Literary Criticism: Narrative Subgenres, p. 460]*. The Hezekiah type-scene is distinguished from the others in that the oracle comes unrequested, is not related to judgment for sin, and ends, unexpectedly, with an extension of life. The extension of the king's life is an acted parable of the life extended to Jerusalem (Wray Beal 2014: 484). The parallels between the Lord's protection of Jerusalem and provision to Hezekiah suggest a similar correspondence between the final vignette (20:12-19) and the national narrative (2 Kings 21-25).

The narrative reports that Hezekiah is at the point of death because of illness (20:1). Isaiah the prophet confirms the prognosis; after an introductory messenger formula (*Thus says the* LORD), he instructs Hezekiah to set his house in order because he is about to die. Hezekiah responds by turning his face to the wall and praying to the Lord (20:2-3). *Walking in faithfulness* (AT: *truth*) is characteristic of David, who instructs Solomon to *walk ... in faithfulness* (1 Kings 2:4; 3:6). Having a fully devoted heart (AT: *heart of shalom*) also characterizes David (11:4; 15:3, 14) *[All His Heart, p. 435]*. Doing *good in the sight of the* LORD (cf. 2 Kings 20:3) is linked to keeping the Lord's commands (Deut 6:17-18). Hezekiah's prayer underscores his close relationship of trust in the Lord but contains no petition regarding his illness or impending death.

God stops Isaiah almost as soon as the prophet has left Hezekiah's chambers with instructions to return to *Hezekiah prince of my people* (2 Kings 20:4; *prince* is a term applied to David in 2 Sam 6:21; 7:8). The oracle reinforces the link with David via an expanded messenger formula from *the* LORD, *the God of your ancestor David* (2 Kings 20:5) and by concluding with an explanation of his motivation to deliver Hezekiah and the city: *for my own sake and for my servant David's sake* (20:6). God *hears* the prayer and *sees* the tears, actions related to divine deliverance (19:16). The Lord promises to *heal* Hezekiah, to *add* fifteen years to his life, and to *deliver* the king and the city *out of the hand [power] of the king of Assyria.* (In the preceding narrative the Assyrians use *deliver* ten times in deriding the Lord's power to save. In his covenant message the Lord says, *[I] will deliver you out of the hand of all your enemies,* 17:39). The final promise reiterates Isaiah's salvation oracle in response to Hezekiah's prayer (20:6; 19:34) *[Literary Criticism: Poetry, p. 460].* The references to David reinforce Hezekiah's positive characterization in the opening royal formula (18:3). The Lord saves *on account of* himself and his servant David without mentioning Hezekiah's claims of faithfulness (20:3). This narrative gap can be interpreted as restraint against a false royal ideology of works righteousness based on Hezekiah's personal faithfulness (Wray Beal 2014: 481) or as promise that walking faithfully in David's example leaves the door open to God's gracious intervention (Cohn 2000: 142). The Lord instructs Isaiah to deliver the oracle (20:4-6). Isaiah prescribes a fig poultice to be applied *to the boil* (20:7; boils, an Egyptian plague, Exod 9:8-12; a Deuteronomic curse, Deut 28:27, 35; Job's ailment, Job 2:7). Hezekiah's request for a sign indicates that he has received the oracle (2 Kings 20:8). Isaiah offers Hezekiah a choice, a sign of an advancing or retreating shadow (20:9). When Hezekiah requests a retreating shadow, Isaiah cries out to the Lord (20:10-11). Just as Hezekiah was sinking into the darkness of death but given miraculous recovery, so the shadow recovers as God miraculously reverses the natural processes.

Hezekiah exhibits trust in the Lord. The Lord works through the prophet Isaiah to deliver Hezekiah and the city from death. Hezekiah, a king like David in doing good in the Lord's sight, receives a gift *for the sake of* the Lord and of David (20:6).

Envoys from Babylon 20:12-19

The indefinite time marker *at that time* and the purpose clause *for he [the king of Babylon] had heard that Hezekiah had been sick* link the Babylonian messengers with the preceding story. Chronological sequence and definitive interpretation are elusive. The narrative places the visit after the illness of Hezekiah, though contemporary annals indicate that Merodach-baladan's reign ended two years before Sennacherib's invasion. Solutions to the chronological problem include an earlier date for the visit, with the assumption that Babylon was seeking a western ally to relieve Assyrian military pressure against them in the east (Long 1991: 243), or reference to Merodach as *king* after the throne had been assumed by his successor (Hobbs: 289).

When the Babylonian envoys arrive with diplomatic correspondence and a present from the king (19:12), Hezekiah shows them the treasure house, including silver, gold, spices (cf. 1 Kings 10:2, 10, 25), good oil, and *his armory* (20:13; *vessels* dedicated in the temple, 1 Kings 7:51; *weapons* of Joash's guards, 2 Kings 11:8). Hezekiah means to demonstrate military capacity as an ally against Assyria (Hens-Piazza 2006: 372; Bodner 2019: 195–97). The references to these treasures parallel Solomon's ostentatious display of wealth to the queen of Sheba (recalling her statement that Solomon's resources were to promote justice, 1 Kings 10:9) [*Mišpaṭ, p. 461*]. Judah pays foreign tribute with wealth from the *storehouses* (20:13; 1 Kings 15:18; 2 Kings 12:18; 14:14; 16:8), including Hezekiah's payment to Sennacherib (18:15; the report fulfilling Isaiah's prophecy that these treasures would be taken by Babylon uses the term *storehouses* twice, 24:13) [*Prophets: Prophetic Word, p. 469*].

Isaiah the prophet interrogates Hezekiah regarding the visitors (20:14). Hezekiah replies that they came from a *distant land* (AT here and in parallels; the Lord warns of judgment from "a distant land," Deut 28:49; 29:22; the Gibeonite ruse is that they are from a "distant land," Josh 9; Solomon's anticipates prayer from exiles in *a distant land*, 1 Kings 8:46). When Isaiah probes further, Hezekiah responds that they have seen all that is in the *house* and all his *storehouses* (20:15). Isaiah responds with an oracle, *Hear the word of the* LORD (20:16-18) [*Literary Criticism, p. 457*]. Prophetic judgment speeches typically open with an accusation that identifies the indictment of sin, but this judgment forecast moves immediately to an announcement that Judah's treasures will be carried to Babylon and that Hezekiah's descendants will become eunuchs in the palace of Babylon. The absence of an accusation of sin leaves a narrative gap. The omniscient narrator reveals Hezekiah's internal reasoning, exposing his self-centered reaction. Hezekiah affirms the Lord's word as *good* (20:19a), reassured in his own mind that he himself will experience *peace and security* (20:19b). Hezekiah's references (20:19) invert his earlier claims to have *walked in faithfulness* (*security*) with a *whole heart* (*peace*) and *done what is good* (20:3). The absence of evaluation of Hezekiah's response allows for interpretive uncertainty. Some readers will find merit in Hezekiah's grateful submission (Nelson 1987: 246). Most will supply the accusation missing from Isaiah's judgment forecast, accusing Hezekiah of false reliance on the Babylonian kingdom like a typical ANE monarch (Park: 108). Others may choose an interpretation acknowledging that Hezekiah, who is lauded for his trust in the Lord, is not perfectly unwavering in that trust yet remains faithful (Wray Beal 2014: 484–85). Still others see in the story a people struggling to understand their own experience in exile, resigned to the reality that even the pious kings Josiah and Hezekiah cannot prevent the destruction, but using the narrative to consider the possibility that human faithfulness can be linked to extended life (Park: 114–17).

Isaiah's judgment alerts the reader to the increasing inevitability of exile. Solomon's dedicatory prayer had assumed that Israel would need to pray from a land of captivity (1 Kings 8:47). The Lord followed the temple dedication by warning that he would cut Israel off from the land and the house if they abandoned him (9:6-9). Israel's exile was foretold in the narrative of their first king (14:15-16) and foreshadows Judah's (2 Kings 17:13, 18-20). The report of the Lord's extension of Hezekiah's life parabolically implies that Judah's life in the land has been extended provisionally. While the pious Hezekiah receives an extension of life, death looms on the horizon. The Hezekiah story dramatizes a confrontation of trust amid political and military conflict (Bodner 2019: 199).

Closing Royal Formula 20:20-21

The closing royal formula includes Hezekiah's deeds and his power, as is customary, as well as reference to the engineering feat that allowed Jerusalem access to its main water supply during time of siege (20:20). Hezekiah's (Siloam) Tunnel was carved through solid rock, connecting the external water source at the Gihon Spring with the Pool of Siloam inside the city of David (*ANET* 321; *ANEP* 85) [*Archaeology: Siloam Inscription, p. 439*].

THE TEXT IN BIBLICAL CONTEXT
Parallel Versions of Hezekiah's Reign (Isa 36–39; 2 Chron 29–32)

A parallel account of Hezekiah prompts questions about the relationship of 2 Kings 18–20 with Isaiah 36–39. Though almost identical, among the differences are the absence of 2 Kings 18:1-12, 14-16 and the addition of Hezekiah's poem (Isa 38:10-20) in Isaiah. It is not clear if the writing of Kings precedes or follows Isaiah or whether both used a preexisting source (Person 1999: 373–79). Hezekiah's poem in Isaiah treats Hezekiah more positively. Second Chronicles 29–31 presents more detail regarding Hezekiah's reform, including an improvised Passover celebration unmentioned in 2 Kings (2 Kings 23:22 characterizes Josiah's Passover as unique). Second Chronicles 32 reports Sennacherib's invasion, with brief reference to the prayer of

Hezekiah and Isaiah and a condensed story of Hezekiah's healing. Each account uniquely contributes to its author's purposes. Throughout, 2 Chronicles' interest in reestablishing worship in Jerusalem is indicated by the focus on reform; the story shows how "right may be done even when there is much that is wrong" (Konkel 2016: 394). Isaiah 36–39 connects the judgment themes in Isaiah 1–39 with the salvation promised in Isaiah 40–66. In 2 Kings the Hezekiah narrative offers hope that repentance and trust open the way for deliverance despite Judah's inexorable path to exile. Passover reform is attributed to Josiah, the model king (2 Kings 23:21-23).

Isaiah and the Plans of God

The disputation between the Lord and Sennacherib focuses on sovereign governance of political events. Sennacherib's rhetoric claims that he is master of his destiny and of the political events of his world. The gods of the nations are powerless before him, he claims.

In Isaiah's taunt song, Yahweh, the Holy One of Israel, challenges Sennacherib, *I determined it long ago[.] I planned from days of old* (2 Kings 19:25). Isaiah 40–55 defends the same theology. Isaiah describes the Lord as seated above the earth, where he controls the princes and rulers of the earth (40:22-23). The Lord summons victors to his service and "tramples kings under foot" (41:2). Also, the Lord challenges the gods to do what he has done: tell what will happen (41:22). Though the Lord has "declared it" (41:27), the gods of the nations fail this test, proving that they "are nothing" and their "work is nothing at all" (41:24). In this long-running apologetic, the Lord challenges the nations to answer the question, "Who among them declared this, and foretold to us the former things?" (43:9). The Lord anointed Cyrus to do his will among the nations (45:1). The Lord challenges the nations to a trial where they present their case, and then asserts that he alone has told of these things "long ago" (45:20-21).

Isaiah's taunt song (2 Kings 19:21-28) and Isaiah 40–55 declare that powerful kings are mistaken to think that they control their own destiny. The Lord raises and discards kings. The Lord alone among the powers knows what is to happen because he controls nations.

Reliance on the Lord

In crisis, Hezekiah *trusts* the Lord, in contrast to the Israelite king likewise clothed in sackcloth who called for the prophet's head (2 Kings 6:30-31; Bodner 2019: 188). There is *no one like* Hezekiah in all the kings that preceded or followed him (18:5). The word *trust* is used nine times in 2 Kings 18–19 but rarely elsewhere in any biblical book prior to Psalms. The word *trust* (*baṭaḥ*) is used most often in Psalms (forty-five times), Isaiah (nineteen times), and Jeremiah (sixteen times), and relatively frequently in Proverbs (ten times). *Trust* depends on both Hezekiah's hope in the Lord (not human power) and the Lord's reliability.

The book of Psalms declares that the Lord is a stronghold for the oppressed who trust in the Lord (9:9-10). Laments include a statement of trust (13:5; 22:4-5, 9; 25:2; 26:1; 31:6, 14; etc.). Wisdom psalms call for trust in the Lord (28:7; 33:21; 37:3, 5; 62:8). The psalmist knows of ill-placed trust in human beings (41:9), weapons (44:6), wealth (49:6; 52:7), oppression (62:10), princes (118:9; 146:3), and idols (135:18). The psalmist trusts in the word of the Lord (119:42).

The book of Proverbs invites trust in the Lord (3:5; 16:20; 28:25; 29:25) and warns against false trust in riches (11:28) or in one's own heart (28:26 KJV). Proverbs pronounces a blessing on the husband of the trustworthy wife (31:11).

Isaiah declares the benefits of trust in the Lord. Because the Lord is his salvation, he trusts and does not fear (Isa 12:2). Peace is the fruit of trust (26:3-4). He warns against false trust in oppression and guile (30:12) and in armaments (31:1) or idols (42:17). Jeremiah speaks out against those who trust in fortified cities (Jer 5:17), deceptive words (7:4, 8), the temple (7:14), other humans (9:4; 17:5), falsehood (13:25; 28:15; 29:31), Pharaoh (46:25), or their own achievements and treasure (48:7; 49:4), but blesses those who trust in the Lord (17:7). The Lord is trustworthy for those in deepest need (e.g., widows, 49:11).

Jesus demonstrates his authority over demons, sin, the Sabbath, and nature (Mark 1:27; 2:9-12; 2:23–3:6; 4:35-41). In the stilling of the storm, the narrator contrasts the "great windstorm" with the "great calm" (4:37, 39; Geddert: 113). Jesus' question contrasts the disciples' "great fear" with absence of trust (4:40; *pistis* is translated as "faith" in NRSV). As in the gospel of John, Mark's story invites trust in Jesus, a relationship, rather than mere assent to a theological confession.

Sennacherib and Solomon under the Vine and Fig Tree

The Rabshakeh promises Jerusalem that they will eat of their *own vine and . . . fig tree* if they surrender to him (2 Kings 18:31). The phrase *vines and fig trees* occurs in one other text in Kings, praising Solomonic bounty (1 Kings 4:25). Both texts claim that the good life is the empire's universal benefit.

The Old Testament links life in the land to fruit of the land, including grapes (or vines) and figs (or fig trees). The terms are first used together in the spies' report of the land (Num 13:23). Vines and fig trees represent the good life, but lack of trust in the Lord and fear of an empire's military blocks Israel's receipt of God's gift. The people quarrel with Moses, describing Egypt, the empire from which God freed them, as superior to their current existence because of its fruit, vines, and figs (Num 20:5). In Israel's deliverance, the Lord strikes the Egyptian vines and fig trees (Ps 105:33).

In contrast to the Rabshakeh's offer, Moses promises a land "of vines and fig trees" as well as grain, olives, pomegranates, and honey (Deut 8:8). Deuteronomy reminds Israel that these are gifts from the God who has liberated them from slavery and warns them not to forget the Lord's gift, not to become proud, and not to neglect care for the marginalized. Figs and vines help create the idyllic context for love (Song of Sol 2:13). Israel is called the Lord's grapes and figs (Hos 9:10).

Prophetic texts mention vines and figs in contexts of judgment (Isa 36:16; Jer 5:17; 8:13; Hos 2:12; Joel 1:7, 12; Amos 4:9). The prophets also use the pair positively. The trees and vines full of fruit are a salvation message (Joel 2:22). The day of the Lord is characterized by life under vine and fig tree (Mic 4:4; Zech 3:10), a bountiful time when vine and fig tree will be blessed (Hag 2:19). Habakkuk calls for faith even when fruit on the vine and fig tree are lacking (3:17). Vines and figs trees are an image that subverts imperial military power, envisioning displacement of the military apparatus and an economic rejuvenation (Brueggemann 1981: 193–94).

The phrase "vine and fig tree" describes abundant life. In Kings, the phrase is linked to imperial justice. The Solomonic scribe glides over the lack of Deuteronomic justice and makes the exaggerated claim that everyone lives under their own *vines and fig trees* (1 Kings 4:20-28). In the mouth of the Rabshakeh, the phrase betrays the counterfeit nature of the promise (2 Kings 18:32). Having one's own vines and fig trees promises the blessed good life of covenant faithfulness; lacking vines and fig trees speaks of judgment.

THE TEXT IN THE LIFE OF THE CHURCH
Model Prayer for the Nation

Psalm 20, a royal psalm, appeals to God to protect the king. Paul instructs Timothy to pray for kings and for those in high positions (1 Tim 2:1-2). Hezekiah prays a model prayer for his nation. Like the psalmist, Timothy, Paul, and Hezekiah, believers today live among governmental authorities that depend on violent threats to retain power.

Hezekiah addresses the Lord as cosmic sovereign and creator (2 Kings 19:15). Isaiah reminds Sennacherib that God raises and lowers empires for strategic purposes (19:23-26). As sovereign, God judges and controls the empires; imperial power is limited and subject to divine judgment. As creator, God cares for the environment. Hezekiah addresses God as the God of Israel; Israel is a dependent covenant partner, committed to God.

In his first petition Hezekiah asks God to see and hear the offenses of the enemy. Naming the wrongs sharpens the perspective of the praying community. The offense includes the violence, mayhem, and injustice of the empire that oppresses those too weak to defend themselves. As we follow Hezekiah's model prayer, our own complicity with imperial injustice may be revealed. The second petition invites God to act. Unless God acts, hope is gone. Following Hezekiah's model, we express our hope that God sees, hears, and acts in ways that redeem humanly impossible problems.

Hezekiah expresses confidence that the kingdoms will know God when they witness God's salvation. The petition acknowledges that the kingdoms will recognize God when God's people give witness regarding the source of salvation. As Paul reiterates, the church gives witness to the powers regarding the mystery of God's salvation (Eph 3:9-11). In prayer, the church joins God in opposing evil structural powers.

Hezekiah also models prayer that extends his life after illness (cf. John 11:4). One friend shares the story of her mother-in-law who prayed that she would live to raise her children; her life was extended many years beyond that. As a young father, when a physician misdiagnosed a tooth infection as lymphoma, I prayed to see my son through high school. Restored to health by a root canal, I have been more grateful for God's gracious gift of life since that moment.

Renewal

Hezekiah's religious renewal affects worship practices, social agenda, and political alliances. Religious renewal transforms individuals and communities. The Great Awakening, an evangelical spiritual revival that swept Protestant Europe and British America in the 1730s and 1740s, fostered deep conviction of need for salvation and commitment to personal morality. Though women were rarely allowed to preach, the movement encouraged women to make independent decisions for Christ and to share their feelings with other women. The awakening brought the message of personal salvation to enslaved Africans and their descendants, who were accepted into Christian congregations and encouraged to learn to read the Bible. The movement provoked schisms between preachers who offered passionate emotional experiences, a pietistic form of Calvinism, and clergy who favored more rationalistic intellectual discourse, stressing orthodoxy and doctrine. Though the American religious landscape was forever transformed (including increased sectarianism because of schisms), social change was limited. Preachers (notably George Whitfield) criticized slaveholders' cruel treatment of enslaved people without working to abolish slavery.

The Reigns of Manasseh and Amon

PREVIEW

The authors of the 2018 article "The Point of No Return for Climate Action" in the journal *Earth Systems Dynamics* seek to answer the question, "At what point will climate change make the planet uninhabitable?" Looking back from exile, the authors of 1–2 Kings recognize that for Judah the reign of Manasseh became the point of no return. Though his grandson Josiah was the best of all kings, Manasseh's transgressions were so great that exile became inevitable. Why?

The reign of Manasseh is pivotal in 1–2 Kings. As 2 Kings 17 interprets Israel's exile from Samaria, 2 Kings 21 attributes Judah's exile to Manasseh (see also 23:12, 26-27; 24:3-4). Second Kings 21 lists the sins of Manasseh that produce the inevitability of Judah's exile. Because the reforms of Manasseh's father, Hezekiah, and his grandson Josiah are evaluated so positively (18:3, 5; 22:2; 23:25), Manasseh's villainous role is essential to the plot. Manasseh is compared negatively to the nations (21:2, 9, 11), to Ahab (21:3, 13), and implicitly to Jeroboam (*caused Judah also to sin*, 21:11; cf. 1 Kings 14:16). Moreover, some of the sins listed in the explanation of Israel's exile (17:16-17) are sins attributed chiefly to Manasseh in Judah. Absent an accounting like 2 Kings 17, Manasseh is the necessary explanation for Judah's exile. The summative report rhetorically replaces the list of Manasseh's abominations with a single code phrase that encapsulates anti-Torah royal practice (21:16). Paraphrasing a mathematical term, Lasine describes the narrative as a "limiting case of a villainous king" for the narrator's creation of a character so extremely evil as to serve as a narratival scapegoat (1993: 163).

OUTLINE

Reign of Manasseh, 21:1-18
 21:1-9 Opening Royal Formula and Evaluative Summary
 21:10-15 Prophetic Judgment Speech
  Accusation against the King (21:10-11)
  Announcement of Judgment (21:12-14)
  Accusation against the People (21:15)
 21:16 Summative Report
 21:17-18 Closing Royal Formula
Reign of Amon, 21:19-26
 21:19-22 Opening Royal Formula
 21:23-26 Conspiracy, Death, and Closing Royal Formula

EXPLANATORY NOTES

Reign of Manasseh 21:1-18

21:1-9 Opening Royal Formula and Evaluative Summary

With minimal narrative plot, the report of Manasseh's reign summarizes his sins with an opening royal formula (21:1-9), a prophetic speech (21:10-15, with accusations against king and people framing the announcement of judgment), a coded summary of the sins of Manasseh and Judah (21:16), and a closing royal formula (21:17-18). The refrain he/they *did . . . evil in the sight of the LORD* is applied to king (21:2, 6) and people (21:15, 16). The list of Manasseh's sins is lengthy and repetitious: committing abominations worse than the nations (21:2, 9-11), rebuilding high places earlier eliminated by Hezekiah (21:3), putting altars for idols and *the host of heaven* in the temple (21:3-5, 7), shedding *innocent blood* (21:16), misleading the people (21:9, 16), and disobeying the Torah (21:8) [*Idolatry, p. 449*]. The opening royal formula introduces Manasseh with standard details. At age twelve, he is among the youngest kings at coronation, and his fifty-five-year tenure is the longest. His mother's name is listed without information about her heritage or birthplace (signaling illegitimate heritage). Though Manasseh's long reign suggests unparalleled political success, 2 Kings regards it as an unmitigated disaster. The exceptionally long opening royal formula lists his unparalleled transgressions. The opening summary is that he *did what was evil in the sight of the LORD* (21:2; 21:6, 15, 16), *following the*

abominable practices of the nations that the LORD drove out (21:2; see also
21:11; 1 Kings 14:24; 2 Kings 16:3). Abominations include cultic transgressions of the nations (Deut 7:25-26) and economic injustice
(25:16) [Evil, p. 446].

Second Kings 21:3-8 itemizes cultic violations. Manasseh rebuilds
the high places and the sacred pole destroyed by Hezekiah (21:3;
18:3; rebuilt [šub] is often translated as repent or restore; e.g., turn from
your evil ways, 17:13). Manasseh, the worst king of Judah, builds
altars for Baal with an Asherah (sacred pole), associating him with
Ahab, the worst king of Israel. The only two kings linked with the
abominations of the Amorite idols (1 Kings 21:26; 2 Kings 21:11) also
shed innocent blood (1 Kings 21:19; 2 Kings 9:7, 26; 21:16;
Schniedewind: 659–60). Outdoing Ahab, Manasseh worshiped and
served all the host of heaven (21:3; the entire pantheon of gods; Micaiah
sees the host of heaven, 1 Kings 22:19; forbidden Canaanite astral deities, Deut 4:19; 17:3; 2 Kings 17:15, 35; Jer 7:18; Cogan and Tadmor:
266). The altars are an affront to Yahweh's name (or honor; 2 Kings
21:4; 1 Kings 9:3).

Introducing idolatrous cultic furnishings into the temple and
making his son pass through the fire (evidently child sacrifice),
Manasseh follows Ahaz (2 Kings 21:5-6a; cf. 16:3, 10-13). The scope of
his false worship (all the host of heaven) infiltrating the whole temple
(in the two courts of the house of the LORD) intensifies judgment (21:3-
5). Manasseh's additional cultic practices (soothsaying, augury,
mediums, and wizards relate to divination and spiritism, all "abhorrent . . . to the LORD," Deut 18:12) imitate the nations driven out by
the Lord (21:6b; Deut 18:9-14).

Manasseh's actions turn God's promises inside out (Nelson 1987:
250). He puts (NIV) a carved image of Asherah in the house where
the Lord had said, I will put my name forever (2 Kings 21:7-8; emph.
added; cf. 21:4; 1 Kings 9:3-5) [House for the Name, p. 449]. The references to David, Solomon, and the house in Jerusalem and to the
promise that Israel would wander no more recall the Davidic and
Solomonic covenant promises (2 Sam 7:10-16; 1 Kings 9:3-4; 2 Kings
21:8). The reference to Solomon, the first time his name is used since
1 Kings 14:26, draws the parallels between the two builders (Manasseh
made and rebuilt the high places, 2 Kings 21:3, 7; Solomon built [the
house] for the LORD but also built a high place, 1 Kings 6:2-3; 11:7;
Leithart: 263).

The opening royal formula is framed by the phrase did what was
evil, applied to Manasseh in the initial summary (2 Kings 21:2) and to
Judah in the summation (21:9; cf. 21:15, 16). The people do not hear

(21:9 AT). *Hear* connotes "obey" and is at the heart of the Lord's covenant (*Hear, O Israel,* Deut 6:4). Like Jeroboam the son of Nebat (2 Kings 17:21-22), Manasseh is indicted for leading the people astray (the only king of Judah indicted for this cause; "every dynasty that makes Israel sin is destroyed, . . . and when Manasseh leads Judah astray, the Davidic dynasty is also judged," Leithart: 264). Manasseh has led the people into more evil than all the nations whom the Lord had *destroyed* (21:9; used twenty-eight times in Deuteronomy, "destroy" describes the Lord's clearing the land for Israel). The opening formula links Manasseh, the worst of Judah, with the sins of Jeroboam, the characteristic and perpetual failure of Israel; and the sins of Ahab, the worst of Israel's kings [*Covenant in Kings, p. 443*].

21:10-15 Prophetic Judgment Speech

The Manasseh judgment speech is the most extensive explanation for the Judean exile (parallel to 2 Kings 17). The Lord's message comes through *the prophets* (21:10, much like a prophetic messenger formula; cf. 17:13, 23) [*Literary Criticism: Poetry, p. 460*]. The judgment is framed with accusations against Manasseh (21:11) and Judah (21:15). The opening accusation repeats the general indictment (21:11): Manasseh has committed *abominations* (21:2) and has *multiplied the evil* (AT) of the Amorites who preceded them in the land (like Ahab, 1 Kings 21:26) and has made Judah sin (like Jeroboam). *Foul idols* is "an invented invective, *gilulim*, from *gelalim*, 'turds'" (2 Kings 21:11; Alter: 599; used previously of Israel in 17:12; of Amon in 21:21).

The messenger formula, *Therefore thus says the LORD* (21:12), followed by the interjection *Behold* (AT), calls readers to the Lord's perspective [*Literary Criticism: Elements of Narrative, p. 458*]. The Lord will bring *evil* upon Jerusalem and Judah that corresponds to their *evil* deeds (21:2, 6, 9, 11, 15-16) [*Evil, p. 446*]. Three metaphors communicate the intensity of judgment. Engaging the sense of hearing, *the ears of everyone who hears of it will tingle* (21:12; *hissing* is judgment for injustice, 1 Kings 9:8; Jer 19:3). The positive architectural metaphor is turned inside out (*measuring line* for covenant building on justice and righteousness, Isa 28:17); Jerusalem is measured for destruction. The measuring line and the plummet reveal that Manasseh is for Jerusalem what Ahab was for Samaria. The third image is domestic: the Lord will *wipe* the city clean as one wipes a dirty dish, turning it over and over to rid it of contamination (to wipe is to "blot out," Deut 29:20). The Lord announces that he will *cast off the remnant of my heritage, and give them into the hand of their enemies*, where they will *become a prey and a spoil* (21:14; Yahweh had promised not to "cast away" his people despite their rejection of him as king, 1 Sam 12:22; Solomon prayed that the Lord not *abandon* his *inheritance*, 1 Kings 8:36, 51, 53, 57; Hezekiah and Isaiah asked the Lord to save the *remnant*, 2 Kings 19:4, 31; Moses pled that the Lord would deliver his "heritage" [AT], his "very own possession," Deut 9:26, 29).

The judgment speech concludes with a sweeping accusation: the people have done evil and provoked the Lord to anger from the exodus until the present (2 Kings 21:15; cf. 21:6). The accusation establishes the Lord's patience and justifies impending judgment. Though the direction had been set earlier, Manasseh has led them deeper into evil, intensifying the cultic transgressions of Judah reported at the beginning of the divided kingdom (Judah did *evil . . . , built . . . high places, pillars, and [Asherim] on every high hill and under every green tree, [and] committed all the abominations of the nations that the LORD drove out*, 1 Kings 14:22-24; cf. 2 Kings 17:8; 21:2). The phrase *the nations that the LORD drove out* impugns Judah for depreciating the Lord's deliverance. Finally, the exodus reference emphasizes how Manasseh (with Judah) has turned the Lord's salvation inside out, rejecting liberation from the gods of Egypt with re-enslaving idolatry. Despite the reforms of Hezekiah and Josiah, Manasseh's sin is so gross as to provoke the Lord's anger. The sin of Manasseh explains the exile of Judah four generations later, a judgment endorsed by Torah (2 Kings 21:8-9), the prophets (21:10-15; 22:16-17), and the narrator (21:16) *[Provoke the Lord to Anger, p. 470]*.

21:16 Summative Report

The summation rewrites the indictment. Like Israel's worst king, Manasseh has exceeded the sins of the Amorites. "The sins of the Amorites" are "completed" (Gen 15:16) by Ahab and Manasseh, the only two kings linked to the Amorites (Leithart: 264). Having developed an unprecedented list of abominations, the narrator uses rhetorical sleight of hand to replace the list with a single charge: like Ahab, Manasseh *shed very much innocent blood, until he had filled Jerusalem from one end to another* (2 Kings 21:16; cf. 1 Kings 21:26). While *innocent bloodshed* can be linked to child sacrifice (Ps 106:38; Jer 19:3-5) or martyred prophets (Jer 26:20-23), *innocent bloodshed* is code for oppression of the orphan, widow, and alien (Isa 59:7; Jer 2:34; 7:6; 22:3, 17). The narrator later repeats the charge of *innocent blood[shed] . . . that fills Jerusalem* to explain the inevitability of the exile (2 Kings 24:2-4). Like Ahab (guilty of social injustice, murdering Naboth, confiscating his ancestral land, 1 Kings 21:17-19; 2 Kings 9:7-10, 26), Manasseh's idolatry ideologically leads to social injustice. Rhetorically, by placing the charge of *innocent bloodshed* at the report's climax, the narrator communicates that this charge outweighs the list of abominations. In Manasseh, the cumulative effects of royal ideological rejection of Torah justice reaches its zenith—and tips the balance toward irrevocable judgment.

21:17-18 Closing Royal Formula

The closing royal formula for Manasseh is anticlimactic. Manasseh's exceptionally corrupt rule is marked by a unique inclusion in the closing formula: *sin that he committed* (21:17). Manasseh sleeps with his ancestors and is buried in the garden of Uzza, where his son will also be buried (21:26). His son Amon succeeds him.

Second Kings 21 presents Manasseh as the most evil character in Kings. Another evaluation of Manasseh is possible. Caught amid empires (Assyrian, Babylonian, Egyptian) that devastate his father, Hezekiah (18:13; 20:17-18), and murder his grandson Josiah (23:29), kings characterized as Judah's most righteous (18:3-6; 23:25), Manasseh's policy protects the small, militarily powerless kingdom of Judah and extends his tenure beyond any other of Judah and Israel (fifty-five years, 21:1). Stavrakopoulou, for example, argues that "Manasseh was one of Judah's most successful kings," citing archaeological support for his assessment (256, 259). According to 2 Chronicles 33, Manasseh repented of his sin, was restored, and prospered (33:14-16; see TBC). The Kings narrator charges that Manasseh's *innocent bloodshed* makes exile inevitable.

Reign of Amon 21:19-26

21:19-22 Opening Royal Formula

The opening royal formula reports Amon's age, brief tenure, and mother's name and origins (21:19). The list intensifies the evil characterization: *did what was evil in the sight of the LORD, walked [as] his father walked, served the idols that his father served, and worshiped them; . . . abandoned the LORD, . . . did not walk in the way of the LORD* (21:20-22). Redundancy reinforces the power of Manasseh's precedent.

21:23-26 Conspiracy, Death, and Closing Royal Formula

Amon is assassinated in a palace coup. The people of the land again support the Davidic dynasty, kill the conspirators, and install Josiah,

son of Amon, as king (19:24) [*People of the Land, p. 464*]. The concluding royal formula cites the Book of the Annals of the Kings of Judah,
identifies Amon's burial place in the garden of Uzza, and reports the
accession of his son Josiah (21:25-26).

THE TEXT IN BIBLICAL CONTEXT
Remnant

Micah the prophet employs the term "remnant" in salvific hope,
promising that God will gather all the remnant (survivors) of Jacob,
put them together like a flock in pasture, lead them, and act as their
king (Mic 2:12-13). Micah promises that on the day of the Lord, the
Lord will make the lame a "remnant" and will make those who were
cast off a strong nation. The Lord will reign in Mount Zion, and the
people will walk in his name (4:5-7). The "remnant," like dew from
the Lord and showers on the grass, will be powerful, a young lion
protected from its foes (Mic 5:7-8). In loyal faithfulness to the ancestors, the Lord will pardon the iniquity of God's "remnant" (7:18-20).
Though Micah uses the term "remnant" most frequently, Isaiah,
Jeremiah, Amos, Zephaniah, and Zechariah look forward to the day
when the "remnant" will enjoy peace (Isa 46:3; Jer 23:3; 31:7; Amos
5:15; Zeph 2:7, 9; 3:13; Zech 8:6, 11, 12). In Romans, Paul cites Isaiah
and refers to Elijah in use of the term "remnant" (9:27; 11:2-5).

Given the positive valence of *remnant* in the prophets (2 Kings
19:4, 31), how are we to understand the announcement that the Lord
will abandon the *remnant* (21:14; Jer 6:9; 8:3; 11:23; 15:9; 24:8; Ezek
5:10; 9:8)? The authors of 1–2 Kings are at pains to explain the exile.
Given the good kings Hezekiah and Josiah, powerful rhetoric is
needed to show that Yahweh, not the imperial Babylonian gods,
orders history and brings exile. Second Kings 21 turns metaphors of
salvation inside out, including the term *remnant*. Manasseh has *provoked the* LORD *with provocations* (23:26 AT). The God who ordered
Assyria to return home without destroying Jerusalem (19:25-28, 35)
is responsible for Jerusalem's destruction because of Manasseh's
regime of bloodshed (24:3-4). No literary stone is left unturned to
make this case that the Lord rules and exile is just.

Manasseh in Chronicles

The account of Manasseh in 2 Chronicles 33 amends 2 Kings 21 significantly. Chronicles also reports that Manasseh led Judah and
Jerusalem to do more evil than the nations that preceded them
(2 Chron 33:1-9; 2 Kings 21:9). The Assyrians deported Manasseh to
Babylon, where he repented, was restored, and "knew that the LORD

indeed was God" (2 Chron 33:10-13). The account ends with a report of Manasseh's successful, faithful reign (33:14-17). Second Chronicles 33:19 refers to the Prayer of Manasseh "written in the records of the seers," a psalm accepted as a deuterocanonical book by Orthodox Christians. The almost irreconcilable contrast between the two biblical reports of Manasseh points to the freedom the narrators had in interpreting events to serve their overall purposes. Chronicles shows that it is never too late to repent and receive pardon. If even the worst of sinners, Manasseh, can be released from exile, surely there is hope for Israel. In 1–2 Kings, Manasseh's sins were so great that exile became inevitable. Kings shows that the reason for exile was rejecting Torah justice. Dillard explains that the tension of the two accounts can be reconciled at a theological level by "the awareness that all that we do is touched both by sin and by the grace of God," which, "taken together[,] display life in its complexity" (270).

THE TEXT IN THE LIFE OF THE CHURCH
Innocent Blood

After listing Manasseh's abominations in repetitive detail, the report concludes, *Moreover Manasseh shed very much innocent blood, until he had filled Jerusalem [with it] from one end to another* (21:16). The narrator explains that the Lord destroyed Judah because of *the innocent blood that [Manasseh] had shed; for he filled Jerusalem with innocent blood, and the LORD was not willing to pardon* (24:4). Rhetorically, the narrator accumulates Manasseh's sins, places them on the balance, then demonstrates that shedding innocent blood outweighs all others. As noted in the commentary above, *innocent blood* refers to unjust practices against the marginalized. Sparing innocent blood requires protecting the most vulnerable.

In *Lest Innocent Blood Be Shed*, Phillip Hallie describes the French Protestant border town Le Chambon, where the pacifist Reformed pastor André Trocmé and his wife, Magda, inspire a village to risk their lives to save thousands of Jews being shipped to Nazi death camps. As a community of faith seeking always to live the gospel, they regard their efforts as ordinary rather than heroic.

Ron Sider, a Mennonite and Brethren in Christ pastor, president of Evangelicals for Social Action, and author of *Completely Pro-Life*, argues that the pro-life stance requires commitment to spare innocent blood everywhere. Protecting innocent life includes the unborn as well as those threatened by weapons of mass destruction, gun violence, poverty, and capital punishment. The church opposes the shedding of innocent blood by promoting the flourishing of human life. Sider teaches followers of Jesus that being completely pro-life means that "we care about peace and justice and freedom and a wholesome environment." Sider calls his stance "pro-life—womb to tomb" (Sider 2016).

2 Kings 22:1–23:30
The Reign of Josiah

PREVIEW

Like a child waiting for Christmas, 1–2 Kings has been awaiting the king promised when Israel seceded (1 Kings 13:2). Josiah fulfills that promise. Not only does he desecrate the Bethel altar, but Josiah does what is right, walks in the way of David, repairs the house of the Lord, makes a covenant with the people to keep the Lord's commands, and celebrates Passover. Josiah is greater than all others in turning to the Lord with his whole being. Despite modeling covenant faithfulness, Josiah's righteousness cannot turn back the Lord's anger provoked by Manasseh, who has brought to a climax the evil done by Judah (and Israel) from the time they left Egypt [*Provoke the Lord to Anger, p. 470*]. The prophetess Huldah confirms the judgment on unfaithful Judah; the narrative reports both the golden age of Josiah's reforms and the ensuing slide into exile.

Though Josiah's initiatives dominate 2 Kings 22–23, the discovery of the book of the Torah is central. This book of covenant has been neglected since the Lord's glory filled the temple at its dedication (1 Kings 8:9-11). The book of the Torah has been hidden from the characters in 1–2 Kings, though Torah has been the basis for condemning the sins of Jeroboam, Ahab's abominations, and Judah's high places. The discovery of the written Torah at this moment underscores that Torah values (justice, righteousness, faithfulness, holiness) and not Israel's institutions (temple, kingship, even prophecy) are foremost in God's engagement with humanity (see McConville 2006).

The opening and closing royal formulas (2 Kings 22:1-2; 23:28-30) frame the account of Josiah's reign. The reforms, dated to his eighteenth year (22:3–23:27), focus on Josiah's five commands: Josiah *sends* Shaphan to oversee temple repairs and recovers the book of the Torah (22:3-11). Josiah *commands* a delegation to inquire of the Lord and receives a double prophetic oracle from Huldah (22:12-20). Josiah *sends* word that all the people are to assemble to hear and renew the covenant (23:1-3). Josiah *commands* Hilkiah the high priest to reform the cultic structure (23:4-20). And Josiah *commands* a Passover as prescribed. After the superlatively positive evaluation of Josiah, the *nevertheless* (23:26 AT; NRSV: *still*) of inevitable judgment stands (23:21-27). Motivated by Torah and undeterred by the inevitable judgment, Josiah models covenant faithfulness.

OUTLINE

EXPLANATORY NOTES

Opening Royal Formula for Josiah's Reign 22:1-2

The standard opening royal formula includes a brief evaluation affirming not only that Josiah *did what was right in the sight of the* LORD (as some other kings, 1 Kings 15:11; 22:43; 2 Kings 10:30; 12:2; 14:3; 15:3, 34; 18:3) and *walked in all the way of his father David* (like Asa, 1 Kings 15:11; and Hezekiah, 2 Kings 18:3), but also that Josiah uniquely *did not turn aside to the right or to the left* (2 Kings 22:2; see also Deut 5:32; 17:11, 20; 28:14; Josh 1:7; 23:6). The formula establishes that Josiah fits the Davidic prototype, unlike any of his predecessors (Joseph: 153). The closing royal formula finds him superior to other kings in turning to the Lord according to the law of Moses (23:25). Josiah sets the standard, unmatched by any other king of Israel or Judah [All His Heart, p. 435].

Discovery of the Scroll 22:3-11
22:3-7 Josiah Sends Shaphan to the Temple

In his eighteenth year as king, Josiah initiates temple renovation. Josiah sends Shaphan . . . , the scribe (KJV) with a message for the high priest Hilkiah (22:3-4; the repeated use of their titles in vv. 3, 4, 8 emphasizes the official nature of the assignment) [Send, p. 476]. Like King Joash before him (12:4-16), Josiah demands action from the high priest, accounting and distribution of the temple income, payment of the temple builders, and confidence that the builders deal honestly (21:7) and need not account for their expenses. Josiah's speech repeats Joash's renovation nearly verbatim, a type-scene giving the surprise discovery of the scroll maximum effect (Cohn 2000: 152; see TBC below).

22:8-11 Hilkiah Reports the Discovery of the Scroll

Temple repair is interrupted by Hilkiah's report to Shaphan: The book of the Torah! I have found it in the house of the LORD (22:8 AT). The discovery reorients the narrative. Immediately Shaphan reads the book. The dramatic tension builds as Shaphan returns to the king, reporting first only temple repair (22:9). Shaphan adds to the report, A book! Hilkiah has given it to me! (22:10 AT). Delaying news of the discovery until after reporting repairs spotlights the announcement. Shaphan reads the book aloud to Josiah. The tension within the narrative builds as the book passes from priest to secretary to king and is read twice without revealing its content. The king's dramatic response, tearing his clothes after he heard the words of the book of the law, reinforces the book's significance (22:11).

Inquiry of the Prophetess 22:12-20
22:12-15 Josiah Sends the Delegation to Huldah

King Josiah commands a five-member delegation (priest, secretary, king's servant, and two named envoys) to inquire of the LORD (22:12-13; inquire is used for health inquiries, 1 Kings 14; 2 Kings 1, 8; Jehoshaphat's battle inquiries, 1 Kings 22; 2 Kings 3; Josiah's inquiries, 22:13, 18). Josiah's concern is for himself, for the people, and for all Judah. Josiah emphasizes that the words of this book that has been found create alarm (22:13). Narrative tension builds as Josiah's mandate reveals that the Lord's great wrath is kindled because of

the ancestors' failure to obey (AT: hear) the words of this book
[Provoke the Lord to Anger, p. 470]. The five-member party (repeating
their names underlines the official status of the group, delays the
inquiry, and builds suspense) speaks to Huldah the prophetess,
wife of a temple official, living in Jerusalem (22:14; that a woman
plays the role of prophet is reported without comment; cf. Exod
15:20; Judg 4:4).

22:16-20 Huldah's Oracles

Huldah issues an oracle: first, judgment on the populace (2 Kings
22:15-17); second, postponement of judgment for the king (22:18-
20). The oracle addresses the man who sent you, emphasizing that
Josiah as king is directing the action (he sends in 22:3, 15, 18; 23:1).
The interjection Behold [Literary Criticism: Elements of Narrative,
p. 458] shifts the perspective to the divine viewpoint. The judgment
oracle announces impending doom (evil upon this place and upon its
inhabitants, 22:16 AT). The indictment reveals some content of the
book that has so distressed the king: Because they have abandoned me
and burned incense to other gods (22:17 AT; cf. 17:16; cf. 21:22). The
people's idolatry has ignited the burning wrath of the Lord, and it
cannot be extinguished, the oracle concludes [Literary Criticism:
Poetry, p. 460].

Turning her attention to the king, Huldah issues a salvation
oracle introduced by a double messenger formula. The oracle
affirms the king's repentance, demonstrated by his public actions of
tearing his clothes and weeping but prompted by internal motivation (Josiah is penitent and humbles himself like Ahab, 22:19; 1 Kings
21:29). Because Josiah hears what the Lord has spoken against
Jerusalem (2 Kings 22:11; unlike the ancestors, 22:13), the Lord has
heard Josiah (22:18-19). Therefore, says the Lord, I will gather you to
your ancestors, and you shall be gathered to your grave in peace (22:20a).
Since Josiah is killed by Pharaoh Neco (23:29-30), scholars are divided about how to read this prophecy. Provan contends that the first
verb refers to Josiah's death and the second to his burial (1988: 149).
Though Josiah's death is violent, he is buried in peacetime, fulfilling
the prophecy. Others suggest that Josiah's violent death confirms
the authenticity of Huldah's misinformed prophecy. Because of his
repentance and reforms, Josiah is granted a temporary reprieve and
will not witness the coming judgment. Despite his repentance, however, judgment looms, with the place and its inhabitants becoming
a desolation and a curse (22:19; cf. Deut 28:15, 37). The envoys carry
the message back to the king.

Covenant Renewal 23:1-3

King Josiah *directs* (*sends*) Jerusalem and Judah to gather for covenant renewal (23:1). In phase 1, Josiah *gathers all the elders* (AT), enlisting leadership support. In phase 2, Josiah ascends to the temple with *all the people of Judah, all the inhabitants of Jerusalem, the priests, the prophets, and all the people, both small and great* (23:2). *All* the people (used five times in 23:1-3), together with the list of assembled participants, emphasizes the community's inclusive commitment to renewal (mirroring Exod 24:3-8; Deut 5:1-5; 29:2-28; 31:9-13; Josh 8:30-35; 24:1-26; 2 Sam 5:3; 2 Kings 11:14-17). The king *reads in their hearing all the words of the book of the covenant*, the third time the text is read (22:8, 10). Though as readers we have not heard any of the content, "the identity of the book is no mystery" (Nelson 1987: 255). The king's reaction of penitent remorse and references to *the wrath of the* LORD *kindled* because of the ancestors' failure to *hear* (22:11-13), the prophetess's reference to *desolation and curse* (22:19), and the king's covenant to keep the Lord's *commandments, his decrees, and his statutes, with all his heart and all his soul* (23:3)—all these leave no doubt that the *book of the Torah* (23:2 AT; *the book of the covenant*) is the book of Deuteronomy (perhaps an edition earlier than the canonical book; Strawn: 33). Covenant renewal involves rehearsing the words of the book (Deut 5:1; 31:11, 28, 30; 32:44; cf. Neh 8:3; 13:1). The king leads in making a covenant to follow the law, *standing* next to the pillar as Joash had done (2 Kings 23:3; 11:14). The three verbs used to describe the commitment to obedience—*follow, keep,* and *perform* (AT: *walk, guard, establish*)—along with the three nouns describing the content of the Torah, and the reference to all the heart and all the soul, are typical Deuteronomic constructions, using a series of synonyms to emphasize the solemnity of this commitment. *All the people joined in the covenant* (*joined* is translated *stood* in the first part of the 23:3) [*Covenant in Kings, p. 443*].

Covenant renewal is at the center of Josiah's reform. Josiah's first renewal act commits the community to covenant. Covenant renewal centers on reading and obeying the book (Deut 31:9-13). Josiah marshals other leaders to support the covenant. Josiah himself is committed heart and soul. All the people join the covenant. Josiah embodies obedience to the charge given first to Joshua (Josh 1:7) and later by David to King Solomon (1 Kings 2:3).

Cultic Reforms 23:4-20

The next two paragraphs describe Josiah's cultic purification, first in Jerusalem and Judah (2 Kings 23:4-14), second in Bethel and Samaria

(23:15-20). The extensive reform brings cultic practices into conformity with Torah: centralization of the cult (Deut 12); rejection of idols (4:15-20) and abhorrent practices of the nations (4:15-20; 18:9-13).

23:4-14 Josiah Commands Reforms for Jerusalem and Judah

Josiah's cultic purification is narrated in detail, demonstrating both the depth of Jerusalem's illicit syncretistic practices and Josiah's commitment to remove the abominations. Josiah is in total control of the purge, the verbal subject throughout the account (Cohn 2000: 156). Three categories of cleansing actions are described: cleansing the temple, purifying cultic personnel, and eliminating cultic sites and practices throughout Judah and Samaria.

Josiah first *commands* the priests to cleanse the Lord's temple of cultic paraphernalia and personnel connected to the idolatrous cults of Baal, Asherah, and the host of heaven (23:4-7, reversing the sins of Manasseh, 21:3). The articles are *burned* (Jehu *burned* the Baal pillars, 10:26). Josiah *burns* the image of Asherah, the chariots of the sun, the Asherah at Bethel, and human bones, with the ashes carried to Bethel and to people's graves (23:4, 5, 6, 11, 15, 16, 20). Josiah *deposes* idolatrous priests appointed by the kings of Judah to sacrifice to Baal and the astral deities (23:5). He demolishes the houses of the *holy ones* where the women weavers honor Asherah (23:7 AT) *[Idolatry: Holy Ones/Cult Prostitutes, p. 451]*. It is unlikely that the *holy ones* were temple prostitutes; yet the cultic personnel promised fertility—an affront to the Lord's covenant promises (Deut 7:12-16; 23:18-19; 1 Kings 15:12; DeVries: 185; Wray Beal 2014: 204–5; Cogan 2001: 387).

Josiah *defiles* and *breaks down* the high places. "Defile" refers to cultic defilement two hundred times in Leviticus, Numbers, and Ezekiel (2 Kings 23:8, 10, 13). Though the term "defilement" (uncleanness) deals primarily with ritual purity in the Torah, the prophets apply it to ethical concerns (Lev 18:21; 19:31; Isa 6:5; 64:6; Jer 2:23; Yamauchi: 350). Israel has defiled the land through murderous bloodshed (Lam 4:13-15), idolatry (Ezek 22:3-4), and following the abominable practices of the nations that occupied the land before Israel (2 Kings 21:2, 11). Josiah's ritual defilement corresponds to the people's unethical behavior, associating the illicit cultic articles with unclean items, including dead bones (23:16). God allows the land to be polluted because of Israel's apostasy (Ps 79:1; Averbeck: 372). Josiah removes the personnel of the high places in Judah as far away as Geba (near Judah's northern border) and Beersheba (to the far south; 2 Kings 23:8-9). These priests were not allowed to stay at the Jerusalem temple, but remained among their kinfolk (Provan 1995: 275–76).

Josiah turns toward the demolition of cultic centers in the environs of Jerusalem and the temple precincts (23:10-14). Starting in the valley of Ben-Hinnom, southwest of Jerusalem, Josiah *defiles* the Topheth associated with child sacrifice (23:10; cf. 16:3). In the Jerusalem temple, Josiah *removes* horses dedicated by the kings of Judah to the sun and *burns* the *chariots of the sun* (23:11) *[Idolatry: Chariots of the Sun, p. 452]*. He *pulls down* the altars erected by Ahaz and Manasseh in the temple, breaks them in pieces, and throws them on the garbage heap (23:12). Moving eastward, Josiah *defiles* the high places set up by Solomon to honor the gods of the nations (23:13). Josiah destroys, defiles, burns, and disposes of these monuments and locations dedicated to cultic apostasy by the kings who preceded him (23:14).

23:15-20 Josiah Cleanses Bethel and Samaria

Josiah extends purification to Bethel and Samaria, fulfilling the prophecy of the man of God from Judah (23:15-18; cf. 1 Kings 13:2). Josiah *pulls down* the shrine (2 Kings 23:7, 8, 12) associated with *the sins of Jeroboam* (23:15). Josiah's demolition is thorough, all in fulfillment of the proclamation of the man of God at Jeroboam's inaugural festival (23:15-16; 1 Kings 13:1-3).

When Josiah learns of a monument for the man of God from Judah who predicted Josiah's actions, he orders that his bones *rest* (23:17-18; cf. Deut 5:14; Josh 12:44; 2 Sam 7:11; 1 Kings 13:29, 30-31). Reference to *the prophet who came out of Samaria* underscores his prophecy that *the word of the LORD against the altar in Bethel, and against all the high places that are in the cities of Samaria, shall surely come to pass* (1 Kings 13:11-32). In Samaria, Josiah removes the shrines of the high places that provoked the Lord. Throughout his violently iconoclastic reforms, Josiah has spared human life thus far. But in Samaria, Josiah slaughters *the priests of the high places* and desecrates those altars by burning human bones on them. Josiah's return to Jerusalem marks the end of his destruction of the idolatrous cult *[Prophets: Prophetic Word, p. 469]*.

Celebration of Passover, Reform, Judgment 23:21-27

23:21-23 Josiah Commands the Jerusalem Passover

In Jerusalem, Josiah *commands* the people to celebrate the Passover *as prescribed in this book of the covenant*, a Passover centralized in Jerusalem rather than local observances (23:21; Deut 16:5-7). Not since the time of the judges had Israel observed a Passover like the one celebrated in the first year of Josiah's reform (2 Kings 23:22-23). The claim that Josiah's Passover is uniquely faithful to the Torah does not exclude the historicity of Hezekiah's Passover (2 Chron 30:1-12). Both compositions use their material for theological purposes. Second Chronicles shows "how right may be done even when there is much that is wrong" (Konkel 2016: 394). Second Kings holds up Josiah as the model in observing Torah.

23:24-27 Josiah's Commitment to the Law of Moses

The narrative summarizes Josiah's thorough reform (23:24): Josiah removes the mediums and the wizards (Manasseh's practices, 21:6) in addition to eliminating teraphim, idols, and all the abominations (following Deut 18:9-12) [Idolatry: Teraphim, p. 452]. Josiah establishes [performs in 2 Kings 23:3] the words of the law written in the book that the priest Hilkiah has found (confirming that the newly discovered book is the Torah). The superlative evaluation of Josiah uses the language of Deuteronomy 6:5: he turned to the LORD with all his heart, with all his soul, and with all his might, according to all the law of Moses (2 Kings 23:25). No other king was as devoted to the Lord and the law.

The praise of Josiah's reform is superlatively positive. The long catalog of actions eliminating the personnel and practices of the ungodly kings, the timeline (from Solomon through Jeroboam and Ahaz and Manasseh), and the geographic completeness (from Beersheba, throughout Jerusalem, and into Bethel and Samaria) underscore its thoroughness. He himself acts with heart, soul, and might. Josiah hears, establishes, commands, reads, keeps the words of the book of the Torah and the covenant. He renews covenant and celebrates Passover. Josiah remodels the temple. Though the prophetess has warned that the reprieve from judgment is only temporary, the reader may become "buoyed by the rosy evaluation" (Cohn 2000: 162).

The adverbial particle Nevertheless (23:26 NIV; NRSV: Still) is jolting. Despite Josiah's turn to the LORD (23:25), the LORD did not turn from the fierceness of his great wrath . . . kindled against Judah, because of all the provocations with which Manasseh provoked the Lord (emph. added). Jeroboam, Ahab, the sins of Israel and Judah, and Manasseh are said to provoke the Lord (1 Kings 14:9, 15; 2 Kings 23:19, 26) [Theology of Exile, p. 479]. The cumulative effect of Israel's sin—from the time they entered the land, fueled by the specific actions of such kings as Solomon and Ahaz, then carried to a nadir by

Manasseh—*provokes with provocation* (AT) the wrath from which the Lord does not *turn*. The Lord's speech concludes the reflection on Israel's exile (17:35-39); here the Lord's judgment speech punctuates the announcement of Judah's doom: *I will remove Judah . . . as I have removed Israel; and I will reject this city that I have chosen* (23:27). *Remove* predicts the most severe judgment: exile. In 2 Kings 17 the Lord announces that he has *removed* Israel because Israel has not *removed* (*departed from*) the sins of Jeroboam (17:18, 22, 23). Though Josiah had *removed* all the shrines in Samaria and Judah, the Lord was bound to *remove* Judah (23:19, 27). *Reject* involves the broken covenant relationship. Because Israel *rejected* the Lord's covenant, the Lord *rejected* all Israel (17:15, 20; Israel first rejected the Lord by choosing a king, 1 Sam 8:7; 10:19). By rejecting Jerusalem and the *house* where the Lord had promised his name would remain, the Lord declares the covenant relationship broken (2 Kings 23:27; 1 Kings 9:3) [*House for the Name, p. 449*].

Despite Josiah's unrivaled reforms, the die is cast. The people have provoked the Lord to wrath. As the people have failed to *remove* the abominations of cultic perversion (until Josiah), the Lord will *remove* them from the land. As the people have rejected the Lord in choosing the ways of the kings, the Lord has finally rejected them, the chosen city, and the temple.

Closing Royal Formula for Josiah 23:28-30

The closing royal formula references the Book of the Annals of the Kings of Judah but is interrupted by Josiah's death notice (23:28-29). King Josiah goes to *meet* Pharaoh Neco II (king of Egypt, 610–595 BCE; ANET 350) on the Egyptian's way to join Assyria to battle Babylon. *Meet* is used of military confrontation as often as it is used for ordinary encounters between persons, and its use here is ambiguous. The narrative does not explain whether Josiah was paying a courtesy visit, responding to Pharaoh's summons, defending Megiddo from an enemy, or (more likely) blocking Pharaoh's advance as part of his revolt against Assyria (cf. 2 Chron 35:20). The text enigmatically states, *And he killed him in Megiddo when he saw him* (2 Kings 23:29 AT). The report of Josiah's reign concludes with the report that Josiah's servants brought his corpse back to Jerusalem for burial in his own tomb (23:30; cf. EN on 22:20 for Huldah's prophecy that Josiah would be buried in peace).

The *people of the land* take the initiative one last time, *anointing* Jehoahaz the son of Josiah as king in place of his father (23:30; Jehoiakim taxes the *people of the land* to pay tribute to Pharaoh Neco,

23:33, 35; see 11:14, 17-18; 21:24 for coronations by the people of the land; cf. Jehu's *anointing*, 9:6). The actions of the people of the land suggest instability, perhaps reflecting dissatisfaction with Josiah's reforms *[People of the Land, p. 464]*.

The last spark of renewal dies with Josiah. Josiah has freed the land of idolatry and anti-Torah influences. Despite Josiah's faithful policies, the sins of Manasseh have set a trajectory of judgment, provoking the wrath of the Lord.

THE TEXT IN BIBLICAL CONTEXT
Josiah and Joshua

Josiah's career mirrors Joshua's. "Joshua was the pioneer who fulfilled the aspirations of Josiah" (Nelson 1981b: 538). Josiah fulfills the initial injunction given Joshua: "Act in accordance with all the law . . . ; do not turn from it to the right hand or to the left" (Josh 1:7; 2 Kings 22:2). Emphasis on *the book of the law* (eleven times in 2 Kings 22–23) is found elsewhere only in the book of Joshua (five times; Nelson 1981b: 534–35; Matties: 397). Nelson suggests that Joshua's entry into the land was more of a triumphal procession than a bloody battle, an unopposed march through a land at Israel's feet (Josh 1:10-15; cf. 2:9), a precursor of Josiah's triumphant, peaceful recovery of ancestral territory vacated by Assyria's withdrawal (Nelson 1981b: 537). Like Joshua, who tears his clothes when Israel fails to take Ai because of its sin (7:6), Josiah tears his clothes at the people's failure to keep the words of this book (2 Kings 22:11-13). Joshua celebrated Passover upon entry into the land (Josh 5:10-12), and renewed a covenant eliminating worship of other gods (Josh 24); Josiah began his reform with covenant commitment (2 Kings 23:2-3), reversed the Canaanization program of earlier kings (23:4-20), and concluded with a Passover celebration (23:21-23). Josiah undoes Jeroboam's cultic center and reunites Israelite worship (Leithart: 268–69).

Joshua's paradigmatic obedience prefigures Josiah as the ideal Davidic king, who keeps the law and is faithful to covenant (see Introduction, "Composition: Authorship and Date"; Nelson 1981b: 533–34, 538–39; Matties: 397). McConville urges caution, pointing out that "the match is by no means perfect" (2006: 107–9). The focus of Joshua is on a people faithful to the covenant and the Torah (113). Matties argues that this strengthens, rather than weakens, the parallel between Joshua and Josiah because the point of their stories is that readers are to practice covenant faithfulness (not search for an ideal king; 398).

Jehoash and Josiah

Jehoash (= Joash) is the first king to direct temple repairs (2 Kings 12:4-16); Josiah is the second (and last) to do so (22:3-10). Both became king as youths (seven and eight years old, 11:21; 22:1) after the assassinations of their fathers (9:27; 21:23). Jehoash and Josiah *did what was right in the sight of the* LORD (12:2; 22:2). The people of the land support their coronation (11:17-18; 21:24). Both renew the temple repair after the midpoint of their reigns (12:6; 22:3), working with the *great priest* (12:10; 22:8 AT). The repairs are reported almost identically: *all the money that was brought into the house of the* LORD and entrusted to those *who guarded the threshold* (12:9; cf. 22:4), who *give the money . . . into the hands of the workers who had the oversight of the house of the* LORD (12:11; cf. 22:5). Neither king *asks an accounting from those into whose hand they delivered the money . . . for they dealt honestly* (12:15; cf. 22:7). Jehoash is *instructed* (the verb is of the same root in Hebrew as the word *Torah*) by the priest Jehoiada (12:2); Josiah receives the book of the Torah discovered by the priest Hilkiah (22:8).

Covenant renewal marks the coronation of Jehoash as he stands by the pillar, followed by destruction of the Baal cult (11:14, 17, 18). Covenant renewal marks the revival of Josiah as he stands by the pillar, followed by removal of the vessels made for Baal (23:3-4). Josiah excels not only Jehoash but also all his predecessors as a reformer. He defiles the pagan high places (contrast Jehoash, 12:3) and deposes their priests, institutes Passover, and turns to the Lord with all his heart like no other king (23:5, 8, 21-25). Both Jehoash and Josiah are bested by foreign enemies (12:17-18; 23:29), events that lead to violent death, though each is buried in his own tomb in Jerusalem and succeeded by his son (12:20-21; 23:29-30). Building on the legacy of Jehoash (Barré argues that this is a literary strategy to support Josiah's reforms [141]), Josiah excels as righteous king.

The closely paralleled stories present a problem for the interpreter. Though 1–2 Kings is often criticized for an overly simplistic reward/retribution schema [*Kings in the Hebrew Canon: Kings in the Deuteronomistic History, p. 453*], these two righteous kings suffer violent deaths. Piety is no guarantee of long life and prosperity. Deuteronomy calls on the reader to choose life by obeying the covenant (30:15-20), but Jehoash and Josiah die violently despite covenant faithfulness. The stories show that historical factors cannot be ignored. Jehoash and Josiah operate in worlds upset by the folly of their predecessors. Both are dominated by formidable military foes. Jehoash and Josiah, like Christian martyrs, testify that living out the vocation of righteousness may be costly [*Theology of Exile, p. 479*].

Do Not Trust Deceptive Words (Jer 7; 2 Kings 22:20)

The temple sermon of Josiah's contemporary Jeremiah warns, "Do not trust in these deceptive words: 'This is the temple of the LORD, the temple of the LORD, the temple of the LORD'" (7:4). The words are deceptive when they lead people to think that the temple is a talisman against judgment for those who disregard the Torah. Worshipers cannot transgress and then enter the temple with relieved assurance: "We are safe!" For those who depend on a slogan, even a true statement can become self-deception. They worship the address rather than the inhabitant!

Second Kings 22–23 corrects the deceptive belief that the Davidic covenant is unconditional. Deuteronomy teaches that life in the land is conditional upon covenant faithfulness (30:15-20). "Choose life!" Moses argues, but he warns of death for those who fail to keep covenant. In 2 Samuel 7 the Lord tells David that he will always have a son on the throne. Disobedience will be met by punishment, but not removal of the Lord's "steadfast love" (7:14-15). "The throne shall be established forever" (7:16). The *lamp* for *David* through his sons endures *forever* (2 Kings 8:19). Second Kings 22–23 counters the "We are safe" theology; the sins of Manasseh have brought the sins of Judah to fulfillment. Exile is inevitable. Provoking the Lord's anger negates covenant promises.

The surprise death of Josiah, killed in a military skirmish with Pharaoh Neco, runs counter to what appears to be Huldah's ironclad promise, *You shall be gathered to your grave in peace* (22:20). Josiah is faithful to the Lord like no other king. He seeks to atone for the sins of the kings of Judah that preceded him. Huldah's promise seems irrevocable. The reader is left to reconcile that promise with Josiah's violent death. Does Josiah go to the grave in peace? Is it possible that Josiah begins to believe he has a "We are safe" card that he can play at any moment? If Josiah meets Pharaoh Neco with the intent to use military force against him, does he undertake this action with confidence that the promise he will die peacefully protects him from negative consequences? Although Huldah's prophecy does hold and Josiah does not see *all the disaster that I will bring on this place* (22:20), Josiah apparently is killed by Neco because he takes a foolish risk—misreading the promise that he will die peacefully. In her analysis of Huldah's prophecy, Hamori points out that the Chronicler attributes Josiah's death to his refusal to listen to an updated prophecy of the Lord through Neco (2 Chron 35:22; Hamori: 842) [*Kings in the Hebrew Canon: Kings and Chronicles, p. 455*].

First and Second Kings teach that life in the land is conditioned on covenant faithfulness. Failure to keep covenant has consequences. Despite what seem to be unconditional promises from the Lord, humans forfeit them by doing wrong. Foolish risks may have disastrous consequences. Even in exile, however, the Deuteronomic promise offers hope. Moses anticipates not only exile but also return "because the LORD your God is a merciful God" (Deut 4:25-31; 30:1-5).

Josiah's Reform and Jeremiah

The absence of the prophet Jeremiah within the narrative of 1–2 Kings is puzzling. Jeremiah seems to be an ally of Josiah and at odds with Josiah's successors. Doorly suggests that Jeremiah authors 1–2 Kings and seeks to strengthen his case by remaining absent as a character (32; cf. Peterson: 294–95).

Josiah's focus is on cultic reform. He restores the temple, removes the idolatrous worship systems, and leads a Passover second to none. The argument of this commentary has been that the Lord's justice is primary, but justice is hidden in Josiah's report. Does Josiah focus only on cultic matters, or is the king committed to justice? Second Kings 23:3 suggests the broader agenda. Though Josiah spares no effort to reverse cultic sin, his commitment is to Torah covenant (23:3). Josiah promises to follow the Lord in keeping his commandments, his decrees, and his statutes. Thus Josiah not only demolishes the Manasseh cult but also defiles Topheth, where innocent blood has been shed.

Jeremiah preaches that Josiah's reform includes the Lord's justice. Jeremiah's lone reference to Josiah comes when the prophet confronts Josiah's son Shallum (Jehoiakim) for his unjust practices in building elaborate buildings without paying his workers fair wages (Jer 22:13-14). Jeremiah argues that Shallum's father (Josiah) did "do justice and righteousness" by providing justice for "the poor and needy" (22:15-16). Shallum, contrary to Josiah, seeks dishonest gain and sheds innocent blood (22:17).

Jeremiah testifies that Josiah's reform goes beyond worship practices to include justice for the marginalized. Since the author of Kings is silent about Jeremiah, the text simply alludes to Josiah's justice. Josiah's covenant commitment leads him to "do justice and righteousness. . . . He judged the cause of the poor and needy; then it was well. Is not this to know me? says the LORD" (Jer 22:15-16).

THE TEXT IN THE LIFE OF THE CHURCH

Cultic Iconoclasm

Josiah is zealous for Torah faithfulness. When he finds the lost Torah, he renews a covenant to keep the entire law, destroying all forms prohibited by Deuteronomy. The post-Josiah cultic stage must be nearly empty but for the temple furniture. In wholehearted faithfulness, Josiah rejects the idolatrous structures of his predecessors.

The Radical Reformers of Zurich emerged in conversation with Ulrich Zwingli, initially a mentor and eventually a mortal foe. The Zwinglian Reformation was radically iconoclastic, emptying the churches of art and precious metals. In full-hearted commitment to biblical faithfulness, Zwingli threw out the art of the Catholic Church. When the Radicals extended simple biblicism to the Lord's Supper and baptism, Zwingli branded them heretics. The Radicals had excluded civil authority from ecclesial deliberations.

Radical commitment to faithfulness divides. Paul and Barnabas split over a personnel issue (Acts 15:39-40). Regarding worship, Paul acknowledges that "there have to be factions among you . . . so it will become clear who among you are genuine" (1 Cor 11:19). Deciding whether to honor the American flag before sporting events divides Brethren and Mennonite college campuses. Faithfulness leads some to radical hospitality that includes committed LGBTQ couples, who may be excluded by those committed to traditional mores. Christian politicians use Romans 13 to defend deporting asylum seekers as lawbreakers while other Christians offer the same people sanctuary, seeking to obey God rather than human authorities (Acts 4:19). James appeals for "mercy [that] triumphs over judgment" (James 2:13).

Women in Ministry

Discussions about women in pastoral leadership, long settled in many church communities but debated in others, often focus on Paul's instructions to first-century congregations. How would the conversation change if our only biblical source were 1–2 Kings? What might the books of Kings indicate about women in leadership in the reign of God?

Despite the patriarchal context and the gender-exclusive title of the books of "Kings," women figure prominently [Women in Kings, p. 485]. The notorious Omride queens Jezebel and Athaliah and the Solomonic harem leading to idolatry are not the only women mentioned in Kings. Positive, prominent speaking roles are given to the queen of Sheba (1 Kings 10:6-9) and the prophetess Huldah (2 Kings 22:15-20), supporting roles to the widow of Zarephath (1 Kings 17:8-24) and the woman of Shunem (2 Kings 4:8-37; 8:1-6), and brief yet positive parts to Naaman's slave girl (5:2-4) and Joash's aunt Jehosheba (11:2-3). The messages of the queen of Sheba and of Huldah are rhetorically significant. The queen reminds Solomon of his vocation to carry out justice and righteousness. Huldah confirms judgment but affirms Josiah's reforms.

A theology of leadership in Kings must acknowledge that both women and men are susceptible to misusing power. Kings also demonstrates that God uses women to proclaim the most important messages in the book. God speaks through women in patriarchal Israel and gifts women for pastoral leadership in contemporary communities.

People of the Book

Jesus roots righteousness and justice in Old Testament Scripture, Torah and the prophets (Matt 5:17-20). The emphasis on Torah, God's teaching, dominates the book of Deuteronomy and "is picked up prominently only in Joshua and Kings" (Matties: 462). Joshua becomes the "prototype" for Josiah (463). Torah is God's instruction, modified, supplemented, and applied to each context (compare God's instruction regarding non-Israelites in Deut 7:1-5; 10:17-19; Josh 2:12-14; Acts 11:1-18; 15:19-20). Josiah consults the prophets for revelation from Torah (2 Kings 22:14-20), but after the exile "scripture has become the vehicle of new revelations, and exegesis is the means of new access to the divine will" (Fishbane: 442; see Neh 8:13-18).

The Reformers based their faith on biblical authority, stressing *sola scriptura*, the Bible alone. In contrast to the Roman Catholic Church, the Reformers placed responsibility for reading the text with the people rather than just with the church hierarchy, though tradition also played a role in biblical interpretation, as shown by their adoption of various creeds. Scripture was primary but was not alone. The Zurich Radicals split from Zwingli, insisting on following Scripture when it disagreed with state officials.

Anabaptist hermeneutics was centered in following the life of Jesus as inspired by the Spirit. Hans Denck famously wrote, "No one may truly know Christ except one who follows him in life." Influenced by Luther, Menno Simons came to understand the Scriptures as his authority, the Word of God, and the cornerstone of his work. His writings are filled with Bible quotations. Menno's approach to interpretation is Christ-centered. Every book he authored bears his motto: "For no one can lay any foundation other than the one that has been laid; that foundation is Jesus Christ" (1 Cor 3:11).

Legend describes early American Mennonites as people of the book, having a bulging pocket where they carried a copy of the New Testament. When interrupted by pressing church questions while doing farm labor, they are said to have taken out the Bible and pursued "what the Bible says." Editors of contemporary confessions of faith found that when stumped for wording acceptable to all, using scriptural language was often a solution. Hilkiah's discovery of the Torah in the temple is an invitation to recover the Bible in church life.

2 Kings 23:31–25:30

The Reign of Josiah's Descendants

PREVIEW

The "Saigon evacuation" photo published in the *New York Times* on April 30, 1975, portrays the collapse of the American-supported regime of South Vietnam. The *Times* photo captures the moment when the last few lucky ones escaped unconditional surrender. The symbols of power—flags, soldiers, and monuments—had been destroyed.

Symbols of political power demonstrate the legitimacy of royal authority. The report of Solomon's reign identifies propaganda tools that served the Davidic dynasty, including the temple, the palace complex, the walls around Jerusalem, horses and chariots, labor and taxation bureaucracy, treasures of gold and silver, and a judiciary (1 Kings 1–11). Second Kings 24–25 narrates the demolition of royal infrastructure. The military was uselessly weak against Babylon. The tax system served the foreign empire but not Judean royal power. Jerusalem's walls were breached, effectively undermining confidence in the king. Destruction of palace and temple marked the dissolution of independent Judah and the Lord's abandonment of the Davidic dynasty.

Josiah's death signals the end of Judean independence. Four of Josiah's heirs, three sons and one grandson, occupy the throne in Jerusalem but are unable to exercise independent foreign policy. These forgettable puppets of imperial power reign for about twenty

418   2 Kings 23:31–25:30

years. Each is characterized as doing evil as (most of) his *ancestors* had done (e.g., 23:32). Dominated first by Egypt and later by Babylon, they survive only by paying heavy tribute to the imperial power. Twice Babylon carries the ruling elite and their treasures to exile. The highly compressed narrative of the final kings of Judah is much like the description of Israel's final years (Mullen 1993: 281). The regime collapses, Judah is exiled, and the history of the kings of Judah ends.

OUTLINE

Reign of Jehoahaz, 23:31-34
Reign of Jehoiakim, 23:35–24:7
Reign of Jehoiachin, 24:8-17
Reign of Zedekiah, 24:18–25:7
Destruction of Jerusalem and the Temple, 25:8-21
Appointment of Gedaliah and Flight to Egypt, 25:22-26
Release of Jehoiachin, 25:27-30

EXPLANATORY NOTES

Reign of Jehoahaz 23:31-34

The people of the land *anoint* Jehoahaz to succeed Josiah, perhaps choosing the younger half-brother to continue Josiah's anti-Egyptian policies (23:30; his mother's hometown in Libnah in southwest Judah suggests ascendancy of a faction concerned about an Egyptian threat; Sweeney 2007a: 451). The opening royal formula names the king, his age, his brief three-month tenure, and the name and origins of his mother (23:31). Jehoahaz is evaluated negatively, doing evil as his fathers had done (23:32). Pharaoh Neco, who killed Josiah, confines Jehoahaz at Riblah, imposes heavy tribute on the land, and enthrones Eliakim, a second son of Josiah, in place of his half-brother, treating Judah as a vassal state (23:33-34). Neco demonstrates his sovereignty by changing Eliakim's name to Jehoiakim (customarily, God would confer a new throne name at accession; Gray: 751). Jehoahaz is imprisoned in Egypt, where he dies. The lack of a closing royal formula underlines the chaotic state of Judah's affairs.

Reign of Jehoiakim 23:35–24:7

Powerless to do otherwise, Jehoiakim taxes *the people of the land* to pay tribute to Pharaoh (23:35). Each pays according to his *assessment* (*'erek*, the standard term for taxation, 2 Kings 12:5; Lev 5:15), and Jehoiakim pays Pharaoh. The tribute-payment report precedes the opening royal formula, which includes the name and ancestry of

Jehoiakim's mother (different from the mother of his half-brother Jehoahaz; 2 Kings 23:36-37). The text evaluates Jehoiakim as it did Jehoahaz: doing evil. Babylon under Nebuchadnezzar replaces Egypt as the dominant power. Nebuchadnezzar invades Judah, and Jehoiakim capitulates. After three years as vassal, Jehoiakim rebels, likely by withholding tribute and perhaps consistent with his alliance with a pro-Egyptian, anti-Babylonian faction in Judah, as suggested by his mother's hometown in Galilee, a region more likely threatened by Babylon than Egypt (24:1; Sweeney 2007a: 452). An editorial explanation interrupts the report (24:2-4). The sovereign Lord intervenes to judge Manasseh. Unlike the longer explanation of Israel's exile (2 Kings 17), the report of Judah's demise is repeatedly interrupted to explain that Manasseh's sins have motivated the judgment (21:10-16; 23:26-27; 24:2-4; 24:20). The repetition creates an echo effect. The Lord (not Nebuchadnezzar) *sends* Chaldean, Aramean, Moabite, and Ammonite marauders. The Lord *sends* (the verb typically describing the action of kings is repeated) *[Send, p. 476]* to *destroy* Judah, according to the word of the Lord spoken *by his servants the prophets* (24:2; see Deut 28:47-51, 63; 2 Kings 17:13; 21:10-12) *[Prophets: Prophetic Word, p. 469]*. The judgment falls because of the sins of Manasseh, who has filled Jerusalem with innocent blood—emphasizing social injustice (21:16) *[Mišpaṭ, p. 461]*. The uncharacteristic phrase *innocent blood* (24:4) alludes to exploitative internal violent policies against the poor and disadvantaged (Mic 3:9-11; Jer 7:5-6; 22:17-18 links this sin to Jehoiakim; Brueggemann 2000: 571). The explanation concludes that the Lord is unwilling to *forgive* (NIV; see also rejection of Solomon's request in the dedicatory temple prayer, Deut 29:20; 1 Kings 8:30, 34, 36, 39, 50).

The standard closing royal formula notes that Jehoiakim's *son* Jehoiachin succeeds him, a unique occurrence among Josiah's royal descendants (24:5-6). Another parenthetical explanation notes the transfer of imperial power from Egypt to Babylon (24:1, 7). The Lord executes judgment on Judah through imperial power plays.

Reign of Jehoiachin 24:8-17

The narrative resumes the report of Judah's last kings shuffling indistinguishably into exile. The standard opening royal formula includes Jehoiachin's mother's name and background and the negative evaluation also given his father and his uncles (24:8-9; see 23:32, 37). Like Jehoahaz, the other descendant of Josiah who succeeded his father without foreign intervention, Jehoiachin is exiled after a three-month rule.

Though this Judean deportation is narrated as an event directed by Nebuchadnezzar (24:10-17), the report radiates around a declaration at the center: *all this as the LORD had foretold* (24:13; the chapter also concludes, as it began, with a reminder that the Lord expels the people from Jerusalem and Judah in anger, 24:3-4, 20). King Nebuchadnezzar dominates the action. After his servants *came up to lay siege* to Jerusalem, Nebuchadnezzar *came, took prisoner, carried off, cut up, carried away* Jerusalem, *carried away* Jehoiachin, *brought captive, made Mattaniah (Jehoiachin's uncle) king*, and *changed his name* (24:10-17 AT). In his only reported royal act, King Jehoiachin, the queen mother (Jer 29:2), and the palace officials surrender (2 Kings 24:12). The event is dated in Babylonian time, *the eighth year of the reign* of the Babylonian king (597 BCE).

Nebuchadnezzar carries off all the treasures of the temple and the palace, fulfilling the word spoken by Isaiah to Hezekiah (20:13, 15-18) *[Prophets: Prophetic Word, p. 469]*. The spoils include golden vessels of Solomon. The temple has been emptied of its golden treasures repeatedly (taken by Pharaoh Shishak; Asa sent them to Aram; Jehoash sent them to Aram; seized by Jehoash of Israel; Ahaz sent them to Assyria; Hezekiah sent them to Assyria, 1 Kings 14:25-26; 15:18; 2 Kings 12:18; 14:13-14; 16:8, 17-18; 18:15; 25:13-17). *Solomon* is a rhetorical reminder of Judah's shameful history in contrast to Solomon's imperial splendor. Nebuchadnezzar exiles ten thousand officials, military men, artisans, and smiths, until only the poor people of the land remain (24:14). He carries away the king, queen mother, and officials, including the king's wives (24:15). The Babylonian king also takes captive seven thousand military and one thousand artisans and smiths fit for battle (24:16). Nebuchadnezzar replaces Jehoiachin with his uncle Mattaniah, a third son of Josiah. Demonstrative of his authority, Nebuchadnezzar changes Mattaniah's name to Zedekiah ("righteousness of Yahweh"; see Jer 23:5-6 for ironic commentary).

This first exile report marks the end of independent Judah and Jerusalem. Persons and possessions of highest value are removed. Only the poor and a puppet king remain in Jerusalem. Babylon has wiped Jerusalem clean. Jehoiachin goes into exile; the omission of a closing royal report gives silent testimony to chaos greater than death that pervades the land.

Reign of Zedekiah 24:18–25:7

The standard opening royal formula (Hamutal is mother of Zedekiah and his full brother Jehoahaz, 23:31) suggests return to normal with a new king in place (24:18-19). The royal data follows form, though the evaluation compares evil Zedekiah only with Jehoiakim, who also ruled eleven years before rebelling against the Babylonians. The parenthetical editorial comment, *Jerusalem and Judah so angered the* LORD *that he expelled them from his presence* (24:20), echoes the Deuteronomic curses and reference to the *anger* provoked by the sins of Manasseh (Deut 11:17; 13:17; 29:20, 23, 24, 27, 28; 31:17; 2 Kings 23:26) *[Provoke the Lord to Anger, p. 470]*. In the ninth year of his reign, Zedekiah rebels against Nebuchadnezzar (24:20–25:1). Zedekiah withstands Nebuchadnezzar's siege for eighteen months until food runs out for the people of the land and the wall is breached (25:2-4). Zedekiah tries to escape but is captured, presented to Nebuchadnezzar, and is sentenced to witness the slaughter of his children, to have his eyes put out, and to be carried in fetters to Babylon (25:4-7).

Destruction of Jerusalem and the Temple 25:8-21

Jerusalem's destruction is reported in three movements (and in imperial time—the nineteenth year of Nebuchadnezzar, or 586 BCE). First, Nebuzaradan, the captain of the Babylonian bodyguard (the title means "butcher" or "hatchet man," Wray Beal 2014: 527), enters Jerusalem four weeks after Zedekiah's capture; he *burns* the city, including the temple, the palace, and all the great houses. He *breaks down* the wall of the city and *exiles* those who remain in the land, except a few poor people left for agricultural labor (25:8-12). Second, the Chaldeans remove the remaining gold, silver, and bronze from the house of the Lord before it is burned (25:13-17). The razing of the temple mirrors the building process (1 Kings 7:15-45), including the massive bronze pillars that are cut up for transport, an amount of bronze too great to be weighed. The loss of the pillars, significant for the covenant renewal ceremonies of Joash and Josiah (11:14; 23:3), signals that the covenant is in ruins. The imperial power of Solomon has been reversed, usurped by Nebuchadnezzar of Babylon (Brueggemann 2000: 596–98). Third, the report identifies priests, officials, and sixty people of the land who are arrested, taken to the king of Babylon at Riblah, and executed (25:18-21). The loss of the power symbols of Jerusalem and Judah extinguishes the light of David in Jerusalem (1 Kings 15:4), though the Davidic line still flickers in exile (2 Kings 25:27-30). The massive brutality is recounted without theological comment. The text laconically summarizes the event with the words *So Judah went into exile out of its land* (just four words in Hebrew; 25:21; the same phrase used of Israel, 17:23; cf. Deut 28:63-64) *[Covenant in Kings, p. 443]*.

Appointment of Gedaliah and Flight to Egypt 25:22-26

Nebuchadnezzar appoints Gedaliah of the family of the royal scribe Shaphan to oversee the people who remain (25:22; 22:3; Jer 36:10-12). Militia leaders who have evaded capture when the military was exiled meet Gedaliah at Mizpah, about seven miles north of Jerusalem (a gathering place during the time of the judges, Judg 10:17; 11:11; 20:1; 21:5; 1 Sam 7:5; rebuilt by Asa as a fortress, 1 Kings 15:22). Gedaliah seeks to reassure the assembly that they have nothing more to fear from the Babylonians and that they can submit to Babylon and do well (2 Kings 25:24). Jeremiah 40–41 narrates the intrigue resulting in the assassination of Gedaliah by Ishmael (2 Kings 25:25). All the people flee to Egypt to escape Babylonian retribution (25:26). The military commanders take the remnant, including Jeremiah and Baruch, to Egypt (Jer 43:5-7). Judah returns to the imperial power where the exodus liberation began (Jer 42–44) [Egypt, p. 445].

Release of Jehoiachin 25:27-30

In an intriguing epilogue, after thirty-seven years in prison, King Jehoiachin of Judah is elevated to the table of Evil-merodach, in his first year as king of Babylon (25:27). The king speaks well to Jehoiachin, elevates him above the other kings at the table where he dines regularly, and gives him a regular allowance (25:28-30; ANET 308) [Archaeology: Jehoiachin's Ration Tablets, p. 439]. The conclusion to 1–2 Kings is ambiguous. The land is emptied of the people; the king is powerless, sitting in exile in Babylon under house arrest and subject to the authority of the Babylonians, yet the Davidic royal house retains a living representative in the palace of the imperial sovereign. One may read the ending as the annulment of the Davidic covenant, or one may discern hope for Davidic restoration. McConville suggests a muted hope, with no specific expectation of return from exile (1993: 138). Janzen suggests that ambiguity suits the composition (58). The story has ended and yet continues.

Based on the Deuteronomic vision that God would continue to care for Israel, our reading of 1–2 Kings finds assurance in God's promise to deliver from exile (Deut 4, 29–30; cf. Jeremiah 31:31-34; 1 Kings 8). The creation-inspired human vocation to practice justice and righteousness supersedes Israelite national identity, the land promises, kingship, prophets, temple and cultic officers, and even Torah. Despite exile, God calls humans to live in the image of God.

THE TEXT IN BIBLICAL CONTEXT
Jeremiah and Kings

From the thirteenth year of Josiah into the exile, Jeremiah prophesies against Josiah's descendants (Jer 1:1-3; chs. 21–22, 24–29, 32–38). In agreement with 1–2 Kings, Jeremiah proclaims that idolatry, rejection of Torah, and violation of justice are intertwined [Mišpaṭ, p. 461]. The prophet exhorts "the king of Judah" to "act with justice and righteousness"; to protect "the alien, the orphan, and the widow"; and to not "shed innocent blood" (Jer 22:1-3). Jeremiah addresses Josiah's successors, who have failed to follow Josiah's commitment to justice and the cause of the oppressed (22:11-30). The prophet announces judgment against Jehoahaz (Shallum), declaring that he will never return from exile (22:11-12). Condemning Jehoiakim's self-indulgence and injustice, Jeremiah threatens him with an ignoble death (22:13-19; cf. 2 Kings 24:4). Jehoiakim's priests and temple prophets condemn Jeremiah, but he is protected by Judean officials and elders, including Ahikam, son of Shaphan (Jer 26; 2 Kings 22:12, 14). As the officials reread Jeremiah's dictation, Jehoiakim "cuts" the scroll in pieces and burns it in the brazier (Jer 36:23-24; cut is the word for Josiah's tearing his clothes in repentance, 2 Kings 22:11); Jeremiah records additional judgment upon Jehoiakim (Jer 36:32). He declares that Jehoiachin (Coniah) and the queen mother will be exiled to Babylon, never to return (22:24-30; 2 Kings 24:15-16; 25:27-30).

Jeremiah 27–28, 32–34, and 37–38 report his exchanges with his primary opponent, Zedekiah. When the king and the people renege on their promise to release slaves (Deut 15; Jer 34:8-11), Jeremiah passes judgment (34:12-22). Zedekiah refuses to heed Jeremiah but requests prayer (37:1-3). Despite Jeremiah's unremitting message of judgment, Zedekiah inquires of Jeremiah and intervenes to improve the prophet's prison conditions. Jeremiah's report of the fall of Jerusalem recalls 2 Kings 25 (Jer 39:1-10). Jeremiah 40–44 adds detail about the people not taken into Babylonian exile. Jeremiah 52 repeats 2 Kings 24–25 nearly verbatim.

Jeremiah's justice message resonates with our reading of 1–2 Kings, raising the question why the prophet Jeremiah is absent from 1–2 Kings. Doorly argues that Jeremiah's absence as a character in Kings is a literary strategy and that Jeremiah or his scribe, Baruch, authors both Jeremiah and Kings (26). Both texts reinforce the biblical message that the universal human vocation is doing justice and righteousness, whether led by prophets, priests, or kings. Godly administration of justice rules out unjust royal administration (McConville 1993: 138).

THE TEXT IN THE LIFE OF THE CHURCH
Speaking Prophetically to Powerful Politicians

With a courageous witness of integrity, Jeremiah confronts the kings of Judah. Jeremiah's faithful proclamation demonstrates exclusive loyalty to the Lord in the face of threats, torture, and imprisonment. Without compromising, Jeremiah establishes rapport with the king against whom he delivers judgment. The king requests that Jeremiah pray for him, seeks his counsel, and intervenes to ameliorate Jeremiah's difficult prison conditions (Jer 37–38). Both aspects of Jeremiah's approach are worthy of appropriation by contemporary prophets. First, commitment to the justice of the Lord in the face of political pressure is essential for a clear message. Second, Jeremiah's respect for the person of the political opponent is exemplary.

Jeremiah's courage is matched by his deep grief. In grief, he addresses people numbed to the pain of loss and denying the immanence of judgment. Jeremiah grieves for the end of his people because, like God, he cares for these people. He also grieves that no one listens to his efforts to overcome the people's deception by the powerful status quo. Jeremiah penetrates the numbness of royal consciousness with his articulation of grief. Following Jeremiah's pathos and Isaiah's hopefulness, Jesus leads Christians into prophetic consciousness. Experience of pain is an essential element for repentance. Resurrection hope is equally essential for community faithfulness (Brueggemann 2001a: 46–48).

Divine Judgment or YHWH War?

The DtrH theology ascribes the destruction of Israel (2 Kings 17) and Judah (2 Kings 24–25) to divine judgment [Kings in the Hebrew Canon: Kings in the Deuteronomistic History, p. 453]. Pilgram Marpeck, like other early Anabaptists, looked with hope for God's judgment on the enemies of the Radical Reformation. Anticipating Jonathan Edwards's "Sinners in the Hands of an Angry God," Marpeck wrote, "Although mercy triumphs over judgment, it does not do so over all men and their sins. It is dangerous to fall into the hands of men, but it is much more dangerous to fall into the hands of God" (336).

Latvus rejects retributionist theology as an explanation for modern political events, asserting that wars and their outcomes must be explained in terms of superpower geopolitics rather than divine intervention (93). Although DtrH explains exile because of divine intervention, Babylonian imperial ambition resulted in the destruction of Jerusalem. Western imperialism, not idolatry by Native peoples, is responsible for the genocide of Indigenous people of North America. Recognizing that various biblical texts interpret God's intervention differently illumines contemporary theological reflection. Unjust human systems exacerbate disasters. Humans are "judged" for unenforced building codes when earthquakes, typhoons, and hurricanes devastate urban housing, a judgment that falls disproportionately on the poor. Inadequately treated mental illness is epidemic after reduced government subsidy for treatment programs. Add widespread access to automatic firearms, and "judgment" results in massive loss of human life. "Sooner or later transgressions find a target, and somebody pays for it—unfortunately too often somebody from the least guilty part of society, thanks to structural injustice" (Latvus: 93). Reinterpreting these disasters as consequences of evil in a fallen and broken world—but not as direct judgment for the sinful actions of the victims themselves—affords an opportunity to provide pastoral care that gives witness to God's compassion. Brethren Disaster Ministries and Mennonite Disaster Service offer humble comfort rather than judgmental condemnation.

Acknowledgments

I am indebted to a supportive community in preparation of this commentary. The commentary editorial council, chaired by Doug Miller, entrusted me with this opportunity; Gordon Matties was particularly generous with timely editorial suggestions. Editor David Baker coaxed and coached my best efforts, and proved to be a faithful companion throughout the process. Early readers, John Toews, Roger Fast, Tom Voth, and Dora Dueck, gave support, encouragement, and valuable insight. Fresno Pacific Biblical Seminary granted a sabbatical leave in Fall 2017 which proved invaluable to the progress of this work. Peer reader and colleague Terry Brensinger made helpful suggestions. Herald Press editors, particularly David Garber, made significant changes to improve the readability, consistency, and accuracy of the work. Colleagues took time to encourage, inquire, and offer support, and I am grateful for each, especially Steve Varvis, Tim Geddert, Mark Baker, Wade French, Kaela Wade, and Mariah Cushing. The Fresno Pacific librarians, Kevin Enns-Rempel, Hope Nisly, and David Hasegawa, worked quickly and efficiently to access resources. Students in several courses that engaged 1-2 Kings helped me recognize the contemporary relevance of the biblical material. To these and many others who gave encouragement I am indebted and grateful.

Outline of 1–2 Kings

PART 1: SOLOMON AS KING
1 Kings 1:1–11:43

Solomon's Business with Hiram, King of Tyre   **5:1-18**
Solomon's Proposal to Hiram   5:1-6
Hiram's Response   5:7-12
Solomon's Conscripted Labor   5:13-18

Solomon's Construction Projects   **6:1–7:51**
Exterior Temple Structure   6:1-10
Message of the Lord to Solomon   6:11-13
Interior Temple Construction   6:14-38
Palace Complex Construction   7:1-12
Temple Furnishings   7:13-51

Temple Dedication   **8:1-66**
A Narrative Introduction   8:1-13
    B Solomon's Blessing of the Assembly   8:14-21
        C Solomon's Dedicatory Prayer   8:22-53
    B^1 Solomon's Blessing of the Assembly   8:54-61
A^1 Narrative Conclusion   8:62-66

Temple Postscript   **9:1-25**
The Lord's Appearance to Solomon   9:1-9
Narrative Report regarding Temple Building   9:10-25
    Business with Hiram   9:10-14
    Account of Forced Labor   9:15-23
    Conclusion   9:24-25

Solomon's Commercial Enterprise   **9:26–10:29**
Maritime Trade   9:26-28
Visit of the Queen of Sheba   10:1-13
Solomon's Accumulation of Wealth   10:14-29
    Trade and Treasure   10:14-22
    Tribute Exchanged for Wisdom   10:23-25
    Import-Export of Horses and Chariots   10:26-29

Solomon's Reign Assessed   **11:1-43**
Judgment of King Solomon   11:1-13
    Foreign Wives Turn Solomon's Heart to Other Gods   11:1-8
    The Lord's Judgment of Solomon   11:9-13
Solomon's Opponents   11:14-40
    Hadad of Edom and Rezon of Aram   11:14-25
    Ahijah Appoints Jeroboam, Son of Nebat   11:26-40
Concluding Royal Formula for the Reign of Solomon   11:41-43

PART 2: THE DIVIDED KINGDOM
1 KINGS 12–2 KINGS 17

PART 3: THE SOUTHERN KINGDOM TO JUDAH'S EXILE
2 KINGS 18–25

Essays

ALL HIS HEART *Heart* (*mind* translates Heb. *lebab*), used forty-four times in 1–2 Kings, refers to one's conscious, rational, and volitional process, not emotion. David is the standard of the true *heart*, characterized by truth, righteousness, uprightness, obedience to the Lord's commandments, and wholeness (1 Kings 3:6; 9:4; 14:8; 15:3, 14). Of the seventy-four verses mentioning David in 1 Kings, sixteen link him with a right heart or with walking according to Torah (2:2-4; 3:3, 6, 14; 6:12; 8:25; 9:4; 11:4-6, 33-34, 38; 14:8; 15:3, 5, 11; note the exceptional *matter of Uriah the Hittite*, 15:5; cf. 2 Kings 14:3; 16:2; 18:3; 22:2). Ahijah's judgment of Jeroboam establishes that to follow with *all his heart*, one keeps God's commandments, doing what is right in God's eyes and rejecting evil and idolatry (1 Kings 14:8-9) [*Evil, p. 446; Idolatry, p. 449*].

Alison Joseph posits that the narrator recasts David as the paradigm for the kings, that the David in 1–2 Kings is a literary construction created via his portrayal in his speech to Solomon (1 Kings 2:3-4) and in Solomon's reference in the inaugural dream (3:6-7). Kings Asa, Hezekiah, and Josiah are like David when they direct their whole heart to the Lord; Jeroboam, Ahab, and Manasseh are anti-types (226–32).

The Solomon story repeatedly raises the issue of a true heart, particularly in the temple dedication, where Solomon refers to David's *heart* for building the temple (8:17) and asks God, who knows the *heart* (8:38, 39), to hear when people pray with all their *heart* (8:48) and incline their *hearts* to God (8:58, 61). The Lord responds that his name, eyes, and *heart* will be in the temple and conditions additional blessing on Solomon's *integrity of heart* (9:3-4). Solomon's *heart* turns away to idolatry (11:2, 4, 9).

In 1–2 Kings, three kings are said to have a *heart* that is devoted to the Lord. The narrator says that Asa *did what was right in the sight of the LORD* and that *the heart of Asa was true to the LORD* (1 Kings 15:11, 14). Asa brought devoted (MT: *holy*) items of gold and silver into the temple (15:15). In prayer Hezekiah claims that he has *walked in the truth with wholehearted*

435

devotion; the Lord heals Hezekiah and extends his life (2 Kings 20:3, 6 AT). The prophetess Huldah declares that the Lord hears Josiah because *his heart is penitent and he has humbled* himself (22:19 AT). There was no king before or after Josiah *who turned to the* LORD *with all his heart,* . . . *according to all the law of Moses* (23:25).

Kings who walk before the Lord with all their heart reject idols and keep the Torah. David is the standard of the true heart. Josiah excels all other kings in turning to the Lord with all his heart.

ARCHAEOLOGY The quotation cited by Matties in his essay "Archaeology and Joshua" is just as apt for archaeology and Kings: "The biblical text preserves remarkable memories . . . [and] raises major questions on topics where archaeologists disagree with archaeologists, biblical scholars with biblical scholars, historians with historians." These different perspectives are "inevitably subject to revision in the near future" (Matties: 389, quoting S. A. Meier, "History of Israel 1: Settlement Period" in *Dictionary of the Old Testament: Historical Books*, 433). This commentary emphasizes literary and theological dimensions, not the resolution of historical issues, based on the understanding that Kings and DtrH elicit a theological challenge to the reader rather than modern historiographical judgment (Matties: 389–90). A brief introduction to some artifacts involving the characters of the biblical story connects us with archaeological data from the first millennium BCE in the ANE.

Judgments regarding biblical historicity are based on several factors, including archaeological finds. Archaeologists do not agree on how archaeological discoveries inform the story of Israel. Archaeological analysis ranges across a spectrum from "minimalists" to "maximalists." Minimalists minimize the value of Scripture in determining facticity of events and find minimal archaeological evidence to support the biblical record. Maximalists maximize Scripture in recovering historicity and tend to identify artifacts that support biblical historical reliability. The spectrum includes scholars who reject the extremes, holding to the basic historicity of the story line without necessarily accepting details in the biblical record. This text is written with sympathy for the judgment that "information regarding the historical integration of Judahite and even Israelite history is . . . generally reliable" and "recollection of foreign kings . . . is also accurate" (Halpern and Lemaire: 136).

One example illustrates judgments regarding historicity. In the summer of 1993, Avraham Biran found a ninth-century BCE inscription referring to "the house of David" and the "king of Israel" at the ancient site of Dan; the item is called the Tel Dan Inscription/Stele. Maximalists saw evidence that David's kingdom was well known throughout Palestine, proving the historicity of the biblical text. Minimalists raised questions about that interpretation. On the basis of their differing interpretation and their presuppositions, they rejected the find as evidence of the biblical David. Archaeological finds in themselves are insufficient to prove the historicity of the events described.

Solomon's Gates and Stables Excavations at Hazor, Megiddo, and Gezer reveal six-chambered gates and extensive horse stalls dated to the time of Solomon by Yigael Yidal when he unearthed them in the 1950s. Their similarity in structure, masonry, and function makes it likely that they were constructed in a single project, and their substantial size necessitates that their builder had significant resources. While excavations of the three cities indicate unbroken habitation throughout the time of Kings, archaeologists are divided regarding the dating of the gates and stables. All three locations were used as fortifications by Ahab. Recent scholarship attributes stables to the time of Jeroboam II. While the dating of construction is unresolved, the three cities were important frontier fortresses in battle and in protecting the trade routes on the Way of the Sea (along the coast) and on the King's Highway (along the edge of the desert) from the Euphrates to the Nile (Gray: 245).

Ahab the Builder The closing royal formula of Ahab, referencing the Annals of the Kings of Israel, attributes to Ahab an ivory house and additional cities ("well attested by archaeology," Gray: 456). "The archaeological picture revealed in the cities of the Israelite kingdom . . . firmly supports Ahab's title of 'builder of cities'" (E. Stern: 21). Archaeological work in Samaria attests to the luxurious, highly decorated palace with ivory paneling, carved figures, furniture, and storerooms (Shanks 1985: 45–46; Avigad; Beach; Grabbe: 66–68). Located in the hills, Samaria was not suitable for garrisoning Ahab's extensive chariotry. The new center established by Ahab at Jezreel provided a central location on important highways, on a dominating summit, near the water, barley, and straw needed for warhorses. Ahab built Jezreel concurrently with Samaria, but its enclosure and buildings, though including a palace, emphasized strong fortifications (Ussishkin: 306–7). Impressive building projects attributed to Ahab include the great fortifications of Hazor (with a large storage building and a water system), the monumental gate and central high place at Tel Dan, four-chambered gates at Beth-Shean and Gezer, and construction at Dor (E. Stern: 21–22) and Tirzah (Mazar: 414–15).

Kurkh Monolith of Shalmaneser III The Kurkh Monolith, an archaeological artifact discovered in modern Turkey in 1861, mentions Israel (the second of only four ancient extrabiblical inscriptions to do so; the Merneptah Stele of Egypt, dated 1209 BCE and now at the Egyptian Museum in Cairo, is the earliest extrabiblical reference). The monolith includes the Assyrian version of the Battle of Qarqar in 853 BCE against eleven allied kings led by Hadadezer of Aram and Ahab of Israel. The inscription credits Ahab with a large force of ten thousand foot soldiers and two thousand chariots (*ANET* 277–81). Though the Assyrian king Shalmaneser claims victory, no further Assyrian advance is reported, and none of the allied kings loses his seat of power. Made of limestone and inscribed in Akkadian cuneiform, the monolith is on display at the British Museum in London.

Mesha Stele   The Mesha Stele (Moabite Stone), discovered in 1870 in Jordan, is considered authentic by most archaeologists. It references Israel and possibly "house of David" as well as "house of Omri." The story told on the stele dates from about 840 BCE and the time of King Mesha of Moab and King Jehoram (son of Ahab) of Israel. The stele appears to refer to an incident preceding 2 Kings 3 or perhaps that biblical event from Moab's perspective. As the Bible tells the story, King Mesha of Moab, facing Jehoram and two allies, prevails after sacrificing his oldest son to the Moabite deity Chemosh. The stele refers to Mesha's successful rebellion and his building projects in honor of Chemosh. Though the stele was discovered intact and a papier-mâché "squeeze" (impression) was made of the stele, it was broken shortly after discovery. Most of the pieces and the inscription were recovered and are on display at the Louvre in Paris. The archaeological evidence of Omri and Israel in conflict with the kingdom of Moab substantiates the biblical story in a significant way (*ANET* 320–21).

Tel Dan "House of David" Inscription   The Tel Dan Stele, discovered in northern Israel in 1993–94, references Israel and "house of David" and is dated later than the Mesha Stele. The broken inscribed stone had been repurposed in a wall, but originally it celebrated the victory of an unknown Aramean (Syrian) king (perhaps Hazael) over Joram of Israel and a king from the "house of David." Though other translations have been suggested, most scholars consider the find and the reading authentic. This early reference is the strongest extrabiblical evidence for the Davidic dynasty.

Black Obelisk of Shalmaneser III   The Black Obelisk (erected in 825 BCE and discovered in Nimrud, Iraq, in 1846) depicts twenty kings paying tribute to Shalmaneser, including one scene with a king of Israel, probably Jehu, bowing in submission. The scene is thought to be the earliest contemporary visual depiction of a biblical character. In Assyrian cuneiform, the stele describes how Jehu brought tribute in 841 BCE, severed alliances with Tyre and Judah, and became subject to Assyria. Jehu is referred to (incorrectly) as son of Omri, who was perhaps king when Assyria first encountered Israel. The black limestone stele, displayed in the British Museum, is nearly two meters in height (*ANET* 282).

Sennacherib's Prism   The annals of the Assyrian king Sennacherib are found in nearly identical form on three clay prisms, discovered in 1830 in Nineveh. In Assyrian cuneiform the annals describe the Assyrian siege of Jerusalem during the reign of Hezekiah in 701 BCE (2 Kings 18:13–19:37). Though the perspective is different from that of 2 Kings, the annals significantly corroborate the events as recorded in the Bible. Second Kings 17 reports that Samaria was destroyed and the people deported; then 18:13-16 says that Sennacherib captured all the fortified cities of Judah and that Hezekiah paid a heavy tribute to induce Sennacherib to withdraw. The Assyrian annals report that forty-six walled cities were conquered; 200,150 people deported; and the conquered territory divided among the Philistines. The annals say about Hezekiah, "I shut him up like a caged bird in his capital city of Jerusalem"; they mention Hezekiah's tribute, but do not claim that Jerusalem was taken. The prisms are displayed in the British Museum, the Oriental Institute of Chicago, and the Israel Museum in Jerusalem (ANET 287–88).

Siloam Inscription Discovered in 1880, the Siloam Tunnel Inscription tells how two crews tunneled through bedrock to bring water from a source outside the walls into Jerusalem. One crew started at the Gihon Spring outside the city, while the other started from within the city walls. The inscription was chiseled out and remains in the Istanbul Archaeological Museum; it describes the engineering feat of an eighteen-hundred-foot tunnel. Though the assertion is disputed by some, many scholars identify the site as Hezekiah's Tunnel, the conduit reported in 2 Kings 20:20, likely in preparation for the siege described in 2 Kings 18–19 (Rollston).

Lachish Lachish was a major political and military city in Judah mentioned in the book of Kings, located about forty miles southwest of Jerusalem. Taken by Joshua in the conquest (Josh 10), Lachish figures most prominently in the Assyrian invasion of Judah that threatened Jerusalem during the reign of Hezekiah (2 Kings 18–19). The Assyrian account of the events is found on Sennacherib's Prism (see above). The contemporaneous Lachish reliefs depict the siege ramp that led to the Assyrian destruction of the city (ANEP 372–73). Among significant finds in situ include the storage jars with the king's seals and pottery shards with military messages during the final battle (Williamson 635–38).

Jehoiachin's Ration Tablets Discovered in about 1900 and held in the Pergamon Museum in Berlin, several clay tablets in Akkadian cuneiform describe rations of oil and barley for various captives, including the deposed Judean king Jehoiachin, given by Nebuchadnezzar from the royal storehouses. The tablets confirm the biblical account that reports Jehoiachin as a prisoner of Babylon, released, and given rations by the king (2 Kings 25:27-30; ANET 308).

CHRONOLOGY The framework of 1–2 Kings records the reigns of the kings of Israel and Judah chronologically. Thus 1–2 Kings synchronizes chronologies in the divided kingdom by reporting the reign of one king as beginning, then moving back in time to identify the reign of the other kingdom's monarch who came to rule a few years earlier (Nelson 1987: 8). This synchronizes the reigns of the divided kingdom into a "relative chronology" in which the reigns in one kingdom are related to those of the other. Such a presentation contrasts with an "absolute chronology," tying the reigns to our calendar (see the table at the end of this essay). Chronologies synchronized with neighboring kings were a feature of the Assyrian and Babylonian annals (Gray: 56).

Opening and Closing Regal Formulas Each report begins with the introductory royal formula, with the names of the king and his predecessor (often father), date of accession with synchronization to the corresponding king of the other kingdom, length and place of reign, and appraisal. The age of the king at coronation and the name of the mother of the king, her father, and her hometown are typically included for the kings of Judah. Following the historical narrative, the report ends with the concluding royal formula with reference to contemporary sources, additional historical notes, death and burial notices, succession information, and in a few instances an addendum. The sources cited are the Annals of the Kings of Judah and of Israel. No extrabiblical evidence has been found for these sources. By referring to the "rest of the acts" of the king, the citations raise the question about the material presented regarding each of the kings. Scholars have not determined whether the reports are parallel to the royal annals, a commentary on them, or identifying additional deeds not found in the sources (Leuchter: 131–32).

Exceptions to the typical pattern include lack of introductory royal formula for Solomon, Jeroboam, and Jehu, who ascend to the throne in unusual circumstances. A closing royal formula is missing for Ahaziah, Jehoram, Hoshea, Jehoahaz, Jehoiachin, and Zedekiah, whose reigns end in coup or exile. Athaliah (2 Kings 11) has neither introductory nor concluding royal formula, an indication of her illegitimacy as a monarch.

Synchronization Synchronization of the king with his contemporary is difficult to harmonize, complicated by approximation, differing calendars in Israel and Judah, differing systems for counting the year of accession, changing systems, coregencies, discrepancies in reporting, and ancient versions (MT/LXX). Approximate dates for the reigns of the kings are included in the table at the end of this essay (Thiele; Hayes and Hooker; Cogan 1992). Because simply adding the years ascribed to each reign results in implausible totals of years, some adjustment is needed. Thiele; Albright; and Hayes and Hooker have developed arguments that suggest resolution to knotty chronological problems. The table follows suggestions of Hayes and Hooker to accept the number of years in the biblical text as the length of the king's life after inauguration (not necessarily his tenure). Adjustments are made for Asa (reign ended prematurely because of his diseased feet, 1 Kings 15:23); Ahab (tenure counted from the founding of Samaria); Jehu (Hayes and Hooker calculate his twenty-eight-year reign from the death of Ahaziah, not Jehoram); Jehoash of Judah (Hayes and Hooker contend that he abdicated, then was assassinated; 2 Kings 12:17-20; 14:1-2); Amaziah (arrested, replaced, 14:13, 17-19); Azariah (Uzziah, retired with leprosy, 15:5); Pekah (tenure began as a rival kingdom east of Jordan, reunited with Israel after Pekahiah's death, 15:25-27).

Two summary remarks guide this commentary. "Although any attempt to map an accurate chronology from the citation of each individual king's length of tenure fails, these opening citations successfully craft an impression of simultaneous periodization" (i.e., of overlapping reigns; Hens-Piazza 2006: 149). The important historical problem of the chronology "does not have a significant effect on the narrative character of the stories of the kings" (J. T. Walsh 1996: 206).

Kings Ahaziah and Jehoram An example of the complexities of harmonization involves two Israelite kings and their Judean namesakes. Both kingdoms have kings named Ahaziah and Joram (= Jehoram). Ahaziah of Israel, son of Ahab and Jezebel, dies without heirs, succeeded by his brother Joram of Israel (1 Kings 22:52–2 Kings 1:17). Ahaziah of Judah, son of Jehoram (Joram) of Judah, is killed by Jehu, succeeded by his mother, Athaliah, and later by his son Joash (Jehoash; 2 Kings 8:25-29; 9:21-29; 11:1-8). Jehoram of Judah, son of Jehoshaphat, marries Athaliah, daughter of Ahab, uniting the house of Omri with the house of David (1:17; 8:16-24). The NIV distinguishes the two by referring to the Judean king as Jehoram and the Israelite king as Joram. Joram of Israel, son of Ahab and Jezebel, is the last Omride (1:17; 3:1-27; 8:16, 25, 28; 9:26). Another complication is that Joram of Israel is synchronized with Jehoram of Judah by dating his accession in Jehoram's second year (1:17), but later the synchronization places the accession of Jehoram of Judah in the fifth year of his namesake, Joram of Israel (8:16). Another hypothesis is that only one Jehoram (son of Jehoshaphat) ruled Israel in the stead of his ailing brother-in-law, Ahaziah (Hayes and Hooker: 33). In the chart below the family tree shows fathers in rectangular shapes and (apparent) mothers in rounded shapes and shows that Jehoash is both Omride (italicized) and Davidide (underlined) in ancestry.

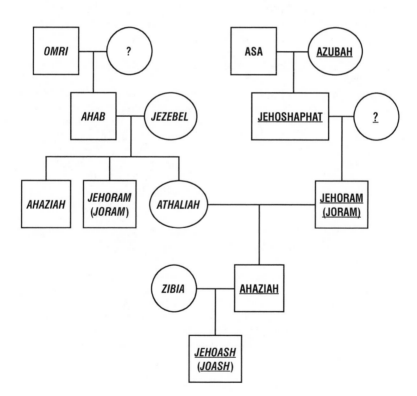

Joash and Jehoash Later contemporary kings of Judah and Israel have the same name—and identical alternate spellings of the name—Joash/Jehoash (2 Kings 11:1-13:13; 14:15-16). Jehoash (Joash) of Judah succeeds his grandmother Athaliah (11:1-3). Jehoash, son of Jehoahaz of Jehu's dynasty in Israel, begins to reign in the thirty-seventh year of Joash of Judah (13:9-10). Joash (Jehoash) of Israel has the rare distinction of two separate (nearly identical) closing royal formulas (13:12-13; 14:15-16).

Complicated Hezekiah Chronology Based on archaeological evidence dating the Assyrian Sennacherib's invasion to 701 BCE (in Hezekiah's fourteenth year, 2 Kings 18:13), some scholars date Hezekiah's accession to 715 BCE. If so, the synchronization to Hoshea's third year (18:1) can be read as a literary technique juxtaposing righteous Hezekiah alongside wicked Hoshea (exiled in 722 BCE). Hezekiah's chronology is further complicated in that the Lord adds fifteen years to Hezekiah's life (20:6). Since Hezekiah reigns twenty-nine years, this would place both Hezekiah's miraculous recovery and Sennacherib's invasion in his fourteenth year. Also perplexing are three separate Assyrian demands for Hezekiah to surrender (18:13-16; 18:17–19:7; 19:8-35). Hayes and Hooker posit that Hezekiah's reign began in 729 BCE, before Hoshea's exile, accounting for multiple Assyrian military campaigns in Palestine, and suggest that scribal confusion explains misdating Sennacherib's invasion in the year of Hezekiah's healing (71–80). Historical explanations vary. This commentary gives primary attention to the story line of the book of Kings.

Reigns of Kings in Judah and in Israel Saul was the first king of the united monarchy, reigning ca. 1020–1000 BCE. Next was David, ca. 1000–961 (1–2 Samuel), then Solomon, ca. 961–925. Shortly after Solomon's son Rehoboam began as king, the split left the tribe of Judah with most of the Benjaminites as the Southern Kingdom and the other tribes as the Northern Kingdom, called Israel (1–2 Kings; all years in this table are BCE).

Judah (Southern Kingdom)	*Israel (Northern Kingdom)*
Rehoboam (926–910)	Jeroboam (927–906)
Abijah/Abijam (909–907)	Nadab (905–904)
Asa (906–878) [d. 866]	Baasha (903–882) [d. 880]
Jehoshaphat (877–853)	Elah (881–880)
	Zimri (7 days)
	Omri (879–869)
	Ahab (868–854)
Jehoram/Joram (852–841)	Ahaziah (853–852)
Ahaziah (840)	Jehoram/Joram (851–840)
Athaliah (839–833)	Jehu (839–822)
Jehoash (832–803) [d. 793]	Jehoahaz (821–805)
Amaziah (802–786) [d. 774]	Jehoash (804–789)
Azariah/Uzziah (785–760) [d. 734]	Jeroboam II (788–748)
Jotham (759–744)	Zechariah (6 months)
	Shallum (1 month)

Ahaz (743–728)

Hezekiah (727–699)
Manasseh (698–644)
Amon (643–642)
Josiah (641–610)
Jehoahaz (3 months)
Jehoiakim (608–598)
Jehoiachin (3 months)
Zedekiah (596–586)
Fall of Judah (586)
Gedaliah (governor, 585–582)

Menahem (746–737)
Pekahiah (736–735)
Pekah (734–731)
Hoshea (730–722)
Fall of Samaria (722)

COVENANT IN KINGS Covenant is a formal commitment between two parties to act with loyalty. Apparently adopting the form of thirteenth-century Hittites or seventh-century Assyrian political treaties, the Old Testament covenant between the greater (God) and lesser partner (Israel) is characterized by a mutual obligation to love the other. The book of Deuteronomy, itself shaped by the covenant form and values [*Kings in the Hebrew Canon: Kings and Deuteronomy, p. 453*], establishes the standards for evaluating Israel and its kings. To keep covenant with the Lord is to love and obey the God of gods and Lord of lords, who makes justice for orphans and widows and loves strangers (Deut 10:12-19). God's covenant with Abraham (Gen 15, 17) is centered in the human vocation of doing justice and righteousness (18:19). For a complete review of covenant in the Old Testament, see "Covenant and Treaty" (Matties: 416–21).

Not counting the *ark of the covenant* (1 Kings 3, 8), political treaties with Tyre and Aram (1 Kings 5, 15, 20), and the *book of the covenant* (2 Kings 23), the Hebrew term *berit* (covenant) appears fourteen times in 1–2 Kings (1 Kings 8:23; 11:11; 19:10, 14; 2 Kings 11:4, 17; 13:23; 17:15, 35, 38; 18:12; 23:3 [three times]), and a related term (ʿedut) four times (1 Kings 2:3; 2 Kings 11:12; 17:5; 23:3; also used for the stone tablets of the Ten Commandments in the ark of the covenant, Exod 32:15; 34:29; 40:20). Even when the term itself is absent, the covenant obligation to do justice [*Mišpaṭ, p. 461*] and obey and worship the Lord is primary. David calls Solomon to covenant obedience (1 Kings 2:1-4). Solomon uses typical covenant vocabulary—steadfast love, faithfulness, righteousness, and uprightness—in asking God for justice (3:5-9). The Lord reminds Solomon that covenant obedience is the condition for God's presence (6:11-13; 9:2-9). Solomon's dedicatory temple prayer celebrates God's covenant faithfulness (8:23-26). The Lord condemns Solomon's covenant failure (11:11, 33-35) and offers Jeroboam an unending covenant conditioned on covenant faithfulness (11:31, 38). Elijah laments that Israel has broken covenant in practicing injustice and worshiping Baal (19:10, 14, 18). After the Omride usurper Athaliah, the priest Jehoiada renews covenant with the Lord, the king (Joash/Jehoash), and the people (2 Kings 11:4, 12, 17). Though the Lord extends mercy to disobedient Israel because the Lord remembers his covenant (13:23), Israel's covenant failure results in exile (17:15, 35, 38). Hezekiah's *trust* is unsurpassed (18:5-6), but the covenant failure of his son Manasseh makes exile inevitable (21:8, 14-16). Josiah, Judah's most exemplary king, finds the book of the covenant and leads radical covenant renewal (2 Kings 22–23). Despite Josiah's reforms, Manasseh's transgression makes the covenant curses inevitable; exile can no longer be averted (24:3-4).

Covenant in Kings corresponds to Deuteronomic Torah. Blessings and curses are conditioned on covenant faithfulness, obedience to the law, the human vocation of justice. Despite Israel's failure as evidenced by exile, the Deuteronomic covenant promises that God's faithfulness is greater than human failure (Deut 4:27-31; 30:1-5).

ECONOMICS IN ANCIENT ISRAEL Basic to the ancient Israelite economy, land is the primary capital resource. Labor is the human resource essential for land use. The Deuteronomic law code declares that the Lord has given the land to Israel and prescribes statutes that describe full life in the land (Deut 6:23-24). Deuteronomic egalitarian economics is put to the test in 1–2 Kings.

Though the law of the king warns against accumulation (Deut 17:16-17), the royal elite lived with the constant temptation of Canaanite mythology, exploitative affluence in violation of Deuteronomic justice. Deuteronomy teaches Israel to integrate misplaced persons lacking kinship ties—the orphan, widow, and stranger (e.g., 10:18)—into the social, juridical, liturgical, and economic life of the covenant community through the father's house (Glanville: 81, 91)

Central to the strategy of the royal elite is latifundialization, the process of concentrating land ownership in the great estates of a powerful few. This is accelerated by centralized urban military power, luxury lifestyles (dependent on grain, oil, and wine, the cash crops valued for trade that replace subsistence farming optimal for the producer), increased taxation and forced labor resulting in indebtedness to urban creditors, and international trade and commerce (Chaney 2014: 35–40). DtrH reports land grants for service to the crown (2 Sam 9); taxation to provide for the court (1 Kings 4:20-28); forced labor (5:13-18; 9:15-22); militarization (4:26-28; 10:26); export of agricultural products (5:11); luxury lifestyle (10:14-22); growing urban centers and fortifications (3:1; 7:1; 9:15); and centralized political administration (4:1-19). Jeroboam I, Omri, and Ahab transfer these policies to Israel through their urban construction projects (1 Kings 12:25-32; 16:24, 32; 22:39); centralization; military establishment (18:5); and alliances (16:31)—all substantiated by archaeological artifacts (Premnath: 39–41) *[Archaeology, p. 436]*. The process reaches its zenith during the long reign of Jeroboam II (2 Kings 14:23-27; see the prophets Amos, Hosea, Isaiah, Micah). Centralized state bureaucracy results in urban luxury and impoverishment of rural peasants (Premnath: 43).

Militarization allows control of trade routes, including the Via Maris (Way of the Sea), running along the coast, around the east side of Mount Carmel, and through the Jezreel valley (Premnath: 46–47); and the King's

Highway, going through the Transjordan and along the edge of the desert—routes dominated by Israel during the reigns of Solomon, Ahab, and Jeroboam II (48–55; Master 504, 509). Successful trade further polarized the economy between the powerful urban elite and the rural poor.

Prophets Amos, Micah, Hosea, and Isaiah protest these policies during the reigns of Jeroboam II and Uzziah, in the second quarter of the eighth century, a period of relative peace and prosperity (Chaney 2014: 35). The invasion of Tiglath-pileser III of Assyria exacerbates the problems as the urban elite extract payment of imperial tribute from the peasant poor (2014: 36).

The Latter Prophets (Isaiah, Jeremiah, Ezekiel, the Twelve) address the socioeconomic conditions in Kings directly *[Prophets, p. 465]*. With the call for justice (1 Kings 10:9) *[Mišpaṭ, p. 461]*, the prophets address the evils inherent in land accumulation by the rich (Isa 5:8-10), urbanization (Amos 3:9-11), militarization (Hos 10:13-15), extraction of surplus (Amos 5:11-12), luxurious lifestyle (Amos 6:4-7), foreign trade and commerce (Isa 2:6-7), debt slavery (Amos 2:6-8; cf. 2 Kings 4:1), and unjust judicial courts (Mic 3:1-4, 9-12; Premnath: 99–179). The systems benefit the upper class, the royal house, and the urban elite, who extract wealth at the cost of vulnerable folks' livelihood (those served by the prophetic community) *[Prophets: Sons of the Prophets, p. 467]*. The conflict between royal policy and Deuteronomic egalitarianism, evident in the report of Solomon's wealth and in Ahab's expropriation of Naboth's vineyard, characterizes the royal policies of Israel and Judah.

EGYPT *Egypt* is mentioned thirty-three times in 1–2 Kings and signifies the ancient imperial order from which God liberated Israel (cf. Exodus). References to Egypt in 1–2 Kings name an ancient political entity contemporary with Israel and Judah in the international power structure (e.g., marking boundaries, 1 Kings 4:21; 8:65; Solomon's ally, 3:1; a trading partner, 10:28-29; a military power, 2 Kings 7:6; 24:7; an ally, 1 Kings 9:16; 2 Kings 17:4; 18:21, 24; a foe, 1 Kings 14:25; 2 Kings 23:29, 34; a safe haven for Solomon's adversaries, 1 Kings 11:17-18, 21, 40; 12:2; a land of wise sages, 4:30). Following Deuteronomy's message, 1–2 Kings treats Egypt as a sign of anti-Yahweh power. In the law of the king, Egypt represents the past to be avoided, the ideology reliant on military might (Deut 17:14-20). Egypt is often referenced within a citation of the Lord's liberation of Israel from slavery (1 Kings 6:1; 8:9, 16, 21, 51, 53; 9:9; 12:28; 2 Kings 21:15). Ironically, the story of Israel ends where it began, in Egypt (2 Kings 25:26). Israel's sin is an affront to the Lord because it reverses the Lord's primary agenda: liberating Israel from the powers, the gods of the nations, the anti-justice power agents *[Mišpaṭ, p. 461]*.

In the Solomon narrative (1 Kings 3–11) the motif of "returning to Egypt" is significant. All but two of the references to Egypt in 1 Kings are found within the Solomon narrative. The two exceptions refer to the *gods . . . who brought you up out of the land of Egypt* (12:28) and the Shishak invasion (14:25). While the Lord's deliverance of Israel from Egypt is mentioned, Egypt most frequently represents imperial values that seduce Solomon. He "returns" to Egypt for his wife (1 Kings 3:1; 9:16, 24; 11:1), for wisdom (2:6; 4:30), and for horses and chariots (10:28-29). Using a "retro-active re-evaluation technique," Jeon shows that the nature of Solomon's corruption in returning to Egypt is developed in the "literary device" of *Pharaoh's daughter* (40). Though his reign was to be the culmination of the exodus (6:1), "Solomon not only spoils the redemptive ending of the Exodus story, [but also] reverses it, forcing his people to relive its bondage in Egypt" (Weitzman 96).

EVIL *Evil (ra^c)* appears sixty times in 1–2 Kings (about one-tenth of the OT occurrences). *Evil* refers to a range of negatives, from Ahab as the wicked-est of all kings of Israel (1 Kings 16:30-33) and Manasseh the worst of Judah's kings (2 Kings 21:11) to bad food and drink, impotable water (2:19), and toxic stew (4:41). Though used occasionally to refer to something bad without moral connotations, the term has theological significance in 1–2 Kings, with its categorical evaluation of kings and others as either good or evil.

Solomon's inaugural dream is the occasion for God's first appearance to Solomon. When God offers Solomon anything he desires, Solomon requests a listening heart to do justice; he asks to be able to discern between good and evil (1 Kings 3:9). Recalling Eve's desire for fruit from the tree of the knowledge of good and evil (Gen 3), Solomon's request points toward wis-dom (a primary motif in the Solomon narrative) *[Wisdom in Kings, p. 484]*, ethics (choosing the good of justice over the evil of self-aggrandizement), and the God-Solomon relationship (*the LORD, the God of Israel, who had ap-peared to him twice* was angry that *Solomon did what was evil in the sight of the LORD*, 1 Kings 11:6-10).

Doing *evil* is an affront to the Lord. Thirty times, kings *do evil in the eyes of the LORD* (from Solomon in 1 Kings 11:6 to the last king, Zedekiah, in 2 Kings 24:19). Doing evil is associated with Jeroboam (twelve times), Ahab (four times), the house of Ahab (three times), and Manasseh (five times). To worship false gods is to do *evil* (note the frequent reference to the sins of Jeroboam). Ahab and Manasseh, the wickedest kings of Israel and Judah, do *evil* by shedding innocent blood (1 Kings 21:19-21, 25; 2 Kings 21:16; 24:3-4).

Ten times the Lord brings judgment (evil), the calamity that comes in consequence for doing evil (1 Kings 9:9; 22:23; 2 Kings 21:12; 22:16). Thus 1–2 Kings attributes judgment to the Lord's anger (2 Kings 21:15) *[Provoke the Lord to Anger, p. 470]*. Judgment comes as an inevitable result of *provoking him with provocations* that the Lord could not pardon (2 Kings 23:26 AT; 24:4).

While kings are cited most frequently for doing evil, six times Israel and Judah collectively do evil (1 Kings 14:22; 2 Kings 17:11, 13, 17; 21:9, 15-16). In the Lord's appearance to Solomon after the temple dedication, the Lord links the consequences of Solomon's idolatry to the fate of the people (1 Kings 9:6-9). Though the urban elite benefit directly from royal injustice at the expense of the poor, the entire nation suffers corporate evil (2 Kings 17:21-23; 25:11-12).

Evil is associated with death, but Elisha's miracles function as parables to demonstrate that God brings life to land and people associated with evil and death. At Jericho (the city founded under the curse; 1 Kings 16:34), the location was good but the water bad (evil; 2 Kings 2:19). After Elisha acts, the Lord declares that he has healed the water and banishes death and miscarriage (2:21). At Gilgal some wild gourds introduce death into the stew of the prophets. Elisha intervenes, and the evil is removed. The miracles are acted parables, with the hopeful message that evil need not have the last word.

HORSES AND CHARIOTS *Horses and chariots* is the biblical metonym (figure of speech representing another term) for military/political power (like modern missiles and tanks). Horses and chariots are markers of raw, royal power. This figure of speech describes the imperial splendor of Solomon, royal Israelite military transport, the military superiority of Israel's enemies, and the superior power of the Lord over physical armies. Chariots are a standard expression of the question whether the king trusts in military power or in the Lord (Ps 20:7; Deijl: 159).

Solomon's political, military, and economic power is closely associated with his chariots and horses (1 Kings 4:26-28; 9:19, 22; 10:26-29). Though no battles are reported in his reign, Solomon's imperial peace is guaranteed by his large chariot force. Solomon's wealth is the product of the import-export business he conducts in moving military hardware from Egypt and Kue to the Hittites and Aram. In a subversive reading, the economics raises flags. Feeding (4:26-28) and stabling (9:19, 22) horses is enormously costly. The horse-and-chariot trade appears profitable, but the identification of the import price and its absence regarding the exports may signal the venture's unprofitability (10:26-29). The negative political outcome of the trade becomes evident as the Arameans rebel in Solomon's time (11:23-25) and torment Solomon's successors militarily (e.g., 15:18-20; chs. 20, 22). Above all, Solomon violates the law of the king prohibiting the acquisition of many horses and a return to Egypt for horses (Deut 17:16).

Horses and chariots provide transport for Israel's kings and are part of their armed forces (1 Kings 16:9). Adonijah communicates his royal pretensions by assembling chariots and horsemen (1:5). In a battle against Aram's cavalry, Ahab goes disguised as an ordinary charioteer (22:29-36). For Ahab, the war equipment becomes a chariot of death, with his blood filling the chariot (22:35-38). Ahab, who was renowned in extrabiblical sources for his great chariot force [*Archaeology: Kurkh Monolith of Shalmaneser III, p. 437*], dies much as prophesied by the Lord (21:19; 22:37-38). Edom's revolt against Joram of Judah succeeds despite Joram's chariots (2 Kings 8:21). Jehu's successful revolt against the Omrides depends on his military advantage, including his daring as a charioteer (*he drives like a maniac*, 9:16-20; also 9:27, 33; 10:15). Jehu defeats Joram, Ahaziah, and the house of Ahab despite their dependence on horses and chariots (9:21-28; 10:2-3). Jehu's son Jehoahaz suffers defeat at the hands of the Aramean kings Hazael and his son Ben-hadad, who decimate his forces (13:3, 7). Israel's dependence on horses and chariots repeatedly results in defeat of the royal house.

Aramean military and political superiority is linked to their advantage in horses and chariots, but despite their superiority, they serve as foils for the Lord's power. When Ben-hadad attacks Ahab with *horses and chariots*,

Israel sues for peace in the face of the Aramean superiority (1 Kings 20:1). The Lord intervenes, empowering Israel to defeat Aram and their king, who escapes on horseback (20:20-21). When Aram rebuilds and changes tactics to take better advantage of their horses and chariots, the Lord again miraculously routs the superior foe (20:25-30). Naaman's pretentious demand for a leprosy cure is supported by his intimidating chariot force (2 Kings 5:9), but his healing comes only when he submits to the Lord's superior power. The unnamed king of Aram is incensed by Elisha's military intelligence that protects Israel from ambush attacks, and he sends an army of horses and chariots against the unarmed prophet, only to be bested again by the Lord and his prophet Elisha (6:15). When the entire Aramean army mounts a siege against Samaria that leaves the city on the verge of starvation (6:24-25), the Arameans panic as they think they hear chariots and horses, sounds caused by the Lord; they flee, leaving behind horses and donkeys and military equipment in their haste (7:6-7, 15).

Similarly, the Assyrians mock Hezekiah and Judah for their inability to provide riders for a cavalry even if the Assyrians were to provide the horses, as well as for their purported reliance on Egyptian horses and chariots (2 Kings 18:23-24; Deut 17:16). Isaiah composes a taunt song ridiculing the Assyrian chariots (2 Kings 19:23-28), and the angel of the Lord strikes down the army (19:35). In Kings, the enemies of Israel and Judah threaten God's people with overwhelming superiority of horses and chariots, only to be repeatedly thwarted by the Lord's miraculous intervention. Horses and chariots are no match for the Lord of Israel—even when Israel fails to follow the Lord. Often the Lord's actions bring peace and avoid violence.

Three references to the Lord's horses and chariots underscore the theme (2 Kings 2:11-12; 6:17; 13:14). In the first and third of these reports, the witness of God's power exclaims, *My father, my father! The chariots of Israel and its horsemen!* in conjunction with the authority of Elijah and Elisha (2:12; 13:14). Sandwiched between the exclamations (*the chariots of Israel*), the Lord demonstrates superior power over Aram (6:14-17). The Lord limits military violence and brings peace through his saving action tied to horses and chariots.

Elsewhere, this figure of speech expresses the Lord's ultimate power. In the exodus the Lord defeats the imperial horses and chariots of Egypt (mentioned nine times in Exod 14–15). Deuteronomy not only warns against returning to Egypt for horses (17:16) but also recalls the destruction of Egypt's forces in the exodus (11:4; cf. Josh 24:6) and reassures Israel when facing horses and chariots in battle (Deut 20:1). When Jabin's coalition "with very many horses and chariots" threatens (Josh 11:4), the Lord delivers Joshua, who eliminates horses and chariots (11:6-9; cf. 2 Sam 8:4). Several psalms declare that God's power is superior to dependence on horses and chariots (20:7; 33:16-17; 76:6, 12; 147:10-11). Isaiah proclaims woe to those who rely on imperial Egypt's horses and chariots (31:1), and Micah announces judgment on "your horses . . . and . . . your chariots" (5:10). Zechariah 9:10 anticipates the day when the Lord will replace horses and chariots with peace.

Matties's Joshua commentary provides an apt summary here:

Horses and chariots come to represent, therefore, the grasping kind of power that prevents trust in the Lord (Ps 20:7; cf. Deut 20:1-4). Isaiah presents them in various contexts alongside gold, silver, and idols, all sources of pride that prevent Israel from trusting God (2:7; 31:1; 36:9). It is God alone who is sovereign over horses and chariots, who calls them to fulfill his purposes, and who brings them to nothing (Isa 43:17; Jer 50:37; 51:21; Ezek 39:20; Hag 2:22). (Matties: 436–37)

HOUSE FOR THE NAME The phrase *a house for the name of the* LORD, or *the place the* LORD *will choose for his name to dwell,* is an Israelite theological strategy to explain how God is present at the place of worship (Brueggemann 2000: 76). "Name theology" distinguishes between God's real dwelling in heaven and the earthly place of worship where God's name dwells. The phrase in Deuteronomy describes the divinely designated place of worship (12:5, 11, 21; 14:23-24; 16:2, 6, 11; 26:2). When David proposes to build a temple, the Lord declares that David's son will "build a house for my name" (2 Sam 7:13). The phrase *a house for the name of the* LORD (or *for my name;* 1 Kings 3:2; 5:3, 5; 8:16, 17, 18, 19, 20, 29, 43, 44, 48; 9:3, 7; 2 Kings 23:27) and the related phrase that the Lord has chosen *Jerusalem . . . to put my name* (1 Kings 11:36; 2 Kings 21:4, 7) appear nearly twenty times in 1–2 Kings. In Israel, the *name* communicates the essence of the person (e.g., Gen 32:28; cf. Exod 3:14-15; 34:5-7); the designation *the Name* substitutes for the personal name *Yahweh* in Judaism. *Name* communicates essence, ownership, presence. Affirming that God's name is in the temple recognizes that God cannot be restricted to a particular place (1 Kings 8:27; Widmer: 262). The phrase *a house for the name of Yahweh* seeks to avoid making Yahweh so remote that the Lord is not present in the temple and to avoid making Yahweh fully present, available, and on call (Brueggemann 2000: 76). This phrase is the characteristic way of speaking of God's ownership of God's sanctuary (cf. 1 Kings 3:2; 8:17) and enables God to identify with the temple and to reject it if he pleases (1 Kings 9:2-9; J. Davies 2012: 187) *[Temple Theology, p. 477].*

IDOLATRY Idolatry is a major problem in Kings because of the strong Deuteronomic prohibition. Deuteronomy forbids the worship of gods other than Yahweh (5:7), the making and worship of images or heavenly bodies (5:7-10; 4:15-28), and worship in pagan shrines such as high places, spreading trees, and preexisting Canaanite altars to Baal and the goddess Asherah, with the related poles and sacred stones (worship is forbidden anywhere other than "the place the LORD your God will choose to put his Name," 12:1-7). Deuteronomy requires Israel to demolish the hills and trees and break down the altars and pillars (*Asherah/im;* 12:3).

Idol worship is problematic in several ways. First, the Lord demands exclusive devotion as the one God. Worship of any other is an affront to this holy God. Second, humans alone are created in the image of God. To create another image is an affront not only to God the creator (who alone has authority to create in the image of God) but also to humans (creating other images gives those images false authority over humankind). Third, idolatry is ideological, a polytheistic system where myth and cult reinforce distorted, unjust values. Whether worship of the golden calves erected by Jeroboam [*Sins of Jeroboam, p. 476*] or worship of the gods of the empires or of the Canaanites (Amorites), cultic activity reinforces an ideology opposed to the Deuteronomic egalitarian justice of the Lord [*Mišpaṭ, p. 461*]. Morgenstern summarizes the position: "The rejection of monotheism and the embrace of idolatry promote disregard of the religious and moral practices that had previously defined Israelite society and supported the basic values of equality and respect for all individuals regardless of their social or economic origins" (liii). Idolatry "symbolizes a totally negative attitude to everything that God has done or given to the Israelites" (Latvus: 86). First and Second Kings denounces kings and people for idol worship, condemning both the cultic activity and the falsifying ideology opposed to the Lord's righteousness and justice.

Idol worship defaces the image of God (Bates: 155). Idolatry derives from a basic "misconstrual of reality" (Bates: 153). Idols are false, fraudulent, deceptive, vain. Idolatry leads to human harm because their creators "trust their own creation" (Hab 2:18). Idols are used to rationalize self-serving interests. Idolatry damages humans, who become what they worship. Idolatry is a move away from the domain of the real, causing an inability to perceive reality accurately (Bates: 153–55; see "Idolatry" in TLC for 1 Kings 12–14).

The Old Testament opposes the polytheism and fertility cult practices of the Canaanite religion in favor of exclusive worship of the Lord, the God of Israel. The Old Testament appropriates elements of Canaanite religion and uses them within Old Testament faith (e.g., Yahweh not Baal brings fertility to the land, Hos 2:10, 16). Although the Old Testament consistently opposes syncretism, both biblical texts (e.g., people's limping between Baal and the Lord, 1 Kings 18) and archaeological evidence (e.g., inscriptions at cultic centers Khirbet el-Qom and Kuntillet Ajrud) suggest that the people's religion incorporated elements of Canaanite religion in a popular Israelite cult (J. Day 1992b).

High Places In 1–2 Kings, high places are the most common affront to the Lord in Judah. Though high places were prohibited by Moses (Num 33:52; Deut 12:3, 11), Samuel worshiped at the high place in Zuph (1 Sam 9) and Solomon at Gibeon, excused *because no house had yet been built for the name of the LORD* (1 Kings 3:2-4). Solomon is condemned for building high places for the gods of his wives (11:7). Committing the abominations of the dispossessed nations, Judah did evil in the sight of the Lord and provoked him by building high places, pillars, and Asherim (14:23). The positive evaluation of the Judean kings Asa, Jehoshaphat, Joash, Amaziah, Azariah, and Jotham is tarnished by their tolerance of high places (15:14; 22:43; 2 Kings 12:3; 14:4; 15:4, 35). The wicked kings of Judah named Ahaz and Manasseh are condemned for the cultic high places (2 Kings 16:3-4; 21:3). The reforms of Hezekiah and Josiah eliminate the high places (18:4; 23:5).

The cultic sins of Israel include worship of other gods at the high places (1 Kings 12:31-32; 13:2-32; 2 Kings 17:9, 11, 29, 32). High places have altars for sacrifice and burning incense. Asherah stones or pillars are characteristic of high places. A temple structure with steps leading up to the altar indicates a more elaborate cultic site. The high places were administered not only by non-Levitical priests (1 Kings 12:31) but also by Levites (2 Kings 23:9).

Holy Ones/Cult Prostitutes Deuteronomy prohibits the daughters and sons of Israel from being *temple prostitutes* (23:17), a term repeated four times in 1–2 Kings. These *holy ones* (1 Kings 14:24 AT) are appointed by the people of Judah but removed by Asa, Jehoshaphat, and Josiah (1 Kings 15:12; 22:46; 2 Kings 23:7). The function of these illicit cultic functionaries is not described except that they are connected to the abominations of the nations in the land before Israel (1 Kings 14:24). Though it is unlikely that the male and female *holy ones* were temple prostitutes, they were cultic personnel in the ancient, non-sanctioned religious places, and their practices were designed to ensure fertility—an affront to the Lord who had promised prosperity (Deut 7:12-16; 23:18-19; 1 Kings 15:12; 22:46; 2 Kings 23:7; DeVries: 185; Wray Beal 2014: 204–5; Cogan 2001: 387).

Idols The Hebrew term for *idols* is an invented invective, *gilulim*, coined from *gelalim* (turds; Alter: 5). First mentioned in Kings in Asa's reform (1 Kings 15:12), *idols* refers to the sins of Ahab (21:26) and Manasseh (2 Kings 21:11, 21), the sins of Israel at exile (17:12), and sins eliminated in Josiah's reform (23:24). The most common figurines found at ancient shrines and in domiciles are female figures a few inches tall, shaped as pillars below the waist and with large breasts, indicating a fertility cult with a mother-like goddess who provides life for her children.

Canaanite Myth A primary extrabiblical source for Canaanite culture and religion is Ugarit (modern Ras Shamra) on the northern Syrian coast, with archaeological texts and artifacts dating from the second millennium (fourteenth–thirteenth centuries BCE). Though El is the chief god in the Canaanite pantheon (council of gods), Baal is the most active. The Baal myth includes a repeated annual cycle of his conflict with Yam, the sea god; the building of Baal's temple; and Baal's conflict with Mot, in which Baal dies and rises again. Both Anat and to a lesser extent Ashtoreth are consorts of Baal, allied in conflict with the other gods (Day 1992b: 831–37).

Baal *Baal* (lord, owner; used ninety times in the OT, twenty-three times in 1–2 Kings; also known as *Hadad*) is a Canaanite deity symbolized by the bull calf and often identified with the territory of his domain (city or mountain; 2 Kings 1:2). As god of wind and weather, Baal shows his power over clouds and storm, lightning and thunder; he dispenses dew, rain, and snow while attending to the fertility of the soil, particularly to produce oil, wine, and grain. Baal guarantees annual vegetation, so when he disappears to the underworld in autumn, vegetation dies. Baal is a fertility god, king of his devotees, defender of his cities, and god of sex and procreation. Baal protects against the forces of destruction: the god of the sea, Yam; and the god of death, Mot. People experience the seasons with the return of fertility in the fall and winter rains as an act of Baal's power (Herrmann). Baal worship is reported within Israel in Judges (eleven times) and 1 Samuel (two times), but Ahab, influenced by his marriage alliance with Sidon though Jezebel, institutionalizes the Baal cult (1 Kings 16:31). So 1–2 Kings records the struggle that Yahwism had with Baal. The stories of Elijah (1 Kings 18–19), Jehu (2 Kings 10:18-28), and Jehoiada (who has the people destroy the Baal temple and kill Mattan the priest of Baal in Jerusalem, 11:18) attest to the popularity and persistence of the Baal cult among Israelites and Canaanites. The summary of the sins of Israel leading to exile mentions Baal explicitly (17:16). Manasseh erects altars to Baal (21:3), later destroyed by Josiah (23:4-5).

Asherah Associated with sacred wooden pillars or trees, the Asherah is a Canaanite goddess of the nations in the land before Israel (Deut 7:5; 12:3; 16:21; Judg 3:7). Asherah is prominent in Gideon's reforms, where she is associated with Baal worship (Judg 6:25, 26, 28, 30). In 1–2 Kings, Asherah is evidence of syncretism, associated with Jeroboam (1 Kings 14:15), Judah (14:23), Ahab (16:33; 18:19), Israel's sins leading to exile (2 Kings 17:10, 16), and Manasseh (21:3, 7). Hadley concludes that the pairing of Asherah and Baal is a Deuteronomistic attempt to discredit her cult and worship (207; so also Olyan: 22). The reformers Asa, Hezekiah, and Josiah remove Asherah (1 Kings 15:13; 2 Kings 18:4; 23:4, 6, 7, 14, 15), suggesting that Asherah was associated with the worship of Yahweh, though not among the reforming kings and the 1–2 Kings narrator. Inscriptions at two cultic centers in southern Judah, Khirbet el-Qom and Kuntillet Ajrud, associate Yahweh with the Asherah, leading to the possibility that some consider the Asherah as a consort of Yahweh (N. Wyatt; Day 1992a).

Nehushtan Hezekiah removes and breaks in pieces Nehushtan, the bronze serpent fashioned by Moses to bring healing from snakebites (Num 21:4-9; 2 Kings 18:4). An old Jebusite symbol, the bronze serpent was used generally in Palestine, Egypt, and Mesopotamia in the fertility cult with Asherah, the mother goddess, and believed to have powers of healing (Jones: 562).

Chariots of the Sun The sun chariot carried the mythical Assyrian sun god Shamash across the sky daily, drawn by four white horses that were also associated with the gods Ashur and Sin. Introduced by Ahaz, Manasseh, and Amon, the Mesopotamian cult gained popularity in Judah. Josiah removed and burned these chariots (2 Kings 23:11; Cogan and Tadmor: 288).

Teraphim Teraphim are household gods ranging in size from miniature to nearly life-size figures that pertained to household headship (Gen

31:19, 34-35; 1 Sam 19:13, 16; 2 Kings 23:24). Teraphim are associated with wizards and mediums (2 Kings 23:24) and divination (Judg 17-18; 1 Sam 15:23; Ezek 21:21).

KINGS IN THE HEBREW CANON

Kings and Deuteronomy The book of Deuteronomy is pivotal in the biblical narrative and foundational for understanding Kings. Deuteronomy, the last book of Torah, restates the creation mandate that humans do righteousness and justice (Gen 1:27; 18:19) to prepare God's people for life in the land. Deuteronomy—with its covenant stipulations, blessings, and curses—anticipates Israel's entry into Canaan, setting the standard for the teaching of the books that follow, Joshua, Judges, Samuel, and Kings (DtrH): love God by keeping covenant in practicing justice (Deut 5:1-21; 6:4-9; 10:12-21).

Deuteronomic justice draws the marginalized into the covenant people. God's people are to integrate misplaced persons lacking kinship ties into their social, juridical, liturgical, and economic community. Orphans, widows, and strangers are incorporated through the basic social unit in ancient Israel, the house of the father (*bet ab*). Every Israelite house is to welcome strangers in daily economic and social intercourse (Deut 15:1-17), in festival celebrations (16:11, 14; 26:11-15), and in covenant renewal (31:9-13; Glanville: 101, 107). Deuteronomic justice, *and only justice*, is the basic covenant stipulation, measured by how well Israel cares for marginalized people (16:19-20).

Anticipating kingship, Deuteronomy's "law of the king" prohibits accumulation of power, weaponry, and wealth and requires the king to practice Torah (17:14-20) *[Law of the King, p. 456]*. Deuteronomy enjoins centralized worship as a safeguard against idolatry, the ideological basis for typical royal justice, which is the antithesis of Deuteronomic justice (12:29-32). Because kings exercise primary influence over religious order, 1-2 Kings focuses on royal behavior regarding idolatry, exercise of power, and Torah faithfulness. Samuel warns that the monarchy ties the fortunes of the people to the faithfulness of their kings (1 Sam 12:14-15; 2 Kings 17:7-8, 21-23) *[Idolatry, p. 449]*.

Deuteronomy demands that Israel's institutions, centralized worship, king, priest, prophet, and Torah interpretation all contribute to Deuteronomic justice. The institutions themselves are subservient to, but not essential for, the practice of justice. Because the human vocation is articulated in creation itself prior to kingship and even Torah (Gen 1:27-29; 18:19), the narrative demonstrates that justice, not any institution, is foundational (McConville 2006). Before Israel enters the land, Deuteronomy presupposes that life in Palestine will end in exile: "when all these things have happened" (Deut 29:28; 30:1). Deuteronomy foresees not only exile but also restoration (30:2-5).

Kings in the Deuteronomistic History (DtrH) The writing of 1-2 Kings is the final installment of Israel's epic narrative known as the Former Prophets in the Hebrew canon. Scholars posit a Deuteronomistic History

(DtrH), proposing that Joshua, Judges, Samuel, and Kings narrate Israel's royal history, as informed by the covenant in Deuteronomy. The book of Joshua dynamically interprets Deuteronomic Torah for life in the land (Matties: 26). Torah reinterpretation welcomes nonethnic Israelites into the covenant people (Rahab and the Gibeonites, Josh 2, 6, 9; cf. Deut 7:1-5). Joshua, royal ideal for the reformer king Josiah, renews the covenant as his crowning achievement (Josh 24; 2 Kings 22–23). The book of Judges reports repeated periods of apostasy. Idolatry leads the people into subjection to enemies, followed by repentance, then divine deliverance (2:11-23). This downward trajectory (18:1; 19:1; 21:25) foreshadows the exile in 1–2 Kings. First and Second Samuel sets the stage for kingship. The elders request a king like the nations to lead them in battle (1 Sam 8). Warning about "the ways of the king" (*mišpaṭ*), Samuel insists that both king and people must obey the Lord. In 1–2 Kings, David is an exemplar; yet in 2 Samuel *the matter of Uriah the Hittite* (1 Kings 15:5) foreshadows judgment (i.e., "the sword will never depart from your house," 2 Sam 12:10).

Israel's failure to practice institutional justice kindles the Lord's anger, sending Israel to exile, as anticipated (Deut 29–30). Though 1–2 Kings concludes in exile, Moses' promise of return ameliorates hopeless despair (Deut 30:1-5). Thus 1–2 Kings invites Israel to reboot covenant faithfulness and fulfill the divine vocation of making justice.

Kings and the Prophets Prophets play a primary role in 1–2 Kings *[Prophets, p. 465]*. The most prominent, Elijah and Elisha, oppose Baal worship and proclaim Yahwistic justice. Two canonical writing prophets, Jonah and Isaiah, appear in 2 Kings. Jonah proclaims salvation for the wicked Jeroboam II, a message consistent with the canonical book (2 Kings 14:25-27; Jon 4:2). Isaiah's prominent role during Hezekiah's reign is narrated in nearly identical parallels (2 Kings 18–20; Isa 36–38). In this text resistance to Assyrian imperial pretension replaces cultic reform as the test of faithfulness. Jeremiah's ministry spans the time of Josiah's economic, political, and religious reform made possible by Assyrian withdrawal, and to the time preceding and including exile from Jerusalem (Jer 1:1-3; Martens 1986: 16). In addition to judgment oracles spoken during the time of and against Jerusalem's final kings, the book of Jeremiah narrates Jeremiah's interaction with Jehoiakim (Jer 26–27, 35–36) and Zedekiah (Jer 21, 32–34, 37–39) and the postexilic assassination of Gedaliah and flight to Egypt (Jer 40–44), supplementing 2 Kings 24–25.

The similarity between Jeremiah and 1–2 Kings suggests that the same editorial processes influenced both books and that Jeremiah and his scribe, Baruch, were leaders of the Deuteronomic theology movement. We find persuasive Doorly's hypothesis that the prophet Jeremiah is the author of 1–2 Kings, yet absent from 1–2 Kings to avoid raising issues that would distract from his theological aims (147).

Though not mentioned in 1–2 Kings, the canonical prophets Hosea, Amos, Micah, and Zephaniah prophesy between 750 BCE and the exile. These latter prophets proclaim the message of 1–2 Kings: humans are to pursue righteousness, justice, peace, and covenant loyalty.

Kings and the Writings The Writings (the Ketuvim in the Hebrew Bible) interest the reader of Kings as the source of Solomonic wisdom [*Wisdom in Kings, p. 484*] and because Chronicles retells the story of the kings of Judah, apparently using 1–2 Kings as a source. Proverbs provides examples of the thousands of Solomon's proverbs (1 Kings 4:32; Prov 1:1; 10:1; 25:1). Ecclesiastes identifies its author as *Qoholeth* (Heb. for "teacher" or "assembler"), "son of David, king in Jerusalem" (Eccl 1:1). Though Solomon's name does not appear in the book, the autobiographical musings fit the genre of "royal testimony" of one who finds success "vain" (1:12–2:26; Brueggemann 2005: 202). Reflecting on the vanity of a life of accomplishment, Qoholeth concludes with a call to fear God, obey God's commands, and accept that God is judge (12:13–14). Song of Songs may be associated with Solomon because of his large harem (1:1; 1 Kings 11:3). According to one interpretation, Song of Songs criticizes Solomon's commodification of love while celebrating the beauty of committed romance (Brueggemann 2005: 212–13). Psalm 72, labeled "of Solomon," calls for justice, including the care of the poor, needy, and oppressed, reinforcing the call to justice in 1–2 Kings.

Kings and Chronicles First and Second Chronicles overlaps substantially with the historical period reported in Kings, raising questions about the relationship between them. The distinct audiences and contexts of the two texts leads to distinct purposes. Kings is composed for the immediate exile, accounting for the reason Jerusalem was destroyed and Judah exiled. Chronicles addresses returned exiles about a century later, offering them hope by showing how individual kings repent and are restored (Schweitzer: 125). The author(s) of Chronicles, called the Chronicler, reworks material found in Kings, offering reassessment of past stories. While Kings gives primary attention to the divided kingdom and the prophets Elijah and Elisha, Chronicles focuses on David and Solomon. Unlike the portrayal of Solomon in 1 Kings 1–11, Chronicles depicts Solomon as exemplary in building the temple. Manasseh, whom 2 Kings 21–24 holds responsible for the Judean exile, is portrayed as a repentant king who did much to restore Judah (Konkel 2016: 24). The temple is treated differently in Kings and in Chronicles. In Kings the temple is located chronologically, its construction placed midway between the exodus from Egypt and the exile in Babylon (1 Kings 6:1). Chronicles emphasizes the temple location spatially, connecting it with God's covenant with Abraham and the test of his faith on Mount Moriah and with David's sacrifice on the threshing floor of Ornan (2 Chron 3:1; Gen 22:17-18; 1 Chron 21:28). Chronicles emphasizes that the temple is the vehicle for change, hope, and new possibilities (Schweitzer: 133–35).

Structurally, Chronicles differs from Kings by opening with genealogies and family lists from the inception of human existence with Adam (1 Chron 1–9), retelling the death of Saul and the reign of David (chs. 10–22, 28–29), and listing temple and palace officers (chs. 23–27). Kings concludes with a postscript about the king's place in Babylonian exile (2 Kings 25:27-30); Chronicles concludes with Cyrus's proclamation to restore

Jerusalem and Judah (2 Chron 36:21-23). Canonically, Chronicles is the final book in the Hebrew Bible, following the report of postexilic activities in Jerusalem in Ezra and Nehemiah. Second Chronicles reports the reign of Solomon (chs. 1–9), Israel's rebellion against Rehoboam (chs. 10–11), and the rest of the kings of Judah (chs. 12–36), almost without reference to Israel (Ahab's death is an incident in Jehoshaphat's reign, ch. 18). Prophets play significant roles in both Kings and Chronicles, with each reinterpreting Hebrew prophecy in ways that are "faithful representations of the broader traditions' interpretation of prophets and prophecy in the monarchic period" (Person 2013: 198–99). Though scholars debate whether the source of Chronicles was an earlier edition of 1–2 Kings or a source common to both, there is consensus that Kings was written before Chronicles.

Ancient history writing considers God's control of history and the faithfulness of God's people in covenant as primary causes for present circumstances, with lessons to be learned from past actions (Konkel 2016: 23). The Chronicler uses midrash to create new meaning from old texts, an interpretation of his sources through his own theological perspective to provide hope for the fifth-century Persian province Yehud (formerly Judah and Jerusalem). According to Konkel, the community faces several primary questions: "How could they be true to their ancestral faith as a subordinate people, permanently under the control of an imperial power? How can a subject people be the people of God? What did the promise of the eternal throne of David mean under these circumstances?" (2016: 26). In answer, the Chronicler explains why the kingdom of David had failed and how the struggling state of Yehud in the mighty Persian Empire can become the promised kingdom of David (2016: 32). The Chronicler helps the community maintain hope for the realization of the promise to David in historical terms, using the fixed points of proper and legitimate patterns of institutions and their personnel: the monarchy of David, the priesthood of Zadok, the city of Jerusalem, the temple of Solomon (2016: 34–35). The primary concerns are proper worship that takes place in the temple, the center of the Lord's kingdom on earth, purity among the holy worshiping community, and obedience to the word of God (2016: 36–37). God's people are the religious community worshiping at the Jerusalem temple (Nelson 1998: 78). Sweeney concludes that both DtrH (Kings) and the Chronicler appear to have their basis in history; both display theological perspectives that interpret events (2007b: 276).

LAW OF THE KING The law of the king outlines the Deuteronomic ideal for kingship (Deut 17:14-20). The law is organized in three parts. Part 1: Moses gives permission for eventual kingship (17:14-15). Part 2: three prohibitions limit the scope of kingship (17:16-17). Part 3: the king's positive requirement is that he keep Torah (17:18-20).

With the expectation that Israel will establish kingship like the nations, part 1 requires that the king be chosen by the Lord, a *brother*, not a foreigner (17:14-15). The law warns against having a "king like the nations," an anti-egalitarian despot who exercises power with ANE administrative strategies. Samuel warns the people that the king's administration *[Mišpaṭ, p. 461]* will be one of accumulation (1 Sam 8:10-18). The word *brother* warns against foreign alliances or domination and anticipates egalitarian administration. To be a *brother* distinguishes the Israelite king from the ANE potentates who proclaim themselves divine (Morgenstern: li). The law shapes how royal responsibility is fulfilled (Gerbrandt 2015: 334).

Part 2 prohibits accumulation that characterizes "a king like the nations." First, the law prohibits acquiring many "horses"; chariots and horses represent the military establishment, requiring a costly infrastructure (17:16) *[Horses and Chariots, p. 447]*. Second, an excessive number of wives is prohibited, not as sound marital advice, but because the king's "heart will turn away" (17:17). Foreign alliances were sealed with marriage. With foreign wives came worship shrines functioning much as foreign embassies. Third, accumulation of material resources is forbidden (17:17). Deuteronomy requires Israel to share wealth; the administrative aim of the ANE monarch is to accumulate wealth and power. The Israelite king is to protect the marginalized, not create a system of economic inequality.

Part 3 requires the king to make a copy of Torah and to read it every day to learn to fear the Lord and to keep the law (17:18-20). The king is to support worship in the place the Lord designates and to provide justice. Torah requires king and people to live out their human vocation by practicing justice for the marginalized.

The law of the king is the standard for measuring kings in 1-2 Kings. King Solomon fails at every turn. Despite warnings to keep the law, he breaks all three prohibitions in grand scale and gives little evidence of reading Torah. The kings of both Israel and Judah build up their military and accumulate wealth. Only a few reformer kings in Judah (notably Hezekiah and Josiah) give attention to Torah. DtrH uses Hezekiah and Josiah as models for kingship, ascribing two very significant roles to the king: covenant administrator and leadership in times of military crisis, guiding Israel to trust in the Lord (Gerbrandt 1986: 115–16, 190). Assuming for the law a seventh-century BCE context in the shadow of the Assyrian Empire, Dutcher-Walls argues that the law of the king served the interests of nonroyal Judean elites who were trying to avoid further Assyrian domination (2002: 615–16). Almost without exception the kings of both nations fail to meet the standard of the law of the king.

LITERARY CRITICISM Kings is mainly recorded in prose. As a subgenre of prose, lists are embedded in narrative descriptions of Solomon's administration (1 Kings 4:1-19) and temple building (7:41-45, 48-50). Poetry is also found within embedded speeches (e.g., 2 Kings 19:21-34). The literary matrix in which these subgenres are found is narrative.

Narrative

The work of 1-2 Kings narrates the story of Israel from Solomon to Judah's exile in Babylon. The study of narrative includes plot (a story that resolves a problem), characterization, theme, and point of view. Thus 1-2 Kings is historiography, relating the story of Israel and Judah during the period of its kings. A primary question of historiography is, Did it happen? The citation of sources—primarily the Book of the Annals of the Kings of Judah (e.g., 1 Kings 14:29) and the Book of the Annals of the Kings of Israel (e.g., 14:19)—of years and dates, and of contemporary nations and kings, creates verisimilitude, the appearance of history. One typical feature of Hebrew narrative is that the plot is carried by dialogue (e.g., 1 Kings 14:4-16), distinguishing it from modern history writing. By its nature, historiography is an interpretive enterprise characterized by selection of events worthy of notice, organization (chronological), and causation (including both sociological and supernatural causes in Kings; Nelson 1998: 21-24). "Happenedness" is complicated by the problems of selection of material, meaning, point of view, and fact (Fretheim: 1983: 28-29).

Elements of Narrative

Plot and tension. Plot moves in linear arc from equilibrium through tension (destabilization) to new stability. "*Tension is what impels a plot: What happens next?*" (J. T. Walsh 2009: 14; italic in the original). Individual units (episodes or scenes) exhibit similar dynamics in service to the larger narrative arc (2009: 14). The plotline of 1-2 Kings moves from the reign of David's heir Solomon (1 Kings 1-11), through the divided kingdom (1 Kings 12-2 Kings 16), to the exiles of Israel (2 Kings 17) and Judah (2 Kings 18-25). The tension of the plot is how the nation moved from covenant promises to exile. The perspective of Kings is that the exile was the Lord's righteous judgment on a disobedient people. An example of how a scene exhibits plot that serves the larger narrative arc is the story of Solomon's judgment of the two mothers (1 Kings 3:16-28). The immediate question has to do with identifying the mother of the living baby, but when the narrator tells the audience who the mother is, the question shifts to how Solomon discerns the mother. The story serves the larger plot of Solomon's reign: Will Solomon rule wisely and justly (1 Kings 2:4-9)? This in turn serves the larger narrative arc of Kings: Will Israel live faithfully in covenant with the Lord?

Characterization. Characters are revealed primarily through actions and speech. The kings are the primary characters and tend to either do right or do evil, with some mitigating issues. The other human characters are the prophets, notably Elijah and Elisha. Though at first reading both prophets seem to be reliable characters, one reading raises questions about the reliability not only of Elijah and Elisha but also of all prophets (Kissling: 96-199). Prophetic deceit may be a narrative strategy questioning prophetic reliability (e.g., 1 Kings 13:8; 22:20-23; Kissling: 132-35). God, the Lord, communicates directly with Solomon and the prophets and through the prophets and the narrator to other characters and the readers (e.g., 2 Kings 17:35-39). Other recurring characters include priests, prophets and sons of the prophets, the people, and the people of the land. Women characters with speaking roles are prominent, including Bathsheba, two women who are prostitutes, the queen of Sheba, the widow of Zarephath, the Shunammite, the Israelite girl who serves Naaman's wife, the mother of the cannibalized son, Jezebel, Athaliah, and the prophetess Huldah. Other women are silent, including several wives, concubines, and queen mothers [Women in Kings, p. 485].

Point of view. The point of view of the narrator is often omniscient, able to recount conversation that God has with other characters as well as self-talk (e.g., Jeroboam in 1 Kings 12:26-27; J. T. Walsh 2009: 47–50). Within a scene the point of view may alternate, as in 1 Kings 3:16-28, from omniscient, to the king, to the women, and back to omniscient. The narrator reports most action without evaluative interpretation. The account of the exile and the royal formulas are the primary elements of the narrative, with explicit evaluation of the characters.

One means of conveying shifts in point of view is the term traditionally rendered *Behold!* The Hebrew interjection *Behold!* (*hinneh*) is a demonstrative particle used more than one hundred times in 1-2 Kings (e.g., 1 Kings 1:22; 3:21). The term expresses surprise and indicates a change in perspective by putting the reader in the perspective of one of the characters, showing readers the scene through the character's eyes (Bar-Efrat: 36; J. T. Walsh 2009: 49).

Divine speeches. In 1-2 Kings the Lord's speech reinforces Deuteronomic theology. When God speaks directly to Solomon (3:11-14; 6:11-13; 9:1-9; 11:11-13) and in judgment of Solomon through the prophet Ahijah (11:31-39), the vocabulary echoes the book of Deuteronomy, using such phrases as *keep my statutes and my commandments/ordinances* (1 Kings 3:14; 9:4); *walk in my statutes, obey my ordinances, and keep all my commandments by walking in them* (6:12); *[keep] my covenant and my statutes that I have commanded you* (11:11); *[walk] in my ways, doing what is right in my sight and keeping my statutes and my ordinances* (11:33, 38). Though no prophet addresses Solomon, the narrator employs speeches of the Lord to articulate the Deuteronomic perspective.

Literary devices. Another term, *please*, used nearly fifty times in Kings (e.g., 1 Kings 1:12; 2:17), also is frequently untranslated; it indicates respect or submission. One Hebraism that is not readily translated is the infinitive absolute, a doubling of the verb to indicate intensity. Wordplays, such as homonyms, are difficult to translate (artful intentionality is also difficult to ascertain). While wordplays in English are often weak attempts at humor (puns), in Hebrew the form is not play but a "reflection of the profound interconnectedness of all reality" and "ties together disparate texts" (J. T. Walsh 1996: xvi). An example is the narrative play on the name Solomon (*Shelomoh*) when Ahijah speaks of the torn garment (*salmah*) that doubles *as* a sign of Solomon's torn kingdom (1 Kings 11:29-32).

Narrative Subgenres

Legend. Legend is a biblical genre purportedly arising from oral folklore and storytelling and is aimed at edification concerned with the wondrous, miraculous, or exemplary (Long 1985: 252). Scholars often characterize the miracle stories of Elijah (1 Kings 17–19) and Elisha (2 Kings 2:19-23; 4:1-7, 38-44; 6:17; 13:20-21) as prophetic legend (see "Miracle stories" below). At times, legend connotes fiction rather than a historical event, avoiding the scandal of prophetic violence (1 Kings 18:40; 2 Kings 2:24), but this connotation is not always present, thus leaving this scandal unresolved. In form criticism, the label identifies short stories that come from oral collections used to characterize the antiroyal message of the prophets. The folkloric legend often employs two exact repetitions followed by a third that deviates from the first two (e.g. 2 Kings 1; Alter: 531).

Miracle stories. Miracle stories (see "Legend" above) follow an intuitive form: problem identified, solution offered, evidence of the miracle, human response. A miracle that follows the form is Elijah's raising of the widow's son (1 Kings 17:17-24). The widow informs Elijah that her son has died (problem; 17:17-18). Elijah prays and the boy's life returns (solution; 17:19-22). Elijah returns the boy to his mother (evidence: 17:23). The woman confesses the truth regarding the Lord and his prophet (response: 17:24).

Type-scene. A basic convention of biblical narrative, a type-scene is a fixed situation where several prominent elements are included in repetitive compositional patterns, such as the betrothal of a girl at the well (Alter: 358). In 1–2 Kings the type-scene of a king receiving a prophetic oracle predicting death occurs four times (Jeroboam, 1 Kings 14; Ahaziah, 2 Kings 1; Ben-hadad, 2 Kings 8:7-15; Hezekiah, 2 Kings 20:1-7). The variation from the repetitive pattern typically points to the unique message: for example, Hezekiah alone recovers after receiving the prophetic death oracle.

Poetry: Prophetic Oracles

Unlike biblical books with freestanding poems (e.g., Psalms), the poetry in Kings is embedded, usually in speeches occurring during the flow of narrative.

Judgment speech typically follow a simple pattern: messenger formula (*Hear the word of the* LORD), accusation (or indictment: naming the offense or sin of the accused), announcement of judgment (sentence: consequences), often concluded with an abbreviated messenger formula (*says the* LORD). An early prophetic judgment oracle is delivered by the old prophet of Bethel to the man of God from Judah (1 Kings 13:21-22).

Salvation oracles follow this typical pattern: self-declaration (fulfilled by messenger formula, *Thus says the* LORD); assurance (*Fear not! I am with you*); promise (*I will deliver* X *into your hand*). The false prophets of Ahab offer a counterfeit salvation oracle (1 Kings 22:12).

Lament is the most common prayer form in the Psalms. Prayers in Kings are typically laments. The form usually includes address ("O LORD"), complaint (an enemy threatens), plea (invocation of the Lord's deliverance), statement of confidence, and praise. The first three elements of the lament are evident in Elijah's prayer for the widow's son (1 Kings 17:20-21). Elijah address the Lord (*O* LORD), issues a complaint (*Have you brought calamity . . . by killing her son?*), and makes a plea (*Let this child's life come into him again*).

Mišpaṭ The Hebrew word *mišpaṭ* (justice) describes what is right in Israel, equity and compassion for the powerless, an orientation that protects the cause of marginalized person in society (J. P. Walsh: 31). *Mišpaṭ* refers "to the restoration of a situation or environment which promoted equity and harmony (*shalom*) in a community" (Mafico: 1128). The verb *šapaṭ* (to judge) means upholding the rights due every individual in the community (Malchow: 16). J. P. Walsh connects the term to the exercise of power, "the way people dealt with one another, especially in the economic and political sphere" (31). Walsh offers the shorthand definition "having the say" and places the term within a word cradle that includes relationship (covenant), the moral consensus (righteousness), and the ideal world (shalom; 31). Biblical justice is social justice, concerned with restoration of equilibrium to society by aiding the needy; though not excluding the juridical sense of the word, it is relevant for the sociopolitical leaders who create and execute laws (Weinfeld 1995: 43-44).

Biblical justice is Yahwistic justice, protection of the marginalized, but the biblical story presents the issue of justice as a contested value, aware that "having the say" in the exercise of power need not result in obedience to the Lord's command to protect the weak. "Royal justice," a counter-justice system, neglects the marginalized to the advantage of the violent, the wealthy, the powerful. "Each king had to decide between acting as a just ruler who adjudicated disputes of all kinds (1 Kgs 3) and a ruinous tyrant who looted the country for political gain (1 Kgs 21; 2 Kgs 15:19-20)" (Master: 516).

Righteousness and justice (a hendiadys: word pair with a single meaning) are implicit in the creation mandate to humans created in the image of God to *have dominion* (McConville 2006: 32). Genesis reinforces this focus at key junctures (7:1; 12:3). The Lord declares that Abraham "shall become a great and mighty nation, and all the earth shall be blessed in him . . . that he may charge his children and his household after him to keep the way of the LORD by doing righteousness and justice" (18:18-19). The human vocation, doing righteousness and justice, precedes Moses' call to Israel in Deuteronomy; justice-doing is essential to the universal human vocation. Informed by that vocational mandate, reading the story from Genesis to

Kings clarifies the purpose of 1–2 Kings (McConville 2006: 32; Peckham: 519). The issue of 1–2 Kings is not the future of the Davidic dynasty, not the place of the Torah as the constitution for Israel, not the possibility of return to the land from exile, nor any of the other crucial questions implicitly raised by 1–2 Kings. The interpretive key is that the human mandate to do justice is broader than questions of Israelite institutions (royalty, Torah, land, prophets, temple; McConville 2006: 163).

Deuteronomy equates justice with prioritized care for the marginalized (orphan, widow, alien). Deuteronomy 10:12-22 articulates that the Lord "executes justice" for the marginalized. Israel is to love, serve, and obey the Lord by acting on the Lord's *mišpaṭ* priority for the alien. To "do justice" (Ps 10:18) and to love God are inseparable acts. Covenant stipulations demand generous treatment of the poor (e.g., Deut 15:1-18). The "law of the king" enjoins the king to read Torah and to abstain from accumulation of wealth, weapons, and wives (creating hardships for a populace constrained to support such policies; 17:14-20) *[Law of the King, p. 456]*.

The concept of just dealing is greater than the single term most often translated *justice*; the richness of the term is communicated in the commentary by using the Hebrew transliteration. The noun *mišpaṭ* occurs 24 times in 1–2 Kings (of 241 times in the OT). The corresponding verb *šapaṭ* is used 8 times in Kings (OT uses: 203 times). English translations frequently seek to convey the meaning with words or phrases that fit the context but dull the point of the Hebrew term. For example, the theme of *mišpaṭ* is advanced in the narrative of the elders' request for a king who will "govern" (*špṭ*) like the nations (1 Sam 8:4-9). Though Samuel objects, the Lord orders him to listen to them—and to show them "the ways" (*mišpaṭ*) of the king. Samuel tells the people, "These will be the ways [*mišpaṭ*] of the king," warning that the king will accumulate at the people's expense (1 Sam 8:10-18). Competing royal and Yahwistic administrative strategies are conveyed by the Hebrew word *mišpaṭ*. Though frequently masked in English, the ironic use of the term *mišpaṭ* deconstructs the imperial power play in 1–2 Kings.

In his charge to Solomon, David is the first to use the term *mišpaṭ* in Kings. David seeks to motivate faithful covenant partnership with the Lord. He tells his son Solomon to *keep the charge of the LORD your God, . . . keeping his statutes, his commandments, his mišpaṭ* [pl.], *and his testimonies, as it is written in the Torah of Moses"* (1 Kings 2:2-3 AT). *Keeping [guarding] mišpaṭ* requires Deuteronomic exercise of power. (Ironically, David shifts abruptly to counsel the *wise* Solomon to eliminate his enemies, 2:5-9.)

In the inaugural dream, God appears to Solomon to offer him anything he desires (3:1-15). Solomon asks for a *listening heart to špṭ [govern; do justice for]* the people (3:9 AT). God approves, commending Solomon for asking for skill to do *mišpaṭ* (3:11). The words of King David (2:2-4) and of the Lord (3:11) set the agenda: royal success depends on doing godly *mišpaṭ*. Whitelam argues that the concept of godly royal justice (the just king) is fundamental to understanding monarchy (219). The ideal royal judge cares for the underprivileged, but "monarchical judicial authority was 'alien' to Israelite society," and "the monarchy gave rise to new categories," including Solomonic "internalization of God-given justice within the king," replacing other judicial institutions (220). The English translations make the centrality of *justice* apparent in two texts. First, immediately after the dream narrative, royal wisdom resolves a case of criminal justice where two marginalized women (prostitutes) are fighting over the death of an infant (3:16-28). The king's wisdom is harnessed to the task of *doing justice*—the noun *mišpaṭ* and the verb *špṭ* are used together in the conclusion (3:28). Second, the powerful foreigner, the queen of Sheba, after witnessing Solomon's great accumulation of wealth and wisdom, reminds the king that his wisdom has been given for doing *mišpaṭ* and righteousness (10:1-13). The first story demonstrates that *mišpaṭ* protects marginalized members of the kingdom; in the second a foreign woman reminds Solomon that royal rule succeeds when God's justice prevails.

Yet English translations mask other uses of the word *mišpaṭ*. First Kings 4:1-28 describes Solomon's administration, listing royal officials (4:1-19) and reporting Solomon's imperial magnificence (4:20-28). The report attributes royal wealth to tribute payments delivered by subservient nations, contributing to peace and prosperity throughout Judah and Israel (4:21, 24). The report clarifies that *those officials* (over the twelve districts in Israel, 4:7-19) supply provisions (4:27-28). The English translation of the sentence concludes that these provisions are brought *each according to his charge* (NRSV; NIV: *quotas*), muting the Hebrew, *each according to his mišpaṭ*. The *mišpaṭ* of 1 Kings 4:1-28 is imperial Solomon's accumulation, a mockery of the Deuteronomic justice demanded by the Lord. Seibert attributes the use of *mišpaṭ* here as well as other ironies in 1 Kings 1–11 to "subversive scribes."

The Lord's speech to Solomon regarding temple construction prioritizes *mišpaṭ* (6:11-13). *As for this house that you are building* (6:12 AT), the Lord begins. Instead of expected instruction related to temple construction, the speech veers from the temple toward covenant keeping, continuing, *If you will walk in my statutes, obey my ordinances* [*mišpaṭ* pl.]*, and keep all my commandments by walking in them, then I will establish my promise with you* (6:12). The Lord concludes that he will *dwell among* the people, without additional reference to the house (6:13). Though the building report takes up the middle third of the Solomon narrative, the Lord's interest is in Torah and its *mišpaṭ*, not the temple. After the temple dedication, the Lord appears to Solomon again (9:1-9). The Lord declares that he has consecrated the house (9:3), continuing, *As for you, if you will walk . . . , keeping my statutes and my ordinances* [*mišpaṭ* pl.]*, then I will establish your royal throne over Israel forever* (9:4-5). The speeches function as bookends, bracketing the temple construction and dedication, prioritizing *mišpaṭ* and Torah over the temple.

The word *mišpaṭ* appears twice more in the temple-building report, first reporting that it was finished *according to all its specifications* (*mišpaṭ* in 6:38), and later both verb (*špṭ*) and noun (*mišpaṭ*) refer to the construction of a hall of justice (7:7). Though Solomon's practice of *mišpaṭ* may be suspect, the construction report confirms that the king's role includes a judicial function.

The most concentrated use of *mišpaṭ* and *špṭ* occurs in the dedicatory temple prayer (8:32, 45, 49, 58, 59 [twice]). McConville provides the key to understanding *mišpaṭ*. He notes that Israel is the covenant people whom God has delivered from imperial domination (8:51). He declares that this reveals the vocational identity of the people of God, arguing that vocational identity, not survival of the people in the land nor the temple nor the Davidic line nor even the Torah itself, is central. This use of *mišpaṭ* reveals that the true nature of Israel depends on commitment to justice (8:51; McConville 2006: 163). The blessing that follows asks that the Lord incline Israel to keep the *mišpaṭ* (ordinances) and that the Lord execute the *mišpaṭ* of his servant and his people (8:59). The prayer concludes by emphasizing that Israel's faithfulness to its vocational identity (doing *mišpaṭ*) will reveal to all the peoples of the earth that the Lord is the one God (8:60).

Ahijah's oracle to Jeroboam indicts Solomon for idolatry and rejecting the Lord's Torah (*mišpaṭ*, 11:33). The other gods are linked with royal *mišpaṭ* and thus are in opposition to the Lord's *mišpaṭ [Idolatry, p. 449]*. False worship links the kings with the gods, authorizing royal control of community resources. The people's rejection of Rehoboam is linked to imperial social policy of high taxes and forced labor (1 Kings 12).

The contest on Mount Carmel contrasts the *custom* (*mišpaṭ*) of the Baal prophets (1 Kings 18:28) with Elijah's confession that the Lord is God. The king falls into the prophet's trap by declaring *mišpaṭ* (*judgment*) on himself (20:40). King Ahaziah asks about *what sort [mišpaṭ] of* man the prophet (Elijah) is (2 Kings 1:7). King Joash stands by the temple pillar *according to the custom [mišpaṭ]* as the priest Jehoiada renews covenant with the Lord, the people, and the king (11:14). The verb *špṭ* is used to report that King Jotham *governs* in place of his father (15:5) and refers to the period of judges (23:22).

The analysis of the Israelite exile uses *mišpaṭ* eight times (2 Kings 17:26 [twice], 27, 33, 34 [twice], 37, 40). The immigrants who resettle Samaria are ignorant of the *mišpaṭ* of the Lord, mixing the *mišpaṭ* of the gods of the nations with that of the Lord (*mišpaṭ*; 17:26-34). The Lord recalls that he had delivered Israel from Egypt, made a covenant with them, and given them his *mišpaṭ* (17:35-39). The chapter concludes by reporting that the new immigrants continued to practice their former customs (*mišpaṭ*).

The reading of 1–2 Kings in this commentary centers on *mišpaṭ*. Exercise of political power from Genesis to Kings is defined by *mišpaṭ*. Created in God's image, humans represent God's rule on earth by governing ("having the say") as the Lord does. Deuteronomy defines *mišpaṭ*, political and economic order that protects the marginalized, grounded in the practices of the Lord meant to be followed by the people (Deut 10:12-22; Dempsey: 84). Thus 1–2 Kings evaluates both the kings and the people based on their pursuit of the justice of the Lord.

PEOPLE OF THE LAND The people of the land appear in the narrative with no introduction, suggesting either that they may be a group familiar to the reader or that the term may be a general expression with no technical meaning (Nicholson: 66). The political agenda of *the people* (the term used fourteen times in 1 Kings 12) is to coronate kings, preferably Davidides with covenantal limits (Deut 17:14-20; 2 Sam 5:3; 1 Kings 1:39-40; 12:1-2; 2 Kings 11:12; 23:3). The Davidic preference accounts for Jeroboam's fears that *this people* will turn to Rehoboam (1 Kings 12:26-27).

One suggestion is that the people of the land are landed tribal traditionalists whose interests oppose powerful officials and high-placed pressure groups, which are "the feudal administration of Jerusalem as a crown estate" (Gray: 577–78; Reviv: 146). If that description is apt, the opponents of these tribal traditionalists would be the king's servants, beneficiaries of royal land grants who receive crown land—land secured from conquest, political rivals, and judicial action—in return for political loyalty (2 Sam 5:7-25; 8:1-14; 9:7, 9; 16:4; 19:29; 1 Kings 21). The interests of the people of the land correspond with the elders who demanded kingship (1 Sam 8). Having learned from Samuel's description of "the ways [*mišpaṭ*] of the king" (8:9-18), from covenants made with Saul (10:25) and David (2 Sam 5:3), and from Solomon's administrative policies (1 Kings 4:20-28; 5:13-18; 12:4), *the people of the land* favor Davidic royal reformers who abide by the Deuteronomic covenant. These rural landowners apparently support prophets who condemn the "manifest destiny" engineered by the palace elite, absentee urban landlords who have "added land to land" (Isa 5:7-9 AT; Doorly; Premnath). Another suggestion is that *the people* are "an elite social group, probably wealthy, whose loyalty was necessary to secure the new regime" (Cohn 2000: 80).

On this issue, 1–2 Kings itself describes the people of the land as a sociopolitical element loyal to David's line who intervene to block coups by palace officials and ensure the accession of the rightful king (e.g., Joash against Athaliah, 2 Kings 11:1-16, 20; Amaziah over Joash's servants, 12:19-21; Azariah over Amaziah's conspirators, 14:19-21; perhaps Azariah/Jotham, 15:5; Josiah over Amon's conspirators, 21:23-24; Jehoahaz son of Josiah, 23:30). Supportive of the covenantal temple reformers Joash and Josiah, the people of the land "embody a conservative political constituency sympathetic to Josiah's Torah religion and anti-Egyptian politics" (Brueggemann 2000: 567). The people of the land have sufficient resources to be patrons of burnt offerings (16:15) and to finance tribute demanded by Pharaoh (23:35) but are decimated in Jerusalem's collapse (24:14; 25:3, 19-21).

PROPHETS Prophets are spokespersons for God. Deuteronomy prescribes leaders for Israel, including Levites, judges, kings, and prophets (Deut 16:18–18:22). The Lord tells Moses that he will raise up prophets like Moses who will speak to the people everything that the Lord commands (18:15-22). As a counterweight to kings, prophets are political actors coterminous with monarchy and function in response to kings (Hanson: 218). They demand a return to Torah (219). Of the 316 times the word *prophet* (*nabiʾ*) is used in the Old Testament, half are found in Jeremiah (85 times) and 1–2 Kings (74 times).

Wilson posits that central prophets function inside the accepted political and religious power structures while peripheral prophets do not have court or cult credentials (1980: 184). As the father of the nation of Israel, Moses is a central prophet who mediates covenant, produces law, directs cultic practices, and speaks with God face-to-face. He limits the office of king (Deut 17:14-20). As a central prophet, Samuel acts as priest (1 Sam 7:3-11), military leader (7:7-14), and judge (7:15). Samuel establishes the monarchy (8:19-22; as seer, 9:9). He contrasts the mišpaṭ of the king to that of the Lord (8:10-18) and makes a covenant that sets mišpaṭ between the king and the people (10:25-26) [Mišpaṭ, p. 461]. Samuel anoints the first king, Saul (chs. 8–12), then deposes him (chs. 13–15) and anoints David his successor (chs. 15–16). With access to David, the "central" prophets Gad (22:5; also a seer, 2 Sam 24:11-12) and Nathan (7:2; 12:25) mediate the word of the Lord to David in critical moments. Nathan delivers the Lord's promise of covenant and a long dynasty to David (7:4-17) and helps install Solomon, David's successor (1 Kings 1:11-27, 32-40).

After the coronation of Solomon reported in the Succession Narrative (1 Kings 1–2), prophets are absent from the Solomon report and assume a peripheral, antagonistic posture to kingship (3:1–11:25). Ahijah the prophet of Shiloh, a kingmaker in the tradition of Samuel, announces that Solomon's rule over Israel is torn from him because he fails to administer mišpaṭ; Ahijah names Jeroboam as Solomon's successor with ten of the tribes (11:26-40). Shiloh, like Shechem and Anathoth, is a traditional tribal home of Levitical priests and prophets outside the central religious establishment in Jerusalem; they limit royal power through covenant stipulations demanding mišpaṭ (Deut 17:14-20; Josh 24:1; 1 Sam 3:21; 1 Kings 2:26; 11:29; 12:1; Wilson 1980: 185). Shemaiah the man of God, who demands Rehoboam's retreat (12:21-24), is characterized as a member of the central religious establishment (2 Chron 12:5-15; Wilson 1980: 187).

The dramatic tale of the peripheral prophets (the man of God from Judah and the old prophet of Israel) and Jeroboam interrupts the political history to establish that royal power is subject to the word of the LORD (1 Kings 13:1-32) [Prophets: Prophetic Word, p. 469]. Ironically, the death of the disobedient man of God authenticates his message, foreshadowing its fulfillment through Josiah (2 Kings 23:15-16; Wilson 1980: 190).

Throughout the story of Israel (1 Kings 13–2 Kings 17) the man of God/ prophet from the periphery confronts and limits centralized royal power and that of its false prophets. Ahijah announces judgment against Jeroboam and exile for Israel because of his sins (1 Kings 14:6-14). Another kingmaking prophet, Jehu son of Hanani, proclaims judgment against the Israelite kings Baasha and Elah because they follow the ways of Jeroboam (16:1-13).

Elijah and his protégé Elisha dominate most of the story in 1 Kings 17–2 Kings 13, roughly one-third of the narrative of Kings. As peripheral prophets opposed to the centralized Baal cult, Elijah and Elisha are foils to the kings of Israel. They counter the mišpaṭ of Baal (and of Jeroboam) with the mišpaṭ of the Deuteronomic covenant. Elijah is the lone prophet who opposes the false prophets of Baal and Asherah on Mount Carmel (1 Kings 18:19-40). Elisha's ministry is closely associated with the prophetic guild. Elijah and Elisha are each identified as a man of God (the term applies as well to anonymous characters who bring prophesy during their ministry, 17:18, 24; 20:28; 2 Kings 7:17, 18, 19; 8:2, 4, 7, 8, 11) and as a *prophet* (also of their anonymous allies, 1 Kings 18:4, 13, 22, 36; 19:10, 14, 16; 20:13, 22, 35, 38, 41).

Sons of the Prophets The *sons of the prophets* (company of prophets) are participants in an association with an undefined structure that includes Elijah and Elisha as members and likely leaders. They are impoverished, often food insecure (each miracle story resolves a problem of material need). The prophets apparently support systems that provide for the marginalized rather than the enrichment of the elite (see 1 Kings 12). Though neither Elijah nor Elisha is a Levite, motifs such as offering sacrifice (18:30, 38) and their concern for worship of Yahweh as God of creation and God of Israel associate them with priestly beliefs and practices (Sweeney 2013: 48–49). This political and theological stance may contribute to their marginalization (see Obadiah and Jezebel's conflict about the prophets in 1 Kings 18).

The *sons of the prophets* (AT) are mentioned eleven times in 1–2 Kings (1 Kings 20:35; 2 Kings 2:3, 5, 7, 15; 4:1, 38 [twice], 5:22; 6:1; 9:1). The first reference is to one of the sons of the prophets who independently confronts the king of Israel for sparing the life of King Ben-hadad of Aram (1 Kings 20:35-43). This reference is an outlier, the only report of an action initiated by one of the sons of the prophets in confronting a king. The other ten references to the sons of the prophets mention them in relation to Elisha. In the only other reference to their activity related to kings, Elisha commands one of the sons of the prophets to anoint Jehu (2 Kings 9:1-10). Within those two framing narratives, the references allude to community life. As Elijah and Elisha travel through Bethel and Jericho to cross the Jordan, groups of the sons of the prophets meet them at each stop (2:3, 5, 7). The third contingent of prophets numbers fifty men of valor who later insist on searching for Elijah (2:7, 15-18). Each of the remaining stories related to the sons of the prophets assumes that Elisha leads and helps provide for them. Elisha empowers a widow facing debt slavery to pay her debts (4:1-7). He feeds the sons of the prophets facing famine (4:38-44). Elisha accompanies them on a project to increase their living space and helps one of them recover a lost ax head (6:1-7). From these stories we learn that at least some of the prophets are married and have children, live in rural/village communities, and are economically marginalized. Deuteronomic hospitality characterizes rural village life but is resisted by the urban elite, who support royal administrative injustice. The sons of the prophets thrive during the ministry of Elisha and, not insignificantly, during the last half of the Omride dynasty.

The sons of the prophets are but one of the groups of prophets mentioned in the Old Testament. Saul meets "a band of prophets" in a prophetic frenzy (1 Sam 10:5, 9-13). The poverty and the marginalization of the prophets hidden and fed by Obadiah also characterize the sons of the prophets (1 Kings 18:4). Ahab has a group of prophets to guide his decisions (22:6; cf. the 450 prophets of Baal and 400 prophets of Asherah associated with Jezebel in 18:19). Jeremiah speaks judgment against "the prophets" (Jer 23:9-40; cf. 29:1).

Rentería proposes that the sons of the prophets are a group of villagers disenfranchised by the political and economic policies of the Omride period (115). In the stratified system of advanced agrarian society, the great mass of people are peasants and "expendables" unable to eke out a living unless they are young and healthy (G. Lenski and J. Lenski: 203). Although the group may have included those who gave up their income to join a Yahwistic religious community, Rentería considers it more likely that they are motivated by loss of patrimonial lands to political elites because of Omride interference. Elisha responds to their petitions by empowering them in forming a community to help themselves. Rentería suggests that the Elisha stories were collected to reinforce strong community norms about obligations to vulnerable widows and orphans. In the stories the prophet helps those without other resources find solutions to seemingly insurmountable problems, liberating them from poverty and resignation. The proposal is based on the presupposition that Yahwist egalitarian justice as outlined in Deuteronomy contests the Baal ideology promoting royal hegemony *[Mišpaṭ, p. 461]*. The sons of the prophets follow Deuteronomic instruction to integrate misplaced persons lacking kinship ties—the orphan, widow, and stranger—into the social, juridical, liturgical, and economic life of the covenant community (Glanville: 262–63).

The last two named male prophets in 2 Kings are associated with canonical books, Jonah son of Amittai (14:25) and Isaiah son of Amoz (2 Kings 19–20). Little is narrated regarding Jonah, who speaks the word of the Lord to Jeroboam II, bringing a restoration of borders to Israel (14:25). Isaiah is portrayed as a central figure during the reign of Hezekiah, interceding for Judah (19:1-7), delivering a taunt song against the Assyrians (19:14-34), providing healing for Hezekiah (20:1-11), and predicting exile (20:12-19). Hezekiah, who submitted to the reforms demanded by Deuteronomic values, and Isaiah, who had access to central power, are portrayed as models for future kings and prophets (Wilson 1980: 216).

Huldah the prophetess delivers the Lord's oracle to Josiah when the Torah discovered in the temple is read to Josiah (22:15-20). Though her gender is not an issue in the narrative, Huldah is the lone named prophetess in 1–2 Kings. She declares judgment on Judah (22:15-17) and shalom for Josiah (22:18-20).

Huldah is portrayed as a central prophet, perhaps associated with the priests of Anathoth. Her husband, Shallum, bears the name of Jeremiah's uncle (2 Kings 22:14; Jer 32:7), and Jeremiah's father is Hilkiah (Jer 1:1), the name of the high priest who found the Torah (2 Kings 22:8). Wilson characterizes these connections as "inferential" but says "there is no particular reason to deny" that these are the same individuals (1980: 223).

Subject to Torah, the prophets speak what the Lord commands (Deut 18:15). Israel goes to exile because they have failed to listen to the Lord's warning *by every prophet and every seer* (2 Kings 17:13). After Manasseh, Judah's exile is inevitable, as the Lord declares *by his servants the prophets* (21:10-15). The prophets are "torah police," warning people of the consequences of failing to keep the Lord's revealed commands (Edelman: 69). In sum and as a group, the prophets in 1–2 Kings (1) are the faithful persecuted minority when the king is evil, (2) are aware that Israel's history of evil warrants exile, (3) have tried unsuccessfully to bring Israel to the Lord, (4) embody the reminder of Israel's history of rejecting the Lord, and (5) associate with Yahweh's teaching (Zvi: 567).

Prophetic Word Fulfillment of the prophetic word is a central theme in 1–2 Kings (Konkel 2006: 28). The promise/fulfillment narratives demonstrate that the future of the kingdom is determined by the will of the Lord as expressed by the prophet. This schema is used "to lend authority to their [prophets'] presentation of Deuteronomic torah theology" (O'Brien 2013: 185). Divine agency in history rather than proof of prophetic inerrancy is the focus (Matties: 403). Fulfillment of the prophetic word communicates the Lord's sovereign power. God's sovereignty is so crucial to Kings' theology that the text frequently provides specific notice of fulfillment (Wray Beal 2014: 51–52). Though fulfillment demonstrates that the Word of God is effective and does not fail (Konkel 2006: 28), the prophetic word does not operate mechanistically to seal the people's fate. As demonstrated by God's response to Hezekiah's prayer (2 Kings 20:1-6) and God's delay of Ahab's judgment after repentance (1 Kings 21:27-29), God's mercy triumphs over judgment. The future remains open until the prophetic word is fulfilled (Fretheim 1999: 12).

More than thirty cases of fulfillment of prophecy can be identified in Kings. The first two citations of fulfilled prophecy reach back to 1–2 Samuel. After Solomon banishes Abiathar from priesthood, the narrator marks the event as *fulfilling the word of the LORD that he had spoken* (1 Kings 2:27; see 1 Sam 2:30-36). Solomon claims that his succession of David and the temple construction fulfill prophecy (1 Kings 5:5; 8:15, 20, 24; see 2 Sam 7:12-13).

Prophetic denunciations that cut off royal houses demonstrate that the Lord through his prophet exercises superior authority. After Ahijah announces Solomon's loss of Israel (1 Kings 11:29-40), the narrator declares that Israel's rebellion *was a turn of affairs brought about by the LORD that he might fulfill his word* (12:15). The houses of Jeroboam and Baasha are cut off (15:29; 16:11), fulfilling the words of the prophets Ahijah (14:12, 14) and Jehu (16:1-4). During Ahab's reign the deaths related to rebuilding Jericho fulfill a word spoken by Joshua before the Israelite conquest (Josh 6:26; 1 Kings 16:34). The deaths of Ahab, Jezebel, and their house fulfill Elijah's prophecy (1 Kings 21:21-29; 22:38; 2 Kings 1:16-17; 9:25-28, 30-37; 10:7-10, 14; 11:16; cf. 22:17).

The prophetic word leads to miracles. Elijah promises food to the widow of Zarephath (1 Kings 17:14-16). Elijah's prophecies of drought and rain are fulfilled (17:1; 18:1, 45). An unnamed prophet twice prophesies the Lord's victory in battle (20:13, 28; fulfilled in 20:20-21, 29-30). Elisha's promises are fulfilled by miracles (2 Kings 2:21-22; 3:17-20; 4:16-17, 43-44; 5:10, 14; 7:1, 16-20; 13:19, 25) and an assassination (8:10-15). Isaiah prophesies deliverance from Assyria for Jerusalem and fifteen additional years of life for Hezekiah (2 Kings 19:7, 35-37; 20:3-6).

The prophetic word central to Kings is narrated with exquisitely complex storytelling: Ahijah prophesies Israel's exile (1 Kings 14:15-16) centuries before it is fulfilled (2 Kings 17:13; 25:21). Having symbolically *torn* the kingdom from Solomon and conditionally given it to Jeroboam's *enduring house* (1 Kings 11:29-40), Ahijah not only prophesies exile but also produces a sign-act prophecy of the death of Jeroboam's son Abijah (14:7-18) that portends the end of Jeroboam's house (15:29-30). This is not the first prophetic announcement of judgment against Jeroboam. The man of God from Judah gives the signs of the broken altar and the dried and restored hand to enact the prophecy that Josiah would desecrate Jeroboam's altar (13:1-6; 2 Kings 23:15-20), only to himself become a sign that disobeying the Lord's command ends in death (1 Kings 13:11-32). Josiah indeed fulfills the prophecy (2 Kings 23:15-20), only to become a sign of inevitable exile himself when Huldah's prophecy that he would be buried in peace is fulfilled after he is murdered by Pharaoh (22:20; 23:29-30). The suspense and artistry of the prophecy/fulfillment theme positively influences the narrative of Kings; yet more significantly, it plays the central theological role of demonstrating the Lord's sovereignty over kings and history. The book of Kings makes the theological claim that the exile expresses the sovereignty of Yahweh, who uses the nations to accomplish his aims, countering the alternative that the gods of the nations have prevailed because of their superiority.

Though not mentioned by name in 1–2 Kings, the editorial prefaces to the canonical prophets Hosea, Amos, Micah, and Zephaniah place them between about 750 BCE and the exile. The Latter Prophets explicitly reinforce the implicit message of 1–2 Kings: live out the human vocation of pursuing righteousness, justice, peace, and covenant loyalty.

PROVOKE THE LORD TO ANGER Divine anger is rooted in God's jealousy for Israel. The anger of the Lord is expressed in 1–2 Kings within the Deuteronomic covenantal concept of blessings and curses. When Israel did evil and worshiped other gods, "the anger of the LORD was kindled.... The LORD uprooted them from their land in anger, fury, and great wrath, and cast them into another land" (Deut 29:27-28; see also 27:15-26; 29:24-26, 29; 2 Kings 17:16-18; 21:6, 15-16; 23:26-27; 24:3-4, 20). God's anger expresses God's sovereignty; divine judgment corresponds to violation of covenant fidelity (Kaminsky: 54; Latvus: 90; Matties: 386). Anger is "a theology of experience, . . . the collective experience of an exiled generation" (Latvus: 86–87). The term explains the disaster that has fallen on Israel and Judah. DtrH seeks to convince readers that "the disaster of exile was a fully justified punishment by the God of Israel of his own people" because of apostasy (Barton: 28). God's anger is mentioned in the biblical text three times as often as human anger (Kaminsky: 56–57).

Provoking the LORD's anger (cf. 1 Kings 15:33) expresses more than divine displeasure. God's relationship in covenant is marked with passion. In Scripture, "the wrath of God is a theologically rich concept that reflects an understanding of a God who cares, hears, and responds to the plight of those facing oppression and tribulation" (Friesen: 456). God is deeply invested in the future of God's people. Thus God grieves the sinfulness of humanity (Gen 6:6); the sins of Israel provoke divine emotion.

Five Hebrew terms for God's anger used in Deuteronomy appear in 1–2 Kings. The phrase *provoking the LORD to anger* (*ka'as*) is the most common term in Kings, where it appears twenty times (seven times in Deuteronomy), always with rebellious, idolatrous Israel as the subject. The *anger* of the Lord is kindled (*'anap*, 1 Kings 8:46; 11:9; 2 Kings 13:3; 17:18; 23:26; 24:20; seventeen times in Deuteronomy) or burns (*ḥemah*, 2 Kings 22:13, 17; five times in Deuteronomy). *Wrath* or fury (*qeṣep*; six times in Deuteronomy) refers to the Lord's wrath (2 Kings 3:27). The verb *punish* (1 Kings 8:35; 11:39; 2 Kings 17:20; seven times in Deuteronomy) involves affliction (1 Kings 2:26) or humbling through difficulty (Deut 8:2, 3, 16). While the range of meanings for this troubling term includes humbling affliction, the term associates an image of violent sexual violation with divine judgment (rape; Deut 21:14; 22:24, 29; Judg 19:24; 20:25).

Two-thirds of the references to divine anger in 1–2 Kings use the expression *provoking the LORD to anger*. Israel *provokes God to anger* with idol worship (or *with the work of his hands*, referring to Jeroboam, 1 Kings 16:7). The *sins of Jeroboam provoke the LORD to anger* seven times (1 Kings 14–16); Ahab's idolatry and injustice three times (16:33; 21:22; 22:53); Israel's sins leading to exile two times (2 Kings 17); Manasseh's sins four times (21:6, 15; 23:26, 26). The emotion is a marital metaphor (related to provoking the Lord to jealousy as Judah does, 1 Kings 14:22). Intensely personal, the image focuses on faithfulness in covenant relationship (Fretheim 1999: 92–93). Idol worship damages humanity's relations with the Lord; idolatry distorts the human vocation implicit in being created in God's image (doing what is right and just) [*Idolatry, p. 449*]. Israel provokes divine anger by transgressing covenant faithfulness, breaking relationship with God. The consequence of covenant transgression is exile. *The LORD was not willing to pardon the sins of Manasseh and the innocent blood that he shed*, which so *angered the LORD that he expelled them from his presence* (AT; 2 Kings 23:26-27; 24:3-4, 20). Deuteronomic theology expresses the consequences of sin as the divine wrath stored up until it is released upon the generation that pushes God over the limit, then spreads beyond the guilty to consume all within its vicinity (Kaminsky: 59) [*Theology of Exile, p. 479*].

A puzzling reference to *wrath* is a term used once in Kings (*qeṣep*; 2 Kings 3:27). Unlike the terms described above, *wrath* is impersonal, a response not to apostasy but to a violation of the creation order. *Wrath* so disrupts a military situation where Israel has the upper hand that they withdraw. Fretheim suggests that this wrath is related to Israel's degradation of the environment, a violation of the war law (2 Kings 3:13, 19, 25; cf. Deut 2:9; 20:19-20; 1999: 143).

After Israel worshiped the golden calf at Mount Sinai, the Lord said to Moses, "Let me alone, so that my wrath may burn hot against them and I may consume them" (Exod 32:10). After Moses' appeal, the Lord relented, agreed to travel with Israel, and passed by Moses, saying, "The LORD, the LORD, a God merciful and gracious, slow to anger, and abounding in steadfast love and faithfulness, ... yet by no means clearing the guilty" (34:6-7).

The Sinai narrative encapsulates the conflict in Deuteronomy and the DtrH between God's mercy and God's just wrath. God's self-confession does not imply that mercy cancels punishment resulting from God's wrath but rather implies that mercy is more enduring and eventually prevails (Matties: 389). Though 2 Kings ends in exile, Moses promises that the Lord will gather Israel back to the land if they return to the Lord (Deut 30:1-5). Thus 1-2 Kings uses the image of divine wrath to describe the people's experience of exile, which they interpret as judgment for covenant violation.

QUEEN MOTHER The introductory royal formulas for the kings of Judah (except Jehoram and Ahaz, 2 Kings 8:16; 16:1) include the name of the mother of the king. Typically, these women are not mentioned again in the report of the king. The mother's place of origin or father is often included, perhaps providing a clue about how regional differences influence policy. Two Israelite queen mothers are named. Zeruah, mother of Jeroboam, is a widow (1 Kings 11:26). Jezebel, wife of Ahab and mother of Ahaziah (22:51-52) and apparently Jehoram (2 Kings 1:17; 3:2) and possibly Athaliah (8:26; 11:1), is associated with the worship of Baal and Asherah (16:31; 18:19), thus in opposition to Elijah (1 Kings 19:1). Jezebel is assassinated by Jehu (2 Kings 9:30-37). Solomon's mother, Bathsheba, twice speaks to King David during the accession of Solomon, addressing him on behalf of Solomon (1:11-31). She intercedes for Adonijah to Solomon (2:13-25). Athaliah, descendant of Omri and mother of the king of Judah Ahaziah (2 Kings 8:26), usurps the throne of Judah after her son's death, kills all her grandchildren but one (Joash), and rules for seven years until she herself is executed in a coup (11:1-16). Babylon exiles Nehushta, mother of Jehoiachin (24:8, 12). The fate of Hamutal, mother of Jehoahaz and Zedekiah (23:31; 24:1), is uncertain (25:7, 11). Though such king's mothers as Bathsheba, Jezebel, and Athaliah exercise considerable influence, the narrator does not use a formal title to link their power to an official role.

The Hebrew term translated *queen mother* (*gebirah*) is used three times in 1-2 Kings (Pharaoh's wife, 1 Kings 11:19; Asa's mother, 15:13; 2 Chron 15:16; and Jezebel, 2 Kings 10:13). The term may refer to an official royal position. Jeremiah addresses the king and the "queen mother" (Jer 13:18) and identifies Jehoiachin's mother with the term (29:2). The term can also refer to the "mistress" of a maidservant (Gen 16:4, 8, 9; 2 Kings 5:3; Ps 123:2; Prov 30:23; Isa 24:2). Twice Isaiah refers to Babylon as "mistress" (47:5, 7).

Scholars have defended three positions regarding the role of queen mother. Andreasen describes the position as royal counselor, with limited social and political influence. Based primarily on the biblical text, Ben-Barak argues that the queen mother exercises influence through proximity to power and personality. Ackerman posits a powerful queen mother who represents the Asherah in the official Judean royal cult. The king's status as adoptive son of Yahweh is strengthened by the queen mother representing Asherah, according to Ackerman. The queen mother exercises both political and cultic influence.

Mothers of kings may be associated with rival factions vying for power (Bathsheba, 1 Kings 1:11-31). The people of the land tend to support kings whose mothers come from the provinces (2 Kings 11:14, 20; 21:23-24; 23:30) [People of the Land, p. 464]. Two of Josiah's sons appear to follow alliances based on the birthplace of their mothers. Jehoahaz, though not the oldest heir, may have been chosen to continue Josiah's anti-Egyptian policies (2 Kings 23:30; his mother's hometown in Libnah in southwest Judah suggests ascendancy of a faction concerned about an Egyptian threat; Sweeney 2007a: 451). His successor Jehoiakim rebels against Babylon, perhaps consistent with his alliance with a pro-Egyptian, anti-Babylonian faction in Judah, as indicated by his mother's hometown in Galilee, a region more likely threatened by Babylon (24:1; Sweeney 2007a: 452).

We conclude that the term *queen mother* refers to what was apparently a position of some influence, but we cannot assume that the mother of a king held the position unless it is stipulated. Extrabiblical ANE sources attribute state and cultic functions to the queen mother, who may continue in office after her husband's death. Queen mother Maacah used her influence to support the cult of Asherah (1 Kings 15:13; Ben-Barak; Ackerman). Bowen argues that the mother's birthplace influences the king's evaluation. Kings with positive appraisal have mothers with connections to Judah or Jerusalem; those with negative appraisal have no mother mentioned, or the mother comes from outside Judah. She argues further that the translation *queen mother* is confusing and would better be rendered *great lady* (618).

READING STRATEGIES Reading strategies describe methods, patterns, and approaches for interpretation of a written text (Nelson 1998: 44–63). Historical criticism, seeking to understand what the author meant, aims to get *behind the text*. Literary criticism, understanding what the text means, seeks to read *within the text*. Reader-response criticism, exploring the world *in front of the text*, finds meaning in the impact of the reading among contemporary readers (J. T. Walsh 2009: 3–5).

Historical Criticism: Reading behind the Text Readers can view 1-2 Kings as an ancient historical document to present the factual record. Historical writing is shaped by the conventions of its time. The narrative of 1-2 Kings bears the marks of ANE historiography, including divine speeches and interpretation of events shaped by God's intervention (Matties: 22).

History writing analyzes past and present circumstances of a people. National history like 1-2 Kings seeks to assess responsibility for past actions and their consequences and establish a corporate identity regarding what a nation is and what it stands for (Konkel 2016: 469; Van Seters: 4–5). Although the role of kings is significant, the history of Israel expresses a wider perspective, including the identity of the people Israel.

Since Noth, scholars have read the story of Israel from entry in the land to exile as Deuteronomistic History (DtrH), with dependence on Deuteronomy and as developed in Joshua, Judges, Samuel, and Kings

[Kings in the Hebrew Canon: Kings in the Deuteronomistic History, p. 453]. This reading strategy assumes that the author, the Deuteronomist, used ancient sources to pursue theological themes developed in Deuteronomy, including commitment to a covenant with Yahweh. DtrH is marked by speeches attributed to the Deuteronomist, notably Solomon's dedicatory prayer in 1 Kings 8 and the explanation of the exile in 2 Kings 17 (Matties: 26–27; Richter: 228).

Socio-scientific Criticism   A contemporary multidisciplinary criticism drawing on the social sciences, especially anthropology and sociology. Socio-scientific criticism is concerned with the historical world *behind* the text rather than the historical world *in* the text.

Ideological Criticism   Seeks to identify the narrow interests of those who produce the texts, naming both oppressive ideology and perspectives that are liberative and prophetic. Seibert analyzes 1 Kings 1–11 from the perspective of "subversive scribes" who cleverly embed, within what appears to be positive propaganda supporting Solomon, narrative elements that undercut his position. The accommodating reading celebrates Solomon as imperial leader who excels all his contemporaries in God-given wisdom, wealth, and glory (Seibert: 259).

Literary Criticism: Reading within the Text   Readers can take 1–2 Kings as literature. *Literary criticism* reads the text as story, treating the text in its finished form without regard to history of origin or historical events (Nelson 1998: 48). Literary criticism treats the text as a unit, notes such elements of good storytelling as narrative structure and composition, plot development, themes and motifs, characters, characterization, dialogue, suspense, humor, and irony, reading it as a novella. Narrative issues include the reliability of the narrator, the question of authorial intent (expressed in terms of the context where the text was written and its presumed intended audience), and the implications of multiple interpretations, recognizing that narrative is capable of more than one interpretation and being aware of the implications of each. Narrative (literary) criticism approaches the text as a story without concern about historical reference.

Literary approaches discover artistic design based on rhetoric, form, or reader response. These approaches are not all mutually exclusive (Seow: 22), nor do they preclude our interest in reading the text as Scripture, with its primary concern that humans created in the image of God should pursue their God-given vocation of doing justice and righteousness. Sometimes called *canonical criticism*, this reading pattern asks how the final form of the text relates to the larger canon, addressing questions about God's nature and God's relationship with humanity (Nelson 1998: 62–63).

Rhetorical Reading   This approach takes a special interest in the relationship between the biblical text and its intended audience within the context of the communal life setting. Rhetorical criticism asks how the text *functions* for its audience, including especially its original audience: to teach, persuade, guide, exhort, reproach, or inspire, and it identifies and explains the techniques in the text itself and the relevant features of the cultural setting (see esp. the next two subsections).

Reading with the Grain This approach corresponds to the accommodating reading informed by imperial values. Reading against the grain (see below) is prompted by Deuteronomy and corresponds to the liberative reading with *suspicion* of the imperial values *[Mišpaṭ, p. 461]*. Reading with the grain, scholars propose that 1 Kings 3–10 narrates King Solomon's reign approvingly. The narrator "presents Solomon's reign, in 1 Kings 3–10, as a monarchical golden age, setting off these chapters from the negative view of Solomon which precedes and follows them" (Jobling: 57; Provan 1999: 163). The most widely held "opinion is that the narrator is favorable to Solomon" in 1 Kings 1–10 and "speaks disparagingly of him only" in 1 Kings 11 (J. T. Walsh 1995: 471–72).

Reading against the Grain This approach identifies a critique that finds within the positive view of Solomon "the seeds of his own destruction" (Provan 1995: 46), "a clever piece of ironical writing" (Newing: 247). The canonical perspective enriches the positive portrayal of Solomon's reign with criticism of the royal propagandistic interpretation of wealth as God's blessing of Solomon's piety. This reading weighs Solomonic governance on the scale of Deuteronomic justice, appreciating that the surprising condemnation of Solomon in 1 Kings 11 can be anticipated by careful reading.

Reader-Response Criticism: Reading in Front of the Text Reader-response criticism is a literary theory that focuses on the reader and on the interpretive strategy or processes that readers use to create meaning. Reading "in front of the text" focuses on the reader's engagement with the text. One variation of the approach argues that the final form preserves a variety of readings, allowing "liberative readings [to] jostle with more accommodating ones" (McConville 2006: 5). A reading community creates meaning (interpretation) by using the interpretive strategies and presuppositions of that community.

Bennett challenges the notion that Deuteronomy advocates for the weakest members of society, to protect them from exploitation by the powerful: he argues that the text is produced by the intellectual elites to avoid peasant revolts (11). Bennett seeks to create a suspicious hermeneutical community that reads with the oppressed to deconstruct this bias. Knight adds that the powerful elite can construct laws that hide their self-interest and manipulate the reader (2011: 2). Gerbrandt, while agreeing that readers can ally themselves with the powerful, contends that the Deuteronomic code is the result of a renewal movement that sought social justice (2015: 20). This discussion illustrates how a reading community shapes meaning in reading a text. Anabaptists have traditionally practiced this type of community hermeneutic, developing church order that includes biblical teaching tested within the local congregation (Murray: 162, 164). Thus, reading in front of the text produces a theological reading similar to the TLC sections found in this commentary.

SEND The act of *sending* expresses royal power. In David's abuse of power against Uriah the Hittite and Bathsheba, the king "sends" Joab to war (2 Sam 11:1), "sends" messengers to take Bathsheba (11:3-4), "sends" to Joab with orders to "send" Uriah (11:6), and "sends" to bring Bathsheba to his house after Uriah's death (11:27). The story turns when the Lord "sends" Nathan to David to confront him for his sin (12:1). Solomon *sends* to establish his throne against his rivals five times in 1 Kings 1–2, for example. In 1–2 Kings the verb *send* is used over one hundred times, with the king as actor in about 80 percent of the cases. The Lord or his prophet *sends* more than one-tenth of the time.

It is noteworthy that all Israel *sends* for Jeroboam (1 Kings 12:3, 20) in deliberations about royal policies. Jezebel, the powerful queen of Ahab, *sends* to threaten Elijah (19:2) and to have Naboth killed to take possession of his vineyard (21:8, 11; cf. 21:14). The king of Aram *sends* messengers to the king of Israel with demands for surrender (20:2, 5, 7, 17). In his conflict with Elijah, King Ahaziah *sends* messengers to inquire of Baal and captains to arrest Elijah (2 Kings 1:2, 6, 9, 11, 13, 16). In the story of the cleansing of Naaman, the balance of power shifts when Elisha interrupts the *sending* of the king of Aram (5:5, 6, 7) by *sending* word to the king of Israel (5:8) and to Naaman (5:10). King Joram's efforts against Jehu are futile: he *sends* messengers who are powerless to return when they meet the rebel Jehu (9:17-19).

Israel goes into exile when they reject the Lord, who *sends* prophets (17:13) and later lions (17:25-26) to teach the people justice. Though kings often signal their intent to take initiative and control their own destiny by *sending* word, messengers, or bribes, the word *send* is used for the last time in 2 Kings 24:2, when the Lord *sends* armed bands against Judah to destroy it. *Send* is code for exercising royal power.

SINS OF JEROBOAM The *sins of Jeroboam* characterize Israel and its kings. When the people continue in the sins of Jeroboam, the Lord sends Israel into exile (2 Kings 17:7, 22-23). The sins of Jeroboam involve not only the golden calf cult but also a royal ideology that transgresses the Deuteronomic covenant (Deut 10:12-22), breaks faith with the Levitical priests, and moves the capital to Penuel, away from Shechem (whose elders have rejected Rehoboam's policies of increased taxation and unremitting corvée, unpaid labor, 1 Kings 12) [*Mišpaṭ, p. 461*]. Jeroboam rejects the egalitarian vision of Deuteronomy promoted by the Levitical priests, and the sins of Jeroboam produce systemic injustice, embraced by the powerful elite in Israel, who benefit (2 Kings 17:7, 21-22).

The *sins of Jeroboam* set the direction for the northern kingdom of Israel, establishing a precedent that characterizes fifteen of Jeroboam's seventeen successors and results in Israel's exile (2 Kings 17:21-22). Even Zimri, who rules for seven days, and Zechariah, who reigns for six months, are guilty of the *sins of Jeroboam* (Ahaz of Judah also *walked in the way of the kings of Israel*, 16:3). Only Hoshea (the last king of Israel, whose evil was *not like the kings of Israel who were before him*, 17:2) escapes censure related to the *sins of Jeroboam*. The exile was caused by the rebellion initiated by Jeroboam and continued by people and leaders across the generations (Kaminsky: 45–46).

Twice the narrator says of Jeroboam that *this thing [word, matter] became a sin* (1 Kings 12:30; 13:34). In the first case, Jeroboam sins by failing to trust God's promise: *If you . . . walk in my ways, . . . [I] will build you an enduring house, . . . and I will give Israel to you* (11:38; Bodner 2012: 93). Jeroboam's lack of trust leads him to build/fortify Shechem and Penuel, erect golden calves, make houses on the high places, and appoint non-Levitical priests (12:25-31). His extensive building program requires the return to Solomonic and Egyptian imperial taxation and forced labor (Deut 17:16; 1 Kings 9:10-22; 11:28, 40). In the second case, the phrase *This thing [matter] became a sin* is associated with rejection of the Levitical priests (and their covenant values; 1 Kings 13:33-34). Jeroboam transgresses the Deuteronomic commandments that forbid idol worship (Deut 5:8), rejects a single place for worship (12:2-7), and appoints non-Levitical priests (10:8-9; 16:18–18:22).

Jeroboam's rejection of Deuteronomic Torah upsets political, economic, and sociological values (in addition to the cultic transgression, idolatry; Doorly: 19–35) *[Idolatry, p. 449]*. Doorly contends that when Jeroboam *went out from there [Shechem] and built Penuel* (12:25), the king moved the capital to distance himself from the Levitical centers at Shechem and the nearby Shiloh (12:29-31), champions of the egalitarian Deuteronomic value system of the elders, prophets, and Levites opposed to the Solomonic royal justice of Rehoboam (12:14-15, 18). The *sins of Jeroboam* describe his break with Levitical values to pursue the imperial structures of ANE kings.

TEMPLE THEOLOGY Traditional Jerusalem temple theology is centered on Zion symbolism, evocative of the kingship of Yahweh (Ollenburger: 145–62). Ollenburger distinguishes between Davidic tradition (responsibility for security is shared between earthly and heavenly kings) and Zion tradition (the Lord as creator and deliverer of slaves, the ground of Zion's security for the trustful community of the poor). Faith in Yahweh's lordship is the criterion for evaluating leadership in Jerusalem (148). Ollenburger's "order of the real world" is the dynamic equivalent of the *mišpaṭ* of Deuteronomic theology *[Mišpaṭ, p. 461; Kings in the Hebrew Canon: Kings and Deuteronomy, p. 453]*.

Much as royal administrative policies counter Deuteronomic egalitarian values, temple theologies in Kings clash with Zion tradition. Eslinger exposes Solomonic temple theology as a rhetorical attempt articulated in the temple dedication address to regain the Lord's unconditional patronage, God's establishment of Solomon's rule (1 Kings 8:14-21; Eslinger: 178). Jeremiah's temple sermon offers essentially the same critique of temple theology: "You say, 'The temple of the LORD, the temple of the LORD, the temple of the LORD' and think you are safe. Safe to do what? Practice violence and injustice!" (AT and paraphrase of Jer 7:4-10). Solomonic temple theology seeks a divine guarantee that the temple has become the Lord's eternal abode, obligating him to support Jerusalem's king (1 Kings 8:12-13). "While, in theory, Zion theology may be quite distant from royal theology, in practice they are deeply intertwined, . . . an extravagant arena from which to exhibit and verbalize and insist upon royal claims" (Brueggemann 2000: 108).

Between the polar extremes of Yahwistic Zion tradition and Solomonic temple security lies a spectrum of temple theological expressions. The Lord rejects David's plans to build a temple because it would limit the Lord's freedom to "move about among" this people (2 Sam 7:4-7). Addressing Solomon concerning this house that you are building, the Lord commands that he obey my ordinances (mišpaṭ; 1 Kings 6:11-13). Solomon recognizes limits of his temple strategy, admitting that the highest heaven cannot contain [God], much less this house that I have built! (8:27). Solomon's prayer, declaring that the Lord's name is with the temple but his dwelling place is in heaven, suggests "a formula [that] seeks to adjudicate the tricky affirmation of presence in the midst of Yahweh's freedom" (Brueggemann 2000: 110). While Yahweh promises to put his name, eyes, and heart at the temple for all time, the Lord conditions promises to Solomon's dynasty on keeping my statutes and ordinances (mišpaṭ; 9:1-5). The Lord's name indicates his presence, identity, and power, but the Lord warns that Israel's disobedience will result in the house becoming a heap of ruins (9:7-8). The temple is also viewed as a place of prayer, confession, and forgiveness (8:31-53). Gillmayr-Bucher argues that Solomon, the praying king, is a model for the exilic community (143) [House for the Name, p. 449].

Israel's rejection of Jerusalem worship leads to worship of golden calves in Bethel and Dan: this thing became a sin for Israel (12:28-30). The man of God from Judah spoke by the word of the LORD and proclaimed against the altar of Jeroboam (13:1-2). Even the Yahwist Jehu, who is commended by the Lord for opposing Ahab, is negatively evaluated for his failure to turn from Jeroboam's sins (2 Kings 10:29-31). Following the Deuteronomic ordinance of a single place of worship in the land (Deut 12), 1–2 Kings condemns Israel's alternative cult.

In Judah without exception, the kings from Solomon until Hezekiah are evaluated negatively for their failure to suppress the high places, allowing rival cultic practice to flourish. The reforming kings Joash and Josiah link covenant renewal with temple repair, though the narrator does not explicitly commend them (2 Kings 11–12, 22–23). The political and economic implications of centralizing the cult in Jerusalem and suppressing high places are not explicitly considered in Kings. Though Manasseh is faulted for placing an image in the temple, it is his sins, particularly shedding much innocent blood, which make Judah's exile inevitable (21:6-7, 14-16). Manasseh's sins lead the Lord to conclude, I will reject this city that I have chosen, Jerusalem, and the house of which I said, my name shall be there (23:26-27). Injustice results in abandonment and destruction of the temple.

In sum, orthodox temple theology follows the Zion tradition outlined by Ollenburger. Sovereign God orders society to protect the poor. Prophets support the Zion tradition by shaping their message according to the Torah. Huldah's message to Josiah the temple reformer is founded on submission to Torah (2 Kings 22:14-20). Though the Lord's name rests in the temple, the Lord conditions life, including temple worship, on Torah obedience, rejecting Solomon's royal temple theology with its aim to use the edifice as a guarantee of divine favor (1 Kings 6:11-13). While DtrH rejects as heterodox all non-temple worship, the suppression of the high places and removal of Jeroboam's altar in Bethel (2 Kings 23) are insufficient to overturn judgment of Manasseh's sins of shedding innocent blood. Zion tradition trumps royal temple theology.

THEOLOGY OF EXILE In Deuteronomy, Yahweh gives Israel the Torah and land as covenant signs. When Israel follows Torah, the Lord blesses Israel with life in the land. Exile is the curse threatened for covenant disloyalty. A primary agenda of the book of Kings is to consider Israel's exilic fate, why it was exiled, and what its identity and mission are as an exiled people.

Exile from the land because of Israel's covenant unfaithfulness is threatened throughout 1–2 Kings, a primary element of a theology of retribution often assumed in the interpretation of Kings (see "Blessings and Curses in a Theology of Retribution" in TBC for 1 Kings 8). The theology of retribution grows out of a deterministic reading of covenant blessings and curses as the inevitable result of human behavior. This reading is reinforced by mechanistically interpreting texts that assume Israel's ultimate exile and attribute exile to punishment for covenant failure (Deut 4:26-28; 1 Kings 8:34; 2 Kings 17:7-23; 24:3-4, 20).

A sociological approach to the problem of exile considers the devastating human cost for loss of life and home for refugees (exiles). Smith-Christopher argues that Kings explores culturally appropriate means to deal with the catastrophic event of exile and PTSD-like experiences for deportees (103). Suggesting that penitential prayers contend with shame of exile by offering narrative repair, Smith-Christopher sees the temple prayer of 1 Kings 8 as a call for nonconformity, rejecting the royal paradigm that led to exile and a recommitment to covenant ethics (120–21). Shame is a mark of honesty, allowing for transformation by offering hope that the new way will correct past mistakes (122).

Klein's theological approach to exile leads to a similar result. Arguing that Noth's theology of retribution—claiming that DtrH explains exile as covenant failure resulting in divine judgment, with no hope for the future—fails to appreciate the hope for repentance explicit in Deuteronomy (4:25-31; 30:10), Klein sees DtrH as a call to repent, to acknowledge God's justice and obey Torah (43). Klein summarizes his theological analysis of Israel in exile with the following:

Exile is God's judgment against idolatry.
Exile places God's people in a new home, a new place for living out true vocation.

Exile requires the work of rebuilding identity by renewing covenant
loyalty to God.
Exile is a time for hope, for new obedience, a catalyst for translating
faith into a new context.
Exile is a time for prayer, self-examination, and returning to faith.
(Klein: 150–54)

VIOLENCE IN KINGS   Political conflict often leads to violence in
1–2 Kings. Violence characterizes royal succession, war, and divine judgment. Human-to-human violence is unsanctioned in 1–2 Kings, but
Yahweh employs violence through war and other means. Elijah and Elisha
and the sons of the prophets operate in a liminal space (on both sides of a
boundary); their violent acts of judgment are reported without approbation or condemnation [*Prophets: Sons of the Prophets, p. 467*].

Violence of Solomon   Solomon perpetrates coercive force in three primary arenas. First, Solomon orders the execution of political rivals—
Adonijah (1 Kings 2:24-25), Joab (2:28-34), and Shimei (2:41-46)—and seeks
the death of Jeroboam, who escapes (11:40). References to Solomon's
political control before and after these assassinations implicitly criticize
his violence (2:12, 46). The threat to Jeroboam contravenes divine prophecy (11:26-39). Second, Solomon accumulates a large chariot force, contrary to the law of the king (4:26-28; 9:19; 10:26; Deut 17:16). Third,
Solomon uses the threat of force to gain tribute and extort unpaid labor
(1 Kings 4:21, 24; 5:13-18; 9:15-22). Solomon's mission to do justice is
inconsistent with his return to imperial Egypt (10:9, 28-29) [*Egypt, p. 445*].

Violence between Israel and Judah   When Israel revolts against
Rehoboam and assassinates his overseer of forced labor, Rehoboam mobilizes troops against Israel (1 Kings 12:18, 21-24). The man of God Shemaiah
orders Rehoboam to turn back. Rehoboam complies. Coming at the outset
of the divided kingdom, the prophetic oracle demonstrates that warfare
between Judah and Israel transgresses the Lord's will.
    The prophetic judgment on Jeroboam's altar includes violent actions
attributed to the Lord's word or plan, though the narrative itself raises
doubts about the reliability of both the Israelite prophet and the Judean
man of God, who attribute violence to the Lord (13:2, 26). The prophet
Ahijah announces judgment against Jeroboam and Israel: *I will cut off from
Jeroboam every male.... The* LORD *will strike Israel,... root up Israel..., scatter
them ..., give Israel up* (14:10, 15-16). The prophet declares that Israel's
exile can be attributed to divine intervention, not political circumstance.
    War is reported between Jeroboam (king of Israel) and Rehoboam and
his son Abijam (of Judah), and between Asa (of Judah) and Baasha (of
Israel), yet without narrative evaluation (14:30; 15:7, 16). Asa's tribute of
temple treasures to Aram is also reported without evaluation (15:18-19).
The narrative separates Asa's positive evaluation (15:11-15) from his reliance on the violent intervention of Aram (15:16-20), indicating that the
military violence falls outside Asa's commended acts.

Though Baasha's violent conspiracy against the house of Jeroboam occurs *according to the word of the LORD . . . because of the sins of Jeroboam* (15:29-30), the narrator condemns Baasha not only for being evil like Jeroboam but also *because he destroyed* the house of Jeroboam (16:7). The explicit condemnation of the perpetrator of divinely ordained judgment distinguishes violent consequences of evil behavior from divine sanction of human violence. In Judah, Joash and Amaziah are assassinated in palace coups (2 Kings 12:20-21; 14:19-20). Amaziah is commended for limiting punishment by not killing the murderers' children, in accord with the Torah (14:5-6). The narrational perspective condemns violent conspiracies.

Violence Involving Elijah and Elisha The conflict between Elijah and the prophets of Baal and Asherah with their patron Jezebel (1 Kings 18:19) involves bloodshed, both Jezebel's killing the Lord's prophets (18:4) and Elijah's slaughter of 450 prophets of Baal (18:40). When Jezebel and Ahab violently grab Naboth's ancestral land, Elijah delivers a divine judgment oracle predicting that violence will rebound onto Ahab's family (1 Kings 21). Though elsewhere Elijah is portrayed as a faithful man of God who follows Yahweh's word, no divine word is reported to mandate execution of Baal prophets (18:40). Obadiah's protection of the prophets of the Lord suggests a peaceful alternative (18:4, 13). Perhaps the Lord's mandate that Elijah anoint successors who will wield the sword and his reassurance of a remnant of Yahweh worshipers further indicate that Elijah's violence does not have divine approval (19:17-18). Elijah violently eliminates two companies of fifty men without explicit divine sanction (2 Kings 1:9-12). Though not explicitly condemned, Elijah's violence is not approved.

Elisha's prophetic ministry begins and ends with the exclamation "*My father, my father! The chariots of Israel and its horsemen!*" (2:12; 13:14), a confession that Yahweh trumps royal violence [*Horses and Chariots, p. 447*]. Three narratives associate Elisha with violence, all reported without evaluation. Though Elisha himself does no violence to the boys of Bethel, cursing his nemeses appears to be out of character for a shalom agent (2:23-25). Before battle, Elisha predicts military victory for Israel and ecological devastation for Moab without endorsing or condemning it. The battle ends with Israel suffering wrath, presumably the Lord's judgment upon terror which they inflicted (3:16-19, 27). The three military victories Elisha predicts for Joash of Israel depend on human initiative and divine support typical of ANE war reports (13:14-19, 25).

In contrast to these reports, Elisha typically reduces violence. Elisha heals enemy Naaman and sends him off with shalom (2 Kings 5). Elisha protects Israel from Aram's ambushes, then defuses military conflict by feeding the enemy (6:8-23). The Aramean siege is broken by *the sound of chariots and of horses, the sound of a great army*—but without violence (7:6). When Elisha appoints Hazael and predicts his war atrocities, Elisha expresses deep grief (8:11-12). Elisha instructs one of the *sons of the prophets* to anoint Jehu as king of Israel (9:3), yet he does not condone the violence mandated by the young prophet, who exceeds Elisha's instructions and

Elijah's prophecy (9:1, 6-9; cf. 1 Kings 19:16-18). The sons of the prophets are also associated with violence when they initiate action in an Aramean battle (1 Kings 20). Through the prophet, the Lord gives Israel victory so that the king of Israel *shall know that I am the* LORD (20:13, 28) *[Prophets: Prophetic Word, p. 469]*. One of the sons of the prophets condemns the king for sparing the king of Aram (20:42).

Both Elijah and Elisha promote life. Typically, their violent acts arise from their own initiative. The narrator does not evaluate the violence, freeing the reader to weigh the reliability of these men of God and the morality of their actions. These violent acts, all done without divine approval, are inconsistent with the canonical vocation of righteousness.

Violence of Ahab and Jezebel Ahab and Jezebel have a running battle with Elijah and other prophets. Jezebel kills prophets of the Lord, and Ahab and Jezebel threaten Elijah's life (1 Kings 18:4, 9-10, 13; 19:2). Jezebel executes a plot to kill Naboth and take his ancestral land for Ahab's benefit (21:15-16). Ahab initiates battle at Ramoth-gilead, imprisons Micaiah when he prophesies unfavorably, and dies in battle much as prophesied (22:2-4, 26-28, 37-38). No king does more evil than the violent Ahab, encouraged by the violent Jezebel.

Violence of Jehu Jehu's bloody coup, annihilating the Omrides, concludes with divine endorsement spoken privately to Jehu: *You have done well in carrying out what I consider right, and in accordance with all that was in my heart have dealt with the house of Ahab* (2 Kings 10:30). Narrative clues raise questions about the reliability of the word. First, when Jehu justifies his violence by citing divine oracles attributed to Elijah, he modifies the original to his advantage (9:25-26; 10:10). Second, Jehu alone hears the young prophet who goes beyond Elisha and Elijah in endorsing violence (9:6-10). The lack of witnesses raises suspicion about the reliability of Jehu's report of the messages. Third, the contrast between the extreme violence of Jehu's coup with the relatively nonviolent coup against Athaliah and Mattan, the priest of Baal (2 Kings 11) implies criticism. Fourth, Hosea condemns Jehu's bloodshed (Hos 1:4-5). The absence of additional witness to the divine approbation raises doubt regarding its reliability. The narrative reports that Jehu violently eliminates the house of Ahab but signals reservations; elsewhere, biblical prophecy explicitly condemns Jehu's violence (Hos 1:4-5).

Devoted to Destruction (Ḥerem) The Lord demands the total annihilation (ḥerem) of the Canaanites when Israel takes the land (Deut 7:2), including spoils from them (13:17). God's aim is to protect the people from contact with and corruption by false religion. John Walton and Jonathan Walton interpret ḥerem as "elimination of identity," suggesting repudiation of a militaristic identity reliant on horses and chariots (179–80). Solomon extracted forced labor from descendants of the people who were not totally destroyed (ḥerem; 1 Kings 9:21). Though the term is not used, Hiel's violation of ḥerem is associated with the death of his sons when he rebuilds Jericho (Josh 6:26; 1 Kings 16:34). Assyria threatens total destruction of Jerusalem as it has done to other nations (2 Kings 19:11).

When the king of Israel spares the king of Aram, who has been *devoted to destruction*, one of the sons of the prophets condemns the king of Israel to death (1 Kings 20:42). Elements of the Aramean battle reflect Yahweh war reports (1 Kings 20). First, the battle belongs to the Lord, who directs Israel's actions. Second, Israel's military weakness demonstrates that the strength is the Lord's, not Israel's (as with Gideon, Judg 7). Third, the purpose of the battle is that Israel would learn to know the Lord. Fourth, the spoils (*ḥerem*) belong to the Lord; war is not to produce economic advantage or be used to stockpile weapons.

Leithart describes the Aramean battle as "reenactment" of the battle of Jericho (Josh 6). Divine intervention fells walls (Josh 6:20; 1 Kings 20:30). Like Joshua, Israel *strikes* horses and chariots rather than stockpiling weapons (Josh 11:6-11; 1 Kings 20:21). When he fails to devote the enemy to destruction, Ahab, like Achan, is the *troubler of Israel*, failing to practice *ḥerem* (1 Kings 18:18; Josh 7:25; Leithart: 150). Ahab fails to practice *ḥerem*, instead embracing Aramean royal values (via treaty and trade; J. H. Walton and J. H. Walton: 214).

Violence and Israel's Exile Second Kings 15 reports Israel's last chaotic decades of conspiracies and assassinations. The Assyrians carried Israel into exile without the text attributing the violence to the Lord (17:5-6). The exile is the Lord's judgment on Israel's transgression, concluding that *the* LORD *removed Israel out of his sight, as he had foretold through all his servants the prophets* (17:7-23) [*Theology of Exile, p. 479*].

Violence Leading to Judah's Exile After the Israelite exile, the two exemplary kings of Judah, Hezekiah and Josiah, conduct military incursions into territory formerly controlled by the Philistines and Israel (2 Kings 18:8; 23:15-20). No specific violence is reported for Hezekiah's Philistine invasion. Elsewhere, Hezekiah depends on the Lord to deliver a defenseless Judah from Assyrian imperial dominance, including the angel's slaughter of 185,000 in the Assyrian camp (19:35). Josiah's final act against Israelite cultic apostasy is the *slaughter* (*sacrifice*) of the priests of the Israelite hill shrines (23:20). Huldah had predicted Josiah's peaceful burial, but Josiah's death at the hands of Pharaoh corresponds to Josiah's violence (22:20; 23:29). Judah's exile is sealed by the sins of Manasseh, filling Jerusalem with innocent blood, meaning oppressive violent royal policies against the *innocent* (21:16; 24:4). The deportation to Babylon includes the note that *Jerusalem and Judah so angered the* LORD *that he banished them from his sight* (24:4, 20 AT) [*Provoke the Lord to Anger, p. 470*].

Summary Divine sanction of violence is more restricted in 1–2 Kings than it is in the rest of DtrH [*Kings in the Hebrew Canon: Kings in the Deuteronomistic History, p. 453*]. Although human characters attribute violence to the Lord (e.g., the prophet of Bethel, 1 Kings 13:26; Ahijah: 1 Kings 14:15), the narrative itself is parsimonious in attributing violence to the

Lord. The Lord promises to give Aram into Israel's hand; the battle report attributes killing to Israel (20:20-21, 29-30). In response to the taunts of Sennacherib, the Lord strikes down the Assyrian camp to deliver Hezekiah (2 Kings 19:35). The two cases reporting the Lord's intervention share the common factor that the events reveal the Lord's sovereignty to Israel, to Judah, and to the powerful nations. The narrative reports the deportations of Samaria and Jerusalem as judgment from the Lord.

Political violence in Israel is common—and condemned. War is not glorified, but violence begets more violence. Though the prophets use their God-given powers to curse and to kill, the text never endorses prophetic violence. The sons of the prophets stand out by initiating and endorsing royal assassination of tyrants.

Yet 1–2 Kings treats nonviolent resolution of conflict positively and either raises questions about or condemns violence. Though the Hebrew *shalom* occurs more than thirty times in 1–2 Kings, it rarely describes peaceful relationships. More characteristic are the queries directed to Jehu on his way to slaughter Ahab's family (2 Kings 9:11, 17, 18, 19), the one-word question, *"Shalom?"* and the ambiguous *"Shalom"* of Elisha in response to Naaman when he asks pardon for his idolatry (2 Kings 5:19). Absent Yahwistic justice, peace is a rare commodity.

WISDOM IN KINGS In 1–2 Kings the word *wisdom (ḥokmah) is used more than twenty times, all but one referring to* Solomon, who is known for unrivaled wisdom (1 Kings 3:12; Hiram, *the artisan in bronze* from Tyre, is also wise, 7:14). Wisdom is associated with Solomon in 2 Chronicles 1; 2; 9; Proverbs 1:2; 10:1; 25:1; Ecclesiastes; Song of Solomon; and the deuterocanonical Wisdom of Solomon. God gives Solomon wisdom (1 Kings 3:12; 5:12), a *listening heart* (3:9 AT) and a *wide heart* (4:29; "largeness of vision and perspective beyond self-interest," Brueggemann 2000: 67). Solomon's wisdom, compared superlatively with ANE wisdom, includes encyclopedic knowledge of natural science and artistic skill (4:29-34). Solomon's wisdom attracts monarchs who travel to test him and pay gold for the privilege (4:34; 10:1-9, 23-25). Hiram king of Tyre marvels at Solomon's wisdom (5:7), which results in peaceful international relations (5:12). "Wisdom include[s] statecraft and craftsmanship" (Brueggemann 2000: 97). For Solomon, wisdom pays enormous financial dividends. Like Joseph, who used his wisdom to appropriate Egypt's wealth, land, and populace for Pharaoh in Egypt, Solomon, through his association with Pharaoh, exploits his wisdom to enrich the state (Gen 41:33-36, 39-49; 47:13-26; 1 Kings 4:34; 10:23-25). Unlike the wise, innocent, yet wealthy Job (Job 28), Solomon cannot claim to have "worn" righteousness and justice by providing for the poor, orphans, and widows (Job 29:11-16).

David's advice to Solomon foreshadows the outcome of Solomon's reign (1 Kings 2:1-9). First, David enjoins Solomon to keep the Torah, promising success if he is faithful (2:2-4) *[Kings in the Hebrew Canon: Kings and Deuteronomy, p. 453]*. Second, David calls Solomon to act *with wisdom* by violently eliminating enemies (2:6, 9). When God promises Solomon wisdom, he replaces the third gift that Solomon might have selected, *the life of your enemies* (3:11), with life for Solomon, contradicting David's violent royal wisdom (Hens-Piazza 2006: 39-40). David and the Lord present opposing options: covenant faithfulness for life or deadly royal wisdom. Solomon's "wise justice" confuses the distinction by threatening to kill the living baby with a sword (3:24-25; Brueggemann 2000: 54). The purpose of God's gift of wisdom is just governance (1 Kings 3:9-12). The people rejoice when Solomon uses godly wisdom (the skill to listen, 3:9, 22-23) while enacting justice for the marginalized (3:28). The queen of Sheba calls Solomon to use his wisdom to execute justice and righteousness (10:7, 9). Yet Solomon fails to use his God-given wisdom in service of justice (11:11) *[Mišpaṭ, p. 461]*. Cook notes the "progression" of Solomon's wisdom from hearing the Lord (3:14) to hearing the people in order to exercise judicial wisdom (3:16-29), then to speaking the wisdom of encyclopedic information to be heard by people from all nations (4:34; 10:23-25), noting that Solomon's wisdom no longer serves the people but himself, his court, and his royal audience. Listening to God, to Torah, and to the people fades (Cook: 83). Fox observes the inadequacy of such wisdom: "Solomon's wisdom is an instrumental faculty used in the achievement of his goals, not a general principle for right living. . . . Solomon's fate proves that it is not enough to be wise" (189-90).

Elsewhere, Hebrew *wisdom* refers to skill, including divination, craftsmanship, social etiquette, military maneuvers, political craft, even duplicity (2 Sam 13:3) and evil (Jer 4:22). Hebrew wisdom can describe either instrumental (skills) or moralistic virtue (godliness). Biblical wisdom, skill for living, is associated with skilled craftmanship (sixteen times referring to tabernacle craftsmen in Exod). Godly wisdom empowers the wise to know right from wrong, to judge justly, and to act for the good of others (Prov 1:1-7). The fear of the Lord is the source of wisdom (Prov 1:7; Job 28:28). Wisdom rejects evil (Job 28:28; Prov 3:7). Fools behave as atheists, maltreating the poor (Pss 14:1, 6; 53:1, 4).

WOMEN IN KINGS Women play a prominent role in Kings. Twelve women have speaking roles—one-fifth of the speakers in Kings (more than any other OT book). Female characterization can be assessed by such categories as (1) named/unnamed, (2) quoted speakers/nonspeakers, (3) Israelite/Judean/foreign, (4) evil/good, (5) active/passive (queen mothers named in relation to royal sons), and (6) power agents/marginalized.

Named women tend to relate to Jerusalem royalty. Fifteen Judean queen mothers are named *[Queen Mother, p. 472]*. Bathsheba plays a critical role in influencing David to honor a promise and in implicating Adonijah in a plot for the throne (1 Kings 1:11-31; 2:13-25). Bathsheba's reliability as a character is ambiguous. Though presented as virtuous, her motives (and integrity) may be impugned because she benefits from her intervention. Maacah's characterization is evil (15:2, 10, 13). Associated with David's rebellious son Absalom (Abishalom), she is removed from office by her son the king because of her cultic transgression. Her identification as mother of both Abijam and his son Asa may raise suspicion of incestuous relations with Abijam. Athaliah is also characterized unambiguously as evil (2 Kings 8:18, 26-27; 11:1-16, 20). A daughter of Ahab, she is foreign to Judah and largely responsible for the transgressions of both husband and son. The narrator quotes her speech only when she interrupts the covenant coronation of her hidden grandson Joash (11:14). A usurper who murders her grandchildren, nearly extinguishes the Davidic royal house, and worships Baal, Athaliah is depicted as the most evil woman to live in Jerusalem. She is the last queen mother with an active role. (Abishag [David's nurse] and Zeruah [Jeroboam's mother] are noteworthy as women named though their sons are not Davidic kings; Jeroboam succeeds a Davidic king, 1 Kings 1:1-4; 11:26.)

Ahab's wife, the notorious Jezebel, epitomizes evil by killing Yahweh's prophets and providing for false prophets (1 Kings 16:31; 18:4, 13, 19). In three speeches, Jezebel threatens to kill a prophet (19:1-2), engineers Naboth's death and loss of inheritance (21:5-15), and mocks the Lord's chosen Jehu (2 Kings 9:30-37). A dynamic character, she influences policy to advance royal power, and is so powerful that in her death not only is she silenced and killed but also her body is "disappeared" (9:35-37). She is one of three women identified by the technical term translated *queen mother* (10:13; cf. 1 Kings 11:19 MT; 15:13).

The speech of the prophetess Huldah is the rhetorical parallel of the narrator's analysis of Israel's exile (2 Kings 17:7-41; 22:14-20). The last prophetic voice of Kings, Huldah delivers the judgment speech that condemns Judah to exile. While questions may linger regarding the reliability of male prophets and their deceptive words, Huldah's speech foretells the exile and Josiah's peaceful burial (Kissling: 130-40).

The speech of the unnamed foreign queen of Sheba may be the most rhetorically significant in Kings. After touring Solomon's royal opulence, she reiterates the Lord's purpose not only for kings but also for the human vocation. She declares that Solomon is in power *to execute justice and righteousness* (1 Kings 10:9). According to Ethiopian tradition, Solomon's son by the queen of Sheba transported the ark of the covenant to Ethiopia, where it remains hidden.

The narrator gives voice to marginalized female characters, a stunning rhetorical move testifying to the Lord's justice. Prostitutes give witness to Solomon's wisdom and justice (1 Kings 3:16-28). The widow of Zarephath saves Elijah and testifies to the power of the Lord's word (17:8-24). A prophet's widow cries out for saving justice and follows Elisha's instructions to save her sons from slavery (2 Kings 4:1-7). The wealthy Shunammite wife persuades her husband to provide for Elisha, then persuades Elisha to revive her dead son, testimony to her influence and to God's power over life and death (4:8-37). Ken Stone notes parallels between the widow of Zarephath and the woman of Shunem. Both act independently of men and confront the prophet, achieving a gender role reversal in a patriarchal society (241). The little Israelite maid gives witness to God's healing power, which then restores the great Aramean general Naaman (5:2-4). After a distraught mother cries out for help, God delivers Samaria from a deadly siege (6:26-30). In the face of distress and loss, these female characters witness to God's salvation. Two female characters give silent witness to God's plans. Jeroboam's wife follows her husband's orders to enquire of the prophet Ahijah. Before she can speak, Ahijah charges her with a judgment speech that foreshadows the exile (1 Kings 14:1-17). The king's daughter Jehosheba preserves David's line by saving Joash from his murderous grandmother Athaliah (2 Kings 11:1-3).

Although the queen of Sheba and the widow of Zarephath are among the foreign women characterized positively, the narrative characterizes the women of Solomon's harem negatively. Pharaoh's daughter (1 Kings 3:1; 7:8; 9:16, 24; 11:1) and many of Solomon's wives and concubines are foreign women, who turn Solomon's heart away from the Lord (11:1-8; 14:31). Under their evil influence Solomon builds high places and sacrifices to their gods.

Hens-Piazza challenges the characterization of Jezebel, who, she says, "receives the lion's share of the criminal credit, although she is not the primary culprit. . . . She serves as the scapegoat" (2006: 295). Noting that violence is both insidious and contagious, Hens-Piazza invites reflection on the vilification of outsiders like Jezebel and the perspective that assigns outsider status because of gender, ethnic identity, or status, characterizing them as the "other" and undeserving of forgiveness (2006: 296–97). Athaliah receives similar treatment (2 Kings 11). Jezebel and Athaliah are not the only females to suffer violence related to gender. The first female character in 1 Kings is Abishag, chosen (likely against her will) for (and characterized by) her physical appearance ostensibly to provide David warmth but perhaps more likely to test the king's virility (1:3-4). The prostitutes in Solomon's court suffer the threat of physical violence (and death) of an infant child (3:24-26). The women of Solomon's harem, delivered up by their royal families for political expediency (alliances), are locked away as political pawns. Though all Israel returns to normalized economy within the day, two mothers who have cannibalized a child continue to suffer for violence done by them and to them (2 Kings 6:26-30; 7:1-20). The narrative does not shy away from using violence against women to advance the story. This misogynistic attitude goes unexamined in DtrH. Crowell investigates the origins of the DtrH perspective on foreign women, attributing it to a postcolonial perspective that mimics imperial culture. He posits further that the scheme was developed to promote an identity of loyalty to the Lord (15–16).

Bibliography

Ackerman, Susan
    1993   "The Queen Mother and the Cult in Ancient Israel." *Journal of Biblical Literature* 112/3:385–401.

Adam, Klaus-Peter
    2005   "Warfare and Treaty Formulas in the Background of Kings." In Adam and Leuchter, 35–68.

Adam, Klaus-Peter, and Mark Leuchter, eds.
    2005   *Soundings in Kings: Perspective and Methods in Contemporary Scholarship.* Minneapolis: Fortress.

Albright, William Foxwell
    1945   "The Chronology of the Divided Monarchy of Israel." *Bulletin of the American Schools of Oriental Research* no. 100 (Dec. 1945): 16–22.

Alter, Robert
    2019   *The Hebrew Bible: A Translation with Commentary.* New York: Norton.

Amit, Yairah
    1987   "The Dual-Causality Principle and Its Effects on Biblical Literature." *Vetus Testamentum* 34/4:385–400.

Andreasen, Niels-Erik A.
    1983   "The Role of the Queen Mother in Israelite Society." *Catholic Biblical Quarterly* 45:179–94.

Averbeck, Richard E.
    1997   "ṭmʾ." In *New International Dictionary of Old Testament Theology and Exegesis*, edited by Willem A. VanGemeren, 2:365–76. Grand Rapids: Zondervan.

Avigad, Nahman
    1993   "Samaria [City]." In *The New Encyclopedia of Archaeological Excavations in the Holy Land*, edited by Ephraim Stern, 4:1304–6. New York: Simon and Schuster; Jerusalem: Israel Exploration Society and Carta, the Israel Map and Publishing Co.

Bar-Efrat, Shimon
1989   *Narrative Art in the Bible.* New York: T&T Clark.
Barré, Lloyd M.
1986   *The Rhetoric of Political Persuasion: The Narrative Artistry and Political Intentions of 2 Kings 9–11.* Washington, DC: Catholic Biblical Association of America.
Barton, John
2007   "Historiography and Theodicy in the Old Testament." In *Reflection and Refraction: Studies in Biblical Historiography in Honour of A. Graeme Auld,* edited by Robert Rezetko, Timothy H. Lim, and W. Brian Aucker, 27–33. Leiden: Brill.
Bates, Matthew W.
2017   *Salvation by Allegiance Alone: Rethinking Faith, Works, and the Gospel of Jesus the King.* Grand Rapids: Baker Academic.
Beach, Eleanor Ferris
1993   "The Samaria Ivories, Marzeaḥ, and the Biblical Text." *Biblical Archaeology* 56:94–104.
Beck, John A.
2003   "Geography as Irony: The Narrative-Geographical Shaping of Elijah's Duel with the Prophets of Baal (1 Kings 18)." *Scandinavian Journal of the Old Testament* 17:291–302.
Ben-Barak, Zafrira
1991   "The Status and Right of the *gebîrâ.*" *Journal of Biblical Literature* 110:23–34.
Bennett, Harold
2002   *Injustice Made Legal: Deuteronomic Law and the Plight of Widows, Strangers, and Orphans in Ancient Israel.* Grand Rapids: Eerdmans.
Bloch-Smith, Elizabeth
2018   "The Impact of Siege Warfare on Biblical Conceptualizations of YHWH." *Journal of Biblical Literature* 137:19–28.
Bodner, Keith
2012   *Jeroboam's Royal Drama.* Oxford: Oxford University Press.
2016   "The Rule of Death and Signs of Life in Kings." In *The Oxford Handbook of Biblical Narrative,* edited by Danna Nolan Fewell, 204–14. Oxford: Oxford University Press.
2019   *The Theology of the Book of Kings.* Cambridge: Cambridge University Press.
Boling, Robert G., and Edward F. Campbell Jr.
1987   "Jeroboam and Rehoboam at Shechem." In *Archaeology and Biblical Interpretation,* edited by Leo G. Perdue, Lawrence E. Toombs, and Gary Lance Johnson, 259–72. Atlanta: John Knox.
Bowen, Nancy R.
2001   "The Quest for the Historical *Gĕbîrâ.*" *Catholic Biblical Quarterly* 63:597–618.
Boyd, Gregory A.
2012   "The Strategic-Level Deliverance Model." In *Understanding Spiritual Warfare: Four Views,* edited by James K. Beilby and Paul Rhodes Eddy, 129–72. Grand Rapids: Baker Academic.

2017   *The Crucifixion of the Warrior God: Interpreting the Old Testament's Violent Portraits of God in Light of the Cross.* 2 vols. Minneapolis: Fortress.

Brandfon, Fredric R.

1992   "Beth-Shemesh." In *ABD*, 1:696–700.

Brueggemann, Walter

1981   "'Vine and Fig Tree': A Case Study in Imagination and Criticism." *Catholic Biblical Quarterly* 43:1–18.

1982a   *1 Kings.* Atlanta: John Knox.

1982b   *2 Kings.* Atlanta: John Knox.

1988   "The Social Nature of the Biblical Text for Preaching." In *Preaching as a Social Act: Theology and Practice*, edited by Arthur Van Seters, 127–65. Nashville: Abingdon.

1991   *Interpretation and Obedience: From Faithful Reading to Faithful Living.* Minneapolis: Fortress.

1997   *Theology of the Old Testament: Testimony, Dispute, Advocacy.* Minneapolis: Fortress Augsburg.

2000   *1 & 2 Kings.* Macon, GA: Smyth and Helwys.

2001a   *The Prophetic Imagination.* 2nd ed. Minneapolis: Fortress.

2001b   *Testimony to Otherwise: The Witness of Elijah and Elisha.* St. Louis: Chalice.

2004   *A Social Reading of the Old Testament: Prophetic Approaches to Israel's Communal Life.* Minneapolis: Fortress.

2005   *Solomon: Israel's Ironic Icon of Human Achievement.* Columbia: University of South Carolina.

2008   "Stereotype and Nuance: The Dynasty of Jehu." *Catholic Biblical Quarterly* 70:16–28.

2010   *Journey to the Common Good.* Louisville: Westminster John Knox.

2013   *Truth Speaks to Power: The Countercultural Nature of Scripture.* Louisville: Westminster John Knox.

2014a   *From Whom No Secrets Are Hid: Introducing the Psalms.* Louisville: Westminster John Knox.

2014b   *Reality, Grief, Hope: Three Urgent Prophetic Tasks.* Grand Rapids: Eerdmans.

2018a   "The Ancient Conflict between *Techne* and *Metis*." Ellul Lectures. http://ellul.org/wp-content/uploads/2018/07/The-Ancient-Conflict-Between-Techne-and-Metis-Full-Paper.pdf.

2018b   "Jesus Acted Out the Alternative to Empire." *Sojourners*, June 22, 2018. https://sojo.net/articles/walter-brueggemann-jesus-acted-out-alternative-empire.

Chaney, Marvin L.

2014   "The Political Economy of Peasant Poverty: What the Eighth-Century Prophets Presumed but Did Not State." In *The Bible, the Economy, and the Poor*, edited by Ronald A. Simkins and Thomas M. Kelly, 34–60. Journal of Religion and Society Supplement Series 10.

Claiborne, Shane, and Michael Martin

2019   *Beating Guns: Hope for People Who Are Weary of Violence.* Grand Rapids: Baker.

Cogan, Mordechai
1992 "Chronology." In *ABD* 1:1102–11.
2001 *1 Kings: A New Translation with Introduction and Commentary*. New York: Doubleday.

Cogan, Mordechai, and Hayim Tadmor
2007 *2 Kings: A New Translation with Introduction and Commentary*. New Haven: Yale University Press.

Cohen, Chaim
1979 "Neo-Assyrian Elements in the First Speech of the Biblical Rab-Šāqē." *Israel Oriental Studies* 9:32–48.

Cohn, Robert L.
1983 "Form and Perspective in 2 Kings V." *Vetus Testamentum* 33:171–84.
2000 *2 Kings*. Berit Olam. Collegeville: Liturgical Press.

Collins, James C.
2006 *Built to Last*. New ed. New York: Collins.

Cook, Sean E.
2017 *The Solomon Narratives in the Context of the Hebrew Bible: Told and Retold*. London: T&T Clark.

Coote, Robert B.
1991 *In Defense of the Revolution: The Elohist History*. Minneapolis: Fortress.

Cross, Frank Moore
1968 "The Structure of Deuteronomic History." *Perspectives in Jewish Learning* 3; Chicago: 9–24. Repr. as "The Themes of the Book of Kings and the Structure of the Deuteronomistic History." In *Canaanite Myth and Hebrew Epic: Essays in the History of the Religion of Israel*, 274–89. Cambridge, MA: Harvard University Press, 1973.

Crouch, Andy
2013 *Playing God: Redeeming the Gift of Power*. Downers Grove: InterVarsity Press.

Crowell, Bradley L.
2013 "Good Girl, Bad Girl: Foreign Women of the Deuteronomistic History in Postcolonial Perspective." *Biblical Interpretation* 21:1–18.

Culpepper, R. Alan
1999 "The Gospel of Luke." In *The New Interpreter's Bible*, edited by Leander E Keck, 9:1–490. Nashville: Abingdon.

Davies, John A.
2011 "Discerning between Good and Evil: Solomon as a New Adam in 1 Kings." *Westminster Theological Journal* 73:39–57.
2012 *1 Kings*. Darlington: Evangelical Press.

Davies, Philip R.
1992 *In Search of 'Ancient Israel': A Study in Biblical Origins*. Sheffield: Sheffield Academic.

Davis, Dale Ralph
2002a *1 Kings: The Wisdom and the Folly*. Rosshire: Christian Focus Publications.

2002b   *2 Kings: The Power and the Fury.* Rosshire: Christian Focus
         Publications.
Day, John
1992a   "Asherah." In *ABD*, 1:483–87.
1992b   "Canaan, Religion of." In *ABD*, 1:831–37.
Deijl, Aarnoud van der
2008   *Protest or Propaganda: War in the Old Testament Book of Kings and
         in Contemporaneous Ancient Near Eastern Texts.* Boston: Brill.
Dempsey, Carol J.
2008   *Justice: A Biblical Perspective.* St. Louis: Chalice.
de Ries, Hans
1618   *Short Confession of Faith and the Essential Elements of Christian
         Doctrine.* 40 articles. Available as "A Short Confession of Faith
         by Hans de Ries," *translated and edited by Cornelius J. Dyck,
         Mennonite Quarterly Review* 38 (January 1964):5–19, https://
         gameo.org/index.php?title=Confession_of_Faith_(Hans_de_
         Ries,_1618).
DeVries, Simon J.
2003   *1 Kings.* 2nd ed. Waco: Word.
Dietrich, Walter
1972   *Prophetie und Geschichte.* Göttingen: Vandenhoeck and Ruprecht.
Dillard, Raymond B.
1987   *2 Chronicles.* Waco: Word.
Doorly, William J.
1994   *Obsession with Justice: The Story of the Deuteronomists.* Mahwah:
         Paulist Press.
Dorsey, David A.
1991   *The Roads and Highways of Ancient Israel.* Baltimore: Johns
         Hopkins University Press.
Dubovský, Peter
2006   "Tiglath-pileser III's Campaigns in 734–732 B.C.: Historical
         Background of Isa 7; 2 Kgs 15–16 and 2 Chr 27–28." *Biblica*
         87/2:153–70.
2008   "Assyrian Downfall through Isaiah's Eyes (2 Kings 15–23): The
         Historiography of Representation." *Biblica* 89/1:1–16.
2014   "Why Did the Northern Kingdom Fall according to 2 Kings 15?"
         Biblica 95/3:321–46.
Dutcher-Walls, Patricia
1991   "The Social Location of the Deuteronomists: A Sociological
         Study of Factional Politics in Late Pre-Exilic Judah." *Journal for
         the Study of the Old Testament* 52:77–94.
1996   *Narrative Art, Political Rhetoric: The Case of Athaliah and Joash.*
         Sheffield: Sheffield Academic.
2002   "The Circumscription of the King: Deuteronomy 17:16–17 in Its
         Ancient Social Context." *Journal of Biblical Literature* 121:601–16.
Dyck, Cornelius J.
1964   "Short Confession of Faith by Hans de Ries." *Mennonite Quarterly
         Review* 38/1:5–19.

Dyck, Peter, and Elfrieda Dyck
  1991   *Up from the Rubble.* Scottdale, PA: Herald Press.
Edelman, Diana
  2013   "Court Prophets during the Monarchy and Literary Prophets in
          the So-Called Deuteronomistic History." In Jacobs and Person,
          51–73.
Ellul, Jacques
  1972   *The Politics of God and the Politics of Man.* Translated and edited
          by Geoffrey W. Bromiley. Grand Rapids: Eerdmans.
Enns, Fernando
  2007   *The Peace Church and the Ecumenical Community: Ecclesiology and
          the Ethics of Nonviolence.* Translated by Helmut Harder.
          Kitchener, ON: Pandora.
Epp-Tiessen, Dan
  2006   "1 Kings 19: The Renewal of Elijah." *Direction* 35/1:33–43.
Eslinger, Lyle
  1994   *House of God or House of David: The Rhetoric of 2 Samuel 7.* Sheffield:
          Sheffield Academic.
Fanwar, Wann M.
  1992   "Sela." In *ABD*, 5:1073–74.
Fewell, Danna Nolan
  1986   "Sennacherib's Defeat: Words at War in 2 Kings 18.13–19.37."
          Journal for the Study of the Old Testament 34:79–90.
Fishbane, Michael
  1992   *The Garments of Torah: Essays in Biblical Hermeneutics.*
          Bloomington: Indiana University Press.
Flannery, Frances
  2008   "'Go Back by the Way You Came': An Internal Textual Critique
          of Elijah's Violence in 1 Kings 18–19." In *Writing and Reading
          War: Rhetoric, Gender, and Ethics in Biblical and Modern Contexts*,
          edited by Brad E. Kelle and Frank Ritchel Ames, 161–73.
          Atlanta: SBL Press.
Fox, Michael V.
  1995   "The Uses of Indeterminacy." *Semeia* 71:173–92.
Franklin, Norma
  2013   "Why Was Jezreel So Important to the Kingdom of Israel?" The
          Bible and Interpretation. https://bibleinterp.arizona.edu/
          opeds/2013/11/fra378006
Fretheim, Terence E.
  1983   *Deuteronomic History.* Nashville: Abingdon.
  1991   *Exodus.* Interpretation. Louisville: John Knox.
  1999   *First and Second Kings.* Louisville: Westminster John Knox.
Friesen, Ivan D.
  2009   *Isaiah.* Believers Church Bible Commentary. Scottdale, PA:
          Herald Press.
Fritz, Volkmar
  2003   *1 and 2 Kings.* Minneapolis: Augsburg Fortress.
Frykholm, Amy
  2015   "Ending Extreme Poverty." *Christian Century* 133/12:32–34.

Gardner, Richard B.
1991 *Matthew*. Believers Church Bible Commentary. Scottdale, PA: Herald Press.

Gawande, Atul
2014 *Being Mortal*. New York: Metropolitan Books.

Geddert, Timothy J.
2001 *Mark*. Believers Church Bible Commentary. Scottdale, PA: Herald Press.

Geoghegan, Jeffrey C.
2005 "The Redaction of Kings and Priestly Authority in Jerusalem." In Adam and Leuchter, 109–18.

Gerbrandt, Gerald E.
1986 *Kingship according to the Deuteronomistic Historian*. Atlanta: Scholars Press.
2015 *Deuteronomy*. Believers Church Bible Commentary. Harrisonburg, VA: Herald Press.

Gillmayr-Bucher, Susanne
2019 "Glory and Remorse: Transitions in Solomon's Prayer (1 Kgs 8)." In *Prayers and the Construction of Israelite Identity*, edited by Susanne Gillmayr-Bucker and Maria Häusl, 125–46. Atlanta: SBL Press.

Gilmour, Rachelle
2014 *Juxtaposition and the Elisha Cycle*. New York: Bloomsbury T&T Clark.

Glancy, Jennifer A.
2011 *Slavery as Moral Problem in the Early Church and Today*. Minneapolis: Fortress.

Glanville, Mark
2018 *Adopting the Stranger as Kindred in Deuteronomy*. Atlanta: SBL Press.

Goff, Stan
2015 *Borderline: Reflections on War, Sex, and Church*. Eugene: Cascade Books.

Grabbe, Lester L.
2010 "Omri and Son, Incorporated: The Business of History." In *Congress Volume Helsinki 2010*, edited by Martti Nissinen, 61–83. Boston and Leiden: Brill.

Gray, John I.
1977 *I and II Kings*. Philadelphia: Westminster.

Greenwood, Kyle
2015 "Late Tenth- and Ninth-Century Issues: Ahab Underplayed? Jehoshaphat Overplayed?" In *Ancient Israel's History: An Introduction to Issues and Sources*, edited by Bill T. Arnold and Richard S. Hess, 286–318. Grand Rapids: Baker Academic.

Hadley, Judith M.
2000 *The Cult of Asherah in Ancient Israel and Judah: Evidence for a Hebrew Goddess*. New York: Cambridge University Press.

Hallie, Phillip
1979 *Lest Innocent Blood Be Shed*. New York: Harper and Row.

Halpern, Baruch
2001 *David's Secret Demons: Messiah, Murderer, Traitor, King.* Grand Rapids: Eerdmans.
Halpern, Baruch, and André Lemaire
2010 "The Composition of Kings." In *The Books of Kings: Sources, Composition, Historiography and Reception,* edited by André Lemaire and Baruch Halpern, 123-51. Leiden and Boston: Brill.
Hamilton, Jeffries
1994 "Caught in the Nets of Prophecy? The Death of King Ahab and the Character of God." *Catholic Biblical Quarterly* 56:649-63.
Hamori, Esther J.
2013 "The Prophet and the Necromancer: Women's Divination for Kings." *Journal of Biblical Literature* 132:827-43.
Hanson, Paul D.
2015 *A Political History of the Bible in America.* Louisville: Westminster John Knox.
Hayes, John H., and Paul K. Hooker
1988 *A New Chronology for the Kings of Israel and Judah and Its implications for Biblical History and Literature.* Atlanta: John Knox.
Hens-Piazza, Gina
1998 "Forms of Violence and the Violence of Forms: Two Cannibal Mothers before a King (2 Kings 6:24-33)." *Journal of Feminist Studies in Religion* 14/2:91-104.
2006 *1-2 Kings.* Nashville: Abingdon.
Herrmann, Wolfgang
1999 "Baal." In *Dictionary of Deities and Demons in the Bible,* edited by Karel van der Toorn, Bob Becking, and Pieter W. van der Horst, 132-39. 2nd ed. Grand Rapids: Eerdmans.
Hobbs, T. R.
1985 *2 Kings.* Waco: Word.
House, Paul R.
1995 *1, 2 Kings.* Nashville: Broadman and Holman.
Hubmaier, Balthasar
1526 *A Brief Apologia.* In *Balthasar Hubmaier: Theologian of Anabaptism,* edited by H. Wayne Pipkin and John Howard Yoder, 296-313. Scottdale, PA: 1989.
Hyman, Ronald T.
1995 "The Rabshakeh's Speech (2 KG 18-25): A Study of Rhetorical Intimidation." *Jewish Bible Quarterly* 23:213-20.
Jacobs, Mignon, and Raymond F. Person Jr., eds.
2013 *Israelite Prophecy and the Deuteronomistic History: Portrait, Reality, and the Formation of a History.* Atlanta: SBL Press.
Janzen, David
2008 "An Ambiguous Ending: Dynastic Punishment in Kings and the Fate of the Davidides in 2 Kings 25.27-30." *Journal for the Study of the Old Testament* 33:39-58.
Jemielity, Thomas
1992 *Satire and the Hebrew Prophets.* Louisville: Westminster/John Knox.

Jeon, Yong Ho
  2011   "The Retroactive Re-evaluation Technique with Pharaoh's
         Daughter and the Nature of Solomon's Corruption in 1 Kings
         1–12." *Tyndale Bulletin* 62/1:15–40.
Jeter, Joseph
  2003   *Preaching Judges.* St. Louis: Chalice.
Jobling, David
  1991   "'Forced Labor': Solomon's Golden Age and the Question of
         Literary Representation." *Semeia* 54:57–76.
Jones, Gwilym H.
  1984   *1 and 2 Kings.* Grand Rapids: Eerdmans.
Joseph, Alison L.
  2015   *Portrait of the Kings: The Davidic Prototype in Deuteronomistic
         Poetics.* Minneapolis: Fortress.
Kaminsky, Joel S.
  1995   *Corporate Responsibility in the Hebrew Bible.* Sheffield: Sheffield
         Academic.
Katulka, Chris
  2013   "Palestinian Liberation Theology." Friends of Israel, October
         13, 2013. https://www.foi.org/free_resource/palestinian
         -liberation-theology/.
Kimelman, Reuven
  2014   "Prophecy as Arguing with God and the Ideal of Justice."
         Interpretation 68/1:17–27.
Kinnaman, David
  2007   *UnChristian: What a New Generation Really Thinks about Christianity
         . . . and Why It Matters.* Grand Rapids: Baker Books.
Kissling, Paul J.
  1996   *Reliable Characters in the Primary History: Profiles of Moses, Joshua,
         Elijah and Elisha.* Sheffield: Sheffield Academic.
Klein, Ralph W.
  1979   *Israel in Exile: A Theological Interpretation.* Philadelphia: Fortress.
Knight, Douglas A.
  2011   *Law, Power, and Justice in Ancient Israel.* Louisville: Westminster
         John Knox.
Knoppers, Gary N.
  1993   *Two Nations under God: The Deuteronomistic History of Solomon and
         the Dual Monarchies.* Atlanta: Scholars Press.
  1995   "Prayer and Propaganda: Solomon's Dedication of the Temple
         and the Deuteronomist's Program." *Catholic Biblical Quarterly*
         57:229–54.
Koba, Mark
  2013   "A Hungry World: Lots of Food, in Too Few Places." CNBC,
         July 30, 2013. https://www.cnbc.com/id/100893540.
Konkel, August H.
  2006   *1 & 2 Kings.* NIV Application Commentary. Grand Rapids:
         Zondervan.
  2016   *1 & 2 Chronicles.* Believers Church Bible Commentary.
         Harrisonburg, VA: Herald Press.

Kröller, Eva-Marie
1995   Afterword to *The Blue Mountains of China*, by Rudy Wiebe. Toronto: McCelland and Stewart.

LaBarbera, Robert
1984   "The Man of War and the Man of God: Social Satire in 2 Kings 6:8–7:20." *Catholic Biblical Quarterly* 46:637–51.

Lallanilla, Marc
2020   "The Effects of War on the Environment." *Treehugger*, June 30, 2020. https://www.treehugger.com/the-effects-of-war-on-environment-1708787.

Lasine, Stuart
1991   "Jehoram and the Cannibal Mothers (2 Kings 6.24-33): Solomon's Judgment in an Inverted World." *Journal for the Study of the Old Testament* 50:27–53.
1993   "Manasseh as Villain and Scapegoat." In *The New Literary Criticism and the Hebrew Bible*, edited by J. Cheryl Exum and David J. A. Clines, 163–83. Sheffield: Sheffield Academic.
2001   *Knowing Kings: Knowledge, Power, and Narcissism in the Hebrew Bible*. Atlanta: SBL Press, 2001.
2011   "'Go in Peace' or 'Go to Hell'? Elisha, Naaman, and the Meaning of Monotheism in 2 Kings 5." *Scandinavian Journal of the Old Testament* 25:3–28.

Latvus, Karl
1998   *God, Anger and Ideology: The Anger of God in Joshua and Judges in Relation to Deuteronomy and the Priestly Writings*. Sheffield: Sheffield Academic.

Leithart, Peter
2006   *1 & 2 Kings*. Grand Rapids: Brazos.

Lenski, Gerhard, and Jean Lenski
1970   *Human Societies: An Introduction to Macrosociology*. New York: McGraw-Hill.

Leuchter, Mark
2005   "The Sociolinguistic and Rhetorical Implications of the Source Citations in Kings." In Adam and Leuchter, 119–34.

Liechty, Daniel, trans. and ed.
1994   *Early Anabaptist Spirituality: Selected Writings*. New York: Paulist Press.

Long, Burke O.
1985   *1 Kings: With an Introduction to Historical Literature*. Grand Rapids: Eerdmans.
1991   *2 Kings*. Grand Rapids: Eerdmans.

Lowery, Richard H.
1991   *The Reforming Kings: Cult and Society in First Temple Judah*. Sheffield: Sheffield Academic.

Mafico, Temba L. J.
1992   "Just, Justice." In *ABD*, 3:1127–29.

Malchow, Bruce V.
1996   *Social Justice in the Hebrew Bible: What Is New and What Is Old*. Collegeville: Liturgical Press.

Marpeck, Pilgram
1978   *The Writings of Pilgram Marpeck.* Translated and edited by William
        Klassen and Walter Klaassen. Scottdale, PA: Herald Press.
Martens, Elmer A.
1986   *Jeremiah.* Believers Church Bible Commentary. Scottdale, PA:
        Herald Press.
2015   *God's Design: A Focus on Old Testament Theology.* 4th ed. Eugene,
        OR: Wipf and Stock. 1st ed. Grand Rapids: Baker, 1981.
Master, Daniel M.
2010   "Institutions of Trade in 1 and 2 Kings." In Halpern and
        Lemaire, 501–16.
Matties, Gordon
2012   *Joshua.* Believers Church Bible Commentary. Harrisonburg, VA:
        Herald Press.
Mazar, Amihai
1990   *Archaeology of the Land of the Bible, 10,000–586 BCE.* New York:
        Doubleday.
McConville, J. Gordon
1993   *Grace in the End: A Study in Deuteronomic Theology.* Grand Rapids:
        Zondervan.
2006   *God and Earthly Power: An Old Testament Political Theology,
        Genesis-Kings.* New York: T&T Clark.
McKenzie, Steven L.
1991   *The Trouble with Kings: The Composition of the Book of Kings in the
        Deuteronomistic History.* Leiden: Brill.
2006   "Kings, First and Second Books of." In *New Interpreter's
        Dictionary of the Bible,* edited by Katharine Doob Sakenfeld,
        Samuel E. Ballantine, and Brian K. Blount, 3:523–32. Nashville:
        Abingdon.
Menno Simons
1956.   *The Complete Writings of Menno Simons c. 1496-1561.* Translated by
        Leonard Verduin. Edited by John Christian Wenger. Scottdale,
        PA: Herald Press.
Mettinger, Tryggve N. D.
1971   *Solomonic State Officials: A Study of the Civil Government Officials of
        the Israelite Monarchy.* Lund: CWK Gleerup.
Miller, Douglas A.
2010   *Ecclesiastes.* Believers Church Bible Commentary. Scottdale, PA:
        Herald Press.
Miller, Geoffrey
2014   "The Wiles of the Lord: Deception, Subtlety, and Mercy."
        Zeitschrift für die Alttestamentliche Wissenschaft 126:45–58.
Moberly, R. Walter L.
1992   *The Old Testament of the Old Testament: Patriarchal Narratives and
        Mosaic Yahwism.* Minneapolis: Augsburg Fortress.
2003   "Does God Lie to His Prophets? The Story of Micaiah ben Imlah
        as a Test Case." *Harvard Theological Review* 96/1:1–23.

Mobley, Gregory
   2009   "1 and 2 Kings." In *Theological Bible Commentary*, edited by
           Gail R. O'Day and Robert L. Petersen, 119–43. Louisville:
           Westminster John Knox.
Moore, Michael S.
   2003   "Jehu's Coronation and Purge of Israel." *Vetus Testamentum*
           53/1:97–114.
Morgenstern, Mira
   2017   *Reframing Politics in the Hebrew Bible: A New Introduction with
           Readings.* Indianapolis: Hackett.
Mulder, Martin J.
   1998   *1 Kings.* Leuven: Peeters.
Mullen, E. Theodore, Jr.
   1992   "Crime and Punishment: The Sins of the King and the
           Despoliation of the Treasuries." *Catholic Biblical Quarterly*
           54:231–48.
   1993   *Narrative History and Ethnic Boundaries: The Deuteronomistic
           Historian and the Creation of Israelite National Identity.* Atlanta:
           Scholars Press.
Murray, Stuart
   2000   *Biblical Interpretation in the Anabaptist Tradition.* Kitchener, ON:
           Pandora; Scottdale, PA: Herald Press.
Murray, Stuart, and Sian Murray Williams
   2012   *The Power of All: Building a Multi-Voiced Church.* Harrisonburg:
           Herald Press.
Nelson, Richard D.
   1981a   *The Double Redaction of the Deuteronomistic History.* Sheffield:
           Sheffield Academic.
   1981b   "Josiah in the Book of Joshua." *Journal of Biblical Literature*
           100:531–40.
   1987   *First and Second Kings.* Atlanta: John Knox.
   1998   *The Historical Books.* Nashville: Abingdon.
Newing, Edward G.
   1994   "Rhetorical Art of the Deuteronomist: Lampooning Solomon in
           First Kings." In *Old Testament Essays* 7:247–60.
Ngan, Lai Ling Elizabeth
   1997   "2 Kings." *Review and Expositor* 94:589–97.
Nicholson, E. W.
   1965   "The Meaning of the Expression *Am ha-Aretz* in the Old
           Testament." *Journal of Semitic Studies* 10:59–66.
Noth, Martin
   1991   *The Deuteronomistic History.* 2nd ed. Sheffield: Sheffield
           Academic.
O'Brien, Mark A.
   1998   "The Portrayal of Prophets in 2 Kings 2." *Australian Biblical
           Review* 46:1–16.
   2013   "Prophetic Stories Making a Story of Prophecy." In Jacobs and
           Person, 169–86.

Ollenburger, Ben C.
    1987   *Zion, the City of the Great King: A Theological Symbol of the Jerusalem Cult.* Sheffield: Sheffield Academic.
Olley, John W.
    1998   "YHWH and His Zealous Prophet: The Presentation of Elijah in 1 and 2 Kings." *Journal for the Study of the Old Testament* 80:25–51.
    2011   "2 Kings 13: A Cluster of Hope in God." *Journal for the Study of the Old Testament* 36/2: 199–218.
Olson, Dennis T.
    1994   *Deuteronomy and the Death of Moses: A Theological Reading.* Overtures to Biblical Theology. Minneapolis: Fortress.
Olyan, Saul M.
    1988   *Asherah and the Cult of Yahweh in Israel.* Atlanta: Scholars Press.
Park, Song-Mi Suzie
    2015   *Hezekiah and the Dialogue of Memory.* Minneapolis: Fortress.
Parker, Julie Faith
    2013   *Valuable and Vulnerable: Children in the Hebrew Bible, Especially the Elisha Cycle.* Providence: Brown Judaic Series.
Peckham, Brian
    1993   *History and Prophecy: The Development of Late Judean Literary Traditions.* New York: Doubleday.
Person, Raymond F., Jr.
    1999   "II Kings 18–20 and Isaiah 36–39: A Text Critical Study in the Redaction History of the Book of Isaiah." *Zeitschrift für die Alttestamentliche Wissenschaft* 111:373–79.
    2013   "Prophets in the Deuteronomic History and the Book of Chronicles: A Reassessment." In Jacobs and Person, 187–99.
Peterson, Brian Neil
    2014   *The Authors of the Deuteronomistic History: Locating a Tradition in Ancient Israel.* Minneapolis: Fortress.
Philips, Dirk
    1559   "Concerning Spiritual Restitution." In Liechty: 218–47.
    1564   "The Enchiridion." In *The Writings of Dirk Philips: 1504-1568,* edited by Cornelius J. Dyck, William E. Keeney, and Alvin J. Beachy, 49–440. Scottdale, PA: Herald Press, 1992.
Piper, John
    1986   *Desiring God: Confessions of a Christian Hedonist.* Portland: Multnomah Press.
Premnath, D. N.
    2003   *Eighth Century Prophets: A Social Analysis.* St. Louis: Chalice.
Provan, Iain
    1988   *Hezekiah and the Books of the Kings: A Contribution to the Debate about the Composition of the Deuteronomistic History.* Berlin: W. de Guyter.
    1995   *1 and 2 Kings.* Peabody, MA: Hendrickson; Carlisle, UK: Paternoster.
    1999   "On 'Seeing the Trees While Missing the Forest.'" In *In Search*

of *True Wisdom: Essays in Old Testament Interpretation in Honour of Ronald E. Clements*, edited by Edward Ball, 153–73. Sheffield: Sheffield Academic.

Quine, Cat
2016 "On Dying in a City Gate: Implications in the Deaths of Eli, Abner and Jezebel." *Journal for the Study of the Old Testament* 40:399–413.

Rainey, Anson F.
1970 "Compulsory Labor Gangs in Ancient Israel." *Israel Exploration Journal* 20:191–202.

Reis, Pamela Tamarkin
1994 "Vindicating God: Another Look at 1 Kings XIII." *Vetus Testamentum* 4:376–86.

Rentería, Tamis Hoover
1992 "The Elijah/Elisha Stories: A Socio-Cultural Analysis." In *Elijah and Elisha in Socioliterary Perspective*, edited by Robert B. Coote, 75–126. Atlanta: Scholars Press.

Reviv, H.
1979 "The Structure of Society." In *The World History of Jewish People*, vol. 4, bk. 2, *The Age of Monarchies: Culture and Society*, edited by A. Malamat and I. Eph'al, 125–46. Jerusalem: Massada Press.

Rice, Gene
1990 *Nations under God: A Commentary on the Book of 1 Kings*. International Theological Commentary. Grand Rapids: Eerdmans.

Richardson, John, and Darren Duerksen
2019 "Learning from the 'Nones' and 'Dones.'" *Christian Leader* 82/2:10–11.

Richter, Sandra
2005 "Deuteronomistic History." In *Dictionary of the Old Testament: Historical Books*, edited by Bill T. Arnold and H. G. M. Williamson, 219–30. Downers Grove: InterVarsity Press.

Rofé, Alexander
1988 "The Vineyard of Naboth: The Origin and Message of the Story." *Vetus Testamentum* 38:89–104.

Rohr, Richard
2018 *Essential Teachings on Love*. Edited by Joelle Chase and Judy Traeger. Maryknoll: Orbis Books.

Roi, Micha
2012 "1 Kings: A 'Departure on a Journey' Story." *Journal for the Study of the Old Testament* 37:25–44.

Rollston, Christopher
n.d. "The Siloam Inscription and Hezekiah's Tunnel." Bible Odyssey, accessed November 9, 2019. https://www.bibleodyssey. org:443/en/places/related-articles/siloam-inscription-and -hezekiahs-tunnel.

Root, Andrew
2019 *The Pastor in a Secular Age: Ministry to People Who No Longer Need a God*. Grand Rapids: Baker Academic.

Rösel, Hartmut N.
2009   "Why 2 Kings 17 Does Not Constitute a Chapter of Reflection in
        the 'Deuteronomistic History.'" *Journal of Biblical Literature*
        128:85–90.
Rost, Leonhard
1982   *The Succession to the Throne of David.* Translated by Michael D.
        Rutter and David M. Gunn. Sheffield: Almond.
Rudman, Dominic
2000   "Is the Rabshakeh Also among the Prophets? A Rhetorical
        Study of 2 Kings XVIII 17–35." *Vetus Testamentum* 50:100–110.
Russell, Stephen C.
2014   "The Hierarchy of Estates in Land and Naboth's Vineyard."
        Journal for the Study of the Old Testament 138:453–69.
Sakenfeld, Katharine Doob.
1985   *Faithfulness in Action: Loyalty in Biblical Perspective.* Philadelphia:
        Fortress.
Sandoval, Timothy J.
2007   "A Prophet's (Re-)call and Recollection: The Case of Elijah in
        1 Kings 19." *Chicago Theological Seminary Register* 94/2–3:12–16.
Schenker, Adrian
2010   "The Septuagint in the Text History of 1–2 Kings." In *The Books
        of Kings: Sources, Composition, Historiography and Reception*, edited
        by André Lemaire, Baruch Halpern, and Matthew Joel Adams,
        3–17. Boston: Brill.
Schipper, Jeremy
2010   "Embodying Deuteronomistic Theology in 1 Kings 15:22–24."
        In *Bodies, Embodiment, and Theology of the Hebrew Bible*, edited
        by S. Tamar Kamionkowski and Wonil Kim. New York: T&T
        Clark.
Schniedewind, William M.
1993   "History and Interpretation: The Religion of Ahab and
        Manasseh in the Book of Kings." *Catholic Biblical Quarterly*
        55:649–61.
Schweitzer, Steven J.
2011   "The Temple in Samuel–Kings and Chronicles." In *Rewriting
        Biblical History: Essays on Chronicles and Ben Sira in Honor of
        Pancratius Beentjes*, edited by Jeremy Corley and Harm van Grol,
        123–38. Berlin: de Gruyter.
Seibert, Eric
2006   *Subversive Scribes and the Solomonic Narrative: A Re-reading of
        1 Kings 1–11.* New York: T&T Clark.
Seow, Choon Leong
1999   "The First and Second Books of Kings." In *The New Interpreter's
        Bible*, edited by Leander E. Keck, 3:3–295. Nashville: Abingdon.
Shanks, Hershel
1985   "Ancient Ivory—The Story of Wealth, Decadence, and Beauty."
        Biblical Archaeology Review 11/5: 40–53.
Sider, Ronald J.
1987   *Completely Pro-Life: Building a Consistent Stance on Abortion, the*

Family, Nuclear Weapons, the Poor. Downers Grove, IL: InterVarsity Press. Repr., Eugene, OR: Wipf and Stock, 2010.

2012   *Just Politics: A Guide for Christian Engagement.* 2nd ed. Grand Rapids, Brazos Press.

2016   "Womb to Tomb: Imagining a Completely Pro-Life Politics." Plough Quarterly No 10, October 12, 2016. https://www .plough.com/en/topics/justice/culture-of-life/womb-to-tomb.

Simons, Menno.
(*see* Menno Simons)

Simundson, Daniel J.
2015   "Pharaoh, the Bad King of Exodus 5, and the Antimonarchical Strains of the Story of King Jeroboam (1 Kgs 11–12)." In *A King like All the Nations? Kingdoms of Israel and Judah in the Bible and History*, edited by Manfred Oeming and Petr Sláma, 193–98. Zurich: LIT.

Smend, Rudolf
1971   "Das Gesetz und die Völker: Ein Beitrag zur deuteronomistischen Redaktionsgeschichte." In *Probleme biblischer Theologie*, edited by H. W. Wolff, 494–509. Munich: Kaiser.

Smith, James K. A.
2016   *You Are What You Love: The Spiritual Power of Habit.* Grand Rapids: Brazos.

Smith, W. Alan
1994   "Naaman and Elisha: Healing, Wholeness, and the Task of Religious Education." *Religious Education* 89:205–19.

Smith-Christopher, Daniel L.
2002   *A Biblical Theology of Exile.* Minneapolis: Augsburg Fortress.

Smucker, Barbara
1952   *Henry's Red Sea.* Scottdale, PA: Herald Press.

Snyder, C. Arnold, and Walter Klaassen
2001   *Sources of South German/Austrian Reformation.* Kitchener, ON: Pandora.

Stavrakopoulou, Francesca
2007   "The Blackballing of Manasseh." In *Good Kings and Bad Kings: The Kingdom of Judah in the Seventh Century* BCE, edited by Lester L. Grabbe, 248–63. New York: T&T Clark.

Stern, Ephraim
1990   "Hazor, Dor and Megiddo in the Time of Ahab and under Assyrian Rule." *Israel Exploration Journal* 40/1:12–30.

Stern, Philip D.
1990   "The ḥerem in 1 Kgs 20,42 as an Exegetical Problem." *Biblica* 71/1:43–47.

Sternberg, Meir
1985   *The Poetics of Biblical Narrative: Ideological Literature and the Drama of Reading.* Bloomington: Indiana University Press.

Stone, Ken
2006   "1 and 2 Kings." In *Queer Bible Commentary*, edited by Deryn Guest, Robert Goss, Mona West, and Thomas Bohache, 222–50. London: SCM.

Stone, Suzanne
  2009   "Between Truth and Trust: The Prophet as Self-Deceiver?"
          Hebraic Political Studies 4:337–66.
Strawn, Brent A.
  2017   "Reading Josiah Reading Deuteronomy." In *Reading for Faith
          and Learning: Essays on Scripture, Community, and Libraries in
          Honor of M. Patrick Graham*, edited by John B. Weaver and
          Douglas L. Gragg, 31–47. Abilene: Abilene Christian University.
Suderman, W. Derek
  2017   *"Conversion to Wisdom." In Quest for Respect: The Church and
          Indigenous Spirituality*, edited by Jeff Friesen, *109–13*. Winnipeg:
          Mennonite Church Canada.
Sweeney, Marvin
  2007a   *I & II Kings: A Commentary*. Louisville: Westminster John Knox.
  2007b   "King Manasseh of Judah and the Problem of Theodicy in the
          Deuteronomistic History." In *Good Kings and Bad Kings: The
          Kingdom of Judah in the Seventh Century* BCE, edited by Lester L.
          Grabbe, 264–78. New York: T&T Clark.
  2013   "Prophets and Priests in the Deuteronomic History: Elijah and
          Elisha." In Jacobs and Person, 35–49.
Terrien, Samuel
  1978   *The Elusive Presence*. New York: Harper and Row. Repr., Eugene:
          Wipf and Stock, 2000.
Thiele, Edwin
  1951   *The Mysterious Numbers of the Hebrew Kings*. 1st ed. New York:
          Macmillan. 3rd ed. Grand Rapids: Zondervan/Kregel, 1983.
Thompson, Thomas L.
  1999   *The Mythic Past: Biblical Archaeology and the Myth of Israel*.
          London: Basic Books.
Toews, Wesley I.
  1993   *Monarchy and Religious Institution in Israel under Jeroboam I*.
          Atlanta: SBL Press.
Trafton, Joseph L.
  1996   "Burial." In *Baker's Evangelical Dictionary of Biblical Theology*,
          edited by Walter A. Elwell, 78. Grand Rapids: Baker.
Twisck, P. J., and Sijwaert Pietersz
  1617   *The Confession of Faith*. 33 articles. https://anabaptistwiki.org/
          mediawiki/index.php?title=The_Confession_of_Faith_(P.J._
          Twisck,_1617).
Uehlinger, Christoph
  1999   "Nisroch." In *Dictionary of Deities and Demons in the Bible*, edited
          by Karel van der Toorn, Bob Becking, and Pieter W. van der
          Horst, 631. 2nd ed. Grand Rapids: Eerdmans.
Ussishkin, David
  2007   "Samaria, Jezreel, and Megiddo: Royal Centres of Omri and
          Ahab." In *Ahab Agonistes: The Rise and Fall of the Omri Dynasty*,
          edited by Lester L. Grabbe, Sharon Keller, and Claire Gottlieb,
          293–309. New York: Bloomsbury Academic.

van Braght, Thieleman J.
1950   *The Bloody Mirror, or Martyrs Mirror of the Defenseless Christians.* Translated from the original 1660 Dutch edition by Joseph Sohm. Scottdale, PA, and Waterloo, ON: Herald Press.
Van Seters, John.
1997   *In Search of History: Historiography in the Ancient World and the Origins of Biblical History.* Winona Lake: Eisenbrauns.
Vasholz, Robert I.
2007   "The Wisdom of Bathsheba in 1 Kings 2:13-25." *Presbyterion* 33/1:49.
Veijola, Timo
1975   *Die ewige Dynastie. David und die Entstehung seiner Dynastie nach der deuteronomistischen Darstellung.* Helsinki: Suomalainen Tiedeakatemia.
Vogt, Peter T.
2006   *Deuteronomic Theology and the Significance of Torah: A Reappraisal.* Winona Lake: Eisenbrauns.
Waldman, Nahum M.
1994   "Sound and Silence." *Jewish Bible Quarterly.* 22:228–36.
Wallace, R. S.
1957   *Elijah and Elisha: Expositions from the Book of Kings.* Achimota: Africa Christian Press.
Wallis, Jim
2005   *God's Politics: Why the Right Gets It Wrong and the Left Doesn't Get It.* San Francisco: Harper San Francisco.
Walsh, James P. M.
1987   *The Mighty from Their Thrones: Power in Biblical Tradition.* Minneapolis: Augsburg Fortress.
Walsh, Jerome T.
1992   "Methods and Meanings: Multiple Readings of 1 Kings 21." *Journal of Biblical Literature* 111:193–211.
1995   "The Characterization of Solomon in First Kings 1–5." *Catholic Biblical Quarterly* 57:471–93.
1996   *1 Kings.* Berit Olam: Studies in Hebrew Narrative and Poetry. Collegeville: Liturgical Press.
2009   *Old Testament Narrative: A Guide to Interpretation.* Westminster John Knox.
Walton, John H., and Jonathan Harvey Walton
2017   *The Lost World of Israelite Conquest: Covenant, Retribution, and the Fate of the Canaanites.* Downers Grove: InterVarsity Press.
Walton, Joshua T.
2018   "Trade in the Late Bronze and Iron Age Levant." In *Behind the Scenes of the Old Testament,* edited by Jonathan S. Greer, John W. Hilber, and John H. Walton, 416–22. Grand Rapids: Baker Academic.
Way, Kenneth C.
2009   "Animals in the Narrative World: Literary Reflections on Numbers 22 and 1 Kings 13." *Journal for the Study of the Old Testament* 34:47–62.

Weinfeld, Moshe
  1995   *Social Justice in Ancient Israel and in the Ancient Near East.*
          Minneapolis: Fortress.
Weingart, Kristin
  2018   "'My Father, My Father! Chariot of Israel and Its Horses!'
          (2 Kings 2:12 // 13:14): Elisha's or Elijah's Title?" *Journal of
          Biblical Literature* 137:257–70.
Weitzman, Steven
  2011   *Solomon: The Lure of Wisdom.* New Haven: Yale University Press.
Wells, Samuel
  2014   "A Different Way to Pray." *Christian Century*, April 30, 2014, 51.
Westbrook, Raymond
  2005   "Elisha's True Prophecy in 2 Kings 3." *Journal of Biblical
          Literature* 124/3:530–32.
White, Andrea C.
  2018   "God Revealed in Blackness." *Christian Century*, May 16, 2018.
          Available online at https://www.christiancentury.org/arti-
          cle/critical-essay/james-cone-looked-evil-face-and-refused-
          let-it-crush-his-hope.
Whitelam, Keith W.
  1979   *The Just King: Monarchical Judicial Authority in Ancient Israel.*
          Sheffield: Sheffield Academic.
Widmer, Michael
  2015   *Standing in the Break: An Old Testament Theology and Spirituality of
          Intercessory Prayer.* Winona Lake: Eisenbrauns.
Williamson, H. G. M.
  2005   "Lachish." In *New International Dictionary of the Old Testament:
          Historical Books*, edited by Bill T. Arnold, 685–88. Downers Grove:
          InterVarsity Press.
Wilson, Robert R.
  1980   *Prophecy and Society in Ancient Israel.* Philadelphia: Fortress.
  1995   "The Former Prophets: Reading the Books of Kings." In *Old
          Testament Interpretation: Past, Present, and Future*, edited by
          David Petersen, Kent H. Richards, and James Luther Mays,
          83–96. Nashville: Abingdon.
Wiseman, Donald J.
  1993   *1 & 2 Kings.* Leicester: Inter-Varsity.
Witherington, Ben
  1994   *Jesus the Sage: The Pilgrimage of Wisdom.* Minneapolis: Fortress.
Wray Beal, Lissa M.
  2007   *The Deuteronomist's Prophet: Narrative Control of Approval and
          Disapproval in the Story of Jehu (2 Kings 9 and 10).* New York: Brill.
  2013   "Jeroboam and the Prophets in 1 Kings 11–14: Prophetic Word
          for Two Kingdoms." In *Prophets, Prophecy, and Ancient Israelite
          Historiography*, edited by Mark J. Boda and Lissa M. Wray Beal,
          105–24. Winona Lake: Eisenbrauns.
  2014   *1 & 2 Kings.* Downers Grove: InterVarsity Press.
Wright, N. T.

1996 *Jesus and the Victory of God*. Minneapolis: Fortress.

Wyatt, Nicolas
1999 "Asherah." In *Dictionary of Deities and Demons in the Bible*, edited by Karel van der Toorn, Bob Becking, and Pieter W. van der Horst, 99–105. 2nd ed. Grand Rapids: Eerdmans.

Wyatt, Stephanie
2012 "Jezebel, Elijah, and the Widow of Zarephath: A Ménage à Trois That Estranges the Holy and Makes the Holy Strange." *Journal for the Study of the Old Testament* 36:435–58.

Yamauchi, Edwin
1980 "ṭāmê." In *Theological Wordbook of the Old Testament*, edited by R. Laird Harris, Gleason L. Archer Jr., and Bruce K. Waltke, 1:349–51. Chicago: Moody Press.

Zucker, David J.
2013 "The Prophet Micaiah in Kings and Chronicles." *Jewish Bible Quarterly* 41/3:156–62.

Zvi, Ehud Ben
1990 "Who Wrote the Speech of Rabshakeh and When?" *Journal of Biblical Literature* 109/1: 79–42.
2004 "'The Prophets'—Generic Prophets and Their Role in the Construction of the Image of the 'Prophets of Old' within the Postmonarchic Relationships of the Book of Kings." *Zeitschrift für die Alttestamentliche Wissenschaft* 116:555–67.

Selected Resources

Commentaries

Recommended for pastors, Sunday school teachers, and Bible study leaders

*Brueggemann, Walter. *1 & 2 Kings*. Smyth & Helwys Bible Commentary. Macon, GA: Smyth and Helwys, 2000. Engaged with the artistry and imagination of the Old Testament and pondering the ways that issues of power in the ancient texts pertain to contemporary times, the author maneuvers between flat history and absolute faith. Includes resources such as photography, classic works of art, and maps.

Cohn, Robert L. *2 Kings*. Berit Olam: *Studies in Hebrew Narrative and Poetry*. Collegeville, MN: Liturgical Press, 2000. Unfolds the literary dimensions of 2 Kings, analyzes the strategies through which words create a world of meaning, and examines tales of prophets, political intrigue, royal apostasy, and religious reform as components of larger patterns. Treats the text as powerful history that creates memories and forges identities for its Jewish readers.

*Davies, John A. *1 Kings*. Darlington: Evangelical Press, 2012. Drawing on the author's translation, introductory paragraphs connect each chapter to the developing, overarching story, followed by commentary, and concluding with brief application. Links redemptive history, the grand themes of the Bible, and Old Testament history with new covenant perspective.

*DeVries, Simon J. *1 Kings*. Word Biblical Commentary. 2nd ed. Waco: Word, 2003. Scholarly commentary with analysis of textual, linguistic, structural, and theological evidence in the framework of biblical theology.

*Fretheim, Terence E. *First and Second Kings*. Westminster Bible Companion. Louisville: Westminster John Knox, 1999. Gives close attention to the text, its rhetoric, and its theology, interspersed with several short essays to illuminate problems raised in the text.

Fritz, Volkmar. *1 and 2 Kings*. Continental Commentary. Minneapolis: Augsburg Fortress, 2003. Readable introduction appropriate for the student, pastor, or scholar. Combines historical, literary, and archaeological approaches. Addresses issues of the Deuteronomic redaction but does not become bogged down in technical discussions that might overshadow the holistic interpretation of the text.

*Hens-Piazza, Gina. *1-2 Kings*. Abingdon Old Testament Commentaries. Nashville: Abingdon, 2006. Compact, critical commentary for theological students and pastors, amplifying the biblical resonances of the contemporary by disclosing how God's Word is made known by those who are least expected.

*Hobbs, T. R. *2 Kings*. Word Biblical Commentary. Waco: Word, 1985. Scholarly commentary with analysis of textual, linguistic, structural, and theological evidence in the framework of biblical theology.

*Konkel, August H. *1 & 2 Kings*. The NIV Application Commentary. Grand Rapids: Zondervan, 2006. Addresses the original meaning of the biblical text in its historical, literary, and cultural context, bridges the biblical world with contemporary life, and explores relevant application of the biblical messages.

*Leithart, Peter. *1 & 2 Kings*. Brazos Theological Commentary on the Bible. Grand Rapids: Brazos, 2006. With a succinct summary of each chapter or section to assist in preaching through the book, the author draws together the disciplines of biblical and theological studies to offer contemporary applications.

Long, Burke O. *1 Kings: With an Introduction to Historical Literature*. Grand Rapids: Eerdmans, 1985.

———. *2 Kings*. Grand Rapids: Eerdmans, 1991. Introduced with a discussion of the nature of historical literature and a survey of its important genres, including list, report, story, and history, the author focuses on the text as historical literature, analyzing the book as a whole as well as unit by unit.

McKenzie, Steven J. *1 Kings 16–2 Kings 16*. International Commentary on the Old Testament. Stuttgart: Kohlhammer, 2019. After translation with notes, synchronic analysis of the final form of the text with attention to canonical and literary features, followed by diachronic analysis of redactional reworkings.

*Nelson, Richard D. *First and Second Kings*. Interpretation. Atlanta: John Knox, 1987. Treats the text as theological literature, emphasizing its literary impact. Treats Kings as a useful though uncritical source of historical information with a purpose to transform the beliefs of its first readers to get them to reevaluate their identity before God.

*Provan, Iain. *1 and 2 Kings*. Understanding the Bible Commentary. Peabody, MA: Hendrickson; Carlisle, UK: Paternoster, 1995. Using the full range of critical methodologies and practices, provides historical context and complete expositions of each chapter, explains important issues, and includes notes to explain key phrases, persons, and places.

*Seow, Choon Leong. "The First and Second Books of Kings." In *The New Interpreter's Bible*, edited by Leander E. Keck, 3:3–295. Nashville: Abingdon, 1999. Detailed commentary of the text, aided by maps, with reflections on the contemporary application for preaching, teaching, and daily living.

Sweeney, Marvin. *I & II Kings: A Commentary*. Louisville: Westminster John Knox, 2007. A close reading of the historical books, concentrating on not only issues in the history of Israel but also the literary techniques of storytelling. Discussions of textual difficulties in the books of Kings as well as compelling narrative interpretations.

Walsh, Jerome T. *1 Kings*. Berit Olam: Studies in Hebrew Narrative and Poetry. Collegeville, MN: Liturgical Press, 1996. Explores the narrative world created by the ancient Israelite author: the people who inhabit it, the lives they live, the deeds they do, and the God revealed in their stories. Explores how the rich traditions of Hebrew narrative and the Hebrew language affect one's reading.

*Wray Beal, Lissa M. *1 & 2 Kings*. Apollos Old Testament Commentary. Downers Grove, IL: InterVarsity Press, 2014. Pursues historiographical, narrative, form, structural, and theological questions, including the relation of each chapter's themes to biblical theology with attention to complex historical issues.

Other Resources

Barré, Lloyd M. *The Rhetoric of Political Persuasion: The Narrative Artistry and Political Intentions of 2 Kings 9–11*. Washington, DC: Catholic Biblical Association of America, 1986. Compares Jehu's violent coup against Ahab's family in Israel with the relatively nonviolent transition to Joash in Judah.

Bennett, Harold. *Injustice Made Legal: Deuteronomic Law and the Plight of Widows, Strangers, and Orphans in Ancient Israel*. Grand Rapids: Eerdmans, 2002. Challenges the perspective that Deuteronomic law protects the needy, arguing instead that the powerful elite used the law to enhance their own material condition and maintain the dehumanization of widows, strangers, and orphans.

Bodner, Keith. *Jeroboam's Royal Drama*. Oxford: Oxford University Press, 2021. A close reading of the Jeroboam narrative revealing a literary achievement of great subtlety and complexity. Contends that Jeroboam's portrait is far more nuanced than is often realized and yields a host of surprises for the engaged reader. Issues include questions of power, leadership, and the role of the prophetic office in national affairs.

———. *The Theology of the Book of Kings*. Cambridge: Cambridge University Press, 2019. A reading of the narrative attentive to its literary sophistication and theological subtleties, as the characters are challenged to resist the tempting pathway of political and spiritual accommodations and called instead to maintain allegiance to their covenant with God.

Bodner, Keith and Benjamin J. M. Johnson, eds. *Characters and Characterization in the Book of Kings*. London: T&T Clark, 2020. Sixteen studies using an array of narratological approaches to analyze such characters as Hezekiah, Solomon, Athaliah, Elijah, and Bathsheba.

Brueggemann, Walter. *Solomon: Israel's Ironic Icon of Human Achievement*. Columbia: University of South Carolina, 2005. Examines assertions about Solomon's wealth, wisdom, and power, noting an irony that invites critique of accepted beliefs. Through close attention to nuances of the biblical text, exposes the competing interpretive voices that claim to offer a reliable rendering of Solomon. Suggests a conflicted pluralistic attempt to sort out the reality of human power in the matrix of covenantal faith.

———. *Testimony to Otherwise: The Witness of Elijah and Elisha.* St. Louis: Chalice, 2001. Shows how the memories of Elijah and Elisha took on an authority of lasting testimony by exhibiting a world open to the gifts, energies, and visions given by God and summoning Israel to a radical either/or decision.

———. *Truth Speaks to Power: The Countercultural Nature of Scripture.* Louisville: Westminster John Knox, 2013. Examines the biblical stories of Moses, Solomon, Elisha, and Josiah to reveal that "power that has been founded on something other than truth [e.g., deception, violence] is exposed as fraudulent, delegitimized."

Doorly, William J. *Obsession with Justice: The Story of the Deuteronomists.* Mahwah: Paulist Press, 1994. Accessible introduction to the authors of Kings, particularly their motivation to pursue biblical justice.

Galvin, Garrett. *David's Successors: Kingship in the Old Testament.* Collegeville, MN: Liturgical Press, 2016. Challenges negative view of kingship among contemporary readers of 1–2 Kings with comparison to 1–2 Chronicles and Royal Psalms.

Gerbrandt, Gerald E. *Kingship according to the Deuteronomistic Historian.* Atlanta: Scholars Press, 1986. Analysis of the positive evaluation of the reigns of Hezekiah and Josiah linked to Mosaic and Davidic covenant and the king's role in upholding the Torah.

Glanville, Mark. *Adopting the Stranger as Kindred in Deuteronomy.* Atlanta: SBL Press, 2018. Investigates how Deuteronomy fosters the integration of displaced, vulnerable people as kindred into the community of Israel. Informs the meaning of "justice" in the book of Kings.

Goldingay, John. *Do We Need the New Testament? Letting the Old Testament Speak for Itself.* Downers Grove, IL: InterVarsity, 2015. A biblical theological case for reading the "First Testament" on its own terms.

Hayes, John H., and Paul K. Hooker. *A New Chronology for the Kings of Israel and Judah and Its Implications for Biblical History and Literature.* Atlanta: John Knox, 1988. Offers one explanation for the chronological issues related to dates of royal tenure.

Joseph, Alison L. *Portrait of the Kings: The Davidic Prototype in Deuteronomistic Poetics.* Minneapolis: Fortress, 2015. Through an examination of the narrative techniques that are used to characterize the kings of Israel, shows that 1–2 Kings instructs readers about the consequences of covenant disobedience.

Kissling, Paul J. *Reliable Characters in the Primary History: Profiles of Moses, Joshua, Elijah and Elisha.* Sheffield: Sheffield Academic, 1996. Using reader-response theory, an examination of prominent Israelite heroes that calls upon the reader to consider the subtle means used to give evidence for the decidedly negative aspects in their portrayals.

Lowery, Richard H. *The Reforming Kings: Cult and Society in First Temple Judah.* Sheffield: Sheffield Academic, 1991. Examines the economic and political motivations for cultic reformations of Ahaz, Hezekiah, Manasseh, and Josiah.

McConville, J. Gordon. *God and Earthly Power: An Old Testament Political Theology, Genesis–Kings.* New York: T&T Clark, 2006. Contends that the center of Old Testament political theology is faithful response to the human vocation: created in the image of God, called to represent God's priority of providing justice for the marginalized; relegates institutions such as kings, temple, prophets, or even Torah to supporting status.

Park, Song-Mi Suzie. *Hezekiah and the Dialogue of Memory.* Minneapolis: Fortress, 2015. A study of the stories of Hezekiah, a king understood both as a positive reformer of the pagan ways of the country and as a sinner responsible for the threats and disasters that befell Judah. Elucidates the ways in which biblical stories foster continual dialogue, dispute, and discussion.

Parker, Julie Faith. *Valuable and Vulnerable: Children in the Hebrew Bible, Especially the Elisha Cycle.* Providence: Brown Judaic Series, 2013. A new methodology of "childist" interpretation applied to the Elisha cycle and its forty-nine child characters.

Provan, Iain. *Hezekiah and the Books of the Kings: A Contribution to the Debate about the Composition of the Deuteronomistic History.* Berlin: W. de Guyter, 1988. Argues that Hezekiah was the ideal royal model in the time of Josiah.

Rentería, Tamis Hoover. "The Elijah/Elisha Stories: A Socio-Cultural Analysis." In *Elijah and Elisha in Socioliterary Perspective*, edited by Robert B. Coote, 75–126. Atlanta: Scholars Press, 1992. A socio-economic analysis of the conflict between the royal interests of the house of Omri and the prophetic community of Elijah and Elisha supporting disenfranchised people.

Seibert, Eric. *Subversive Scribes and the Solomonic Narrative: A Re-reading of 1 Kings 1–11.* New York: T&T Clark, 2006. Considers 1 Kings 1–11 through the optics of propaganda and subversion with primary attention to subversive readings of the Solomonic narrative. Explores the social context in which scribal subversion was perhaps necessary and examines texts that covertly undermine the legacy of Solomon.

Walsh, James P. M. *The Mighty from Their Thrones: Power in Biblical Tradition.* Minneapolis: Augsburg Fortress, 1987. Theological evaluation of Israel's history rooted in a biblical view of social justice. Popularization of peasant revolt model. Defines justice as authority or power.

Weinfeld, Moshe. *Social Justice in Ancient Israel and in the Ancient Near East.* Minneapolis: Fortress, 1995. Citing ancient Near Eastern parallels, the author makes the case that justice and righteousness involve not only fair execution of laws but also legislation that protects the marginalized.

Wray Beal, Lissa M. *The Deuteronomist's Prophet: Narrative Control of Approval and Disapproval in the Story of Jehu (2 Kings 9 and 10).* New York: Brill, 2007. Narrative analysis of the story of Jehu's revolt in 2 Kings 9 and 10 and the tensions and ambiguities surrounding the evaluation of Jehu.

Palestine for 1&2 Kings

Sidon
Damascus
Mt. Lebanon • Mt. Hermon
Tyre
ARAM
Dan

Acco
Hazor•
BASHAN

Sea of
Galilee
Wadi Yarmuk

Mt. Carmel
Mt. Tabor
Beth-shan
GILEAD

Megiddo
Jezreel•

ISRAEL

Samaria•
Shechem•
Aphek•
EPHRAIM
Joppa
Shiloh•

AMMON

BENJAMIN
Bethel
Mizpah
Ai
Jericho
Rabbath-Ammon
Ekron
Gibeon
Ramah
Heshbon
Jerusalem
Anathoth (Anata)
Mt. Nebo
Ashdod
(Zion)
Medeba
Beth-shemesh
Beth-hakkerem
Baal-meon
Gath
Bethlehem
Ashkelon
Lachish
Tekoa
Gaza
Hebron
Dibon

Mediterranean Sea

Jordan River

The Arabah

Dead
Sea
Aroer
Wadi Arnon

JUDAH

MOAB

Beer-sheba

Kir-hareseth
Honoraim

The Negev

Zoar•
Ije-abarim
Wadi Zered

0 10   MILES   50

The Arabah

EDOM
Bozrah

N
W E
S

513

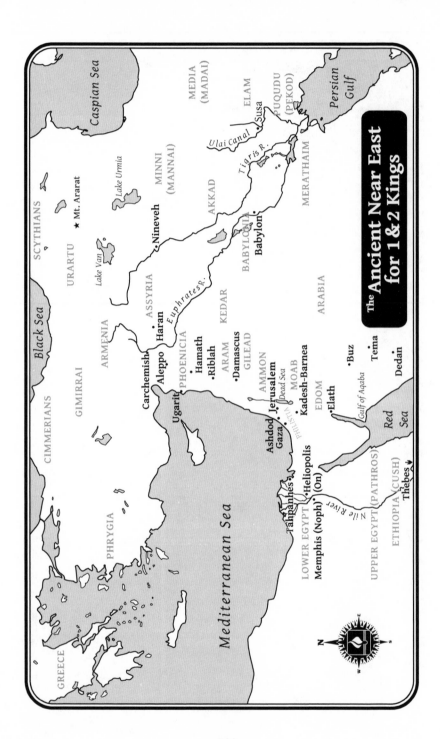

The Ancient Near East for 1 & 2 Kings

Index of Ancient Sources